Endtime Warriors
Ideology and Terror of the SS

Catalog accompanying the permanent exhibition
"Ideology and Terror of the SS"
at the Wewelsburg 1933 – 1945 Memorial Museum
of the Kreismuseum Wewelsburg
Burgwall 19, 33142 Büren-Wewelsburg
www.wewelsburg.de

Editors
Wulff E. Brebeck
Frank Huismann
Kirsten John-Stucke
Jörg Piron

Authors
Wulff E. Brebeck
Norbert Ellermann
Matthias Hambrock
Frank Huismann
Kirsten John-Stucke
Sabine Kritter
Markus Moors
Andreas Neuwöhner
Oliver Nickel
Moritz Pfeiffer
Dana Schlegelmilch
Jan Erik Schulte

Archive and Documentation
Doris Bohm
With assistance from
Andy Jung
Jürgen Ratajczak

Design
Weidner Händle Atelier, Stuttgart
With assistance from
Friederike Schlenz

Index of Names
Daniel Westermann

Copy Editors
Isabel Hartwig, Deutscher Kunstverlag
Birgit Olbrich (original German publication)
Laura McGuire

Translated by
Matthias Goldmann
Nicholas Marder
Thomas Raab
Consulting historian:
Peter Black

Editing of the English Text
Jörg Piron
James Bell
With assistance from
Cressida Joyce
Jonathan Lutes
Wendy Wallis

Printed by
Druckerei Rösler, Schorndorf

Published by
Deutscher Kunstverlag GmbH Berlin München
ISBN 978-3-422-02396-3
The Deutsche Nationalbibliothek lists
this publication in the Deutsche Nationalbibliografie;
detailed bibliographic data are available on the Internet:
http://dnb.ddb.de.

KREISMUSEUM
Wewelsburg

Publication series of the Kreismuseum Wewelsburg
Volume 8
Edited on behalf of the District of Paderborn
by Kirsten John-Stucke

Endtime Warriors
Ideology and Terror of the SS

Edited by
Wulff E. Brebeck
Frank Huismann
Kirsten John-Stucke
Jörg Piron

DEUTSCHER KUNSTVERLAG

Preface

The District of Paderborn, as the legal successor to the former District of Büren, assumed ownership of Wewelsburg Castle in 1975, and the responsibility for how to deal with the National Socialist past at this location. At this juncture, the District Administration decided to document the history of the National Socialist era and embed it in the overall history of Wewelsburg Castle. Developed by Paderborn University Professor Karl Hüser, the documentation center and memorial site "Wewelsburg 1933–1945. Cult and Terror Site of the SS" opened on March 20, 1982. Both the conflict-ridden story of the origins of this institution at Wewelsburg and its documentary form of presentation were typical of the approach taken in the early 1980s to dealing with the sites of National Socialist crimes. Under the direction of Wulff E. Brebeck, the documentation project developed in the following decades into an active, historical-political educational institution for young people and adults. The memory of the victims of SS crimes in Wewelsburg was kept alive. Twenty-eight years later, after ten years of planning and restructuring, the District of Paderborn opened the "Wewelsburg 1933–1945 Memorial Museum" with the new permanent exhibition "Ideology and Terror of the SS." With its three-dimensional original artifacts and numerous media modules, this exhibition meets the conceptual standards of a modern, museum-style memorial site. It has been adapted to the expectations of today's visitors, who no longer need any proof of the ruthless, criminal activity of the SS at Wewelsburg during the years 1933 to 1945, and whose knowledge about National Socialism and the SS has already been shaped by modern media. With this new exhibition, the District of Paderborn renews its commitment to educational work that raises political awareness by conveying the history of the SS in this place. As the agency that administers the only concentration camp memorial on North Rhine-Westphalian soil, the District of Paderborn recognizes the responsibility for preserving the legacy of the victims of SS terror. At the same time, the worldview of the SS manifests itself in Wewelsburg. Coming to terms with the historical site where *Reichsführer-SS* Heinrich Himmler ruthlessly deployed concentration camp prisoners to build a meeting place of gigantic proportions for his *SS-Gruppenführer* to reinforce their elitist and racist self-image is fraught with tension. It is precisely this ideologically, mythically charged component that distinguishes this site from other concentration camp memorials – and even from other so-called perpetrator sites, where today historical exhibitions reflect the National Socialist past.

Minister of State Bernd Neumann, Federal Commissioner for Culture and the Media, Berlin, recognized the special quality of the historical site of Wewelsburg and deemed the project worthy of financial support through federal funding as a memorial site. I particularly want to thank him for his sponsorship. I would also like to express my gratitude to the State of North Rhine-Westphalia for financial support of the project through North Rhine-Westphalia's State Agency for Civic Education and Ministry of Building and Transport. Furthermore, I thank the Regional Association of Westphalia-Lippe in Münster for its financial sponsorship of the project as well as the scholarly guidance we received from the Westphalian Museum Office. We also extend our appreciation to the European Union for sponsoring the reconception of the Wewelsburg 1933–1945 Memorial Museum through the "Leader +" program.

The scholarly and conceptual development of the new exhibition was completed under the project management of Wulff E. Brebeck and Kirsten John-Stucke. We extend our heartfelt thanks, once again, to the academic project group and all others involved in preparing the exhibition. From 2006, the project group received support from an academic advisory panel. I thank Professor Stefan Baumeier, Dr. Detlef Garbe, Angela Genger, Professor Detlef Hoffmann, Professor Hans Ottomeyer, Professor Waltraud Schreiber, Dr. Johannes Tuchel, and Professor Wolfgang Wippermann for their expertise and their readiness to support the project.

In this volume we present the historical site of Wewelsburg, the concept behind the exhibition, and the majority of its exhibits and texts. Our thanks goes out to the editors Wulff E. Brebeck (deceased: June 2011), Frank Huismann, Kirsten John-Stucke, and Jörg Piron for their elaborate and painstaking work to commit to paper the broad range of subjects covered by this exhibition.

As the district responsible for this institution, we are conscious of the expectations that are placed on us and the tasks that lie ahead. The completion of the exhibition marks the end of the project, but not of our work: We are committed to the task of communicating the history of a location that is fraught with tension and aim to inform and educate visitors through this new exhibition. Our goal is to appeal to the willingness of visitors to take responsibility for themselves and their actions in society. It is important to point out the possibilities to take action in today's world. The exhibition intends, among other things, that visitors learn from the racist, criminal, and unjust behavior of the National Socialists; that they be on the lookout and become aware of what is happening in their surroundings; that they notice injustice, exclusion, and xenophobia; and that they engage themselves for peace, human rights, and integration.

Manfred Müller
District Administrator

Endtime Warriors –
A Foreword by the Editors

The notion of an "endtime" is found in many religions. As a rule, it revolves around expectations in an entirely positive sense. This endtime, in which the world as we know it ceases to exist, is connected with the dawning of a new, peaceful, and divine world. Particularly in Christianity, the endtime is also a time of struggle against evil, before the Judge of the World comes and the new paradise is erected.

Thus, the term "endtime warrior" can be used to denote a person who – often entirely detached from the Christian religion – firmly believes in his destiny of fighting against (alleged) evil and harbors the expectation of a new and better world. This expression also points to some central elements in the history of the Protection Squadron (*Schutzstaffel* or SS). Complementing the attitude of permanent struggle, a quasi-religious, ideological component permeated the organization. Many SS men believed they were surrounded by evil and expected the – in their view – inevitable victory would be followed by the dawn of a new and glorious National Socialist world. An striking representation of this worldview is found in Hans Lohbeck's designs for a triptych that he was to create for Wewelsburg Castle. While in the War version, the battle for a new future still rages, the gouache titled *Peace* clearly depicts what this "endtime" could look like: soldiers parading, farmers tilling their fields, mothers with their children, and – high above all in the background, crowning the scene – Wewelsburg Castle. The original gouaches are on display in the new exhibition.

To the SS and especially Heinrich Himmler, it was indisputable that the battle against the supposedly evil could and had to be fought outside of the normal rules of morality. The SS man could murder and still "remain pure," Himmler explained in his infamous Posen speech on October 4, 1943. The "final battle" denotes a completely ideological war that can only end in total triumph or downfall and which, unlike "normal wars," cannot be settled through mediation. To this day, extreme right-wing publications espouse similar notions of a final battle and the rising of the "black sun," which with its power will create a new world. Tellingly, such a final battle is fought at the gates of Wewelsburg Castle in the novel *Die Schwarze Sonne von Tashi Lhunpo* (The Black Sun of Tashi Lhunpo) by Russell McCloud, which became a bestseller on the right-wing scene in the early 1990s.

Certainly, the SS man was not per se an endtime warrior; for that the SS was too diverse, too heterogeneous in its composition. Not every SS man was an enthusiastic warrior, nor did all members of Himmler's organization subscribe to pseudo-religious beliefs. Even the vision of fighting for a new world likely only formed in the minds of many SS men with the onset of World War II. But the ideal type of SS man – the fanatically fighting, ideologically drilled, and fully committed soldier who subordinated himself absolutely to the cause – was a wishful notion of the SS leadership. This also characterized the ideal type of National Socialist – at least in the minds of the key SS leaders, which is why the SS could view itself as spearheading the "movement." From the beginning, this elitist claim of the SS was conveyed to the public by means of propaganda. Those who joined the SS usually knew what was expected of them. That many nonetheless joined out of completely different motives doesn't make this less true.

The SS stylized itself as the champion of alleged good against evil. This "battle," however, had to be won through terror and murder. Extermination of the "other" (those who were different) was the goal.

The basic ideology of serving as front-line warriors in a world filled with enemies led the SS to participate in virtually every criminal and murderous action of the regime. Some SS leaders practically saw it as their task to be the first in line to kill. At no point in time can the self-image of the SS be separated from the murderous terror inflicted by its men. Even those in the SS who held "desk jobs" or worked as academics at Wewelsburg Castle had to reckon with being detailed to a police operation or a combat mission. Participation in acts of terror became the binding tie linking all parts of the organization. Thus, every one of its members was called upon to become a "warrior" and in a certain sense, an "endtime warrior."

Opened in April 2010, the permanent exhibition "Ideology and Terror of the SS" represents the world's first museum presentation on the history of the SS. The permanent exhibition is part of the Wewelsburg 1933 – 1945 Memorial Museum, a branch of the Kreismuseum Wewelsburg, which is operated by the District of Paderborn. The exhibition not only documents the local history of Wewelsburg Castle during National Socialism, it also gives a comprehensive account of the development of the SS, the National Socialist Party organization that under the leadership of Heinrich Himmler rose from being Adolf Hitler's personal security detachment to become one of the most powerful organizations of the Third Reich and responsible for the murder of millions.

This catalog accompanying the exhibition presents the museum exhibits in its twelve chapters, with introductory essays by Wulff E. Brebeck and Kirsten John-Stucke providing information on the locality of Wewelsburg and the exhibition concept.

The location of the exhibition "Ideology and Terror of the SS" in a historical building meant that exhibition planners had to consider the different sizes and properties of its rooms. Together with the exhibition's intended thematic focal points, this resulted in certain spatial arrangements with numerous sub-sections. For improved clarity and readability, this publication was arranged according to its own chapter structure. Topical breaks that could not be translated into spatial transitions in the exhibition are implemented in the catalog. Conversely, coherent sections that had to be arranged across two exhibition rooms due to the available space are now brought together in one chapter.

Furthermore, the presentation in book form is subject to different principles than a three-dimensional exhibition with its spatial experience, original artifacts, and audiovisual media. Thus, additional adaptations needed to be made. Where multiple possible perspectives and associations of objects or captions with each other arose, care was taken that they followed a logical linear narrative structure that is basic to the medium of the book.

This adaptation was aimed at producing a publication that could be read as an independent work and did not require a visit to the Wewelsburg permanent exhibition. A selection from the extensive material available was made accordingly.

The exhibit texts were written by a number of authors, who, as a team, were responsible for the exhibition subject matter. These texts, marked with the author's initials, were taken directly from the exhibition, with only a few being edited for brevity. The texts introducing the main chapters and their subsections were jointly developed by the project group and are therefore not marked with the authors' names. They have been revised for this publication in order to correspond with the changed division of the chapters.

As is common in contemporary exhibitions, the new permanent Wewelsburg exhibition explores the possibilities of modern media in the form of audio stations, films, and interactive media units. In some cases these media are essential for understanding the narrative and their contents have thus been included, whole or in part, in this catalog. Excerpts from interviews with survivors of the Niederhagen Concentration Camp were transcribed.

We thank the District of Paderborn for its financial support of our project and its readiness to publish the exhibition catalog as part of the publication series of the Kreismuseum Wewelsburg. Our heartfelt gratitude is extended to Berthold Weidner and his team for their patience and dedication to the book's design and layout, as well as to Esther Zadow and Luzie Diekmann from Deutscher Kunstverlag for the painstaking care they have invested in this publication.

The editors

Wewelsburg – About the Historical Site

Wulff E. Brebeck, Kirsten John-Stucke

Wewelsburg Castle
Photograph: Henke, 2003
Kreismuseum Wewelsburg,
Fotoarchiv

Wewelsburg Castle with its triangular ground plan was built in the Renaissance period during the early seventeenth century as a secondary residence of the prince-bishops of Paderborn. Scarcely known outside the region, it caught the attention of SS leader Heinrich Himmler (*Reichsführer-SS*) during the Third Reich and would become an important place for our understanding of the history of the SS (*Schutzstaffel*).[1] Heinrich Himmler endeavored to turn Wewelsburg Castle (which he envisioned as a "*Burg*" or medieval stronghold) into a central meeting place for the SS, intending to create an environment around the castle where his *SS-Gruppenführer*, the organization's ranking officers, were supposed to gain a sense, from a mythical perspective, of their supposedly historic role as the racial and military ruling elite of the National Socialist regime. At the same time, the SS presence here comprised an exceptionally broad group of representatives of its various units and manifestations.[2] Among others, this included members of the Death's Head Units (*Totenkopfverbände*), who operated a concentration camp here from 1939. The concentration-camp prisoners were used for construction work at the castle, which the SS sought to give a fortress-like character. Niederhagen Concentration Camp, a main camp within the state-run system, existed on the outskirts of Wewelsburg from 1941 to 1943.

Village residents were affected in various ways by the presence of the SS, which repeatedly threatened the familiar normality of their everyday lives. In the end, they saw themselves faced with the threat of having to give up their houses and hometown to make room for the conversion plans of the SS. Since 1945, the village of Wewelsburg and its surrounding Paderborn countryside have become paradigmatic for the difficulties and hardships, but also for the new beginnings that have marked the process in the Federal Republic of Germany of coming to terms with National Socialism and its crimes.

Wewelsburg Castle was pointed out to Heinrich Himmler by National Socialists from Westphalia in November 1933. Early in the year, he had commissioned a search for a castle stronghold for the SS in the Westphalia-Lippe surroundings of the Hermannsdenkmal (Hermann Monument) and the rock formation of the Externsteine. Here, he sought to realize key ideological goals of the SS. In his understanding, this region was "Germania's heartland." The then District of Büren, which ran a community center, youth hostel, and local history museum at Wewelsburg Castle, was in financial difficulty and sought a tenant. In 1934, Himmler rented the building and, from that point on, pursued two objectives: the first was

the establishment of a school for the upper echelons of the SS, the second was the creation of a prestigious venue for gatherings of top SS leaders, albeit one that was also shielded from public view. The first of these aims led to the designation Wewelsburg SS School as of 1935 and would shape staffing at the castle until the second half of the 1930s. Young academics in fields ranging from folklore to archeology were hired and a museum with a focus on archeology and a library concentrating on cultural and legal history were created.[3] On the other hand, the artistic furnishings, room layout of the complex, and, at a later point, its restaffing and architectural development were adapted to achieve the second objective of creating an exclusive central meeting place for the *Gruppenführer* corps. In a November 1938 speech, Himmler announced that in the future he intended to conduct an annual *Gruppenführer* meeting at Wewelsburg Castle, in the course of which newly promoted *Gruppenführer* were to be sworn in.[4] As part of an effort to associate tradition with this location, one hall was to be furnished with the coat of arms of *Gruppenführer* and the death's head rings (*Totenkopfringe*), special rings awarded to SS leaders for outstanding merit, were to be placed in a shrine upon the bearer's death.[5] In times of war, art treasures from all occupied countries were to be stored at Wewelsburg Castle. Works of art representative of SS ideology were also acquired or commissioned.[6]

Although Himmler had invited several high-ranking *Gruppenführer* to Wewelsburg Castle as early as May 1938,[7] only a single important *Gruppenführer* meeting was ever held subsequently – contrary to his November announcement. It took place between June 12 and June 15, 1941, just a few days before the attack on the Soviet Union. The hand picked participants included several *Gruppenführer* who were to play a leading role in the planned campaign of extermination against the indigenous Jewish and Slavic populations. The gathering was intended to provide the *Gruppenführer* with a relaxed environment, assure them of their elite position, and let them reflect on the historic significance of the coming battle. Here, all elements of Himmler's imagination concerning the Wewelsburg location converged in a political and mythological perspective.[8]

Starting in 1940, development plans were expanded under Himmler's chief architect Hermann Bartels. Previously, the construction activity of the SS had been limited to work on the castle to lend it the appearance of a medieval castle and on new buildings in its immediate vicinity. The SS guard building on the forecourt had been constructed in 1937. Now, plans foresaw a gigantic new castle complex arranged in concentric circles around Wewelsburg Castle's

The former SS guard building on the forecourt of Wewelsburg Castle
Photograph:
Johannes Büttner, 2011
Kreismuseum Wewelsburg, Fotoarchiv

View from the new staircase in the former gym and fencing hall
Photograph:
Matthias Groppe, 2010
Kreismuseum Wewelsburg, Fotoarchiv

northern tower and a settlement for SS members in the surrounding area. The old village was to disappear entirely. The northern tower itself was to house large rooms on three floors, including a "crypt" (*Gruft*) and an *Obergruppenführer* Hall. Financing of the enormous complex was to be secured largely through loans, and building costs were to be kept as low as possible. In a move typical of the SS, concentration camp prisoners were therefore used.[9] By May 1939, a small prisoner detachment from Sachsenhausen Concentration Camp had already been established in Wewelsburg. For a time, it consisted almost exclusively of Jehovah's Witnesses, which explains the importance of the camp for this religious community.[10] In view of the new planning perspectives, the enlarged work detachment was first upgraded to a subcamp and, in September 1941, was integrated into the state-run system of concentration camps as a main camp, which was now named "Niederhagen." The prisoners had to work at numerous construction sites in the village. Aside from the above-mentioned rooms in the northern tower, however, the "big projects" had not even been initiated yet. After the Battle of Stalingrad, construction work was halted; the concentration camp was dissolved in the spring of 1943. Until the end of the war, a small prisoner detachment subordinate to Buchenwald Concentration Camp remained in Wewelsburg. Out of a total of some 3,900 prisoners from Germany and nearly all occupied countries, including over 2,000 from the Soviet Union,[11] at least 1,285 were killed.

Concentration camp memorials are set in locations where SS crimes were committed or were built on the sites of historic decisions or actions, as is the case, for instance, with the Topography of Terror Museum and the Memorial to the German Resistance in Berlin. In contrast, the former guard building, the current exhibition building at Wewelsburg Castle, played only a minor role in the historical events in the locality. Although the SS pursued various goals during its presence there,[12] it saw Wewelsburg as a space of action and power where it could increasingly reign supreme and overall, with it's scope comprising the areas of the castle with its neighboring guard building, the village, and – from 1939 – the concentration camp. From this perspective, it is aptly termed a "historical site." The extent to which relics of historical significance are extant in this space of action has hinged on several factors: What meaning was ascribed to individual sites after 1945? What impact did these attributions develop on public communication and decision-making processes?[13] That is to say, why were the Führerhaus I, the villa of architect Hermann Bartels, or the former village community center preserved, while the offices of the SS

Construction Management at the Marx farm or the barracks on the grounds of the former concentration camp were razed? The different meanings ascribed to them in the postwar period significantly influenced decisions on village development. What is more, since the 1950s, Wewelsburg Castle has also become the object of various projections, fantastical conceptions, and, as of the 1990s, symbolic attributions by various groups of society. Reference to the long history of Wewelsburg Castle as the bearer of symbolic meaning was not taken into consideration.[14]

The History of the Exhibition Site
The five-story guard building, which the SS referred to by an antiquated term for sentry house (*Wachtgebäude*) is situated on the forecourt of Wewelsburg Castle. Built in from 1936 to 1937 on the hillside site of four of the village's residential and outbuildings, it served as an SS administration and social center. Among others, it housed the castle administrator's service apartment, administrative offices, for a time the Construction Management entity, the gym and fencing hall, and a staff canteen. The staff building, an additional administration building adjoined to the south side of the guard building, was built between 1939 and 1941. From 1941 to 1942, prisoners had to construct the "north terrace," a two-story annex north of the guard building. Together with Wewelsburg Castle, this group of buildings was demolished by the SS on March 31, 1945.

In contrast to the neighboring staff building, the ruins of which were razed in 1957, the guard building was preserved because it now served a new purpose. Youths made homeless by wartime events renovated it with public funding in 1948. It served as a hostel and training center for boys, operated by the Assistance to German Catholic Youth Association, until the home's closure in 1952. Beginning in the following year and for the next two decades, the building served as the St. Catherine Old-Age Home for Refugees, run by the sisters of the Warmian Catholic Order of Saint Catherine. Franz Josef Tusch (1883–1971) died here – he served as Wewelsburg's parish priest from 1934 to 1958 and played a vital role in shaping public opinion in the village.

In the course of discussions about the establishment of a historical documentation center in the second half of the 1970s, attention turned to the vacant building. After acquiring it from the Catholic Church, the District of Paderborn opened the documentation center "Wewelsburg 1933–1945. Cult and Terror Site of the SS" on its ground floor in 1982. Furthermore, the former guard building housed the museum

administration, a restaurant, and a youth center run by the town of Büren, among others. In 1984, the second permanent historical exhibition, *Deutsche im östlichen Mitteleuropa. Kultur – Vertreibung – Integration* (Germans in Eastern Central Europe. Culture – Expulsion – Integration), opened its doors to the public. A second phase of construction saw the storage rooms and workshops relocated from Wewelsburg Castle to the newly converted basement floors of the guard building in 1993. Starting in 2007, in connection with the redesign of the exhibition "Wewelsburg 1933–1945," the guard building as a whole was converted into the Wewelsburg 1933–1945 Memorial Museum, an exhibition building with museum educational spaces.

Since April 2010, the guard building's two basement floors have been the site of the new permanent exhibition, "Ideology and Terror of the SS." In the exhibition rooms, several details relevant to the building's history are highlighted on information panels with reproductions of the original building plans from the 1930s and texts.

The first exhibition room, one-and-a-half stories high, is designated as a "gym and fencing hall" in the 1936/1937 designs drawn up by SS architect Hermann Bartels for the construction of the guard building. At least in intent, the Wewelsburg contingent was supposed to engage in physical training to demonstrate military toughness and hone their fencing skills as an expression of the elitist image the SS had of itself. It is unclear whether the hall was ever used for the purpose it was built to serve. According to eyewitness accounts, it served as a warehouse during World War II, housed workshops in the days of the youth home, and functioned as a laundry room during the period of the home for the elderly.

The visitor tour leads from the gym and fencing hall via a newly built staircase to the castle tavern. The building plans also had a staircase there. Eyewitnesses maintained that a few days prior to the arrival of American troops in March 1945, prisoners from the concentration camp's "remaining detachment" had to stow and wall in paintings and carpets hoarded by the SS at Wewelsburg Castle underneath a staircase in the gym and fencing hall. It was rumored among the prisoners engaged in this work that they would be shot because they knew of this hiding place. If there ever was such an order, it was not carried out. During the postwar period, no evidence of the staircase could be found and for a long time its existence was doubted. A study of the construction history of the building later confirmed that a staircase had existed at that location. The room is divided into three aisles by an arcade

and is called a "canteen" in the 1936 plans and a "castle tavern" in 1941. However, it served not only as a dining room, but also as a tavern, for both the staff of the Wewelsburg SS School and – during the war – members of the concentration camp guard units. In 1938 and 1939, the SS castle administration's carnival event was staged here. The wives of SS members and female employees were also welcome at the castle tavern.

On one of the pillars an element characteristic of SS architecture in Wewelsburg is visible. The supporting structures were often built from modern materials such as reinforced concrete, but surfaces were faced with undressed stones or ashlar. The ostensibly ancient, undressed-stone archways, for instance, were made of concrete and subsequently veneered with natural stones to create a faux "castle atmosphere."

In a second construction phase from 1941 to 1942, a two-story terrace annex was built on the north side of the guard building. The newly created spaces were intended to house storerooms and domestic work rooms. Extending over both stories, the triple-arched portico arcade formed the north end of the front side of the guard building, which was built on a slope facing the valley. It also opened the adjoining castle tavern to the garden. Among other elements, the oculi windows on the ground and upper floor as well as the ceiling design of the hallway, which was bordered by sandstone molding, show how architect Hermann Bartels was striving to develop the stylistic features of the existing administration building into a splendid country style. As with all SS buildings in Wewelsburg during World War II, he deployed prisoners of Niederhagen Concentration Camp on this construction project. Bartels acquired the granite used for the floor covering of open spaces and the stairs from the quarry of Flossenbürg Concentration Camp in Upper Palatinate [Bavaria].

At the height of the war, the prisoners were also made to construct a wine cellar. At least the clay tubes in the tower-like end of the terrace building suggest it was used as one. Apparently, ample supplies of wine and liquor were basic to the culture of comradeship that was prevalent in rooms such as the castle tavern. But they were also part of the cliché of the "stronghold of the *SS-Gruppenführer*" that Wewelsburg Castle was designed to represent. For a time, the permanent staff included a "cellarer." Numerous eyewitnesses reported that looting of the castle following its attempted demolition on March 31, 1945, turned up large amounts of wine and champagne in the cellar of the southwestern tower. The local chronicle puts the number of bottles in this cache at forty thousand.

Exhibition Room 16 in the former air-raid shelter of the guard building
Photograph: Matthias Groppe, 2010
Kreismuseum Wewelsburg, Fotoarchiv

The new access bridge with a chimera
Photograph: Matthias Groppe, 2010
Kreismuseum Wewelsburg, Fotoarchiv

The last exhibition room was part of a former air raid bunker. From 1937 on, air raid protection laws required new buildings to have air raid shelters. Their windows and doors had to be gas and shatterproof. Walls and ceilings in the guard building were also reinforced. One of the bunker's former two entry doors still exists and is displayed in the room. Wall inscriptions reading "No Smoking" and "Keep Calm" also refer to the former function of the room. During bombing alerts, not only SS members, but also the village residents gathered in the air raid shelter.

The surviving rooms of the northern tower are included in today's visitor tour, which passes through the wine cellar and up a steep stairway. Visitors reach the castle moat through a vaulted hallway faced with undressed stone. This hallway connected the garden fronting the arcade of the north terrace with the gardens of Wewelsburg Castle. This passageway to the moat was walled up after the war and only reopened fifty years later in 2010 after the completion of renovations begun in 2009 for the new exhibition. The visitor is led to the northern tower on a newly laid path in the moat, along the castle's eastern façade, which is where its entrance gate is located. This measure achieved two things with regard to access to the building: The rooms in the northern tower, the crypt and *Obergruppenführer* Hall, with their ideologically charged architecture were thus integrated into the exhibition tour, from which they had previously been excluded. Inside the tower, however, a connecting staircase had to be installed. The second achievement lies in the possibility of rendering visible, from the individual visitor's point of view, the changes the SS made to the structural fabric of the Renaissance building. The bottom of the moat lies two floors below the traditional principal visual perspective from the access road that leads to the inner courtyard of Wewelsburg Castle. The design of the main entrance gate, which is aligned with the bridge, and above it the oriel with the coat of arms, title, and motto of builder-owner Dietrich von Fürstenberg, is dominated by imagery signifying the recatholicization of the state of Paderborn in the early seventeenth century.[15] The walk along the castle moat also leads visitors past information displays with historic photos that point them to traces of SS construction measures. The goal of Himmler and his architect Hermann Bartels was to transform – as far as possible – the appearance of the dilapidated Renaissance castle of the Paderborn prince bishops into that of a "German castle" of earlier times. To this end, painstaking work was undertaken to remove the exterior plaster surfacing, because walls of exposed stone belonged to the generic image of a medieval

stronghold. As the uncovered surfaces were not very attractive, large sections of the walls had to be refaced, something that is still visible in various seams in the building's exterior.

The moat, which over the centuries had filled with soil, was cleared and deepened to emphasize the fortified character of the building. It was also augmented by the construction of a new access bridge with a sculptural "chimera" in the medieval tradition (1934). From 1939, concentration camp prisoners were forced to work on these building projects. On the east façade, the traces of a construction shed have survived, with a photograph confirming that this was a prisoner workplace. The marks are remnants of the structure's tarred roof that firmly abutted the wall. A surviving measuring stick on the northern tower marks the line to which the prisoner detachment tore down the upper stories of the tower ruin in 1942. Finally, visitors can look around the now overgrown quarry area and the former train path of the former narrow gauge railway at the foot of the castle hill, which conveys an idea of the harshness of forced labor.

Visitors enter the northern tower through an entrance dating from 1949. Following the conversion of Wewelsburg Castle and the near completion of the interior furnishings in the "Nordic style," Hermann Bartels turned in 1938 to plans for the northern tower, which had been gutted by fire caused by a lightning strike in 1815. Presumably, the three planned rooms were initially intended only as venues for the most important ceremonial events at Wewelsburg Castle. From 1940 at the latest, however, together with the northern tower, they were designed to form the topographical center of a new "SS castle and settlement." In the annual reports of the Society for the Preservation and Promotion of German Cultural Monuments – the SS association that acted as the building developer in Wewelsburg – they appear, from bottom to top, as "crypt," "*Obergruppenführer* Hall," and "*Gruppenführer* Hall." There is no information about their intended use – at most, it can be inferred from Himmler's ideas for Wewelsburg Castle. In all likelihood, they would have played a role in the overall function of the castle, serving as a central venue for meetings and oath-taking ceremonies for the *Gruppenführer* corps. Even the two largely finished lower rooms were never completed and thus never used for any kind of gatherings or ceremonies. They remained under construction until 1945. The planned multistory *Gruppenführer* Hall on the upper stories was to be built on the stump of the old tower following its demolition, but its construction was never begun.

In 1939, concentration camp prisoners had to demolish the complicated vaulted basement ceiling that rested on two pillars before they could begin to remove approximately 4.4 vertical meters (ca. 14.5 ft.) of bedrock. Because they were equipped with inadequate tools, work in the damp, dark space was protracted. Furthermore, since they had undermined sections of the foundations, it proved necessary to stabilize the tower with shotcrete.

The crypt was a 9.50-meter (ca. 31 ft.) high dome hall that was modeled on the tombs of Mycenae. It was probably designed to serve as a hall of the dead. The dome shell was made of reinforced concrete, which was faced with limestone from the local quarries. At the dome's apex, a swastika is embedded in a meander ornament; the openings of shafts are visible between its arms. Twelve round pedestals are positioned on the edge of the floor in front of niches, which were already closed off again during the construction period. At the center of the dark Anröchte limestone floor, three steps lead into a round basin with a circular area at its center. According to oral accounts, the two pipes leading to its edge had to do a gas flame, presumably symbolizing an "eternal flame," in a bowl in the middle of the room. Outside light shines into the middle of the room through four shafts – a fifth one was completed but closed after the war. Because it is a domed hall, the room has acoustic properties such as echo effects.

The discrepancy in the alignment of the steps to the basin and today's entrance shows that a different entrance had been planned. Himmler and Bartels intended to make the crypt accessible from the castle's inner courtyard. From there, a monumental outside staircase was supposed to lead down to the basement floor. In 1940, the top Prussian conservator of historic buildings and monuments – to whom the plans had to be submitted, as stipulated by the 1925 agreement on conveyance of the property from the Prussian state to the District of Büren – rejected the outside staircase on the grounds that it compromised the courtyard. Dr. Robert Hiecke was unaware that plans already existed in which this outside staircase and the crypt marked the end of a miles-long axis, which would provide access to the new castle and settlement of the large-scale project that he had not been informed of. These plans were described by Hermann Bartels in 1941 as follows:

"The starting point of the entire design is the center of the northern tower of Wewelsburg Castle, which has a layout in the shape of an isosceles triangle. The height of this isosceles triangle is the direction of the main access road, which will run in a straight line for two kilometers in a northwesterly direction up to the castle and is to be designed as a splendid boulevard with four rows of trees. ... The castle grounds proper are enclosed within a ¾-circle with a 430-meter [ca. 1410 ft.] radius closed off by a wall with 18 towers. Within these castle grounds a larger number of buildings will be erected, which will exclusively serve the purposes of the Reichsführung-SS. The main street of the future village will pass around the center of Wewelsburg Castle's northern tower at a radius of 635 meters [ca. 2083 ft.]. This main road will be linked to the castle grounds by three radially aligned streets and special gates. ... In future, the provincial road will ... bypass around the village in a semicircle with a radius of 1,115 meters [ca. 3658 ft.]."[16]

Not only was this excessive endeavor never realized, the crypt was never completed either. Until the late 1940s, a huge hole yawned at the site of today's entrance, lending an additional gloomy touch to the castle complex that had been demolished on Himmler's order on March 31, 1945. The opening was only closed and the room fitted with an arched entrance when the District of Büren decided to rebuild the castle ruins. Without engaging in local political discussions, the district administration launched an effort to reinstate the situation existing before 1933. The youth hostel was reopened in the east wing, the local history museum returned to the cellar of the west wing, while other parts of the building initially remained vacant. In the course of reopening of the edifice to the public on June 19, 1950, a memorial had been created in the crypt. At the suggestion of the honorary chairman of the Society for the Preservation of the Wewelsburg, Dr. Aloys Vogels, who as district administrator of Büren had negotiated the acquisition of Wewelsburg Castle from the Prussian state in 1925, the young Büren painter Josef Glahé was commissioned with the creation of ten large-format paintings addressing the destructive effects of National Socialism, including prison labor at Wewelsburg Castle.[17] In a time when commemorative stones were erected almost exclusively by victims groups themselves or German decision-makers under pressure of the Allied forces, the founding of a memorial for victims of National Socialism by an independent association of citizens stood out as a remarkable exception. The expressionistic paintings, however, met with general disapproval. A defensive attitude towards the truly shocking content of the cycle of paintings manifested itself in the cloak of art criticism. Following a complaint, the painting titled *Verschleppt, vergast, ausgelöscht* (Displaced, Gassed, Extinguished), which shows naked, emaciated people, was removed on the grounds that it "offended public decency." The cycle of paintings attracted less and less attention, and a tradition of commemoration did not take shape. Even less consideration was given to Vogels's farsighted proposal to integrate commemorative activities into an overall concept of the politics of memory and to establish in Wewelsburg a "political educational institution in a truly democratic sense."[18]

By 1973, the damp climate of the crypt had seriously affected the paintings. On the instructions of the district's chief administrative officer, they were removed and placed in a storeroom. That this was not primarily a preservation measure is clear from the simultaneous instruction to remove a commemorative plaque. The latter had been put up in the castle's inner courtyard in 1965 by the Union of Persecutees of the Nazi Regime following a proposal by a survivor of the Wewelsburg concentration camp and with financial support from the District of Büren. With the revision of this decision, the chief administrator had complied with repeated criticism from Wewelsburg dignitaries and personnel in his own cultural section, who had argued that the wording of the plaque could create the impression that the concentration camp had been located inside Wewelsburg Castle.

Considered particularly problematic were questions asked by participants of the International Youth Festival Week, a pan-European folklore festival that had been staged biannually in Wewelsburg since 1953. District officials wanted to remove the source of these inquiries. The time of "non-commemoration," however, did not last even two years. In 1975, in the course of local government reorganization, Wewelsburg Castle was transferred to the ownership of the District of Paderborn and thus received broader attention than before. The absence of any sign of commemoration was conspicuous. Demands for a memorial, first voiced by the German Communist Party (DKP) and later seized on by the Social Democratic Party of Germany (SPD), were initially rejected outright by the Christian Democratic Union of Germany (CDU), the majority party in the district council, and subsequently turned down in the proposed form. Already during the decision prepared by a working group to recommend against the establishment of a memorial, after an unsuccessful search for a suitable site, fierce criticism from the public was to be heard. The decision of the district council on July 6, 1977, not to create a memorial but to establish a permanent exhibition in the form of a historical documentation provoked, in addition to a large flurry of media responses across the country, Klaus Thüsing, then the SPD representative for Paderborn in the federal parliament, to mount, on his own initiative, a new commemorative plaque in the inner courtyard on November 9, 1977. A few days later, the plaque was removed by young people and brought to the nearby Böddeken Military Cemetery. Thus, they pointed the way for the district administrator of Paderborn. One year later, on November 8, 1978, he dedicated a memorial to all victims of the war and tyranny in the military cemetery's so-called Valley of Peace, where predominantly SS men were buried. Commemoration ceremonies are staged here twice a year: on the People's Day of Mourning (*Volkstrauertag*) – a public holiday in Germany – by the War Graves Commission (*Volksbund Deutsche Kriegsgräberfürsorge*), and on September 1 by the Confederation of German Trade Unions.[19]

The district council's decision of 1977 also resulted in the establishment of the above-mentioned historical documentation center and memorial "Wewelsburg 1933–1945. Cult and Terror Site of the SS" in the guard building. The exhibition that provided the foundation for the commemorative activities that shape the profile of the Kreismuseum Wewelsburg to this day was opened on March 20, 1982.

What had initially been intended as an extension of the District Museum of Local History increasingly became the focus of efforts that attracted attention beyond the region. Following revisions and the 1967 relocation to the east and south wings, the museum in the castle was also redesigned and its existing collections were significantly expanded in the late 1970s. After a costly partial conversion of Wewelsburg Castle, the museum's exhibition space was enlarged, and it reopened as the Historical Museum of the Prince-Bishopric of Paderborn on August 24, 1996. On September 23, 2001, there followed the completion of the second installation phase of this regional history museum of the District of Paderborn. Its name still reflected the regional historical perspective, the term "prince-bishopric" exuding the authority of the old Prince-Bishopric.[20]

Approaching the northern tower on their way through the castle moat, visitors today again see it in its original height. It was rebuilt as part of the expansion of the youth hostel between 1973 and 1975. Ascending the above-mentioned new staircase from the crypt, visitors climb two and a half stories inside the tower to reach the *Obergruppenführer* Hall.

The *Obergruppenführer* Hall on the ground floor of the northern tower has common elements with local and regional traditions. Like today's room, which Bartels built into the empty tower, the Baroque chapel of the prince-bishops also had twelve pillars – it was destroyed in 1815 and is documented only by a single piece of evidence from the early nineteenth century. We have no knowledge of whether this was a continuation of a medieval tradition (such as copies of the Church of the Holy Sepulcher in Paderborn and Helmarshausen). A photograph taken during the construction work, however, provides evidence that details were changed, just as in the crypt. The Anröchte green sandstone pillars are connected to round-arch arcades faced with the same material. They separate a gallery with groin vaults (faced with local lime-sandstone slabs) from the large interior space with its flat, stuccoed ceiling panel. There is a niche in every section of the gallery; eight of them have large elongated rectangular windows created in that period.[21]

The structure of the room is punctuated by the ornament at the center of the marble floor. This is a sun wheel with twelve spokes, which are shaped as inverse sig runes, each pointing in the direction of a pillar or niche. The ornament was modeled on an Alamannic fibula from the seventh century.[22] There is no record of an authentic interpretation of the sun wheel from the time before 1945.

Even though the *Obergruppenführer* Hall had served as a chapel from 1971 to 1985, it stood vacant for quite some time after 1945. Since the 1973 removal of the Glahé paintings, the crypt had also not been used. Aside from the fact that the rooms had remained nearly unscathed by the 1945 demolition, this may have been the reason why they became a magnet for fantasies and projections at an early stage. Relatively harmless and geared towards educational purposes, it seems, were attempts by the then castle management to breathe life into the crypt in the form of all kinds of "Germanic" SS customs and traditions.[23] It remains inexplicable to what extent this was perhaps done in reference to misunderstood research in contemporary history.[24]

Since the 1950s, Wewelsburg castle has been featured as an icon of a number of fantastic-literature books. Particularly popular are works that are referred to as "crypto-historiography" because, disregarding historical facts, they attribute the policies of the Third Reich to the dark machinations of secret societies. As a rule, medieval myths in the tradition of the "Holy Lance" or the "Holy Grail," popularized by Richard Wagner, play a prominent role here. This literature, especially the book *The Spear of Destiny* by Trevor Ravenscroft,[25] spawned interpretations that Himmler kept a replica of the so-called Holy Lance at Wewelsburg, and that for this reason the main building of the planned "new Wewelsburg Castle" was designed in the form of a spear. The "Holy Lance" is taken to be the (Ottonian) Vienna Spear, which was part of the imperial insignia of the Holy Roman Empire of the German Nation. Kept in Nuremberg from 1938 to 1945, it is presently exhibited in Vienna. It is said to be the spear used by the Roman soldier Longinus to pierce the side of the deceased Jesus, as mentioned in an Apocrypha (a Gospel not included in the Bible). Some of the authors in this genre are former SS members or avowed anti-Semites such as Wilhelm Landig[26] or Miguel Serrano.[27] They place the SS in the tradition of the descendants of the population of the lost continent Atlantis (Himmler searched for its traces in Tibet). They stylize it as a positive force in a cosmic struggle against the powers of interbreeding, plutocracy, egalitarianism, and internationalism. In this world, Wewelsburg Castle is the SS's "place of initiation." Published in 1991 under the pen name Russell McCloud, the political thriller *Die schwarze Sonne von Tashi Lhunpo* (The Black Sun of Tashi Lhunpo)[28] marked the apex of this type of Wewelsburg Castle mythologization. It contains all the elements of extreme right-wing crypto-historiography. Sympathy for a positive tradition of the SS, however, is presented much more cautiously than in the works of the above-mentioned authors. Wewelsburg Castle becomes the scene of the last battle between the SS as the bearers of the "good" tradition (Tashi Lhunpo is a Tibetan monastery where the "positive secret knowledge" of the ex-Atlanteans was preserved) and the "evil" of the U.N. and the superpowers. The story also mentions – and this is a novelty – the sun wheel intarsia in the northern tower's *Obergruppenführer* Hall as the central symbol of a secret association of former SS members: the "Black Sun." This novel became a bestseller throughout the right-wing scene. The publisher produced a "Thule watch" with the Wewelsburg sun wheel on its face. A full-fledged market for "black sun devotional objects" emerged: T-shirts, scarfs, flags, tablecloths, lamps, among other things, have been decorated with this sign ever since. It also became the symbol of extreme right wing and esoteric music bands, which frequently extol ostensibly mystical experiences connected with Wewelsburg Castle.[29] The structure has repeatedly been exposed to extreme right wing incursions. In 2002, a political occupation of the venue by right-wing extremists was prevented by the Federal Court of Justice, which, as the court of final appeal, prohibited a demonstration by the Initiative of the White Race under the motto "glory and honor to the *Waffen-SS.*"

The crypt
Photograph:
Matthias Groppe, 2010
Kreismuseum Wewelsburg,
Fotoarchiv

The *SS-Obergruppen-führer* Hall
Photograph:
Matthias Groppe, 2010
Kreismuseum Wewelsburg,
Fotoarchiv

The memorial on the
former roll call area of
Niederhagen/Wewelsburg
Concentration Camp
Photograph:
Johannes Büttner, 2011
Kreismuseum Wewelsburg,
Fotoarchiv

Wewelsburg Castle also plays a role in connection with Satanism. In 1982, Michael A. Aquino, founder of the Temple of Set, performed a ritual that went down in the history of elitist Satanism as the "Wewelsburg Working." In contrast, a number of women have provided accounts of Satanist practices and horrific personal experiences, which allegedly took place at the castle.[30] Members of a complex set of esoteric groups, on the other hand, see Wewelsburg Castle as a "place of power."[31] The institutional approach to such a place and such an audience faces a variety of challenges. Already at its opening in 1982, the documentation center was equipped with surveillance cameras. In 2006, new house rules were adopted, which prohibited the wearing of anti-constitutional symbols, clothing brands coded as extreme right-wing, as well as expressions of xenophobic and racist opinion. Both measures have successfully prevented expressions of extreme right-wing views and sentiments on the exhibition premises.

Early on in the process of redesigning the memorial museum it became clear that the rooms in the northern tower should become part of the exhibition tour, and a solution had to be found as to how this could be done. Extensive discussions on the associated conceptual questions were conducted in the planning group, with the interior architects, and at a specially organized 2005 workshop with experts from various academic fields. In the case of the *Obergruppenführer* Hall, considerations included an interior design in the vein of a counter-architecture offsetting its monumental appearance or the Hall's integration into the exhibition's topical canon with a deliberate extension of the exhibition architecture across the "black sun" symbol to "deflect" its possible effect. It was also contemplated whether the exhibition section "Crimes of the SS" should be shown here to create the strongest possible contrast of subject matter and surroundings. Eventually, the realization set in that these attempts were inadequate, born of desperation, and poorly conceived from a didactic viewpoint. In the case of the crypt, the climatic conditions precluded integration into the sequence of exhibition topics. Here, it was debated whether the spatial impression could be transformed through new lighting. In the course of the workshop, the question was raised for the first time whether a reinterpretation of the room or a "refraction" of its alleged impact could be achieved through a reconstruction of the Glahé cycle.

In the end, it was decided against having a contrasting interior design as well as against integration into the sequence of exhibition topics in the case of the *Obergruppenführer* Hall, but in favor of a contemporary adaptation of the Glahé cycle in the crypt.

In both cases, following extensive consultations by the project group and advisory council, the effects of this architecture and its reception history seemed so strong that everything spoke against including the rooms in the sequence of exhibition topics as quasi "normal" exhibition spaces. Consequently, communication strategies were chosen that came down to an account of the building history, an interpretation of the architecture, and an outline of its reception history. In the case of the crypt, this information is presented in the form of two short films on the wall, which, aside from depicting prison labor, include attempts at bringing life to the room through pseudo-Germanic customs and traditions. Due to the, in part, crude reception of the room, however, it was anticipated that visitors could misunderstand these narratives. Thus a "historically legitimized" counterinterpretation of the room was reactivated through the paintings cycle. This was done in a manner, however, that also implied the limits and the historical failure of the cycle as a memorial. The original paintings were not returned to the crypt and are now shown in a separate exhibition room in the guard building. Original-format prints are displayed in the crypt, albeit not in their historical locations on pedestals, but between them and with new lighting.

Regarding the *Obergruppenführer* Hall, it was decided at an early point that the problematic chapter of the history of its influence – the mythologization of the "black sun" – would be told in a separate exhibition area in the context of an examination of the SS past. This opened up the option of focusing on the building's history and on interpretations of its architecture. The central objective, however, was to prevent visitors from moving to the center of the floor ornament soon after entering the room. Observations over the past decades have shown that this visitor behavior was displayed not only by those whose attention had been focused on this symbol prior to entering the hall, as in the case of right-wing extremists, but also by many groups of visitors who seemed to "automatically" gather in the center of the room. This generated an unwelcome correspondence between the authoritarian architecture of the SS and the orientation of visitors. Thus, to achieve a modified perception of the room opportunities needed to be provided for visitors to respond differently. The entire mood had to be changed – in the simplest possible manner. It appeared that a relaxed posture was most effective: "slouching" instead of "standing at attention." This required adding appropriate furniture. Thus, beanbag chairs and stools were arranged around the floor. Document folders were placed on small tables. Two

additional factors contributed to the rapid success of this solution: Once visitors have climbed the many stairs to the room, they are inclined to sit and rest. Furthermore, they look for information that is, in a literal sense, easy to grasp. It is readily available on the tables. The seating is loosely arranged around the room, so that the space's center does not immediately attract attention. It is put into perspective in an unpretentious manner and without overtly didactic overtones. What is more, the beanbag chairs and stools not only invite visitor groups to glean information from the document folders, but also to engage in conversation. The hall thus serves as a communication zone within the exhibition.

The Use of the Camp Grounds in Niederhagen

While rebuilding of Wewelsburg Castle after the war was never politically questioned and soon commenced, the other buildings erected by the SS in both of the other above-outlined areas of the SS's activities underwent various alterations and developments driven by conflicts surrounding Wewelsburg Castle.

Following the dissolution of Niederhagen Concentration Camp in the spring of 1943, the remaining prisoners moved to the workshop barracks of the industrial area on the grounds of the concentration camp. The abandoned barracks of the SS guard units were used as accommodations for ethnic Germans (*Volksdeutsche*) from Eastern Europe by the SS Ethnic German Liaison Main Office (*SS-Stabshauptamt Volksdeutsche Mittelstelle* or VOMI) in the fall of 1943. The "VOMI Camp" was relocated to the former prisoner camp in October 1944.[32] Subsequently, a military preparedness training camp of the Hitler Youth was set up in the SS barracks. Here, adolescents received military training under the command of SS members. They fought until the last days of the war against U.S. troops.[33] Following their liberation in 1945, many ethnic Germans were able to return to their Eastern European homelands; those remaining were distributed among the nearby villages. The barracks camp at Niederhagen served as a "DP camp" (displaced persons camp) from the summer of 1945 to the fall of 1946, where forced laborers from Eastern Europe were accommodated centrally prior to their repatriation.[34] From the fall of 1946, refugees and expellees from the former eastern territories of the German Reich moved into the former concentration camp.[35] Because it had the barracks camp at its disposal, the Wewelsburg community had to take in some one thousand refugees and expellees.[36] In 1951, twenty-six buildings of the former camp still stood. In the mid-1950s, work began to tear down the wooden barracks and replace them with stone houses. Gradually, a small residential and commercial area developed on the grounds. The last barracks were torn down in 1965. Only a few of the solidly constructed buildings of the concentration camp were retained: The gatehouse was converted into a spacious residential and commercial building. The prisoner kitchen and canteen together with part of the adjoining roll call area were legally designated as historic buildings in 1988. Presently, they house a fire station equipment depot and public housing units. In 1958, the SS garages on the former industrial area were taken over by a factory; the crematorium, temporarily used as a residential building, was integrated into a new factory hall. The former laundry is now a barn. These buildings remained as relics of SS buildings on the grounds of the former camp because they could quickly be used for housing and business purposes.

In the late 1980s tempers flared about the use of the not yet redeveloped area of the former roll call area. A citizens' initiative group from the village opposed any reconstruction work and commemorative plaques in the entire area of the village of Wewelsburg. In the end, it was agreed that there would be no rebuilding on the roll call area, which would be cultivated as a grassy field. The layout of the first two barracks' foundations and the former camp road were marked with paving stones. A plaque or symbol of commemoration was not put up. It was only thanks to the initiative of a group of young Wewelsburgers, who had formed the April 2nd Day of Remembrance Work Group (*Arbeitsgruppe Gedenktag 2. April*),[37] that the village population's reservations about a symbol of commemoration at the authentic site were finally overcome at the end of the 1990s. Ultimately, in 2000, a natural stone memorial dedicated to the victims of the dictatorship and shaped like the triangular patch (*Häftlingswinkel*) worn by the concentration camp prisoners was inaugurated on the former roll call area of the Niederhagen/Wewelsburg Concentration Camp.

Traces of SS Buildings in the Village of Wewelsburg

From the mid-1930s, the SS increasingly began to use the village of Wewelsburg as a projection screen for its ideological and architectural plans. In addition to the newly built guard and staff building on the castle forecourt, other buildings were converted or replaced by new ones and are still visible today as structural vestiges of the SS era in Wewelsburg. For example, between 1935 and 1937, SS architect Walter Franzius converted an old, half-timbered farm building, the old Hofstelle Thiele (today's Ottens Hof), into the "National Socialist village community center."[38] A janitor's cottage and the enclosed porch of the private house across the street were integrated into the building decoration that comprised symbols and runes. They are an impressive manifestation of the way in which SS architects visualized their "Blood and Soil" ideology. The ensemble, which was to form the new center of National Socialist-style village life, housed an agricultural girls' school after the war. The ensemble is now a historic landmark, with the former village community center housing an inn.

Hermann Bartels, the SS architect responsible for the gigantomanac conversion plans for the Wewelsburg, had concentration-camp prisoners build a splendid villa (the Führerhaus I, or Villa Bartels) for his use on the Kuhkampsberg from 1939 to 1942. After the war, the building was taken over by the Protestant Church and serves to the present day as a parish hall and church. Between 1940 and 1942, concentration camp prisoners had to construct the "Waldsiedlung" (Forest Development) below Villa Bartels: seven single-family houses for SS members that – refurbished and expanded – are now in private hands. For months, the Waldsiedlung labor detachment was run as one of the feared disciplinary work details. Both Villa Bartels and the Waldsiedlung houses were residential buildings designed to reflect the landscape and promote the SS leaders' programmatic "taking root" on Westphalian soil.[39] In 1940, the SS took over the farmstead of the Marx family, who had traded their ancestral estate for a larger farm in Silesia. Concentration camp prisoners were forced to convert the buildings into a U-shaped complex that subsequently housed the SS Construction Management, which had grown to a staff of more than fifty. In the postwar period, these offices were also used to accommodate refugees and expellees. The church-based refugee organization Catholic East Welfare turned the vacant building into an old-age home (Altenheim St. Josef). For years, it was plagued by unacceptable sanitary conditions because, like the barracks camp, it was not connected to the sewer system.[40] In the early 1970s, the building complex lost its function and was razed.

On the orders of Adolf Haas, commandant of the concentration camp, architect Bartels had concentration camp prisoners build a shooting range in the Oberhagen forest in 1941. The SS used it not only for target practice, but also as the execution site of Soviet prisoners of war and persons held by the Gestapo. The victims also included fifteen forced laborers, who in March 1945 were shot by Gestapo members and buried in a shallow grave at the shooting range. Presumably, the dead forced laborers were fourteen Russians and one Pole who had been arrested in Paderborn for alleged looting. The American military government ordered that their bodies be exhumed by former NSDAP members and interred at the Wewelsburg Parish Graveyard on May 4, 1945. The entire village population between the ages of nine and seventy had to attend the so-called atonement funeral (*Sühnebegräbnis*). The dead were reburied once more in 1961. The Russians lie today in the Soviet Military Cemetery in Stukenbrock/Senne; the Polish forced laborer is buried in the Foreigners' Cemetery, Sennelager. After the war, the shooting range was demolished and filled in. It then served as a garbage dump. The former SS shooting range first became the focus of commemorative work in 1988. Volunteers participating in an international work camp organized by Aktion Sühnezeichen e. V. (Action Reconciliation Service for Peace) cleared the overgrown shooting range. For a few years now, the Kreismuseum Wewelsburg regularly organizes youth work camps to secure the structural remnants of the former shooting range and gradually to uncover it. Since 2008, a plaque has commemorated the history of this place and the victims who were murdered here during the SS era.

The various uses and preservation of former SS buildings in the three outlined areas of activity and the historical site of Wewelsburg, as well as the conflicts surrounding the establishment of a memorial for the victims of SS atrocities render one thing clear: the preservation or destruction of National Socialist buildings is an expression of the development of historical awareness and the result of political decisions.[41] Despite widespread objections and resistance, a responsible-minded, democratic culture of commemoration, remembrance, and learning from history has formed in Wewelsburg over the past sixty years.

1
Karl Hüser, *Wewelsburg 1933–1945. Kult- und Terrorstätte der SS. Eine Dokumentation* (From a series by the Kreismuseum Wewelsburg; 1), Paderborn, 1982, 2nd rev. ed., Paderborn, 1987.

2
Jan Erik Schulte, "Die SS in Wewelsburg: Weltanschauliche Hybris – terroristische Praxis: Auf dem Weg zu einer Gesamtdarstellung," in *Gedenkstättenarbeit und Erinnerungskultur in Ostwestfalen-Lippe. Ein Projektbericht*, Juliane Kerzel (ed.), Paderborn, 2002, pp. 208–220.

3
Regarding the library see: Markus Moors, "'Die SS als geistiger Stoßtrupp?' Dr. Hans-Peter des Coudres, Schulungsleiter der 'SS-Schule Haus Wewelsburg'" 1935–1939, in *Die SS, Himmler und die Wewelsburg*; Jan Erik Schulte (ed.) (From a series by the Kreismuseum Wewelsburg; 7), Paderborn, 2009, pp. 180–195; idem, "Von der 'SS-Schule Haus Wewelsburg' zum 'Kommandostab Reichsführer SS.' Rudi Bergmann und Bernhard Frank zwischen Forschung und Vernichtungskrieg," ibid., pp. 227–241; Beate Herring, "Wilhelm Jordan. Der Archäologe auf der Wewelsburg," ibid., pp. 196–208; Frank Huismann, "Wilhelm Jordan. Als Wissenschaftler im besetzten Osten," ibid., pp. 209–226.

4
Speech from November 8, 1938, in Bradley F. Smith, Agnes F. Peterson (ed.), *Heinrich Himmler. Geheimreden 1933–1945*, Munich, 1974, p. 26.

5
Markus Moors, "Das 'Reichshaus der SS-Gruppenführer.' Himmlers Pläne und Absichten in Wewelsburg," in *Die SS, Himmler und die Wewelsburg*, Jan Erik Schulte (ed.), (as in note 3), pp. 161–179.

6
Dina van Faassen, "Himmlers Wewelsburger Gemäldesammlung," in *Die SS, Himmler und die Wewelsburg*, Jan Erik Schulte (ed.), (as in note 3), pp. 242–272.

7
Peter Longerich, *Heinrich Himmler. Biographie*, Munich, 2008, p. 305.

8
Jan Erik Schulte, *Himmlers Wewelsburg und der Rassenkrieg. Eine historische Ortsbestimmung*, in *Die SS, Himmler und die Wewelsburg, idem*, (as in note 3), pp. 3–22.

9
Kirsten John[-Stucke], *"Mein Vater wird gesucht …" Häftlinge des Konzentrationslagers in Wewelsburg* (Historical series by the Kreismuseum Wewelsburg; 2), 4th ed., Essen, 2004.

10
Kirsten John-Stucke, "Die Zeugen Jehovas im Konzentrationslager in Wewelsburg und ihre Geheimdruckerei," in *Die SS, Himmler und die Wewelsburg*, Jan Erik Schulte (ed.), (as in note 3), pp. 337–354.

11
Andreas Neuwöhner, "Radikalisierung und Expansion. Der Wandel der Häftlingsgesellschaft im Jahr 1942: Zwangsarbeiter aus Osteuropa als neue Häftlingsgruppe im KZ Niederhagen-Wewelsburg," in *Die SS, Himmler und die Wewelsburg*, Jan Erik Schulte (ed.), pp. 355–378.

12
Cf. Markus Moors, "Das 'Reichshaus der SS-Gruppenführer,'" in *Die SS, Himmler und die Wewelsburg*, Jan Erik Schulte (ds.), (as in note 3), pp. 161–179.

13
Regarding the connection between development decisions and communication cf. Alexander C. T. Geppert, Uffa Jensen, and Jörn Weinhold (eds.), *Ortsgespräche. Raum und Kommunikation im 19. und 20. Jahrhundert*, Bielefeld, 2005.

14
Cf. Wulff E. Brebeck, "400 Jahre Schloss Wewelsburg – Kultureller Aufbruch in die Gegenwart," in *400 Jahre Wewelsburg – Rückblick und Ausblick*, Förderverein Kreismuseum Wewelsburg (ed.), Paderborn, 2010, pp. 12–19.

15
Wulff E. Brebeck, *Die Wewelsburg – Geschichte und Bauwerk im Überblick*, 2nd ed., Munich/Berlin, 2009, p. 31 ff.

16
Landesamt für Agrarverordnung, Arch. Nr. 302, Aufsichtsakte Bl. 58, quoted after Karl Hüser, *Wewelsburg 1933–1945* (as in note 1), p. 62 f.

17
Angelika Gausmann, Iris Schäferjohann-Bursian, "Das vergessene Mahnmal Josef Glahés – Kunst als Mittel der Auseinandersetzung mit dem Nationalsozialismus im Bürener Land (1949–1974)" in *Westfalen* 71/1993, pp. 121–138.

18
Meeting minutes of the Society for the Preservation of Wewelsburg Castle, June 29, 1949, Kreismuseum Wewelsburg, AS. 18/3/1.

19
Wulff E. Brebeck, "Erhaltung oder Zerstörung von NS-Bauten? Historisches Bewusstsein und politische Prozesse, dargestellt am Beispiel der SS-Kult- und Terrorstätte Wewelsburg," in *Denkmalpflege und Architektur in Westfalen 1933–1945*, Edeltraud Klüting (eds.), Münster, 1995, p. 130; cf. Wulff E. Brebeck, "Von langer Dauer. Zum Streit um eine Mahnmal für die NS-Opfer in Wewelsburg seit 1945," in *Dörfliche Gesellschaft und ländliche Siedlung. Lippe und das Hochstift Paderborn in überregionaler Perspektive*, Uta Halle et al. (eds.), (From a series by the Kreismuseum Wewelsburg; 5), Bielefeld, 2001, p. 300 ff.

20
Cf. Wulff E. Brebeck, *Das Historische Museum des Hochstifts Paderborn. Geschichte – Ausbau – Konzeption*, Paderborn, 2001.

21
Wulff E. Brebeck, *Die Wewelsburg*, (as in note 15), pp. 76–78.

22
Cf. Dorothee Renner, *Die durchbrochenen Zierscheiben der Merowingerzeit*, Mainz 1970, p. 72. Cf. also Rüdiger Sünner: *Schwarze Sonne. Entfesselung und Missbrauch der Mythen im Nationalsozialismus und rechter Esoterik*, 2nd ed., Freiburg im Breisgau, 1999, p. 148.

23
Cf. the appearance of *Burgwart* (castle manager) Kemper on a TV show by Angela Joschko and Peter Milger: "Den Lebenden zur Mahnung," part 1, aired by Hessischer Rundfunk (Hessian Broadcasting) on January 29, 1978.

24
Cf., for instance, Heinz Höhne, *Der Orden unter dem Totenkopf. Die Geschichte der SS*, Gütersloh, 1967, p. 141 ff. Cf. also, in particular, Karl Hüser, *Wewelsburg 1933–1945*, (as in note 1), p. 6 f.

25
Trevor Ravenscroft, *Der Speer des Schicksals. Die Geschichte der Heiligen Lanze*, Munich, 1988.

26
Wilhelm Landig, *Götzen gegen Thule. Ein Roman voller Wirklichkeiten*, Hanover, 1971; idem, *Wolfszeit um Thule*, Vienna, 1980; idem, *Rebellen für Thule. Das Erbe von Atlantis*, Vienna, 1991.

27
Miguel Serrano, *Das Goldene Band. Esoterischer Hitlerismus*, Wetter, 1987.

28
Russel McCloud, *Die schwarze Sonne von Tashi Lhunpo*, novel, 4th ed., Engerda, 1999.

29
Wulff E. Brebeck, *Die Wewelsburg*, (as in note 15), p. 92 f.

30
"Höllenleben. Eine multiple Persönlichkeit auf Spurensuche," a documentary film by Liz Wiskerstrauch (director) p.p. NDR/ARD, first broadcast December 2001, part 2, 2003.

31
For the full spectrum of the meaning of Wewelsburg Castle in its various depictions cf. Daniela Siepe, "Die Rolle der Wewelsburg in der phantastischen Literatur, in Esoterik und Rechtsextremismus nach 1945," in *Die SS, Himmler und die Wewelsburg*, Jan Erik Schulte (ed.), (as in note 3), pp. 488–510.

32
See Norbert Ellermann, "Erfahrungen im Umsiedlungslager der Volksdeutschen Mittelstelle in Wewelsburg von 1943–1945," in *Himmler, Wewelsburg und die SS*, Jan Erik Schulte (ed.), (as in note 3), pp. 196–313.

33
See Norbert Ellermann, "Zur Erforschung der Geschichte des früheren Konzentrationslagers Niederhagen von 1943–1946," in *Gedenkstättenarbeit und Erinnerungskultur in Ostwestfalen-Lippe. Ein Projektbericht*, Juliane Kerzel (ed.), Paderborn, 2002, pp. 268–272.

34
See Norbert Ellermann, *Zur Erforschung der Geschichte des früheren Konzentrationslagers* (as in note 33), p. 272 ff.

35
For in-depth information on the situation of refugees in the village of Wewelsburg see Andreas Lüttig, *Fremde im Dorf. Flüchtlingsintegration im westfälischen Wewelsburg 1945–1958* (Historical series by the Kreismuseum Wewelsburg; 1), Essen, 1993.

36
Regarding the conflict between the community of Wewelsburg and the State of North Rhine-Westphalia over the complicated question of ownership of the camp see Wulff E. Brebeck, Karl Hüser, and Kirsten John-Stucke, *1933–1945. SS-Größenwahn und KZ-Terror*, Münster, 2007, p. 58 f.

37
Sonja Büttner, "Die Arbeitsgruppe 'Gedenktag 2. April' in Wewelsburg," in *Gedenkstättenrundbrief* 86/1998, pp. 21–24.

38
Walter Franzius, "Ein westfälisches Dorfgemeinschaftshaus," in *Heimat und Reich* 5/1938, pp. 442–448; idem, "Schatzkammer Westfalen. Sinnbilder in alter und neuer Volkskunst," in *Heimat und Reich* 6/1939, pp. 51–58.

39
Wulff E. Brebeck, "Erhaltung oder Zerstörung von NS-Bauten?", (as in note 19), p. 123.

40
Andreas Lüttig, *Fremde im Dorf* (as in note 35), p. 125.

41
Wulff E. Brebeck, "Erhaltung oder Zerstörung von NS-Bauten?" (as in note 19), p. 134.

Origins, Conceptual Principles, and Structure of the Exhibition "Ideology and Terror of the SS"

Kirsten John-Stucke

The Origins and Development of the Wewelsburg 1933–1945 Memorial Museum

In April 2010 the Wewelsburg 1933–1945 Memorial Museum opened with its permanent contemporary-history exhibition "Ideology and Terror of the SS," replacing the documentation center and memorial, Wewelsburg 1933–1945. Cult and Terror Site of the SS, in existence since March 1982. In the wake of a long and controversial public debate on how to deal with the SS past in Wewelsburg, the Paderborn district assembly had decided in the late 1970s in favor of establishing a documentation center "as a cautionary message for the living and a commemoration of the victims of Niederhagen Concentration Camp."[1] University of Paderborn Professor Karl Hüser, who had been tasked with the center's basic research, presented his findings in the exhibition in the former SS guard building and an extensive companion volume.[2] Both the conflict-ridden history of its origins and the factual, documentary character of the exhibition were typical of the public debate in the 1980s about the sites of National Socialist crimes.[3] The exhibition consisted of wall displays with numerous texts, documents, and photographs, complemented by just a few artifacts in individual showcases.[4] The documents were intended to show that the events had actually occurred in Wewelsburg as described. With the opening of the documentation center, the Kreismuseum Wewelsburg in the role of a memorial initiated its intensive educational work with adolescent and adult visitors.[5] Wewelsburg's population gradually overcame its initial widespread reticence, with individuals increasingly coming forward to provide personal accounts of their experiences in the National Socialist era. For these visitors, the exhibition became the site of an intensive examination of their own history.[6] The documentation center took on the function of a memorial, even though the exhibition space was located outside the grounds of the former concentration camp, in a place entirely associated with the perpetrators. First unveiled in 1992, a plaque with the names of 1,285 documented concentration camp victims was welcomed by many visitors as a mutual public place of commemoration in the otherwise fact-laden exhibition. The center's staff interpreted their workplace as an "active" or "working" memorial site and set themselves apart from the old-school image of the memorial as a quiet place of ritualized commemoration.[7] They sought to establish contact with survivors of the concentration camp and the families of victims. In 1992, a first meeting of survivors was held in Wewelsburg. The memories of former prisoners were documented and recorded, personal documents and photographs collected, and conversations between contemporary witnesses and youth as well as with village residents were organized.[8] In addition to keeping in touch with survivors and engaging in historical and political educational activity, which in recent years has also been informed by aspects of human-rights education and the topics of right-wing extremism and civil courage,[9] the documentation center and memorial site's ongoing tasks also included academic research.[10]

In the 1990s, the permanent exhibition, particularly the section on the concentration camp, was expanded to reflect the current state of research. The film room was moved out of the exhibition and the space dedicated to a museum display. Initially this exhibit showed the "desk of chief architect Hermann Bartels" with a "view of the quarry," an arrangement that has led to great controversy even among the staff itself. Only when the desk was subsequently juxtaposed with a pile of stones as a perceptible representation of prisoner labor and accompanied by quotes from perpetrators and victims did a successful contextualization of the displayed objects result. The introduction of the exhibit in the mid-1990s corresponded to the general trend towards the "auratic" at memorial sites. Without reconstructing the historical reality, the symbolic testimony – the "aura" of authentic objects – was to be singled out as a vehicle of communication.[11]

In the late 1990s, it became apparent that the permanent exhibition needed to be reconceived. An accelerated decline in visitor numbers made clear that the exhibition's text-heavy, austere presentation was no longer in step with the public's expectations. There were requests for the use of new media in the form of audio stations and audiovisual media, with the exhibition also being expanded to include additional topics. The experience of the past years had shown that visitors were primarily interested in the ideological aspects of the SS and the subjective experiences of the concentration camp prisoners. Participation in the "ExpoInitiative East Westphalia-Lippe," a regional cultural sponsorship program launched by the state government, made it possible to draw up the first concrete plans for a reconception of the exhibition. On the occasion of the Expo 2000 world's fair in Hanover, the state of North Rhine-Westphalia sponsored regional cultural projects focused, among other things, on the research and representation of subjects related to National Socialism. Beginning in 2000, the District of Paderborn together with the district of Gütersloh conducted the two-year "Planning Workshop on the Culture of Memory," which undertook initial research on previously little-scrutinized subjects: the understanding of art and culture in the SS, the organization's

occult and ideological origins, biographies of SS perpetrators, and the use of the concentration camp grounds after 1943.[12] At the end of the Planning Workshop, the project's academic advisory committee[13] made specific recommendations for the further development of the revised exhibition concept. It concluded that Wewelsburg Castle was "*the* historic site for an exemplary, in other words, unique exhibition on the subject of the SS" and recommended that the Kreismuseum Wewelsburg apply to the state of North Rhine-Westphalia and the federal government for project funding.[14]

On the basis of the considerations developed to date by the Planning Workshop, the Kreismuseum Wewelsburg submitted a grant application to the federal government and the state of North Rhine-Westphalia in October 2002[15] and received principal approval in summer 2003. The reconception was embedded in a museum development plan for the Kreismuseum, which provided for the former SS guard building to be used exclusively as an exhibition space. To this end, two new buildings needed to be constructed first: a low storage building along the rear of the former guard building as well as an administration building (with an area for special exhibitions) on the foundations of the former SS staff building. The workshops, storage space, and museum administration could subsequently be moved out of the guard building. Historical research was begun by an interdisciplinary project group, which presented its findings to the public at a June 2005 academic conference accompanied by workshop discussions.[16] Starting in October 2005, the conceptual considerations based on the historical research findings were discussed with representatives of the panel of experts that advises the Federal Commissioner for Culture and the Media, the competent federal authority. In the spring of 2006, the District of Paderborn additionally appointed an academic advisory council, which comprised representatives from different universities as well as museum and memorial site professionals.[17] In the fall of 2006, experts from various fields together with members of the academic advisory council and the project group participated in a workshop that considered the presentation of objects from the lifeworld of the SS and how to deal with the rooms in the northern tower of Wewelsburg Castle that had been converted during the SS period. A revised concept was presented on the basis of these deliberations and received final approval from the office of the Federal Commissioner for Culture and the Media in December 2007. In the following two and a half years a partially reconstituted project team working together with the academic advisory committee implemented the exhibition concept

in the converted space of the guard building. The exhibition design had already been entrusted to the Hanover-based Ikon planning office, in 2005, and the graphic design was developed by Atelier Weidner/Händle in Stuttgart. On April 15, 2010, the new exhibition, "Ideology and Terror of the SS," opened in the presence of three survivors of Niederhagen Concentration Camp, numerous relatives of former concentration camp prisoners, Minister of State and Federal Commissioner for Culture and the Media, Bernd Neumann, the then President of the Central Council of Jews in Germany, Dr. Charlotte Knobloch, and the President of the Central Council of German Sinti and Roma, Romani Rose. Those attending also included several diplomatic representatives and honored guests from political life as well as professionals from museums and memorial sites. The new educational section (with audio visual projection space, seminar rooms, and computer work stations) of the Memorial Museum is located on the top floor; the terrace floor houses a visitor restaurant. The costs of the redesign, including all structural measures, amounted to seven million euros and were covered by funds provided by the federal government, the State of North Rhine-Westphalia (Ministry of Building and Transport and State Agency for Civic Education), the Regional Association of Westphalia-Lippe, and the District of Paderborn.

The Concept Fundamentals

The title of the new permanent historical exhibition, "Ideology and Terror of the SS," points to its broad thematic scope. The Protection Squadron (*Schutzstaffel*), or SS, is documented in its multiplicity of forms and increasingly radicalizing development, from its beginnings to the collapse of the National Socialist regime in 1945. The exhibition documents numerous aspects of the SS, including its organization and structure, its ideological origins, its concept of art and culture, and its notions of religion and history. The crimes of the SS cannot be viewed separately from its racist and destructive worldview. Aside from the extensive examination of SS crimes in regard to their progressively worsening nature, a main focus is on the micro level of developments in the concentration camp in Wewelsburg, taking as a point of departure the local events in Wewelsburg, the site of a Renaissance castle that was intended to become a central meeting place for Himmler's SS. The exhibition is thus also a memorial to the victims of SS violence in Wewelsburg and continues to pursue the main goals of the earlier documentation from 1982. As the only concentration camp memorial site in North Rhine-Westphalia, the exhibition seeks to inform and educate about the criminal system of National Socialist concentration camps and the specific development of Nieder-hagen Concentration Camp and its prisoner society. The coming to terms with the SS past and the commemoration of the victims are addressed at the end of the exhibition, with local events and conflicts in Wewelsburg serving as a paradigm for the overall development in the Federal Republic of Germany.

The Historical Site

The historical site of Wewelsburg proves to be particularly suited for an exhibition with this mission.[18] Wewelsburg ranks among the places that Volkhard Knigge referred to as "places of negative commemoration." These are sites of historic crimes or places of suffering from the point of view of a society comprised mainly of perpetrators, supporters, and the indifferent. Such locations call up the "memory of and confrontation with crimes committed, crimes to answer for, rather than those suffered."[19] A culture of history and memory is inconceivable without spatial points of reference. In a time when mass media, electronic data communication, and virtual networks seem to be bringing places and events around the world closer together, people search for precisely this type of fixed reference point. The physical visit to an "authentic" historical site is experienced as extraordinary, especially when visitors inform themselves beforehand using the virtual Internet presentations. At these "original" locations, memory – and thus the past – become tangible and perceptible. This is also true for places of negative commemoration.[20] The historical place of Wewelsburg has, therefore, been more strongly integrated into both the exhibition concept and the didactic communication. Information on the few surviving structures of the SS around the village is available to visitors on a video-guided tour of these sites that reveals and explains the significance of these building remnants. The new exhibition was intentionally set up on the basement floors of the preservation-listed former SS guard building because here, in particular, one can detect architectural traces of the SS project that are characteristic of the organization's ways of thinking and acting.[21]

Diversity of Perspective

Chronology is the characteristic organizational element of collections in historical museums.[22] The Wewelsburg exhibition, too, largely generally follows an a sequential narrative, beginning with the founding of the SS in the 1920s and ending with the establishment of a memorial in 2000 symbolizing remembrance of the victims of SS violence in Wewelsburg. The narrative does not progress in a strictly linear fashion, but is divided into individual exhibition themes presented in a fashion that both documents and reasons.[23] These sections are presented from different points of view. The escape of a concentration camp prisoner, for example, is told first from the perspective of the prisoner, then from the viewpoint of the SS man responsible for the manhunt, and finally through the eyes of a farm boy on whose farm the SS captured the escaped prisoner. This approach seeks to emphasize the fragmentary nature of transmitted history and is informed by the current discussion in museum circles asserting that the "grand narratives" (Jean-Francois Lyotard) have failed in the "second modernity" and been superseded by a wide range of discourses, rendering the hermetic interpretations found in museums obsolete in the process.[24] The openness of historical developments and their relation to universal values, such as self-determination and human rights, conforms to the prevalent outlook of "reflexive modernization." Attention is directed towards the micro level, diversity of experience, and personal perspectives. The biographical approach and presentation of survivors' subjective recollections as commemorative elements in the Wewelsburg exhibition support the self-reflexive processes of individualization,[25] with the biographical method demonstrating the principle of multiperspectivity particularly well. Presenting the triad of SS staff, concentration camp prisoners, and villagers on the level of local Wewelsburg history reveals the wide range of perceptions of the SS and of National Socialism as a whole. The exhibition tour initially focuses primarily on the biographies of SS men with their diverse personal backgrounds, processes of socialization, and ambitions. The exhibition subsequently shifts its attention to the former concentration camp prisoners, their lives prior to their imprisonment, the grounds for their arrest, their camp experiences, and their lives after their incarceration. In parallel, it documents the village population's perceptions of SS activities and the presence of the camp in Wewelsburg.[26] The different biographical approaches make it clear that there is not one single history, but rather one composed of diverse remembered narratives that can be experienced from different angles.[27]

Original Objects

An important criterion of the "Ideology and Terror of the SS" exhibition is the presentation of authentic exhibits. The documentation center and memorial site initiated in 1982 showed hardly any such objects. Twenty-eight years later the character of the presentation has changed considerably, with the new exhibition consistently following a museum-style presentation. Concentration camp memorials are increasingly developing into contemporary history museums,[28] recognizing the need to collect and preserve original objects for posterity, while not neglecting their humanitarian tasks.[29] The memorial's integration into the Kreismuseum Wewelsburg meant that the principles of museum practice were consistently applied at the Wewelsburg memorial, assuring that the collection and proper preservation of original objects from the concentration camp grounds and the perpetrators' living environment commenced at an early stage. The latter items are mostly objects from SS members' personal estates, such as ceremonial swords, documents, photographs, or diaries – including one penned by chief castle administrator Manfred von Knobelsdorff – and from the SS castle administration's furnishings for Wewelsburg Castle, such as furniture, lamps, dinnerware, and silver cutlery. The museum collection also comprises ideologically significant art, such as drawings, paintings, and SS jewelry, as well as porcelain and ceramics from the SS-owned Allach Porcelain Manufactory (Porzellanmanufaktur Allach), from which Himmler had a collection of samples created at Wewelsburg. The storage at the castle also held weapons, parts of uniforms, and everyday objects from life under National Socialism and from mass propaganda, including badges of the Winter Relief Agency (*Winterhilfswerk*), flags, "people's radios" (*Volksempfänger*), and books.[30]

Some of the contemporary objects entered the collection when the District Museum of Local History reopened in 1950. These were items left behind at Wewelsburg Castle following its attempted demolition and the flight of the SS castle administration. Several items of SS furnishings, however, have only been given to the Kreismuseum in recent years. For the most part, these were objects that residents of the village or the region had taken following the destruction of the castle and kept in their homes for decades. Many objects were acquired at auctions or from dealers in recent years in connection with the exhibition redesign. This includes, among others, Heinrich Himmler's personal appointment calendar from 1940, which lists a visit by Albert Speer in Wewelsburg in March of that year. Since the reopening of the exhibition, both donations from private individuals and offers from dealers regarding items of importance to the exhibition have increased. The significance of the Kreismuseum Wewelsburg

Display units showing biographies of members of the Wewelsburg SS castle administration in the first exhibition room
Photograph: Matthias Groppe, 2010
Kreismuseum Wewelsburg, Fotoarchiv

as a secure repository for original objects from the SS environment or the everyday world of National Socialism appears to have increased. The history of the collection containing objects from the concentration camp in Wewelsburg is an altogether different story. A wealth of original objects similar to the one left behind by the perpetrator society could never emerge from this other world of deprivation and terror. Due to the later use of the concentration camp barracks as a resettlement camp (*Volksdeutsche Mittelstelle*, Ethnic German Liaison Office), displaced persons (DP) camp, and refugee camp, only a small number of original objects from the period of the concentration camp survived on site, and it is difficult to determine whether later discoveries on the premises really date from the time of the concentration camp. Thus, the orgin of small items, such as textile, shoe, and rubber remnants, buttons, and fragments of brushes found in a collapsed cesspit on the former grounds of the camp in 2002 could not be assigned to a specific camp. In 2005, wall segments of a former barracks in Niederhagen Concentration Camp were salvaged from a farm in the neighboring village, preserved, and put into storage. They had been dismantled in the 1960s on the former camp grounds and served as a chicken coop for decades. For the exhibition, two segments were restored. In order to illustrate the successive functions the building served, part of an exterior wall is now presented in the section dedicated to the history of the concentration camp, while part of an interior wall – complete with remnants of wall paper – points to the structure's postwar use as a refugee barracks. The bundle of prisoners' clothes donated to the memorial in 2007 deserves special attention. Following his liberation, a member of the "remaining detachment" took home twelve items of winter and summer clothing and stowed them away. Owing to the still legible prisoner numbers it was possible to irrefutably identify which members of the Wewelsburg remaining work detachment the items belonged to.[31] In addition to the original documents, letters from the concentration camp are of particularly great significance in the new exhibition, because they were often the only contact the prisoners had with the world outside for years. As memorials have increasingly taken on the character of museums, a stronger focus on material culture has ensued. The importance of originality and authenticity of objects has long been a point of discussion in museums.[32] It was deemed important that the new Wewelsburg exhibition forego replicas and present original objects, to avoid creating distorted or fictional impressions.[33] The earlier exhibition, for example, contained a replica of a flogging table, and its effect on visitors proved controversial. The new exhibition now documents violence and punishment at the concentration camp by showing original prisoner index cards, which list the reasons for punishments, as well as their type and severity. The photograph of a historical flogging table in a drawer has replaced the former three-dimensional reproduction.

An aura of authenticity is attributed to the original objects,[34] which invests them with a special power of persuasion within the sphere of sensory perception. This raises the question of how to treat original objects in the Wewelsburg exhibition. Is a multilayer decryption of complex structures of meaning using a contextualization of original objects necessary to reveal their historical background,[35] or should the genuine "aesthetic language" of authentic objects be brought to bear without interpretation and commentary, so as not to weaken their effect?[36]

Presentation Strategies

If we proceed from the thesis that exhibitions are not only places of experience or learning but also always sensory spaces to be perceived individually, an exhibition concept must also take into consideration context creation, the neighboring objects, and the means of presentation.[37] This task resulted, in particular, because the new exhibition required the increased presentation of realia from the SS realm of experience together with objects from the living environment of the victims. The majority of these realia are ideologically charged, "affirmative" objects. In this context, the term is used to denote original objects that affirm and endorse National Socialism and, specifically, the worldview of the SS. The great importance of a proper presentation of affirmative objects was recognized at the start of the exhibition redesign process. A "workshop exhibition" held within the framework of the Planning Workshop on the Culture of Memory showed initial trial presentations intended to clarify the approach being sought for dealing with SS artifacts.[38] The possible effect and appeal of these artifacts, which were very important for community building within the SS, and the appropriate manner of presenting these artifacts was also vigorously debated within the academic project group on the exhibition's redesign and discussed at a workshop. The exhibition organizers and specialists from different fields agreed that the objects should be exhibited in a bid to inform the public about the ideology of the SS and to demystify the objects. At the same time, it was deemed necessary that affirmative objects not be shown without comment and that the educational intent of the exhibition organizers be made clear.[39] A responsible contextualization would be needed to help prevent not only fetishization, but also a naive dehistoricization

The display units in Room 3 resemble storage cabinets
Photograph:
Matthias Groppe, 2010
Kreismuseum Wewelsburg,
Fotoarchiv

Clothes of concentration camp prisoners in Room 12 of the exhibition
Photograph:
Matthias Groppe, 2010
Kreismuseum Wewelsburg,
Fotoarchiv

of the objects.[40] It was, therefore, necessary to develop responsible presentation strategies that considered the original objects as well as their interplay with neighboring objects and their position in the room.

The Principle of Storage Facility Arrangement

The showcases are integrated into plain exhibition display units, which are designed to resemble storeroom cabinets and are covered with panels in different shades of white. The functional, neutral storage in the display cases is intended to strip the objects of any hint of a supposed "magic of the mysterious." The display units of various sizes are designed in the style of a modular system. They can generally be viewed from several sides, thus allowing the objects to be viewed from different angles: there is no fixed, preconceived view of the exhibits, just as there is no predefined perspective on the history of the SS. Silver jewelry, such as that adorned with runes, as well as original documents and original photographs were placed on light gray, acid-free cardboard. It was important not to highlight them with accent lighting. The "genuine" death's head ring (*Totenkopfring*) is shown together with a fake one in a wall-mounted display cabinet without any accentuation, giving it the appearance of an unspectacular small silver ring. The ideological and political meaning it formerly held for the SS only becomes apparent through additional documents on exhibit and the labels on the display case glass or in the drawers.

The Principle of Obscuring but not Concealing

The SS uniforms or pieces of Wewelsburg furniture with swastika emblems shown in the display cases are partially obscured by frosted screens affixed to the glass in order to disrupt any potential fascination they might possess. The partial covering of display cases hinders an unobstructed view of the artifacts. This method of obscured presentation is particularly obvious in the hanging of an oil painting depicting Oswald Pohl, head of the SS Economic and Administrative Main Office, as a medieval knight in a splendid uniform. Instead of allowing a full view of the painting in a slightly elevated position where it would achieve its intended effect, it can today only be seen from the side through the glass of a display case. The image can now neither fascinate nor impress. All artifacts are kept inside depot-style display cases, and this also applies to large-format objects such as chairs or floor candle sticks. It was calculated that these could not be viewed in their entirety, but that they would perhaps be covered in part with a blind.

The Principle of Massification

Several items that were mass-produced as National Socialist everyday objects, such as the badges of the Winter Relief Agency, are exhibited in large quantities and presented in acid-free archival cardboard boxes. They do not appear as individual objects of value but in the way they were conceived under National Socialism – as mass produced propaganda materials, which now are in storage, as if in a depot.

The Principle of Contrast

A portrayal of the SS worldview was sought that presented not only the organization's self-promoted claim, but also everyday reality. The intended role of women as mothers within the SS community of kin is illustrated by a porcelain figure from the Allach Porcelain Manufactory that shows a vigorous figure of a mother with two small sons. The figure draws attention to the SS's ideological concept of life. Contrasting this image, the reproduction of a statistical analysis of the birth rate of SS families inscribed on the glass of the display case highlights a reality in the Third Reich: compared to other families in National Socialist Germany, the birth rate in SS families was below average.

The Principle of Responsible Contextualization

This measure requires that objects be displayed with documents and photos to prevent a glorification of ideologically charged objects. The presentation of the Yule Lantern (*Julleuchter*) illustrates this approach: Heinrich Himmler made gifts of these ceramic candle holders with runes to married SS men. The candle was lit at the Yuletide (*Julfest*), the celebration to replace the Christian one of Christmas. It thus epitomizes the creation of an ersatz religion. The exhibition places the prescribed use of the candlesticks in the context of their production. That is, they were first produced by the SS-owned Allach Porcelain Manufactory and later by prisoners in the brickworks of Neuengamme Concentration Camp. The seemingly harmless candlestick is thus seen in the context of SS atrocities – in this case the exploitation of concentration camp prisoners. The presentation of all topics and objects takes into account the genuinely criminal character of the SS.

In contrast to the fact-oriented presentation of affirmative objects from the SS environment, original artifacts from the concentration camp were deliberately exhibited in a manner that initially lets the "language of the aesthetics" of original objects affect exhibition visitors. Only with a second look do they become aware of the object descriptions, which are not attached to the display glasses but to their frames. The display case captions do not obscure the objects, with the storage-style arrangement being consciously abandoned. The artifacts are shown in wall displays that surround and protect them. Warm accent light distinguishes individual items. This lighting extends to the document drawers as well, where original letters from the concentration camp and the original printed pamphlets of the remaining detachment are presented in dark mats.

Some objects are presented separately, for emphasis, in individual display cases, including the original record created illegally by a Jehovah's Witness and the "Russian boxes" (*Russenkästchen*) that Soviet forced laborers gave as a token of gratitude or in exchange for additional food. The display of these artifacts is complemented by additional audio stations where contemporary eyewitnesses relate the history of the objects.

The Transition from Communicative to Cultural Memory

Within the collective memory of National Socialism, an inexorable transition is occurring. Jan Assmann developed in this regard the thesis that with the death of the last contemporary witnesses, experiential knowledge will transition from communicative memory of contemporary witnesses – that is, those who experienced events personally – to the cultural memory of society. In the early 1990s, he anticipated that "what today is still living memory … will be communicated tomorrow only through media."[41] As a consequence of this shift in the collective memory, the new exhibition uses more media presentations of interviews with witnesses of the times: in the past, it was in personal conversations conducted by memorial staff with survivors and visitor groups as part of the pedagogical work, that recollections from autobiographical memory of the witnesses were compiled anew every time. What visitors perceive today are excerpts compiled by the memorial staff from media recordings of witness accounts that have already become a part of cultural memory.

Conversations with contemporary witnesses have been conducted since the inception of the documentation center and memorial museum in 1982. This includes interviews with concentration camp victims and their relatives, inmates of the neighboring National Socialist camps and subsequent refugee camp, villagers who lived in Wewelsburg during the war, persons who worked for the SS, and descendants of SS members. There are interviews with 21 concentration camp survivors that could be used in the exhibition. They were conducted with survivors from Germany, Austria, Belgium, Poland, Russia, Ukraine, and the United States who were incarcerated as political prisoners and Jehovah's Witnesses.[42] Most conversations were structured as biographical interviews and recorded during the gathering of survivors at Wewelsburg. With some of these witnesses, two or more conversations were conducted over a longer period of time.[43]

As in the case of the three-dimensional original artifacts, the selected oral history sources[44] are taken seriously in the exhibition and presented, as much as possible, in their "original" form. The excerpts of filmed conversations with foreign survivors are not dubbed in German but are augmented with translated subtitles. Transitions of topic between the interview excerpts are communicated with captions. Longer passages of biographical interviews with survivors of Niederhagen Concentration Camp are available at the exhibition's thematic transition from the end of the SS to the postwar period. Under the title "The Survivors Tell Their Stories," the victims are given space to convey their own personal

interpretation of their memories. In this section it was deemed important that survivors no longer be presented as victims but as human beings who have regained their freedom and dignity. The interview excerpts do not serve to clarify historical facts, but they can help to better understand events from the perspective of concentration camp victims. This insight guided the design of the room dedicated to prisoners' experiences: the personal perceptions of individuals – their subjective memories – are at the center of their testimony.[45] At an audio station, visitors can listen to statements by survivors on different aspects of life at the camp. Visitors gain insight into the camp world via the memories of former concentration camp prisoners, memories that are linked to selected original artifacts from the world of the camp, for example a barracks wall. Many years after the war, the smell of a Henkel brand glue reminded a former concentration camp prisoner from Ukraine of the hunger he had to suffer at Niederhagen Concentration Camp: fellow prisoners in his labor detachment had sniffed this glue to overcome their constant hunger. He donated a tube of the glue, which is now marketed under the name "Moment" in Ukraine, to the Memorial Museum. Survivors talk about other aspects of camp life, such as illness and death, without connection to specific artifacts.

The victims of the persecutory apparatus of the SS and contemporary witnesses from the village have the chance to speak at other thematic audio stations located at central locations throughout the exhibition, for instance, about the conditions at the resettlement camp, or about the end of the war.

Audio documents of quotes by SS members are not included in the exhibition. The domain of the spoken word is withheld from them for two reasons. For one thing, former SS members themselves were not prepared to participate in contemporary-witness conversations, and for another, original recordings of speeches by Himmler or other prominent SS figures were deliberately done without. The focus of the exhibition's depiction of the perpetrators is to be found in original artifacts and documents, while the perspective of oral history sources plays an important part in portraying the victims – precisely because it was a lack of documents that made research on the history of the concentration camps and their inmates so difficult. Neither relics nor documents of the camp administration can represent the personal views of victims. Documents written or censored by the perpetrators distort our view of events. For instance, the cause of prisoner deaths given on death certificates was frequently falsified to play down the conditions in the camp or to avoid legal consequences. It is also impossible to infer from SS documents any evidence on the internal structure of prisoner groups or the relationships among inmates. Even the evidentiary value of letters by concentration camp prisoners is limited because of SS censorship. Thus, the perspective of survivors plays an ever-greater role in research on the concentration camps. For this reason, the new exhibition not only draws on and presents the few extant written records, diaries, and accounts by survivors, but also places stronger emphasis on verbal accounts and conversations with witnesses of the events.

Visitors' Habits of Perception

The historical awareness of future generations of visitors to museums and memorial sites is shaped by the processes and radical changes society has undergone in connection with a second modernity.[46] Faced with the demand to create his or her own identity reflexively, to construct a subjective identity,[47] individuals are increasingly called upon to decide for themselves in ever more spheres of life how to shape their lives and which stand to take with respect to society, culture, and history. They are faced with a "patchwork of interpretations, views, and divergent attributions of meaning"[48] that they must choose from. The design of the new exhibition seeks to do justice to these habits of perception and calls for visitors to engage in self-reflection. The exhibition's layered approach to information provides visitors the opportunity to deepen their knowledge and gain multiple perspectives through, for instance, documentary films, document drawers or folders, interactive media stations, and communication zones. The modular display units themselves have multiple functions. They present the exhibition texts and reproductions of photographs and documents while also serving as storage for the objects and original documents and photographs kept in their drawers. Although the structures still stand in precise formation in the first exhibition room, their modules are rearranged in the style of building blocks in the following rooms to suit the individual topics. Document folders, documentary films, and interactive media stations at numerous locations throughout the exhibition supplement individual subjects with in-depth information, motivating visitors to form their own notion of the exhibition's content. The array of offerings[49] does not provide a fixed interpretation of history, but is intended to stimulate visitors to discover history themselves.

The increased use of media in the exhibition is likewise the result of broader societal processes.[50] Complementing traditional print, audio, and visual media, the new electronic media offer enormous storage capacity and individual means

The organization of the SS
into General SS, SS and
Police, and Armed SS
in Room 2
Photograph:
Matthias Groppe, 2010
Kreismuseum Wewelsburg,
Fotoarchiv

View of the former
SS mess hall
Photograph:
Matthias Groppe, 2010
Kreismuseum Wewelsburg,
Fotoarchiv

of access and are increasingly being used as repositories for the collective memory.[51] The exhibition taps the broad potential of new media. Aside from image series navigated via touch screens, interactive media units offer large amounts of information in a compact space. Documentary films make it possible to add expert commentary to historical footage. Contemporary witness accounts are presented at audio stations or in the form of interview videos. Lastly, at the end of the exhibition, selected websites of human rights organizations and educational institutions can be accessed on Internet workstations. A multilingual video guide gives visitors from abroad access to the exhibition.

The Structure of the Exhibition

The organization of the "Ideology and Terror of the SS" exhibition was adapted to the architecture and former significance of the space on the basement floors of the guard building. The color design derives from a conscious decision not to use the black-and-white contrasts or gray-in-gray schemes frequently seen at memorials. It was not conceived as a "dark" exhibition, but as one conveying the impression of a bright, friendly atmosphere. The color selection – blue, mauve, orange – is also not intended to communicate messages, rather, it is designed to express the rooms' various moods and point out the changes of perspective in the exhibition's three main areas.

The exhibition begins in the former SS gym and fencing hall with a thematic approach: The pivotal year 1941 is suited to elucidate key, locally and supra-regionally significant aspects of the SS presence in Wewelsburg. First, the meeting of top SS leaders in June 1941, directly preceding the beginning of the racial war of extermination against the Soviet Union, is addressed. The event clearly illustrates the importance of Wewelsburg Castle as a central meeting place for the SS, serving to solidify its self-image as a racial elite. In the same year, the gigantic scale of the planned building project at Wewelsburg became publicly known. Selected objects shine a light on efforts by the SS at mythologizing self-glorification and the ideological importance of Wewelsburg Castle in the overall structure of the SS. The reorganization of the external prisoner detachment as a state-run main camp, Niederhagen Concentration Camp, in September 1941, ultimately increased the exploitation of prisoners there, confirming the use of terror by the SS. A chronological overview of events from 1923 to the present follows, outlining the dynamic development of events both on the micro level of Wewelsburg and the

macro level of the overall development of the SS. The chronological overview provides the historical framework for understanding the following sections of the exhibition, which are not chronologically arranged but thematically structured.[52]

An understanding of the exhibition topic "The Social Structure and Organization of the SS" is offered using biographical material. The lives of the Wewelsburg SS castle administration provide a picture of the socialization processes, personal backgrounds, and ambitions of SS members. The diverse views and career paths of the SS men highlight the heterogeneity of the SS. Likewise, the organization of the SS into General SS (*Allgemeine SS*), SS and Police, and Armed SS (*Bewaffnete SS*) is also explained through the introduction of biographies of the responsible SS leaders.

Three rooms follow addressing the "Worldview, Mindset, and Crimes of the SS," beginning in the former SS officers' mess. The ideological dimension of the SS was based on the National Socialist ideology, which was marked by community building (of the *Volksgemeinschaft*, or ethnic community) and exclusion. Thus, notions of art, religion, and history, as well as ambitions aimed at community formation within the SS, were as early as the 1930s always associated with ostracism, discrimination, and persecution. The SS concept of art is the theme of a collection of selected figures from the Allach Porcelain Manufactory.[53] Though part of the SS economic empire, the porcelain manufactory did not succeed as planned in permeating the living environment of the SS with its porcelain figures. Its methods of operation, however, were consistent with typical SS working methods aimed at the exploitation and extermination of concentration camp prisoners.[54]

Supported by its own structural dynamic, the terroristic practices of the SS became ever more apparent with the beginning of World War II. Continuing escalation of SS violence is documented in Room 4, which is located beneath the north terrace and no longer shows any historical architectural features. Four identical interactive media stations document SS crimes in war, in the conquered eastern territories as well as in the remaining European countries and the German Reich.

The impact of the loss of constraint in the SS's thinking becomes apparent on the local level when one considers the SS Construction Management organization's ever expanding plans for the Wewelsburg project. In the arcade beneath the north terrace, the plans for the gigantomanic building project

A summary account of the crimes of the SS during the war is provided at media stations
Photograph: Matthias Groppe, 2010
Kreismuseum Wewelsburg, Fotoarchiv

The exhibition section on "Concentration Camps in Wewelsburg"
Photograph: Matthias Groppe, 2010
Kreismuseum Wewelsburg, Fotoarchiv

are presented in plastic film mounted on the window panes – against a view of the village that would have been destroyed under these plans. Passing the moat on their way to the northern tower, visitors are able to grasp the transformation by the SS of the former secondary residence of the prince-bishops into what the organization held to be a "German castle." The ideologically charged architecture of the historical rooms – the crypt and the *Obergruppenführer* Hall – makes them structural exhibits in their own right.[55]

Once again in the guard building, the first basement floor takes up the subject of the "Concentration Camp in Wewelsburg." These rooms were constructed by concentration camp prisoners; the change in perspective in the exhibition becomes apparent in a change of colors, from blue to mauve. First, the integration of the concentration camp in Wewelsburg into the overall system of National Socialist concentration camps is outlined. While the view of the camp from outside or from the perspective of the SS perpetrators predominates in Room 11, the perspective changes in Room 12. Here, quotations by survivors of Niederhagen Concentration Camp about their working and living conditions are linked with the few extant camp relics, with the focus placed on the subjective memories of former prisoners. In the next room, the relationship of the village population to the concentration camp is documented using the example of two escape attempts during the early phase of the camp. In Room 14 the final phase of the "remaining work detachment" in Wewelsburg is juxtaposed with the development of the concentration camp system as a whole. Although the prisoners of the Wewelsburg external work detachment experienced some improvement in their living conditions, hunger, mass murder, and death marches threatened the lives of most inmates of the National Socialist concentration camp system.

The third large exhibition aggregate covers the process of coming to terms with the past. The atmosphere of the spacious Room 15 is bright, transparent, and marked by an orange bench that encompasses the individual themes of the room like a bracket. The room begins with a review of the end of the war in Wewelsburg. Society's treatment of the victims and perpetrators is conveyed through postwar biographies of concentration camp survivors and former SS members. The judicial system's insufficient scrutiny of National Socialist crimes is pointed out.

The last theme of the exhibition is concerned with the struggle over memory of National Socialism, both in Wewelsburg and throughout Germany. The controversy over memorials occurring since 1945 informs the different modes of remembrance. The decades-long fight for a responsible culture of commemoration in Wewelsburg was successful, despite conflict and resistance. Nevertheless, the historical site of Wewelsburg is in particular danger of being misused by occultists and right-wing extremists as a projection screen for supposedly positive aspects of National Socialism. The exhibition ends with an open forum, where visitors are encouraged to contemplate their role in society as well as their involvement in their communities. Information and support is provided for self-determined, democratic action on behalf of a peaceful present and future.[56]

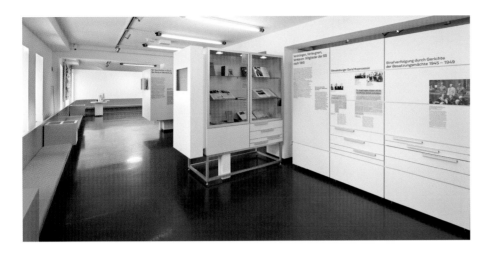

View of Room 15
Photograph:
Matthias Groppe, 2010
Kreismuseum Wewelsburg,
Fotoarchiv

1
Excerpt from the July 6, 1977, meeting minutes of the District Council (Kreismuseum Wewelsburg, AS, No. 18/6/4/1)
2
Karl Hüser, *Wewelsburg 1933–1945. Kult und Terrorstätte der SS. Eine Dokumentation* (From a series by the Kreismuseum Wewelsburg), 2nd revised ed., Paderborn, 1987.
3
Wulff E. Brebeck, "Gedenkstätten für NS-Opfer im kollektiven Gedächtnis der Bundesrepublik," in *Den Opfern gewidmet – auf Zukunft gerichtet. Gedenkstätten für die Opfer des Nationalsozialismus in NordrheinWestfalen*, Arbeitskreis für NS-Gedenkstätten (ed.), 4th ed., Düsseldorf, 1998, p. 21 f; cf. Volkhard Knigge, *Die Zukunft der Erinnerung. Gedenkstätten und Museen in Verbrechen erinnern. Die Auseinandersetzung mit Holocaust und Völkermord, idem* and Norbert Frei (eds.), Munich, 2002, p. 383.
4
The exhibition was designed by museum architect Heinz Micheel of Cologne.
5
A number of slide shows and CD-ROMs were developed (some in English) in cooperation with the State Media Center of Westphalia. They provide an educational approach to the history of Wewelsburg in the years between 1933 and 1945.
A selection: Wulff E. Brebeck and Karl Hüser, *Wewelsburg 1933–1945. Kultstätte des SS-Ordens*, 3rd ed., Münster, 1998; Wulff E. Brebeck, Karl Hüser, and Kirsten John-Stucke, Wewelsburg 1933–1945. *Das Konzentrationslager*, 3rd ed., Münster, 1998;
Wulff E. Brebeck, Karl Hüser, and Kirsten John-Stucke, *Wewelsburg 1933–1945. Größenwahn und KZTerror*, CD-Rom with brochure, Münster, 2007.
6
Cf. Wulff E. Brebeck, "Wewelsburg – Zum Umgang der Bevölkerung mit der Erfahrung eines Konzentrationslagers im Dorf," in *Opfer und Täter. Zum nationalsozialistischen und antijüdischen Alltag in Ostwestfalen-Lippe*, Hubert Frankemölle (ed.), Bielefeld, 1990, pp. 175–202.

7
Wulff E. Brebeck, "Von langer Dauer. Zum Streit um ein Mahnmal für die NSOpfer in Wewelsburg seit 1945," in *Dörfliche Gesellschaft und ländliche Siedlung. Lippe und das Hochstift Paderborn in überregionaler Perspektive*, Uta Halle, Frank Huismann, and Roland Linde (eds.), (From a series by the Kreismuseum Wewelsburg; 5), Bielefeld, 2001, pp. 312–314.
8
Iris Schäferjohann-Bursian, "Eine besondere Begegnung. Bericht über das Treffen der Überlebenden des KZ Niederhagen vom 14.–17. Mai 1992 im Kreis Paderborn," in *Gedenkstättenrundbrief 50*, 1992, pp. 5–9.
9
This theme is considered because since the 1990s, following with the publication of the book *Die schwarze Sonne von Tashi Lhunpo* (The Black Sun of Tashi Lhunpo) by Russel McCloud (Engerda, 1991), Wewelsburg Castle and its sun-wheel floor inlay in the North Tower have increasingly drawn the attention of the right-wing extremist scene. Cf. Daniela Siepe, "Die Rolle der Wewelsburg in der phantastischen Literatur, in Esoterik und Rechtsextremismus nach 1945," in *Die SS, Himmler und die Wewelsburg*, Jan Erik Schulte (ed.), (From a series by the Kreismuseum Wewelsburg; 7), Paderborn, 2009, pp. 488–510.
10
A selection: Irmhild K. Jakobi, *Die Wewelsburg 1919–1933. Kultureller Mittelpunkt des Kreises Büren und überregionales Zentrum der Jugend und Heimatpflege*, Paderborn, 1991; Andreas Lüttig, *Fremde im Dorf. Flüchtlingsintegration im westfälischen Wewelsburg 1945–1958*, Essen, 1993; Kirsten John[-Stucke], *"Mein Vater wird gesucht …" Häftlinge des Konzentrationslagers in Wewelsburg* (Historical series by the Kreismuseum Wewelsburg; 2), 4th ed., Essen, 2004; Andreas Pflock, *Gerrit Visser (1894–1942) – Von Hengelo nach Wewelsburg. Lebensstationen und Briefe des niederländischen Gewerkschafters aus nationalsozialistischer Gefangenschaft* (German/ Dutch) (Historical series by the Kreismuseum Wewelsburg; 6), Münster, 2005; Norbert Ellermann, "Erfahrungen im Umsiedlungslager der Volksdeutschen

Mittelstelle in Wewelsburg 1943–1945," in *Die SS, Himmler und die Wewelsburg*, Jan Erik Schulte (ed.), (as in note 9), pp. 296–313.
11
Olaf Mußmann, "Die Gestaltung von Gedenkstätten im historischen Wandel," in *Museale und mediale Präsentationen in KZ-Gedenkstätten, KZ-Gedenkstätte Neuengamme* (ed.) (From the series *Beiträge zur Geschichte der nationalsozialistischen Verfolgung in Norddeutschland*; 6), Bremen, 2001, p. 17.
12
Kirsten John-Stucke, "Neukonzeption der zeitgeschichtlichen Ausstellung – Entwicklung und Perspektiven," in *Gedenkstättenarbeit und Erinnerungskultur in Ostwestfalen-Lippe. Ein Projektbericht*, Juliane Kerzel (ed.), p. 200.
13
Prof. Volkhard Knigge, director of the Buchenwald and Mittelbau-Dora Memorial Foundation, took over the chair of the academic advisory committee. Vice chairs were Prof. Reinhard Rürup, then director of the Topography of Terror Foundation, Berlin, and Adj. Prof. Bernd Walter, director of the Institute for Westphalian Regional History at the Regional Association of Westphalia-Lippe in Münster. Paul Spiegel, at that time president of the Central Council of Jews in Germany, agreed to become the patron of the project.
14
"Empfehlungen des wissenschaftlichen Beirates für die 'Dokumentation Wewelsburg 1933–1945. Kult und Terrorstätte der SS,'" in *Projektbericht*, Juliane Kerzel (ed.), (as in note 12), pp. 291–296.
15
This was a 220-page proposal, which contained initial research results and conceptual considerations, cf. Kirsten John-Stucke, in: Juliane Kerzel, Projektbericht (see note 12), p. 195–207.
16
Jan Erik Schulte published the results in an anthology: Jan Erik Schulte (ed.), *Die SS, Himmler und die Wewelsburg* (as in note 9).

17
The members of the academic advisory committee included: Prof. Stefan Baumeier, former head of LWLOpen Air Exhibition in Detmold, Westphalian State Museum for Folklore; Dr. Detlef Garbe, head of the Neuengamme Concentration Camp Memorial in Hamburg; Angela Genger, at that time head of the Düsseldorf Memorial Site; Prof. Detlef Hoffmann of the formerly existing Institute for the Study of Culture – Textiles – Media at the University of Oldenburg; Prof. Hans Ottomeyer, former general director of the German Historical Museum in Berlin; Prof. Waltraud Schreiber, Professor of Theory and Didactics at the Catholic University in Eichstätt-Ingolstadt; Dr. Johannes Tuchel, head of the Memorial Site for German Resistance in Berlin; Prof. Wolfgang Wippermann, Friedrich Meinecke Institute for Area Studies, History and Culture, at Freie Universität in Berlin.
18
Like the academic advisory committee of the Planning Workshop on the Culture of Memory before it, representatives of the Federal Commissioner for Culture and the Media panel of experts, which evaluated grant applications, recognized the unique characteristics of Wewelsburg as a historical location. Regarding the significance of the historical site see the contribution to this catalog by Wulff E. Brebeck and Kirsten John-Stucke.
19
Volkhard Knigge and Norbert Frei (eds.), Introduction in *Verbrechen erinnern* (as in note 3), p. XI. Knigge states that since the reunification of Germany, a process of nationalization of negative commemoration has been completed. Perpetrated crimes or those for which responsibility must be assumed, have become a permanent part of the collective memory of the Germans. *Idem*, "Statt eines Nachworts: Abschied der Erinnerung. Anmerkungen zum notwendigen Wandel der Gedenkkultur in Deutschland," in *Verbrechen erinnern, idem* and Norbert Frei (eds.), (as in note 3), p. 423.
20
Wulff E. Brebeck, "Wewelsburg 1933–1945. Ansätze und Perspektiven zur Neukon-

zeption der Dauerausstellung," in *Erinnerungsarbeit kontra Verklärung der NS-Zeit. Vom Umgang mit Tatorten, Gedenkorten und Kultorten*, Wulff E. Brebeck and Barbara Stambolis (eds.) (Historical series by the Kreismuseum Wewelsburg; 7), Munich, 2008, p. 128.
21
Thus, the use of granite from Flossenbürg Concentration Camp calls attention, for example, to the large-scale SS economic empire against the backdrop of the SS system of persecution and extermination. For more on the construction history of the Guard Building see Wulff E. Brebeck and Kirsten John-Stucke's text in this catalog.
22
Jana Scholze, *Medium Ausstellung. Lektüren musealer Gestaltung in Oxford*, Leipzig, Amsterdam und Berlin, Bielefeld, 2004, p. 27.
23
Volkhard Knigge considers the narrative approach inadequate for memorials that aim to inform and educate about the crimes of the National Socialist state, because it permits only one perspective. In contrast, "documenting and reasoning" exhibitions present original objects as triggers for historical imagination and interpretation as well as for the translation of the products of imagination into results of reasoning, without losing sight of the objects' sensory and emotional basis. Cf. Volkhard Knigge, "Gedenkstätten und Museen in Deutschland," in *Verbrechen erinnern, idem* and Norbert Frei (eds.), (as in note 3), p. 385.
24
The term "second modernity" was coined by art historian Heinrich Klotz in the early 1990s. He sought to describe the changes resulting from the collapse of the old order of the first modernity and the resulting impact on art and architecture. In the field of sociology, these theses are also applied to the radical changes in economic, social, and political developments, for instance in globalization.
25
Rosmarie Beierde Haan, *Erinnerte Geschichte – Inszenierte Geschichte*, Frankfurt a.M., 2005, p. 29.

26
Moritz Pfeiffer, "'Ideologie und Terror der SS': Zur neuen Dauerausstellung in der 'Erinnerungs und Gedenkstätte Wewelsburg 1933–1945,'" in Gedenkstättenrundbrief 157, 10/2010, Stiftung Topographie des Terrors (ed.), p. 25.
27
Cf. Omer Bartov, "Der Holocaust. Von Geschehen und Erfahrung zu Erinnerung und Darstellung," in Geschichtskultur in der Zweiten Moderne, Rosmarie Beier[de Haan] (ed.), Frankfurt a.M., 2000, p. 104 ff.
28
Olaf Mußmann, "Die Gestaltung der Gedenkstätten im historischen Wandel," in Museale und mediale Präsentationen in KZGedenkstätten, KZGedenkstätte Neuengamme (ed.), (as in note 11), p. 26.
29
Volkhard Knigge, "Statt eines Nachworts: Abschied von der Erinnerung," in Verbrechen erinnern, idem and Norbert Frei (eds.), pp. 388 and 430 f. Knigge calls for research on original objects to be professionalized and its approach made more critical in order to avoid their elevation to the status of relics, which one grants credence to without scrutiny.
30
Wulff E. Brebeck, "Wewelsburg 1933–1945," in Erinnerungsarbeit kontra Verklärung, idem and Barbara Stambolis (eds.) (as in note 20), p. 133.
31
On the history of clothing see Kirsten John-Stucke, "Häftlingskleidung des Wewelsburger 'Restkommandos.' Symbol und historische Quelle zugleich," in Die SS, Himmler und die Wewelsburg, Jan Erik Schulte (ed.), (as in note 9), pp. 533–542.
32
Jana Scholze, Medium Ausstellung (as in note 22), p. 16 f. Cf. Spencer Crew and James E. Sims, "Locating Authenticity. Fragments of a Dialogue," in Exhibiting Cultures: The Poetics and Politics of Museum Display, Ivan Karp and Steven D. Lavine (eds.), Washington, D.C., 1991, pp. 159–175.

33
Jörn Rüsen, "Über den Umgang mit den Orten des Schreckens. Überlegungen zur Symbolik des Holocaust," in Das Gedächtnis der Dinge. KZ-Relikte und KZ-Denkmäler 1945–1955, Detlef Hoffmann (ed.), Frankfurt a.M./New York, 1998, p. 333 f.
34
Rosmarie Beier-de Haan, Erinnerte Geschichte – Inszenierte Geschichte (as in note 25), p. 186.
35
Olaf Mußmann, "Die Gestaltung der Gedenkstätten," in Museale und mediale Präsentationen, KZ-Gedenkstätte Neuengamme (ed.), (as in note 11), p. 27. According to Gottfried Korff, the "re-contextualization" of artifacts that comes to us only in a fragmentary form is appropriate as a means of making historical statements; cf. Gottfried Korff, "Bildwelt Ausstellung. Die Darstellung von Geschichte im Museum," in Orte der Erinnerung, Denkmal, Gedenkstätte, Museum, Ulrich Borsdorf and Heinrich Theodor Grütter (eds.), Frankfurt a.M./New York, 1999, p. 331 f.
36
Rüsen argues in favor of giving the genuine "aesthetic language" of original artifacts at memorials a chance to speak for itself and not let the language of interpretation, which is determined by predefined concepts of historical analysis, defamiliarize and suppress it; Jörn Rüsen, "Über den Umgang mit den Orten des Schreckens," in Gedächtnis der Dinge, Detlef Hoffmann (ed.), (as in note 33), p. 333. Michael Fehr has taken a critical view of "recontextualization" (Korff), arguing that exhibition organizers thereby strip original artifacts of their characteristics and impose too much discipline on the framework of interpretation; Cf. Michael Fehr, "Das Museum als Ort der Beobachtung Zweiter Ordnung. Einige Überlegungen zur Zukunft des Museums," in Geschichtskultur in der Zweiten Moderne, Rosmarie Beier[-de Haan] (ed.), (as in note 27), p. 150 f. [see note 24, above].
37
Jana Scholze, Medium Ausstellung (as in note 22), p. 274.

38
Thus, a white porcelain German shepherd from the SS-owned Porcelain Factory Allach, for instance, was shown next to information panels, which documented the role of the German shepherd in concentration camp guard detachments and provided commentary on the ideological aspects of the "German shepherd." The exhibition was developed by then project manager Andreas Pflock; see Kirsten John-Stucke, "Neukonzeption," in Projektbericht, Juliane Kerzel (ed.), (as in note 12), p. 201.
39
Responding to Michael Fehr's argument, Rosmarie Beier-de Haan maintains that this process does not mean exhibition managers overly interfere with possible interpretations, because exhibits or entire exhibitions cannot be read as "texts" with unambiguous interpretations. Even if the intention of an exhibition is didactically unambiguous, its effects are multi-dimensional. Visitors retain their own perceptions and capabilities for alternate interpretations. What is shown at an exhibition always also has a dimension of aesthetics and staging; cf. Rosmarie Beier-de Haan, Erinnerte Geschichte – Inszenierte Geschichte (as in note 25), p. 184.
40
Wulff E. Brebeck, "Wewelsburg 1933–1945," in Erinnerungsarbeit kontra Verklärung, idem and Barbara Stambolis (eds.), (as in note 20), p. 133; on fetishization cf. Jana Scholze, Medium Ausstellung (as in note 22), p. 127, and Henje Richter, "'Ich weiß zwar, dass es kein Original sein muss, aber dennoch …': Fetischistische Grundlagen von Authentizität musealer Objekte," in Authentizitätsfiktionen in populären Geschichtskulturen, Eva Ulrike Pirker et al. (ed.) Bielefeld, 2010, pp. 47–60.
41
Jan Assmann, Das kulturelle Gedächtnis. Schrift, Erinnerung und politische Identität in frühen Hochkulturen, 6th ed., Munich, 2007, p. 51.

42
Footage of interviews with contemporary witnesses is held at the media archive of the Kreismuseum Wewelsburg. The quality of the audio varies. Some of these conversations were recorded on cassette or mini-disc, others are available as video footage shot by film professionals. It turned out that it was difficult for some of the witnesses to confront and relive the memory of their suffering. In these cases the interviews were interrupted or canceled.
43
On the methodology of conducting interviews with contemporary witnesses cf. Waltraud Schreiber and Katalin Árkossy (eds.), Zeitzeugengespräche führen und werten. Historische Kompetenzen schulen (In the series Themenhefte Geschichte; 4), Neuried, 2009. Schreiber maintains that contemporary witnesses in their role as the bearers of the historical narrative live with, rearrange, and reinterpret it. Later experiences exert influence on the memory of earlier ones. This is not about biased historical accounts, but about interpretation or retrospective attribution of meaning (p. 23).
44
The term oral history refers to a method of historiography based on the memory of living witnesses that has been recorded through oral conversations, cf. Lutz Niethammer, Lebenserfahrung und kollektives Gedächtnis. Die Praxis der "Oral History," Bodenheim, 1987.
45
On new approaches to brain research regarding interviews with living witnesses, cf. Harald Welzer, Das kommunikative Gedächtnis. Eine Theorie der Erinnerung, Munich, 2008. Welzer emphasizes the subjectivity of memory: "The significance of autobiographical memory does not lie in the veracity of the remembered experiences and events, but in the subjective conviction that they are true and, thus, belong to 'me,'" (p. 219).
46
Wulff E. Brebeck, "Wewelsburg 1933–1945," in Erinnerungsarbeit kontra Verklärung, idem and Barbara Stambolis (eds.), (as in note 20), p. 131.

47
Anthony Giddens, Modernity and Self-Identity, Stanford, California, 1991, p. 52.
48
Rosmarie Beier[-de Haan] (ed.), "Geschichtskultur in der Zweiten Moderne. Eine Einführung," in Geschichtskultur in der Zweiten Moderne (as in note 27), p. 13 f. Beier-de Haan stresses the point that the reflective construction of identity has become a specific characteristic of modernity.
49
Cf. Detlef Hoffmann, "Spur, Vorstellung Ausstellung," in Geschichtskultur in der Zweiten Moderne, Rosmarie Beier[-de Haan] (ed.), (as in note 27), p. 178.
50
Wulff E. Brebeck, "Wewelsburg 1933–1945," in Erinnerungsarbeit kontra Verklärung, idem and Barbara Stambolis (eds.), (as in note 20), pp. 131, 135.
51
Rosmarie Beier[-de Haan] (ed.), "Geschichte, Erinnerung und Neue Medien. Überlegungen am Beispiel des Holocaust," in Geschichtskultur in der Zweiten Moderne (as in note 27), p. 300. Beier-de Haan stresses the point that an unprecedented abundance of recollections of the Holocaust have established a presence in public spaces.
52
For detailed information on the presentation of chronological exhibitions see Jana Scholze, Medium Ausstellung (as in note 22), pp. 89–141.
53
In the conception of the SS, art was to serve the interests of politics. Through the SS-owned Porcelain Manufactory Allach, the SS wanted to establish an ideologically charged understanding of art as a concept that countered the "bourgeois enjoyment of art." Ranging from political figures of the movement to figures in traditional costume, and extending to porcelain animals, the factory's various production schedules were meant to achieve a "total" immersion in the SS living environment. The exhibition shows, among other items, an SS fencer, a Hitler Youth member, a member of the League of German Girls, a woman wearing traditional Frisian costume, and three dog figures. These ambitious plans failed, however, because the figures, particularly those of animals,

served the relaxation of consumers rather than the establishment of a new worldview. Further pieces from the porcelain factory product line, such as the Julleuchter (Yule Lanterns) or Germanic urns, are shown as manifestations of SS notions of religion and historical narrative. On the "Germanic ceramics" products see Gabriele Huber, Die Porzellan-Manufaktur Allach-München GmbH. Eine "Wirtschaftsunternehmung" der SS zum Schutz der "deutschen Seele," Marburg, 1992, pp. 124–138.
54
Gabriele Huber, Die Porzellan-Manufaktur Allach-München GmbH (as in note 53), p. 142.
55
For detailed information on the design of the two rooms in the North Tower see Wulff E. Brebeck and Kirsten John-Stucke's contribution in this catalog.
56
This intention behind the exhibition is in line with Rosmarie Beier-de Haan's assessment of the manner in which modern exhibitions react to the process of individualization in the second modernity: In a world of individualization, exhibitions must be conceived as events that foster a sense of community by supporting standards and values that should be universally recognized, such as human rights; Rosmarie Beier-de Haan, Erinnerte Geschichte – Inszenierte Geschichte (as in note 25), p. 174 f.

Wewelsburg Castle offers particular insight into the mindset and history of the Protection Squadron (*Schutzstaffel* or SS). During the Third Reich, the Renaissance castle played a crucial role in the plans of *Reichsführer-SS* Heinrich Himmler. In order to accomplish the Wewelsburg project, the SS created a microcosm in the village that is exemplary of the worldview, personnel, and organization of the SS. The exhibition begins with the pivotal year 1941. Events of that year serve to highlight developments that structure the entire exhibition. This includes the intertwined histories of Wewelsburg Castle, the SS as a whole, and the local Niederhagen Concentration Camp.

The chronology provides an overview of the history of Wewelsburg Castle and the SS. It is divided into six phases that trace the increasingly rapid expansion and radicalization of the SS and its terror.

1 Introduction

1.1
The Pivotal Year 1941

A few days before the military campaign against the Soviet Union commenced in June 1941, Himmler held a gathering at Wewelsburg Castle of his most important *SS-Gruppenführer*, the highest-ranking officers in the SS. This meeting highlights the special role Wewelsburg Castle was meant to play in the ideological preparation of the war.

Himmler sought to establish Wewelsburg Castle as a main venue for *SS-Gruppenführer*. His goal was the invention of a political myth that would lend the SS community meaning and a future. To this end, the historical narrative was altered and falsified according to his own beliefs. Wewelsburg was not about decision-making, but about strengthening the SS leadership's political, racist, and militaristic self-image with its aim of terror and destruction.

To expedite conversion works on Wewelsburg Castle through the use of concentration camp prisoners, Himmler converted what had been a sub-camp of Sachsenhausen Concentration Camp into Niederhagen Concentration Camp, a main camp in the state-run system, in September 1941. From that point on, it had the same organizational status as the large National Socialist concentration camps. Niederhagen stands as an example of the local entrenchment of the SS system of terror and its practice of exploitation.

No. 1-1, No. 1-2
**The *Gruppenführer* Meeting
at Wewelsburg Castle
Photographs: Privately owned
Mid-June 1941**
The castle's east facade is visible in the background. The photograph on the left shows the participants in the meeting on their way to the castle and Hermann Bartels, the architect in charge of the conversion of Wewelsburg Castle, approaching the photographer. In the photograph on the right, castle administrator Siegfried Taubert, wearing a peaked cap, looks towards the camera. Reinhard Heydrich is seen on the far left; head of domestic services at Wewelsburg Castle, Elfriede Wippermann, is on the far right. jes

Kreismuseum Wewelsburg, Fotoarchiv

From June 12 to 15, 1941, the top SS commanders of the impending attack against the Soviet Union met at Wewelsburg Castle. Contrary to Himmler's expectations, this would be the only *Gruppenführer* meeting ever staged at this location.

Two photographs document the meeting at Wewelsburg Castle and show some of its participants. Little is known about what was discussed at the gathering, with surviving sources providing little information on the matter. Presumably, no special orders were issued regarding the impending war, as preparations for the campaign were largely complete. Rather, the conference had to do with the self-affirmation of its participants and the mythologization of the battle against the Soviet Union, which was seen as pivotal, and against an enemy vilified as "Judeo-Bolshevist." Wewelsburg Castle served Himmler as a place of self-assurance and as the link between planning and action. Its political and ideological significance stems from this context. jes

No. 1-3
Heinrich Himmler
1900 – 1945
Himmler assumed the office of *Reichsführer-SS* (RFSS) in 1929. He developed the SS into a formation that saw itself as a political, social elite closely tied to the person of Hitler. At the time of the Wewelsburg meeting, Himmler ranked as one of the most influential National Socialist leaders. He wielded undisputed control over all branches of the SS and the police. From 1939, he organized extensive settlement and expulsion measures. He had already been given wide-ranging authority for the impending war against the Soviet Union. The SS was to play a pivotal role in ruling the occupied territory and in the war of extermination against the civilian population, especially the Jews. jes
Bundesarchiv Koblenz, Bildarchiv,
Bild 183-S62673

No. 1-4
Reinhard Heydrich
1904 – 1942
The *SS-Gruppenführer* and police lieutenant-general headed the Reich Security Main Office (*Reichssicherheitshauptamt*). At the time of the Wewelsburg conference, he was responsible for four deployment groups (*Einsatzgruppen*) of the Security Police (*Sicherheitspolizei*) and the SS Security Service (*SS-Sicherheitsdienst*, or SD) that stood ready for the campaign against the Soviet Union. After the war began, the *Einsatzgruppen* began to murder civilians, prisoners of war, and, in an increasingly systematic manner, the Jewish population in the western Soviet Union.

In addition to Himmler, Heydrich, together with Kurt Daluege and Karl Wolff, had conducted negotiations with the *Wehrmacht* (armed forces) in the spring of 1941 on the deployment of SS units during the planned campaign against the Soviet Union. jes
Bundesarchiv Berlin
SSO Reinhard Heydrich

No. 1-5
Kurt Daluege
1897 – 1946
The *SS-Obergruppenführer* and police general commanded the entire uniformed police force. As the chief of the Order Police Main Office (*Hauptamt Ordnungspolizei*), he commanded the police and reserve police battalions that were to take part in the war of aggression. Like the Deployment Groups (*Einsatzgruppen*), these police units also participated in the mass murder of civilian populations, particularly the Jews, in the Soviet Union. jes
Bundesarchiv Koblenz, Bildarchiv,
Bild 183-2007-1010-502

No. 1-6
Karl Wolff
1900 – 1984
A close confidante of Himmler, the *SS-Gruppenführer* and chief of the Personal Staff of the *Reichsführer-SS* had already been a frequent guest at Wewelsburg before 1941. With the beginning of World War II, Himmler sent him to Hitler's headquarters as the SS liaison officer to the Führer. In 1964 Wolff was sentenced to fifteen years in prison, of which he served six. jes
Bundesarchiv Berlin,
SSO Karl Wolff

The Supporters

No. 1-10
Oswald Pohl
1892 – 1951
At the time of the conference, the *SS-Gruppenführer* and lieutenant general of the *Waffen-SS*, stood at the helm of two SS Main Offices, "Administration and Economy" and "Budget and Construction." He supplied administrative staff and construction units for the military campaign against the Soviet Union. Pohl controlled numerous SS-owned companies and oversaw the forced labor of concentration camp prisoners. As the chairman of the Society for the Promotion and Care of German Cultural Monuments, he was in charge of the administration and financing of Wewelsburg Castle. Pohl was one of the most important supporters of Himmler's plans and of the expansion of the SS's claim to power. jes
Bundesarchiv Koblenz, Bildarchiv,
Bild 183-R64926

No. 1-11
Werner Lorenz
1891 – 1974
Lorenz was an important functionary in carrying out National Socialist "ethnic policy." In 1937, the *SS-Obergruppenführer* was already at the helm of the Ethnic German Liaison Office (*Volksdeutsche Mittelstelle*, or VOMI), the National Socialist Party's (NSDAP) central coordination agency for the so-called *Volksdeutsche*, in other words, minorities living outside of Germany considered to be ethnic Germans. Following the 1941 transformation of the VOMI into an SS Main Office, Lorenz lost political significance, but continued to hold major responsibility for the resettlement or settlement of ethnic German populations. jes
Bundesarchiv Berlin,
SSO Werner Lorenz

No. 1-12
Johannes (Hanns) Johst
1890 – 1978
A friend of Himmler's and a National Socialist poet, Johst launched a career in the National Socialist state that secured him a top position in the cultural administration. In 1935, he was appointed president of the Reich Literature Chamber (*Reichsschrifttumskammer*). The *SS-Brigadeführer* was viewed as the "chronicler of the SS." It was in this role that he participated in the Wewelsburg conference. He was to idealize the SS-*Gruppenführer* meeting and craft the political myth that Himmler sought to attach to Wewelsburg Castle. jes
Siegfried Casper, *Hanns Johst*,
Verlag Langen Müller, Munich 1940

No. 1-13
Hans Albin Rauter
1895 – 1949
The Austrian right-wing extremist fled to National Socialist Germany in 1933 and joined the SS as a Higher Leader in 1935. Rauter was a willing enforcer of the SS's politics of terror and murder. During the entire occupation from 1940 to 1945, he held the office of Higher SS and Police Leader and Commissar General for the Security Forces at the Reich Commissariat for the Occupied Dutch territories. In this position, he was responsible for the deportation of 110,000 Jewish residents of the Netherlands. The reason for his presence at Wewelsburg Castle remains unclear and it is documented only in a testimony by Bach. jes
Bundesarchiv Koblenz, Bildarchiv,
Bild 183-1982-1021-509

The Implementers

No. 1-7
Erich von dem Bach-Zelewski
1899 – 1972
The *SS-Gruppenführer* and major general of the police was one of three Higher SS and Police Leaders designated to shape future occupation policy in the German-occupied territories of the Soviet Union. At the start of the war, he was posted to the middle sector of the "Eastern Front." Together with Prützmann and Jeckeln, Bach ranks as one of the most important implementers of the racist genocide against the Jews and the reign of terror visited on the civilian population in the occupied territories. After the war, Bach testified as a chief witness for the prosecution in the Nuremberg Trials, which saved him from prosecution by the Allies. jes

Bundesarchiv Koblenz, Bildarchiv
Bild 183-S73507

No. 1-8
Hans-Adolf Prützmann
1901 – 1945
Like Erich von dem Bach-Zelewski, the former Free Corps man belonged to the high-ranking regional SS commanders of the prewar period. As a Higher SS and Police Leader, *SS-Gruppenführer*, and police lieutenant-general, Prützmann actively participated in the campaign of extermination against the Jewish population, first in the Baltic region (as Higher SS and Police Leader North), then in Ukraine (as Higher SS and Police Leader South). jes

Bundesarchiv Berlin,
SSO Hans-Adolf Pruetzmann

No. 1-9
Friedrich Jeckeln
1895 – 1946
Until shortly before the Wewelsburg conference, the *SS-Obergruppenführer* and police general had resided in Düsseldorf as Higher SS and Police Leader West. In the attack against the Soviet Union he was to act as Higher SS and Police Leader Russia South (Ukraine) and was later posted to the Baltic as Higher SS and Police Leader North, replacing Prützmann. Jeckeln was one of the most radical regional SS commanders and continually developed initiatives of his own to expand the practice of extermination in the occupied Soviet Union. jes

Bundesarchiv Koblenz, Bildarchiv
Bild 183-S45466

No. 1-14
Siegfried Taubert (1880 – 1946)
The *SS-Gruppenführer* served as castle administrator at Wewelsburg Castle from early 1938 until the end of the war. Forging a career in the SS, he had previously served as chief of staff of the SS Main Sector East under Daluege and subsequently held the same function at the SD Main Office under Heydrich. Immediately after the start of World War II, he temporarily also functioned as inspector general of the Reinforced Death's Head Regiments. These units served as guards at concentration camps, and were responsible in the occupied territories for numerous murder and terror operations against civilians, especially Jews. Wherever organizational skills and military demeanor were in demand, Taubert was able to successfully and unscrupulously make his mark. jes

Bundesarchiv Berlin,
SSO Siegfried Taubert

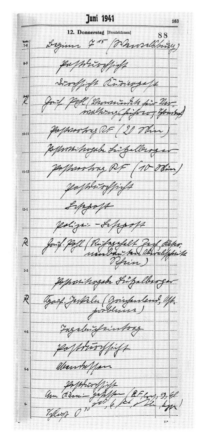

No. 1-15
Page for June 12, 1941, from the service diary of the department *Reichsführer-SS* within the Personal Staff of the *Reichsführer-SS*; head *SS-Sturmbannführer* Dr. Rudolf Brandt
This service diary was kept by Brandt.

Bundesarchiv Berlin, NS 19/2957, p. 88

Hour:		
7-8		Begin 7:15 (Wewelsburg)
8-9		Mail screening
		Screening courier mail
9-10	*Gru[ppen]f[ührer]* Pohl	(Wounded for
R[ücksprache?]		administrative officer; Schondorf)
[consultation?]		
10-11		Mail report *R[eichs]F[ührer-SS]* (20 min)
		Mail passed on to Lützelberger
11-12		Mail report RF (10 min)
		Mail screening
12-1		Reading of mail
		Reading of police mail
1-2		
R		*Gru[ppen]f.[ührer]* Pohl (retirement pay Zech, barracks Main Sector Rhine)
2-3		Mail passed on to Lützelberger
3-4		*O[ber]gru[ppen]f[ührer].* Jeckeln
R		(Greece, east. problems)
4-5		Diary entry
		Mail screening
5-6		Dinner
		Mail screening
		Sat at fireplace (RF, [Lorenz], [Bach], [Wolff], [Heydrich], [Pohl], [Taubert], [Jeckeln], [Prützmann])
6-		Conclusion 030

Wewelsburg Castle as *SS-Gruppenführer* Stronghold

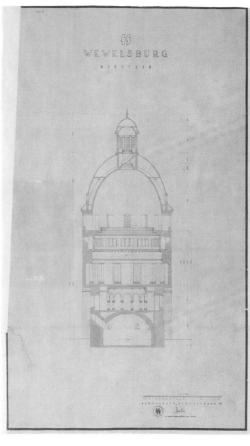

No. 1-19
Construction Management at the Wewelsburg SS School, October 1, 1941
Colorized blueprint, paper, stamp of the SS Construction Management,
signed by Bartels
Scale 1:100
The SS had leased Wewelsburg Castle in 1934 and soon officially named it "Wewelsburg SS School." From 1937/1938 at the latest, however, Himmler focused efforts on transforming the castle into an exclusive venue for SS-Gruppenführer. It was intended to provide top SS officers with a place to meet and retreat that was shielded from public view. Himmler and his architect Hermann Bartels developed numerous ideas and plans for the interior and exterior design of Wewelsburg Castle. From the beginning of World War II, Bartels worked on plans to redesign the entire Wewelsburg village for the purposes of the SS. The focus of the planned gigantic three-quarter circular castle complex was to be the converted northern tower at the tip of the triangular Wewelsburg Castle mm

Kreismuseum Wewelsburg, plan no. 130

No. 1-20
Construction Management of the Wewelsburg SS School, October 1, 1941
Colorized blueprint, paper, stamp of the SS Construction Management,
signed by Bartels
Scale 1:100
In the SS plans, the cellar vault was designated as the "crypt," intended to serve as a venue for funeral rites. The names "*Gruppenführer* Hall" (above, with dome) and "*Obergruppenführer* Hall" (below) were chosen for the upper floors. What specific purpose was foreseen for these rooms is unknown. With their central location, their grand and sacred architecture, the rooms of the northern tower were meant to strengthen the SS-*Gruppenführers'* awareness of belonging to the chosen elite within the National Socialist Reich. mm

Kreismuseum Wewelsburg, plan no. 129

No. 1-18
Hans Lohbeck (1909 – 1974): *War*, study for a Wewelsburg triptych
Gouache on paper
1939 – 1941
In January 1939, eight months before the beginning of World War II, Himmler commissioned an altar-style, three-panel painting with the following motifs for Wewelsburg Castle: "a) an assault by SS troops in battle"; "b) a field in a new country, being ploughed by a soldier-peasant, an SS man"; "c) the newly founded village with the family and numerous children." The triptych, however, was never realized. This study was created between 1939 and 1941. Lohbeck's proposed image allegorizes the SS's political self-image and a utopian society in which National Socialist "shock troops" take part in the planned military conquest and racist settlement of "*Lebensraum* in the East." Wewelsburg Castle rises in the background of the middle panel, appearing as the detached grand fixed point in this SS devotional picture glorifying violence. A depiction of what amounts to the National Socialist version of a "Holy Family" forms the focus of the image. mm

Kreismuseum Wewelsburg, inv. no. 13634

No. 1-16

Chair from the "Grand Courtroom" on the ground floor of Wewelsburg Castle
Oak, leather upholstery, brass fittings, double sig rune impressed into the backrest, band of swastikas imprinted on the uprights of the backrest
1935 – 1939

From the outset, the SS aimed to convey its conception of the course and meaning of history to its guests at Wewelsburg Castle. In the setting of the "castle," the SS-Gruppenführer, in particular, were supposed to conceive of themselves as outstanding representatives of an Aryan, Nordic "race," which since time immemorial and for all eternity was destined to fight, create culture, and rule. In this context, furniture, too, was invested with ideological meaning. As with this leather-upholstered oak chair with sig runes (SS insignia) and bands of swastikas, the choices of material, form, and ornaments were not meant to express modernity and individuality, but pragmatism, permanence, and the National Socialist view of Germanic culture and the Middle Ages. The chair originally stood in a room that carried the grand-sounding, if apparently wholly empty name of "Grand Courtroom." mm

Kreismuseum Wewelsburg, inv. no. 1076

"I intend to introduce and schedule two regular major meetings of Gruppenführer, one on November 8, here in Munich ..., and the other, which will handle other matters, each spring at the Wewelsburg."

"I have requested the following:
1. An picture of a Tree of Life, of an Ash Tree of Life for the Courtroom.
2. An image of Marienburg Castle for the hall with the Teutonic Knights theme.
3. A large triptych for the forecourt in front of the leader's quarters, with the following three panels:
a) An assault by an SS unit in battle, for which I can even imagine a fallen or mortally wounded SS stalwart, a married man, to show that new life sprouts even from the death of a married man.
b) A field in the new lands, being plowed by a soldier farmer, an SS man.
c) The newly founded village, with the family and numerous children.
4. The Reich Eagle for the Courtroom, in ceramic (already contracted to Allach).
5. A large gray carpet with red edge pattern, made of rayon, for the Courtroom.
6. In addition, when feasible, a long, narrow tapestry for the *Reichsführer-SS* room, with the figure of a fully-grown, virginal girl, a future mother."

"I will have ... the coat of arms of the deceased *Gruppenführer* displayed in the *Gruppenführer* Hall, where, when Wewelsburg Castle is ready, the *Gruppenführer* meetings, with the exception of that of November 8/9, shall always be held. This will insure that those who come after us always deliberate beneath our plaques, and must answer for doing things the way we did them."

"There is a shrine there where these rings will be kept, and I think it will be a marvelous memory for coming generations to know that those rings were worn by generations of SS officers in times easy and hard, good and bad. I believe that with this we can let a piece of tradition gradually grow. ... I believe that these inner things from the heart, from honor, from the soul of the truest, deepest worldview are indeed those which, in the end, give us the strength for today, and will give us the strength for every struggle, every fateful hour that Germany, and perhaps we, personally, shall face over the next 30, 50, or 100 years."

Speech to *SS-Gruppenführer* in Bad Tölz, February 18, 1937

Speech to *SS-Gruppenführer* in Munich, November 8, 1938

From a speech by Himmler in 1938

Translation of notes made from Himmler's comments during a visit at Wewelsburg Castle, January 15 – 18, 1939

No. 1-17
Statements by *Reichsführer-SS* Heinrich Himmler from the years 1937 to 1944 on the purposes of Wewelsburg Castle and its furnishing for the *SS-Gruppenführer*
There are few known contemporary sources providing specific information on the intentions and objectives of the SS in Wewelsburg. Of special significance are the surviving statements by Heinrich Himmler about the project. The conversion of Wewelsburg Castle for SS purposes was, above all, a personal interest of the *Reichsführer-SS*. With his growing power in the Third Reich, Himmler increasingly emerged as the actual driving force in Wewelsburg. It is not coincidental that his publicized programmatic statements on the *SS-Gruppenführer* stronghold date from the period following Himmler's appointment to Chief of the German Police, in June 1936. mm

"In future …, I will perform the swearing-in ceremony of uninitiated *Gruppenführer* at Wewelsburg Castle. Next year I will also invite to that event at Wewelsburg Castle the *Gruppenführer*, who through their covenant as Gruppenführer have forever committed their lives to upholding the laws of Race and Blood."

"His harried *Gruppenführer*, chasing around in the struggle for Germany, could not be gathered in training camps to be drilled, but required a more comfortable venue, one which would also stimulate them ideologically."

"The Reichsführer-SS responded that regular castle visits were out of the question. If anyone were invited, this had to be seen as a very special honor for the concerned party; for example, some general or other would be invited at a later date. Furthermore, the leading figures in the National Socialist Party (*Reichsleiter*) would occasionally have to be periodically invited, as they could not appear to have a lower status than the *SS-Gruppenführer*. Asked whether anything about the castle should be made public, the *Reichsführer-SS* declared categorically that this was absolutely out of the question: The press, that "hyena," would have no chance to publicize this gem. The *Reichsführer-SS* explained to *SS-Gruppenführer* Taubert that he wished to see special facilities built to house a gold and silver treasure; first, for reasons of tradition, and second – let this be clear to all – as a necessary reserve for hard times."

"Now, I would not like it that individual ideas or thoughts about the future that come to me, including that of Wewelsburg Castle, should be forgotten. In the context of these thoughts, it occurred to me that in peacetime we could best define Wewelsburg Castle as follows: 'Wewelsburg Castle – Reich House of the SS-Gruppenführer.' I request that you resubmit this record to me upon the 'outbreak of peace.'"

Notes from Himmler's comments during a visit at Wewelsburg Castle, January 15 – 18, 1939

Speech to *SS-Gruppenführer* in Munich on November 8, 1938

Himmler, as quoted in von Knobelsdorff's diary

Translation from a letter to the chief administrator of Wewelsburg Castle, *SS-Obergruppenführer* Siegfried Taubert, February 26, 1944

1.1.3
The Reclassification of the Wewelsburg Concentration Camp as "Niederhagen Concentration Camp"

No. 1-22
Wooden gatehouse
Ca. 1941
Intially a wooden gatehouse was built at the entrance to the protective detention camp, through which the concentration camp prisoners marched into the camp. After a fire, the structure was replaced by a larger stone gatehouse. Both the layout and the organization of the self-administered concentration camp in Wewelsburg complied with the regulations prevailing throughout the concentration camp system. The barracks were aligned on the grounds in a grid pattern so the SS guard units could better oversee the camp. The preventive detention camp was surrounded by an electric, triple layer barbed-wire fence. The SS compound for the guard units was built later in the vegetable field across from the gatehouse. kjs
Kreismuseum Wewelsburg, Fotoarchiv

No. 1-23
Concentration camp inmate working in the castle moat
Ca. 1939 – 1943
This is the only known photograph showing a concentration camp prisoner doing construction at the northern tower. Apparently the prisoner and guard were only included in the photograph unintentionally. Located in the moat were construction sheds where prisoners carried out preparations for enlarging the basement to construct the crypt. For example, the wooden frames to cast the concrete dome were built there, and the quarried stone to clad it was also dressed in the sheds. With backbreaking effort, the prisoners had to extract and transport the stone from several local quarries. Conditions in these work details, as well as those at other local worksites, were extremely debilitating and dangerous, frequently resulting in injury and death. kjs
Kreismuseum Wewelsburg, Fotoarchiv

No. 1-24
SS Order no. 388
Posted in the *Waffen-SS* decree gazette
October 15, 1941
With his order of October 15, 1941, Heinrich Himmler clarified the initially inconsistent designation of the new main camp at Wewelsburg. Whereas up to that point, the camp had repeatedly been referred to as "Wewelsburg Concentration Camp," the designation "Niederhagen Concentration Camp" was now specified. With this name, Himmler made reference to the historical landscape where the camp had been built. Presumably, he wished to avoid any connection between the concentration camp and his construction project.

Following its reclassification as a main camp (*Hauptlager*), Niederhagen Concentration Camp eventually got its own vital statistics office, where the death register was maintained, as well as its own crematorium, to be able to cremate the increasing number of dead prisoners on site. The Gestapo central offices in Westphalia/Lippe used the camp as a location to execute their prisoners. kjs
Bundesarchiv Berlin

- 13 -

ℋ-Obersturmbannführer Bartels) ist im Rohbau fertiggestellt. Ausserdem wurden mehrere Strassenbauarbeiten durchgeführt, so wurde der
Platz vor dem Wachgebäude mit roten Wesersandsteinen gepflastert.

Zur Verringerung der Unkosten der Gesellschaft wurde das Häftlings-
lager Wewelsburg auf das Reich übernommen und ist als KL Niederhagen selbständig. Nach Entscheidung des Hauptamtschefs blieb die
Bauleitung für das KL Niederhagen bei der Bauleitung der ℋ-Schule.
Die Abrechnung erfolgt über das Amt W VIII mit der Inspektion der
Konzentrationslager. Obwohl auch für das in die Dringlichkeitsstufe
2 U 1 Münster eingestufte Bauvorhaben des KL Niederhagen Baustoffe
im Berichtsjahr vom Amt II nicht zur Verfügung gestellt wurden,
konnte die Errichtung und der Ausbau mit geringen Verzögerungen
durchgeführt werden.

3) Dringlichkeitseinstufung und Rohstoffbeschaffung
Eine Dringlichkeitseinstufung für das Bauvorhaben Wewelsburg selbst
wurde Ende des Jahres 1940 vom RF-ℋ beim G.B.-Bau, Reichsminister
Dr. Todt beantragt, aber von diesem zu Beginn des Berichtsjahres
unter Verweisung an den Reichsschatzmeister abgelehnt. Dieser konnte
ebenfalls keine Baustoffe zur Verfügung stellen. Bis zum 30.6.
wurden trotzdem von der Rohstoffstelle, ℋ-Obersturmbannführer Kloth,
ausreichend Kennziffern zur Verfügung gestellt. Die Kennzifferzu-
teilung stockte sodann vollständig nach der erfolgten Neuorganisa-
tion der Rohstoffstelle. Gegen Ende des Berichtsjahres wurde der
Reichsführer durch den Hauptamtschef über diese Rohstofflage unter-
richtet. (Vor kurzem ist die Antwort von Obergruppenführer Wolff
eingegangen. Die von diesem gewünschten Verhandlungen mit Standartenführer Kloth laufen).

4) Umsiedlung und Grunderwerb
Das Umsiedlungsverfahren wird von dem Kulturamt in Soest durchgeführt. Durch Vermittlung von ℋ-Gruppenführer Willikens im Reichs-
ernährungsministerium wurde erreicht, dass dem Kulturamt die hier-

- 14 -

No. 1-26
Excerpt from the 1941 annual report of the Society for the Promotion and Care of German Cultural Monuments
Translation on page 440

To provide financial relief to the Society for the Promotion and Care of German Cultural Monuments (GEFÖ), which until the summer of 1941 was responsible for construction and maintenance of the concentration camp, Heinrich Himmler and Oswald Pohl, head of the Economic and Administration Main Office as well as chairman of the GEFÖ, reclassified the camp in Wewelsburg, which had been a subcamp of Sachsenhausen Concentration Camp, as a main camp in the state-run system of concentration camps. This transferred the costs of running the concentration camp to the German Reich. The reimbursement to the GEFÖ amounted to 600,000 Reichsmarks. kjs

Landesarchiv NRW, Abteilung Ostwestfalen-Lippe, Detmold, D 70 no. 160, p. 13

No. 1-25
Not shown
Unused envelope, concentration camp administration
November 3/4, 1941

This unused envelope was to be used to return death certificates from the local police agency in Büren to the concentration camp administration. The initially inconsistent designation of the main camp is apparent in the concurrent use of a stamp with the imprint "K.L. Wewelsburg" and the address "K.L. Niederhagen, Dept. II," which appears on the return envelope. "K.L." was the official contemporary abbreviation for "concentration camp." "Department II" is given as the addressee for the death certificates, denoting the camp administration's political department, which was run by a member of the Gestapo and in charge of the intake and release of prisoners. Other administrative departments were: I. Commandant Staff, III. Protective Custody Camp, IV. Administration, V. Camp Physician. The stamp also documents that the concentration camps were an institution of the *Waffen-SS*. In the spring of 1941, Himmler had assigned the Death's Head guard battalions to the Waffen-SS. kjs

Stadtarchiv Büren, Polizeiakte/Kreismuseum Wewelsburg, 16699

No. 1-21
Cap
Undyed recovered wool with blue stripes (Rayon, cotton, wool)
Rayon lining
Ca. 1939 – 1945

Prisoners usually wore striped suits made of wool-blend fabric in winter, cotton-blend fabric in summer. During the war, simple substitute fabrics were increasingly used. The clothing did not provide prisoners adequate protection in rain or in winter, resulting in illness and frostbite. The resemblance of the concentration camp prisoners' striped outfits to the clothing then worn by convicts was a conscious ploy by the SS to foster the impression among the general population that concentration camp and penal imprisonment were identical, and that concentration camp inmates were common criminals. kjs

Kreismuseum Wewelsburg, Nachlass Wettin Müller, inv. no. 15541

1.2
The SS and Wewelsburg / A Chronology

Few months after the National Socialist seizure of power, *Reichsführer-SS* Heinrich Himmler decided to make the imposing Wewelsburg Castle near Paderborn a central venue of his organization. Much of what the SS stood for generally was now also reflected in the village of Wewelsburg: intense ideological activity, increasing megalomania, and – with the building of a concentration camp – exploitation and extermination.

The legacy of the SS survived the war. To this day, it compels the locality and German society as a whole to confront the National Socialist past.

At the founding of the SS, very little presaged that one of the most powerful organizations of the Third Reich would develop from a handful of men who came together in Munich in the spring of 1923 to protect the chairman of the NSDAP, Adolf Hitler.

The principal tasks of the SS included providing security at Party events, hawking National Socialist publications, and serving as informers. But above all, the SS actively participated in the right-wing campaign against the democratic Weimar Republic.

In January 1929, agronomist Heinrich Himmler assumed the position of *Reichsführer-SS*, the organization's highest rank. He then set about transforming the organization into a group structured along strict ideological lines. The SS owed its growing importance within the NSDAP to its reputation for special loyalty to the party leadership. mh

No. 1-27
The "Hitler Shock Troop" in Munich, on its way to "German Day" in Bayreuth
Photograph: Heinrich Hoffmann, September 20, 1923
Bayerische Staatsbibliothek, Munich, Fotoarchiv Heinrich Hoffmann, 6569

Security Corps and Civil War

1923 – 1932
Wewelsburg Village and Castle during the Weimar Republic

As a seat of secular and ecclesiastical power, Wewelsburg Castle had since the Middle Ages exerted a powerful influence on life in the East Westphalian village of the same name. In 1925, property of the three-hundred-year-old erstwhile secondary residence of the prince-bishops of Paderborn passed from the State of Prussia to what was then the District of Büren. The latter established a museum of local history and a youth hostel in the castle, while making it available as a conference center and venue for meetings and gatherings. With its marked Catholic and peasant background, Wewelsburg thus became an attractive interregional venue for varied cultural activities during the last years of the Weimar Republic. Catholic youth organizations, in particular, conducted their (occasionally national) meetings at Wewelsburg Castle until 1933. Here, in 1931, the Peace League of German Catholics explored the possibilities of a European peace order. mm

No. 1-32
Aerial photograph of the castle and village of Wewelsburg from the north
1920s
Kreismuseum Wewelsburg, Fotoarchiv

No. 1-28
"Hitler Putsch," November 1923: Members of the "Adolf Hitler Shock Troop" arrest Social Democratic and Communist parliamentary representatives in Munich
Photograph: Heinrich Hoffmann, November 9, 1923

Wilfried Bade, *Deutschland erwacht. Werden, Kampf und Sieg der NSDAP*; Cigaretten-Bilderdienst, Altona-Bahrenfeld, 1933

No. 1-29
Hitler in the circle of the Leadership Guard, founded by his chauffeur, Julius Schreck, in the spring of 1925; from left to right: Julius Schaub, Julius Schreck, Adolf Hitler, Hansjörg Maurer, Friedrich Schneider
Original photograph, ca. fall 1925; postcard version with signatures, presumably from later years

Bayerische Staatsbibliothek, Munich, Fotoarchiv Heinrich Hoffmann, 6685

No. 1-31
Reichsführer-SS Heinrich Himmler at an open-air mass on the occasion of the "Congress of the National Opposition" in Bad Harzburg
October 11, 1931

Ullstein Bilderdienst, 00021545

No. 1-30
SS men handing out leaflets on Schelling Straße, Munich, close to NSDAP headquarters
Ca. 1930

Stadtarchiv Munich, WRep-0004

No. 1-34
Placing a wreath at the Wewelsburg memorial for fallen soldiers of World War I behind the parish church (original inscription: "Honoring Heroes")
Photograph: Josef Buben, probably 1927

Kreismuseum Wewelsburg, Fotoarchiv

No. 1-33
Opening ceremony at the Wewelsburg Museum of Local History, view into the inner courtyard and to the ruined northern tower
Photograph: Josef Buben, May 31, 1925

Kreismuseum Wewelsburg, Fotoarchiv

No. 1-35
Tent camp at the annual congress of the Catholic association, "New Germany," in Wewelsburg
August 1 to 5, 1925

Kommission für Zeitgeschichte, Bonn: Archiv Bund Neudeutschland

No. 1-36
Interior of the Museum of Local History in the basement of Wewelsburg Castle's west wing after its inauguration in 1925
1925–1932

Kreismuseum Wewelsburg, Fotoarchiv

No. 1-37
Wewelsburg Catholic priest (1907–1934) Johann Pöppelbaum (1845–1934), on the 60th anniversary of his ministry, surrounded by guests at the festivities in the inner courtyard of Wewelsburg Castle
March 12, 1930

Kreismuseum Wewelsburg, Fotoarchiv

After the National Socialists came to power in January 1933, Heinrich Himmler initially became Munich's chief of police, and shortly thereafter, commander of the Bavarian Political Police. In the following years these positions proved useful springboards for him and the SS from which to consolidate their power.

From the summer of 1934, Himmler commanded all political police forces of the German states, along with the concentration camps, which existed from the beginning of the Third Reich. Himmler now wielded the decisive instruments for the control of society as well as of his own party. In July 1934, the SS played a crucial role in the bloody purge of the highest echelon of the Storm Detachment (*Sturmabteilung* or SA), around its chief of staff, Ernst Röhm. In return, Hitler declared the SS an "independent organization within the framework of the NSDAP," and authorized it to build up its own armed formation, the *SS-Verfügungstruppe* (Special Service Troop).mh

No. 1-38
Confiscation by the SS of Social Democratic Party offices at Reichenbach im Vogtland in March 1933
The SS converted the building to a concentration camp, leaving only the letters "SS" from the original inscription "*Volkshaus*."
Stadtarchiv Reichenbach

No. 1-39
Heinrich Himmler as acting Munich Police President March 1933
Hoover Institution, Stanford University

Pillars of Power
1933 – 1936
Between Ideological Academy and Elitist Venue

In the year 1933, the SS leadership launched the search for a "castle" in the area of the Externsteine and the Hermann Monument. In November 1933, on the advice of architect Hermann Bartels, Himmler chose Wewelsburg Castle. Initially, various vaguely defined, competing notions were considered: one foresaw converting Wewelsburg Castle into a form of high-level ideological academy for SS officers.

Another concept envisioned the castle as a protected and insulated meeting place reserved for the highest circles of the SS leadership and their guests. Himmler followed the research activities of the Wewelsburg SS castle administration with interest and support, yet he and his architect, Hermann Bartels, kept the main focus on developing Wewelsburg Castle into a grand, elitist meeting place. mm

No. 1-46
Heinrich Himmler (third from left) with Adolf Hitler (far left) at Grevenburg Castle during the Lippe state elections Early January, 1933
Ullstein Bilderdienst, 60061

No. 1-44
First construction work in the castle moat, with personnel from the Voluntary Labor Service Photograph: Gieshoidt, Wewelsburg, March 1934
This photograph appeared on March 10, 1934, in the *Bürener Zeitung*.
Kreismuseum Wewelsburg, Fotoarchiv

No. 1-40
The first prisoner transport at the entrance gate of Dachau Concentration Camp
March 22, 1933
Stadtarchiv Munich, NS-322

No. 1-41
SA and SS men in front of the Wertheim department store in Berlin, during the anti-Jewish boycott
April 1, 193
The sign reads: "Germans! Defend yourselves! Don't buy from Jews!"
Bundesarchiv Koblenz, Fotoarchiv, Bild 183-R7035

No. 1-42
Chief of Staff of the *Sturmabteilung* (SA), Ernst Röhm, between Adolf Hitler and Heinrich Himmler Kiel, May 1933
Still from the film *Der Appell der SA-Gruppe Nordmark in Kiel 1933*
Bundesarchiv Berlin, Filmarchiv, M 808/24065

No. 1-43
Secret State Police Offices, Gestapo headquarters in Berlin, Prinz Albrecht Straße 8
1934
Bundesarchiv Koblenz, Fotoarchiv, Bild 102-03788

No. 1-45
Construction sheds in front of Wewelsburg Castle, with posters and banners for the *Reichstag* "election" of March 29, 1936
Early 1936
Kreismuseum Wewelsburg, Fotoarchiv

No. 1-47
The head of "Construction Management at the Wewelsburg SS School," Hermann Bartels (left), with Heinrich Himmler (right) and Bochum building contractor Fritz Scherpeltz (center) at a site inspection
Ca. 1936/1937
Kreismuseum Wewelsburg, Fotoarchiv

No. 1-48
The "Grand Courtroom" on the ground floor of the west wing
Mid-1930s
Kreismuseum Wewelsburg, Fotoarchiv

With his appointment as Chief of the German Police by Reich Chancellor Adolf Hitler, Himmler secured control of all police formations. He proceeded to bind them closely to the SS in personnel and ideological terms, and to employ them as instruments of ever more radical persecution.

Whereas political adversaries had constituted their principal victims immediately after the National Socialist seizure of power, the SS and police apparatus now gave increasing attention to Jews, Sinti, and Roma, and generally to all people viewed as "foreign to the community" or "antisocial."

To internally consolidate an organization whose rapid growth imperiled its cohesion, Himmler redoubled his efforts to stabilize the SS ideologically. Unique rituals and ideological training were supposed to strengthen elitist consciousness and prepare for a ruthless war of conquest. mh

No. 1-49
Adolf Hitler appoints Heinrich Himmler Chief of the German Police in the Reich Chancellery
Photograph: Scherl, June 17, 1936
Süddeutsche Zeitung Photo, 99713

No. 1-50
On the occasion of the fourth anniversary of the National-Socialist takeover, Hitler's bodyguard regiment, the SS-Leibstandarte, marches past Adolf Hitler, Heinrich Himmler, and Josef Dietrich, the regiment's commander
Wilhelm Straße, Berlin
January 30, 1937
Ullstein Bilderdienst, 00076378

No. 1-51
Reich Physician-SS Ernst Robert Grawitz, executive president of the German Red Cross, at a reception given by Hitler
Photograph: Heinrich Hoffmann, January 1938
Das Deutsche Rote Kreuz, Vol. 2 (Jan. 1938)

Expansion and Radicalization
1936 – 1939
Himmler's Stronghold for SS-Gruppenführer

The more Himmler's power grew within the National Socialist state, the more pressing his demands became that Wewelsburg Castle be transformed into a secrecy-shrouded retreat, screened from public view and with a particular allure for the highest SS leadership.

For its part, the SS castle administration initially sought to reshape the locality of Wewelsburg into a model village in keeping with the National Socialist ideology of a racially exclusive community. Taking a contrary approach, architect Bartels soon began to use ever larger areas of the village to fulfill Himmler's ideas and to initiate construction. The official designation for the SS school in Wewelsburg, the "SS School [at] House Wewelsburg," used until the collapse in 1945 primarily served Himmler's need to disguise the project. It was also to this end that the SS took over the financing of its Wewelsburg building projects in 1936. Ultimately, the withdrawal of the Reich Labor Service from Wewelsburg in 1938 also served Himmler's interests. In place of compulsory laborers supplied by the government, the SS now deployed prisoners from their own concentration camp erected at Wewelsburg to do forced labor. mm

No. 1-57
Heinrich Himmler (fourth from left) and guest Robert Ley (fifth from left, chief of the German Labor Front), inspecting excavations by the Wewelsburg SS School in Böddeken State Forest
Photograph: E. Hiebel, Wewelsburg SS School, January 4 – 6, 1937
Kreismuseum Wewelsburg, Fotoarchiv

No. 1-56
Construction work by the Reich Labor Service in front of the nearly finished "Village Community Center"
Photograph: Walter Franzius, early 1937
Kreismuseum Wewelsburg, Fotoarchiv

No. 1-58
May Day celebration 1937 with the Wewelsburg folk dance group
Photograph: Wewelsburg SS School, May 1, 1937
Among the spectators, the SS castle administration staff (front right) and the Reich Labor Service unit stationed in Wewelsburg (rear right).
Kreismuseum Wewelsburg, Fotoarchiv

No. 1-52
The flag of the SS is raised for the first time at Flossenbürg Concentration Camp
May 1938
Bundesarchiv Berlin, formerly the Berlin Document Center, SSO Theodor Eicke

No. 1-55
Heinrich Himmler conferring in Berlin with the chiefs of the Gestapo and Criminal Police (*Kriminalpolizei*) following the assassination attempt on Adolf Hitler by carpenter Georg Elser
Photograph: Heinrich Hoffmann, November 9, 1939
From left to right: Franz Josef Huber, Arthur Nebe, Heinrich Himmler, Reinhard Heydrich, Heinrich Müller; in the background, a painting of Wewelsburg Castle.
Bayerische Staatsbibliothek, Munich, Fotoarchiv Hoffmann, 28780

No. 1-54
Soon after the incorporation of the Sudetenland into the German Reich, political opponents were arrested and taken away by the police
Graslitz (Sudetenland), October 1938
Ullstein Bilderdienst, Archiv Gerstenberg, 00684524

No. 1-53
Himmler and the SS leadership lay a wreath at the tomb of King Henry I in the crypt of Quedlinburg Abby
Photograph: Scherl, July 2, 1938
Süddeutsche Zeitung Photo, 38897

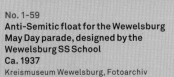
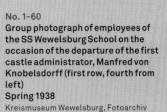
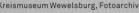

No. 1-59
Anti-Semitic float for the Wewelsburg May Day parade, designed by the Wewelsburg SS School
Ca. 1937
Kreismuseum Wewelsburg, Fotoarchiv

No. 1-60
Group photograph of employees of the SS Wewelsburg School on the occasion of the departure of the first castle administrator, Manfred von Knobelsdorff (first row, fourth from left)
Spring 1938
Kreismuseum Wewelsburg, Fotoarchiv

No. 1-61
Covertly taken photograph of the first temporary Wewelsburg concentration camp in the Alme Valley, below the castle
June 29, 1939
Kreismuseum Wewelsburg, Fotoarchiv

Immediately after the start of World War II, the SS, the police, and the so-called *Einsatzgruppen*, brought ideologically inspired terror to the occupied territories in the wake of advancing German troops. Within just a few years their firing squads killed millions of civilians, in particular in the eastern regions of Europe.

After the end of 1941, Jews, as well as Roma and Sinti (also known as Gypsies), were deported from the German Reich and the conquered West European countries to occupied areas in the east, where they were systematically murdered in extermination camps set up for that purpose. The mass murder was part of a "great Germanic population policy," just like the gigantic settlement plans, which Himmler's subordinates developed in the same period to settle or resettle members of the ethnic German minorities (the so-called *Volksdeutsche*) in the conquered territories.

The armed units of the SS also took part in the war. Known since the end of 1939 as the *Waffen-SS*, they participated in regular combat operations as well as in innumerable crimes. mh

No. 1-63
Deportation of Roma and Sinti families, Asperg (Württemberg)
May 22, 1940
Bundesarchiv Koblenz, Fotoarchiv, R 165 Bild-244-43

No. 1-62
The *Waffen-SS* in combat operations
Herbert König and Ludwig Pröscholdt, *SS im Kampf*, for the *Reichsführer–SS Main Office* Nordland Verlag, Berlin, 1942

No. 1-64
Heinrich Himmler inaugurates the exhibition "Reconstruction and Planning in the East" at the State University of Fine Arts, Hardenberg Straße, Berlin
March 20, 1941
Present are Hitler's deputy, Rudolf Hess (center), and the head of the *Führer*'s chancellery, Philip Bouhler (left, next to Hess), among others.
Ullstein Bildarchiv, 00024539

War and the Dissolution of Boundaries

1939 – 1942

Megalomania and Criminal Acts

Against a background of the racist war of conquest, the dimensions of the projected SS architecture in Wewelsburg became increasingly gargantuan. Hermann Bartels designed an enormous castle complex in multiple concentric circles. The village of Wewelsburg shrunk to a mere planning obstacle for the SS in charge. Yet, unlike in the conquered territories of Eastern Europe, the SS were forced to resort to judicial means and enticing offers to cajole their Wewelsburg "racial comrades" into abandoning their ancestral home.

On the periphery of Wewelsburg, the SS erected Niederhagen Concentration Camp, which provided the forced labor for its building projects. About 3,900 people, including over 2,000 Soviet prisoners of war and forced laborers, several hundred Poles, along with numerous Jehovah's Witnesses, were interned here between 1939 and 1945. Imprisonment and work conditions, as well as mistreatment and executions at the hands of SS guards, resulted in the deaths of 1,285 prisoners in Wewelsburg. mm

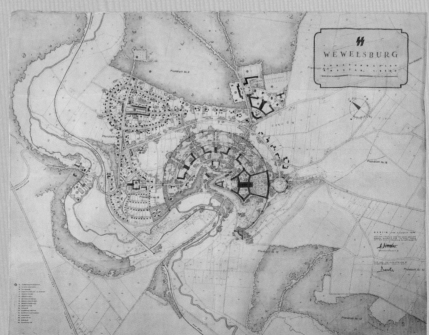

No. 1-68
SS development plan for Wewelsburg by Hermann Bartels, approved by *Reichsführer-SS* Heinrich Himmler
August 5, 1940
Kreismuseum Wewelsburg, Fotoarchiv

No. 1-69
View of the projected *Gruppenführer* Hall in the upper stories of the northern tower (model)
Ca. 1942
Kreismuseum Wewelsburg, Fotoarchiv

No. 1-65
Special train of the SS Immigration Central Office (*Einwanderer-zentralstelle*)
Ca. 1941
Bundesarchiv Koblenz, Fotoarchiv, Bild 146-1972-041-03

No. 1-66
SS men in front of Soviet prisoners of war at the roll call area of Mauthausen Concentration Camp
October 1941
Bundesarchiv Koblenz, Bildarchiv, Bild 192-050

No. 1-67
"Executions of Jews conducted by Einsatzgruppe A," appendix to the second report by the commander of *Einsatzgruppe* A, Dr. Franz Walter Stahlecker, for the period from October 16, 1941 to January 31, 1942
U. S. Holocaust Memorial Museum, Washington D.C., Photo Archives, 03550

No. 1-70
Northern tower with scaffolding shortly before its partial demolition; construction sheds and building materials in the castle moat
Summer 1941
Kreismuseum Wewelsburg, Fotoarchiv

No. 1-71
Niederhagen Concentration Camp viewed from the west
Between 1940 and 1943
Kreismuseum Wewelsburg, Fotoarchiv

No. 1-72
Concentration camp prisoners at work in the stone quarry below Wewelsburg Castle
1940/1941
Kreismuseum Wewelsburg, Fotoarchiv

No. 1-73
SS guard unit at Niederhagen Concentration Camp
Ca. 1941
Kreismuseum Wewelsburg, Fotoarchiv

After the Battle of Stalingrad, in early 1943, the German armies were in continuous retreat. Meanwhile, the National Socialist regime further intensified its reign of terror. Systematic murder reached its peak; in the extermination camps alone, about three million people perished before the end of the war. To supplement an insufficient workforce, primarily in the armaments industry, the SS Economic and Administrative Main Office (*SS-Wirtschafts-Verwaltungshauptamt*) assigned concentration camp prisoners as forced laborers.

The SS leadership sought to make up for increasing personnel shortages in the *Waffen-SS* and police by recruiting men from other European countries, eventually even loosening its racist selection standards.

To the very last days of the war, well after the combat had reached the territory of the German Reich, the SS and police continued with their terror; only the total defeat of Germany finally ended its devastating impact.mh

No. 1-75
Prisoners of Dachau Concentration Camp doing forced labor in an armament plant
1943
Bildarchiv Preußischer Kulturbesitz, Berlin, 30023281

No. 1-74
Deployment of task force under SS Brigadeführer Walter Schimana in the Soviet Union
Photograph: May, ca. 1942/1943
Order Police soldiers in front of a burning building
Bundesarchiv Koblenz, Bildarchiv, Bild 146-1993-025-03

No. 1-77
Arrival and selection of Hungarian Jews in Auschwitz-Birkenau
May 1944
In the foreground (center), concentration camp physician Dr. Horst Fischer
Yad Vashem, Jerusalem, Auschwitz Album, 268-35

Terror During the Downfall of the Third Reich

1943 – 1945
"Final Victory" Fantasies and Collapse

The turn of the war's tide in spring 1943 led to the SS having to abandon its ideological construction project in Wewelsburg for the benefit of the German war effort. Niederhagen Concentration Camp was disbanded and the prisoners, apart from a 42-man work detachment, were sent to other concentration camps. The Niederhagen Camp grounds were subsequently used by the SS as a relocation camp for ethnic Germans from southeastern Europe, and as a military preparedness training camp, to ready members of the Hitler Youth for combat. Nevertheless, the SS leadership and the local construction management under Hermann Bartels continued their planning for the transformation of Wewelsburg. Following a German "final victory," the project was to take about twenty years to complete. A few days before American troops reached the village of Wewelsburg on April 2, 1945, and liberated the last remaining prisoners, Himmler had the castle blown up. mm

No. 1-83
Occupants of the Wewelsburg Relocation Camp under the "Ethnic German Liaison Office"
Winter 1943 – 1944
Kreismuseum Wewelsburg, Fotoarchiv

No. 1-84
Prisoners of the former Wewelsburg external detachment of Buchenwald Concentration Camp, a few weeks after their liberation by American troops
Early May, 1945
Kreismuseum Wewelsburg, Fotoarchiv

No. 1-81
Model of the planned SS castle complex
1944
LWL-Amt für Denkmalpflege in Westfalen

No. 1-78
Himmler with the 14th *Waffen-SS* Infantry Division, also known as the Galician SS Division, consisting mainly of Ukrainian soldiers
Photograph: SS war correspondent Markert, ca. 1944
Left, behind Himmler, the division commander Fritz Freitag, *SS-Brigadeführer* and *Waffen-SS* major general
Weltkriegsbücherei, Stuttgart, neg. no. 131/12A

No. 1-80
SS guards of Buchenwald Concentration Camp in American captivity April 1945
U.S. Holocaust Memorial Museum, Washington, D.C., Photo Archives, 04748

No. 1-76
***Lebensborn* Home 1943**
SS Leitheft, vol. 9, no. 3 (1943)

No. 1-79
Removal of the body of a prisoner who died after the liberation of Flossenbürg Concentration Camp
Photograph: U.S. Army Signal Corps, May 3, 1945
National Archives, Washington, D.C., 111-SC-207008

No. 1-82
Wewelsburg Castle in camouflage paint 1944
Kreismuseum Wewelsburg, Fotoarchiv

No. 1-85
American soldiers and a Wewelsburg shepherd in the Alme Valley in front of the ruin of Wewelsburg Castle, blown up by the SS April 7, 1945
National Archives, Washington, D.C., Signal Corps photo 407883

On September 30, 1946, the Nuremberg International Military Tribunal ruled that the SS, the Security Service of the *Reichsführer SS* (SD), and the Gestapo were "criminal organizations."

Over the following decades, atrocities committed by the SS and police were repeatedly the object of court proceedings in Germany and elsewhere. Most of the former perpetrators, however, got off lightly or remained unknown. For many years, veterans of the *Waffen-SS* held their reunions unmolested; subsequent generations of right-wing extremists perpetuate the use of SS symbols and slogans to this day.

Countering this is an increasing social engagement by those who critically confront the legacy of the National Socialist past in many ways, and keep alive the memory of the victims. mh

No. 1-86
Session of the International Military Tribunal in Nuremberg; issuing the indictment against National Socialist organizations, including the SS, Gestapo, and the SD
Photograph: Ray d'Addario, December 19/20, 1945
Ullstein Bilderdienst, 00522731

No. 1-88
"Comradeship meeting" of former members of the *Waffen-SS* Karlsburg, July 1957
At center, the former commander of the SS division *Hitlerjugend*, Kurt Meyer; to his right, sitting, former commander of the SS division *Das Reich*, Paul Hausser
Bundesarchiv Koblenz, Bildarchiv, Bild 183-48645-0003

No. 1-87
Buchenwald monument from 1958, with a statuary group by sculptor Fritz Cremer
Photograph: Matthias Hambrock, June 1990
Kreismuseum Wewelsburg, Fotoarchiv

The Aftermath

After 1945

The Aftermath in Wewelsburg

After 1945, there was a desire among numerous long-time residents of Wewelsburg to return to life as it existed before 1933. Many felt that they, too, were victims and thus rejected any serious examination of the consequences of National Socialist rule. The first memorials were initiated from outside the region, and were soon removed.

Myths portraying Wewelsburg Castle as, for example, a "home" for "racially desirable, illegitimate newborns" developed in parallel to media fancies, which designated the castle as the location of spiritualist séances by SS leadership. Serious investigation of the history of the SS did not start until the 1970s. This effort has included the cultivation of contact with surviving concentration camp prisoners since the memorial was founded at the Kreismuseum Wewelsburg in 1982. Academic research and pedagogical work took on new significance at the close of the twentieth century, when Wewelsburg Castle became a kind of projection screen for any number of extreme-right-wing, esoteric, and satanic fantasies. The villagers' perception of the past was also evolving, as demonstrated by the erection of a memorial on the former concentration camp roll call area by younger members of the Wewelsburg community in 2000. mm

No. 1-93
The former gatehouse of Niederhagen Concentration Camp, seen from the former roll call area
Photogaph: Adolf Porsch, probably 1949
Kreismuseum Wewelsburg, Fotoarchiv

No. 1-95
On the day marking the reopening of the District History Museum and the youth hostel, visitors view the cautionary memorial cycle by Jo Glahé in the former crypt of the northern tower
June 29, 1950
Kreismuseum Wewelsburg, Fotoarchiv

No. 1-94
A dance company in the Alme Valley, below the castle, during the first "International Festival" in Wewelsburg
June 18 to 25, 1954
Kreismuseum Wewelsburg, Fotoarchiv

No. 1-89
Cover of *Der Spiegel*, January 29, 1979, at the time of the first German broadcast of the American television series *Holocaust*
January 29, 1979
Spiegel-Verlag

No. 1-90
Public protests following the announcement of the verdict in the Düsseldorf Madjanek trial
June 29, 1981
Ullstein Bilderdienst, 00131572

No. 1-92
The SS leader unmasked
Front cover of the book by Joachim Lerchenmüller and Gerd Simon, *Maskenwechsel. Wie der SS-Hauptsturm-führer Schneider zum BRD-Hochschulrektor Schwerte wurde und andere Geschichten über die Wendigkeit deutscher Wissenschaft im 20. Jahrhundert*. [Change of Masks: How SS-Hauptsturmführer Schneider Became University Rector Schwerte, and Other Tales of Flexibility in German Academia during the 20th Century]
Verlag der Gesellschaft für interdisziplinäre Forschung, Tübingen 1999

No. 1-91
Demonstration by right-wing extremists in Halbe (Brandenburg)
November 13, 2004
In the foreground, two participants with the opening lines of the SS hymn printed on their T-shirts.
Ullstein Bilderdienst, 00761937

No. 1-96
Group photograph of former prisoners from Niederhagen Concentration Camp on the former roll call area on the occasion of their first official reunion in Wewelsburg after 1945
May 1992
Kreismuseum Wewelsburg, Fotoarchiv

No. 1-98
Tour of the exhibition "Wewelsburg 1933–1945. SS Cult and Terror Site" by former Niederhagen Concentration Camp prisoners, their families, and young people
April 3, 1998
Kreismuseum Wewelsburg, Fotoarchiv

No. 1-99
Dedication of the memorial to victims of Niederhagen Concentration Camp on the former roll call area
Photograph: Stephan Sagurna, **April 2, 2000**
LWL-Medienzentrum für Westfalen

No. 1-97
Floor ornament in the *Obergruppenführer* Hall of the northern tower; known internationally since the 1990s as a "black sun"
Kreismuseum Wewelsburg, Fotoarchiv

The SS was a diverse organization; its development was dynamic. The following subject area offers insight into the central aspects of its history and structure. Selected biographies of SS members active in Wewelsburg reveal the diversity of social backgrounds, careers, and functions represented in the SS. The organization, which from outside appeared monolithic, is shown to be a heterogeneous group of individuals.

2 The SS in Wewelsburg – Biographical Approaches

2.1
Organizational Status and Financing of Wewelsburg Castle

During the first two years, reconstruction of Wewelsburg Castle for the SS was financed by the Prussian state and the NSDAP, as well as with private donations. Organizationally, the project was initially under the control of the SS Race and Settlement Main Office, which was responsible for the ideological training of the SS. In 1935, Himmler transferred the castle administration personnel to his staff. In order to circumvent state and party financial controls, he and six other SS leaders founded the Society for the Promotion and Care of German Cultural Monuments (GEFÖ) on February 1, 1936. The organization was subsequently integrated into the economic and administrative institutions of the SS, remaining in charge of the Wewelsburg SS project until 1945. Over time, the GEFÖ took out bank loans amounting to 13 million Reichsmarks – from the Dresdner Bank in particular – as well as other private organizations. Repayment was to be made from the profits the SS planned to generate from forced labor in the concentration camps.

No. 2-1
Organizational chart for financing and status of Wewelsburg in the SS organization 1934 – 1945

Reichsführer-SS
Heinrich Himmler

	Administration of SS School House Wewelsburg		Administration and organization of SS construction projects in Wewelsburg
	1934 – 1935	1935 – 1945	Until 1939
Central SS institutions	**SS Race and Settlement Office** (Main Office since 1935) Chief until 1938: Richard Walter Darré	**Staff Reichsführer-SS** Subsequently: **Personal Staff Reichsführer-SS** As of 1939; retroactive to 1936, established as a Main Office Head: Karl Wolff	**SS Administration Office** All SS construction operations in Wewelsburg were managed as of February 1, 1936, by the: **Society for the Promotion and Care of German Cultural Monuments** Chairman: Heinrich Himmler Business Manager: Oswald Pohl
The SS in Wewelsburg	1934/1935 **Reichsführer School SS** As of 1935 officially named: **SS-Schule Haus Wewelsburg (Wewelsburg SS School)** As of 1942, at the latest: **Department Wewelsburg SS School at the Personal Staff RFSS Main Office** Chief castle Administrators: 1934 – January 30, 1938: Manfred von Knobelsdorff January 30, 1938 – 1945: Siegfried Taubert		1934 – 1945 **Construction Management of Wewelsburg SS School** Head: Hermann Bartels
Non-SS participants			**Non-SS construction contractors:** Private construction companies and craftsmen firms 1934 – 1938, workforce from the Labor Service – until 1935 the Volunteer Labor Service (FAD), then the Reich Labor Service (RAD)

1 Bergmann
2 Franzius
3 von Knobelsdorff
4 des Coudres
5 Jordan
6 Frank

No. 2-2

Group photograph, personnel of the Wewelsburg SS School in the castle moat Spring 1938

This photograph of the academic and operations staff of the Wewelsburg SS School was taken in the spring of 1938, on the occasion of the departure of the castle's first chief administrator, Manfred von Knobelsdorff from Wewelsburg Castle (front row, 4th from the left).

During this period, the SS castle administration experienced a phase of profound disorientation. Himmler questioned the continued existence of Wewelsburg Castle's research facilities, because he wanted "his castle" put entirely at the disposal of the SS-Gruppenführer. The leading "ideological instructors" would all leave the SS school within the coming year. Von Knobelsdorff turned out to be an inadequate leader, resulting in lax discipline. Although the stability sought by the SS hierarchy did return under the next chief castle administrator, Siegfried Taubert, his staff as such lost practically all significance for the development of the SS project in Wewelsburg. mm

Kreismuseum Wewelsburg, Fotoarchiv

1939–1942	From March 1942
Main Offices of Administration and Economy & Budget and Construction Main Department for Special Tasks Section HS I	**SS Economy and Administration Main Office (WVHA)** Department W (business enterprises) including Department VIII: Special Tasks Chief administrator for all of the above: Oswald Pohl

	Development of the concentration camp at Wewelsburg
May 1939 – January 7, 1941	External detachment of Sachsenhausen Concentration Camp
January 7, 1941 – August 31, 1941	Subcamp of Sachsenhausen Concentration Camp
September 1, 1941 – April 1943	Independent Niederhagen Concentration Camp
April 1943 – April 2, 1945	External detachment of Buchenwald Concentration Camp
Detachment and camp leaders:	
May 1939 – June 1940	Wolfgang Plaul
June 17, 1940 – April 1943	Adolf Haas
May – December 1943	Otto Jacob
January – October 1944	Schiering
November 1944 – April 1945	Johann Skupy

Lenders to the SS:
Banks, primarily Dresdner Bank
The German Red Cross
The German Labor Front
Private donors
Initially government grants as well

Official property developer 1934–1936
The National Socialist German Workers' Party (NSDAP), the Treasurer

2.2
Biographies of SS Men in Wewelsburg

The Wewelsburg SS biographies illuminate how and by what means men from all walks of life came to the SS. The discernible personal traits of the SS men presented here and the peculiarities of Wewelsburg demonstrate that one cannot view the SS as a homogeneous bloc. The careers represented in Wewelsburg illustrate – despite their individual ruptures – the political, ideological, and violent development of the SS until 1945. They show that the elitist self-perception of the SS cannot be separated from its racist ideology, or its increasingly unrestrained violence.

2.2.1
Nordic Racism and Genealogy: Manfred von Knobelsdorff, the First Chief Administrator of Wewelsburg Castle

No. 2-3
Manfred von Knobelsdorff, photograph from his SS officer file
In 1934, Manfred von Knobelsdorff (1892 – 1965), a 42-year-old commercial agent and ex-officer in the Imperial Army, was chosen for the position of chief administrator and first director of the "SS School" at Wewelsburg Castle. He was an enthusiastic follower of his brother-in-law, Richard Walther Darré, whose notion of an agrarian, racial aristocracy long influenced the ideological orientation of the SS. Supported by his wife Ilse, von Knobelsdorff largely had a free hand in selecting his staff for the castle.

His personal interest in genealogy decisively molded the practical work at the Wewelsburg SS School. In 1938, von Knobelsdorff left full-time service in the SS, disappointed with the organization's ideological direction and increasingly at odds with the duties of a chief administrator at Wewelsburg Castle. mm

Bundesarchiv Berlin; formerly Berlin Document Center, SSO Manfred von Knobelsdorff

Manfred von Knobelsdorff (1892 – 1965)
Chief administrator of the castle and head of the Wewelsburg SS School, 1934 – 1938
June 15, 1892
Born in Heide/Holstein, the fourth son of an aristocratic Prussian military family
1902 – 1910
Basic military training at the Prussian Cadet Institutes at Plön and Lichterfelde/Berlin
1910
Entry into the army as officer cadet in the 85th Prussian Infantry Regiment
1914 – 1918
Front-line officer in World War I, ultimately with the rank of first lieutenant in the Guard Cavalry Rifle Division, he participated in the suppression of the democratic councils movement during the November Revolution in Germany.
1918 – 1920
Activism in national-conservative parties and military officer leagues; active supporter of the right-wing Kapp Putsch in March 1920; politically motivated resignation from the *Reichswehr* with the rank of captain
1920 – 1934
Commercial representative for companies trading in essential oils and perfumes; privately engaged in genealogical research and in publishing historical and racist materials
1923
Marriage to Ilse Darré, sister of later National Socialist ideologue and SS Leader Richard Walther Darré; the marriage produced two sons and a daughter
1931
Foundation in Düsseldorf of a local chapter of the "Nordic Ring" for the promotion of Nordic-Germanic awareness and ideology
1933
Entry into the NSDAP
1934
Entry into the SS and work with the SS Race and Settlement Office, headed by Darré, as commissioner for the ideological training of SS members in and around Düsseldorf; selection as director of a planned SS school in Schwalenburg Castle (Lippe)
1935
Fulltime assumption of the same duties at the *Reichsführer* School SS Wewelsburg
1937
Publication of his book on the genealogical tree of Richard Walther Darré; disciplinary proceedings against von Knobelsdorff and other Wewelsburg SS officers on allegations of maintaining slush funds are inconclusive in the case of the chief administrator
January 30, 1938
Departure as chief castle administrator of the Wewelsburg SS School and end of full time SS service with the rank of *SS-Obersturmbannführer*; professional activity as an editor for the Blut und Boden (Blood and Soil) publishing house of the Reich Food Administration office in Goslar
1939 – 1945
Military service in World War II as a transport and occupation administration officer in the German Armed Forces, in Finland and France, among other places
After 1945
Three-year internment, then resumption of professional activity as a salesman for the perfume industry
July 20, 1965
Death in Bremen mm

No. 2-7
Heinrich Himmler (left) and Manfred von Knobelsdorff in the Wewelsburg Castle gardens
Probably May 8, 1937
Himmler regarded von Knobelsdorff favorably, though without granting special support or promotion. With Darré's diminishing influence upon Himmler, von Knobelsdorff's position in Wewelsburg became less secure. In his interactions with the local Wewelsburg population, he was inept and arrogant. His internal leadership qualities also quickly reached their limits, with his subordinates engaging in various disciplinary violations. He was himself investigated on allegations of maintaining slush funds.

Above all, some of the younger academics in the SS castle administration appear to have thought von Knobelsdorff insufficiently "military" in his bearing, and too "emotional." That he obviously owed his position as chief castle administrator to his personal relationship with Darré contradicted the standards of ideological radicalism and result-oriented practices prevalent among those who had come of age in the elitist right-wing extremist associations. mm

Kreismuseum Wewelsburg, Fotoarchiv

No. 2-4

"Major v. Knobelsdorff in the uniform of the Leib-Grenadier-Regiment Frederick-William III, I. Brandenb. N. 8, with sons Egbert, Arved, Manfred" (translation of original inscription)
Photograph on cardboard, probably 1911 – 1914

From earliest childhood, Manfred von Knobelsdorff's personality was shaped by a combination of Prussian militarism and a sense of aristocratic tradition. He began to wear a uniform as a ten-year old cadet. Like his father and his brothers, he became an officer. He experienced World War I on the Western Front, in France. He fought against the November Revolution of 1918 both in combat – as an officer in a monarchist elite unit – and politics, as a member of nationalistic officer associations. His preoccupation with his own aristocratic family history and with various figures of Prussian history (for example, King Frederick II, "the Great") seems initially to have occupied von Knobeldorff's free time during the Weimar Republic. mm

Loan from private collection
Kreismuseum Wewelsburg, inv. no. 16627

No. 2-5
Not shown

Manfred von Knobelsdorff and his wife Ilse, nee Darré, in the family Opel 4 PS ("Laubfrosch")
Postcard, ca. 1930

Loan from private collection
Kreismuseum Wewelsburg,
inv. no. 16626

No. 2-6

Manfred von Knobelsdorff in white leisure clothing
July 25, 1931

During the Weimar Republic, Manfred von Knobelsdorff and his family lived a life typical of the Rhineland upper middle class, with corresponding status symbols and social activities. In this period, his brother-in-law, Richard Walther Darré, imparted a specifically racist character to von Knobelsdorff's fundamentally anti-republican and anti-democratic outlook. The close relationship to Darré, who as Himmler's ideological sloganeer and first chief of the SS Race and Settlement Main Office was a leading figure in the early SS, put von Knobeldorff in the running for high-level functions within the organization in 1933. mm

Loan from private collection
Kreismuseum Wewelsburg, inv. no. 16624

No. 2-9

Firearms license for Manfred von Knobelsdorff
Büren, July 13, 1935

A set of firearms licenses has survived from the years 1935/1936; they permitted staff of the Wewelsburg SS School to carry pistols. The Büren District Office also issued such a document to the chief administrator of the castle.

On November 9, 1935, Himmler issued the "Law of Honor of the SS Man," which established for every member of the SS "the right and the duty" to "defend his honor by force of arms." The "honor" of the SS man was a construct compounded of racist and militarist, male-society concepts such as "race-consciousness," "loyalty to one's own blood," to one's "comrades in arms" or to the "leaders of the people." The daily habituation to carrying weapons, clothed in unctuous language, constituted a stone in the mosaic of the education to violence in the SS, as also practiced in the Wewelsburg SS School. mm

Kreisarchiv Paderborn, BürA 1388

No. 2–10

Handmade certificate with colored coat of arms of the Darré family. Design by Karl Maria Wiligut (alias Weisthor), execution for Ilse von Knobelsdorff, with an adage from her brother, Richard Walther Darré: "Through leadership and procreation, maintenance of the divine order. Dedicated to my sister, Ilse. Goslar, November 1936" Material: drawing on parchment, red leather binding

Richard Walther Darré dedicated this certificate to his sister Ilse von Knobelsdorff. Designed by Karl Maria Wiligut, it depicts the coat of arms of the Darré family. The motto refers to the racist ideas of the Austrian occultist Wiligut. Naming himself Weisthor, Wiligut was long believed to have decisively shaped Himmler's plans for Wewelsburg Castle. In fact, his ideological influence proved more lasting on Darré and Darré's family and colleagues (including his brother-in-law, Manfred von Knobelsdorff) than on the chief of the SS. Himmler used Wiligut in Wewelsburg merely to resolve practical issues, such as the design of the coats of arms for the *SS-Gruppenführer*, which he wished to have on the wall in the SS stronghold. mm

Loan from private collection
Kreismuseum Wewelsburg, inv. no. 16611

No. 2–12

**Manfred von Knobelsdorff's photograph album, with 14 images of the family apartment in Wewelsburg Castle's south wing, here: "The Upper Hall" (translation of original inscription)
1935 – 1938**

Loan from private collection
Kreismuseum Wewelsburg, inv. no. 16696

No. 2–8
Not shown

**Manfred von Knobelsdorff in an army uniform
February 9, 1941**

At the end of January 1938, Manfred von Knobelsdorff left Wewelsburg Castle and full-time service in the SS, though he nominally remained a member of the General SS. As an employee of a publishing house of the Reich Food Administration, he moved even closer – now also professionally – to his brother-in-law, the Reich Farmer Leader, Darré, who in the meantime had been stripped of power within the SS. During the war, von Knobelsdorff served as a transport and occupation administrative officer in the armed forces. Neither von Knobelsdorff nor the SS leadership appears to have sought his admission to the *Waffen-SS*. mm

Loan from private collection
Kreismuseum Wewelsburg, inv. no. 16625

No. 2–11

Diary of Manfred von Knobelsdorff with entries from March 14, 1938

In 1933/1934 and again in 1938, Manfred von Knobelsdorff wrote diary-like entries – including many from Wewelsburg – in this green notebook. At the end of January 1938, von Knobelsdorff had retired from service as chief administrator of the castle. The events leading to the incorporation of Austria into the German Reich, however, delayed his official discharge by Himmler and the assumption of duties by his successor, *SS-Brigadeführer* Siegfried Taubert, until May 22 of that year. In the interim, the ex-chief administrator continued to reside at Wewelsburg Castle, consigning to the notebook his increasingly ill-tempered and pessimistic observations on developments around the Wewelsburg SS School. mm

Loan from private collection
Kreismuseum Wewelsburg, inv. no. 16401

"Besides, the difference between Taubert and me was unmistakable. It's intellectual in nature. He expressed this quite openly, by the way, on the occasion of his appointment to his position. He bluntly told the Reich Leader: 'Give me a regiment, I can take command; I can also ride horses. I can hunt a buck and sort out military history or a tactical problem. But excavations, ideological things like this [illegible], I understand nothing of these things.' The Reichsführer-SS laughed and remarked: 'Well, if you can understand that much, things I don't even understand yet, then you're sure to handle this business in Wewelsburg.'"

Translation of a transcription excerpt

2.2.2
Propagandist of the "Ethnic Community" in Wewelsburg: Walter Franzius

No. 2-13

Photograph from Walter Franzius's SS file on his engagement and marriage application

Twenty-seven-year-old Düsseldorf architect Walter Franzius (1906 – 1987) was the first to be summoned by chief castle administrator von Knobelsdorff as SS indoctrination leader at Wewelsburg Castle. According to expectations of his superior, Franzius was to provide a "Nordic" orientation to the architectural design of the castle. Unable to prevail over Himmler's favorite, Hermann Bartels, Franzius then directed his energies to an attempt at reshaping the village of Wewelsburg and its inhabitants according to National Socialist ethnic community ideology. In the end, with little to do, he left the Wewelsburg SS School and full-time service in the SS in the spring of 1939. He subsequently sought to realize his ideas of National Socialist (NS) settlement architecture in the service of the NS labor organization, the German Labor Front. Following a short stint in an army artillery regiment, Franzius spent the rest of the war as the construction supervisor of a NS armaments organization in Scandinavia. mm

Bundesarchiv Berlin,
formerly Berlin Document Center, RS Franzius

Walter Franzius (1906 – 1987)
Architect, instruction leader at the Wewelsburg SS School, 1934 – 1939

<u>November 28, 1906</u>
Born in Düsseldorf, the third child in a family of architects

<u>1913 – 1925</u>
Schooling in Düsseldorf, secondary school graduation after the twelfth grade

<u>1922</u>
Membership in the extreme anti-Semitic and nationalist German National Freedom Party (*Deutschvölkische Freiheitspartei*)

<u>1925/1926</u>
Apprenticeship in a Düsseldorf construction firm

<u>1926 – 1929</u>
Study of architecture at the Stuttgart Technical University, under Paul Bonatz, among others

<u>1930</u>
Self-employed architect in Düsseldorf

<u>May 1, 1932</u>
Entry into the NSDAP, employed in the engineering/technical department of the Party

<u>1933</u>
Entry into the SA

<u>Summer of 1933</u>
Beginning of the collaboration with Manfred von Knobelsdorff as employee in the training activities of the SS Race and Settlement Office, SS Sector V (headquarters in Essen)

<u>February 1934</u>
Transfer from SA to SS as indoctrination leader in the region under the 20th SS Regiment (Düsseldorf)

<u>Summer of 1934</u>
Assumption of duties as indoctrination leader at the planned SS School in Wewelsburg, archaeological excavations in the Wewelsburg surroundings: several weeks of training with the SS Special Service Troops in Munich while under contract with the Wewelsburg SS School

<u>Spring of 1935</u>
Research on witchcraft and genealogy for Himmler

<u>July 1935</u>
Rejection of Franzius's position paper "The Communal Village of the SS Settlers" by the SS Race and Settlement Main Office

<u>Fall of 1935</u>
Start of planning for the future Village Community Center in Wewelsburg

<u>1936 – 1938</u>
Design, planning, and execution of National Socialist festive processions, solstice festivities, and village beautification campaigns in Wewelsburg

<u>May 7, 1937</u>
Wedding ceremony at the Wewelsburg Village Community Center, which was constructed under Franzius's supervision and inaugurated the same day in the presence of Himmler

<u>May 1938</u>
Application to the SS's research group "Ancestral Heritage" in the framework of the research project "Forest and Tree in Aryan-Germanic Intellectual and Cultural History" as responsible contributor on topic 15: "The Influence of Wood on the Plastic Arts of the Germanic Tribes" (withdrawn the following year)

<u>March 31, 1939</u>
Departure from Wewelsburg SS School and full-time service in the SS with the rank of an *SS-Hauptsturmführer*

<u>Spring/Summer 1939</u>
Architectural activity at the Homesteading Section of the German Labor Front (DAF) in Hamburg

<u>September 1939</u>
Combat deployment in a *Wehrmacht* army artillery regiment

<u>Summer 1940</u>
Discharge from the *Wehrmacht* following service-related injury, return to DAF Homesteading Section in Hamburg

<u>April 1942</u>
Beginning of activity at *Einsatzgruppe Wiking* of the *Organisation Todt* (OT) with headquarters in Oslo

<u>April 1943</u>
Head of the Finnish central office of OT's *Einsatzgruppe Wiking* in Helsinki

<u>June 29, 1945</u>
"Automatic arrest" (internment) in the British-occupied zone because of officer rank in the General SS, release on March 19, 1947

<u>June 30, 1948</u>
In the denazification process, classification in Category IV ("follower"). Return to professional activity as an independent architect in Düsseldorf, for a time in association with his former SS comrade Norbert Demmel, SS construction supervisor at the Externsteine; Demmel also spent some time at Wewelsburg SS School. Franzius and Demmel built schools and other facilities in the Rhineland and the Ruhr.

<u>June 5, 1987</u>
Death in Düsseldorf mm

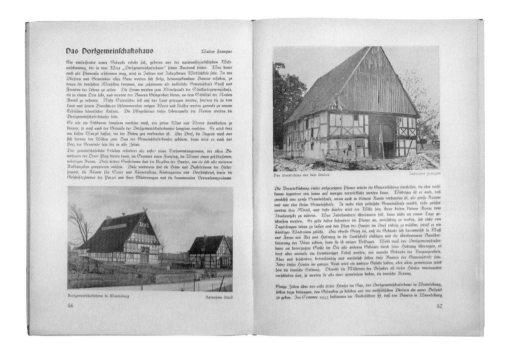

No. 2-15, No. 2-16

Franzius with master carpenter Grote at the construction site
Walter Franzius during construction work for the village community center
Between 1926 and 1929, Franzius studied at the Technical University, Stuttgart, then the most important conservative architectural school in Germany. Its mandatory curriculum included hands-on experience in the building trades. This proved useful to Franzius in working with the craftsmen during construction of the Wewelsburg Village Community Center. The "Stuttgart School" was committed to a building approach that stressed integration into the landscape along with proper application of construction materials and techniques. Its theoretical guidelines presented numerous affinities with the National Socialist propagandistic concept of *Volksgemeinschaft* (ethnic community). Franzius did not limit his interest in creating a National Socialist *Volksgemeinschaft* in Wewelsburg to the Village Community Center; he also organized local festivals and processions on National Socialist holidays, in an effort to convince the villagers of the racial difference between "race comrades" and "strangers to the community," in other words, Jews, opponents of National Socialism, etc. mm
Kreismuseum Wewelsburg, Fotoarchiv

No. 2-14
Not shown

"Mention, in chronological order, of all professional relationships and employment, along with all military service since January 1, 1931"; from the denazification file of Walter Franzius
1947
After 1945, in his denazification questionnaire, Franzius listed the successive stages of his professional and military career since 1930. Here, he reduced his activity in Wewelsburg to that of an architect for "settlement development" in the "SS Settlement Office." In reality, he had been dispatched to the Wewelsburg SS School on the authority of the SS Race and Settlement Office in the official capacity of a "indoctrination leader." In 1935, the SS castle administration was placed under the authority of the Staff of the Reich Leader SS. Franzius had to try his luck as an archaeologist and a researcher into witchcraft and genealogy; in 1935, he spent several weeks in military training with the SS Special Service Troops. His "personal and professional disappointment" sprang from the growing realization in Wewelsburg that under the SS there would be no place for development of his own architectural interpretation of National Socialism. mm
Landesarchiv NRW, Abteilung Rheinland, Düsseldorf, NW 1002-G, No. 60908, Bl. 7r

No. 2-17

Walter Franzius, "Das Dorfgemeinschafts-haus" [The Village Community Center]
Das schöne Dorf im Gau Westfalen-Nord in *Beiträge und Bilder zur Dorfverschönerung* [Articles and Pictures on Village Beautification], Deutsche Arbeitsfront, Gauverwaltung Westfalen-Nord, Münster, late 1938, early 1939, pp. 56 – 66
Franzius published several articles on the Wewelsburg Village Community Center. Here, he attempted to portray the construction, layout, and decoration of the house as a National Socialist continuation of centuries-old "race-bound" Germanic-German folk traditions.

The publisher of the book shown here was the German Labor Front (DAF), the National Socialist unitary federation of German workers and employers. Through one of its suborganizations, the regionally organized Reich Homesteading Office (*Reichsheimstättenamt*), the DAF controlled the public construction of housing settlements in the Reich. In the spring of 1939, Franzius moved from the Wewelsburg SS School to the District (*Gau*) Homesteading Office of DAF in Hamburg. The growing claim to elitist exclusiveness on the part of the SS in Wewelsburg deprived even an advocate of the racist concept of *Volksgemeinschaft* such as Franzius literally of any space for development. mm
Kreismuseum Wewelsburg, inv. no. 12705

2.2.3
From the Wewelsburg SS School to the Heart of the Concentration Camp Administration: August Harbaum

No. 2-18

Photograph from the SS file on August Harbaum's application for engagement and marriage

Twenty-one-year-old commercial clerk August Harbaum (1913 – ?) joined the administrative staff of the Wewelsburg SS School in October 1934. Following repeated disciplinary offenses, he was transferred to the SS guard unit at Sachsenhausen Concentration Camp in November 1937. Having failed at Wewelsburg, Harbaum now made his "career" in the SS concentration camp system. Interim adjutant to the concentration camp commandant at Flossenbürg Concentration Camp, he rose to become adjutant to the Inspector of Concentration Camps (IKL) in Oranienburg in 1940. Following incorporation of the IKL into the SS Economic and Administrative Main Office as Department D, *SS-Sturmbannführer* Harbaum was granted additional responsibility for the deployment of a total of some forty-five thousand members of the *Waffen-SS* in the concentration camps. After making a deposition, while in internment, to the International Military Tribunal in Nuremberg in 1946, Harbaum vanished and is since considered a missing person.mm

Bundesarchiv Berlin, formerly the Berlin Document Center, RS Harbaum

August Harbaum (1913 – unknown)
Administrative employee at Wewelsburg SS School, 1934 – 1937, Adjutant to the Inspector of Concentration Camps, 1940 – 1945

March 25, 1913
Born into a family of weavers in Gütersloh
1919 – 1927
Attended the Protestant primary school in Gütersloh
1927 – 1930
Business apprenticeship in his hometown, followed by alternating periods of unemployment and work as a commercial employee
August 1, 1932
Entry into the NSDAP and the SS
May 1, 1934
Entry into service as adjutant to the 1st *Sturmbann* (battalion) of the 82nd SS Regiment (Bielefeld) in Paderborn
October 29, 1934
Assumption of duties at Wewelsburg Castle
July 12, 1936
Promotion to *SS-Untersturmführer*
Late August 1936
Severe reprimand from Wewelsburg SS chief castle administrator von Knobelsdorff for insulting party comrades and resisting the police who sought to intervene
July 31, 1936
Initiation of disciplinary proceedings on alleged participation in the maintenance of slush funds by employees of the Wewelsburg SS castle administration
September 4, 1937
Suspension from duties with a ban on the wearing of SS insignia for unauthorized extension of leave period
November 22, 1937
Assignment to a six-month "training course" in the 2nd SS Death's Head Regiment "Brandenburg" at Sachsenhausen Concentration Camp with temporary demotion to the rank of simple SS man; a knee injury causes delays
August 1, 1938
Transfer from his Wewelsburg posting to the 2nd SS Death's Head Regiment "Brandenburg" at Sachsenhausen Concentration Camp with the rank of an *SS-Untersturmführer*
November 1, 1938
Transfer to 1st SS Death's Head Regiment "Oberbayern" in Flossenbürg Concentration Camp as platoon leader
March 1, 1939
Appointment as adjutant to the commandant of Flossenbürg Concentration Camp
August 25, 1939
Promotion to *SS-Obersturmführer*
February 20, 1940
Assignment to the Concentration Camp Inspectorate in Oranienburg as adjutant to the Inspector, *SS-Brigadeführer* Richard Glücks
April 20, 1940
Wedding
November 1, 1940
Promotion to *SS-Hauptsturmführer*
March 16, 1942
Head of Main Personnel Office AV/4 of Department D (previously Concentration Camp Inspectorate) in the reorganized SS Economic and Administrative Main Office
June 21, 1944
Promotion to *SS-Sturmbannführer*
March 19, 1946
Disposition at Paderborn-Staumühle internment camp for the Nuremberg International Military Tribunal regarding strength levels and composition of SS personnel in the concentration camps. Since then, whereabouts unknown. mm

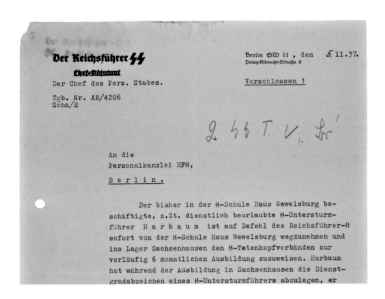

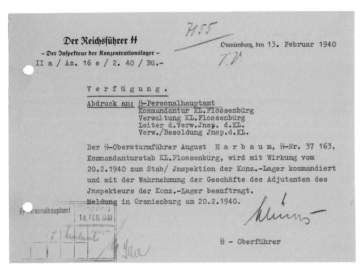

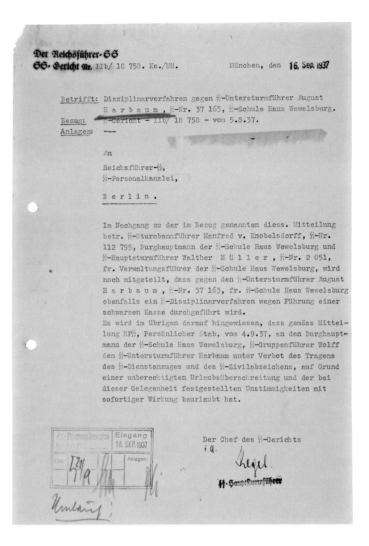

No. 2-20

Letter from Karl Wolff, chief of the Personal Staff to the *Reichsführer-SS*, to the SS Personnel Chancellery ordering Harbaum's immediate transfer from the Wewelsburg SS School to Sachsenhausen Concentration Camp for training in the Death's Head Units

Berlin, November 5, 1937 (excerpt)

Harbaum was not dismissed or downgraded to a lower administrative position. Rather, under temporary demotion, he was detailed from the Wewelsburg SS School to the guard unit at Sachsenhausen Concentration Camp, near Berlin. In accordance with the wishes of Karl Wolff, who as chief of the Personal Staff of the *Reichsführer-SS* had responsibility for Wewelsburg Castle, the uniformed SS administrative employee Harbaum was to be transformed into a broadly deployable, SS-worthy soldier through guarding (i.e., abuse) of concentration camp prisoners. The Harbaum case constitutes an early personal illustration of how closely the ideological sphere of the SS in Wewelsburg was interwoven with the organization's military-police apparatus of persecution. It demonstrates the dominant role played by the peculiar SS conception of the "soldierly" in the canon of values and conduct of the SS. mm

No. 2-21

Order from the Inspector of Concentration Camps, Glücks, concerning the transfer of Harbaum from the commandant's staff at Flossenbürg Concentration Camp as adjutant to the staff of the Concentration Camp Inspectorate in Oranienburg, February 13, 1940

Harbaum's official transfer from Wewelsburg to Sachsenhausen's 2nd SS Death's Head Regiment "Brandenburg" unit occurred on August 1, 1938. Two months later, he was transferred to the 1st Death's Head Regiment "Oberbayern" at Flossenbürg/Oberpfalz Concentration Camp as a platoon leader. On February 1, 1939, after about a year as a concentration camp guard, came his appointment as adjutant to the concentration camp commandant. With that position, the former employee of the Wewelsburg SS School had now achieved a key position within the organizational and administrative structure of a concentration camp, in which he participated in all-important decision-making processes. With his transfer in the same function to the head of the Concentration Camps Inspectorate, the central executive administration for all concentration camps, Harbaum moved up into the circle of the most important desk perpetrators implementing the mass crimes of the SS. mm

No. 2-19

Letter from the chief of the SS Tribunal to the SS Personnel Chancellery, announcing that disciplinary action was being taken against employees of the Wewelsburg SS School, August Harbaum, Manfred von Knobelsdorff, and Walter Müller on suspicion of maintaining illegal slush funds. In addition, by order of the *Reichsführer-SS*, Harbaum was barred from wearing SS insignia and uniforms for having exceeded his authorized leave time.

Munich, September 16, 1937 mm

2.2.4
Elitist Ideas of Soldiering and Careerist Calculation: Hans Peter des Coudres

No. 2-22

Photograph from the SS file on Hans Peter des Coudres's application for engagement and marriage

For 30-year-old librarian Dr. Hans Peter des Coudres, assumption of the duties of the director of the SS Library at Wewelsburg Castle in April 1935 offered an opportunity to combine career interests with political convictions. Molded by the racist and nationalistic youth movement under the Weimar Republic, he saw himself as the leader of the intellectual shock troops of National Socialism within the Wewelsburg Castle administration. The actual development taken by Wewelsburg SS School, however, left him disappointed. Although Himmler wished to promote him within the SS, des Coudres, using his SS connections, instead took a post of chief librarian at a larger state library. During the war, as commander of a *Waffen-SS* artillery unit, he sought to move closer to his ideal of a National Socialist shock troop leader, now in the military realm.

mm

Bundesarchiv Berlin, formerly Berlin Document Center, SSO Harbaum

Dr. Hans Peter des Coudres (1905 – 1977) Head of the "SS Library" at the Wewelsburg SS School, 1935 – 1939

September 27, 1905
Born in Spandau, son of a future Prussian major general whose family hailed from western Switzerland; initially named Jean Pierre

1922
Beginning of political engagement in the nationalist youth movement

1925
High School diploma in Kassel; subsequently study of law and political science in Göttingen, The Hague, and Leipzig

November 1, 1930
Entry into the NSDAP

January 1, 1932
Entry into the SA

January 1933
Graduation with doctorate in Civil and Canon Law (Dr. iur. utr.) under Prof. Erwin Jacobi at Leipzig University

May 1933
Beginning of an internship as an academic librarian at the German National Library in Leipzig; conflict during the entire internship with library management about the compatibility of his training with holding party offices

Fall 1933
Short-term appointment as specialist for youth literature at the Reich Office for the Promotion of German Literature and the Reich Youth Leadership, then Saxony state representative for German literature in the Military League for German Culture; honorary expert at the Leipzig police headquarters for questions on publications on politics and culture

1934
Head of the subdepartment for monitoring publications at the NSDAP district administration (*Gauleitung*) of Saxony

April 1, 1935
Examination in advanced academic library science, passed with grade 2 (good)

April 15, 1935
Assumption of duties as indoctrination leader at the SS School in Wewelsburg; the setting up of the SS Library commences; Germanizes his name to "Hans Peter"

1936
Composition of the essay "The SS as Intellectual Shock Troop"

June 1936
Journey to Iceland in the company of Grailseeker and Catharism expert, Otto Rahn

May 8, 1937
Wedding celebration (together with the Franzius couple) in the newly opened Wewelsberg Village Community Center in Himmler's presence

March 3, 1938
Conversation with former chief castle administrator von Knobelsdorff on his application as director of the State Library in Kassel

April 1938
Earliest possible date of the completion of the progress report "Three Years of the SS Library at Wewelsburg Castle"

May 22, 1938
Himmler and the academic director of the SS research society *Das Ahnenerbe* (Ancestral Heritage), Walther Wüst, announce that the Wewelsburg SS library is to be moved to another location within the framework of *Das Ahnenerbe*.

November 1938
Presumed date of the final decision to accept the position of director at the State Library in Kassel; conflict with Wewelsburg SS archaeologist Wilhelm Jordan; accusation that Jordan did not possess the "ideological demeanor of an SS officer"

December 7, 1938
Himmler expresses his disappointment to Wüst at des Coudres's decision to leave full-time service in the SS

January 14, 1939
Unsent draft of a letter by Wüst addressing Himmler's intention to entrust des Coudres with overall control of all *Ahnenerbe* libraries

March 31, 1939
Exit from Wewelsburg SS School and full-time SS service with the rank of an *SS-Hauptsturmführer*; assumption of duties the next day at the State Library in Kassel

May 1939
Plan for reorganization and the technical modernization of the State Library in Kassel

September 2, 1939
Transfer of twenty of the State Library's most valuable manuscripts to a bombproof underground vault – against the wishes of the National Socialist Party district leader in Kassel

September 1939
Induction into Police Reinforcements, an armed reserve organization for the SS Death's Head Units; from there, application for transfer to the *Wehrmacht*

October 10, 1939
Transfer to the artillery regiment of the SS Death's Head Division, participation in the invasions of France (1940) and the Soviet Union (1941)

January 1942
Three-month home leave for reconstruction of the State Library in Kassel, which had been destroyed in a bombing raid

April 27, 1943
Command of SS Mortar Unit 102; operations in south Russia and the Ukraine, in France after the Allied invasion in June 1944, later at Arnheim

October 1, 1944
Transfer as commander to SS Mortar Unit 505, combat on the Eastern Front, including at the Oder River. After the war and his internment, return to activity as an academic librarian, especially as director of the Library for International and Foreign Civil Law at the Max Planck Institute in Hamburg (until 1972), contacts and collaboration with Ernst Jünger

January 8, 1977
Death in Hamburg mm

Die Schutzstaffel als geistiger Stosstrupp
==

Durchdrungen von der Gewißheit, daß es Gewehre und Bücher sind, deren
Güte und Fertigkeit der Handhabung für die kommenden Zeiten der Aus-
einandersetzungen entscheidend sein werden, hat eine Mobilmachung der
Jugend in diesen beiden Waffen stattgefunden, deren Ausmass umso mehr
zu begrüssen und zu steigern ist, je mehr die Bedrohung unserer Geisteshaltung und Weltanschauung auf der Erde zunimmt.
Das Gewehr übt und führt das Heer zur Sicherheit des Reiches nach aussen.
Das Gewehr übt und führt die Schutzstaffel zur Sicherheit des Reiches
nach innen. Doch das Gewehr kann allein unsere errungene Freiheit so
wenig verteidigen, wie Wissen und Bücher es allein vermögen.

Während der Zweck des Gewehres und der Sinn seiner Übung offenbar
sind, erscheinen Buch und Büchersammlung in Sinn und Zweck zunächst all-
zu umfassend und verworren. Aus diesem Universalismus der Gebrauchs-
möglichkeit des Buches für alle eben nur ausdenkbaren Überlegungen und
leeren Worte soll allein die Kategorie von Büchern herausgehoben sein,
denen ihrer Natur nach Rüstungsfunktionen innewohnen. Hierunter wird
eine Art Schrifttum zu verstehen sein, das alle geistigen Wehrbezirke
unseres Glaubens und Lebens total umfasst.

Die Auswahl des eben gekennzeichneten Schrifttums aus der Sint-
flut des gedruckten, ähnelt durchaus, wenn wir tiefer zu sehen vermögen, der Aufgabe des Truppenführers, der aus einem unendlichen zur Verfügung stehenden Gelände die strategisch wichtigen Punkte zu Angriff
und Verteidigung auszuwählen hat. Hier gibt es eine sich mit der Zeit
ändernde Kriegskunst, die jedoch stets ein und denselben ehernen Grund-
gesetzen unterworfen ist, und so soll auch von einer Kunst des Lesens
und Lernens gesprochen werden, die ebenfalls dem Wechsel und der Ver-
änderung unterworfen, in ihrem entscheidendem Kern sich gleich bleiben
muss. So mag auch das Schwert dem Maschinengewehr gewichen sein, es ist
Symbol der tauglichen und blanken Waffe geblieben, so wie das alte Buch
unabdingbarer Wahrheiten seinen ständigen Platz unter seinen jüngsten
Brüdern und in unseren Herzen behauptet. Es sind weiter zu allen Zeiten

---

der in einem kleinen Zwischenbericht über die
Bibliothek Wewelsburg zum Julfest 1936 dem
Reichsführer SS vorgelegt wurde:
Als 1934 der Reichsführer SS die einstige germanische Feste und spätere Burg der Paderborner
Fürstbischöfe übernahm, da ging Hand in Hand mit
dem Aufbau einer hohen Schule der Schutzstaffel
auch die Errichtung einer Bibliothek auf der
Wewelsburg. Diese Errichtung einer hohen Schule
nordischer Geisteshaltung ist das Gegenteil zu
der Jesuitenakademiegründung Dietrich Theodors
von Fürstenberg, des Erbauers der Wewelsburg
in ihrer heutigen Form. Dieses Mal ist Aufgabe
nicht die Sicherung römischer Machtansprüche
und Dogmen, sondern Festigung und Sicherung
deutscher arteigener Weltanschauung. Hatten die
Jesuiten Philosophie und Theologie als Fächer
von Ewigkeitswert erkannt, so mag die Philosophie
in neuem und weiten Sinne als Weltanschauung
auch Inbegriff der Tätigkeit der neuen hohen
Schule sein. Hier darf Rosenbergs Wort gelten,
daß eine nationalsozialistische Philosophie
einst Königin der Fakultäten einer kommenden
Universität sein wird und daß diese Philosophie
nicht von metaphysischen Spekulationen, sondern
von einer germanischen Wertlehre ihren Ausgang
nehmen wird. So wird auch die Bibliothek der
hohen Schule in Wewelsburg die Werke umfassen,
die dieser germanischen Wertlehre dienen. Da ist
es gewiß, daß nicht nur das Schrifttum und die

No. 2-24
Hans Peter des Coudres: The *Schutzstaffel* as Intellectual Shock Troop
Wewelsburg 1936, p. 1
Translation on page 440
Barely two weeks had passed since his qualifying exams when des Coudres assumed the position of head of the SS Library at Wewelsburg. In the 1936 paper reproduced here, he sought to associate the SS's claim to leadership in the struggle against the internal and external enemies of National Socialism with his own pro-fessional and political identity. For des Coudres, books, no less than guns, were weapons in an ideological war. Like their police and military SS counterparts, librarians like him were charged with maintaining such intellectual "arsenals" and were "intellectual shock troop officers" fighting on the front lines for the triumph of the National Socialist world-view. Not just as an SS man, but also as librarian, des Coudres thus counted himself among the fighting elite of the Third Reich. mm

Bayerische Staatsbibliothek, Munich, sign. 4° 38.355

No. 2-23
Not shown
Jean Pierre (Hans Peter) des Coudres: Implementation of Child Labor Protection Laws
Inaugural dissertation for achieving the doctorate at the University of Leipzig School of Law, 1933, 63 pages
Des Coudres came from a family settled since the eighteenth century in Kassel, where it had produced a number of scholars, painters, and officers. In Janu-ary 1933, National Socialist Party and SA member des Coudres earned his doctorate of law with the work displayed here, under Leipzig constitutional and labor-law expert Ernst Jacobi. He did not appear to have any difficulty with his doctoral supervisor's Jewish origins, nor can any openly National Socialist views be ascertained in the thesis. A few weeks later, des Coudres began a two-year training course as an academic librarian at the German National Library in Leipzig. Here, however, conflicts arose with library management as des Coudres simulta-neously worked as a publications and censorship officer for various National Socialist Party agencies, without showing regard for his status as a person in training. mm

Kreismuseum Wewelsburg, inv.-No. 16267

No. 2-25
"Three Years of the SS Library at Wewels-burg Castle. Progress Report on the Period from 4/1/1935 to 3/31/1938, by SS Captain des Coudres," Chapter II, p. 2
Over time, des Coudres had to recognize that Himmler's concept of a Wewelsburg SS "castle" left less and less room for his own professional and personal devel-opment needs. His desire to achieve recognition within the German library milieu with his SS Library was incom-patible with Himmler's intention to shield Wewelsburg Castle from public view. At the time he composed the 1938 progress report reproduced here, des Coudres himself could no longer have believed that a "higher school of the SS," a "Nordic"-racist SS academy of the arts, should see the light of day here. Shortly afterwards, Himmler informed him that he planned to transfer the Wewelsburg library to another location. By that time, however, des Coudres had already sent out feelers to take over the directorship of a large state library. mm

Bundesarchiv Berlin, NS 48/17

No. 2-26

The des Coudres newlyweds in front of the Village Community Center;
Double wedding of SS members Dr. Hans Peter des Coudres and Walter Franzius on the day of the opening of the Village Community Center
Photograph: Karl Schumacher, Wewelsburg SS School, May 8, 1937

Trained both as a jurist and a librarian, the highly-educated des Coudres presumably found it humiliating that the leadership of Wewelsburg SS School did not rest in the hands of a result-oriented, academically qualified, and ideologically radical SS man of his own caliber, but in those of von Knobelsdorff, a political favorite and untrained lay person. To academically trained colleagues of his age or younger, he attempted to aggrandize himself, more or less successfully, as the genuine authority and point of reference at the SS School. The friendship with Franzius, which began at Wewelsburg Castle, lasted until des Coudres's death. In May 1937, they celebrated their weddings together at the Wewelsburg Village Community Center in the presence of Himmler and his adjutant, Karl Wolff. mm

Kreismuseum Wewelsburg, Fotoarchiv

No. 2-27
Not shown

Letter from the president of *Das Ahnenerbe*, Walther Wüst, to des Coudres conveying Himmler's displeasure at des Coudres' projected career change in spite of his planned appointment as head of all *Ahnenerbe* libraries
Munich, January 1, 1939

In late 1938, Himmler had to abandon his plan to transfer the SS Library from Wewelsburg to a central location for the SS research society *Das Ahnenerbe*. Now, des Coudres was to take over management of all *Ahnenerbe* libraries from his Wewelsburg office. But in the meantime, he had successfully applied for the prestigious position of head of the State Library in his hometown of Kassel – with significant support of higher SS leaders in the Hessian provincial administration. The letter from the academic director of *Ahnenerbe*, the Munich Indo-Germanist Professor Walter Wüst, on January 1, 1939, could do nothing to alter des Coudres' decision. After the downfall of the Third Reich, des Coudres attempted to spin the letter as alleged proof of his early estrangement from Himmler and the SS. mm

Staatsarchiv Hamburg, Best. 221-11, Staatskommissar fur die Entnazifizierung, Nr. 32234 [denazification file on des Coudres], p. 8

No. 2-28

SS Major Dr. Hans Peter des Coudres as commander of SS Mortar Unit 505 with his officer staff in Ebstorf/Uelzen October 1944

On April 1, 1939, library director des Coudres could command respect as master of more than 380,000 books, significant collections of historical manuscripts, and early editions. The SS Library at Wewelsburg, with its 16,000 volumes, paled in comparison. Though the SS Captain had left full-time SS service, the ideological views he had formulated in Wewelsburg continued to guide him in Kassel. During World War II, des Coudres commanded *Waffen-SS* artillery units. His service evaluations described him as a zealous National Socialist, now able to demonstrate his dedication as a "shock troop leader" in the military arena. mm

Archiv G. Reibe/Verlag Gerald Ramm, Woltersdorf

2.2.5
A Ruthless Idealist with Artistic Sensibility
and Intellectual Curiosity: The Archaeologist Wilhelm Jordan

No. 2-29
Wilhelm Jordan with honorary sword
Ca. 1942
Although Wilhelm Jordan had not completed
his studies of prehistoric archaeology,
it was as an archaeologist that he came to
the Wewelsburg in 1936. Enthusiastic
about the opportunities available there,
he used the most hideous aspects of the
system with equanimity: As a Wewelsburg
SS man he exploited the labor of the
concentration camp prisoners, whom he
referred to disdainfully as "rabble."

In the prewar years, as an archaeologist in Wewelsburg, he founded an
SS museum of "German Prehistory" while
organizing the preservation of regional
monuments. During the war, he excavated
archaeological sites at concentration
and forced-labor camps and plundered
Ukrainian museums and private collections
for the SS and "his" museum in Wewelsburg on personal instructions from
Himmler.

As a military geologist during the war,
he prospected for important mineral
resources for the SS, and did not hesitate
to use concentration camp prisoners for
extracting them. In operations against
partisans in the Ukraine, he was presumably personally involved in terrorizing
the local population. ds

Kreismuseum Wewelsburg, Wilhelm Jordan estate,
inv. no. 16619

Wilhelm Jordan (1903 – 1983)
Director of the Geology and Prehistory
Department in Wewelsburg 1935 – 1942,
Military Geologist 1942 – 1945
January 11, 1903
Born in Merseburg/Saale, the eldest
of six children
1915 – 1921
Attended the Sankt Marien zur Pforte
("Schulpforta") High School in Naumburg/
Saale, a secondary school specializing in
the humanities
1920
As a student, brief membership
in the *Lützow Freikorps*
1922 – 1924
Training as an artisan woodturner
in Berlin and Leipzig
1921 – 1923
Concurrent study at the Berlin University
without a diploma examination:
registered for coursework in geology
and paleontology
1923 – 1927
Member of the right-wing *Jungnationaler
Bund* (Young Nationalist Association)
1929
High school diploma; beginning studies
of prehistory combined with classical
archaeology, geology, zoology, and botany
at Marburg/Lahn University
October 1, 1930
Entry into the NSDAP (party no. 313903)
March 2, 1931
Entry into the SA
March 10, 1934
Wedding; the marriage produced five sons
November 15, 1935
Assumption of duties at Wewelsburg
Castle as director of the Department of
Geology and Prehistory, charged with
setting up a museum and conducting
excavations; accompanied by a transfer
from the SA to the SS (SS no. 278248)
January 24, 1938
Appointed honorary state conservator of
historical monuments for the area around
the Wewelsburg; he now was active in
archaeology for both the SS and the state
1939
The only scholar of the SS castle administration to remain in Wewelsburg during
the reorganization and even after the war
began
1942
Induction into military service
February 15, 1942
Basic training at the Signal Intelligence
Replacement Battalion of the *Waffen-SS*
in Nuremberg; then assignment to the SS
Military Geology Battalion in Hamburg
under SS archaeologist Dr. Rolf Höhne
(with whom Jordan was acquainted) as a
specialist officer, permitted to act inde-
pendently in specified spheres of activity
June 15, 1942
Service as military geologist in the sector
of Higher SS and Police Leader (HSSPF)
in the Ukraine, Hans-Adolf Prützmann, in
Kiev; presumably in September 1942,
entrusted with a secret special assignment
by Himmler: the "collection" of cultural
treasures in the Ukraine for the SS by
purchases below market value or plunder
of private and museum collections
May 1943
Reassignment to a "partisan operation"
under the general command of HSSPF
Prützmann

May 1944
Meeting with the German Governor
General of occupied Poland, Hans Frank,
arranged by Himmler; discussion of
exploitation by the SS of a manganese
deposit for arms production
June 1944
Start of an expedition to the manganese
deposits on the northern slopes of the
Eastern Carpathian Mountains (code-
name, "Wieland Project") deploying
concentration camp prisoners
August 1944
Excavation of an urn grave at Krakow-
Plaszow concentration camp
September 1944
Return to the SS Military Geology Battal-
ion in Hamburg, then transfer to Balingen/
Württemberg as "geological advisor" for
the extraction of shale oil; here, excavation of early medieval series of graves
discovered during construction of a prisoner of war camp
April 7, 1945
Taken prisoner by U.S. troops in north
Hesse; subsequent internment in various
prisoner of war camps, the last one
at Neuengamme, near Hamburg
March 5, 1948
Release from internment
28. April 1948
Court proceeding; sentenced to eight
months imprisonment for exploitation of
concentration camp labor in Wewelsburg
and Balingen; no proof of criminal acts
in the East; time served is applied to
sentence, consequently no further prison
time imposed
1948 – 1953
Employment as unskilled laborer in
various occupations; plans to emigrate,
but no country is prepared to admit him
September 8, 1953
Hired as technical draftsman
at the State Geology Office
of Rhineland-Palatinate in Mainz
1964
Divorce and second marriage
1968
Relocation from Mainz to Haaren, a community located eight kilometers from the
Wewelsburg
November 1972
NPD candidate for the electoral
precinct Paderborn in federal
parliamentary elections
1977
Relocation to Hürnheim/Ries
March 4, 1983
Death ds

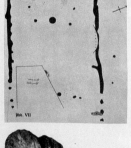

No. 2-30
**Wilhelm Jordan, "Finderglück"
[Finder's Luck]**
FM **Zeitschrift. Monatsschrift der
Reichsführung SS für fördernde Mitglieder
[Monthly magazine of the Reich
Leadership of the SS for sustaining
members], vol. 4, no. 6 (June 1, 1937)**
The excavations of Wilhelm Jordan around
Wewelsburg were of great interest to
Reichsführer-SS Heinrich Himmler. The
discovery of the foundations of a house
classified as "Germanic" at Gut Böddecken,
only a few kilometers from Wewelsburg,
was Jordan's greatest success here, as
the Germanic tribes were considered the
ancestors of modern-day Germans.
Himmler even visited the excavation site in
person, accompanied by official guests
such as Alfred Meyer, the National Socialist Party district leader in North Westphalia and political head of the state of
Lippe, or the Reich Organization Leader of
the National Socialist Party, Robert Ley.

From 1938, Jordan was also honorary
state conservator of historical monuments
for Wewelsburg and environs, giving him
a virtual autonomy for his projects. ds

Loan from the LWL Archeology for Westphalia, Münster

No. 2-31
**Wilhelm Jordan with one of his sons on a
swing in the Waldsiedlung settlement
Ca. 1940**
Even after the war began, the Jordan family lived harmoniously in Wewelsburg.
Though Wilhelm Jordan impatiently awaited
his military service, he was initially
deferred as being "indispensable" and
inducted only in 1942.

This idyllic life stood in stark contrast
to the suffering of the concentration camp
prisoners, who had been forced to work in
Wewelsburg since 1939. The Jordan family
profited from the labor of the prisoners,
who built the houses for SS members in
the so-called Waldsiedlung (Forest
Development). After numerous moves and
rental arrangements, their own house with
garden now offered the Jordans ample
space for the four sons that had been born
by that time. Unmoved by the atrocious
living conditions endured by those he had
dismissed as "rabble" in one of his poems,
Wilhelm Jordan had the leisure in 1941 to
photograph the beauty of autumn fog
looming over pastures of the Alme Valley.
ds

Kreismuseum Wewelsburg, Nachlass Wilhelm Jordan
inv. no. 16687

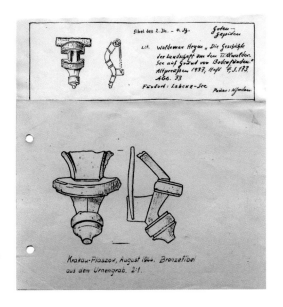

No. 2-32
Fastoff drawing
August 16, 1942

In June 1942, Wilhelm Jordan was sent to Ukraine as an SS military geologist. He decided on his own initiative to accept this assignment after discussing it with Himmler. His role was to develop mineral resources of military significance, and to sketch relevant maps. In Fastov, about a hundred kilometers (ca. sixty-two miles) from Himmler's field command post in Zhytomyr and about seventy kilometers (ca. forty-three miles) from Kiev, Jordan sketched the ravages of war. Barely a year later, in May 1943, Wilhelm Jordan personally took part in a "partisan operation" against the Ukrainian population. What exactly he did there remains unknown, but the involved SS units reported killing 4,018 people, mostly Jews, burning down 103 villages and removing 18,860 persons by force as prisoners of war. In contrast, Jordan reported on these events in a letter as if he had been on an adventurous journey, concluding: "To recount my experiences and observations, including those in terms of folklore, would lead us too far at the moment." ds

Kreismuseum Wewelsburg, Nachlass Wilhelm Jordan
inv. no. 16600

No. 2-34
Blueprint: Drawing of a fibula from the urn grave at Krakow-Plaszow
1944

In order to evaluate the discovery at Plaszow, Wilhelm Jordan used his academic contacts, since he no longer had access to specialized literature. Here, he merely outlined the conditions of the find, focusing mainly on technical questions. By mid-September 1944, Jordan was already engaged at another archaeological site in Balingen/Württemberg, where early medieval discoveries were made during construction of a concentration camp. Yet, the Plaszow urn grave continued to occupy him. He made detailed drawings and searched for comparable finds. He was not able to realize his intention to publish these findings, because the war ended. What became of the finds remains unknown. ds

Kreismuseum Wewelsburg, Nachlass Wilhelm Jordan
inv. no. 16601

No. 2-33
Memorandum by Wilhelm Jordan on archaeological discoveries at Krakow-Plaszow Concentration Camp
September 1, 1944

In August 1944, Wilhelm Jordan, on the order of the Higher SS and Police Leader in Krakow evaluated the archaeological finds made on the grounds of Krakow-Plaszow Concentration Camp. The camp was built in 1940 on the grounds of two Jewish cemeteries; it was considered particularly brutal. Connected to the evaluation of the finds was a brief follow-up excavation at the discovery site. Neither the suffering of the prisoners all around him, nor the fact that the excavation desecrated Jewish graves, seems to have constrained Jordan's research enthusiasm in the least.

It is probable that Wilhelm Jordan had already been to Plaszow before, for in June 1944 he had led the so-called Project Wieland, deploying one hundred Jewish prisoners from this camp as forced laborers. In circumvention of Armaments Minister Speer, the project pursued the extraction of weapons-production-grade manganese deposits from the northeastern slopes of the Carpathian Mountains to benefit the SS. After conclusion of the work, the prisoners were presumably moved from Plaszow to Auschwitz, where they were murdered. ds

Kreismuseum Wewelsburg, Nachlass Wilhelm Jordan,
inv. no. 16852

Wewelsburg, War of Extermination, Obersalzberg
Flexibility in the SS Sense: Bernhard Frank

No. 2-35

**Photograph on the firearms permit
for Bernhard Frank
Büren, November 9, 1936**

Ideologically and professionally, Bernhard Frank was a product of the SS, which he joined in 1933, at the age of 19. An early member of the SS Special Service Troops, he was molded by the *Schutzstaffel* into a National Socialist soldier; as the commissioner for folklore at the Wewelsburg SS School (since 1935), the SS made its mark on Frank as an academic in its racist ideas and elitist self-image. Dr. Frank proved quite versatile for the SS: At Wewelsburg Castle, he was treated as a future leading SS research specialist; in the attack on the Soviet Union, he acted as staff officer for mobile SS killing units operating behind the front lines; for a few months he commanded a front-line battalion of the *Waffen-SS*; and in 1943, he was assigned to command the *Waffen-SS* units deployed to protect Adolf Hitler's residence at Obersalzberg. mm

Kreisarchiv Paderborn, BürA 1388

**Dr. Bernhard Frank (1913 – 2011)
Specialist on folklore at Wewelsburg
SS School, 1935 – 1939;
commander of the *Waffen-SS* units
at the Obersalzberg, 1943 – 1945**

July 15, 1913
Born the third and youngest child – and the only son – of a businessman's family in Frankfurt am Main

December 1918
Death of the mother; soon after, the father remarried; birth of another child

Easter 1932
Diploma from Helmholtz high school in Frankfurt am Main

Summer 1932
Beginning of studies in German Studies and philosophy at Johann Wolfgang von Goethe University in his hometown; switches to economics after one semester

May 30, 1933
Entry into the SS (in a Student Battalion)

June 9, 1934
Selected for participation in an SS officer candidate training program by Himmler during his inspection of the Frankfurt 2nd SS Regiment

October 1, 1934
Beginning of training with the SS Special Service Troops in Ellwangen/Jagst

Spring 1935
Transfer to the SS Officer School (*Junkerschule*) in Braunschweig, from which he was expelled that autumn because of an alleged violation on guard duty; short-term transfer to Dachau

December 15, 1935
Beginning of service as an academic employee at Wewelsburg SS School following an interview in Berlin with chief castle administrator von Knobelsdorff; area of specialization is folklore

1936
Beginning of research on the Wewelsburg toponymy (the subject of his future thesis); establishment of a Folklore Research Office at the Wewelsburg SS School

Fall 1936
Enrollment at Münster University in German and Folklore Studies

November 9, 1938
Oral examinations for the doctorate in Münster

December 17, 1938
Marriage to Tilli Neuhaus in Frankfurt am Main in the presence of Siegfried Taubert, the SS chief castle administrator, and Rudi Bergmann, his friend from the days at the Braunschweig SS officer school.

Beginning of 1939
Served several months as assistant to Prof. Walther Wüst, academic director of the SS research society *Das Ahnenerbe*, in Munich

July 1939
Participated in the selection of new academic researchers for Wewelsburg SS School

August 17, 1939
Letter to the chief castle administrator Taubert requesting, in case of war, to be assigned to an SS unit, with consideration of previous time in service with the SS Special Service Troops and at the *SS-Junkerschule* in Braunschweig

August 28, 1939
Report from Taubert to the Personal Staff of the *Reichsführer-SS* that Frank should be inducted into an army unit as a training non-commissioned officer; the same day, the head of the Personal Staff clears Frank for service in the Reinforced SS Death's Head Units.

September 30, 1939
On Himmler's order, Frank was assigned, effective immediately, to the SS Death's Head Regiments as a platoon leader.

December 1939
Adjutant to the 3rd SS Death's Head Infantry Replacement Battalion in Breslau (now Wroclaw)

December 1940
Beginning of a three-month stay in Wewelsburg to write a memorandum on assignment by Prof. Wüst on the further development of the scholarly work of Wewelsburg SS School

January 21, 1941
Composition of a file memorandum entitled "Suggestions for final planning of the academic buildings at Wewelsburg Castle"

April 25, 1941
Detailed to the newly created Deployment Staff of the *Reichsführer-SS* (later: Commando Staff of the *Reichsführer-SS*), initially as an aide

August 9, 1941
Started keeping the service diary of the Commando Staff

November 19, 1941
Assignment as a company commander (battalion commander) to the SS Volunteer Legion "Niederlande," combat deployment at Volkhov (northern Russia)

June 5, 1942
Notification to the SS's *Das Ahnenerbe* that, due to military deployments, work on the research project "Forest and Tree" was suspended until further notice

September 1942
Return to a staff officer position as head of Department IIa (adjutant's office) of the Commando Staff

1943
Command of an SS anti-aircraft unit in East Prussia

Summer 1943
Command of SS anti-aircraft department "B" at the Obersalzberg within the Commando Staff framework, thus commander of all SS security troops around Berchtesgaden; highest rank, *SS-Obersturmbann-führer*

Early May, 1945
Following military evacuation of the Obersalzberg, captured by U.S. troops near the Chiemsee

Until early 1948
Internment, then return to civilian life as a businessman

Since the 1980s
Publication of autobiographical-historical works and volumes of poetry

June 29, 2011
Death in Schmitten (district of Hochtaunus) mm

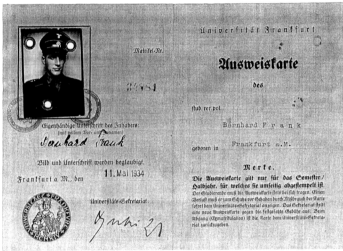

No. 2-38
Bernhard Frank (in service overcoat), a Wewelsburg farmer (with horse and foal), and another SS man in front of the castle garden (in the background, the south wing of Wewelsburg Castle)
Ca. 1938
In Wewelsburg, Himmler himself once again set a task for Frank. On orders from the SS chief, the "folklore specialist" of the Wewelsburg SS School and student at Münster University researched the toponymy of the Wewelsburg district. Frank considered the doctoral thesis that ensued as part of a "German folklore," which contained highly racist elements. Frank was to remain the only employee of Wewelsburg SS School to earn an academic degree during his time of service there.

Though his study at Münster required long absences from Wewelsburg, his research interest brought him into closer contact with the village population than most other SS researchers. Some of these relationships survived the end of the war. mm

Kreismuseum Wewelsburg, Fotoarchiv

No. 2-36, No. 2-37
Frankfurt/Main University ID cards for Bernhard Frank
April 1, 1932 (top), May 11, 1934 (bottom)
His enrollment in the SS student battalion in his hometown, Frankfurt am Main, in May 1933, seems to have been the first political engagement of any significance for the businessman's son, Bernhard Frank. A year later, Himmler himself selected Frank for an officer-training course with the SS Special Service Troops. His assignment to Wewelsburg SS School in December 1935 followed a disciplinary transfer out of the SS officer school in Braunschweig to the SS unit at Dachau Concentration Camp. At the beginning of World War II, Frank, now with a doctorate in folklore studies, requested deployment in what would become the *Waffen-SS*. A constant preparedness to switch roles between ideological SS research and political SS soldiering marked Frank's career until 1945. mm

Universitätsarchiv, Frankfurt/Main, Bestand Studentensekretariat

No. 2-39
Not shown
Bernhard Frank's work plan for the preparation of his postdoctoral thesis for professorship qualification, "The Forest in the Religious Experience and Customs of the Germanic People," within the framework of the research project conducted by the SS research association *Das Ahnenerbe* on the theme "Forest and Tree in Aryan-Germanic Intellectual and Cultural History"
Munich, March 4, 1939
In early 1939, with his doctorate now in hand, Frank moved into the role of the ideal candidate for reorganizing research at the Wewelsburg SS School under the umbrella of the SS research association Das Ahnenerbe. The SS now wished to lend a more respectable image to research conducted on its orders and for its purposes. To groom him for a future leading role at Wewelsburg, Frank was dispatched to the University at Munich as the assistant to the academic director of *Das Ahnenerbe*, Professor Walther Wüst. There, he was to prepare for his qualification to hold a professorship with a work on the subject of "The Forest in the Religious Experience and Customs of the Germanic People." Frank also participated in the selection of new scholars for Wewelsburg Castle. World War II, however, put an end to Frank's academic career and prevented the influx of new SS researchers to Wewelsburg. mm

Bundesarchiv Berlin, formerly the Berlin Document Center, DS/Lehr- und Forschungsgemeinschaft "Das Ahnenerbe," Bernhard Frank, Bl. 75 – 76

No. 2-40

Operations Special Order from the Commando Staff of the *Reichsführer-SS*: Guidelines for screening and patrolling swampland by cavalry units; signed by Himmler; countersigned by Frank "for the accuracy [i.e., of the file copy]"

July 28, 1941

Translation on page 440

Following his stay in Wewelsburg, *SS-Hauptsturmführer* of the Reserves Dr. Bernhard Frank was detailed as staff officer to the newly established Commando Staff of the *Reichsführer-SS*. After the attack on the Soviet Union on June 22, 1941, SS brigades subordinated to the Commando Staff murdered tens of thousands of people in the areas behind the Eastern Front by the end of that year. Most of the victims were Jews and actual or alleged partisans. As an orderly, Frank confirmed the correct transmission of the text of an order from Himmler granting the cavalry units of the Commando Staff virtually a free hand for mass shootings in villages within their area of operation. Shortly afterwards, Frank assumed maintaining the war diary of the Commando Staff. Thus, until the middle of November 1941, he was, at the very least, informed of all murder operations conducted by his units. mm

Central Military Archive in Prague, K 14, A 107, reproduced in *Unsere Ehre heisst Treue.* War diary of the Commando Staff of the *Reichsführer-SS*, activity reports of 1st and 2nd SS Infantry Brigades, 1st SS Cavalry Brigade, and Special Detachments of the SS, Vienna/Frankfurt am Main/Zurich, 1965, pp. 210–213

No. 2-41

SS-Sturmbannführer Bernhard Frank as commander of the *Waffen-SS* at the Obersalzberg

Summer 1944

In 1942, Frank first commanded combat units of the SS Volunteer Legion "Niederlande" in northern Russia. He then returned as an adjutant responsible for officer affairs to the headquarters of the Commando Staff of the *Reichsführer-SS*. The units subordinate to the Commando Staff units alternated between combat deployments and brutal "cleansing operations" behind the lines. To date, Frank's direct participation in their crimes could not be established. In the summer of 1943, he was tasked with command of the *Waffen-SS* security detail around Adolf Hitler's residence at the Obersalzberg near Berchtesgaden. Especially from this last function in the SS before the end of the Third Reich, Frank derived an unshakable belief in his own historical significance, which into his old age remained untouched by any insight into the criminal character of the SS. mm

Original privately owned

2.2.7
Amateur Academic and Ideological Soldier: Rudi Bergmann

No. 2-42

Photograph attached to the firearms permit for Rudi Bergmann
Büren, November 9, 1936
Eighteen-year-old Hitler Youth and SA member Rudi Bergman was enrolled in a business-training program when he transferred to the SS in 1933. Military and political training in the SS Special Service Troop was followed by his transfer to the Wewelsburg SS School at the beginning of 1936. Here, Bergmann, who was not an academic, was offered the opportunity to pursue his hobby of genealogy, on behalf of Himmler and other high SS officers, as an ideologically prestigious principal occupation. At Wewelsburg Castle, Bergmann assumed the position of adjutant to the chief castle administrator, before he joined the SS Death's Head Regiments at the beginning of World War II. While his friend Bernhard Frank monitored the killing actions of the Commando Staff of the *Reichsführer-SS* in the Soviet Union as a staff officer, Bergmann was a company commander in one of the SS infantry brigades subordinate to the Commando Staff that directly participated in the mass shootings. He was killed in action in Russia in December 1942. mm
Kreisarchiv Paderborn, BürA 1388

Rudi Bergmann (1913 – 1942)
Expert in genealogical research at SS School House Wewelsburg 1936 – 1940
January 29, 1914
Born in Berlin, the son of a businessman; attended school until completion of a middle school certificate; two years of vocational school
December 21, 1930
Entry into the Hitler Youth
Fall 1931
Accepted into the SA
June 1933
Transfer to the SS
October 1933
Commercial employee in his father's Berlin automobile company
August 1934
Application for inclusion on the list of authorized "genealogical researchers" with the Expert on Racial Research at the Reich Ministry of the Interior, after 1935 called the Reich Office for Family Research (renamed the Reich Family Office in 1940)
November 2, 1934
Start of officer candidate training at SS Regiment "Adolf Hitler" in Jüterbog
Summer 1935
Enrollment in the SS Officer School (later, SS Junker School) in Braunschweig; processing of "Proof of Arian Descent" for SS officer candidates (*Junker*); beginning of friendship with Bernhard Frank
Early 1936
Transfer to Wewelsburg SS School; here he worked primarily on the genealogical charts of Himmler and Chief Adjutant of the *Reichsführer-SS*, Karl Wolff
1936
Foundation of a genealogical "Bergmann Family Association for the Descendants of Pewter Craftsman Christian Bergmann, from Hameln, ca. 1635 (Right of Citizenship)," and publication of an association periodical (*Der Bergmann*) until 1939
From 1938
Performs the duties of the adjutant to the chief castle administrator, Siegfried Taubert
August 31, 1938
Letter from the chief of the Personal Staff of the *Reichsführer-SS*: In the event of war, Bergmann must immediately report to the SS Death's Head Regiments as platoon leader
May 1940
Writing of the "Wewelsburg Military Postal Service Letters No. 3" as *SS-Obersturmführer* and company commander of an SS Death's Head Infantry Regiment temporarily garrisoned in Weimar-Buchenwald
1941/1942
At the time of the invasion of the Soviet Union: belonged to a unit of the Commando Staff of the *Reichsführer-SS*
December 7, 1942
Killed in action near Velikiye Luki, Russia, as an SS-Hauptsturmführer and company commander on the Staff of the *Reichsführer-SS* mm

No. 2-45

Rudi Bergmann (at center, with turban) during the Carnival celebration at Wewelsburg SS School
March 1, 1938
The 1938 and 1939 Carnival celebrations at Wewelsburg SS School took place in the mess hall of the guard building. In addition to the SS men and their wives, the female domestic staff, the so-called "castle maidens" also participated. The photograph shows Rudi Bergmann with several "castle maidens" at the March 1, 1938, celebration. Around this time, the SS castle administration was going through a time of upheaval: The outgoing chief castle administrator, Manfred von Knobelsdorff, had already given up his post, while his successor, Siegfried Taubert, had not yet taken over. Several indoctrination leaders, such as librarian Hans Peter des Coudres, began to think of moving on. The genealogical researcher and SS soldier Bergmann benefited from these changes. His field of work remained a core function of the SS school, and he rose to become the adjutant to the chief castle administrator. mm
Kreismuseum Wewelsburg, Fotoarchiv

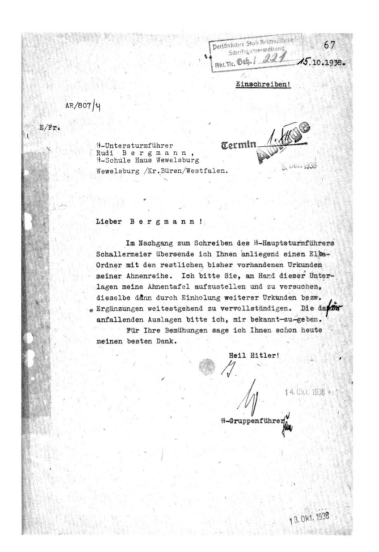

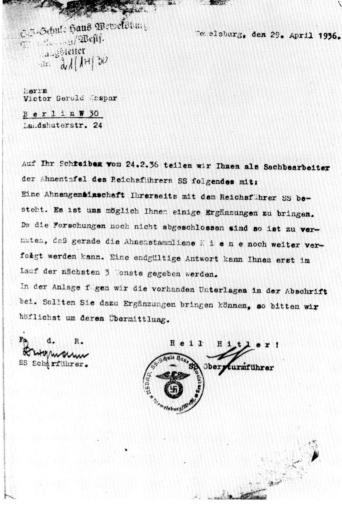

No. 2-43
Not shown
Rudi Bergmann's ID card from the Reich Office for Family Research
October 14, 1934
Initially, the interest of the young National Socialist Rudi Bergmann in genealogical research does not appear to have been politically motivated. Nevertheless, engagement in the history of one's own family and that of others soon became a political issue with the rise to power of the National Socialists in Germany. Due to racist regulations such as the Law for the Reconstitution of the Professional Civil Service of April 7, 1933, submission of proof that one had no Jewish ancestors was required more and more in professional and public life. Only "racially" and politically vetted bearers of the Genealogical Research-er Certificate issued by the Expert for Racial Research (later, the Reich Office for Family Research, or Reich Family Office) were authorized to conduct family research in archival documents and issue Proof of Aryan Descent certificates. mm

Bundesarchiv Berlin,
Zwischenarchiv, Dahlwitz-Hoppegarten,
ZB II/3032, Akte 4

No. 2-46
Letter from the chief of the Personal Staff of the *Reichsführer-SS*, *SS-Gruppenführer* Karl Wolff, to Bergmann, requesting the compilation of a table of ancestors
Aside from *Reichsführer-SS* Heinrich Himmler, other *SS-Gruppenführer* had Rudi Bergmann research their ancestry at Wewelsburg Castle. Among them was the chief of the Personal Staff of the *Reichsführer-SS*, Karl Wolff. Researching the family histories of the top SS officers fit in perfectly with Himmler's increasingly obvious intent to make Wewelsburg Castle a center of tradition for the *Gruppenführer*. Consequently, Bergmann's duties at the "castle" remained relatively unaffected by developments in the more specialized departments of Wewelsburg SS School. mm

Bundesarchiv Berlin, formerly the Berlin
Document Center, SL 63

No. 2-44
Letter from the employees of the Wewelsburg SS School Karlernst Lasch and Rudi Bergmann, in their capacity as preparers of Heinrich Himmler's genealogical chart, to Viktor Gerold K. in Berlin
Wewelsburg, April 29, 1936
At the latest by 1932, proof of "purely Aryan" ancestry back to the eighteenth-century constituted a mandatory requirement for acceptance into the SS. The enthusiasm of Wewelsburg chief castle administrator von Knobelsdorff for family research gave Himmler the idea of having his own family history investigated by personnel at Wewelsburg SS School. During the period of his officer training at the SS Officer School in Braunschweig, Rudi Bergmann had already worked on genealogical research matters for his fellow trainees – without having had professional training for this work. Following his friend Bernhard Frank to Wewelsburg, he became the full-time custodian of Himmler's genealogical chart. In this capacity, his tasks included handling the correspondence with numerous real or alleged distant relatives of the *Reichsführer-SS*. mm

Kreismuseum Wewelsburg

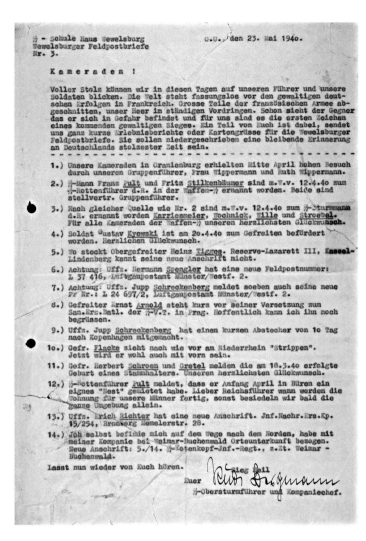

No. 2-47
Wewelsburg Military Postal Service Letters, No. 3, written by *Obersturmführer* and company commander Rudi Bergmann
Weimar, May 23, 1940
Translation on page 441
In addition to his activity as a genealogist, Bergmann served as adjutant to the new SS chief castle administrator Siegfried Taubert from mid/late 1938. When the war began in September 1939, he, like his friend Bernhard Frank, urgently requested assignment to a military unit of the SS rather than to the *Wehrmacht*. In May 1940, he greeted his fellow conscripts from Wewelsburg Castle as a member of the SS Death's Head Infantry Regiment. At the time, he was garrisoned at the SS base adjacent to Buchenwald Concentration Camp. mm
Bundesarchiv Berlin, NS 48/16

No. 2-48
Casualty Report for Rudi Bergmann
Bergmann was killed on December 7, 1942, as commander of the 7th Company, 8th SS Infantry Regiment, 1st Motorized Infantry Brigade. This brigade was subordinate to the Commando Staff of the *Reichsführer-SS* and, since the attack on the Soviet Union in June 1941, had participated intensively in major extermination operations targeting Jews and partisans behind the Eastern Front. In between such operations, the unit was sent to fill gaps on the front. During such a combat deployment Bergmann met his death.

On January 14, 1943 the notice of his death appeared in the SS weekly *Das Schwarze Korps* (The Black Corps). The extent of Bergmann's personal participation in executions has not been clarified. mm
Kreismuseum Wewelsburg, inv. no. 5489/2

Figurehead and Administrator: Siegfried Taubert, the Second Chief Administrator of the Castle

No. 2-49
The chief administrator of Wewelsburg Castle (1938 – 1945), Siegfried Taubert; original inscription: "S. Taubert. *SS-Gruppenführer*, 25. 12. 39"
A former imperial general staff officer and intermittent traveling salesman, Siegfried Taubert was appointed the SS chief administrator of Wewelsburg Castle by Himmler in January 1938. Up to that point, the 57-year-old *SS-Brigadeführer* had built a notable career in SS personnel management. Through his martial demeanor, he was expected to cultivate discipline within the SS castle administration, and his smooth social skills were expected to exert a calming effect on the Wewelsburg population. With the rank of general within the SS he would serve Wewelsburg Castle as a suitable representative befitting a residence for the *SS-Gruppenführer*. As an assessor at the People's Court and a short-term inspector of the Reinforced SS Death's Head Regiments, Taubert personally integrated into the National Socialist apparatus of persecution during his time at Wewelsburg. mm

Kreismuseum Wewelsburg, Fotoarchiv

Siegfried Taubert (1880 – 1946)
Chief Administrator of Wewelsburg Castle
1938 – 1945
December 11, 1880
Born as the son of a Lutheran pastor in Brallentin/Pomerania, educated at home and at Schiller high school in Stettin
1899
Entry as a cadet into the 57th Infantry Regiment in Wesel
1904
Marriage to a Dutch woman, produces three children; one daughter married Dr. Ernst Robert Grawitz, a future physician general in the medical service of the SS
1914
Study at the war college and qualification as general staff officer
1914 – 1918
In World War I: initially company commander; following wounding and illness, staff officer
Early 1919
Freikorps Company Commander
February 22, 1919
Discharge from the *Reichswehr* with the rank of major, purchase of an agricultural estate in Pomerania
1921 – 1924
District managing officer of the *Landbund* (Agrarian League), a nationalist-conservative association of big agriculture, as well as military commander of the *Stahlhelm* (Steel Helmet), a right-wing association of combat veterans, for the Greiffenhagen/Pomerania district; sympathizer of the "National Socialist Freedom Movement"
August 22, 1924
Sale of the estate and start of activity as sales representative for a Berlin piano manufacturer
1926
Membership in the ethnic onationalist *Tannenberg* League
February 1929
Resignation from the *Tannenberg* League
April 1, 1929
Employment at a Swiss life insurance company in Berlin
April 1, 1931
Entry into the NSDAP and the SS in Berlin
October 1, 1931
Beginning of a period of unemployment
January 9, 1932
Transfer as *SS-Scharführer* to the SS Group East under Kurt Daluege; by 1934, promoted seven times, the last to the rank of an *SS-Standartenführer*
December 18, 1933
Appointed *Stabsführer* of the SS Main Sector East under Sepp Dietrich
September 20, 1935
Promotion to *SS-Oberführer*
November 1, 1935
Appointed Stabsführer in the Security Service Main Office
September 13, 1936
Promotion to *SS-Brigadeführer*
January 30, 1938
Appointment to the position of chief castle administrator at Wewelsburg SS School
June 27, 1938
Awarded the hunting rights at the Externsteine by Himmler
September 3, 1938
Confirmation of the right to wear the cuff insignia of an SS department head (Wewelsburg Department of the Personal Staff of the *Reichsführer-SS* Main Office)

September 11, 1938
Promotion to *SS-Gruppenführer*
November 15, 1939
Appointment as chief of staff to the inspector general of the Reinforced SS Death's Head Regiments (Oranienburg Office) – in addition to the position of chief administrator of Wewelsburg Castle
January 22, 1940
As acting inspector, establishment of rules of conduct for members of the *Waffen-SS* in interactions with prisoners in concentration camps
January 29, 1940
Appointment by Hitler as honorary member of the People's Court for five years
May 25, 1940
Appointment as inspector of the Death's Head Regiments
June 26, 1940
End of his service as inspector of the SS Death's Head Regiments
June 21, 1942
Promotion to lieutenant general of the *Waffen-SS* on the occasion of Himmler's (last known) visit to Wewelsburg
August 19, 1942
Taubert suggested to the chief of staff of the Operations Main Office of the *Waffen-SS*, SS-Gruppenführer Hans Jüttner, that a *Waffen-SS* staff office be established in Wewelsburg under his (Taubert's) command, because almost all SS administrative personnel were also members of the *Waffen-SS*.
September 10, 1942
Reprimanded for his suggestion and actions on August 19 by the head of the Personal Staff of the *Reichsführer-SS*, Karl Wolff
January 30, 1943
Promotion to the rank of *SS-Obergruppenführer* and general of the *Waffen-SS*
May 13/14, 1944
Participation as pianist in a benefit concert for the German Red Cross at the Wewelsburg Village Community Center
1944
Takes over leadership of the Staff Department *Waffen-SS* at headquarters of the Personal Staff of the *Reichsführer-SS*
March 30, 1945
Flight from Wewelsburg to Frankenhausen in Thuringia, at the head of the SS castle administration personnel
February 13, 1946
Death in Kiel mm

Aufn.: Hoffmann.

Am 28. Oktober verabschiedete sich Stabsführer, S.S.-Oberführer Taubert von seinen
Kameraden und Mitarbeitern des S.S.-Ober-
abschnitts Ost, um auf Befehl des Reichsführers-
S.S. die gleiche Dienststellung beim S.D.-Haupt-
amt zu übernehmen. Nachdem S.S.-Ober-
gruppenführer Sepp Dietrich in einer An-
sprache die Entwicklung des Oberabschnitts aus
der früheren S.S.-Gruppe Ost dargelegt hatte,
dankte er seinem scheidenden Stabsführer für
seine Tätigkeit und führte dann S.S.-Brigade-
führer Koppe — bisher Abschnittsführer in
Danzig — als Stabsführer und Vertreter des
Oberabschnittsführers ein.

No. 2-50
Siegfried Taubert in the uniform of an *SS-Sturmhauptführer* with the cuff insignia of SS Main Sector East 1933/1934
In contrast to his Wewelsburg pre-decessor von Knobelsdorff, the years of civilian life during the Wei-mar Republic did not seem to have diluted Taubert's bearing as a mili-tary officer. His reputation as a man with General Staff experience in the Imperial Army helped him rise in the organization from SS candidate to the rank of *SS-Brigadeführer* in just five years. His career evolved within the close proximity to the highest SS military and police leaders. As chief of staff in the SS Main Sector East under Kurt Daluege and Sepp Dietrich, as well as at the Security Service Main Office under Reinhard Heydrich, Taubert was responsible for organizing the administration of these offices, but had no involve-ment in their operations. mm
Bundesarchiv Berlin, formerly Berlin Document Center, SSO Taubert

No. 2-53
Taubert leaving the guard building, a military band serenading him on the Monday of the Marksmen's Festival
June 19, 1939
Kreismuseum Wewelsburg, Fotoarchiv

No. 2-52
Not shown
Order of *Reichsführer-SS* Heinrich Himmler for the transfer of Siegfried Taubert from the Security Service Main Office to Wewelsburg as chief administrator of the castle, effective January 30, 1938
January 24, 1938
Himmler appointed Taubert chief castle administrator in January 1938. In this position, Taubert, as an organizer with military training, replaced the somewhat emotional head of training, von Knobelsdorff. With this change at the top, Himm-ler signaled that the SS admin-istration should play an altogether different role at the castle. Up to that point, the staff of Wewelsburg SS School had been able to pursue their individual professional and personal interests relatively un-hindered, which had sometimes led to chaotic conditions at the castle. Now, under Taubert's leadership, they were to understand them-selves first and foremost as a hier-archically organized military formation. Its principal task would no longer be ideological research and indoctrination, but the admin-istration and cultivation of Wewels-burg Castle as the future center of *SS-Gruppenführer*. mm
Bundesarchiv Berlin, formerly Berlin Document Center, SSO Taubert

No. 2-51
Report in the November 7, 1935, issue of the SS newspaper *Das Schwarze Korps* on the departure of Taubert as chief of staff of SS Main Sector East and his assumption of the same duties at the Security Service Main Office
October 28, 1935
The photograph shows Taubert with Sepp Dietrich.
Kreismuseum Wewelsburg, inv. no. 5481/36

DER REICHSFÜHRER ꙮꙮ
Der Generalinspekteur
der verstärkten ꙮꙮ-Totenkopfstandarten

Oranienburg, 22. Januar 1940.

IIa Az. St.Kdo.

Betrifft: Unterrichtung aller ꙮꙮ-Männer über Verhaltungsmass-
nahmen gegenüber Häftlingen.
Bezug : Ohne.
Anlagen : - 1 -

An alle Totenkopfstandarten,
Abteilungen und E-Einheiten.

1./ Alle Häftlinge, die in den Konzentrationslagern untergebracht
sind, sind Staatsfeinde schlimmster Art.

2./ In letzter Zeit ist es zu wiederholten Malen vorgekommen, dass
ꙮꙮ-Angehörige sich von den Gefangenen durch Bettenbau, Stiefel-
putzen und andere Handreichungen bedienen lassen.
Die Verbrecher wurden dann von den ꙮꙮ-Angehörigen durch Zuwendungen von Brot u. a. m. noch belohnt.

3./ Verbrecher und Staatsfeinde sind aus dem Volkskörper ausgeschie-
den und eingesperrt. Die Bewachung dieser Verbrecher liegt in
den Händen des Inspekteurs der K. L.

4./ Es wird hiemit befohlen:
a.) Alle Einheiten in den Totenkopfstandarten, Abteilungen und
E-Formationen sind über das Verhalten gegenüber Häftlingen
eingehend zu unterrichten.
Der Unterricht ist alle 2 Wochen zu wiederholen.
b.) Neu eintreffende Mannschaften sind über das Verhalten
gegenüber den Gefangenen in den 1. Unterrichtsstunden zu
unterweisen.

5./ Verboten wird:
a.) Dass sich ꙮꙮ-Angehörige in irgend einer Form von den Ver-
brechern bedienen lassen.
b.) Gefangene ohne Erlaubnis der aufsichtsführenden ꙮꙮ-Männer
zu Arbeiten heranzuziehen.
c.) Den Häftlingen in irgend einer Form Zuwendungen zu machen.

6./ Werden Häftlinge zu Arbeitsleistungen für die T. V. abgestellt,
so müssen dieselben, wenn kein Posten der K. L. unmittelbar
zur Verfügung steht, durch ꙮꙮ-Männer der T-Einheiten bewacht
werden. Nach Beendigung der Arbeit ist der Gefangene wieder an
den Posten der K. L. abzuliefern.

7./ Gegen alle Angehörige der ꙮꙮ, die sich Gefühlsduseleien zu schul-
den kommen lassen und die Staatsfeinde und Verbrecher nicht
als das ansehen, was sie sind, wird rücksichtslos vorgegangen
werden.

Der Inspekteur der K. L.

gez. Glücks

ꙮꙮ-Oberführer

F.d.R.d.A.
Der Stabskommandant:

ꙮꙮ-Sturmbannführer

Der Generalinspekteur
der verstärkten ꙮꙮ-Totenkopfstandarten

gez. Taubert

ꙮꙮ-Gruppenführer.

DAB NS31/372

No. 2-54

Instructions to all SS men on conduct to be adopted toward prisoners in the concentration camps, issued by the Inspector of Concentration Camps, Glücks, and the General Inspector of the Reinforced SS Death's Head Regiments, signed by Siegfried Taubert

Oranienburg, January 22, 1940

Translation on page 442

In November 1939, Himmler additionally appointed Taubert, Wewelsburg Castle's chief administrator, to the leadership of the Reinforced Death's Head Regiments. These were the SS units that would take the place of the SS Death's Head Guard Units at the concentration camps, if the latter were detailed to reinforce the military SS Special Service Troop deployments. For about nine months, the headquarters of the Inspector of Concentration Camps in Oranienburg became Taubert's second office. Having already worked for one of the central institutions of the persecution apparatus as chief of staff of the SS Security Service Main Office, he now, at the latest, personally became one of the leading desk perpetrators in the SS. In January 1940, moreover, he became an assessor at the National Socialist People's Court; in this capacity, Taubert participated in the National Socialists' system of injustice, from a position outside of the SS. mm

Bundesarchiv Berlin, NS 31/372

No. 2-55

Architect Hermann Bartels, Wewelsburg master carpenter Grote, SS chief castle administrator Taubert, and construction contractor Fritz Scherpeltz at the topping-out ceremony for the SS staff building

September 25, 1940

Taubert's assignment in Oranienburg as Inspector of the SS Death's Head Regiments ended in the summer of 1940. Henceforth, the 60-year-old *SS-Gruppenführer* was to concentrate on day-to-day management of the Wewelsburg SS castle administration, and the reception of high-ranking SS officers and their guests at the castle. Promoted in the end to *SS-Obergruppenführer* and lieutenant general of the *Waffen-SS*, Taubert remained the highest-ranking SS officer in Wewelsburg. Yet, specifically in relations with the SS leadership, and Himmler in particular, he was overshadowed in importance and influence by the chief of the SS's construction management in Wewelsburg, the architect and honorary *SS-Standartenführer* Bartels. Construction Management was not subordinate to the chief castle administrator. On the other hand, Bartels never hesitated to involve Taubert to achieve Construction Management objectives. mm

Kreismuseum Wewelsburg, Fotoarchiv

No. 2-56

Siegfried Taubert, chief castle administrator (second from left), and Karl Elstermann von Elster, staff commander (second from right), with guests, in front of the Wewelsburg Village Community Center

1938/1939

Photograph from private collection

Order Police Official on an SS Mission: Karl Elstermann von Elster

No. 2-57

Karl Elstermann von Elster in the uniform of a police officer

In the summer of 1938, 41-year-old police major and *SS-Sturmbannführer* Karl Elstermann von Elster was appointed to the newly created position of staff commander at Wewelsburg Castle. In concert with the new chief castle administrator, Taubert, he was to provide a tightening of discipline in the castle administration and improve relations between the SS and the local population of Wewelsburg. Previously, Elstermann had assumed numerous political and paramilitary functions in the National Socialist movement. In the mid-1930's, he made the switch to police service. In the summer of 1939, Elstermann himself became the target of SS disciplinary proceedings that led to his transfer out of Wewelsburg. In the first weeks of World War II, by his own account, he led an *Einsatzkommando*, or mobile execution squads, in Poland and therefore participated directly in some of the first actions of the war of extermination mm

Kreismuseum Wewelsburg, Fotoarchiv

Karl Elstermann von Elster (1897 – 1943)
Staff commander of Wewelsburg SS School, 1938 – 1939

September 27, 1897
Born in Frankfurt/Oder, the son of an army captain, secondary education in Königsberg, Berlin, and Frankfurt/Main

August 2, 1914
Entry as cadet into the 3rd Guard Infantry Regiment, Berlin; after being wounded as a lieutenant during World War I, service as an ordnance officer; work in espionage and counterespionage; after the end of the war, service in the 12th Infantry Division, border defense in Upper Silesia

Fall 1919
Discharge from the *Reichswehr*

1919 – 1922
Training in agronomy, then business activity and work as an independent sales representative

1923
First marriage, one daughter, deceased in 1939

October 1, 1930
Entry into the NSDAP

June 1, 1931
Entry into the SA

December 1931
NSDAP-*Sektionsführer* in Berlin-Dahlem

Spring 1932
Discharge from the SA on order of Berlin *Gauleiter* Joseph Goebbels

August 1932
NSDAP-*Ortsgruppenleiter* in Berlin-Zehlendorf

December 1932
Reinstatement in the SA

April 6, 1933
Appointment by Goebbels as head of the ministerial office in the newly created Reich Ministry for Propaganda and Public Enlightenment

1934
Transfer to the *Reichssendeleitung* (Reich Programming Management) of the radio broadcasting service

January 1934
Switch from SA to SS

September 1934
Service under the "chief of training" (initially responsible for military preparedness training of the SA). Following the dissolution of this office:

July 1, 1935
Entry into the Military Police and the municipal police (*Schutzpolizei*); leadership of a company squad of military police in Berlin; transfer to the Municipal Police leadership, Berlin; temporary resignation from the SS

1935
Second marriage, after the death of his first wife in 1930

April 21, 1936
Assumed duty of managing disciplinary matters with the police

August 1936
Deployed at the Olympics in Berlin as escort to film director Leni Riefenstahl

October 19, 1936
Detailed to the staff of the chief of the Order Police, *SS-Obergruppenführer* Kurt Daluege

September 12, 1937
Re-entry into the SS at the rank of an *SS-Hauptsturmführer*

March/April 1938
Deployment as liaison officer between the staffs of the chief of the Order Police (Daluege) and the chief of the Security Police (*SS-Gruppenführer* Heydrich) during the incorporation of Austria into National Socialist Germany

May 1938
Furlough from police service for purpose of a detail, initially to last three months, to the newly created post of staff commander of Wewelsburg SS School (on Himmler's order)

May 24/25, 1938
First visit to Wewelsburg Castle

June 13, 1938
Beginning of service at Wewelsburg and promotion to the rank of major in the Order Police and to that of *SS-Sturmbannführer*

Second half of 1938
Interrogations and investigations within the SS castle administration for prosecution of disciplinary offenses

December 1, 1938
Admission as major of the police to a permanent position in the Berlin police administration concurrent with continuation of the detail to Wewelsburg SS School

First half of May, 1939
Himmler's decision to transfer Elstermann von Elster as police major to the staff of the *Reichsführer-SS*

May 15, 1939
Commander of operation to pursue two prisoners who escaped from the Wewelsburg external detachment of Sachsenhausen Concentration Camp

June 24, 1939
Confirmation of transfer as SS officer from the staff of the SS Main Office to the Personal Staff of the *Reichsführer-SS*, Wewelsburg SS School

June 28, 1939
Suspended from duty by the SS chief castle administrator Taubert after the interrogation of several male castle administration staff and female witnesses related to charges of "behavior unworthy of the SS"

June 29, 1939
Repudiation of the allegations raised against Elstermann von Elster

June 30, 1939
Compilation of a report to the chief of the Personal Staff of the *Reichsführer-SS* concerning Taubert's allegations

July 6, 1939
Assignment to Wewelsburg Castle canceled and one-year prohibition on wearing the SS uniform and the SS runes on the police uniform imposed by Himmler; the *Reichsführer-SS* also sought initiation of police disciplinary proceedings

July 7, 1939
Transfer by Daluege to a hardship post with the municipal police in Munich, effective August 1, 1939

August 1939
Service as sector commander of the Municipal Police in Munich

August 2, 1939
Letter from Daluege to Himmler requesting that the uniform-related penalties only enter into force after the disciplinary proceedings; and that those proceedings be carried out by the SS and not by the police; Himmler agreed to the request

September 1939
After the German attack on Poland, command of an *Einsatzkommando* in Poznan

October 1939
Took command of a battalion in the SS Police Division

December 14, 1939
Interrogation regarding the events in Wewelsburg before the tribunal of the SS Police Division

March 1940
Himmler ordered that the SS disciplinary matter be deferred until after the war

May/June 1940
Participation with his unit in the invasion of France

August 1940
Decision by Himmler that SS disciplinary proceedings be abandoned because of Elstermann von Elster's "bravery in the face of the enemy" demonstrated in combat

June 1941
Transfer to the Colonial Police School in Oranienburg as deputy commander

September 1941
Beginning of a detail of several months in Libya

September 1942
Interim command at the Police School for Foreign Deployment (formerly Colonial Police School) in Oranienburg for one month

March 1943
Assumption of duty as liaison officer to the Italian Colonial Police in North Africa

April 9, 1943
Killed when his plane is shot down off the Tunisian coast

April 15, 1943
Discovery of the corpse on the Tunisian coast

April 20, 1943
Posthumous promotion to lieutenant colonel of the Municipal Police mm

2.2.10
Concentration Camp Commandant: Adolf Haas

No. 2-58
**Adolf Haas in the uniform
of an *SS-Obersturmführer***
Ca. 1935
The baker Adolf Haas commanded
Niederhagen/Wewelsburg Concentration Camp for nearly three years.
Like many of the Wewelsburg camp
personnel, he began his concentration camp service at Sachsenhausen
Concentration Camp, from where he
was transferred to Wewelsburg as
labor detachment commander. With
the reclassification of the subcamp
as the self-administered Niederhagen Concentration Camp, he was
promoted to camp commandant, and
retained this position until the dis-
banding of the camp in the spring of
1943.

His service evaluations were
quite critical. Though his superiors
praised his commanding tone, they
found him to be unsuited for promotion to executive positions because of his inadequate writing
skills. The concentration camp prisoners feared his brutal and un-
predictable behavior. Haas exploited
his power over them and had them
produce art objects and paintings
that he gave as gifts to his family and
superiors. kjs/sk
Kreismuseum Wewelsburg, Fotoarchiv

Adolf Haas (1893 – ?)
**Detachment Commander and concen-
tration camp commandant in Wewelsburg,
1940 – 1943**
November 14, 1893
Born in Siegen/Westphalia,
the son of a Protestant innkeeper
1899 – 1907
Elementary school in Hachenburg,
Westerwald
1907
Apprenticeship as baker and confectioner
in Wiesbaden; at conclusion, employment
in various businesses
October 1913
Enlistment in the navy, deployment to East
Asia from November 1914 to March 1920.
Following the start of World War I, six years
as a Japanese prisoner of war
March 11, 1922
Marriage to Lina Müller; three children
1929 – 1935
Runs a leased bakery in Hachenburg
December 1, 1931
Entry into the NSDAP
(membership no. 760610)
April 1, 1932
Entry into the SS
(membership no. 28943)
April 4, 1933
Commander of the 2nd Company of
the 2nd Battalion, 2nd SS Regiment
January 30, 1934
Promotion to *SS-Untersturmführer*,
appointed commander of 2nd Company of
the 3rd Battalion, 5th SS Regiment
October 10, 1935
Gave up the bakery to enter active career
service with the SS as commander of
the 3rd SS Battalion, 78th SS Regiment
(Limburg)
September 13, 1936
Promotion to *SS-Sturmbannführer*
March 1, 1940
Called up as reinforcement to Sachsen-
hausen Concentration Camp (training on
the job as protective custody camp leader)
June 17, 1940
Transfer to Wewelsburg as labor
detachment commander
September 1, 1941
Appointment as commandant of
Niederhagen Concentration Camp
May 1943
Transfer as camp commandant,
together with 92 SS men, to Bergen-
Belsen Concentration Camp
Early 1944
Investigation of Haas, along with other
SS men, for having his portrait painted by
Jewish prisoners
December 20, 1944
Command of 18th SS Motorized
Infantry Battalion
March 1945
Departure from his place of residence to
Hamburg; considered missing thereafter
August 18, 1950
Official declaration of Haas's death
kjs/sk

No. 2-59
**Adolf Haas as a Japanese
prisoner of war (front, right)**
Ca. 1914
Kreismuseum Wewelsburg,
Fotoarchiv

No. 2-63
Letter of complaint from
***SS-Obergruppenführer* Oswald Pohl**
to Adolf Haas, March 30, 1944
Translation on page 442
Bundesarchiv Berlin, SSO Haas

No. 2-64
Wooden box owned by the Haas family,
front and rear views
Photograph: J. Büttner, 1994
Even though it was officially prohibited,
camp commandant Adolf Haas repeatedly
exploited concentration camp prisoners
to his private advantage. For instance,
while at Niederhagen Concentration Camp,
he had various paintings and wood objects
made for himself. In his family's possession is a wooden box that political prisoner
Kurt Hüter was forced to build for Haas in
1942. Hüter signed the handcrafted item
in a hidden compartment, with the
inscription "Crafted in November 1942
Kurt Hüter master cabinetmaker."

Having his portrait painted with other
SS officers by a Jewish prisoner in Bergen-
Belsen Concentration Camp in 1944 re-
sulted in "severest disapproval" of Adolf
Haas from the highest levels of SS
leadership. kjs/sk

Kreismuseum Wewelsburg, Fotoarchiv

No. 2-60
Camp commandant Adolf
Haas with SS personnel,
presumably of Bergen-Belsen
Concentration Camp
Ca. 1943

Lohamei Hagetaot Kibbutz, Israel

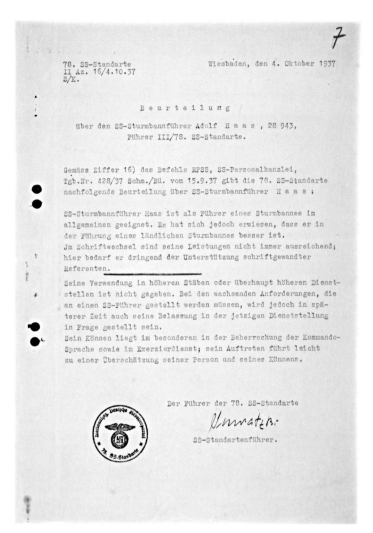

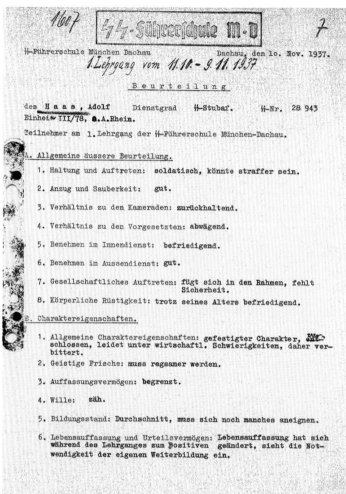

No. 2-61

**Official evaluation for SS Major Adolf Haas,
commander of the 3rd SS Battalion,
78th SS Regiment
October 4, 1937**

Translation on page 443

In their official service evaluation for 1937, Adolf
Haas's superiors noted that his deficient verbal
skills made him suitable only for command of
a rural battalion. In his character assessment
at the Munich-Dachau School for Reich Leaders,
which he attended for a month-long training
course, he was described as "embittered,"
"strong-willed," with "limited powers of compre-
hension." Here too, his level of written and
oral performance was found wanting. In the end,
his evaluation of November 26, 1942 was more
positive; he was evaluated as a "good leader,"
whose "writing abilities," however, "could be better." He proved his mettle "in practical service,"
though he could stand to further educate himself
in the theoretical sphere. Once again, however,
his suitability for executive service was not
confirmed. kjs

Bundesarchiv Berlin, SSO Haas

No. 2-62

**Excerpt from the evaluation of
Adolf Haas for the training course of
October 11 – November 9, 1937,
at the SS Officer Training School in
Munich-Dachau**

Bundesarchiv Berlin, SSO Haas

2.2.11
Guard Unit Commander: Hans Lau

No. 2-65
SS-Untersturmführer **Hans Lau**
1942
SS-Untersturmführer Hans Lau was the commander of the concentration camp guard unit at Wewelsburg from late 1939 to September 1941. He organized and coordinated the guarding of prisoners, assigned SS men to guard duty, and monitored the work of the SS guards. With the rising number of prisoners, the strength of the guard unit under his command also increased, from thirty-five at the start, to almost one hundred SS men.

Even though Hans Lau had not volunteered for duty with the SS Death's Head Units, he performed his concentration camp duties conscientiously, and was convinced on a political and ideological level of the meaning of his work at the concentration camp. Nevertheless, his behavior toward the prisoners was neither violent nor without scruples. His conduct demonstrates that the leeway available to an SS guard – despite National Socialist conviction – permitted more humane behavior. kjs/sk

Kreismuseum Wewelsburg, Fotoarchiv

Hans Lau (1893 – 1943)
SS guard unit commander
in Wewelsburg, 1939 – 1941
June 17, 1893
Born the son of a businessman
1900 – 1908
Elementary and middle school education
1908 – 1911
Training course in business, then employed as business courier
1914 – 1917
Military service during World War I in France and Galicia (wounded by shrapnel)
1919
Discharged from the army, apprenticeship as cabinetmaker
1929 – 1933
Unemployment
1929
Entry into the NSDAP (membership no. 166412) and the SA
1931
Participation in an SA meeting in Braunschweig and entry into the SS (membership no. 10997)
From 1933
Unskilled worker at the local health insurance agency in Quickborn
April 30, 1934
Marriage to Henny Böckmann, 17 years his junior; three children: Herbert, born May 28, 1935, Gretchen, born July 27, 1936, Anneliese, born July 6, 1939
1934
Command of SS Company 4/4 in Hamburg as acting company commander
March 1935
Employee exam before the examination commission of the Higher Insurance Board of Schleswig
Fall 1938
Induction to the reinforcement of the Death's Head Units at Sachsenhausen Concentration Camp for several weeks during the annexation of the Sudetenland
From October 28, 1939
As SS member, obligatory emergency detail as permanent guard at Sachsen-hausen Concentration Camp
December 11, 1939 – September 16, 1941
Commander of the guard unit at the Wewelsburg Concentration Camp; intensive exchange of letters with his wife Henny
May 1, 1940
Promoted to *SS-Untersturmführer* of the Reserve in the *Waffen-SS*
September 17, 1941
Transfer to Dachau Concentration Camp; serves as platoon commander and company commander
1942
Falls ill with tuberculosis, stay at the SS field hospital in Vienna
January 30, 1943
Promoted to *SS-Obersturmführer* of the Reserve in the *Waffen-SS*
March 26, 1943
Death kjs/sk

No. 2-66
Hans Lau with Henny, née Böckmann, at their wedding in Quickborn
April 30, 1934

Kreismuseum Wewelsburg,
Nachlass Hans Lau, inv. no. 16697/4

No. 2-68
Hans Lau with SS guards Escher, Friedsam, Brinkmann, Scheidler, Maus, Vongerichten, and Johanns in Wewelsburg
Ca. 1940

Kreismuseum Wewelsburg,
Nachlass Hans Lau, inv. no. 16697/3

No. 2-67
Hans Lau in front of his office barracks in Wewelsburg
1940
Kreismuseum Wewelsburg,
Nachlass Hans Lau, inv. no. 16697/2

No. 2-69
Hans Lau with unknown comrades
Ca. 1940
Kreismuseum Wewelsburg,
Nachlass Hans Lau, inv. no. 16697/7

The photographs show Hans Lau going about his business at the concentration camp in Wewelsburg. Lau took many photographs of the Wewelsburg camp. He had copies made for his SS colleagues, and sent them to his family in Hamburg to give his wife an impression of his workplace. sk

No. 2-73
Relief carving with a view of Wewelsburg Castle, crafted by a concentration camp prisoner
1940
Despite an official prohibition, many SS men forced prisoners of the Niederhagen Concentration Camp to produce objects for their personal use. Hans Lau also had numerous objects made, such as this woodcut, as a "happy memento" of his period of service at Wewelsburg. In a letter dated October 27, 1940, he enthused about the numerous Christmas presents for his children that the SS had prisoners produce, adding: "our workshops are real industrial concerns: in the wood shop, twelve carpenters and cabinetmakers are at work; in the metalworking shop, six; in the forge, two. There are four painters, two electricians, and so on. ... There is no article of necessity which cannot be produced at the camp." sk
Kreismuseum Wewelsburg,
Nachlass Hans Lau, inv. no. 14231

No. 2-70
Memorial medal for the First of October, 1938
In December 1939, when Hans Lau was transferred from Sachsenhausen Concentration Camp to Wewelsburg, along with 35 other SS men, he already had months of experience in guard duty at Sachsenhausen Concentration Camp. In the fall of 1938, he had been called up to Sachsenhausen for the first time for several weeks as reinforcement to the Death's Head Units. At this time, the SS began to deploy members of the original concentration camp guard units outside the camps. Older men of the General SS took over the vacant positions in the camps, including Hans Lau, then 45.

He received this medal for having worked several days at Sachsenhausen Concentration Camp during the annexation of the Sudetenland. Altogether, the medal was awarded over a million times. sk
Kreismuseum Wewelsburg,
Nachlass Hans Lau, inv. no. 14227

Jn schönen Paderborner Land, juppheidi, juppheida,
Jst mir ein kleiner Ort bekannt, juppheidi, heida.
Da geht's bergauf und geht's bergab,
Da schwitzt man manchmal nicht zu knapp.
Juppheidi, juppheida, juppheidi, heidallala,
Juppheidi, juppheida, juppheidi, heida.

Hier liegt ein Lager wohlbekannt, ——
Kommando Wewelsburg genannt, ——
Da zogen wir zum Wachdienst ein,
Potz Donner, hatten wir ein Schwein. ——

Der Kommandant, das ist ein Mann, ——
Der tut uns Gutes, wo er kann, ——
Wenn man auf Posten sitzen tut,
Dann hat man es noch mal so gut. ——

Und schläfst du dann auf Posten mal, ——
So ist das weiter nicht fatal, ——
Du kriegst dann keinen Urlaubsschein,
Und steckst kein Geld in'n Spartopf rein. ——

Der Führer von dem Schutzhaftlager, ——
Der ist sehr lang und auch sehr hager, ——
Die Posten lobt er aus der Ferne,
Auch trinkt er siessen Kaffee gerne. ——

Als Stratege ist er wohlbekannt, ——
Jn ganzen Wewelsburger Land, ——
Er leistet auch zu nächt'ger Zeit,
Auf dem Burghof gern Spähtrupptätigkeit. ——

Der Führer unseres Wachblocks dann, ——
Das ist ein ganz humaner Mann, ——
Er liebt nicht nur 'ne Flasche Wein,
Er liebt auch kleine Mägdelein. ——

Das Fussballspiel macht ihm Pläsier, ——
Doch kann er wirklich nichts dafür, ——
Lass er, wie es bei ihm ist Brauch,
Sich jedesmal den Fuss verstaucht. ——

Dann ist da noch ein grauer Alter, ——
Jch glaub, er heisst mit Namen Walter, ——
Er kam von Mauthausen her, ——
Und erzählt uns manche schöne Mär. ——
Mit Hermann, unserm Korporal, ——
Hat man so manchmal seine Qual, ——
Jn der Woche zehnmal Stelldichein,
Und immer andere Mägdelein. ——

Den Mack aus Baden jeder kennt, ——
Er hat ein neues Reichspatent, ——
Geruchlos' Gas liefert er in Massen,
Doch Vorsicht ! An die Nase fassen. ——

Der O'scha Kuhn hat viel Malheur, ——
Er kam von Sachsenhausen her, ——
Hat eben seine Maus gefreit,
Und muss nun fort auf lange Zeit. ——

'Ne Wohnung hat er wunderschön, ——
Doch hat er sie noch nie gesehn, ——
Die vier Tage Urlaub war er blind,
Sah nur sein allerliebstes Kind. ——

Wewelsburg, den 8.12.1940.

Mein liebes Muttchen!

Heute Sonntag habe ich wieder Dienst, und da ich inzwischen wieder zwei Briefe und das Paket mit Taschentüchern erhalten habe, muß ich wohl oder übel einen Dankesbrief nach Quickborn senden. Und ich tu es gerne. Also endlich läßt sich meine Frau mal wieder Dauerwellen machen, das ist aber auch Dein Glück, denn sonst wäre ich Weihnachten keinen Schritt mit Dir aus dem Hause gegangen. Ich weiß nur nicht, wie wir alle Besuche bewältigen wollen. Michels, Jüttemeier, Erna hat auch darum gebeten, sie diesmal nicht zu übergehen. Dann sollen wir für einen Sprung zu Wendefeuers kommen. Es ist eigenartig, alle fremden Menschen verfügen über meinen Urlaub, nur ich alleine habe nichts darüber zu bestimmen, und ich komme doch schließlich nach Hause, um mich meiner Familie zu widmen. Ja, wenn es vier Wochen wären, dann könnte man dies und jenes noch nebenbei besorgen, aber so, wo man nur eben acht Tage zur Verfügung hat, man ist eben angekommen, dann kann man auch schon wieder an die Abreise denken. Die ganzen Besuche müssen dann eben innerhalb zweier Tage abgewickelt sein, mehr will ich nicht dafür einbüßen. Es fehlte dann blos noch, daß Erna den genauen Tag wissen will, damit sie sich noch allerhand Besuch einladen kann, um sich mit ihrem Bruder von der Waffen SS dicke zu tun.
Heute habe ich auch wieder das bewußte Paket abgeschickt, endlich sind auch Deine Schuhe dabei, und was ich sonst noch alles hatte. Es ist wieder ein ansehnliches Paket geworden. Aber diesmal gibt es nur wieder ein Pf. Butter, die alte Dame hatte nicht mehr auf Lager. Sie versprach uns aber, daß wir in der nächsten Woche etwas mehr bekommen würden. Zu Weihnachten gibt es dann aber keine Butter, da ich schon in der Mitte der Woche fahren werde, und Ernst W. fährt auch schon am Sonnabend Nachmittag. Wir lassen dann die Butter für die Woche nach Weihnachten zurücklegen, bei dieser Kälte hält sie sich auch lange frisch.
Gestern hatte ich eine unliebsame Attacke mit Plaul. Dieser unverschämte Kerl verlangte von mir, ich sollte schon am zweiten Weihnachtstage wieder zurückkommen, damit er ja rechtzeitig zum Polterabend seiner Schwägerin in Chemnitz sein könnte. Ich habe ihm aber schön heimgeleuchtet, und fand ich auch tatkräftige Unterstützung beim Oberstuf. Haas. Aber so sind die Herren von der Waffen-SS, wenn man ihnen den kleinen Finger reicht, wollen sie nicht nur die ganze Hand, sondern womöglich noch den ganzen Kerl dazu. Unverschämt bis zum Äußersten. Aber ich wußte ja schon lange, wes Geistes Kind der Plaul war, ich bin jetzt ja genau ein Jahr mit ihm zusammen. Am 11.12. feiern wir im kleinen Rahmen unser einjähriges Hiersein. Was hat sich nicht alles in dem einen Jahre hier verändert. Mit 36 Mann kamen wir an, hatten 70 Häftlinge, und jetzt sind wir auf 142 Männer und 500 Häftlinge angewachsen. Und was für Veränderungen wurden hier vorgenommen, man sieht aber nur an unserem Lager, daß etwas praktisches geleistet wurde. An den anderen Arbeitsstellen ist nicht viel geschafft worden, weil die Bauleitung eben eine lange Zeit hindurch keinen Mann an ihrer Spitze hatte, der etwas Verantwortungsgefühl hat. Die Gelder werden aus dem Fenster geworfen, Materialien werden vergeudet, und Hermann Göring ruft immer wieder zur weiteren Sparsamkeit auf allen Gebieten auf. Wenn der den Mist sehen würde, der hier von den vielen Architekten verzapft wird, noch dazu bei einem Gehalt von mindestens 600.- RM der würde den ganzen Laden auflösen, und ihnen allen gestreifte Kittel anziehen lassen. An diesen Brüdern hätte ich auch Lust, meine Wut auszulassen. Die Herren leben einen guten Tag. Aber davon später.
Heute in 14 Tagen bin ich längst daheim. In dieser Hoffnung grüße ich Euch alle und schließe mit vielen Grüßen und einem langen Kuß für Dich
mein Muttchen Dein   14234/129

No. 2-71

"Humor magazine" for the Wewelsburg SS Company party
About 1940

Celebrations constituted an integral part of regular leisure-time activities for the Wewelsburg camp SS. Occasionally, parties were thrown that, in addition to the Wewelsburg concentration camp personnel, brought together the SS castle administration and the villagers. This "humor magazine," in all probability written by Hans Lau, was composed for just such a common celebration at the Wewelsburg Community Center. Aside from humorous verses about individual SS men, it features several references to the political situation, including disparaging remarks about the enemy, England, and about the concentration camp prisoners. sk

Kreismuseum Wewelsburg, inv. no. 16879

No. 2-72

Letter from Hans Lau to his wife Henny
December 8, 1940

Translation on page 443

During his service at the concentration camps Sachsenhausen, Wewelsburg, and Dachau, Hans Lau wrote dozens of letters to his wife, Henny, in which he reported in detail about his duties and of his daily life in the camps. His activities in the concentration camp he depicted as completely self-evident and "normal." In this letter, Hans Lau referred to the wish of the camp SS to organize a party in Wewelsburg on the occasion of the first anniversary of the establishment of the camp. He repeatedly spoke out against camp commander Wolfgang Plaul and criticized Construction Management in Wewelsburg for its wasteful ways. Henny and Hans Lau saved their letters in order to some day show their children what contributions he had made to the construction and consolidation of National Socialist Germany. kjs/sk

Kreismuseum Wewelsburg,
Nachlass Hans Lau, inv. no. 14234/129

The biographies of prominent SS leaders offer a key to the organizational structure of the Protection Squadron (*Schutzstaffel*). This chapter focuses on its three main areas of activity: the organization itself, its merger with the police, and the establishment of its own armed formations. All three areas are more clearly detailed through individual biographies. At the same time, the chapter seeks to illustrate that the areas of responsibility were not sharply defined. The individual SS man could easily engage in all spheres of activity within the SS over the course of his career. The chapter opens with the biography of Heinrich Himmler, whose functions drew together all strands of SS operations.

3 The Organization of the SS – Biographical Approaches

3.1
Heinrich Himmler

As a subdivision of the National Socialist Party, the SS was formally a registered association. For most members, belonging to the SS was a spare-time activity, which they pursued voluntarily, and for which they paid membership dues.

The SS quickly outgrew this limited role when the police were subordinated to Himmler's authority and the SS was tasked with creating quasi-military armed formations. The assumption of sovereign functions secured for the steadily expanding SS organization not only additional funding sources, but also – most importantly – various opportunities to exert ideological influence on society.

The diverse functions and activities of the SS were fused in the person of Himmler. He was known to interfere in the minute details of the personal and official concerns of his subordinates. But Himmler also allowed his men great leeway – as long as they moved in what he considered to be the right direction.

No. 3-1

The tent of *Reichsführer-SS* Heinrich Himmler in Döberitz near Berlin during a roll call of SS Group East
August 11 – 13, 1933

Heinrich Himmler was one of the most influential persons in the National Socialist regime. His power was based on the organizations of the SS and the police, which he single-mindedly merged, and whose scope of responsibilities he shaped like no other. He unremittingly expanded the fields of operation and range of authority for his apparatus.

Himmler's thinking and actions derived from a simplistic worldview based on distrust and implacable images of the enemy: oppositional forces incessantly threatened the "good" world of the family, SS, and ethnic community (*Volksgemeinschaft*). These required protection through ideological decisiveness, biological "selection," a "military" mindset, and the willingness to cross ethical boundaries.

The SS system would have been inconceivable without Himmler, his obsessiveness, and his constant interventions. But he frequently gave his subordinates a free hand, which, as a rule, they readily utilized to realize his vision, up to and including mass murder. mh

Ullstein Bilderdienst, 00006282

Heinrich Himmler (1900 – 1945)
Agronomist, *Reichsführer-SS*
October 7, 1900
Born in Munich
December 1917
Drops out of secondary school to join the Bavarian army as an officer candidate; discharged from the military at the end of 1918
Fall 1919 – summer 1922
After completing high school (July 1919), he studied agronomy at the Technical University in Munich (diploma exam, August 1922), concurrently a member of several Free Corps and right-wing organizations
August 1923
Entry into the NSDAP
November 1923
Participation in Adolf Hitler's coup attempt in Munich
July 1924
Secretary and deputy of Gregor Straßer, district leader (*Gauleiter*) of the National Socialist Freedom Movement, or the Lower Bavarian NSDAP, in Landshut
Late 1925
Entry into the SS
September 1926
Deputy NSDAP Reich Propaganda Leader (until September 1930); moves to the Party headquarters in Munich
Summer 1927
Deputy *Reichsführer-SS*
January 1929
Reichsführer-SS
September 1930
Member of the Reichstag

March 1933
Police president in Munich and Nuremberg-Fürth
April 1933
Commander of the Bavarian Political Police
April 1934
Inspector of the Prussian Secret State Police and Political Police Commander of the States
June 1936
Chief of the German Police
October 1939
Reich Commissar for the Strengthening of German Nationhood
August 1943
Reich and Prussian Minister of the Interior
July 1944
Chief of Army Equipment and commander of the Replacement Army
December 1944 – March 1945
Commander of Army Group Upper Rhine, then Army Group Vistula
April 1945
Expulsion from the Party and dismissal from all offices by Hitler
May 23, 1945
Suicide in British captivity in Lüneburg mh

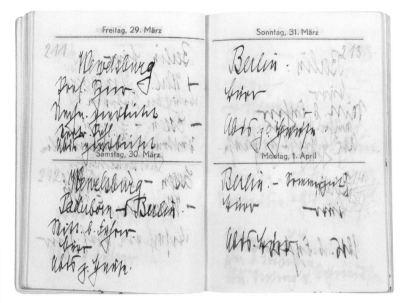

No. 3-4

Photograph of Heinrich Himmler in uniform as *Reichsführer-SS*, presumably from the records of the 1st Battalion (*Sturmbann*), 33rd SS Regiment (*Standarte*) Rhein-Hessen in Mainz

The photograph reproduced above was one of the official photographs of the *Reichsführer-SS* that were hung in SS and police offices. Portraits were in great demand because, in the course of his career, Himmler amassed countless Party and state functions, many outside the SS and police. To each of these fields of activity, a large personnel apparatus was generally attached. Himmler always delegated the management of these personnel to high-ranking SS leaders. mh

Kreismuseum Wewelsburg, inv. no. 15902

No. 3-2

Ticket to a National Socialist Party mass rally in Herford on March 10, 1930, featuring Heinrich Himmler as speaker

From September 1926 until the Reichstag (parliamentary) election in September 1930, Himmler acted as deputy Reich Propaganda Leader for the NSDAP. In this position he had significant influence in shaping the public image of the party. Novel elements included increased political outreach to the rural population and the idea of "propaganda concentration" to saturate the public with speeches, mass rallies, and posters.

As a propaganda organizer and as a speaker, Himmler frequently traveled around Germany and regularly came to Westphalia. However, it appears that he did not give the scheduled speech in Herford. mh

Kreismuseum Wewelsburg, inv. no. 16693

No. 3-5

Heinrich Himmler's 1940 appointment calendar

The pages shown here note Himmler's stay at Wewelsburg from March 28 to March 30, 1940, and a meeting with Hitler's architect, Albert Speer.

Himmler's many appointment books and service calendars testify to his frequent, almost constant travel, which increased during the war. In the period of the Third Reich, he visited Wewelsburg at least twenty-five times, always staying for only a few days. On these occasions, Himmler often hosted guests, mostly high-ranking SS leaders and individuals who were of great use to his organization. The latter included Hitler's architect Albert Speer, who visited Wewelsburg in March 1940. Speer repeatedly worked closely with the SS. As General Construction Inspector for the Reich Capital and, since 1942, as Minister of Armaments, he had concentration camp prisoners and forced laborers deployed to his projects. mh

Kreismuseum Wewelsburg, inv. no. 16287

Friday, March 29 [1940]
211
Wewelsburg
Prof. Speer.
Afternoon: worked
Report by Pohl
Evening: worked

Saturday, March 30
212
Wewelsburg
Paderborn – Berlin.
Lunch with the Führer.
Office
Evening at home.

Sunday, March 31
213
Berlin.
Office
Evening at home

Monday, April 1
214
150
Berlin – daylight-saving time
Office
Evening: office
Translation of a transcription

With consecutive numbers in red, Himmler marked the number of days since the beginning of the war; with green numbers Himmler kept track of his weight (in pounds).

No. 3-3

Heinrich Himmler (MdR), *Der Reichstag 1930. Das sterbende System und der Nationalsozialismus. Nationalsozialistische Bibliothek, Heft 25*, [Heinrich Himmler (MdR), member of the Reichstag), The Reichstag in 1930: The Dying System and National Socialism. National Socialist Library, vol. 25], Gottfried Feder, MdR (ed.), Verlag F. Eher Nachf. GmbH, Munich, 1931

Emerging from the Reichstag election of September 14, 1930, as the second-strongest party in Germany, the NSDAP sent 107 delegates to parliament. One of them was Heinrich Himmler who, as the Deputy Reich Propaganda Leader, had contributed significantly to the electoral success.

Soon after the election, Himmler published *The Reichstag* in 1930, a pamphlet in which he expressed his disdain for the highest level of representation of the German people. In the foreword, he proudly presented himself as a "despiser of the system." Himmler himself did not participate in parliamentary work. He never spoke in parliamentary session, joined no committee, and even neglected his own Party delegation. Nevertheless, as a member of parliament he earned his first reasonable regular income. From now on, he devoted himself, almost exclusively, to the development of the SS, of which he had been the leader since January 1929. mh

Kreismuseum Wewelsburg, inv. no. 16931

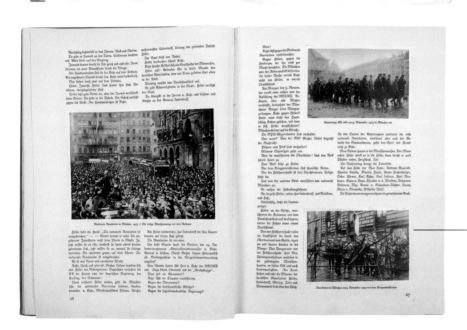

No. 3-6
Heinrich Himmler and Ernst Röhm participate in the "Hitler Putsch"
Deutschland erwacht. Werden, Kampf und Sieg der NSDAP.
[Germany Awakens: Birth, Struggle, and Triumph of the National Socialist Party]
Selection and artistic adaptation of photographs: Heinrich Hoffmann, Munich. Text: Wilfried Bade
Cigaretten-Bilderdienst, Altona-Bahrenfeld, 1933
Album for cigarette cards, first edition, published before June 1934
Directly after the National Socialist seizure of power, illustrated books that glorified the early years of the National Socialist Party as a "time of struggle, courage, and sacrifice," enjoyed widespread popularity. This album for collectible pictures distributed with cigarette packs was one of them. It featured photographs taken by Heinrich Hoffmann, the personal photographer of Adolf Hitler. We see a shot taken on November 9, 1923, in front of the Bavarian

War Ministry in Munich, showing Heinrich Himmler (holding a banner) as a participant in the so-called Hitler Putsch. At the time, he was a member of the right-wing Reich War Flag Military Union, led by the retired army captain Ernst Röhm (third from right, wearing an officer's overcoat). It was Röhm who had introduced college student Himmler to the extremist right-wing circles of Munich, bringing him into the National Socialist Party in the summer of 1923.

With his appointment as SA chief of staff at the beginning of 1931, Röhm became the direct superior of Himmler who, in the meantime, had risen to the position of *Reichsführer-SS*. Until 1934, the SS remained formally subordinated to the SA. mh
Kreismuseum Wewelsburg, inv. no. 12421

No. 3-7
Heinrich Himmler during the "Hitler Putsch" without Ernst Röhm
Deutschland erwacht. Werden, Kampf und Sieg der NSDAP.
[Germany Awakens: Birth, Struggle, and Triumph of the National Socialist Party]
Selection and artistic adaptation of photographs: Heinrich Hoffmann, Munich. Text: Wilfried Bade.
Print run 201,000–300,000, Cigaretten-Bilderdienst, Altona-Bahrenfeld, 1933
Album for cigarette cards, edition published after July 1934
On the face of it, this later edition of the picture book scarcely differed from the first edition. But some photographs were missing and the photographer, Heinrich Hoffmann, had manipulated others. In the Hitler Putsch picture, a beam, apparently jutting out of the barricade, now conceals the face of Ernst Röhm.

After the bloody elimination of the SA leadership at the end of June 1934, which saw Röhm murdered by an SS detachment on Hitler's orders, many photographs used in the public realm were retouched, with the former SA chief of staff, who had fallen out of favor, no longer appearing in the pictures.

Himmler's organization participated decisively in the violent action against the SA and therefore belonged to the winners in this power struggle within the National Socialist Party. Himmler himself later declared the murder of his cherished former sponsor a difficult but necessary test that the SS had passed in a reliable and "clean" manner. mh
Kreismuseum Wewelsburg, inv. no. 4564

End of 1934

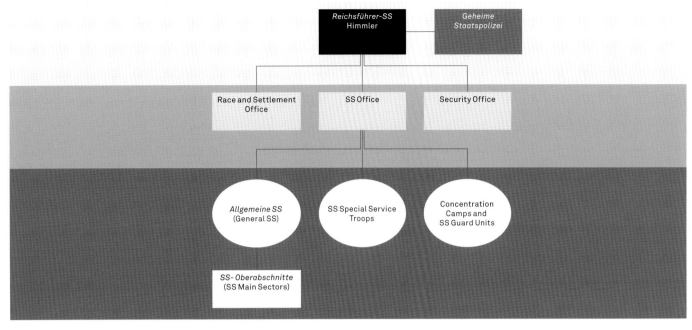

Beginning of September 1939

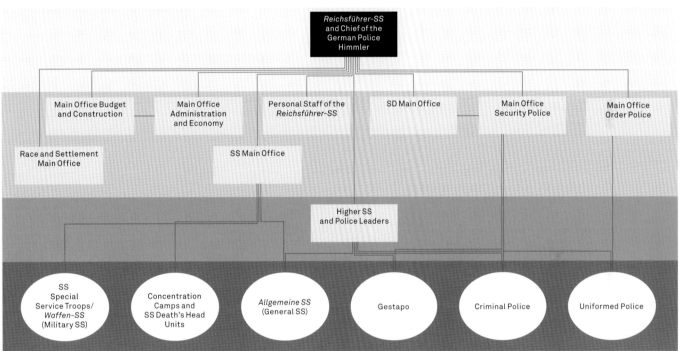

End of 1944

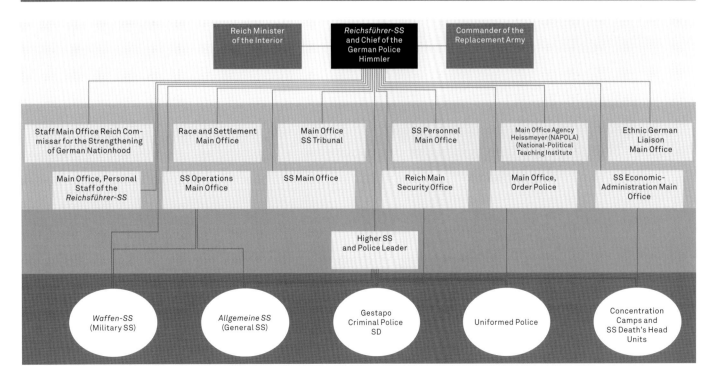

No. 3-8
Chart of the SS Organization
Graphic by
Weidner Händle

3.2
The *Allgemeine SS*

The General SS (*Allgemeine SS*), also known as the Black SS because of the color of its uniforms, was the organizational nucleus from which a large apparatus gradually developed. After 1938, it counted fairly consistently around 250,000 members. The numerous tasks of the SS led to the formation of the most diverse organizational subunits. Two were of crucial importance for the development of the SS:

1

The Race and Settlement Main Office: In the first years of National Socialist rule, this department served both as ideological pillar and experimental laboratory for the ideas of Himmler and his leading planners;

2

The Main Office Administration and Economy (merged, in February 1942, with the Main Office Budget and Construction into the SS Economic and Administrative Main Office). With its countless branches and interconnections, this institution mirrored perfectly the SS as a whole, and became one of its most powerful departments during the war. Here, all the threads of the SS's economic complex came together. In March 1942, the agency gained control of the concentration camp system as well.

No. 3-9
**The black service cap of General (*Allgemeine*) SS units, worn only as part of the "traditional uniform" after 1935
Around 1934**
Kreismuseum Wewelsburg, inv. no. 15022

3.2.1
Oswald Pohl – Economy and Administration

No. 3-10
Oswald Pohl wearing the uniform of an *SS-Obergruppenführer*
1944
Oswald Pohl was one of the most powerful men in the SS. From 1934 until the end of the war, he remained a loyal follower of Himmler. A convinced National Socialist, Pohl sought to quickly rise through the ranks of the SS and therefore gave up his position as a Navy purser in 1934. No independent thinker in ideological questions, Pohl aligned himself completely with Himmler. His unconditional loyalty secured his meteoric rise within the organization. In 1942, he was promoted to *SS-Obergruppenführer* and general of the Armed SS (*Waffen-SS*). Pohl controlled the administration and finances of the SS and *Waffen-SS*; the engineering and construction activity of SS, *Waffen-SS*, and police; and the concentration camps, as well as SS enterprises. From 1942, he led the SS Economic and Administrative Main Office. In a manner typical of National Socialism, Pohl established and sponsored a patronage system with strong personal ties, which was designed to guarantee unity within his organization. jes
Bundesarchiv Koblenz, Bild 183-R64926

Oswald Pohl (1892 – 1951)
Career military man (Naval purser);
***Obergruppenführer* and general of the**
Waffen-SS
<u>June 30, 1892</u>
Born in Hamborn (now Duisburg)
<u>1912</u>
Joined the Imperial Navy; training as navy purser
<u>1914 – 1918</u>
Deployments in the Baltic Sea and off the coast of Flanders
<u>1919/1920</u>
Free Corps fighter according to his own, unsubstantiated account
<u>1920</u>
Continued service as purser in the Reich Navy
<u>1925 – 1934</u>
Member of the SA
<u>1923, 1925 oder 1926</u>
Joined the NSDAP
<u>1925/1927</u>
Swinemünde *Ortsgruppenführer* (local Party group leader)
<u>1931</u>
Expansion of the SA in the Navy in Kiel
<u>1933</u>
Elected to Kiel municipal parliament, acting chairman of the city council
<u>May 22, 1933</u>
Meets Himmler in Kiel
<u>January 31, 1934</u>
Discharged from the Navy at his own request
<u>February 1, 1934</u>
Joins the SS; *SS-Standartenführer* and head of the SS Administration Office
<u>June 1, 1935</u>
SS-Brigadeführer and chief administrator of the SS
<u>January 30, 1937</u>
SS-Gruppenführer
<u>March 1, 1937</u>
Member of the Presiding Council of the German Red Cross
<u>April 1, 1939</u>
Chief of the Main Offices for Administration and Economy and for Budget and Construction
<u>April 20, 1939</u>
Ministerial director in the Reich Ministry of the Interior
<u>February 1, 1942</u>
Chief of the SS Economic and Administrative Main Office (WVHA)
<u>March 16, 1942</u>
Incorporation of the Concentration Camps Inspectorate into the WVHA as *Amtsgruppe D* (Department D)
<u>April 20, 1942</u>
SS-Obergruppenführer and *Waffen-SS* general
<u>July 9, 1942 – March 20, 1943</u>
Replaces Reinhard Heydrich as a member of the Reichstag
<u>April 23, 1945</u>
Goes underground
<u>May 27, 1946</u>
Arrested by allied soldiers in northern Germany
<u>January 13, 1947</u>
Case IV of the Nuremberg Subsequent Trials against Pohl and others commences
<u>November 3, 1947</u>
Sentenced to death
<u>June 7, 1951</u>
Executed at Landsberg prison jes

Kiel, January 24, 1932

Sturmführer Pohl
Marinesturm III/187

a) Why am I a National Socialist and why an SA man?

Because I was a National Socialist before there was a National Socialism, because, due to heredity, upbringing, and environment, the man in me could only find political satisfaction in an idealistic worldview such as offered by National Socialism.
...

No. 3-12
Essay by Oswald Pohl
January 24, 1932
Oswald Pohl was no "follower." He had joined the NSDAP early on and was a member of the Storm Detachment (*Sturmabteilung* or SA) from 1925. As the essay he wrote in 1932 shows, his worldview, however, was not well thought-out and vague. Slogans supplant careful consideration. Affirmations of faith take the place of a genuine analysis of National Socialist ideology. Pohl actively and unscrupulously worked on his SS career. He accepted and promoted its criminal policies. His actions are clearly documented; in contrast, his ideological views are more difficult to pin down. Pohl's biography epitomizes a more general problem: it is often difficult to answer questions about the significance of ideological convictions or even about the motivations for working in the SS and participating in criminal acts. jes
Bundesarchiv Berlin, formerly the Berlin Document Center, SSO Oswald Pohl

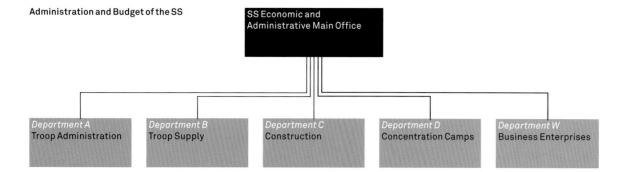

SS Economic and Administrative Main Office

Department A	Department B	Department C	Department D	Department W
Troop Administration	Troop Supply	Construction	Concentration Camps	Business Enterprises

Concentration Camps and the Economy

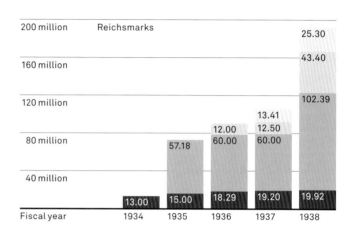

Concentration camps

SS Death's Head Units

SS Special Service Troops

Allgemeine SS

No. 3-11
Organizational chart of the top administrative level in the SS Economic and Administrative Main Office 1942 – 1945

The SS Economic and Administrative Main Office was founded on February 1, 1942. Its complicated name reflects Oswald Pohl's various areas of activity, which had been combined into a single organization. On March 16, 1942, Himmler officially put the Inspectorate of Concentration Camps under Pohl's control. It was now named Department D – Concentration Camps. This agency was in charge of all SS concentration camps. The SS Economic and Administrative Main Office (WVHA) exemplified the expansion of the SS. Its ever-increasing tasks and areas of operation led to the expansion of this originally small organization. At times, up to 1,500 people worked at the Berlin headquarters of the SS. jes

No. 3-13
Not shown
Financing of the SS: minutes of an SS officers' meeting on June 13 and 14, 1931 (excerpt)

Bundesarchiv Berlin, NS 19/1934

No. 3-14
Budget controlled by the SS Administration under Oswald Pohl from 1934 to 1938

Until 1933, the finances of the SS rested on shaky foundations. The modest budget of the organization derived from monthly dues of SS members as well as donations by "sustaining members," who themselves did not belong to the SS. No funding was provided by the NSDAP. Financial irregularities eroded trust in in-house money management. Fear that financial bottlenecks could jeopardize the activities of the SS was realistic.

The organization's financial situation only improved when, after 1933, the SS was entrusted with functions of the state. Police forces, concentration camps, and the armed units of the SS Special Service Troops were funded by public sources. Even the General (*Allgemeine*) SS, the voluntary organization of the SS, now received substantial funding from the NSDAP. The Party, in turn, had obtained these funds from government sources. Access to public funding sources was crucial for the expansion of the SS. jes

Jan Erik Schulte, *Zwangsarbeit und Vernichtung: Das Wirtschaftsimperium der SS. Oswald Pohl und das SS-Wirtschafts-Verwaltungshauptamt 1933 – 1945,* Paderborn, 2001, p. 87

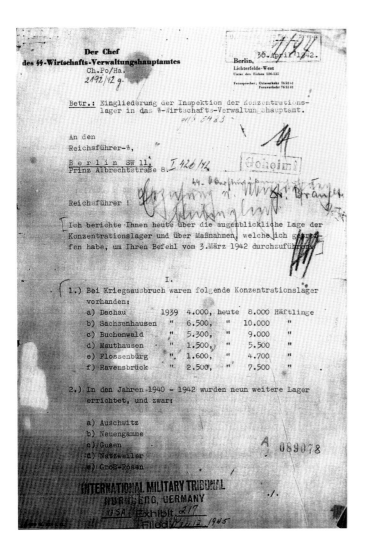

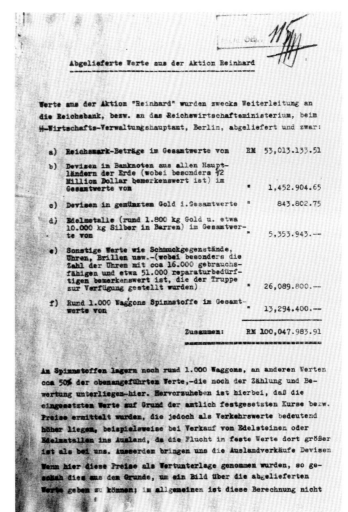

No. 3-15

Takeover of the concentration camps by the SS Economic and Administrative Main Office and the economic tasks of the camps: Pohl's report to Himmler April 30, 1942
Translation on page 444

On March 16, 1942, the SS Economic and Administrative Main Office (WVHA) took over the Inspectorate of Concentration Camps. Himmler had already issued an order to that effect on March 3, 1942. By subordinating the camps to Pohl, Himmler intended to deny the newly appointed Plenipotentiary for Labor Allocation, *Gauleiter* Fritz Sauckel, access to prisoner labor. The SS wanted to use concentration camp prisoners in SS-owned companies and not in the armaments industry. The "economic tasks" mentioned in Pohl's report referred primarily to SS enterprises.

In fact, however, the WVHA had to hand over more and more forced laborers to private enterprises. Only in exceptional cases, however, did deployment in privately owned firms mean an improvement in living conditions. On April 30, 1942, Pohl issued the following order to concentration camp commanders: "This deployment [of concentration camp prisoners] must literally be exhausting in order to achieve maximum productivity." jes
Staatsarchiv Nuremberg, R-129

No. 3-16

Correspondence concerning the administration and accounting of valuables stolen from Jews murdered in Poland Cover letter for a report by *SS-Gruppenführer* Odilo Globocnik 1943
Translation on page 444

No. 3-17

Not shown
Pohl's letter of clearance to Globocnik February 16, 1944

The SS Economic and Administrative Main Office was responsible for balancing accounts related to the valuables stolen from Jews murdered in Poland. The code name "Operation Reinhard(t)" was used to disguise the mass murder primarily committed at the extermination facilities Belzec (Bełzec), Sobibor (Sobibór), and Treblinka.

Odilo Globocnik, SS and Police Leader in the occupied Polish city of Lublin, commanded the murder operation. In 1943, Globocnik submitted a detailed list of stolen valuables as a final accounting report. On February 16, 1944, Pohl officially cleared him for the accounting period ending March 31, 1943. The ostensibly correct accounting of looted goods was a sham. Contemporary witnesses reported that the SS men who administered the valuables on location were corrupt and had personally enriched themselves. jes
Staatsarchiv Nuremberg, PS-4024

3.2.2
Richard W. Darré – "Race" and "Settlement"

No. 3-18
**Richard Walther Darré in the uniform
of an *SS-Gruppenführer***
**Photograph: Studio Bieber/Nather
October 1934**

Like Heinrich Himmler, Richard Walther Darré earned a university degree in agronomy; in the early 1930s, he became the leading agricultural policy expert of the Party and the SS. Appointed Reich Minister for Food and Agriculture as well as Reich Farmers' Leader after the seizure of power, Darré embodied a typical National Socialist blending of party, state, and special interest group representation.

Darré's power base within the SS was the Race and Settlement Main Office (RuSHA), which he founded in 1931 on Himmler's order, and led until 1938. The main tasks of this office consisted of assessing the "racial" reliability of SS men and their wives, as well as to provide their ideological training. The RuSHA employees developed ideas for the "renewal of the German race from the peasantry," which Darré propagated under the slogan of "Blood and Soil."

After 1936, Darré's political influence gradually waned, chiefly because his agricultural ideology did not meet the demands of the war economy. The RuSHA, however, remained actively involved in the radical "Germanization" of occupied territories after the start of World War II, especially in the activity of conducting official expert opinions determining the "race" of individuals. mh

Bildarchiv Preußischer Kulturbesitz, Berlin, 10008182

**Richard Walther Darré (1895 – 1953)
Certified colonial economist and agronomist
Highest SS rank: *SS-Obergruppenführer***
July 14, 1895
Born in Belgrano, near Buenos Aires (Argentina)
1914 – 1918
Volunteer in World War I; highest rank: Lieutenant
1918 – 1925
Degree course in agronomy at the Kolonialschule Witzenhausen, as well as at the University of Halle, specializing in livestock breeding and heredity (graduated in 1925); membership in *völkisch,* nationalist organizations
1925 – 1929
Active as an agricultural expert, chiefly for breeding issues, on behalf of various government institutions
As of 1926
Publication of articles and books with the ethno-nationalist (*völkisch*)-oriented publishing house Julius Friedrich Lehmann in Munich; this included articles for the periodical *Volk und Rasse* (People and Race), as well as his books *Das Bauerntum als Lebensquell der nordischen Rasse* (The Peasantry as Life Source of the Nordic Race, 1929) and *Neuadel aus Blut und Boden* (A New Nobility from Blood and Soil, 1930).
June 1930
Following a meeting with Hitler in the spring of 1930, establishment of an NSDAP "agricultural policy apparatus" (continued after 1933 as Reich Office for Agricultural Policy of the NSDAP)
July 1930
Entry into the NSDAP; in 1931 entry into the SS
December 1931
Establishment of the SS Race Office (later, the Race and Settlement Main Office)
November 1932
Member of the Reichstag
May 1933
Reich Farmers' Leader (until 1945)
June 1933
Reich Minister for Food and Agriculture
September 1933
Hereditary Farm Law, Reich Food Corporation Law (establishment of the Reich Food Corporation under the leadership of the Reich Farmers' Leader)
September 1938
Resignation as head of the Race and Settlement Main Office
May 1942
Suspended as Reich Minister of Food and Agriculture; withdrawal from political life
April 1945
Arrested and indicted by the International Military Tribunal at Nuremberg
April 1949
Sentenced to seven years imprisonment in the "Wilhelmstrasse Trial" against former National Socialist cabinet ministers; pardoned in August 1950 for health reasons; private life in Bad Harzburg
September 5, 1953
Death in Munich mh

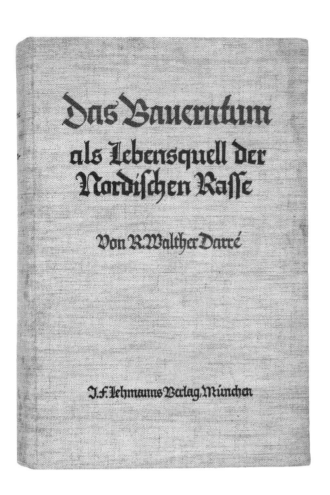

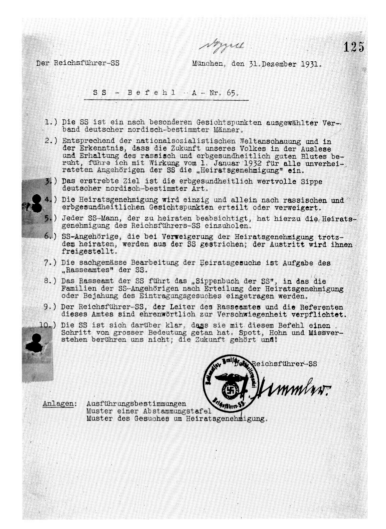

No. 3-19

Richard Walther Darré, *Das Bauerntum als Lebensquell der Nordischen Rasse* [The Peasantry as Life Source of the Nordic Race]

J. F. Lehmanns Verlag, Munich, 1929

Richard Walther Darré was one of the few theoreticians of the SS. The title of his first book *The Peasantry as Life Source of the Nordic Race* in 1929 already revealed the thrust of his racist thought.

Darré harbored a deep aversion to the modern city, liberalism, capitalism, and the Jews. His goal was to reshape German society on the basis of an ethno-nationalist (*völkisch*) ennobled peasantry, systematically resettled in the "East," and thus to create a "new nobility" (reflected in the title of his later book). Such ideas on human breeding and class politics impressed Heinrich Himmler. He commissioned Darré to set up the SS Race Office, later the Race and Settlement Main Office, with the intent of strengthening the ideological reliability of the SS. mh

Kreismuseum Wewelsburg, inv. no. 16521

No. 3-20

"Heirats- und Verlobungsbefehl des Reichsführers SS" [Marriage and Engagement Order of the Reichsführer-SS], SS Order A No. 65

December 31, 1931

Translation on page 444

On December 31, 1931, Heinrich Himmler issued an order in which he redefined his organization as an elite based on biological criteria for the first time. He included the wives of the men in his considerations in order to avoid an impression of the SS as an all-male society.

In order to ensure the "racial superiority" of the "SS kin," every SS man who wanted to get married had to obtain approval from the *Reichsführer-SS*. The SS man and his bride had to undergo an examination conducted "according to racial and hereditary health principles." The "SS Race Office," later the RuSHA, was given responsibility for these examinations, for which purpose the agency had been founded.

The bureaucratic expenditure of this measure was immense, particularly beginning in 1932/1933, as every new SS applicant had to submit to examination by RuSHA "race experts." In all, the office evaluated more than 1.2 million SS men, their wives to be, and female members of the "SS retinue."

In a disputed case Himmler himself got involved as an expert assessor. Consistent with his conception of a large "SS family," Himmler liked to intervene in the private lives of his subordinates. mh

Bundesarchiv Berlin, NS 2/174, Bl. 125

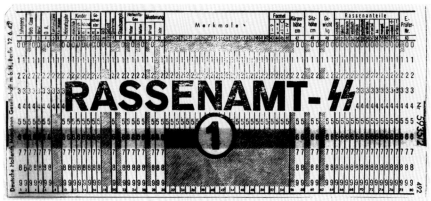

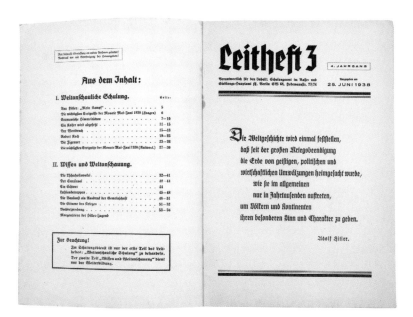

No. 3-22

SS training material: *SS-Leitheft*, published by the *Reichsführer-SS*: Chief of the Race and Settlement Main Office, Berlin

Vol. 4, no. 3 (June 25, 1938)

From 1934 until August 1938, the Race and Settlement Main Office was responsible for the ideological instruction of SS members. The most important didactic tool was the periodical *SS-Leitheft* (SS Guidance Booklet), which RuSHA indoctrination instructors used to prepare weekly classes in the individual SS units. The content of these guides was deliberately kept simple; the aim of the instruction was not to convey useful knowledge but a "deep inner experience." SS men were to be indoctrinated to an "ideologically firm attitude." mh

Kreismuseum Wewelsburg, inv. no. 16949

No. 3-25

Hollerith punch card of the Race Office in the RuSHA for recording data on "race-based features"

In the first years of National Socialist rule, SS settlement projects played no significant role. That changed from 1938 on, with the annexations of Austria, the Sudetenland, and the "Protectorate of Bohemia-Moravia," but above all with the beginning of World War II.

An enormous apparatus was established to achieve a thorough "Germanization" of the populations in these occupied territories. Its key agencies were the Ethnic German Liaison Office (VOMI), numerous police bases and, at the top, Himmler as the Reich Commissioner for the Strengthening of German Nationhood.

The RuSHA also participated in the racist policy of conquest. It was included in the planning and implementation of numerous "settlement projects" and it defined the criteria for the large-scale "racial" survey of the local civilian population. RuSHA "race experts" drew on the same criteria that they had used previously to evaluate SS members. Now their questionnaires, punch cards, and expert assessments decided the fate of millions in the future "Greater Germanic Reich." mh

Bildarchiv Preußischer Kulturbesitz, Berlin, 30011636

No. 3-24

Wall ornament from a hereditary farm: sconce with odal rune from the property of a "hereditary farm family" near Marsberg (Sauerland region)

A key piece of Darré's "blood and soil" ideology was the establishment of so-called hereditary farms (*Erbhöfe*). The aim was to implement a National Socialist-style land reform: Farmsteads were to be indivisible, therefore bequeathable to only one heir, and not exceed a certain size, which could result in land confiscation. Prerequisites for owning a hereditary farm was the "racial" impeccability of both the owner and the heir, who each had to present a "Proof of Aryan Descent" certificate. Only owners of hereditary farms were allowed to call themselves "farmers." Darré declared hereditary farms to be the basis for the "preservation of the health of people and state." mh

Kreismuseum Wewelsburg, inv. no. 16984

No. 3-21
Members of the Race and Settlement Main Office processing "racial" data
1938
Bildarchiv Preußischer Kulturbesitz, Berlin, 30022030

No. 3-23
Odal. Monatsschrift für Blut und Boden [Odal. Monthly Journal for Blood and Soil], R. Walther Darré (ed.)
"Zeitgeschichte" Verlag und Vertriebs-Gesellschaft m.b.H., Berlin, later Verlag Blut und Boden, Goslar
Vol. 6, no. 1 (July 1937)
To editor Darré and other National Socialist agricultural experts, the Odal journal served as a platform for their racial ideological ideas about farming and population policy. The publication was named after the Germanic odal rune, which the National Socialists used as a symbol of "blood and soil." It was the emblem of the hereditary farms and staff of the Race and Settlement Main Office wore it as insignia on the left sleeve of their uniforms.
mh
Kreismuseum Wewelsburg, inv. no. 16962

No. 3-26
Registration of Poles by RuSHA staff at the Central Resettlement Agency's Camp on Wiesenstraße in Litzmannstadt (Łódz)
1940
SS resettlement activities were focused on "ethnic German" communities, in other words, people who spoke German and professed to German culture, but who did not hold German, Austrian, or Swiss citizenship. They lived scattered throughout Eastern and South Eastern Europe (mainly in Poland and the Soviet Union) as well as in Alsace-Lorraine, which had belonged to the German Reich before 1918.

Aiming to build a "racially pure settler society," SS "suitability evaluators" determined the "racial value" of future settlers and of the indigenous population. Until the end of the war, well over 2.5 million people residing in areas beyond Germany's borders had to undergo appraisal by the responsible regional Immigration and Resettlement Central Offices. Classification as "unworthy of Germanization" was often a death sentence for those so judged – or meant at the very least their expulsion from their traditional places of residence or exploitation by the occupiers. From the start, Jews, as well as Sinti and Roma, had no place in this new order. They were "resettled," in other words, deported, crammed into ghettoes, and killed in extermination camps.
mh
U.S. Holocaust Memorial Museum, Washington, D.C., Photo Archives, 70235

3.3
The SS and Police

An ideological missionary zeal, increasing indispensability to the regime as the guarantor of "internal security," as well as a growing number of ambitious staff helped *Reichsführer-SS* Heinrich Himmler gain control of the entire police apparatus within a few years.

In 1936 Himmler restructured the police, previously a matter for the individual states, into a centralized organization. Together with the Criminal Police, the Political Police (now known as the Secret State Police throughout the German Reich) formed the Security Police Main Office. In 1939, the internal intelligence service of the Party, the Security Service of the RFSS (SD), was integrated into the organization, as well. At the same time, Himmler incorporated the uniformed policing executive (*Vollzugspolizei*) – which comprised the municipal police (*Schutzpolizei*) and gendarmerie – into the newly established Order Police Main Office.

Largely removed from the control of the state administration and increasingly merged with the SS in terms of personnel, the German police became the central instrument of a ruthless persecution of the regime's opponents.

No. 3-27
**Shako of Municipal Police officers
after 1933**
Kreismuseum Wewelsburg, inv. no. 16801

No. 3-28
Reinhard Heydrich wearing the uniform of an *SS-Gruppenführer*
Photograph published on August 30, 1940
Former naval officer Reinhard Heydrich was Heinrich Himmler's most important collaborator in implementing the ideological and political goals of the SS. He embodied a combination of efficiency, ambition, and loyalty indispensable for Himmler's aims. Above all, Heydrich shared Himmler's deep distrust in society.

Heydrich established the SS Security Service (SD), which became the sole intelligence service of the National Socialist Party on June 9, 1934. He pushed forward a merger of police and SS and played a crucial role in defining the guidelines and structure of the entire persecution apparatus of the Security Police, which he himself headed.

After the war began, Heydrich, as chief of the Reich Security Main Office (RSHA), coordinated the escalation of the terror in the occupied countries. This included the systematic murder of the European Jews. mh

Ullstein Bilderdienst, 00013329

Reinhard Heydrich (1904 – 1942)
Retired Navy Lieutenant; final SS rank:
***SS-Obergruppenführer* and police general**
<u>March 7, 1904</u>
Born in Halle an der Saale
<u>Since 1920</u>
Active in several far-right and anti-Semitic organizations
<u>1922</u>
High-school graduation; joined the Reich Navy
<u>April 1931</u>
Dishonorably discharged from the navy
<u>July 1931</u>
Entry into the NSDAP and SS; Beginning of the establishment of an SS intelligence service, the later Security Service of the *Reichsführer-SS* (RFSS)
<u>July 1932</u>
Chief of the RFSS Security Service (*Sicherheitsdienst* or SD)
<u>April 1933</u>
Commander of the Bavarian Political Police
<u>April 1934</u>
Director of the Prussian Secret State Police Office (Gestapo)
<u>June 1936</u>
Chief of the Security Police Main Office (Gestapo and Criminal Police)
<u>September 1939</u>
Director of the Reich Main Security Office (Security Police and SD)
<u>July 1941</u>
Göring authorizes Heydrich to implement radical measures against all Jews in territories under German control.
<u>September 1941</u>
Acting Reich Protector of Bohemia and Moravia (concurrent with police functions)
<u>January 20, 1942</u>
Chair of the "Wannsee Conference" (coordination of the Europe-wide mass murder of the Jews)
<u>June 4, 1942</u>
Died as a result of injuries sustained in an assassination attempt by Czech resistance fighters in Prague on May 27, 1942
mh

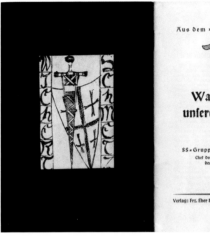

No. 3-29
Reinhard Heydrich, *Wandlungen unseres Kampfes* [Transformation of Our Struggle], by SS-Gruppenführer R. Heydrich, Chief of the Security Main Office of the *Reichsführer-SS*
Print run 87,000 – 96,000
Franz Eher Verlag Nachfolger, Munich/Berlin, 1936
This text had originally been published as a series in the SS periodical *Das Schwarze Korps* (The Black Corps).

Reinhard Heydrich was obsessed with images of the enemy. His booklet *Transformation of Our Struggle* shows that he suspected "hidden foes" and new "hostile elements" everywhere. Consequently, his surveillance and persecution apparatus engaged in a wide range of activities. Officially, suppression of opponents was divided between two branches: The Gestapo was its executive arm while the Security Service of the RFSS (SD), which Heydrich also headed, initially handled the more theoretical field of "research on the enemy." A core task of the SD was the collection of material and information on political and ideological opposition groups.

The influence of the SD grew with its administrative integration into the complex of Security Police and SS. At the end of September 1939, this development led to the establishment of the Reich Main Security Office (RSHA), which coordinated the persecution and terror both domestically and in the occupied territories. With the establishment of the notorious SS *Einsatzgruppen* at the latest the Security Service actively participated in the extermination of human lives. mh

Kreismuseum Wewelsburg, inv. no. 16932

No. 3-30
SS-Brigadeführer Reinhard Heydrich,
head of the Bavarian Political Police, in his
office at the Wittelsbacher Palace, Munich;
standing in the front is his adjutant
Alfred Naujocks
April 11, 1934
Already in 1933, as commanders of the
Bavarian Political Police, the team Himmler-
Heydrich targeted political opponents
and organizations of ideologically defined
enemies, particularly Jews and Catholics.

In Bavaria, Himmler and Heydrich
tested their brand of ruthlessness and systematic tyranny, which they perfected in
the following years as they built up an apparatus of persecution. mh
Bundesarchiv Koblenz, Bildarchiv,
Bild 152-50-05

No. 3-31
**Prussian Minister President Hermann
Göring (right) appoints *Reichsführer-SS*
Heinrich Himmler Inspector of the
Prussian Secret State Police**
Photograph: Bildagentur Scherl,
April 20, 1934
Between autumn 1933 and June 1934,
Himmler gradually succeeded in securing
his appointment as commander of the
Political Police in each of the German
states. One of the last bastions he captured was Prussia, the largest and most
powerful of the German states. Here,
Hermann Göring had long pursued his own
police policy. As Prussian Minister President and Minister of the Interior, he had
created the Secret State Police (Gestapo)
out of the former Prussian Political Police.
With "protective detention" (*Schutzhaft*)
and concentration camps, Göring introduced the same methods of oppression,
which Himmler employed in Bavaria.

Presumably to protect his political
ambitions in other areas and his position
against internal rivals, Göring had finally
struck a deal with Himmler in April 1934.
By appointing Himmler Inspector of the
Prussian Secret State Police, Göring, who
continued to lead the agency, made
Himmler his deputy. From Bavaria Himmler
brought more than thirty of his closest
associates, among them Reinhard Heydrich, whom he installed as the new
Director of the Secret State Police Office
in Berlin. mh
Bundesarchiv Koblenz,
Image Archives, sign. Bild 183-R96954

No. 3-32
**Service medaillion of the
"Secret State Police," nickel
version**
Kreismuseum Wewelsburg,
inv. no. 16570

No. 3-33
Security Police poster: "The Police – Your Friend, Your Helper! Your Thanks: Donate to the WHW on 'German Police Day.'"
Drawing: Helmuth Ellgaard, Berlin, 1938
This poster was displayed in January 1939 to draw attention to the street collection of the German police for the Winter Relief Agency (*Winterhilfswerk*). It shows two Criminal Police officials on a manhunt. On their jacket lapels, both men wear the SS civilian insignia of a double sig rune.

Just as in the case of the Gestapo, Himmler wanted Criminal Police officials to join the SS. In fact, the Criminal Police actually lagged behind the Gestapo with regard to integrating its personnel with the SS. Nevertheless, it fully satisfied the political and ideological expectations of the National Socialist regime.

While the Gestapo was responsible for political and ideological opponents, the Criminal Police hunted for persons allegedly harmful to the "ethnic community" (*Volksgemeinschaft*) itself. With "preventive arrest" (*Vorbeugungshaft*) it had available an instrument of persecution that it exploited extensively and rigorously in a manner similar to the Gestapo's use of "protective detention" (*Schutzhaft*). mh

No. 3-35
Sleeve patch of the Security Service of the *Reichsführer-SS*
This insignia of the Security Service with the acronym "SD" was introduced around 1935. During the war, Gestapo and Criminal Police officials also wore it in the occupied territories, even if they were not members of the SD, as did members of the deployment troops (*Einsatzgruppen*) of the SS and SD. Accordingly, there existed several slightly different variations of the sleeve patch. mh

No. 3-34
**Axel Alt (i.e, *SS-Sturmbannführer* Wilhelm Ihde), *Der Tod fuhr im Zug. Den Akten der Kriminalpolizei nacherzählt*. Neuzeitliche Kriminalromane, Bd. 1
[Death Rode the Train. Told from Documents of the Criminal Police. Modern Detective Novels, Vol. 1]**
Verlag Hermann Hillger, Berlin/Leipzig, 1944
Death Rode the Train was the first in a series of detective novels that appeared in large quantities and sold inexpensively in 1943 and 1944. The Reich Criminal Police Office had encouraged the appearance of the series. It aimed to improve the public perception of the Criminal Police and, above all, achieve public acceptance of the ideological principles upon which they operated. For this purpose, the Reich Criminal Police Office provided the authors with information and police files.

Axel Alt was the pen name of *SS-Sturmbann-führer* Wilhelm Ihde (1899 – 1986). Since 1937, he had been managing director and acting president of the Reich Chamber for Literature, controlled by the Propaganda Ministry. In addition to detective stories, Ihde wrote anti-British war propaganda pieces. In *Death Rode the Train*, a young blond criminal detective solves a series of murders on the Berlin municipal train system in 1940 and 1941. The investigator represents the prototype of the "modern" National Socialist detective. He shows "interest in the race question" and perceives himself as a "surgeon [working] on the body of the German nation," "mercilessly" removing that which is "rotten" in society. mh

No. 3-36
Shooting of Polish hostages by members of an SS-Einsatzgruppe in Kóruik/Kursnik (1939 – 1945: Burgstadt), Reich District Posen/Wartheland October 20, 1939

Bundesarchiv Koblenz, Bildarchiv, Bild 146-1968-034-19A

No. 3-38
Deportation of the Stuttgart Jews to Riga November 1941
Gestapo officials search the hand luggage of a Jewish woman in the Killesberg transit camp near Stuttgart.

Bildarchiv Preußischer Kulturbesitz, 30023016

No. 3-37
Settlement of ethnic German farmers from East Poland in the Wartheland Photograph: Spahn, May 1940
The SS-Scharführer on the right wears the SD diamond patch of the Security Service.

Bundesarchiv Koblenz, Bildarchiv, Bild 137-058157

No. 3-39
Members of the Cologne Gestapo escort eleven "foreign workers" of various nationalities to their public execution Photograph: Georg Schödl, October 25, 1944

Bildarchiv Preußischer Kulturbesitz, Berlin, 30017534

No. 3-40

***SS-Obergruppenführer* Kurt Daluege**
Photograph: Friedrich Franz Bauer/
Agentur Scherl, 1933

In June 1936, the Order Police Main Office was established concurrently with the Security Police Main Office. It was responsible for the uniformed police; this included, among others, the municipal police (*Schutzpolizei*), the gendarmerie (rural police), the fire departments, and the Air Raid Protection Police.

Kurt Daluege, a veteran National Socialist with connections to Hitler, became director of the Order Police Main Office. After the 1933 seizure of power, Daluege had rapidly forged a career in the state police apparatus but had to cut a deal with Heinrich Himmler in order to realize his own leadership ambitions.

As the Main Office chief, Daluege pressed forward the transformation of the Order Police into an instrument of National Socialist power: he armed his forces for the event of war, and promoted its connection to the SS. After 1939, the police forces commanded by Daluege (eventually over three million men) served as an essential pillar of Germany's war of conquest and its racist goals. mh

Ullstein Bilderdienst, 00635125

Kurt Daluege (1897 – 1946)
Civil Engineer; department head and engineer with several municipal companies in Berlin; highest SS rank: *SS-Oberstgruppenführer* and police general
September 15, 1897
Born in Kreuzburg (Upper Silesia)
1916 – 1918
After an accelerated diploma examination (taken in wartime by students about to be conscripted), volunteer and officer candidate in World War I
Since 1918
Free Corps member in Upper Silesia and other locations; later, member of the anti-Semitic Defense and Combat League of the German Race (*Deutschvölkischer Schutz- und Trutzbund*); street fighter in Berlin as leader in the *Frontbann* (a cover organization of the NSDAP and the SA)
1921 – 1924
Civil engineering course at Technical University of Berlin-Charlottenburg
March 1926
Joins the National Socialist Party; co-founder and leader of the Berlin SA
1926 – 1928
Deputy *Gauleiter* (district leader) of Berlin
July 1930
Exit from the SA and entry into the SS; chief of the Berlin SS
1931 – October 1933
Leader of *SS-Gruppe Ost* (Group East)
April 1931
His loyalty during the revolt led by Berlin SA commander Walter Stennes secured him the lasting favor of Adolf Hitler.
1932 – 1933
National Socialist Party delegate in the Prussian state parliament; from November 1933 member of the Reichstag
May 1933
Ministerial councilor and director of the police department in the Prussian Ministry of the Interior; purge of the Prussian police administration of politically undesirable officials
September 1933
Additionally: commander and general of the Prussian State Police (barracked *Schutzpolizei*)
November 1934
Chief of the police division in the Reich and Prussian Ministry of the Interior
June 1936
Chief of the Order Police Main Office and nominal deputy of the Chief of German Police, Heinrich Himmler
June 1942
Additionally: Acting Reich Protector of Bohemia and Moravia
Summer 1943
Relieved of all offices due to illness
May 1945
Arrested by British troops; interned in Nuremberg
May 1946
Extradited to Czechoslovakia by Allied forces
October 23, 1946
Sentenced to death and hanged in Prague mh

No. 3-43
An SS man deployed as auxiliary policeman and a municipal policeman on patrol in Berlin on the day of the Reichstag elections in March 1933
Photograph: Bildagentur Scherl, March 5, 1933
The appointment of SS and SA men as auxiliary police officers was an important feature of the National Socialist seizure of power. mh
Süddeutsche Zeitung Photo, 3634

No. 3-41
Berlin municipal police at a practice for the indoor sports festival at the Sportpalast, performing a shooting drill in a swastika formation
Photograph: Bildagentur Scherl, 1933 or 1934
Süddeutsche Zeitung Photo, 340086

As the state's armed force of order, the municipal police participated directly and from the beginning in the establishment of National Socialist (NS) rule and the persecution of opponents. The systematic integration of the municipal police into the NS system commenced with the foundation of the Order Police Main Office in the summer of 1936: its staff was increased, in some places entire NS formations or auxiliary police units were integrated into the police force. Evidence of firm National Socialist conviction was vetted in the hiring process. Membership in the SS was expected at least for police officers. In later years, "SS suitability" became a job requirement for senior-level police service candidates. From 1937 on, the Order Police was included in the "ideological training" of the SS. mh

No. 3-45
German Order Police officers collect money for Vienna's poor at Heldenplatz shortly after the so-called *Anschluss* [incorporation in the German Reich] of Austria
March 20, 1938
The police official in the middle wears a patch containing the SS runes sewed on to his uniform.
Ullstein Bilderdienst, 00039186

No. 3-44
Patch worn on the uniform of the Order Police with double SS runes
This patch was introduced by a "Führer decision" at the beginning of 1937. Police who were also members of the SS were allowed to add it to their police uniform. mh
Kreismuseum Wewelsburg, inv. no. 17000

No. 3-47
Members of Police Battalion 91 in front of a burning village
The original image caption reads "war against bandits," a term the National Socialists used to refer to the fight against partisans, which often degenerated into brutal retaliatory operations against the civilian population. mh

Landesarchiv NRW, Abteilung Westfalen, Münster, Primavesi No. 282

No. 3-46
German policemen search a Jew in Warthbrücken (Kolo/Warthegau) 1941
Original caption: "After the arrest, a body search follows immediately"

U.S. Holocaust Memorial Museum, Washington, D.C., Photo Archives, 51047

No. 3-42
Not shown
Municipal policemen and Gestapo officials cooperate in hunting down political opponents (film still, presumably made for propaganda or educational puposes)

Süddeutscher Verlag, Image Services, sign. 6149

No. 3-48
Order Police and Security Police on patrol in the east
Poster for the annual collection drive of the Winter Relief Agency (*Winterhilfswerk*) on the "Day of the German Police," 1942
Drawing: Felix Albrecht
This poster shows a Security Police officer on the right (recognizable by the SD patch on his left sleeve) and an Order Police officer on the left.

In the day-to-day operations in the German-occupied territories, the different spheres of the police and the SS merged into a single unity of crime and perpetrator, consisting of the Order Police and Security Police, the SS Deployment Groups (*Einsatzgruppen*), the police battalions, the Reich Security Main Office as the control center of terror, and the Higher SS and Police Leaders as Himmler's powerful deputies, as well as numerous indigenous auxiliary police forces. Together they were agents of a war of aggression driven by ideological principles. They carried on the persecution and extermination of politically or "racially" undesirable population groups as well as the implementation of huge settlement projects, which were intended to lay the foundations of a "Greater Germanic Reich." mh

Bundesarchiv Koblenz, Bildarchiv, Plak 003-025-007

3.4
The Armed Units of the SS

Initially, the SS saw itself as a purely political organization, which was neither equipped nor trained to military specifications. After it participated in the political neutralization of the SA leadership around Ernst Röhm in June 1934, the SS was, however, allowed to establish a limited contingent of armed units.
In the beginning, these co-called SS Special Service Troops lacked a clear purpose; in a vague sense, they were supposed to maintain readiness for "special internal political tasks the Führer might assign to the SS."

Counted among the armed units of SS – although formally relatively independent – were the guard personnel of the concentration camps, which bore the designation "Death's Head Units" as of 1936.

During the preparation for war, the hitherto diffuse orientation of the armed SS formations as a domestic police force transformed to one openly focused on military and foreign affairs. Under the new name of *Waffen-SS* (Armed SS), the armed units participated in regular combat operations during World War II, but frequently also in racially motivated punitive and police operations, consistent with their ideological vocation.

No. 3-49
Steel helmet of the SS Special Service Troops with painted SS runes on the right side and a scratched-out swastika on the left
After August 1935
Kreismuseum Wewelsburg, inv. no. 4500

No. 3-50
SS-Obergruppenführer **Josef "Sepp" Dietrich as commander of SS Regiment "Adolf Hitler"**
Ca. 1937
Sepp Dietrich, a former noncommissioned officer in World War I, was a key figure in the establishment of armed SS units. He joined the SS in May 1928 and quickly forged a career there. A close follower of Hitler, he was solely responsible for the Führer's personal security after February 1932.

In March 1933, Hitler commissioned him to establish an armed leadership protection guard, which became the Leibstandarte-SS "Adolf Hitler" (Personal Bodyguard Regiment) that subsequently formed a core element of the SS Special Service Troops. As commander of the Leibstandarte, Dietrich was promoted into the ranks of the generals, which would have been impossible in the regular army because of his modest family background and lack of education. Towards the end of World War II, Dietrich was one of the two highest ranking officers in the *Waffen-SS*. mh

Süddeutsche Zeitung Photo, 214208

Josef "Sepp" Dietrich (1892 – 1966)
Various occupations; a gas station employee before joining the SS; highest SS rank: *SS-Oberstgruppenführer* **and** *Waffen-SS* **general**
May 25, 1892
Born in Hawangen (Allgäu)
1914 – 1918
After finishing elementary school and several years in various short-term jobs (e.g., in agriculture and the hotel industry), military service in World War I, ending his service in the rank of staff sergeant
February 1920
For a short time, sergeant in the Bavarian State Police; afterwards Free Corps fighter engaged in border fighting in Upper Silesia; since 1925 active in connection with the NSDAP
May 1928
Entry into the National Socialist Party and the SS
August 1928
Commander of the SS Regiment in Munich (*SS-Standarte München*)
Since August 1928
Frequent contact with Adolf Hitler
July 1930
As *SS-Oberführer* South responsible for all SS activities in Bavaria
September 1930
Member of the Reichstag (until 1945)
February 1932
Hitler's personal security officer (SS Escort Commando *Der Führer*)
March 1933
Formation of a leadership guard detail (*Stabswache*), in fall 1933 renamed *Leibstandarte Adolf Hitler* (Personal Bodyguard Regiment), in April 1934 *Leibstandarte-SS Adolf Hitler*
June 1934
Commander of a firing squad that murdered six high-ranking SA leaders
From September 1939
As commander of the Leibstandarte in combat zones in Poland, the Netherlands, France, South Yugoslavia, Greece, and Russia
July 1943
Commanding general of the 1st SS Tank Corps
October 1944
Commander-in-chief of the 6th SS Tank Army
December 1944
Participated in the Ardennes offensive; from February 1945 in Hungary and Vienna
May 1945
Arrested by the US Army
July 1946
In the so-called Malmédy trial at Dachau, Dietrich was sentenced to life in prison for a massacre of American prisoners of war and Belgian civilians by units under his command during the Ardennes offensive.
August 1951
Reduction of sentence to 25 years, pardoned and released from prison in October 1955
May 1958
Sentenced to 18 months of prison by Munich Jury Court for accessory to manslaughter of six SA leaders during the "Röhm Affair"; in February 1959, after six months in prison, released on medical grounds
April 21, 1966
Died in Ludwigsburg mh

No. 3-53
After the "Röhm Putsch": An armed SS detachment stationed in front of the Secret State Police building on Prinz Albrecht Straße in Berlin
Photograph: Röhnert, July 3, 1934
Bundesarchiv Koblenz, Bildarchiv, Bild 183-B0527-01-506

No. 3-51
Not shown
Hitler and his personal security officer, Sepp Dietrich, casting their votes in Königsberg in the Reichstag elections on March 5, 1933
Photograph: Heinrich Hoffmann
Barely two weeks later, Hitler entrusted Sepp Dietrich with the establishment of a "leadership guard." mh
Bayerische Staatsbibliothek, Munich, Fotoarchiv Heinrich Hoffmann, 7677

No. 3-52
Not shown
SS camp in Döberitz near Berlin
Photograph: Heinrich Hoffmann, August 12, 1933
Bayerische Staatsbibliothek, Munich, Fotoarchiv Heinrich Hoffmann, 8181

Shortly after the National Socialist seizure of power, local SS leaders established armed special detachments and bodyguards, the so-called Political Readiness Squads, for their own ends and purposes. These early armed SS formations included the leadership guard detail later renamed *Leibstandarte Adolf Hitler* (Personal Bodyguard Regiment), which was commanded by Sepp Dietrich.

Many of these units participated in the bloody elimination of the SA leadership around Ernst Röhm in the summer of 1934. Dietrich commanded an execution detail consisting of members of the Leibstandarte unit. They shot six high-ranking SA leaders in the Stadelheim Prison in Munich. As thanks, Hitler promoted Dietrich to the rank of *SS-Obergruppenführer* and promised him a "modern, armed troop separate from the *Reichswehr* [German military forces, 1918 – 1935]." This troop materialized on December 14, 1934, when Heinrich Himmler ordered the Political Readiness Squads merged with the *Leibstandarte* to form the new SS Special Service Troops. Himmler had previously worked out the general conditions of this merger with the *Reichswehr* leadership. mh

No. 3-54
**Collar patch of the
SS Special Service Troops
Ca. mid-1930s**
Kreismuseum Wewelsburg, inv. no. 16573

No. 3-57
Not shown
**Celebration of the seizure of power
in Berlin: *The Leibstandarte-SS
Adolf Hitler* (Personal Bodyguard
Regiment) marches in formation
past Hitler, Himmler, and Dietrich
January 30, 1938**
Ullstein Bilderdienst, 00076399

No. 3-55
Not shown
**"Der 9. November 1935 am Königs-
platz in München. Die Leibstandarte
des Führers"
[November 9, 1935, at Königsplatz in
Munich: The Leibstandarte (Personal
Bodyguard Regiment) of the Führer]
Translation of the original caption,
collectible card
Photograph: Heinrich Hoffmann,
November 1935**
Kreismuseum Wewelsburg,
inv. no. 14281/24

No. 3-56
Not shown
**Hitler's visit to the Leibstandarte
barracks in Berlin-Lichterfelde;
next to him is Sepp Dietrich
Photograph: Heinrich Hoffmann,
December 17, 1935**
Adolf Hitler – Bilder aus dem Leben des Führers,
Hamburg-Bahrenfeld: Cigaretten-Bilderdienst,
1936, p. 123

For years, the *Leibstandarte* maintained a
certain independence within the SS
Special Service Troops (*SS-Verfügungstruppe*), a consequence of its special role
as Hitler's personal security detail. It
provided the majority of the male service
staff in the Reich Chancellery and frequently served as an imposing backdrop
for state ceremonies and celebratory
events of the National Socialist Party.

From the beginning of World War II,
the *Leibstandarte*, as well as the three
other SS Special Service Troops Regiments, engaged in military operations. mh

No. 3-58
**Main entrance of the barracks of the
SS Junker School in Bad Tölz
December 1936
From a report on the construction
work**
Bildarchiv Preußischer Kulturbesitz,
Berlin, 50038574

No. 3-59
**Maneuver of the SS Special Service
Troops Regiment "Deutschland"
of the at the Munsterlager military
training grounds in the Lüneburg
Heath in the presence of Hitler and
high-ranking *Wehrmacht* officers
May 1939**
Bildarchiv Preußischer Kulturbesitz,
Berlin, 30027559

No. 3-60
**Theodor Eicke wearing the uniform
of an *SS-Brigadeführer***
Ca. 1934

Theodor Eicke played a decisive role in
shaping the organization of the concentration camp system of the SS and the brutali-
zation of its guard units. After World War I,
the former paymaster of the Imperial Army
served in the police forces of several
communities but was repeatedly dismissed for anti-republican activity. He joined
the National Socialist Party in 1928, and in
1930 the SS, where he initially moved up
the ranks quickly. His repeated defeat in
conflicts with National Socialist functionaries pushed him both politically and
personally to the sidelines. Himmler's influence led to Eicke being appointed commander of Dachau Concentration Camp in
June 1933, enabling him to rise anew
within the SS. Personally close to Himmler,
Eicke remained a loyal follower. In the late
1930s, Eicke expanded the SS Death's
Head Units into a military formation. From
1939 until his death in 1943, he commanded
the SS Death's Head Division. jes

Bundesarchiv Koblenz, Bildarchiv,
Bild 183-W0402-503

Theodor Eicke (1892 – 1943)
**Plant security employee; *SS-Obergruppen-
führer* and general of the *Waffen-SS***
October 17, 1892
Born in Hampont/Alsace-Lorraine
1909
Joins the army as a career soldier
1914 – 1918
Paymaster for the 3rd and 22nd Bavarian
Infantry Regiments
1919
Dismissed from military service in the
position of assistant paymaster
1919 – 1922
Service in several police departments
1923 – 1932
Service in plant security department
at IG Farbenindustrie AG in Ludwigshafen
December 1, 1928
Joins the National Socialist Party
1928 – 1930
Member of the SA
July 29, 1930
Entry into the SS
November 15, 1931
SS-Standartenführer and commander of
10th SS Regiment Rheinpfalz
March 6, 1932
Arrested for illegal possession of explo-
sives and conspiracy to commit murder for
political motives; consequently dismissed
by IG Farben
July 7, 1932
Sentenced to two years' imprisonment
September 1932
Flees to Italy before detention
1933
Returns to Germany; admission to a psy-
chiatric hospital on order of the district
leader (*Gauleiter*) Josef Bürkel; as a conse-
quence temporarily suspended from the
SS; re-admitted by Himmler
June 26, 1933
Commandant of Concentration Camp
Dachau
January 30, 1934
SS-Brigadeführer
May 1934
Inspector of the Concentration Camps
July 1, 1934
Murders SA Chief of Staff Ernst Röhm
July 4, 1934
Inspector of the Concentration Camps and
commander of the SS guard units
July 11, 1936
SS-Gruppenführer
September/October 1939
As a senior SS officer commander of three
SS Death's Head Regiments in the army
rear area during the war against Poland;
SS Death's Head Regiments murdered
hundreds of Polish civilians
October 1939
Commander of the SS Division *Totenkopf*
(Death's Head), later renamed the 3rd *SS-
Panzerdivision Totenkopf*. Formation of
the division at Dachau Concentration
Camp, which was temporarily cleared of
prisoners
November 14, 1939
Lieutenant General of the *Waffen-SS*
April 20, 1942
SS-Obergruppenführer and general
of the *Waffen-SS*
June 26, 1942
Awarded the Oak Leaves to the Knight's
Cross of the Iron Cross by Hitler
February 23, 1943
Killed when his reconnaissance plane
was shot down in eastern Ukraine jes

 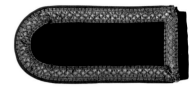

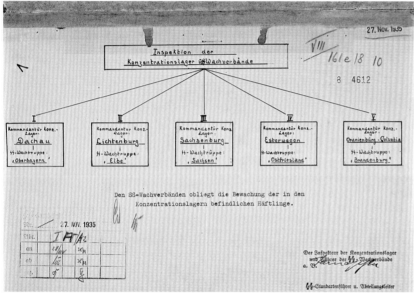

No. 3-61
Theodor Eicke (third from right) visiting the Lichtenburg Concentration Camp
March 1936
U. S. Holocaust Memorial Museum, Washington, D.C., Photo Archives, 51640

No. 3-63
Organization chart of the "Inspectorate of the Concentration Camps and SS Guard Units"
November 1935
Bundesarchiv Berlin, NS 31/256

No. 3-62
Not shown
Letter from Theodor Eicke to the local police authorities in Prettin
May 28, 1934
Gedenkstätte KZ Lichtenburg, Archiv, 678 G

No. 3-64
Not shown
The headquarters of the Inspectorate of the Concentration Camps, Oranienburg
Allied aerial photograph
1944/1945
Known as the T-building because of its architectural shape, the Inspectorate headquarters was located in the immediate vicinity of Sachsenhausen Concentration Camp.

On assignment from Himmler, Theodor Eicke took over the reorganization of the Prussian concentration camps in May 1934. In a letter written on May 31, Eicke for the first time used the title "Inspector of the Concentration Camps," which expressed his claim to leadership of all concentration camps. One month later the SA leadership was essentially stripped of its power. As a result, the concentration camps previously run by the SA came under the control of the SS. On Hitler and Himmler's order, Eicke himself carried out the execution of SA Chief of Staff Ernst Röhm, murdering him in Stadelheim Prison in Munich on July 1, 1934. As chief of the Inspectorate of the Concentration Camps and commander of the SS Guard Units, Eicke controlled the entire concentration camp system. On August 2, 1938 he moved to his new headquarters in Oranienburg. The structures created by Eicke remained in place with minor changes until the end of the war. jes
Johannes Tuchel, Die Inspektion der Konzentrationslager 1938 – 1945, Berlin, 1994, p. 12 f.

No. 3-66
Right collar patch of the SS Death's Head Units with the death's head emblem of *SS-Unterführer*
Kreismuseum Wewelsburg, inv. no. 16578

No. 3-65
Pair of shoulder boards of an *SS-Scharführer* in the SS Death's Head Battalions in the military color of brown (sewn-in, narrow brown borders)
Kreismuseum Wewelsburg, inv. nos. 15269/1 and 15269/2

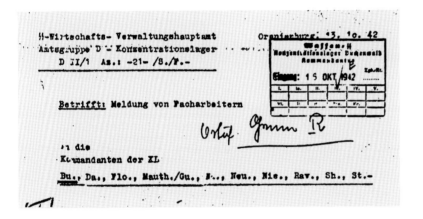

No. 3-70
Letterhead of a letter from Gerhard Maurer to concentration camp commandants, including the commandant of Niederhagen Concentration Camp ("Nie.")
October 13, 1942

Bundesarchiv Berlin,
NS 4 Buchenwald/208

No. 3-68
Not shown
Circular from Richard Glücks and Siegfried Taubert
January 22, 1940

Bundesarchiv Berlin, NS 31/372, Bl. 116

No. 3-69
Not shown
Letter from Richard Glücks to concentration camp commandants
July 3, 1940

Bundesarchiv Berlin, NS 4 Natzweiler/6

No. 3-71
SS guard Herta with her dog "Greif," Ravensbrück Women's Concentration Camp
1944

Mahn- und Gedenkstätte Ravensbrück/Stiftung Brandenburgische Gedenkstätten, 1099

No. 3-67
Richard Glücks wearing the uniform of an *SS-Oberführer*
Ca. 1937 – 1941
On November 15, 1939, *SS-Oberführer* Richard Glücks (1898 – 1945) became the successor of Theodor Eicke as chief of the Inspectorate of the Concentration Camps (IKL). To this point, he had served as Eicke's chief of staff and deputy for more than three years. After World War II began on September 1, 1939, the IKL was subordinate to the SS Main Office and later to the SS Operations Main Office, which was responsible for the organization and for armaments for the *Waffen-SS*. The guard units were temporarily under the authority of the General Inspector of the Reinforced SS Death's Head Regiments, at that time, the chief administrator of Wewelsburg Castle, Siegfried Taubert. In March 1942, Himmler ordered the integration of the IKL into the SS Economic and Administrative Main Office. There it was Department D until the end of the war, commanded by Glücks, who had been promoted to *SS-Gruppen-führer* and lieutenant general of the *Waffen-SS*. At the end of the war, Glücks committed suicide in Flensburg. jes

Bundesarchiv Koblenz, Bildarchiv, Bild 119/2115/11

No. 3-72
Paul Hausser wearing the uniform of an *SS-Obergruppenführer* and general of the *Waffen-SS*.
The picture ostensibly shows Hausser after having been decorated with the Oak Leaves to the Knight's Cross. The photograph, however, was retouched to add the decoration.
Photograph: Büschel, SS-PK [propaganda company] war reporter, July 30, 1943

Paul Hausser was the military figurehead of the Waffen-SS. The son of a Prussian officer and former Reichswehr general, he had built up the SS Special Service Troops since 1934. In 1936, Himmler appointed him inspector of these units. In the campaign against Poland, Hausser commanded the newly formed SS Special Service Division (*SS-Verfügungsdivision*), later renamed 2nd SS Tank Division "Das Reich." As a *Waffen-SS* general he held highest command functions, finally serving as an army and army group commander. Hausser stands as the prototype of an officer from the *Reichswehr* and the *Wehrmacht* who accepted the ideological orientation of the *Waffen-SS* in order to advance his career and to implement his political as well as military ideas. jes

Bundesarchiv Koblenz, Bildarchiv, Bild 101III-Bueschel-152-23A

Paul Hausser (1880 – 1972)
Career officer (Reichswehr general);
SS-Oberstgruppenführer and Waffen-SS general
October 7, 1880
Born in Brandenburg/Havel
1899
Lieutenant in the 155th Infantry Regiment at Ostrow, Posen
1907
Detailed to the military academy
1914 – 1918
General staff officer, lastly in the rank of major
1919
Free Corps
1920
Taken into the *Reichswehr*
1930 – 1932
Major general, *Infanterieführer IV* (infantry commander), and deputy commander of the 4th Infantry Division
1932
Retired in the honorary rank (*Charakter*) of lieutenant general
1933 – 1934
Leader of the *Stahlhelm*, a World War I veterans' league
1934
SA-Standartenführer
November 15, 1934
Joins SS as an *SS-Standartenführer*; preparations for the foundation of SS Officer School Braunschweig
1935 – 1937
Inspector of the SS Officer Schools
May 22, 1936
SS-Brigadeführer
October 1, 1936
Inspector of the SS Special Service Troops
June 1, 1939
SS-Gruppenführer
November 1, 1939
Commander of the SS Special Service Division (*SS-Verfügungsdivision*), later renamed SS Division "Deutschland," again later 2nd SS Tank Division "Das Reich"
October 1, 1941
SS-Obergruppenführer and General of the *Waffen-SS*
1941 – 1944
Commanding general of the 2nd SS Tank Corps
June 26, 1944
Commander of the 7th Army in France
August 1, 1944
SS-Oberstgruppenführer and colonel general of the *Waffen-SS*
January 23, 1945
Commander of Army Group Lower Rhine
January 28, 1945
Commander of Army Group G
1945 – 1948
In custody of Allied forces; testimony at the Trial of the Major War Criminals at Nuremberg and at the Nuremberg Subsequent Trials
After 1948
Member of the Mutual Help Association of Former *Waffen-SS* Members (HIAG) and the Federal Association of Soldiers of the Former *Waffen-SS*; author of *Waffen-SS im Einsatz* (The Waffen-SS in Action) (1953), and *Soldaten, wie andere auch* (Soldiers Just Like the Others) (1966)
December 21, 1972
Deceased jes

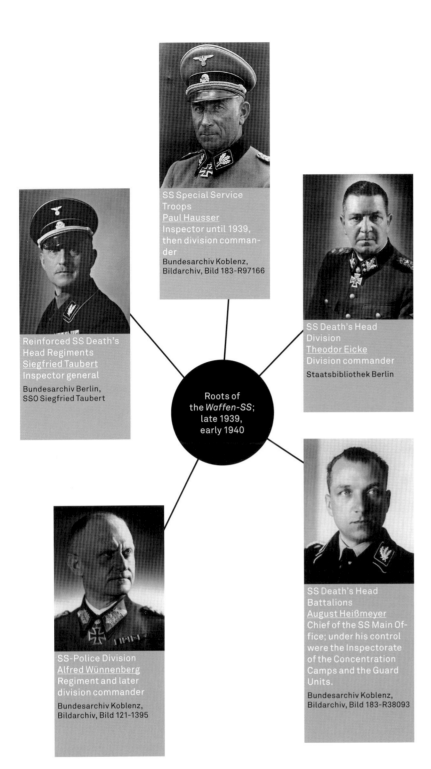

SS Special Service Troops
Paul Hausser
Inspector until 1939, then division commander
Bundesarchiv Koblenz, Bildarchiv, Bild 183-R97166

Reinforced SS Death's Head Regiments
Siegfried Taubert
Inspector general
Bundesarchiv Berlin, SSO Siegfried Taubert

SS Death's Head Division
Theodor Eicke
Division commander
Staatsbibliothek Berlin

Roots of the Waffen-SS; late 1939, early 1940

SS-Police Division
Alfred Wünnenberg
Regiment and later division commander
Bundesarchiv Koblenz, Bildarchiv, Bild 121-1395

SS Death's Head Battalions
August Heißmeyer
Chief of the SS Main Office; under his control were the Inspectorate of the Concentration Camps and the Guard Units.
Bundesarchiv Koblenz, Bildarchiv, Bild 183-R38093

No. 3-76
Patch worn on the left collar lapel with the rank insignia of an SS-Oberscharführer
On loan from LWL-Freilichtmuseum Detmold – Westfälisches Landesmuseum für Volkskunde, WFM 2762-78
Kreismuseum Wewelsburg, inv. no. 17047

No. 3-75
Not shown
Light blue shoulder board with the rank insignia of an SS-Obersturmführer in administrative service
On loan from LWL-Freilichtmuseum Detmold – Westfälisches Landesmuseum für Volkskunde, WFM 2762-78
Kreismuseum Wewelsburg, inv. no. 17049

No. 3-73
Roots of the Waffen-SS
The *Waffen-SS* was formed from a number of different units around late 1939, early 1940. The SS Special Service Troops, including the *Leibstandarte-SS Adolf Hitler*, are generally considered to have been the core of the *Waffen-SS*. Of similar strength in terms of personnel, was the SS Death's Head Division, recruited from the concentration camp guard units. Thirty-six thousand men came from the *Allgemeine SS* (General SS); they were initially allocated to thirteen SS Death's Head Regiments. Siegfried Taubert, chief administrator of Wewelsburg Castle, served temporarily as inspector of these units. In September 1939, the SS Police Division was established with members of the Order Police; it was officially incorporated into the *Waffen-SS* in 1942. At the beginning of the war, the

SS Death's Head Guard Battalions (*SS-Totenkopfsturmbanne*) assumed the guard duties at the concentration camps. They officially became part of the *Waffen-SS* by at least 1941. During its founding period, various different traditions were already represented in the *Waffen-SS*: The political-ideological soldiering mindset of the SS Special Service Troops, the paramilitary experience of the *Allgemeine SS*, the opponent suppression focus of the police, and the inhumanity of the concentration camp guard units. jes

No. 3-74
Not shown
Bright red shoulder board with the rank insignia of an SS-Obersturmführer serving in the artillery
On loan from LWL-Freilichtmuseum Detmold – Westfälisches Landesmuseum für Volkskunde, WFM 2762-78
Kreismuseum Wewelsburg, inv. no. 17048

Und nun fegte von neuem die Brandfackel des Krieges über Bailleul hinweg. Unsere Wagenkolonnen parkten auf dem Marktplatz, umgeben von Trümmern. Eigenes Verschulden brachte zum zweiten Male das Unglück über Bailleul

No. 3-78

Recruitment brochure for the _Waffen-SS_, entitled "Auch Du" [You Too]
Stapled, 32 pgs.
Published during World War II

Kreismuseum Wewelsburg, inv. no. 15903

No. 3-80

Motor pool of the SS Death's Head Division in France
 "The Deployment of the _Waffen-SS_ in the West: Formation site for SS units on the market square in Bailleux [Bailleul, a Franco-Belgian border town]"
Translation of the original caption
Photograph: Ege, SS-PK
(SS propaganda company, or perhaps more precisely, an SS war reporters' company)
Scherl Bilderdienst, May 1940

Bundesarchiv Berlin,
GX 1939-239-Belgien (L11 376)

No. 3-79
Not shown

Swearing in of _Waffen-SS_ members
"Swearing in of young volunteers for the _Waffen-SS_ 12th SS Tank Division 'Hitler Youth' by _SS-Standartenführer_ Kurt Meyer, nicknamed 'Panzermeyer' (in the background with Knight's Cross)"
Translation of the original caption
Ca. 1943/1944

Bundesarchiv Berlin, 73/114/33A

No. 3-82

SS tank in front of Milan Cathedral
"On the front in Italy, September 1943. Following the announcement of the armistice agreement between the Badoglio government and the Western Allies, tanks of the Leibstandarte 'Adolf Hitler' occupy the city of Milan on September 8."
Translation of the original caption
Foto: Rottenstei ... (full name not legible), SS-PK war reporter, September 1943

Bundesarchiv Koblenz, Bildarchiv,
Bild 183-J15480

In late 1939, early 1940, _Waffen-SS_ became widely accepted as the name of the military units of the SS. Contrary to claims made after World War II, the _Waffen-SS_ remained organizationally separate from the _Wehrmacht_. However, the appearance of members of both formations was at first glance quite similar. Both wore nearly identical "field gray" uniforms. Furthermore, the rank insignia and colors of individual branches and categories of service were quite similar, with the bright red of the artillery units, for instance, scarcely differing between the _Wehrmacht_ and the _Waffen-SS_. However, in addition to the death's head on their cap and the SS sig runes on their steel helmets, SS soldiers also wore SS runes or death's head emblems, as well as special rank insignia, on their uniform lapels. Some parts of the uniforms issued to _Waffen-SS_ soldiers were produced in the SS garment workshops by concentration camp prisoners.

The strength of the _Waffen-SS_ personnel grew from 100,000 soldiers in July 1940 to an estimated 800,000 in March 1945. About 310,000 _Waffen-SS_ men lost their lives in World War II. Because the _Waffen-SS_, unlike the _Wehrmacht_, was not permitted to draft recruits at the beginning of the war, it had to focus on recruitment of volunteers. Members of the Hitler Youth were a preferred target of recruiters. After the German defeat at Stalingrad, an entire SS division was established with recruits from the Hitler Youth and placed under the command of former officers and non-commissioned officers of the _Leibstandarte-SS Adolf Hitler_. The requirement that the recruits be volunteers, however, was not always observed. Contemporaneous letters of complaint show that youths were put under massive pressure to join the 12th SS Tank Division "Hitler Youth," which was in the process of formation. jes

No. 3-81
Soldier wearing a face mask
"On guard duty at 25 degrees below zero Celsius; the soldier's breath forms ice crystals on the balaclava covering the entire head except for a narrow eye slit."
Translation of the original caption
Photograph: Wiesebach, SS-PK (i.e., SS propaganda company, or more correctly, SS war reporters' company), January 18, 1942
Weltkriegsbücherei/Bibliothek für Zeitgeschichte, Stuttgart, 51984

No. 3-84
The commander of the 13th *Waffen* Mountain Division of the SS *Hand-schar*, Karl-Gustav Sauberzweig, *SS-Brigadeführer* and *Waffen-SS* major general, talking to a non-commissioned officer in his division
Photograph: Heinrich Hoffmann, March 31, 1944
Translation of the original caption: "Muslims fighting Tito's hordes"
Weltkriegsbücherei Stuttgart/Bibliothek für Zeitgeschichte, 64100

No. 3-83
Volunteer registration office for the *Estland Legion* (Estonia Legion), one of the non-German units that fought within the framework of the *Waffen-SS*
Photograph: Heinrich Hoffmann, September 19, 1942
Translation of the original caption: "Estonia joins the European struggle against Bolshevism"
Weltkriegsbücherei/Bibliothek für Zeitgeschichte, Stuttgart, 56402

No. 3-85
Not shown
Heinrich Himmler visiting the 14th *Waffen* Grenadier Division of the SS, a.k.a. the Galician Volunteer Infantry Division
Photograph: Heinrich Hoffmann, June 3, 1944
On the left, behind Himmler, stands the commander of the division, Fritz Freitag, *SS-Brigadeführer* and *Waffen-SS* major general. jes
Weltkriegsbücherei/Bibliothek für Zeitgeschichte, Stuttgart, 64704

As the war dragged on, the SS recruited not only Reich Germans, "ethnic Germans," and "Germanic" soldiers, but also non-German inhabitants of the territories occupied by the German Reich, primarily in Eastern and South Eastern Europe. Thus, they broke definitively with their own standards of an ideologically and "racial-ly" uniform *Waffen-SS*. Due to the specific motives of their members, some of the new divisions could only be deployed in the homelands of the recruits or against spe-cific enemies. Mutinies and desertions occurred sometimes during training. Almost forty percent of the 38 *Waffen-SS* divisions that existed, at least on paper, belonged in the category of so-called "foreign national" units. jes

No. 3-77
Not shown
Supplement "Für die Waffen-SS" (*1. Folge*) [For the Waffen-SS (1st issue)]
Das Schwarze Korps [The Black Corps], Vol. 5, Issue 49 (December 7, 1939), p. 9 f.
Kreismuseum Wewelsburg, inv. no. 5485

No. 3-86
Right collar patch with the emblem of the 13th *Waffen* Mountain Division of the SS *Handschar*
Kreismuseum Wewelsburg, inv. no. 16580

1

The Netherlands have brought forth many a great man: De Ruyter, Tromp, J.P. Coen, etc. All of them went out into the wide world. For centuries, they have lived on in the collective memory of our people as pioneers and men of action. He who understands that a new future is beginning does not remain at home. He follows his impulse for the new and the unknown, and fights with tens of thousands of other young men to conquer for himself and his people a place in the new Europe. He joins the *Waffen-SS* or the Volunteer Legion!

So sign up before it is too late! Seize this chance and prove that you are a real man. Later, when the war is over, people will say, "He was there!" Then you will be one of us, because you will have fought for your future and the future of your people. You will forever stand head and shoulders above those who stayed home in cowardly fashion and let the others pull the chestnuts out of the fire.

Do you have the courage? Then prove it by action. Your comrades in the *Waffen-SS* and in the Volunteer Legion are counting on you. Together you will be young, will laugh, will live, and fight. That is where your future lies! So come on! Sign up!

2

A Dutch volunteer writes to his mother:
You must not forget, mother, that it is of utmost importance to us, too, that Germany wins this war! We must not be selfish and think only of ourselves, but also of coming generations. Some day, when I return home with my comrades, you will be proud that your son, too, made a contribution to having given people who earn their living by honest and hard work the chance to enjoy the beauty of this world.

3

Sport and play
toughen your muscles

4

And a really delicious
warm meal every day

5

At night, when the work is done,
a relaxing get-together

6

All brave young men join
the *Waffen-SS*

Translation of a transcription

No. 3–87

Poster to recruit Dutch men for the *Waffen-SS*: "Jongens met pit melden sich allen bij de Waffen SS"
The *Waffen-SS* was permitted to recruit German citizens only on a limited basis. The majority of Germans obligated to serve in the military were drafted by the *Wehrmacht*. The SS Main Office, which was in charge of recruitment, therefore initially sought to recruit for the *Waffen-SS* men from areas of German settlement outside the Reich, the so-called *Volksdeutsche* (ethnic Germans), as well as "Germanic" volunteers, from, for instance, the Netherlands, Denmark, and Norway. Racist reasons dictated this choice. For each of the targeted groups, SS propaganda appealed to national patriotism and pride in their country. At the same time it drew upon traditional perceptions of military life, such as comradeship and adventure. The SS promised to supply good food, modern equipment, adequate leisure activities, and, last but not least, female admiration. The SS projected a racially charged body image of physical prowess, which was designed to invite identification as well as to set its members apart from other ethnicities who did not conform to this ideal. jes

Kreismuseum Wewelsburg, inv. no. 16965

No. 3–88

Page from a training guide for concentration camp guards Reproduction of a print from the lithography stone at the Auschwitz-Birkenau Museum
The recruitment of non-German soldiers into the *Waffen-SS* posed specific problems, in particular language barriers. Commands given in German met with incomprehension. In general, communication between foreign units and the German leadership has to be seen as woefully limited. Because non-German soldiers were deployed in all areas of responsibility of the *Waffen-SS*, diverse solutions to the language problem developed. At Auschwitz Concentration Camp, for example, a "picture book: right – wrong" was developed. It was supposed to provide the SS guards with easily understood guidance on their duties and conduct regarding the concentration camp prisoners. It even covered shooting prisoners. jes

Staatliches Museum Auschwitz-Birkenau

With its numerous subunits and tasks, the SS was anything but a homogenous organization. Nevertheless, its members shared many interests and views, which created an outward impression of unanimity. The following chapter focuses on the theme of the organization's ideological and mental prerequisites and illustrates its ambitions to construct, as it were, a life program of its own that encompassed the areas of religion, history, and art. The interior world the SS built to boost its elitist self-image always manifested itself violently. As the organization's dual nature (community – crimes against others) unfolded, so did its horrendous impact, which was also felt at Wewelsburg.

4
Worldview Mindset Crimes

4.1
National Socialist Society and the SS

Founded in 1918/1919, the Weimar Republic, as Germany's first democratic state, had a difficult stand right from the start. It was burdened by the consequences of the defeat of the German Reich in World War I as well as by disappointed nationalism, a peace treaty that was felt to be humiliating, economic crises, and isolation on the international political stage.

The National Socialists were among the fiercest adversaries of the young Republic. Their political program was a clear counter concept that responded to the challenges of a modern society with ostensibly simple solutions. Denial and confrontation replaced arduous negotiations, while radical notions of order were advocated in place of freedom.

With their implacable behavior, the National Socialists met widespread needs for identification and expressions of resentment. The ideal of a *Volksgemeinschaft* (national or racial community), which they attempted to achieve after assuming power in January 1933, was based on broad consent among the population as well as exceedingly aggressive enemy stereotypes.

No. 4-1
**The November Pogroms of 1938
November 10, 1938**
In Baden-Baden, SS and police forces lead Jewish citizens to the synagogue, which was then desecrated and set on fire as they watched.
Bundesarchiv Koblenz, Bildarchiv, sign. Bild 183-86686-0008

Rapidly escalating violence against Jews in November 1938 marked the dramatic culmination of a development that began immediately after the National Socialists came into power in 1933. Old social, cultural, and political prejudices towards society's outsiders suddenly formed the basis of government decisions and publicly tolerated harassment. NSDAP leaders and their rank and file mutually reinforced their prejudices, accelerating a process of continuous disenfranchisement.

In part, acts of persecution, such as the elimination of the political left and measures against the Jews, met with wide approval far beyond the National Socialists. Many people had never accepted the equal legal status of outsiders that had been guaranteed by Weimar Republic's liberal and democratic constitutional order. These groups now saw discrimination as a form of retributive justice. mh

No. 4-2
**Erich Kästner, *Emil und die Detektive* [Emil and the Detectives]
Print run 11,000 – 20,000
Williams & Co. Verlag, Berlin-Grunewald, 1930**
Kreismuseum Wewelsburg, inv. no. 16550

No. 4-3
***Entartete "Kunst"* [Degenerate "Art"]. Exhibition guide.
Compilation of the exhibition by the Central Party Propaganda Office of the NSDAP
Verlag für Kultur- und Wirtschaftswerbung, Munich, 1937**
Kreismuseum Wewelsburg, inv. no. 16525

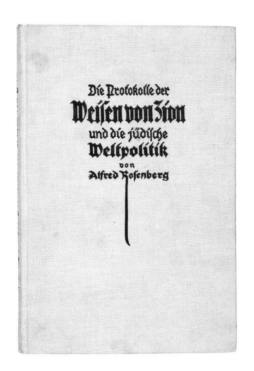

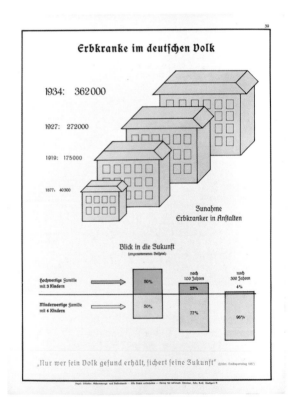

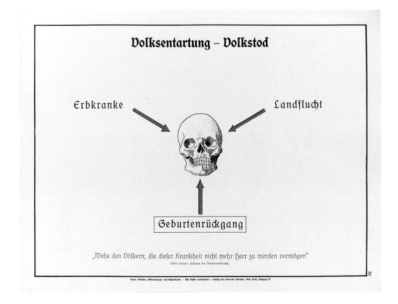

No. 4-4
Alfred Rosenberg, *Die Protokolle der Weisen von Zion und die jüdische Weltpolitik* [The Protocols of the Elders of Zion and Jewish World Politics]
Print run 15,000, Deutscher Volksverlag, Munich, 1923

No. 4-6
Alfred Vogel, *Erblehre, Abstammungs- und Rassenkunde in bildlicher Darstellung* [Heredity, Ancestry, and Race Research, With Illustrations]
2nd extended and revised edition Verlag für nationale Literatur, Gebr. Rath, Stuttgart, 1939

No. 4-5
Der Giftpilz. Ein Stürmerbuch für Jung und Alt. Erzählungen von Ernst Hiemer. Bilder von Fips [i.e., Philipp Rupprecht] [The Poison Mushroom: A Stürmer Book for Young and Old]
Print run 31,000–60,000, Nuremberg, 1938

Forging a Sense of Community

No. 4-7
Harvest Festival Day at the Bückeberg near Hameln; cheering crowd behind an SS cordon
1935
Propaganda photograph that was distributed as a collectible album picture. Original title: "So grüßen die deutschen Bauern ihren Führer Adolf Hitler, Bückeberg 1935" (This is how German farmers welcome their leader Adolf Hitler, Bückeberg, 1935). mh

Kreismuseum Wewelsburg, inv. no. 14279/8

Enthusiastic crowds were a frequent subject of National Socialist-era propaganda images. As much as these pictures had often been staged or manipulated, at their core, they certainly communicated something real. Until the outbreak of World War II, approval of the National Socialist regime rose continually among the German population – and by no means only in response to intimidation and paternalism.

Among the most popular government measures were the steps it took to recover national strength through foreign policy. On the domestic front, the popularity of identifying with a supposedly intact *Volksgemeinschaft* was manifest in countless mass events and in political activism that pledged to satisfy a variety of interests and needs. Those ready to identify as *Volksgenossen* (national or racial comrades) and heed the promises of the National Socialist state were rewarded with opportunities for participation, material benefits, and social advancement. mh

No. 4-9
National Socialist Party (NSDAP) badge
Kreismuseum Wewelsburg, inv. no. 12501

No. 4-8
Volksempfänger (People's Radio), model VE 301 W produced by the Siemens & Halske company
Kreismuseum Wewelsburg, inv. no. 14660

No. 4-10
Bust of Hitler. A gift made to the retiring district leader by the district administration head and the *Ortsgruppenleiter* (local NS leader) of Büren District
April 1938
Kreismuseum Wewelsburg, inv. no. 14325

No. 4-12
Frauenkultur im Deutschen Frauenwerk magazine [Women's Culture in the German Women's Association; the latter was a National Socialist Women's Organization]
Issue 4 (April 1941)
Kreismuseum Wewelsburg, inv. no. 14086/2

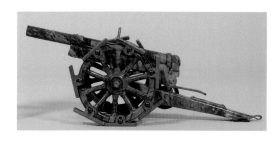

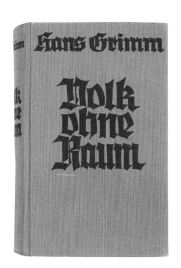

No. 4-11
NS-Frauen-Warte magazine
[Women's Watch]
Vol. 11, issue 15 (May 1943)

Kreismuseum Wewelsburg, inv. no. 14082/5

No. 4-14
Hans Grimm, *Volk ohne Raum*
[A People without Space]
Munich, 1932

Kreismuseum Wewelsburg, inv. no. 14068

No. 4-15
Camouflage-painted toy howitzer
The Märklin company
1945

Kreismuseum Wewelsburg, inv. no. 14205

No. 4-16
"Deutschland" jigsaw puzzle
Verlag Martin Hillger, Berlin
"Showing status of November 1942"

Kreismuseum Wewelsburg, inv. no. 14301

No. 4-13
Figurines and badges sold at street
collections of the *Winterhilfswerk*
(WHW: Winter Relief Agency)

Kreismuseum Wewelsburg,
inv. no. Best. 14220

4.2
Exclusion:
Persecution by the SS
1933 – 1939

A wave of violence accompanied the National Socialist assumption of power. It included attacks on and boycotts of Jews, retaliation against political opponents, abductions, and physical abuse.

Numerous SS members participated in this street terror. However, following the close integration of the SS and regular police forces, Heinrich Himmler gave precedence to the execution of state power. Thus, from the mid-1930s onwards, the Gestapo and criminal police rapidly took the lead in the systematic oppression of the Jews, Sinti, Roma, and, ultimately, all citizens defying the code of conduct imposed by the regime.

Beginning in the summer of 1934, Himmler was also put in charge of all concentration camps. Here, in a particularly obvious manner, the SS combined the direct physical despotism of street terror with violence legitimized by the state.

Political Opponents

No. 4-18
In the spring of 1933, the SA and SS set up makeshift torture sites all over Germany and established several concentration camps, most of which were run by the SA. In the former *Volkshaus* of the Social Democratic Party in Reichenbach/Vogtland, however, it was the SS that set up a "transit camp" for political prisoners, which operated from the end of March until the summer of 1933. Here, 1,200 prisoners were held in "protective detention." One member of the Reichstag, a member of the Communist Party (KPD), was murdered and his body was hung from a chandelier. In order to make the screams of the tortured inaudible to people on the market square in front of the building, SS thugs pressed the faces of their victims into "muffling pillows" donated by the local National Socialist Women's Organization. mh/mm

Stadtarchiv Reichenbach (Vogtland)

No. 4-17
After the *Reichstag* election on March 5, 1933, the actual seizure of power by the National Socialists commenced. Hitler's followers now took revenge for the parliamentary democratic system of the Weimar Republic they had loathed. Everywhere leftist and even more mainstream public officials and functionaries were ousted from their positions. All across Germany, massive terror was launched against the political opponents of the National Socialist Party. SA and SS commandos raided and destroyed the offices of political parties, trade unions, associations, town halls, and newspaper publishers. "Politically undesirable" persons were arrested and abused. At the beginning of March 1933, SS members raided the *Volkshaus* – the office building of the local Social Democratic Party – and destroyed its interior furnishings. Violence against the opposition soon led to the *Gleichschaltung* (forcible coordination) of state and society. By the summer of 1933, all parties except the NSDAP were prohibited. mh/mm

Stadtarchiv Reichenbach (Vogtland)

No. 4-19
"Berliner Schutzpolizei und nationalsozialistische Hilfspolizei durchsuchen das Berliner Judenviertel in der Grenadierstraße und Dragonerstraße nach kommunistischen Flugblättern und lästigen Ausländern!" [Berlin Municipal Police and National Socialist Auxiliary Police search the Jewish quarter of Berlin in Grenadierstraße and Dragonerstraße for Communist flyers and undesirable foreigners!] Original caption Spring 1933
As early as February 1933, Hermann Göring, the Reich Commissar for the Prussian Ministry of the Interior, had several tens of thousands of SA and SS members join Prussia's "auxiliary police" force. From March onwards, all of the other provinces brought into line followed the Prussian example. The terrorist violence of party organizations against dissenters was thus also perpetrated in the name of state authority. Aside from the countless brutal arrest raids of SA and SS during spring of 1933, approximately twenty-five thousand people were taken into "protective detention" in Prussia alone. In all this, political and racial motives played an equal role – the image above shows SS members conducting a raid in Berlin's Scheunenviertel district, which was home to many Jewish and Eastern European immigrants. mh/mm

Bundesarchiv Koblenz, Image Archives, Bild 102-02940A

Sonnenwende — Zeitenwende

Vernichtung der Reaktion in jeder Gestalt   Zeichnung: Mjölnir

No. 4-20
Cartoon by "Mjölnir" (Hans Schweitzer): "Sonnenwende – Zeitenwende. Vernichtung der Reaktion in jeder Gestalt" [*Sonnenwende*, or "sun change," means solstice. Sun Change – Sea Change. Death to Reaction in All of Its Forms.]
Das Schwarze Korps, vol. 1, issue 15 (June 12, 1935), p. 2
Soon after targeting communists, social democrats, and the moderate left, the National Socialist regime extended its persecution measures to conservative persons and institutions. Everyone on the political right who was, or allegedly was, critical of National Socialism was branded "reactionary" and persecuted. During the Night of the Long Knives, when Hitler, strongly supported by the SS, ordered the killing of his rivals within the Party (i.e., the SA leadership) many German nationalists, Catholics, and National Socialist deviationists were also killed. Cartoons like this one from the SS newspaper *Das Schwarze Korps* (The Black Corps) played their role in representing the physical annihilation of opponents as something "normal" and "necessary." Typical of National Socialist polemics, the cartoon shows a clerical politician, a monocle-wearing member of the National German People's Party, and a Jewish man being symbolically burned at the stake.
mh/mm

Kreismuseum Wewelsburg, inv. no. 5481/15

No. 4-21
Arthur Nebe, head of the Reich Criminal Police Department (with SD rhombus), interrogates Georg Elser (would-be Hitler assassin) at the RSHA in Berlin
November 1939
By the mid-1930s, the National Socialist regime had crushed the organizational structures of the political opposition, on both the left and the right. The most determined act of resistance against the Third Reich during the 1930s came from a political lone wolf: On November 8, 1939, carpenter journeyman Georg Elser (1903 – 1945) attempted to assassinate Adolf Hitler by bombing the Bürgerbräukeller in Munich. With his attack, Elser wanted to stop the regime's politics of war. However, the attempt failed, and Elser was arrested the same day. In the subsequent investigation, the Gestapo collaborated closely with the criminal police. Elser was tortured during the interrogations. As a "special detainee," who was to be put on a show trial after the war, Elser was imprisoned at Sachsenhausen Concentration Camp. After his transfer to Dachau, he was shot by the SS on April 9, 1945. mh/mm

Bayerische Staatsbibliothek, Munich, Fotoarchiv Hoffmann, 28880

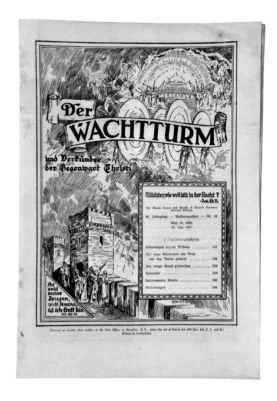

No. 4-22
Der Reichsführer SS. Chief of the Security Office, *Special Report: New Propaganda Forms of Political Catholicism.* Restricted!
Copy no. 105, September 1934

In the years following the NSDAP's seizure of power, the relation between National Socialism and the Catholic Church gradually deteriorated. Party activists often subverted the consensual regulations of the *Reichskonkordat* (Reich Agreement). Vehement opponents of the church among the National Socialists, such as Alfred Rosenberg, the anti-Christian ideologist of the NSDAP, set an even more radical tone. Heinrich Himmler, too, was a professed opponent of Catholicism. As early as the mid-1920s, long before he officially left the church in September 1936, Himmler, a former Catholic himself, had already loosened his connection with the church and its – according to his own statement – "bourgeois Christian ties" in favor of radical racism. The SS as well as the Security Service of the RFSS (SD) took the same stance. Repression against the Catholic Church and surveillance of its members was tightened as of 1935/1936 with the help of the police apparatus, and especially the Gestapo mh/mm

Kreismuseum Wewelsburg, inv. no. 14321

No. 4-23
Cartoon by "Bogner" (Walter Hofmann): "Wir sind im Bilde" [We Have Taken Note]
Das Schwarze Korps, vol. 4, issue 31 (August 4, 1938), p. 1

The hooked nose was an ever-perpetuated anti-Semitic stereotype in the depiction of Jews in National Socialist cartoons. In this drawing from the *Schwarze Korps* magazine, the bishop's crosier is used to suggest that characteristic shape. This caricature was published in the wake of several official statements in which the Vatican had publicly condemned the National Socialist racism. From the perspective of the regime, both the Jewish people and the Catholic Church, on account of their international integration and prevalence, were antagonistic to the German *völkisch* national doctrine. At the same time, this cartoon appealed to the National Socialists' fixed idea that "the Jews" were pulling the strings behind any criticism of the Third Reich mh/mm

Kreismuseum Wewelsburg, inv. no. 5484/31

No. 4-25
Home of the Kusserow family in Bad Lippspringe, with the slogan "Lesen Sie Das Goldene Zeitalter" (Read The Golden Age)

Jehovah's Witnesses defied the ban on their organization in large numbers and continued their gatherings and missionary activities. In open letters from the underground and illegal flyer campaigns, they voiced protest against their persecution by the National Socialist police and judicial system. The authorities reacted with several waves of arrests, which resulted in the collapse of the organizational structure of Jehovah's Witnesses by 1938/1939. On one side of the Kusserows' house in Bad Lippspringe there was a slogan advertising the Jehovah's Witnesses' magazine *Das Goldene Zeitalter* (The Golden Age). The Gestapo had it painted over and terrorized the Kusserows with house searches on several occasions. The family had participated in a nationwide dissemination of protest letters. mh/mm

Photograph from a private collection

No. 4-24
Der Wachtturm [The Watchtower], title page
May 15, 1935

Until 1931, Jehovah's Witnesses were active under the name of *Ernste Bibelforscher* (Serious Bible Researchers). They were a Christian denomination oriented towards missionary work and an eschatological belief in the imminent foundation of the Kingdom of Heaven on Earth. The movement originated in the United States and included around 25 thousand German members in 1933. The state's persecution of Jehovah's Witnesses began soon after the National Socialist seizure of power. From June 1933 on, the community was outlawed throughout Germany. In hundreds of cases, their members lost custody of their children. Those employed in public service were dismissed. It became illegal to publish their publications (such as *Der Wachtturm*) in Germany, so copies had to be smuggled into the country. In 1936 the Gestapo established a department exclusively dedicated to the systematic oppression of Jehovah's Witnesses. mh/mm

Kreismuseum Wewelsburg, inv. no. 17122

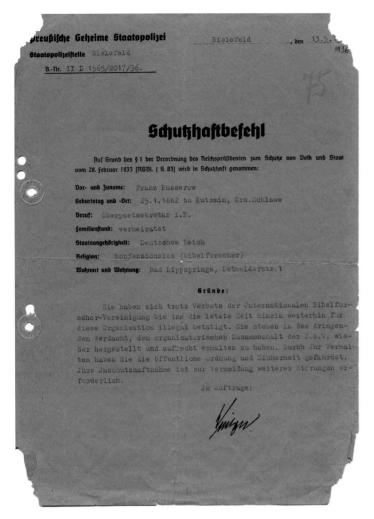

No. 4-26

Protective detention order for Franz Kusserow, dated May 13, 1936

Franz Kusserow, father of eleven children, was already detained and sentenced to several months of prison during the first wave of arrests against Jehovah's Witnesses in May 1936. Under the Third Reich, nine out of the thirteen members of the Kusserow family had to endure imprisonment for their unwavering religious conviction – in total, their sentences amount to almost thirty years. What is more, four family members were not only handed prison sentences but also sent to the concentration camps of Dachau, Ravensbrück, and Sachsenhausen. Two of the sons were executed for conscientious objection to military service. In 1939, the three youngest children were put on a journey of harassment through various National Socialist community homes and conformist foster families. It was only after the end of the National Socialist rule in 1945 that the surviving Kusserows were able to reunite. mh/mm

Original privately owned

No. 4-27

Members of the *Freundeskreis Heinrich Himmler* (Friends of Heinrich Himmler) visit the Freemason Museum of the SD in February 1937

In the eyes of the National Socialists, the Freemasons represented the ideals of Enlightenment and liberalism, and because of alleged identical interests, they were considered "Instruments of the Jews." Government pressure resulted in the gradual closing of lodges, and individual Masons were arrested one after the other. In July 1937, Himmler finally ordered the few remaining lodges to disband. Overall, however, the persecution of Freemasons was less systematic and brutal than that of other groups. The Freemason Museum in Berlin was established by the SD in a former lodge building. It contained objects and documents of several German Mason lodges confiscated by the Gestapo. Adolf Eichmann worked there before continuing his career at the Section for Jewish Affairs. mh/mm

Bildarchiv Preußischer Kulturbesitz, Berlin, 30017400

No. 4-28

Dr. F[ranz] A[lfred] Six, *Freimaurerei und Judenemanzipation* [Freemasonry and Jewish Emancipation] Hanseatische Verlagsanstalt, Hamburg, 1938

Following the dissolution of the lodges, the bulk of their libraries and archives were taken over by the SD, which had assigned several employees to work on a "scholarly" evaluation of Freemasonry. Among them was Franz Alfred Six (1906 – 1975) who had been working full-time at the SD since July 1935 and later became director of the department for *Weltanschauliche Gegnerforschung* (Research on Ideological Enemies) at the Reich security headquarters. The SD took a special interest in this issue because it sought to find proof of sectarian and hostile collaboration between the Jews and Freemasons. This SS department was convinced that the lodges were under the control of Judaism and had assisted their emancipation since the end of the eighteenth century. mh/mm

Kreismuseum Wewelsburg, inv. no. 15557

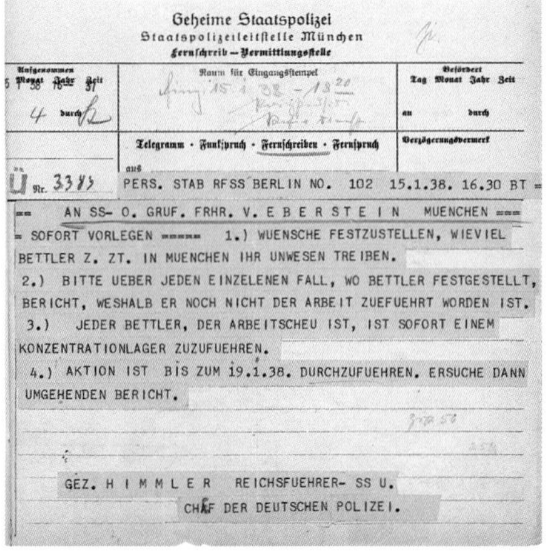

No. 4-30

Telegram sent on January 15, 1938, by Heinrich Himmler to *SS-Obergruppenführer* Karl Friedrich Freiherr von Eberstein, chief of the Munich police, demanding the immediate deportation of beggars in Munich to a concentration camp

The first Reich-wide campaigns to deport countless "antisocial elements" to concentration camps were carried out in 1938, and began with the arrest of several beggars in January 1938. This measure, which was still carried out by the Gestapo, was a direct result of Himmler's initiative. During *Aktion Arbeitsscheu Reich* (the Reich Anti-Work-Shy Campaign), which followed in April 1938, the Gestapo and criminal police arrested some one thousand five hundred to two thousand "work-shy career criminals and persistent offenders." The June Action followed, with yet another wave of arrests now carried out exclusively by the criminal police. Aside from the "work-shy," it also targeted Jews, and particularly many Sinti and Roma. Overall, this last measure resulted in nearly ten thousand individuals being transported to concentration camps, quickly increasing the population in the camps by a quarter. The SS largely used these prisoners as forced laborers in various industries. mh/mm

Bayerisches Hauptstaatsarchiv, Munich,
Minn 71576

No. 4-29

Erich von Liebermann von Sonnenberg, "Großkampf gegen Berufsverbrecher" [The Great Battle against Professional Criminals]
***Acht Uhr Abendblatt*, Berlin,
September 3, 1933**

Before 1933, Detective Erich von Liebermann von Sonnenberg (1885 – 1941) was an SA and SS informant for the Prussian police. After the seizure of power he served as deputy chief of the Berlin criminal police and chief of the Prussian Criminal Police Department. With the backing of his superior Kurt Daluege, he played a crucial role in developing the idea of "preemptive crime control."

As a result, preventive custody was used increasingly and systematically. No longer was it only applied to career criminals, but increasingly also to anyone deemed antisocial or work-shy, in the broadest sense, and who could be deployed into the work force of the war economy. mh/mm

Staatsbibliothek Berlin

No. 4-31

Robert Ritter, *Ein Menschenschlag. Erbärztliche und erbgeschichtliche Untersuchungen über die – durch 10 Geschlechterfolgen erforschten – Nachkommen von "Vagabunden, Jaunern und Räubern"* [A Separate Breed. Medical and Historical Heredity Studies Conducted on Descendants of "Vagabonds, Crooks, and Robbers," Observations over Ten Generations]
G. Thieme, Leipzig, 1937

The progressive expansion of the crime prevention policy was rooted in the belief that an "antisocial environment" was the breeding ground for criminality. As a result, there was a shift away from applying educational discipline to seeing it as a biological problem that could be remedied with permanent detention or extermination. This development was significantly influenced by the physician and psychologist Robert Ritter (1901 – 1951).

Ritter's postdoctoral thesis on the alleged heredity of criminal and antisocial traits earned him an appointment at the *Reichsgesundheitsamt* (Reich Health Office). Working closely with the *Reichskriminalpolizeiamt* (Reich Criminal Police Department) he was able to focus his research on his favorite topic, "the Gypsies," and play a key role in the stigmatization and registration of Sinti and Roma. mh/mm

Kreismuseum Wewelsburg, inv. no. 17053

No. 4-32

Prof. Eckhardt, "Widernatürliche Unzucht ist todeswürdig" [Unnatural Fornication is a Capital Offence]
***Das Schwarze Korps* [The Black Corps], vol. 1, issue 12 (May 22, 1935), p. 13**

Homosexual relations, in particular between men, were already illegal before 1933. The National Socialists systematically excluded this group by inciting the public against "strangers to the community" and antisocial behavior, the SS and police force once again playing a leading role in this development.

Various public hate campaigns were launched, which also included this article by *SS-Unterführer* and legal historian Professor Karl August Eckhardt, published in the SS newspaper *Das Schwarze Korps* in May 1935. The following month, the punishment in Paragraph 175 of the penal code was drastically increased to allow for prison sentences of up to ten years. From July 1940, homosexuals could also be sent to concentration camps. It is estimated that between five thousand and fifteen thousand persons died under both the Gestapo's protective custody decree and the preventive detention order of the criminal police. mh/mm

Kreismuseum Wewelsburg, inv. no. 5481/9

No. 4-33
SS commando marching lawyer Michael Siegel through the center of Munich Photographs: Heinrich Sanden, March 10, 1933
The sign reads: "I will never complain to the police again."

In 1933, two photographs were seen around the world that showed the respected Jewish lawyer, Michael Siegel, being forced to walk through the center of Munich by an SS commando. He had been seized by SS members present at the Munich police headquarters, where he had gone to contest the imprisonment of one of his clients in a concentration camp.

These images are an early indication of an essential feature of National Socialism: The enforcement of its own biased notions of justice and legal concepts in total disregard of the standards and laws of the constitutional democracy that existed previously.

As the text on the original photograph made in 1933 was too faint to be read, it was painted in on subsequent reproductions. Nonetheless, although the precise wording is no longer known, its accuracy has been confirmed by several witnesses. mh

Süddeutsche Zeitung Photo, Munich, 20904 and 20905

No. 4-34
**May Day Wagon in the Courtyard of Wewelsburg Castle decorated with anti-Semitic propaganda: "Die Meckerer nach Palästina" (Send the Whiners to Palestine). Front view of the wagon with a member of the SS
May 1, 1938**
The National Socialists' coup d'état gripped the entire country, was felt in every fibre of the nation, and carried out in full view of the public. Especially the streets became arenas of enduring menace, humiliation, and exposure to excessive violence for political and ideological opponents.

Apart from the SA and other members of the National Socialist Party, the SS was always ready to join in: for instance, for the 1938 May Day procession in Wewelsburg, the SS decorated a wagon with anti-Semitic propaganda; in November 1938, just a few months later, SS men destroyed synagogues and Jewish shops in the nearby towns of Salzkotten and Paderborn. During these raids, the SS and the Gestapo arrested 16 Jewish men from Salzkotten and locked them in the former *Hexenkeller* (witches' dungeon) of Wewelsburg for one night. The next day, the detainees were transferred via Paderborn and Bielefeld to Buchenwald Concentration Camp. mh

Kreismuseum Wewelsburg, Fotoarchiv

No. 4-38
SD Special Forces raid on the Jewish Community in Vienna, March 18, 1938
Left to right: Dr. Josef Löwenherz, director of the Jewish community in Vienna, *SS-Untersturmführer* Herbert Hagen, *SS-Untersturmführer* Adolf Eichmann
When Adolf Eichmann, one of the main men responsible for the mass murder of European Jews, claimed at his trial in Jerusalem in 1961 that he had been powerless and had merely followed orders, he represented in the mind of the public the quintessence of the emotionless and thoughtless *Schreibtischtäter* (desk perpetrator).

As important as the administration was for handling the whole persecution process, there is enough evidence to prove that to no degree did Eichmann or many other National Socialist bureaucrats actually act in an indifferent manner. In fact, they allowed themselves to be guided by colossal prejudices and were well aware of the consequences suffered by their victims.

During World War II, many of these men would regularly leave their desk duties to actively participate in these murderous events as "fighting adminis-trators," as envisioned by Reinhard Heydrich. mh

Bundesarchiv Koblenz, Bildarchiv, Bild 152-65-14A

No. 4-40
Not shown
Der nichtseßhafte Mensch. Ein Beitrag zur Neugestaltung der Raum- und Menschenordnung im Großdeutschen Reich.
[Non-Sedentary Man: An Article on the Reorganization of Regional and Population Policy Planning in the Greater German Reich.] Issued by the Bayerischer Landesverband für Wanderdienst München (Bavarian Association for Vagrancy Control) in cooperation with the Bavarian Ministry of the Interior
C. H. Beck, Munich, 1938

Kreismuseum Wewelsburg, inv. no. 16544

No. 4-39
"Gypsy Research"
Robert Ritter and his assistant Eva Justin collecting a blood sample in the open, Stein in der Pfalz
April 1938
Many scientists and research institutes offered their services to promote racist policies during the National Socialist era. At the behest of government and party-run authorities and with lavish public funding, they contributed to the transfor-mation of common prejudices into recom-mendations and arguments that formed the basis of drastic population policy measures.

This was not only true for "research on ideological enemies" carried out by the Security Service of the *Reichsführer-SS*, which openly expressed its persecutory intentions, but also for the "gypsy re-search" carried out by physician and psy-chologist Robert Ritter (1901 – 1951). He conducted "hereditary biology" research on German Sinti and Roma in close colla-boration with the criminal police. For thousands, his medical reports resulted in forced sterilization, deportation to concentration camps, and death. mh

Bundesarchiv Koblenz, Bildarchiv, Bild 146-1991-014-09

No. 4-37
Publicity campaign for *Das Schwarze Korps* during the Week of the National Socialist Press in January 1936
Photograph: B. Spahn
January 19, 1936

FM-Zeitschrift, vol. 3, issue 3 (March 1, 1936), p. 7
Kreismuseum Wewelsburg, inv. no. 17113

No. 4-35
SS men hand out promotional copies of *Das Schwarze Korps*
Photograph: Böker, February 1937

Das Schwarze Korps, vol. 3, issue 8 (February 25, 1937), p. 3
Kreismuseum Wewelsburg, inv. no. 5483/8

Apart from radio, which was a new mass medium, high-circulation print media reached most of the German population. Following the rapid ban on oppositional newspapers and forcible coordination of the remaining, mostly bourgeois, press, the National Socialist regime were able to completely dominate the shaping of public opinion.

The dissemination of mass propaganda was pioneered via party publications. The SS also had its own channels, the most important of which was the weekly *Das Schwarze Korps* (The Black Corps). Launched in May 1935 with an initial print run of 70,000 copies, its circulation increased to 700,000 during the war, reaching a readership far beyond the SS itself.

Editor-in-chief Gunter d'Alquen (1910–1998), a member of the SS since 1931, was the driving force behind *Das Schwarze Korps*. Although it officially presented itself as the medium of the SS and the *Reichsführung-SS*, it nevertheless liked to emphasize its independence. mh

No. 4-41
"Menschen hinter Gittern" [Men behind Bars]
***Das Schwarze Korps*, vol. 2, issue 43 (October 22, 1936), p. 10**
This article from *Das Schwarze Korps* illustrates the methods used in National Socialist publications to denigrate social outcasts and, at the same time, to lower inhibitions towards using radical measures.

The author addresses the problem with "occasional and career criminals," i.e., repeat offenders. He shares the opinion commonly held at the time that mental illness as well as career criminality and antisocial behavior were hereditary. The article praises the National Socialist regime's Law for the Prevention of Hereditarily Diseased Offspring, i.e. forced sterilization, which he sees as a "truly humanitarian" act because it would ultimately save the "heritage of the nation" and raise the "personal safety of *Volksgenossen* [racial/national comrades]."

To counter possible objections, the author finally states: "Whoever still believes that anyone with a human countenance is equal and should therefore be entitled to the same rights as valuable citizens should carefully consider these pictures and then proceed to pass judgment." This open appeal to the readers' racist prejudices is supported by the overall denunciatory quality of the images, achieved by their selection, cropping, and unfavorable camera angles.

Following the introduction of preventive detention at the end of 1937, the criminal police deported more than 70,000 alleged career criminals and antisocial "elements" to concentration camps, where more than half of them died. The beginning of World War II saw the systematic murder of the mentally disabled and infirm. Their death toll rose to at least 120,000. The true number is very likely much higher. mh

Kreismuseum Wewelsburg, inv. no. 5482/43

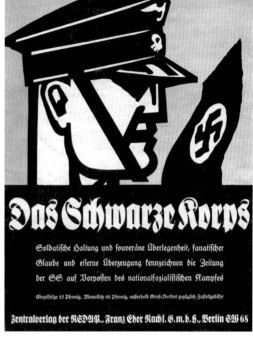

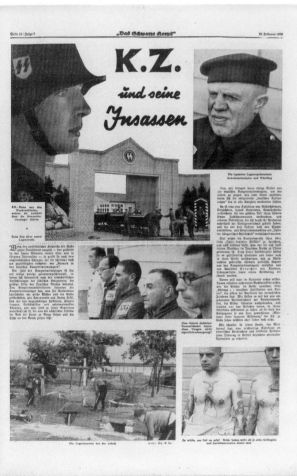

No. 4-43

"K.Z. und seine Insassen" [The Concentration Camp and its Inmates]
Das Schwarze Korps, vol. 2, issue 7
(February 13, 1936), p. 10
The Third Reich press frequently wrote about concentration camps, a subject even covered occasionally by *Das Schwarze Korps*. This article was written in response to ongoing foreign criticism of the German camps. The author dismisses these accusations irritably as the "atrocity propaganda" of German Jewish émigrés. He insists that there are hardly any camps left, and anyone still serving a sentence is there for a good reason. To support his claim, he refers disdainfully to the depicted prisoners, remarking: "Don't these faces speak for themselves?"

The way in which these photographs have been edited combines a number of fundamental image manipulation techniques. Deliberately humiliating shots of tormented and powerless men are contrasted with the image of a strapping, young SS guard. The accompanying captions contain snide remarks and false assertions. In fact, the "Jewish race violators" in the middle photograph were imprisoned at Esterwegen Concentration Camp, where most of the pictures for the article were taken. The camp primarily held political prisoners and people in "protective custody," among whom, for instance, was the (non-Jewish) pacifist and writer Carl von Ossietzky, whose harsh treatment caused an international stir. mh

Kreismuseum Wewelsburg, inv. no. 5482/7

No. 4-42

"Arbeitsscheu!" [Work-Shy!]
Das Schwarze Korps, vol. 4, issue 31
(August 4, 1938), p. 10
Kreismuseum Wewelsburg, inv. no. 5484/31

No. 4-36

Advertisement for
Das Schwarze Korps
The advertising copy reads: "A soldierly attitude and commanding superiority, fanatic belief and iron conviction, are the hallmarks of this SS newspaper in the vanguard of the National Socialist struggle"

FM-Zeitschrift, vol. 3, issue 3
March 1, 1936), p. 12

No. 4-46
Sites of concentration camps and protective custody units from 1933 to 1939
From 1933 to 1934, there were at least seventy concentration camps and thirty protective custody units at prisons and police jails in the German Reich. At various times, up to 50,000 prisoners were imprisoned there.

By November 1935, after the majority had been closed and the Concentration Camps Inspectorate established by the SS, only five remained: Dachau, Lichtenburg, Sachsenburg, Esterwegen, and Columbia(-Haus). With the exception of Dachau, the remaining four were also subsequently closed, while new detention facilities were being set up at the same time. At the beginning of World War II, 21,400 people were imprisoned in the concentration camps of Buchenwald, Dachau, Flossenbürg, Mauthausen, Ravensbrück, and Sachsenhausen. jes

☐ Concentration camps established in 1933

◨ Concentration camps established in 1933 still operating in November 1935

■ Concentration camps in operation in 1939

● Shown for orientation purposes

▦ German border as of December 31, 1937

▦ Border of the Protectorate of Bohemia and Moravia

▦ Territory of the German Reich and the Protectorate of Bohemia and Moravia as of September 1, 1939

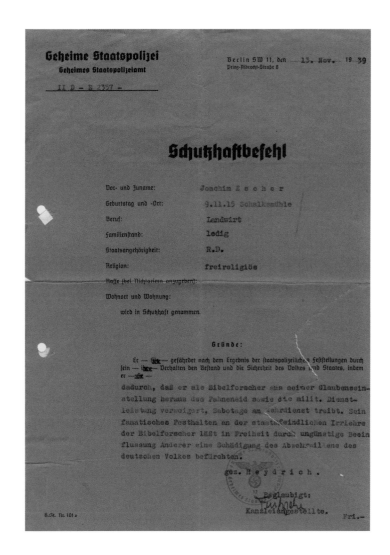

No. 4-44

**Protective custody order issued
by the Berlin Secret State Police office for
Joachim Escher, who was temporarily
imprisoned at Niederhagen Concentration
Camp**
November 13, 1939
Translation on page 445
A protective custody order was commonly
issued by the protective custody department of the Secret State Police (Gestapo)
office in Berlin, its national headquarters,
at the request of the State Police. Arres-
tees had no right of appeal. Furthermore,
the period of protective custody was
unlimited, with the sentence being served
in one of the concentration camps.
The Decree for the Protection of the German People, signed by President Hindenburg on February 4, 1933, had already
included protective custody legislation
that allowed for sentences of specific
duration. After a state of emergency was
declared, and the Reichstag Fire Decree
issued on February 28, 1934, this measure
evolved into an arbitrarily used, and un-
controllable instrument for persecuting
political opponents. In the beginning, such
orders were also imposed by local and
regional police authorities. However, the
Gestapo increasingly gained control of
protective custody sentencing. In April
1934, the Reich minister of the interior
issued the first protective custody decree
for the entire Reich. Above all, it legally
established the protective detainees' lack
of rights. jes
Original privately owned

Der Reichsführer-SS   Berlin, den 8.Februar 1937
             und
Chef der Deutschen Polizei

- B.Nr.1983/37 J.K.L. -

        Wie der Inspekteur der Konzentrationslager und Führer
der SS-Totenkopfverbände, SS-Gruppenführer Eicke, in meinem
Auftrage bereits mündlich dort zum Vortrag gebracht hat,
ist von mir in unmittelbaren Verhandlungen mit dem Reichs-
arbeitsführer, Staatssekretär Hierl, aus politischen Gründen
die Räumung des der Geheimen Staatspolizei gehörenden, an der
deutsch-holländischen Grenze innerhalb des militärischen
Aufmarschgebiets belegenen Konzentrationslagers Esterwegen
und seine Überlassung an den Reichsarbeitsdienst angeordnet
worden. Die Übernahme des 2000-2200 Mann fassenden Lagers
im Moorgebiet der Ems, dessen Kultivierung ursprünglich dem
Reichsarbeitsdienst vorbehalten war, konnte für letzteren
jedoch nur dann in Frage kommen, wenn eine Räumung und Zur-
verfügungstellung des Lagers zum Zwecke der Belegung mit
den Anfang Oktober 1936 einrückenden Arbeitsdienstpflichti-
gen sich bis zu diesem Zeitpunkte ermöglichen ließe. Um
diese Bedingung erfüllen zu können und, nachdem die Wehrmacht
wiederholt ein starkes Interesse an der Errichtung eines
großen Lagers in der nächsten Umgebung von Groß-Berlin mit
umfassenden Erweiterungsmöglichkeiten für den Mob.-Fall zum
Ausdruck gebracht hat, habe ich dem Inspekteur der Konzentrationslager unter den gegebenen Umständen die Weisung
                                    erteilt,

     An
das Reichsjustizministerium
  -z.Hd.des Kammergerichtsrats Hecker-
         in B e r l i n W 8
Sofort!   Wilhelmstr.65
-vertraulich-
         zu III r² 329/37

- 7 -

noch irgend brauchbar, von Esterwegen mitgenommen und
nur einige Ausstattungsstücke unter Selbstanfertigung
im Lager bei denkbar größter Sparsamkeit aus den vor-
handenen laufenden Haushaltsmitteln bestritten werden
konnten.

        Ich bitte, bei Prüfung meines vorstehenden Antrages
auch die von allen Beteiligten in anstrengender, mühe-
und aufopferungsvollster Tages- und Nachtarbeit unter
besonders schwierigen Verhältnissen und Gefahrenmomen-
ten in erstaunlich kurzer Zeit hier vollbrachte Leistung
zu würdigen und darüber hinaus auch anzuerkennen, daß
anstelle des s.Zt. in der ersten Revolutionszeit im
Moorgebiet an der Nordwestgrenze des Reiches gebauten
einfachen Lagers Esterwegen jetzt hier in der nächsten
Nähe der Reichshauptstadt ein vollkommen neues, jederzeit erweiterungsfähiges, modernes und neuzeitliches
Konzentrationslager mit verhältnismäßig geringen Mitteln neugeschaffen worden ist, das allen Anforderungen
und Erfordernissen nach jeder Richtung hin gewachsen
ist und sowohl in Friedenszeiten sowie für den Mob.-Fall
die Sicherung des Reiches gegen Staatsfeinde und Staats-
schädlinge in vollem Umfange jederzeit gewährleistet.

        gez. Himmler

An den Herrn Preußischen Finanzminister - z.Hd. des
Herrn Ministerialrats Rademacher - in Berlin C 2, Hinter
dem Gießhause 2.

        Vorstehende Abschrift übersende ich zur gefälligen
Kenntnisnahme mit der Bitte, meinen Antrag zu unter-
                        stützen

No. 4-45

Letter from Himmler to the Reich Ministry of Justice (excerpt)
February 8, 1937

For the SS, Sachsenhausen was the prototype for a "completely new, always expandable, state-of-the-art concentration camp." The planning and construction of Sachsenhausen Concentration Camp made it clear that Himmler did not see the camps as temporary detention and torture facilities for political opponents. They represented a long-term instrument of terror that symbolized the power of the SS in the National Socialist state. The concentration camp system was never intended to be static; as early as 1937, Himmler had already envisaged its further expansion. jes

Bundesarchiv Berlin, R 2/24006

No. 4-48
Not shown

Account given by protective detainee No. 231 (Kurt Hiller) regarding SS guards at Columbia Concentration Camp, parts VIII and X

Die neue Weltbühne, no. 3, 1935, pp. 40–41

SS member Kramer, the man who punched me on the nose on the evening I was interned, comes to my cell and – without cause, without any semblance of a reason – grins and steps on my toes, shoves me in the chest, slamming me against the wall, and punches me in the face with his fist.

My analysis of the data on the sixty to seventy SS members from all the ranks represented here showed that about fifteen percent are decent people, around fifty-five percent are average in their lack of moral principles, conforming and going along with everything, and about thirty percent are outright sadists.

Translated excerpt

Eicke's Dachau "School of Violence"

No. 4–47
**Theodor Eicke (seated at the table, second from the left) with SS guards from Dachau Concentration Camp
1934**

Andrew Mollo, *Uniforms of the SS*, vol. 4: *SS-Totenkopfverbände 1933–1945*, London, 1971, p. 13

Franz Hofmann
1933–1942: Dachau
1942–1944: Camp leader at Auschwitz Concentration Camp
1944: Camp leader at Natzweiler Concentration Camp

Bundesarchiv Berlin, RS Franz Johann Hofmann

Martin Weiss
1933–1940: Dachau
1940–1942: Commandant of Neuengamme Concentration Camp
1942–1943: Commandant of Dachau Concentration Camp
1943–1944: Commandant of Lublin Concentration Camp
1944–1945: Staff chief for special deployments, Department D (concentration camps) of the WVHA (SS Main Economic and Administrative Department)

KZ-Gedenkstätte Neuengamme, sign. 1998-694 Weiss

Karl Fritzsch
1934–1940: Dachau
1940–1941: Camp leader at Auschwitz Concentration Camp
1942–1944: Camp leader at Flossenbürg Concentration Camp

KZ-Gedenkstätte Flossenbürg

Richard Baer
1933–1934: Dachau
1942–1943: Adjutant of Neuengamme Concentration Camp
1942–1943: Adjutant of Oswald Pohl, Chief of the WVHA (SS Main Economic and Administrative Department)
1944–1945: Commandant of Auschwitz I Concentration Camp
1945: Mittelbau-Dora Concentration Camp commandant

Bundesarchiv Berlin, RS Richard Baer

Hans Aumeier
1934–1938: Dachau
1938–1941: Camp leader at Flossenbürg Concentration Camp
1942–1943: Camp leader at Auschwitz Concentration Camp
1944: Commandant of Vaivara Concentration Camp

KZ-Gedenkstätte Flossenbürg

Rudolf Höß
1934–1938: Dachau
1938–1940: Adjutant and camp leader at Sachsenhausen Concentration Camp
1940–1943 (1944): Auschwitz Concentration Camp commandant
1943–1945: Staff chief of Section D I in Department D (concentration camps) of the WVHA (SS Main Economic and Administrative Department)

U. S. Holocaust Memorial Museum, Washington, D.C., Photo Archives, 34755

Max Koegel
1933–1936: Dachau
1936: Adjutant of Berlin-Columbia-Haus Concentration Camp
1937–1938: Adjutant of Dachau Con. Camp
1938–1939: Commandant of Lichtenburg Concentration Camp
1939–1942: Commandant of Ravensbrück Concentration Camp Ravensbrück
1942–1943: Commandant of Lublin Concentration Camp
1943–1945: Commandant of Flossenbürg Concentration Camp

National Archives, Washington, D.C., RG 549 Cases tried 1945-49, 000-50-46, Box 488, Exhibit D-4

Hans Loritz
1933–1934: Dachau
1934–1936: Commandant of Esterwegen Concentration Camp
1936–1939: Commandant of Dachau Concentration Camp
1940–1942: Commandant of Sachsenhausen Concentration Camp

U. S. Holocaust Memorial Museum, Washington, D.C., Photo Archives, 55778

Franz Xaver Trenkle
1933–1938: Dachau
1942–1944: Assistant camp leader at Dachau Concentration Camp
1944: Camp leader at Bergen-Belsen Concentration Camp

KZ-Gedenkstätte Dachau

Günther Tamaschke
1933–1934: Dachau
1935–1936: Deputy inspector of the Concentration camps
1937–1938: Commandant of Lichtenburg Concentration Camp

Bundesarchiv Berlin, SSO Günther Tamaschke

Many concentration camp commandants and leading camp officials were recruited from the guard units at Dachau Concentration Camp. Eicke commanded his subordinates to treat prisoners with extreme inhumanity. Drawing on postwar writings by Auschwitz commandant Rudolf Höß, the brutalizing effects of Eicke's instructions are referred to as the "Dachau School" or "School of Violence." In this respect, Dachau functioned as a model for the entire concentration camp system. jes

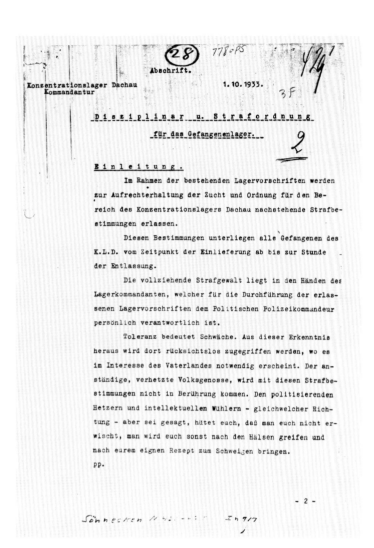

No. 4-49
Office of the Dachau Concentration Camp Commandant: Disciplinary and Penal Regulations (copy), excerpt
October 1, 1933
Translation on page 445
Hauptstaatsarchiv Nürnberg, PS 778, Sheet 570

No. 4-50
Office of the Dachau Concentration Camp Commandant: Service Regulations for SS Guards (copy), excerpt
October 1, 1933
Translation on page 445
Hauptstaatsarchiv Nürnberg, PS 778, Blatt 576

The camp regulations imposed by Theodor Eicke on October 1, 1933, established a brutal regime that aimed to break down the resistance and personality of the prisoners, thwart any attempt at escape, and instill the guard units with a spirit of unquestioning hostility towards inmates. In the disciplinary and penal regulations, the camp commandant openly threatens with the death penalty from his position of absolute power outside the law. The service regulations for escort and guard staff ordered that fleeing prisoners be shot and promised immunity from prosecution for the shooters, thus leaving the door wide open to the random murder of camp inmates. Eicke's Dachau regulations became a model for all subsequent organizational regulations of the SS concentration camp system, with essential elements remaining in effect until the end of the war. jes

4.3
Myths – Rules – Rituals: The Internal World of the SS

The policy of humiliation and exclusion was the exact opposite of the ideal of strength and greatness that National Socialism claimed for itself. This is evidenced in particular by the exclusive parallel world the SS created within National Socialist society.

The invention of its own regulations, symbols, rituals, artifacts, publications, and large-scale building projects, such as Wewelsburg, all served to emphasize the social importance of the SS. Himmler's organization promoted a tradition it had assembled itself from fragments of a perceived heroic Germanic-German past.

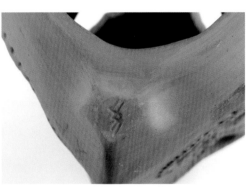

No. 4-51
Julleuchter (Yule lantern)
Clay
Between 1936 and 1944
Kreismuseum Wewelsburg,
inv. no. 4228

No. 4-52
Julleuchter (Yule lantern)
Clay
Possible replica
After 1945
Photograph of the base with
Allach runes
Kreismuseum Wewelsburg,
inv. no. 9639

The *Julleuchter* (Yule lantern) was a central object used by the SS used to strengthen the bond within their community. Himmler was particularly involved in introducing a substitute religion and creating new rites for the SS. This candle holder played a crucial role in this process, and was primarily used during the *Julfest* (Yuletide celebration), which SS units held at the end of the year instead of Christmas. Initially, Yule lanterns were produced exclusively for the SS at the SS-owned Allach factory near Munich. Later, production was transferred to a brick works inside Neuengamme Concentration Camp, where they were manufactured by prisoners.

Himmler gave all married SS men Yule lanterns as presents, which he expected them to use for all family celebrations. Each Yule lantern came with an accompanying certificate claiming it was a replica of a "(piece) from the early history of our people." In fact, Yule lanterns are an exact imitation of a Swedish candle holder from around 1800. web/fh

SS

Liebe Eltern, Frauen und Kinder,

Bräute und Geschwister,

unserer gefallenen SS-Männer!

Euch, den Gesippen unserer gefallenen

lieben Kameraden, die Ihr unserer großen

Familie der Schutzstaffel angehört, über-

sende ich meine herzlichsten Wünsche für

das Julfest und für das Jahr 1945.

Heil Hitler!

H. Himmler

Feldkommandostelle, im Dezember 1944

No. 4-54
Julfeier (Yuletide Celebration) held by the Guard Unit
at Neuengamme
Concentration Camp
1944
KZ-Gedenkstätte Neuengamme

No. 4-53
Yule Lantern Production in
the Brick Works at Neuen-
gamme Concentration Camp
1944
KZ-Gedenkstätte Neuengamme

No. 4-55
Not shown
*Die Gestaltung der Feste im Jahres- und Lebens-
lauf in den SS-Familien*, hrsg. vom SS-Ober-
abschnitt West, verantwortlich für den Inhalt:
**Fritz Weitzel, Wuppertal, ohne Jahr [Celebrations
in keeping with the Seasons and the Lives of SS
Families, issued by SS Main Sector West,
content: Fritz Weitzel, Wuppertal, undated]**
The Yule lantern was supposed to involve the
entire family in the new rite. In his speech at
Dachau on November 8, 1936, Himmler proclaimed: "It is especially women who, when the
myth surrounding the Church is lost, long for
something else that will fill their minds and
hearts, as well as those of their children." All
family celebrations were to be defined by these
new SS customs. Between celebrations, the Yule
lantern was displayed on a table or a chest in a
so-called *Julecke* (Yule corner), together with
Julteller (Yule plates) and similar objects. The
Yule corner was strongly reminiscent of an altar.
   In order to promote the actual use of Yule
lanterns, at the end of each year Himmler had a
so-called *Julkerze* (Yule candle) sent to all SS
men who already had a Yule lantern. Even at the
turn of the year 1944/1945, Himmler still sent
out thousands of Yule candles. web/fh
Kreismuseum Wewelsburg, inv. no. 16438

No. 4-56
Julleuchter (Yule lantern Dedication
Certificate with Heinrich Himmler's
facsimile signature
1941
Translation on page 446
Heinrich W. Schild, "Der Julleuchter der Porzellan-Manufaktur Allach," *Militaria*, vol. 23,
issue 6 (November/December 2000), p. 157

ℍ-Männer!

Sippen der ℍ!

Ich übersende Euch die Julkerze und meine besten Julwünsche für 1945.

Das neue Jahr möge Euch allen Glück und Segen bringen!

1944 hat abermals das gesamte deutsche Volk den härtesten Belastungen ausgesetzt und wiederum haben Heimat und Front die Probe bestanden.

Das Jahr 1945 wird wohl das entscheidende Jahr dieses Krieges sein. Es steht für uns unter der Parole:

„Durch Mütter und Helden —

wird unser der Sieg!"

Wir grüßen in unerschütterlicher Treue und tiefster Dankbarkeit

den uns vom Herrgott gesandten Führer:

ADOLF HITLER!

Feld-Kommandostelle, 21. Dezember 1944.

Germanien

Monatshefte für Germanenkunde zur Erkenntnis deutschen Wesens

1936 — Dezember — Heft 12

Zur Erkenntnis deutschen Wesens:

Julzeit — heilige Zeit

Nordisch-germanischer Gottglaube lebt seit Jahrtausenden in seinen Sinnbildern. Er lebt unzerstörbar in jenen, die diese Sinnbilder schufen und die in ihnen das große Gleichnis von der ewigen Wiederkehr des Seienden und der Unzerstörbarkeit der lebendigen Kräfte erkannten, mit denen sich das All geschmückt. Mit ihrem Blute und Geiste haben sie das Ahnen von dem großen Geheimnis ihren Nachfahren weitergegeben, die aus den Sinnbildern uraltes Erleben immer von neuem erweckten; die in den Gleichnis von dem neugeborenen Kindlein das Gleichnis von der Unvergänglichkeit des Lebens erkannten und in der heiligen Mütternacht, wie die frommen angelsächsischen Heiden sie nannten, sich dem ewigen Urquell allen Lebens nahefühlten.

Sinnbilder sind mehr als Zierat, mehr als Symbole im allgemeinen Sinne. Sie sind Abbilder eines innersten Erlebens, in eine Form geprägt, die geheimnisvoll zu dem sprechen, der Blut vom Blute und Geist vom Geist jener hat, die einst in der Urzeit aus ihrem Welterleben diese Bilder schufen. Darum sprechen sie auch heute noch zu uns, darum wecken sie in uns jenes Urerlebnis, das einmalig und ewig ist, das keiner Psychologie und keiner Entwicklung unterworfen ist, weil es unmittelbar von jenem Punkte der Seele ausgeht, in dem sich das Menschliche mit dem Göttlichen berührt.

Dieses Urerlebnis ist die Geburt des Lichtes.

Dem Germanen ist alles was uns vergänglich erscheint, ein Gleichnis des großen Unvergänglichen, des Allvaters der Welt, des Lebens und unseres Seins. Unter mancherlei Bildern hat er diese ewige Wahrheit begriffen. Er fand sie im Bilde des wegelosen Wanderers wieder, der gewaltig durch die Lande fährt, und der niemals an ein Ziel kommt, weil sein Ziel ewig in ihm selber ruht. Er fand sie zugleich in dem Bilde von dem Kindlein, das in der goldenen Wiege im dunklen Grabe der Ahnen geboren wird — in der Urzeit, da die Aare schrien und heiliges Naß von den Himmelsbergen zur Erde träuft. Diese Urzeit ist ewig in ihm; zeitlos, und nur in den Zeiten der tiefsten Selbstbesinnung zum

24. Germanien — 369

No. 4-57

Letter from Himmler accompanying a Shipment of *Julkerzen* (Yule candles) December 21, 1944

Translation on page 446

In 1937 Himmler declared that all SS men were expected to celebrate the *Julfest* (Yuletide) with their families. On this occasion, SS unit commanders gave additional Yule lanterns to individual SS members, in order to emphasize their importance for the new customs. This award ceremony became a central element during the handing out of presents at "Christmas" celebrations. The event was also called *Sippenabend* (kin evening) and formed the highlight of the year. As with the *Ehrendolch* (honorary dagger), the awarded Yule lantern was also noted on the SS member's *Stammkarte* (SS basic record card). Himmler wanted all married men to eventually own such a lantern. This diminished the initially exclusive character of this prize; it also demonstrated how much importance Himmler attached to its role regarding the new family customs. web/fh

Heinrich W. Schild, "Der Julleuchter der Porzellan-Manufaktur Allach," Militaria, vol. 23, issue 6 (November/December 2000), p. 160

No. 4-58

Hugin und Munin (pseudonym of Joseph Otto Plassmann), "Zur Erkenntnis deutschen Wesens: Julzeit – heilige Zeit" [Understanding the Essence of Being German: Yule Time – Holy Time]
***Germanien*, issue 12 (1936), p. 370 f.**

In this piece Joseph Plassmann explains the National Socialist re-interpretation of Christmas. The propagandized "Nordic-Germanic faith in God," he writes, celebrated a "rebirth of light." He claims that the tale of the *Kindlein in der goldenen Wiege* (the infant in the golden cradle) as well as worship of the *Wintergrüner Baum* (wintergreen tree) had evolved from this supposed belief in light. He also sees the Blessed Virgin as belonging to Germanic tradition, which depicted her locked in a tower from which she emerged, "shining and radiant with new life." Plassmann interprets the *Julleuchter* as a symbol of this tower. The Yule lantern is "decorated with the Wheel of the Year, the holy Yuletide, and the heart, the symbol of the depth of Germanic feeling for God."

Additionally, Plassmann also saw the *Julleuchter* as representing the fight of the SS against threats from the outside world: "Thus, we will only be able to build an iron bulwark against all foreign and Bolshevist subversions if we anchor its fundament in the depths of the German soul." This passage reveals the political dimension of the new rites, especially of the *Julleuchter*.
web/fh

Kreismuseum Wewelsburg, inv. no. 10207

No. 4-60
Black round cap of an *Oberführer* of the *Allgemeine SS* with white piping, eagle over the swastika, and SS death's head (design prescribed since 1934)
Kreismuseum Wewelsburg, inv. no. 4554

No. 4-59
Adolf Hitler with an SA and an SS member Colorized photograph by Heinrich Hoffmann, before 1933
The original caption reads: "The Führer honors a German fighter."

Wilfried Bade: Deutschland erwacht. *Werden, Kampf und Sieg der NSDAP* [Germany Awakes. Origin, Struggle and Victory of the NSDAP], 1st edition, Cigaretten-Bilderdienst, Altona-Bahrenfeld 1933

From the beginning, the National Socialists saw themselves as victims of the loathed democratic "system" of the Weimar Republic and its representatives, of the victorious powers of World War I, of their political opponents, and of the police, with whom they routinely had brawls and street fights.

This feeling of being persecuted and discriminated against was the basis for their readiness to use violence, and continued to be their driving force even after the seizure of power. In order to reinforce their self-image as victims, the National Socialists doggedly cultivated the public memory of their "time of struggle." Special rituals, mass rallies, as well as the design of their uniforms and symbols were intended to make comprehensible past humiliations and the triumph of overcoming them. The SS and the organization preceding it, *Stoßtrupp* (shock troop) *Adolf Hitler*, with its own traditions, always played a prominent role in this cult of remembrance. mh

No. 4-61
Black uniform tunic of an *SS-Untersturmführer* of the Death's Head Units (with a "K" and a death's head on the right collar patch)
This jacket was worn by a member of the commandant staff at a concentration camp.
Kreismuseum Wewelsburg, inv. no. 4552

No. 4-62
Red swastika armband
Kreismuseum Wewelsburg, inv. no. 4555

No. 4-65
Death's head badge Sheet metal
Kreismuseum Wewelsburg, inv. no. 7011

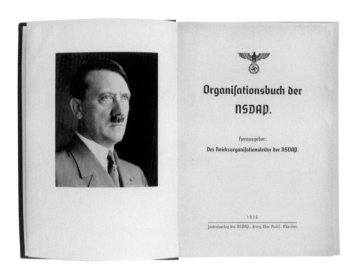

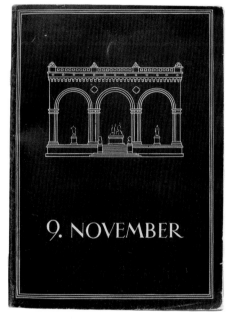

No. 4-63

Der Reichsorganisationsleiter der NSDAP: *Organisationsbuch der NSDAP* [The Reich Organization Leader of the NSDAP, Organization Book of the NSDAP]
Zentralverlag der NSDAP, Franz Eher Nachf., Munich, 1936

Kreismuseum Wewelsburg, inv. no. 16527

No. 4-64

9. November: Sonderdruck für die Gestaltung von Gedenkfeiern in der SS [November 9: Offprint for use at commemoration ceremonies in the SS], brochure, *Reichsführer-SS*, SS Main Administrative Office, n.p. (1943/1944)

Kreismuseum Wewelsburg, inv. no. 16939

No. 4-66

"The Führer consecrates new flags with the *Blutfahne* (Blood Flag)" Photograph: Otto Häckel, Berlin

Friedrich Heiß, *Deutschland zwischen Nacht und Tag* [Germany between Night and Day], 5th expanded edition (Print run 31,000–55,000), Volk und Reich Verlag, Berlin, 1934, p. 146
Kreismuseum Wewelsburg, inv. no. 12423

No. 4-67

"Old fighters" at a commemoration of the failed 1923 Munich Putsch. "November 9, 1934, in front of the Feldherrnhalle. The Führer and his deputy, Rudolf Heß, with old fighters" (Translation of original caption)

Cigarette picture album: *Adolf Hitler – Bilder aus dem Leben des Führers* [Adolf Hitler. Pictures of the Life of the Führer], Cigaretten-Bilderdienst, Hamburg-Bahrenfeld, 1936, p. 118
Kreismuseum Wewelsburg, inv. no. 4231

No. 4-68
August von Mackensen as a lieutenant with the *Leib-Husaren* (Life Hussars)
Undated photograph
Early or mid-1870s
August von Mackensen (1849 – 1945) was one of the most prominent members of the "Death's Head Hussars." From 1893 to 1898 he commanded the *Leibhusaren* (Life Hussar) *Regiment Nr. 1*, and as of 1901 the Life Hussar Brigade in Danzig, which was formed out of the two previously existing regiments. A general field marshal and commander in World War I, Mackensen epitomized in the 1920s and 1930s the old Imperial Army, similar to Reich President Paul von Hindenburg.

In this photograph from early in his military career, Mackensen wears the smaller field cap variant of the death's head badge. After the defeat of the Central Powers in World War I, the Life Hussar regiments were disbanded in the course of general troop reductions, and their now superfluous emblems sold off with other military equipment on the militaria market. mh

Ullstein Bilderdienst, 00672421

No. 4-69
Counter-revolutionary troops enter Munich
A Free Corps armed vehicle marked with a death's head
Postcard with photograph by Heinrich Hoffmann from early May 1919
In early May 1919, *Reichswehr* units, Bavarian troops, and several Free Corps units advanced on the Bavarian capital of Munich. Acting on the orders of the Social-Democrat-led Bavarian government, they brought a bloody end to the Bavarian Soviet Republic established just a few weeks earlier.

In the following period, Munich became a stronghold of the political right, which launched numerous attempts from the city to topple the democratic parliamentary Weimar state. The end of the Munich Soviet Republic also marked the beginning of the political career of the thirty-year-old World War I veteran, Adolf Hitler. Bavaria became a haven for the disbanded Free Corps and right-wing organizations that had been banned elsewhere throughout the Reich. In Bavaria, many of them joined nationalist associations, including the *Nationalsozialistische Deutsche Arbeiterpartei* (NSDAP), or Nazi Party, and its subdivisions, the SA and SS. mh

Bildarchiv Preußischer Kulturbesitz, Berlin, 50056530

No. 4-70
Retired Major Josef Bischoff, commander of the "Iron Division," with the Life Hussars' death's head on his cap
Photograph presumably after May 1919
Under Josef Bischoff, a former infantry regiment commander, the Iron Division took part in the Russian civil war from the end of 1918 until the fall of 1919. It fought in Estonia and Latvia, partly on official order, or at least with tacit consent, of the German government, and partly on its own authority and with varying allies. Its goal was to prevent the advance of Bolshevist troops. The division comprised regular German army units and volunteer formations, as well as local units of Baltic Germans and smaller Latvian contingents. The soldiers of the Iron Division had long made the death's head their emblem and in May 1919 Bischoff also chose to wear the insignia to honor of the division's troops; it was, he told his men, "a decoration well earned in bloody battles." mh

Josef Bischoff, *Die letzte Front. Geschichte der Eisernen Division im Baltikum 1919*, 2nd edition (print run 6,000–9,000), Schützen-Verlag, Berlin, 1935, frontispiece

Wehrwolf-Marinegruppe

No. 4-71

Navy group from the Werewolf paramilitary group with a death's head flag
Photograph: Location and date unknown

The paramilitary group *Wehrwolf* was founded at the beginning of 1923, at almost the same time as the *Stoßtrupp* (shock troop) *Hitler*. It was led by Dr. Fritz Kloppe, a high school teacher, and established mainly out of local groups from the disbanded, far-right *Verband nationalgesinnter Soldaten* (Association of Nationalist-Minded Soldiers) in central Germany. The *Wehrwolf* group saw itself as a *Kampfbund*, or fighting association, uncompromisingly opposed to the Weimar Republic and its "liberal capitalist system." The group's name derived from the title of a highly popular 1910 novel by the regional writer Hermann Löns. The book tells the story of a group of heathland farmers during the Thirty Years' War, who quite brutally defended themselves against plundering mercenary forces. The *Wehrwolf* of the 1920s had nothing to do with the later SS underground organization *Werwolf*, which also took its name from Lön's book. mh

Alfred Bochinski, Paul dall'Asta, and Fritz Kloppe, *Kamerad, weißt du noch? Erinnerungen aus der Geschichte des Wehrwolf 1923 – 1933*, brochure, Berlin-Neukölln, undated [1938]

No. 4-72

John Heartfield, *Das Gesicht des Faschismus* [The Face of Fascism], cover illustration of *Italien in Ketten* [Italy in Chains], published by the German Communist Party
Photomontage, July 1928

John Heartfield (pen name of Helmut Herzfelde, 1891 – 1968) was one of the most prominent artists of the Weimar Republic. During the 1920s and 1930s, he became famous for his political photomontages, which he created primarily for communist newspapers. His 1928 *Face of Fascism* shows the face of Italy's Benito Mussolini with the countenance of a death's head. It was also intended as a warning against the rise of National Socialism in Germany. Following Hitler's seizure of power, Heartfield only narrowly escaped being seized by National Socialist pursuers. He fled to Czechoslovakia at Easter of 1933, and to England in 1938. mh

Bildarchiv Preußischer Kulturbesitz, Berlin, 30001342

No. 4-73

Presentation of a new tank at the Reich Harvest Festival celebration at the Bückeberg near Hameln
Photograph: Arthur Grimm, October 1935

Some *Reichswehr* and subsequent *Wehrmacht* units cultivated a much stronger connection to the past than the SS. They saw themselves as direct successors of the Life Hussars and Braunschweig Hussars and thus wore the death's head as a symbol of tradition. Starting in 1935, the tank forces also wore it on the collar tabs of their black, specialized clothing, and sometimes also on their caps and epaulets. During the war, Allied soldiers in some cases mistook captured tank soldiers for SS men, with fateful consequences. mh

Bildarchiv Preußischer Kulturbesitz, Berlin, 30009360

No. 4-74

Members of the *Waffen-SS-Division Totenkopf* in a Volkswagen utility vehicle
Photograph: Cantzler, Soviet Union, 1941

The SS concentration camp guard units openly emphasized the threatening aspect of the death's head. They not only wore it on their caps, like all other SS formations, but also on their collar tabs (and occasionally on their sleeves). The prominent display of the symbol earned them the name "SS Death's Head Units," a title used informally at first and made their official designation in March 1936. The SS Death's Head Division was recruited from their ranks at the beginning of the war in fall 1939. As part of the *Waffen-SS*, these troops mercilessly carried out the National Socialists' racist policy of annihilation in Poland and other countries. mh

Bundesarchiv Koblenz, Image Archives, Bild 101III-Cantzler-045-05A

"Our new German nobility must, once again, become a vital source of highbred leadership talent. It must have institutions that retain proven blood in inheritance, repel that which is inferior, and constantly ensure the incorporation of new talent emerging from the people."
Italics in the original

No. 4-75, No. 4-76
Richard Walther Darré, *Neuadel aus Blut und Boden* [New Nobility from Blood and Soil]
J. F. Lehmanns Verlag, Munich, 1930
Quote: p. 39 f.
In his 1930 book, *Neuadel aus Blut und Boden*, Darré first elaborated in detail his ideas of a rural leadership caste, with the title of the book boldly proclaiming his programmatic goal. Darré envisioned a corporatively organized society led by a "new association of the nobility" comprised of owners of hunting manors and hereditary farms. His theory of a "new nobility" was not specifically tailored to the SS, but Darré nonetheless saw the SS, and especially the Race and Settlement Main Office he headed, as a means to realize his aims. The SS, however, conformed little to his ideals, and farmers were and remained very underrepresented in the organization. mh

Kreismuseum Wewelsburg, inv. no. 14127

No. 4-77
Hans F. K. Günther, *Adel und Rasse* [Nobility and Race]
2nd revised and expanded edition
Print run 4,000–8,000
J. F. Lehmanns Verlag, Munich, 1927
Author Hans F. K. Günther (1891 – 1968) was a *völkisch* race theoretician and a leading source of National Socialist catchwords. His writings greatly influenced both Richard Walther Darré and Heinrich Himmler. His numerous publications included the 1926 book *Adel und Rasse*. He emphasized the importance of nobility as a stronghold of social and biological selection and as a model for the "new nobility" emerging from a "youth stirred by the Nordic idea."

Unlike Darré, who applied Günther's ideas to farmers, Himmler hardly conceived of the SS as a rural elite – in spite of his penchant for agrarian policy in other areas, for instance that of settlement policy. It was more traditional aristocracy that he took as a model, praising it specifically for its attention to bloodlines and admiring it for its noble conduct and high regard for ancestry. mh

Kreismuseum Wewelsburg, inv. no. 16526

No. 4-81
"Nach Ostland geht unser Ritt" and "Nach Ostland wollen wir reiten" [We are Riding Towards the East Land]
The popular fantasies of the Germanic and heroic knighthood stood against the backdrop of a naïve, romantic glorification of the past, a view that had emerged in the nineteenth century and was then propagated again by the National Socialists in countless historical works, novels, books for children and young people, and songs. Discontent with the present dissipated into a yearning for historical national grandeur and its renewal.

Songs such as "Nach Ostland geht unser Ritt" and "Nach Ostland wollen wir reiten" from 1922 became popular, especially in the Third Reich, because they spoke to the widespread infatuation with the Middle Ages and the warlike ideologies of conquering lands in the east. mh

Lied im Volk. Musikbuch für höhere Jungenschulen, Adolf Strube (ed.), in collaboration with Kurt Benkel, Karl Rehberg, and Kurt Walther; Deutsches Volkslied, vol. 1, Verlag Merseburger & Co., Leipzig, 1942, p. 127
Kreismuseum Wewelsburg, inv. no. 16536

No. 4-78
Erich von dem Bach-Zelewski
wearing the uniform of an
SS-Oberführer
1932/1933
Süddeutscher Verlag Photo, 18280

No. 4-79
Portrait of Josias Erbprinz
zu Waldeck-Pyrmont as an
SS-Obergruppenführer
1936 (or later)
Bundesarchiv Koblenz, Bildarchiv,
Bild 146-1969-041-62

At least since his appointment as *Reichsführer-SS*, Heinrich Himmler actively sought to build ties with members of the German aristocracy to promote the social reputation of the SS. The generous awarding of SS honorary ranks served as a means of winning aristocrats over for the organization. After 1933, the SS did indeed become attractive to aristocrats already sympathizing with National Socialism. Erich von dem Bach-Zelewski (1899 – 1972), for instance, belonged to the petty gentry and had unsuccessfully tried to establish himself in various professions after World War I. The SS provided him with an opportunity to climb back up the social hierarchy.

Josias Erbprinz zu Waldeck und Pyrmont (1896 – 1967) was a member of the wealthy higher nobility. After 1918 he blamed the democratic Weimar Republic for the loss of his family's political influence. In an act of protest, he joined right-wing nationalist organizations, first the Young Germans Order (*Jungdeutscher Orden*), and then the National Socialist Party and the SS. A good friend of Himmler, he became his adjutant in September 1930. Waldeck used his prominent position in the SS to secure his extensive estate and land holdings.

In 1938, both Bach-Zelewski and Waldeck were promoted to the position of High-ranking SS and Police Leader (HSSPF). Within the SS, members of the HSSPF formed a leadership group with an larger-than-average proportion of aristocrats. mh

No. 4-80
SS-Gruppenführer Oswald Pohl
in a suit of armor
Oil on canvas
Ca. 1940
This oil portrait of *SS-Gruppenführer* Oswald Pohl, the powerful leader of the SS's economic, financial, and administrative institutions, shows the extent to which some SS members had internalized the idea of their organization as a knights' order. A former navy purser from a modest background, Pohl underscored his importance in the National Socialist political and ideological system by having himself pictured as a knight from the heroic past. As the chief of SS Main Office Budget and Buildings, Pohl was also responsible for converting the Wewelsburg Renaissance castle into a SS center suggestive of a medieval knight's castle. mh
On loan from the Deutsches Historisches Museum, Berlin, inv. no. 1988/420

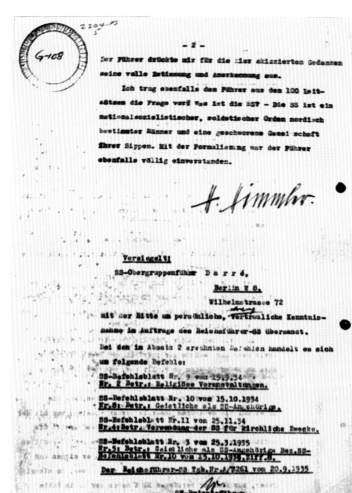

No. 4-82
Alfred Rosenberg
Between 1933 and 1939
On April 27, 1934, National Socialist
Party ideologue Alfred Rosenberg
(1893 – 1946) gave a speech at the
Marienburg (Malbork Castle), the
seat of the grandmaster of the
Teutonic Knights in the Middle
Ages. Under the title "The State of
the Teutonic Order," Rosenberg
developed the idea of a "political
order" as a principle of the order
and leadership of the National
Socialist state. This concept of
orders began to spread after Hitler
had taken it up, even if only for a
short time. The notion drawn on by
Rosenberg was also favored by, in
particular, Robert Ley, National
Socialist Party Reich Organization
Leader who renamed his ideological
training centers for the Party elite
"order castles" (*Ordensburgen*) , as
well as Heinrich Himmler. mh
Süddeutscher Verlag, Photo 97346

No. 4-83
Notes by Himmler made after a personal
meeting with Hitler on November 1, 1935,
p. 2 (excerpt)
Confidential memo for Richard
Walther Darré
November 1935
Over the course of 1935, Himmler worked
on several phrases that would capture the
concept behind his organization. In the
fall, he finally found an adequate formu-
lation. Slightly modifying his former
definition from the "Marriage Order" of
December 1931, he now declared the SS to
be a "National Socialist, soldierly order of
Nordic men and a sworn community of
their kin."

In a personal meeting on November 1,
Himmler presented Hitler with the results
of his search. In his memo Himmler wrote
that Hitler had "completely agreed" with
his proposal. mh
Institut für Zeitgeschichte, Munich, PS-2204

> "We have set forth and are marching, under immutable laws, as a National Socialist, soldierly order of Nordic men, and as a sworn community of their kin, along a path to a distant future, wishing and believing that we shall not only be the grandchildren who fought a better battle but also the ancestors of the latest generations necessary for the eternal life of the German Germanic people."

No. 4-84, No. 4-85
Heinrich Himmler, *Die SS als antibolschewistische Kampforganisation* [The SS as an anti-Bolshevist Combat Organization] Zentralverlag der NSDAP, Franz Eher Nachf., Munich 1936
Quote from p. 31
This booklet featured the transcript of a speech given by Himmler at the Reich Farmer's Day in Goslar on November 16, 1935. On this occasion, Himmler for the first time publicly referred to the SS as an "order." mh
Kreismuseum Wewelsburg, inv. no. 16942

No. 4-86
***Die Ordensgesetze der SS* [Rules of the SS Order], *Obergruppenführer* Fritz Weitzel (ed.) for the SS Main Sector West**
1938
Kreismuseum Wewelsburg, inv. no. 16370

No. 4-87
Not shown
***Erläuterungen der Ordensgesetze der SS* [Annotated Rules of the SS Order], *Obergruppenführer* Fritz Weitzel (ed.) for the SS Main Sector West**
1938
Kreismuseum Wewelsburg, inv. no. 16371

Neither Himmler nor the SS as a whole used the term "order" in a systematic manner, let alone developed a corresponding theory for their organization. The few attempts to do so were usually made on the initiative of individual members. For example, *SS-Obergruppenführer* Fritz Weitzel (1904 – 1940), the chief of police in Düsseldorf, issued two brochures for his area of command in which he renamed the "basic laws," i.e., the principles of the SS, the "laws of the SS order."

Himmler himself repeatedly stated that "the word 'order' was used too frequently." With his inner-party rivals Rosenberg and Ley in mind, he felt obliged to stress, "We are … not the, but a National Socialist soldierly order." mh

No. 4-88
***SS-Leitheft, Reichsführer-SS*, vol. 9, issue 2 (February 1943)**
Art direction: Hans Klöcker
Although Himmler's concept of an order seemed to capture essential features of the SS, it had several flaws that diminished its practical value. Apart from the fact that it was also used by competing National Socialist Party leaders, it had negative connotations: "order" sounded too much like an all-male or Catholic association. After all, monastic vows had been common in the much admired medieval chivalric orders. To make matters worse, Himmler had brought the term into use just as the SS and the Gestapo had initated massive repression against church orders. Nonetheless, the idea of an order continued to resurface within the SS, for instance in the *Leitheft* (Leadership Booklet). Published at the height of the war in February 1943, it invoked the historic importance and military achievements of knights' orders and unashamedly depicted the SS as the culmination of this tradition. mh
Kreismuseum Wewelsburg, inv. no. 6939

"Large parts of the German people as well as many members of the SS often take too lightly the offences and crimes committed against the written and unwritten laws of property. …
I therefore order that effective December 1, 1936, all locks are to be removed from lockers in all quarters of the SS Special Assignment Troops, SS Death's Head Units, and SS officer schools. Within a short period of time, it must become a matter of course to an SS man that he will not take minor or worthless objects, such as a comrade's cigarette, just as he does not take the greatest, most valuable treasure."

No. 4-89
"SS speist Kinder" [SS Feeds Children], propaganda article in the magazine for sustaining members of the SS
Photograph: P. Cortz
FM-Zeitschrift, vol. 3, issue 2 (February 1, 1936), p. 12

No. 4-90
Carnival party in the tavern at the Wewelsburg guard building Wewelsburg, 1938
Kreismuseum Wewelsburg, Fotoarchiv

The SS claimed to be an elite with the aim to act as a model for all of society through physical selection, purity of character, and community ideals, such as "comradeship," discipline, "decency," and selfless care.

In truth, however, the behavior of most SS members followed rather common social patterns. Their ostensible idealism often masked attempts to climb the social ladder, pursuit of personal advantages, the machinations of a male society, and camaraderie. The lines between legitimate and criminal acts became blurred. Personal enrichment, corruption, excessive violence, and alcoholic excesses were quite widespread within the SS.

It was a foregone conclusion that the purview of SS ideals did not extend to social outsiders and – after the beginning of the war – the populations of the occupied territories. mh

No. 4-92
An extra lesson on "loyalty" and "honor": Himmler's "Grundgesetz über die Heiligkeit des Eigentums" [Basic Law on the Sacredness of Property]
November 9, 1936
Quoted from the Bundesarchiv Berlin, NS 19/3902, sheet 145 f.

No. 4-91
Soldiers of the *Waffen-SS* in Cracow, probably during the liquidation of the Ghetto in March 1943
The Institute of National Remembrance, Warsaw, 28651

No. 4-94
Belt buckle for SS leaders. Text around centerpiece: "Meine Ehre heißt Treue" [My Honor is Loyalty] Sheet metal
Kreismuseum Wewelsburg, inv. no. 1853

No. 4-93
SS-Dienstdolch (service dagger) and metal scabbard, lettering etched into blade: "Meine Ehre heißt Treue" (My Honor is Loyalty)
Kreismuseum Wewelsburg, inv. no. 1121

No. 4-95
Stick pin with lettering "Sustaining member of the SS" (left) and honorary silver badge for "Old Fighters" among sustaining SS members (right)
Kreismuseum Wewelsburg, inv. nos. 16572 and 16574

No. 4-96
Julteller (Yule plate) from the SS's porcelain manufactory at Allach, with the inscription "Nur aus Opfern steigt groß das Reich" (Only from sacrifice will the Reich rise)
The Julteller was a popular present within SS circles.
Kreismuseum Wewelsburg, inv. no. 14330

Propaganda and Self-Affirmation: SS Publications

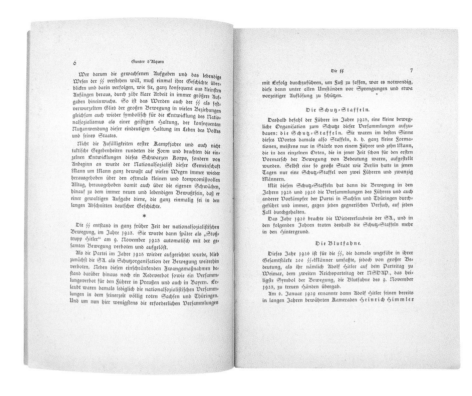

No. 4-99
Das Schwarze Korps [The Black Corps], vol. 1, issue 1 (March 6, 1935), p. 1
Founded in 1935, the SS newspaper *Das Schwarze Korps* was one of the most widely circulated weeklies in the Third Reich and the most important propaganda instrument of the SS. This is the cover of its first issue. mh
Kreismuseum Wewelsburg, inv. no. 5481/1

No. 4-100
Gunter d'Alquen, *Die SS. Geschichte, Aufgabe und Organisation der Schutz-staffeln der NSDAP* [The SS: The History, Tasks, and Organization of the Schutz-staffeln of the NSDAP]
The Reichsführer-SS, Schriften der Hochschule für Politik, Series II, vol. 33
Junker und Dünnhaupt Verlag, Berlin, 1939
Although many books were written and printed in SS circles, none contained a contemporary theory or a comprehensive presentation of the philosophy of the SS. One of the few attempts at such an over-view was published in this small brochure by Gunter d'Alquen (1910 – 1998), the editor-in-chief of *The Black Corps*. mh
Kreismuseum Wewelsburg, inv. no. 16983

In the course of the twelve years the National Socialist regime existed, it produced a vast amount of propaganda texts to disseminate its ideology. A significant number stemmed from the SS. Its publications were intended to promote the organization's standpoint and create internal cohesion. Their production and dispersal was also an economic factor, with the SS running its own publishing house, the Nordland-Verlag, as of 1934. It belonged to the SS business empire and was highly profitable, with print runs sometimes reaching into the millions.

Its publications included fiction, literature claiming to be scientific, and political pamphlets as well as picture and children's books. The entire range of SS ideological interests was represented, from an edification of a Germanic past, adoration of Hitler, and glorification of war to nutrition matters and a deliberate cultivation of conspiracy theories and enemy stereotypes.

Many Nordland-Verlag authors were SS members and a number of them worked for the Security Service of the *Reichsführer-SS* or the Reich Main Security Office. mh

No. 4-97
Not shown
SS-Leitheft, vol. 6, issue 2b (1940), war edition, published by SS Main Administrative Office –
Office of Education, Berlin
The thematic focus of this issue was "German settlement policy in the East." Initially, the *SS-Leitheft*e had served as internal training material. In later years, however, they aimed to present ideological content in the more sophisticated style of a cultural journal. mh
Kreismuseum Wewelsburg, inv. no. 6936

No. 4-98
Not shown
SS-Leitheft, vol. 8, issue 5 (1942), published by SS Main Administrative Office, Berlin
This *Leitheft* was dedicated to the subject of "peasantry."
Kreismuseum Wewelsburg, inv. no. 6938

No. 4-101
**Wulf Sörensen, *Stimme der Ahnen.
Eine Dichtung* [Ancestral Voices:
A Poem], Nordland-Bücherei
[Nordland Library], vol. 1, cover
drawing by August Ibing, Düsseldorf
Print run 35,000–40,000,
Magdeburg, ©1935**
Wulf Sörensen was a pen name of
the author Frithjof Fischer, who for
a time served as head of the Nord-
land-Verlag.

Kreismuseum Wewelsburg, inv. no. 14008

One of the most popular and successful segments of the SS book
business was the *Nordland-Bücherei* (Nordland Library). This was a
series of handily-sized, often
bibliophile books claiming literary
quality. Its volumes predominantly
offered poetry and fiction communicating National Socialist ideology, intellectual hardening for
battle, and rallying calls in the guise
of literature. mh

No. 4-102
**Heinz Ballensiefen, *Juden in Frankreich. Die
französische Judenfrage in Geschichte und
Gegenwart* [Jews in France: The French Jewish
Problem Past and Present], *Bücher zur Judenfrage* [Books on the Jewish Question]
Print run 1,000–5,000, Berlin, 1939**
Heinz Ballensiefen (born 1912) had a doctorate in
history and was a typical advocate of "research
into the Jewish Question" motivated by anti-
Semitism. He combined, as it were, academic
qualification with practical application. As an
"expert on Jews," he took part in establishing
several "institutes for research on Jews" in
Germany and in the occupied territories. He was
also a consultant for the Security Service (SD)
Office on "Jewish affairs." In the name of its
Amt VII (Enemy Ideology) of the Reich Main
Security Office, he confiscated valuable book
collections and literary estates, primarily from
Jewish owners. mh

Kreismuseum Wewelsburg, inv. no. 16533

No. 4-103
Not shown
**Adolf Roßberg, *Freimaurerei und Politik im
Zeitalter der Französischen Revolution* [Free-
masonry and Politics in the Age of the French
Revolution], *Quellen und Darstellungen zur
Freimaurerfrage* [Sources and Presentations
on the Free Masonry Question], vol. 2,
Berlin, 1942**
Roßberg's 1940 postdoctoral thesis was one of
several academic qualification studies produced
by young SS scholars using material collected in
the SD archives on Freemasonry. They were published in a Nordland-Verlag book series
dedicated to this field. mh

Kreismuseum Wewelsburg, inv. no. 16523

The ideological orientation of the Nordland-Verlag was overly apparent in several
special book series intended to provide
background information on the National
Socialists' fight against the three of their
main political and social opponents – the
Jews, religious institutions (particularly
the Catholic Church), and the Freemasons.
A series on Marxism was planned. The
series' "educational" aspect consisted in
part of pseudo-scientific studies and in
part of collections of quotations by prominent poets and thinkers. mh

No. 4-107
Otto Rahn, *Luzifers Hofgesind*
[Lucifer's Court]
Schwarzhäupter-Verlag,
Leipzig/Berlin, 1937
Writer Otto Rahn was a proponent of esoteric doctrines. His main interest was the
study of the legend of the Holy Grail, which
he associated with the medieval Christian
sect of the Cathars and their Château de
Montségur in France. From 1935, Rahn
worked at the SS Race and Settlement
Main Office. Following disputes with other
SS members, he was assigned guard duty
at the concentration camps Dachau and
Buchenwald in 1937 and 1938. His alcoholism and, presumably, fear that his ho-
mosexuality would be exposed led him to
commit suicide in 1939. ds
Kreismuseum Wewelsburg, inv. no. 16937

No. 4-104
Not shown
Jakob Wilhelm Hauer (ed.),
Deutscher Glaube. Zeitschrift
für arteigene Lebens-
gestaltung, Weltschau und
Frömmigkeit **[German Faith:**
Journal of Race-Specific
Conduct of Life, Worldview,
and Piety), December, 1942
Kreismuseum Wewelsburg, inv. no. 16725

No. 4-119
Cover of the SS-owned newspaper
Nordland, **vol. 5, issue 2**
(January 15, 1937), p. 1
This article from 1937 illustrates the religious significance Adolf Hitler had for
many *völkisch* believers. It depicts the
seizure of power by the National Socialists
on January 30, 1933, as a form of religious
awakening and stylizes Hitler as a champion of the *völkisch* community. This one-
sided view suppresses the fact that prior
to 1933 the *völkisch* movement had been
quite diverse. It had seen considerable
controversy, especially with regard to the
leadership role of the NSDAP as a political
party and to Hitler himself. Old rivalries
continued to play a role after 1933, with
some of these *völkisch* religious groups
being outlawed or having their activities
severely restricted. The best known
among them was the *Tannenbergbund* and
associated *Deutschvolk* group, which was
led by General Erich von Ludendorff and
his wife Mathilde. Ludendorff had been a
prominent army officer in World War I and
had collaborated with Hitler during the
1920s, jointly leading the Munich Beer Hall
Putsch with him in 1923. Afterwards their
relationship transformed into one of
competition for the leadership role in the
völkisch movement. It was only in 1937
that the two finally cleared up the matter.
Ludendorff's *Bund für Gotterkenntnis* was
then officially approved again – and it still
exists today. ds
Staatsbibliothek, Berlin

The works presented here are from authors within the SS who were interested
in which form the pagan religion of ancient Germanic peoples – the supposed
forbears of the Germans, might have had prior to the spread of Christianity.
This thematic perspective provided the basis for the creation of a new pagan
religion similar to the one Heinrich Himmler envisioned as an ideological
foundation of the SS. The *Reichsführer-SS* thus initiated and fostered work
in this area of enquiry. It made little difference to Himmler whether the
authors were scholars or esoterics acting as layman researchers. Many of
these ideologically motivated writers had already been dabbling in this field
before 1933 and it was their reputation in that area that led Himmler to bring
them into the SS. While he did not issue any specific guidelines for their
"research," they all based their work on the same fixed premises of a racist,
anti-Semitic, and anticlerical ideology. The Germans, they believed, formed
a "master race" that stood above all others. Their research, therefore, only
focused on which religious practices their "ancestors" had engaged in. Of
course, the lack of sources on pre-Christian religious ideas in North and Central Europe left them plenty of room for interpretation and speculation. ds

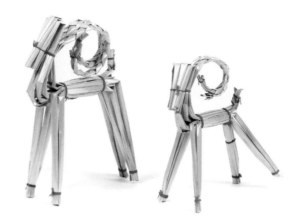

No. 4-106
Not shown
Karl August Eckhardt, *Irdische Unsterblichkeit. Germanischer Glaube an die Wiedergeburt in der Sippe* [Worldly Immortality: The Germanic Faith in Rebirth within the Kin] *Studien zur Rechts- und Religionsgeschichte* [Studies on Legal and Religious History], vol. 1 Böhlau Nachf. Verlag, Weimar, 1937
In 1937 law professor Karl August Eckhart began teaching Germanic History of Law at Bonn University. As head of the "Deutschrechtliches Institut des *Reichsführers-SS*" (Department of German Law of the *Reichsführer-SS*) he was a member of Himmler's Personal Staff. ds
Kreismuseum Wewelsburg, inv. no. 16612

No. 4-105
Not shown
Otto Huth, *Die Fällung des Lebensbaumes. Die Bekehrung der Germanen in völkischer Sicht* [Felling the Tree of Life: The Conversion of the Germanic Peoples from a Völkisch Perspective], *Das deutsche Leben* [The German Life], vol. 2 Widukind Verlag, Berlin-Lichterfelde, 1936
Otto Huth held a doctorate in religious studies and a university professorship as of 1942. He headed the "Institute for Indo-Germanic Religious History," a department of the SS research society Das Ahnenerbe, and on the staff of its journal *Germanien*. ds
Kreismuseum Wewelsburg, inv. no. 16902

The proponents of *völkisch* religious notions also aimed to "Germanize" the private celebration of Christmas as well. Decoration of the *Julbaum* (Yule tree) was to be kept as simple as possible, consisting of apples, nuts, candles, and a symbolically shaped pastry known as the *Gebildbrot*. The new customs, however, also included glass *Julkugeln* (Yule orbs) showing various symbols and runes. The examples shown here were probably originally transparent and later "beautified" with color.

The two straw *Julböcke* (Yule rams) illustrate that the SS drew inspiration for the design of their new traditions from Scandinavia, a region they considered to be particularly authentic and pagan. In addition, the perception existed in these circles that many rural customs were old Germanic traditions that the church had simply taken over and reinterpreted, which now needed to be restored to their original meaning. In this vein, the celebration of Thanksgiving, which were intended to demonstrate the connection of the German farmer with their ancestral "blood and soil," played an important role in the National Socialist calendar.

Even the *Dreihasenfenster* (Window of Three Hares) in Paderborn Cathedral, which symbolizes the Holy Trinity, was declared a pagan symbol. Easter was no longer dedicated to Christ's resurrection but to a goddess named Ostara. ds

No. 4-109
Advertisement in the SS newspaper *Nordland* for the book *Die Gestaltung der Feste im Jahreslauf* [The Arrangement of Celebrations in the Course of the Year], Sigrune Verlag, Erfurt *Nordland*, vol. 8, issue 41 (October 12, 1940), p. 7
Lippische Landesbibliothek, Detmold, 2 St 2315

No. 4-108
Two *Julböcke* (Yule rams) from the estate of an *SS-Obersturmbannführer* Straw 1930s/1940s
Kreismuseum Wewelsburg, inv. nos. 15682/1 and 15682/2

No. 4-111
Harvest Crown from the estate of an *SS-Obersturmbannführer* Straw 1930s/1940s
Kreismuseum Wewelsburg, inv. no. 15681

No. 4-110
Not shown
Allgemeine Richtlinien für die Feier zur Sommersonnenwende bei den Ausbildungshundertschaften, Schutzpolizeihundertschaften, mot.[orisierten] Gendamerie-Bereitschaften und Schutzpolizei und Gendamerieschulen [Guidelines for the summer solstice celebrations staged by various police organizations] May 12, 1938
The SS also involved itself practically in the arrangement of their neo-pagan customs. Within the Race and Settlement Main Office, a special department was responsible for defining the appearance and procedures of the particular festivities. Based on the assumption that the ancient Germanic tribes had adhered to a pagan sun cult and the winter and summer solstice celebrations, in particular, could be traced back to pagan rituals, the SS placed great importance on these two events in their newly developed traditions. Those in Berlin responsible for planning these events specified all of their aspects in great detail. Even the stacking of logs for the solstice fire was precisely regulated. Instructions were given on how to handle winds from various directions, which marching routes to take on arrival, and how to sing songs.

The winter solstice celebration on December 21 was followed by the so-called *Julfeier* (Yule celebration), which the SS members celebrated as a unit, together with their *Sippenangehörigen* (members of kin). ds
Niedersächsisches Landesarchiv, Hauptstaatsarchiv Hannover, 122a no. 2625, *Polizei – Allgemeines und Verschiedenes*, vol. 3, p. 307

Zur Herstellung des "U r g l a u b e n s" , der nie den Fortschritten allen Wissens und der Naturerkenntnisse zu widersprechen vermag, sind folgende Maßregeln seitens des Staates in k l u g e r Aufeinanderfolge nötig:

1. Vollster Denkmalschutz für alle Museen (auch sogenannte private !), Kunsterzeugnisse aller Art (insbesondere solche aus vorgeschichtlicher Zeit bis ins 17.Jahrhundert),Bauten, Höhlen,Denksteine, Felsgebilde, Kirchen, Kapellen und Wallanlagen, sowie für alle Funde aus dem Boden.
Die Denkmal-Schutz-Vorschriften sind wiederholt und regelmäßig im Jahre überall zu verlautbaren !

2. Erfassung aller Kirchenbesitze, zuerst in Evidenz. Dann "Ausgleich" dieser nach den derzeitigen Verhältnissen der Gläubigenzahl, da z.B. viele protestantisch oder deutschgläubig u.s.w. wurden und daher vollberechtigten Anspruch auf Anteil eines "Kirchenbesitzes" zu haben, der ihnen durch Glaubenswechsel in den Übergangszeiten verloren ging......

3. Allmähliche Aufhebung der Klosterschulen nach gleichem Gesichtspunkte. (Bei Neubauten von Kirchen und Klöstern ist deren Notwendigkeit dem Staate durch Namens- und Adressen-Anführung aus den betreffenden Gemeinden, Bezirken, Gauen u.s.w. genauest nachzuweisen!)

4. Allen Berufsausbildungen zu Priestern hat stets die staatliche voranzugehen und darf vor dem 24.Lebensjahre überhaupt nicht angetreten werden !

5. Sodann hat die Auflösung aller männlichen und weiblichen Klöster platzzugreifen, wobei man vorher mit einer genauen Kontrolle der Staatsangehörigkeit in allen Klöstern vorgehen und alle "Nicht Teutschen" ausweisen kann. Nur die einem charitativen Zwecke dienenden sind anfangs zu belassen.

6. Sodann sind auch die humanitären Zwecken dienenden Anstalten in staatlichen Besitz und Betrieb überzuführen, wobei man anfangs die dortselbst tätigen Personen bis zum Tode belässt, aber keine Neuaufnahmen von Geistlichen oder Nonnen duldet.

7. Energische Maßregelung von Geistlichen, die"Proselyten" zu machen, sich evtl. Kirchenaustritten entgegenstellen oder gegen Andersdenkende öffentlich oder von den Kanzeln auftreten.

8. Beschlagnahme aller Kirchenvermögen ohne Unterschied, Verbot aller"Erbschaften" für Kirchenzwecke, wobei solche Testamente als ungiltig erklärt werden und solche testierte Vermögen sofort dem Staate zuzufallen haben.

9. Unschädlichmachung von Geistlichen aller Grade mittels der dem Staate zur Verfügung stehenden Mittel.........

10. Alle Glaubens-Vereinigungen haben ihre Funktionäre aus diesen jährlich neu zu bemessenden Mitteln selbst zu erhalten !
Die Glaubensvereinigungen finanzieren sich also ausschliesslich aus eigenen Mitteln aus Beiträgen!

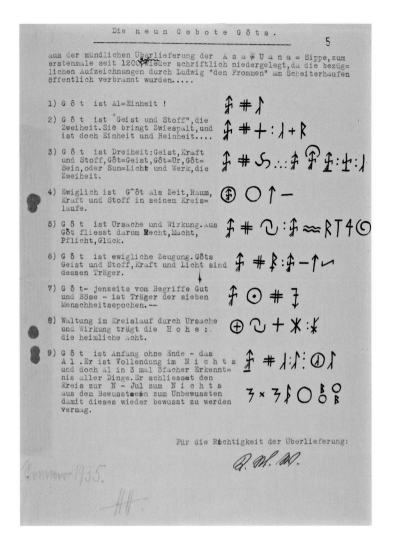

aus der mündlichen Überlieferung der A s a ᛉ U a n a = Sippe,zum erstenmale seit 1200 Jahre schriftlich niedergelegt,da die bezüglichen Aufzeichnungen durch Ludwig "den Frommen" am Scheiterhaufen öffentlich verbrannt wurden.....

1) G ô t ist Al=Einheit !

2) G ô t ist "Geist und Stoff",die Zweiheit.Sie bringt Zwiespalt,und ist doch Einheit und Reinheit....

3) G ô t ist Dreiheit:Geist,Kraft und Stoff,Gôt=Geist,Gôt=Ur,Gôt= Sein,oder Sun=Licht und Werk,die Zweiheit.

4) Ewiglich ist Gˆôt als Zeit,Raum, Kraft und Stoff in seinem Kreis= laufe.

5) G ô t ist Ursache und Wirkung.Aus Gôt fliesst darum Recht,Macht, Pflicht,Glück.

6) G ô t ist ewigliche Zeugung.Gôts Geist und Stoff,Kraft und Licht sind dessen Träger.

7) G ô t- jenseits vom Begriffe Gut und Böse - ist Träger der sieben Menschheitsepochen.--

8) Waltung im Kreislauf durch Ursache und Wirkung trägt die H o h e : die heimliche Acht.

9) G ô t ist Anfang ohne Ende - das A l .Er ist Vollendung im N i c h t s und doch Al in 3 mal 3facher Erkennt= nis aller Dinge.Er schliesst den Kreis zur N - Jul zum N i c h t s aus dem Bewusstsein zum Unbewussten damit dieses wieder bewusst zu werden vermag.

Für die Richtigkeit der Überlieferung:

No. 4-114
Karl Maria Wiligut, "Zur Herstellung des Urglaubens" [On the Establishment of the Original Faith], with Wiligut's stylized signature
Undated
Translation on page 447
Bundesarchiv Berlin, NS 19/3670, p. 1

No. 4-115
Karl Maria Wiligut, "Die neun Gebote Gôts"
[The Nine Commandments of Gôt]
Lower left: Heinrich Himmler's initials, indicating he had read and approved the text.
1935
Wiligut's concept of religion was based on a blend of various esoteric teachings. He proclaimed the existence of an "Irminic" religion, which saw the ancient Germans had been worshipping a Germanic god named "Krist" some twelve thousand years before Christ. Only later, he claimed, did Christian churches adopt this god as their Christ. The ancient Germans, Willigut wrote, went through a schism, in the course of which the followers of the German pagan diety Wotan attacked the Irminic believers. At the height of the war between the two groups, the Irminian prophet Baldur-Krestos was crucified in Goslar. Ultimately, the Wotanists succeeded in destroying the Irminic belief's religious center in Goslar, after which the Irminic believers founded a new temple at the Externsteine near Detmold. Wiligut identified "Gôt" as the primal principle and an eternal spiritual power. This doctrine represented a modified version of the teachings of the Ariosophy founder, Guido List, who promoted a religious nature mysticism and belief in the Germanic god Wotan. ds
Bundesarchiv Berlin, NS 19/3671, p. 5

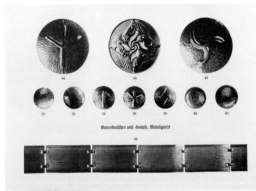

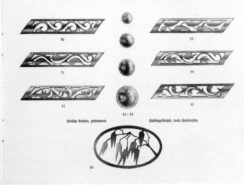

No. 4-112
Karl Maria Wiligut, alias Weisthor, in the uniform of an *SS-Brigadeführer*. The rune on his sleeve identified him as an employee of the SS Race and Settlement Main Office. Photograph: Atelier Bieber/Nather Berlin, September 13, 1935
A former Austrian army officer, Karl Maria Wiligut, also known as Weisthor, was a *völkisch* esoteric who influenced both Heinrich Himmler and Richard Walther Darré, the head of the SS Race and Settlement Main Office. Wiligut joined the SS in 1934 and was already promoted to the high rank of *Brigadeführer* in 1935. The 1938 letter shown is a testament to the mutual respect of Himmler and Wiligut. The latter adhered to the so-called Ariosophy, a radical, racist doctrine based on mystic and occult ideas. He believed he was descended from a long line of Germanic sages reaching back to the ancient Germanic "Asen" gods. Williqut claimed the ability of "ancestral memory," which enabled him to intuit the world of the old Germanic culture. The disclosure in 1939 that Wiligut had spent from 1924 to 1927 in a psychiatric institution in addition to his increasingly evident alcoholism resulted in Wiligut having to leave the SS. ds
Bildarchiv Preußischer Kulturbesitz, Berlin, 10017758

No. 4-113
**Karl Maria Wiligut
(1866 – 1946)**
Kreismuseum Wewelsburg, Fotoarchiv

No. 4-117
Cardboard box, glued-in descriptions of the brooches
Kreismuseum Wewelsburg, inv. no. 15149

No. 4-118
**Brooch with triskele
Non-ferrous metal**
Kreismuseum Wewelsburg, inv. no. 15147

No. 4-116
**Catalog from Helmut Greif Goldsmiths
1938**
Kreismuseum Wewelsburg, inv. no. 16829

No. 4-121
Not shown
**Cross erected by the citizens of Lügde in 1935
1938**
Kreismuseum Wewelsburg, inv. no. 16805

No. 4-120
The 72nd SS Regiment Detmold escorts the *Osterrad* (Easter Wheel) of Lügde with the inscription "Ein Volk Ein Reich Ein Führer" (One People One Reich One Führer) April 17, 1938
Kreismuseum Wewelsburg, inv. no. 16805

The adaptation of Christian customs by the SS is epitomized by the traditional rolling of "Easter wheels" on Easter Sunday in the city of Lügde in the Lippe district. To this day, the people of Lügde send straw-stuffed burning oak wheels rolling down from the mountain into the valley. The wheels are decorated with pious phrases celebrating the resurrection of Jesus Christ. The SS, however, re-interpreted the ceremony as a relic of a prehistoric Germanic sun cult. In 1937, the SS took over the organization of the event, against the will of parts of the population. The Party had already tried earlier to co-opt the festivity, and in 1935, in an attempt to resist such moves, some Lügde residents had erected a large wooden cross on the private lot where the wheels were launched downhill, to profess quite publicly their faith in traditional Christianity. Ultimately, however, they were unable to stop the takeover by the SS. ds

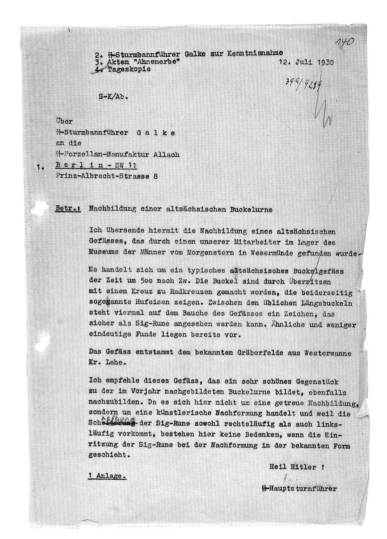

No. 4-124
Cinerary urn/*Buckelurne*
with sig runes from the Allach
Porcelain Manufactory
Brown glazed clay
1936 – 1945
Kreismuseum Wewelsburg,
inv. no. 14671

No. 4-123
"Bowl with Germanic
Motives," Allach Porcelain
Manufactory, catalog no. K 6.
The catalog describes the
bowl as "clay, brown,
diameter 25 cm, 7 Reichs-
mark"
1938/1939
Kreismuseum Wewelsburg,
inv. no. 17185

Reichsführer-SS Heinrich Himmler strongly believed in the significance of the past
for the present – to the extent that he had
his office furnished with archeological
artifacts. In the same spirit, the SS-owned
Allach Porcelain Manufactory (PMA)
started producing an inexpensive series
under the name *Germanische Keramik*
(Germanic Ceramics) in 1938. The design
of the pieces was a reinterpretation of
that of original artifacts, as is evident in
the two urns shown here. This urn form
from the third to fifth centuries was
attributed by archaeologists to the Saxon
tribe. The decoration with swastikas and
sig runes was developed by the PMA. ds

No. 4-122
Letter from Wolfram Sievers,
general secretary of the SS-Ahnen-
erbe, to *SS-Sturmbannführer* Galke
July 12, 1938
Translation on page 447
This letter shows the readiness of
the SS Ahnenerbe management to
modify the planned replica of an
ancient Saxon Buckelurne from
Westerwanna in the Lehe district to
make the sig runes clearly discernible. This falsification is described
as "artistic recreation." ds
Bundesarchiv Berlin, former Berlin Document
Center, Sievers, Wolfram, Ordner 1, p. 140

No. 4-129
Not shown
Herman Wirth, *Führer durch die*
erste urreligionsgeschichtliche
Ausstellung "Der Heilbringer."*
Von Thule bis Galiläa und von Galiläa
bis Thule
[Guide to the First Exhibition on the
History of Ancient Religion:
"The Savior." From Thule to Galilee
and from Galilee to Thule.]
Organized by the Research Institute
for Ancient Intellectual History Bad
Doberan i.[n] M.[ecklenburg],
Directed by Prof. Herman Wirth
Koehler und Amelung Verlag,
Leipzig, 1933
Exhibition dates: May 2 to 15, 1933
Kreismuseum Wewelsburg,
inv. no. 16552

No. 4-128
Wilhelm Teudt, *Germanische Heiligtümer, Beiträge zur Aufdeckung der Vorgeschichte, ausgehend von den Externsteinen, den Lippequellen und der Teutoburg* [Germanic Sanctuaries: Contributions to the Discovery of Prehistory, Beginning with the Externsteine, the Lippe Springs, and the Teutoburg]
4th revised and expanded edition
Eugen-Diederichs-Verlag, Jena, 1936
Kreismuseum Wewelsburg, inv. no. 14639

No. 4-130
Not shown
Declaration of membership in the Ahnenerbe Society
Kreismuseum Wewelsburg, inv. no. 16830

No. 4-131
Not shown
Special order of the Race and Settlement Main Office to establish a registration office for archeological artifacts under its Department for Pre- and Ancient History
May 11, 1935
Bundesarchiv Berlin, NS 2/152, p. 6

Until 1936, most historical policy departments of the SS were part of the Race and Settlement Main Office (RuSHA), which was also responsible for ideological training. Heinrich Himmler also employed historical consultants on his staff. The growing power of the SS along with ever new initiatives resulted in parallel SS departments with similar orientations. Himmler, therefore, restructured the allocation of tasks in 1937. The integration of the Ahnenerbe Society into the Personal Staff of the *Reichsführer-SS* marked the beginning of its upgrading. From 1938 onwards, both existing and newly formed research departments came under its control, with responsibilities ranging from archeological excavations to applied research into "military science" which was carried out using concentration camp prisoners. In the process, amateur *völkisch*, or "folk," researchers were dismissed from prominent positions and replaced by SS members with established reputations in science. ds

No. 4-126
Wilhelm Teudt (in civilian clothes) talking to the first administrator of the Wewelsburg Castle, Manfred von Knobelsdorff
Both esoteric amateur researchers and academically trained cultural studies scholars participated in the SS's search for the Germans' "Germanic heritage." This resulted in a constant tension between the esoteric quest for meaning and the claim to academic standards within its Germanic studies.

The "intuitive approach" to the past was represented within the SS in a publicity-counscious manner by Herman Wirth and Wilhelm Teudt, in particular. Both had already been active prior to 1933 as völkisch "founders of religion." Together with Himmler and Richard Walter Darré, head of the Race and Settlement Main Office, Herman Wirth established the SS research society Das Ahnenerbe in 1935. Wilhelm Teudt transferred his research activities at the Externsteine (a rock formation he considered a Germanic shrine) to the SS.

In 1938 both Wirth and Teudt had to leave the SS-Ahnenerbe. The research entity's increased collaboration with academic researchers made the presence of dilettantes in prominent positions inopportune. Teudt and Himmler parted ways, but Herman Wirth continued to receive SS research grants until 1945. ds
Landesarchiv NRW, Abteilung Ostwestfalen-Lippe, Detmold, D 72 (Wilhelm Teudt), no. 14

No. 4-125
Archeologist Alexander Langsdorff giving a speech before the *Leibstandarte Adolf Hitler* on the premises of the Staatliches Museum für Völkerkunde (State Museum of Ethnology), Saarlandstraße, Berlin
Photograph: Scherl, 1935
Professor Alexander Langsdorff served as a curator at the Staatliches Museum für Vor- und Frühgeschichte (State Museum of Pre- and Ancient History) in Berlin, which ranked as one of the world's leading institutions of its kind in the 1930s. Langsdorff belonged to the squad of academically trained scholars within the SS. Irrespective of their different approaches, Langsdorff and all SS members were convinced of a fundamental proposition that excluded any possibility of scientific method regarding their subject of research: the chosenness of the "Germanic" race as forbears of the Germans, who were superior to all other peoples. ds
Bundesarchiv Koblenz, Bildarchiv, 183-2008-0229-500

No. 4-127
Not shown
Invitation to a lecture at the Detmold branch of the *Deutschbund*
1928
Many in the ethno-nationalist (*völkisch*) movement believed that the original homeland of the Aryans was the legendary continent of Atlantis, the first mention of which is found in the writings of Greek philosopher Plato. Atlantis was considered synonymous with the mythical island of Thule. The *Deutschbund* was one of the first *völkisch* groups, having already been founded in 1894. Its followers came predominately from the middle class, with many being prominent members of society. In 1928, the Detmold branch of the *Deutschbund* was led by amateur *völkisch* researcher and former Protestant pastor Wilhelm Teudt. That same year, Teudt founded the "Vereinigung der Freunde germanischer Vorgeschichte" ("Association of the Friends of Germanic Prehistory"), which was active at the Externsteine. ds
Kreismuseum Wewelsburg, inv. no. 16831

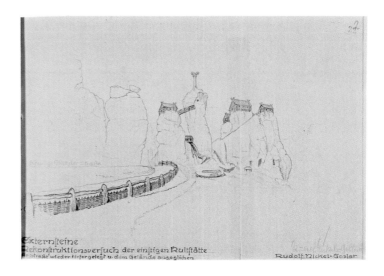

No. 4-134

Memorandum by the Head of the Cultural Department of the Administration of Rhine Province, Hans Joachim Apfelstaedt, on a conversation with Heinrich Himmler
July 10, 1935

According to this memo, Himmler considered the hill fort on the Erdenburg near Cologne, a structure dating from the first century B.C., to be a Germanic cult site. The existence of such sanctuaries was a central theme in the mindset of the *Reichsführer-SS*. Their excavation and redesign by the SS was to serve as ideological training. Himmler's emphasis on "exact scientific research" points to the increasing activity of academically trained researchers within the SS as of 1935. This, however, did not mean that the ideological element was neglected.

The letter also illustrates that the field of prehistoric research was marked by fierce competition, particularly with the group around Alfred Rosenberg. As the "Representative of the *Führer* for the Oversight of the Complete Intellectual and Ideological Training and Education of the NSDAP," Rosenberg also sought to gain control of the cultural policy activities in the field of "Germanic research." ds

Archiv des Landschaftsverbandes Rheinland, Provinzialverband 11399

No. 4-132

Reconstruction sketch of the "cult site" at the Externsteine, including the erected Irminsul column

Bundesarchiv Berlin, NS 19/1631, p. 2

On the basis of theories developed by the local amateur researcher Wilhelm Teudt, the SS declared the Externsteine, near Detmold in the Lippe district, to be an ancient cult site. This led to large-scale excavations intended to establish the site's ancient age and significance as a prehistoric astronomical observatory, as well as the location of the so-called Irminsul – the alleged holy column of the Saxons. The excavations were so ideologically charged that their findings dating the site to the Middle Ages were not published. This, however, did not hinder the propagandistic redesign and exploitation of the surroundings. The Externsteine became a tourist attraction offering guided tours for private guests as well as National Socialist Party organizations, with the SS also staging summer solstice festivals there. ds

No. 4-133

"Haltet Ruhe am Heiligtum der Ahnen!" (Maintain quiet at the ancestral shrine!)

LWL-Freilichtmuseum Detmold – Westfälisches Landesmuseum für Volkskunde, Sammlung Wolf

The importance the SS attached to the Externsteine was reflected in the fact that the Detmold Germanic Lore Protective Society (*Pflegstätte für Germanenkunde*), which was founded in 1936 and took over maintenance of the Externsteine in 1937, was slated to become the headquarters of the Ahnenerbe after the war. Himmler, however, also promoted other cult sites. The SS, for example, took over patronage of the *Widukind-Gedächtnisstätte* (Widukind Memorial Site) in Enger. In Verden, the SS designed the so-called *Sachsenhain* (Saxons' Grove), where 4,500 boulders were placed to commemorate the pagan Saxons allegedly murdered there by Charlemagne. ds

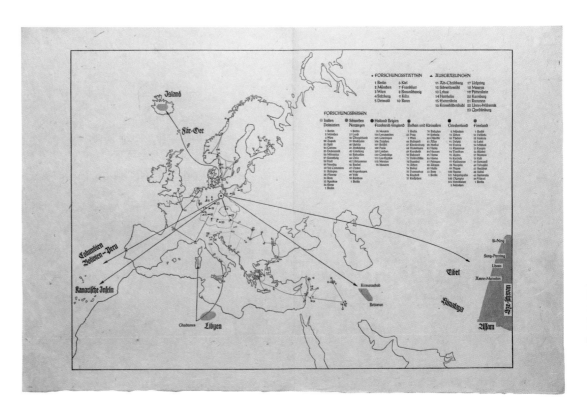

No. 4-137
Edmund Kiss, *Das Sonnentor von Tihuanaku und Hörbigers Welteislehre* [The Sun Gate of Tihuanaku and Hörbiger's World Ice Theory]
Koehler und Amelung Verlag, Leipzig, 1937

Kreismuseum Wewelsburg, inv. no. 16808

No. 4-136
***Geheimnis Tibet: Erster Bericht der Deutschen Tibet-Expedition Ernst Schafers 1938/1939* [The Secret of Tibet: The First Report of Ernst Schafer's German Tibet Expedition 1938/1939]**
Bruckmann Verlag, Munich, 1943

Kreismuseum Wewelsburg, Inv. Nr. 16647

No. 4-135
Map of the realized and planned expeditions of the SS-Ahnenerbe
***Die Forschungsgemeinschaft Das Ahnenerbe: Werden, Wesen, Wirken* [The Ahnenerbe Research Institute: Becoming, Being, Effecting], Offenbach, 1939**

This map illustrates both the global reach of Ahnenerbe society research planning and the limits to what was actually achieved. The map includes all planned expeditions canceled upon the onset of war.

These global plans were based on the assumption that there had once been a primeval Aryan race, which had colonized the entire world and from which modern Aryan Germans descended. Ahnenerbe Researchers suspected to find traces of this race in all parts of the world.

Two expeditions epitomize these SS-sponsored ventures: one by Edmund Kiss to Bolivia, which was slated for 1940 but never realized, and Ernst Schäfer's expedition to Tibet.

In 1938 and 1939 the Tibet expedition explored the region of the Himalayas. Its participants documented fauna and flora but also conducted racial measurements on the Tibetan population. The anthropologist in charge, Bruno Beger, hoped the results would lead him to traces of the primeval Aryan race. The Tibet expedition became a media sensation, and spawned the successful 1943 film *Geheimnis Tibet* [The Secret of Tibet].

While the work of the Tibet explorers was acknowledged by fellow scientists, the methods Edmund Kiss applied in Bolivia were disputed. Kiss believed in the World Ice Theory (*Welteislehre*), which not only postulated that the entire universe developed from ice, but also that all weather and astronomical phenomena derive from ice. This theory enjoyed much popularity but was debunked by fellow scientists. Kiss nevertheless held the opinion that in the distant past, ice moons had collided with the Earth and triggered massive climate catastrophes. The primeval Nordic race would thus have been forced to retreat to the Andes, Himalayas, and Ethiopian highlands. In 1928, Kiss had already visited Tihuanacu, a city in the Andes that had existed from 2000 to 1200 B.C. As he did not believe the Natives capable of building such impressive structures, he declared it to be a town founded by Nordic-Germanic peoples. Based on a building referred to as the "Sun Gate," whose ornamentation was interpreted as a calendar, Kiss concluded that the migration to this area by the primeval Aryans had occurred several million years ago. ds

Original in the public domain

König Heinrichs Gruft in Quedlinburg

KOENIG HEINRICH I·

er war der Erfte unter Gleichen, und es wurde ihm eine gröfiere
und wahre menfchliche Ehrfurcht entgegengebracht, als fpäter
Kaifern, Königen und Fürften, die fie nach volksfremdem byzanti-
nifchen Jeremoniell forderten, je zuteil wurde· er hieß Herzog
und König und war ein Führer vor taufend Jahren·

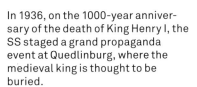

In 1936, on the 1000-year anniversary of the death of King Henry I, the SS staged a grand propaganda event at Quedlinburg, where the medieval king is thought to be buried.

King Henry of Saxony (876–936) played a significant role in the National Socialist view of history. His campaigns against Hungarians and Slavs, and the subsequent settlement of territories east of the Elbe and Saale with German subjects, were interpreted by many historians as the first German colonization of the East, which resonated with the National Socialist ideology encompassing the German Drang nach Osten (drive toward the East).

Up until 1944, the SS annually reprised the King Henry Celebration, hailing Quedlinburg as a "national site of consecration." Because in 1936 the location of the tomb of Henry I was still unknown, the SS proceeded with excavations beneath Quedlinburg cathedral. In 1937, in due time for the second King Henry Celebration, Rolf Höhne, the employee at the Race and Settlement Main Office tasked with the search, unveiled what were claimed to be the skeletal remains of Henry and his wife Mathilda, which were subsequently reburied as part of a pompous ceremony. ds

No. 4-139
Excerpt from a speech by Heinrich Himmler in Quedlinburg
Das Schwarze Korps [The Black Corps], vol. 1938, issue 52 (December 23, 1938), p. 11

King Henry I.
The first among equals, he was shown more sincere reverence than later emperors, kings and princes, who demanded it according to Byzantine ceremonial foreign to their subjects. He was called duke and king and was leader a thousand years ago.
Reichsführer-SS Heinrich Himmler

Translation of a transcription

No. 4-138
Not shown
Speech by the *Reichsführer-SS* at Quedlinburg cathedral on July 2, 1936, special printing
Nordland Verlag, Magdeburg 1936

Kreismuseum Wewelsburg, inv. no. 16648

No. 4-141
Brooch with Viking ship motif
Silver, possibly from a Scandinavian workshop
Probably after 1936

Kreismuseum Wewelsburg, inv. no. 15266

No. 4-142
Brooch with Viking ship motif
Silver, presumed to be a replica, produced at the Gahr workshop, of the Scandinavian original.
Probably after 1936

Kreismuseum Wewelsburg, inv. no. 15265

No. 4-143
Thor's hammer
Silver
Gahr workshop (?)
Ca. 1934

Kreismuseum Wewelsburg, inv. no. 15263

No. 4-144
Wolfgang Willrich, *Thorshammerträgerin aus Siebenbürgen* [Woman from Transylvania wearing Thor's Hammer]
The drawing appeared as an illustration in Wolfgang Willrich/ Richard Walther Darré, *Bauerntum als Heger deutschen Blutes* [The Peasantry as the Keeper of German Blood]
Blut- und Bodenverlag, Goslar, 1935

Kreismuseum Wewelsburg, inv. no. 14470

Beginning in 1938, the excavations at the Haithabu Viking settlement in Schleswig were turned into an SS-Ahnenerbe showcase project. The cultic classification of Haithabu as a central Viking site also found artistic expression. Jewelers Otto and Karolina Gahr, frequent recipients of SS commissions, produced the silver replica of a so-called Thor's hammer after an original from Haithabu. In the ethnonationalist (*völkisch*) movement, Thor's hammer represented an avowal of new pagan beliefs. The image, by the prominent völkisch painter Wolfgang Willrich, depicts a young woman from Transylvania, in Romania.

The two Viking ship brooches displayed here represent an original one, presumably from a Scandinavian workshop (1), and a replica from the Gahr workshop (2). While the prototype depicts a mythical creature blowing into the sail, the replica shows no such figure. Moreover, Gahr changed the swastikas of the original to the Olaf Cross, adopted by Norway's fascist Nasjonal Samling party in an effort to place it within the Viking tradition. The Vikings were the epitome of the fearless, heroic Germanic warriors and explorers, and were alleged to have been conscious of their race.

Since its founding in 1933, Nordland-Verlag, the publishing house under the auspices of the SS, had also used the Viking ship as its signet. ds

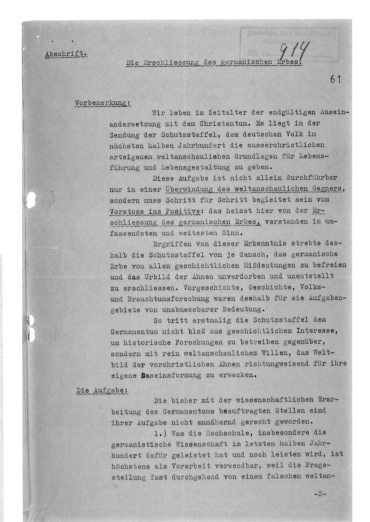

No. 4-140
Nordland-Verlag bookmark
Kreismuseum Wewelsburg, inv. no. 16826

No. 4-145
Plan for development of the Germanic heritage
1937
The document is a draft for a 1937 SS research project. The plan rests upon the notion that a racially defined Germanic heritage is preserved in German folklore and can again be exposed by removing the various layers of falsifying sediment. The church was designated as the primary adversary for allegedly having suppressed the original nature of the Germanic peoples through Christianization.

The plan was shared with various SS researchers active in this field, who for the most part found it exceedingly ambitious and wished to see the project entrusted to their own organizations. The SS-Ahnenerbe was ultimately granted the job of producing an encyclopedia of Germanic studies over the course of several years. ds
Bundesarchiv Berlin, NS 19/2241. pp. 61–63

No. 4-149
Not shown
Headquarters of the SS-Ahnenerbe (Ancestral Heritage Research Institute) at the aryanized villa at Pückler Straße 16 in Berlin-Dahlem
1940
Bildarchiv Preußischer Kulturbesitz, Berlin, 30019004

No. 4-150
Entrance of the Villa at Pückler Straße 16; note the tapestry with the Ahnenerbe emblem
1940
Bildarchiv Preußischer Kulturbesitz, Berlin, 30019002

No. 4-146
Not shown
"Die Forschungs- und Lehrgemeinschaft 'Das Ahnenerbe'" [Ahnenerbe Research and Teaching Community], *Die Forschungsgemeinschaft Das Ahnenerbe: Werden, Wesen, Wirken* [The Ahnenerbe Research Institute: Becoming, Being, Effecting], Offenbach, 1939
This commemorative publication was made available only to a select group. Heinrich Himmler gave one to Adolf Hitler on his birthday in 1939. ds
Original in the public domain

On July 1, 1935, *Reichsführer-SS* Heinrich Himmler, Richard Walther Darré – Reich Peasant Leader and head of the Race and Settlement Main Office (RuSHA) – and the amateur scientist Herman Wirth founded the non-profit institution Studiengesellschaft für Geistesurgeschichte Deutsches Ahnenerbe e. V. (Society for the Study of Primeval Intellectual History, German Ancestral Heritage). Initially under the auspices of RuSHA, this institution became affiliated with the newly formed Personal Staff of the *Reichsführer-SS* in 1936. It was renamed the Forschungs- und Lehrgemeinschaft Das Ahnenerbe e. V. (the Ancestral Heritage Research and Teaching Association) in 1937, at which point Herman Wirth left the organization. He was replaced as president by Professor Walther Wüst, a linguist from Munich.

Under the leadership of Wüst and General Secretary Wolfram Sievers, and in ongoing consultation with Heinrich Himmler, the Ahnenerbe expanded to become a far-reaching organization with teaching and research facilities throughout the Reich. Ahnenerbe functioned on multiple levels, bringing together academic scholars while also integrating integrated laymen, who contributed historico-cultural collections from the fields of anthropology and prehistory.

From an organizational standpoint, Wolfram Sievers integrated the Ahnenerbe ever more firmly into the SS; it was only in 1939, however, that it achieved the status of an official SS agency.

With the onset of World War II, the Ahnenerbe expanded its activities to encompass the natural sciences and medicine as fields of military importance which included research on concentration camp prisoners. Furthermore, the Ahnenerbe also played a substantial role in organizing the plunder of cultural treasure from occupied countries. ds

Dieses Blatt ist eine Original-Handmalerei, gefertigt in der Malstube der Heilkräuterkulturen Dachau von einem Häftling des Konzentrationslagers Dachau.

Die Heilkräuterkulturen in Dachau sind eine Schöpfung der Reichsführung ℋ Sie stellen mit über 200 Morgen bebauter Fläche die größte Anlage dieser Art im Reiche dar. Angeschlossen sind eine Pfeffermühle zur Herstellung eines deutschen Pfeffergewürzes und ein Forschungsinstitut.

Die Anlage dieser Heilkräuterkulturen erfolgte, um Häftlinge des Konzentrationslagers produktiv und erzieherisch ansetzen zu können.

In der Malstube der Heilkräuterkulturen malen Häftlinge alle bekannten Heil- und Gewürzpflanzen nach der Natur. So ist auch diese Malerei entstanden.

Sie stellt die Eberwurz dar.

Die Heilkraft dieser Pflanze liegt in der Wurzel. Ihr Extrakt wirkt innerlich bei Erkrankungen des Magens und der Nieren, äußerlich bei Zahn- und Hauterkrankungen.

220

No. 4-148

General secretary of the SS-Ahnenerbe, Wolfram Sievers
1937/1938

As a schoolboy, Wolfram Sievers was already active in ethno-nationalist (*völkisch*) causes. This involvement led him to leave school early, rendering him unable to pursue higher education. Opting instead for a business career, he audited courses at Stuttgart Technical University in his free time. As part of his *völkisch* quest for meaning, he joined forces with Herman Wirth in 1932. Although Sievers would soon part ways with him in the spring of 1933, Wirth recommended the businessman for the post of general secretary of the newly founded the Ahnenerbe Society. In this capacity, Sievers proved a forceful leader, imparting to the Ahnenerbe its elitist character and showing that he was more than able to assert himself with the academics in his role as scientific manager. ds

Bundesarchiv Berlin, formerly Berlin Document Center, SSO III

No. 4-147

President of the SS-Ahnenerbe, Prof. Walther Wüst
1944

Walther Wüst studied Indo-Germanic linguistics, with a focus on Indology, in Munich, and was awarded his doctorate with honors in 1923. In 1926, he began teaching at the university in Munich as an assistant professor, becoming full professor in 1932 at the age of 31. While at the university he promoted the cause of National Socialism, serving most notably as the campus representative of the SS Security Service (SD). In 1935, he was appointed dean of faculty for philosophy. It was in this context that he made the acquaintance of *Reichsführer-SS* Heinrich Himmler, who, in 1936, appointed him head of the Department of Lexicography at the Ahnenerbe. Finally, in 1937, Himmler called upon him to become the president of the Ahnenerbe. Wüst's academic reputation would lend the Ahnenerbe the prestige to attract additional scientists to the SS.

Wüst's own university career also benefited: In 1941, he became *Führerrektor* of Munich University. In this capacity, he was later involved in the arrest of members of the resistance group "White Rose." ds

Ullstein Bilderdienst, 00293609

No. 4-154

Karl Otto Bäcker/Rudolf Lucass, *Der Kräutergarten. Ein Führer durch die spezielle Heilpflanzenkunde. Zugleich eine Zusammenstellung aller Heil- und Gewürzpflanzen, die auf deutschem Boden ihren natürlichen Standort haben oder angebaut werden können* [The Herb Garden. A Guide to the Study of Special Medicinal Plants. With a Compendium of All Medicinal and Aromatic Plants Growing Naturally in Germany, or Feasible for Cultivation There]
Berlin, Nordland-Verlag, 1943

Bäcker and Lucass were both active at the Dachau medicinal herb garden.

Kreismuseum Wewelsburg, inv. no. 16804

No. 4-152
Not shown

Prisoners at work in Dachau Illegal photograph by the prisoner Karl Kašak
1944

In 1940, *Reichsführer-SS* Heinrich Himmler ordered the establishment of agricultural research stations at concentration camps – including Dachau, Ravensbrück, and Auschwitz – that utilized biological dynamic production. Camp operations overseen by the SS German Research Institute for Nutrition and Food banished artificial fertilizers and heeded phases of the moon and the movements of stars for sowing, cultivation, and harvesting, thus following the practices of Anthroposophy while ignoring its accompanying doctrine.

Dachau Concentration Camp housed the largest of these centers, which included a medicinal plant garden with associated processing facilities as well as a research institute. Its principal product was a blend of spices serving as a pepper substitute, which the institute hoped would contribute to Germany's economic independence. The war spelled considerable profits for the Dachau spice production, which also supplied *Waffen-SS* units. ds

KZ-Gedenkstätte Dachau, sign. Da 16.432

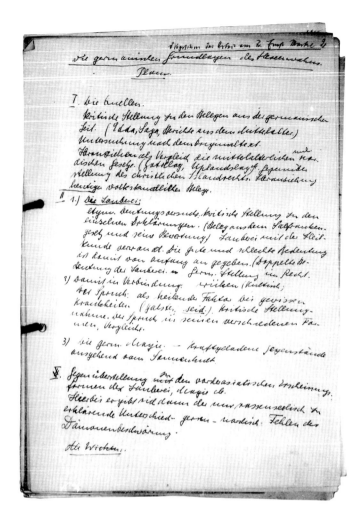

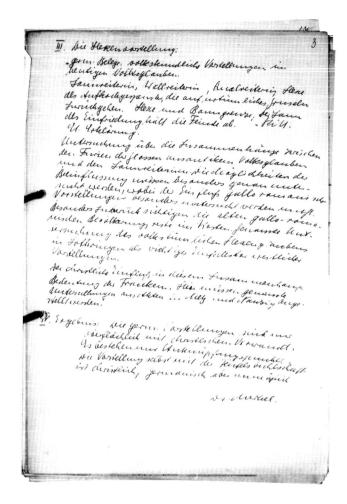

No. 4-155
Ernst Merkel, *Die germanischen Grundlagen des Hexenwahns* [The Germanic Foundations of Belief in Witches]
Probably 1939/1940
Ernst Merkel was on the staff of Special Project H. His doctoral thesis at the University of Gießen was titled "The Devil in Hessian Witch Trials." ds

Bundesarchiv Koblenz, Fsg. 2/1-F, Kartotheka no. 3

Preoccupation with history was a key element of SS ideology. The SS Security Service (SD) also engaged in historical pursuits. The department of "Enemy Research" studied movements that had been opposed to, or persecuted by, the Christian church throughout the centuries. The persecution of witches, particularly in the seventeenth century, was given special attention. In 1935, Heinrich Himmler initiated Special Project H, for which the SD was responsible. It involved three high-ranking SS leaders and thirteen full-time SS employees who while working with archives and libraries usually pretended to be researchers from Leipzig University. They amassed an extensive library and conducted archival research in setting up a "witch register." The results of Special Project H were to be exploited in propaganda films and novels disparaging the Catholic Church. A collection of sources edited according to scientific standards was also planned for publication. For Special Project H, however, the term "scientific" was defined as "strictly for political utility and impact."
ds

No. 4-153
Herb box
The logo of the German Research Institute for Nutrition and Food – Dachau Plant was designed by prisoners at Dachau Concentration Camp. ds

Kreismuseum Wewelsburg, inv. no. 150022

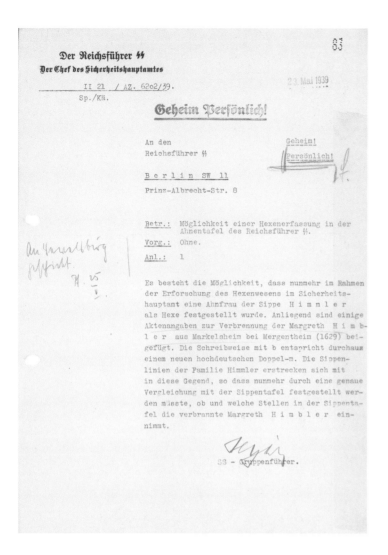

No. 4-151
Not shown
Wulf Sörensen, "Hexenverbrennungen"
[Witch Burnings]
***Nordland*, vol. 2, issue 21**
(November/Nebelung 11, 1934)
This article from the SS magazine *Nordland* illustrates how, within *völkisch* religious circles, persecution of accused witches was seen as connected to race issues and anti-church agitation. In both the image and the text, the woman persecuted as a witch is exalted and the church's role as persecutor is emphasized.

"It sufficed for a girl, a woman, to be beautiful, with blond hair and blue eyes, to become considered a witch, to be accused of coupling with the Devil and be burned at the stake. In such a way were the Nordic mothers of our race systematically murdered. And in the shadows always lurked the cross and the priest."

The SS defined women as the overall sustainers of the race, while witches were seen as something more: vessels for pagan-Germanic ritual and ancient therapeutic wisdom. Despite historical sources claiming otherwise, the persecution of witches was attributed exclusively to the church, which stood accused of having carried out the eradication of the "Germanic ideal." ds
Kreismuseum Wewelsburg, inv. no. 16802

No. 4-156
Letter from the head of the Reich Security Main Office, Reinhard Heydrich, to Heinrich Himmler
May 23, 1939
Translation on page 448
On May 23, 1939, the head of the Reich Security Main Office, Reinhard Heydrich, informed *Reichsführer-SS* Heinrich Himmler of a woman who was accused of witchcraft and burned at the stake near Stuttgart in 1629. It was conceivable, he explained, that the woman, named Margreth Himbler, was an ancestor of the Himmler family. The handwritten note, with name and date to the left of the text, is from Himmler's personal secretary and mistress, Hedwig Potthast; it states "Sent to Wewelsburg Ph. 25. V." The SS castle administration at Wewelsburg, in particular genealogist Rudi Bergmann, was assigned the task of establishing Himmler's family tree. ds
Bundesarchiv Koblenz, Nachlass Himmler,
N 1126/23

No. 4-157
Staff of the State Office of Racial Affairs, with a fold-out chart
Ca. 1937
Gedenkstätte Buchenwald, 373.014

No. 4-158
Not shown
Kinship chart developed by Karl Astel
The basis for research at the State Office for Racial Affairs was provided by the so-called kinship chart developed by Karl Astel. It included first and last names, social or professional status, age at time of death, cause of death, body type, and health conditions of all relatives, including all four grandparents. Beginning in elementary school, children learned to record information on their ancestry. The method developed by Astel was successful to the extent that it was adopted by the SS Race and Settlement Main Office. ds
Kreismuseum Wewelsburg, inv. no. 16449

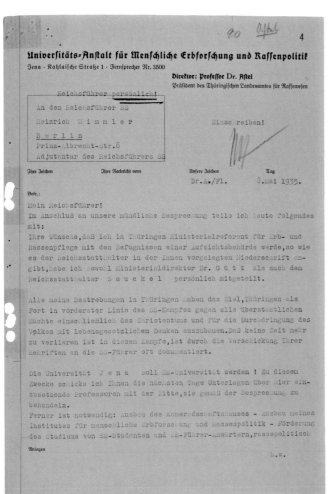

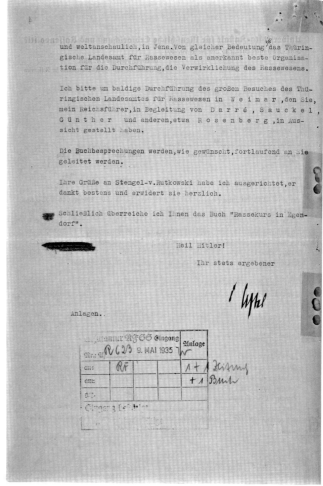

No. 4-159

Letter from Karl Astel to Heinrich Himmler

May 8, 1935

The State Office for Racial Affairs in Weimar was institutionally linked to Friedrich Schiller University in Jena; from 1939, the director of the office, Karl Astel, was also rector of the university. In this capacity, he pursued the objective, formulated as early as 1935, of converting the school into an SS university. This involved the ideological orientation of the faculty by means of a correspondingly selective hiring policy, which he was able to implement with the support of Heinrich Himmler. Like his colleague Lothar Stengel von Rutkowski, Karl Astel had long been acquainted with the *Reichsführer-SS*. Students were also subjected to increased ideological pressure, and the SS base in Jena benefited as a result. ds

Bundesarchiv Berlin, NS 19/1838, v. 1. p. 4

No. 4-160

"Brennpunkt rassegesetzlichen Denkens" [Focus on Legal Theories of Race] *Das Schwarze Korps* [The Black Corps], vol. 28 (July 15, 1937), p. 3

Kreismuseum Wewelsburg, inv. no. 5483

The Promise for Wife and Family: The SS Community of Kin

No. 4-161
Two wedding cups
White porcelain, glazed, marked on underside, with relief decoration around the circumference; inscription in capital letters: "As your rings are without beginning or end/So may your kin be without beginning or end"
Allach Porcelain Manufactory
Between 1935 and 1944

Kreismuseum Wewelsburg,
inv. nos. 15870/1 and 15870/2

No. 4-162
Bread plate, with maxim carved into rim: "Honor the land. It gives us bread."
Ash wood

Kreismuseum Wewelsburg, inv. no. 15888

The SS was not intended as a men's association, but rather a "community of kin." Women would join by marrying SS men. Because SS members were expected to sever their association with the Christian church, religious weddings were replaced by "marriage consecrations." These were intended to provide a ceremonial framework for civil weddings, thereby introducing the newly wedded couple into the SS community of kin.

The details of this marriage consecration were not fixed; it was to be a sober, yet impressive affair, above all a clear departure from religious ceremonies. In 1936, Himmler recommended presenting the newly wedded couple with two cups as a gift from the SS, a practice which seems never to have caught on. The cups shown here, presumably produced models, are the only known pair.

However, the practice of presenting the bridal pair with bread and salt gained general currency within the SS. The displayed bread plate served this purpose. web/fh

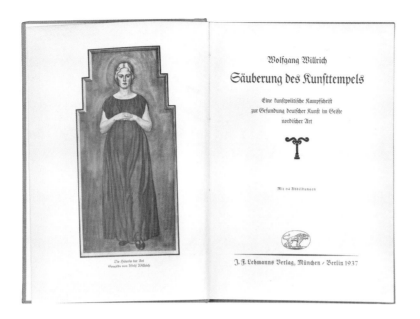

No. 4-179
"Hitlerites Adopt Rules To Regulate Marriages"
Associated Press
February 3, 1932
This U.S. newspaper article from 1932 reports that marriages in a Germany under Hitler would be controlled by a race commission. The article cites the Marriage Order of December 31, 1931, in which Himmler outlined his intention to rate marriage partners according to physical, moral, and racial criteria. This was to be the first step in implementing the fascist theory of the superiority of the Nordic man. Although the article notes that the order would only apply to members of the SS, it assumes subsequent measures for the general population. There follows an English translation of the engagement and marriage order. Citing the founding of National Socialist parties outside Germany, the article concludes by warning of a racialist bloc comprising all traditionally Nordic nations. web/fh

Bayerisches Hauptstaatsarchiv, Munich, PrASig, Rehse 329

No. 4-163
Wolfgang Willrich, *Säuberung des Kunsttempels. Eine kunstpolitische Kampfschrift zur Gesundung deutscher Kunst im Geiste nordischer Art* **[Purging the Temple of Art. A Polemic for the Rehabilitation of German Art in the Spirit of the Nordic Race]**
Munich, Berlin, 1937
Shown here is the painting titled *Hüterin der Art* [Guardian of the Race], by Willrich, a favored artist of the SS. The work hung in Wewelsburg beginning in 1940. web/fh

Kreismuseum Wewelsburg, inv. no. 16234

No. 4-169
Not shown
Cardboard postcard with a painting by Karl Diebitsch: *Mother*
The postcard was issued for the Great German Art Exhibition of 1939. A version of the painting hung at Wewelsburg from 1943 onward. web/fh

Kreismuseum Wewelsburg, inv. no. 16202

No. 4-171
Not shown
Letter from Heinrich Himmler to the leadership of the Ahnenerbe regarding a Friedelehe (a legally inferior form of marriage practiced in the Middle Ages)

Helmuth Heiber, *Reichsführer! Briefe von und an Himmler* [Reichsführer! Letters from and to Himmler], Munich, 1970, p. 356

No. 4-172
Heinrich Himmler and Hedwig Potthast, together at an official function
The SS woman was to bear as many children as possible. Yet, the SS offered a field of experimentation for novel social roles. Although traditional marriage remained generally unchallenged in deference to the prevailing moral orientation of the population, "racial selection" was the guiding principle within the SS. Himmler thus repeatedly called for the acceptance of an officially sanctioned second marriage, which, in reference to alleged ancient Germanic practice, he called *Friedelehe* (marriage without property transfer).

In this instance, Himmler preached what he practiced. Beginning in 1938 he conducted an openly acknowledged relationship with his secretary Hedwig Potthast that produced two children, while his wife Margarete maintained her status of "first wife" within the SS community. This conformed to Himmler's hierarchical conception of double marriage, with special privileges accorded the first wife. Other high-ranking SS leaders also conducted disclosed second relationships. web/fh

Peter-Ferdinand Koch, *Himmlers Graue Eminenz. Oswald Pohl und das Wirtschaftsverwaltungshauptamt der SS* [Himmler's Gray Eminence. Oswald Pohl and the SS Main Economic and Administrative Department], Hamburg, 1988, reprinted in Gudrun Schwarz, *Eine Frau an seiner Seite. Ehefrauen in der "SS-Sippengemeinschaft"* [A Woman at His Side: Wives in the SS Community of Kin], Hamburg, 1997, p. 85

No. 4-165
Motherhood Brooch, initial version, in silver with six horse heads
Gahr workshop, 1936, or replica
As was the case in National Socialism as a whole, a cult of motherhood existed within the SS. The married mother with as many children as possible was to be honored and rewarded. She was the perfect representative of the community of kin. Himmler initially envisioned a motherhood brooch, which the SS husband would give his wife upon the birth of their first child. The brooch accomplished a dual purpose: the woman felt respected as a mother while the brooch identified her as a member of the SS community of kin.

The contract for design of the brooch was awarded to the Gahr silver workshop in Munich, which submitted several prototypes. However, development of the brooch dragged on until 1939 and Himmler tabled the project once the war began. web/fh

Kreismuseum Wewelsburg, inv. no. 16441

No. 4-166
Motherhood Brooch, second version, in silver with sig runes in hagel rune configuration
Gahr workshop, 1939

Kreismuseum Wewelsburg, inv. no. 15003

No. 4-167
Motherhood Brooch, third version, in silver with four horse heads
Gahr workshop, probably from 1939; replica by the Peichl company from the 1980s or 1990s

Kreismuseum Wewelsburg, inv. no. 15261

Beginning in 1905, engraver Otto Michael Gahr (1876 – 1932) ran a small workshop in Munich. He was personally acquainted with Hitler and Himmler, and gained notoriety in 1922 with his creation of the NSDAP standard *Deutschland Erwache* (Germany awake), which Hitler claimed to have designed himself. After his death, Otto Gahr's wife, Karolina Gahr (1881 – 1969), carried on the business. The Gahr workshop primarily designed and produced silver products for the NSDAP and SS, including the death's head ring, the SS sword and dagger, civilian insignias, as well as special orders. Otto and Karolina Gahr worked closely with SS and NSDAP leaders and artists. Like the SS-owned Allach Porcelain Manufactory, the Gahr workshop marked its pieces destined for the SS with intertwined sig runes. At the Gahr workshop, the runes were framed by an octagonal escutcheon. web/fh

No. 4-164
Mother with two children
White porcelain, after a design by Karl Diebitsch
Allach Porcelain Manufactory, 1939

Kreismuseum Wewelsburg, inv. no. 15427

No. 4-168
Not shown
Mother Pendant
Silver
Used by the 72nd SS Regiment in Detmold
Possibly by the Gahr workshop, between 1936 and 1939

Kreismuseum Wewelsburg, inv. no. 15004

No. 4-176
Das Mütterheim Steinhöring des Vereins Lebensborn [Steinhöring Home for Mothers of the Lebensborn organization]
Das Schwarze Korps [The Black Corps], vol. 1937, issue 1 (January 7, 1937)
According to Heinrich Himmler and other National Socialists, what mattered most was not a loving relationship between man and woman, but the breeding of "appropriate" offspring. This moved Himmler to found the *Lebensborn* organization in 1935. All members of the SS were also compulsory members of this organization, which was essentially financed through membership dues.

In the organization's homes for expectant mothers, an unmarried woman who had been impregnated by an SS man could give birth anonymously and then put her baby up for adoption by an SS family. This of course only applied to women who had undergone thorough racial and ideological vetting.

The young women were thus able to evade stigma by the mainstream and its rejection of extramarital pregnancies. Nonetheless, the SS was evidently forced to act firmly in repressing popular rumors that the homes for mothers were indeed "copulation centers." web/fh
Kreismuseum Wewelsburg, inv. no. 5483/1

No. 4-175
Not shown
Dr. U., "Erbgesund – Erbkrank" [Hereditarily healthy – Hereditarily ill]
Das Schwarze Korps [The Black Corps], vol. 1935, issue 5 (April 3, 1935)
Engaged couples wishing to obtain SS marriage authorization faced two hurdles of existential significance: Jewish ancestry and hereditary disease.

A certificate of family lineage could prove that neither of the candidates had Jewish ancestors. If the prospective marriage partners could not clearly document all their ancestors dating back to 1800, they were not entered into the great SS Book of Kin. Their offspring would thus not be granted automatic acceptance into the SS, or authorization to marry a member of the SS. Himmler's own genealogical tree showed gaps, though he himself was exempted from the strict rules, which were otherwise rigidly applied. Examination by an SS physician, along with questionnaires, were to ensure that the families of the marriage partners would remain free of hereditary diseases, including deformities, deafness and blindness.

SS men who married without permission, or, worse, defied an explicit prohibition from marrying, were excluded from the organization. web/fh
Kreismuseum Wewelsburg, inv. no. 5481/5

No. 4-180
Candleholder with frieze of children
White porcelain, after a design by Theodor Kärner (frieze) and Richard Förster (ornamentation on the base designed by Karl Diebitsch)
Allach Porcelain Manufactory, 1943 – 1944
Kreismuseum Wewelsburg, inv. no. 15393

No. 4-181
Candleholder of Life
Porcelain with dark brown glaze, after a design by Karl Diebitsch
Allach Porcelain Manufactory, 1938
Kreismuseum Wewelsburg, inv. no. 11455

No. 4-183
Silver cup as godparent gift with engraved inscription
1941
The goblet was a gift from an SS officer to his godchild, born to a police officer in Rambonnet, France. web/fh
Kreismuseum Wewelsburg, inv. no. 15872

No. 4-184
Not shown
Henrik Herse, *Fünf Wiegen und noch eine* [Five Cradles and One More], Berlin, 1943
Issued by the SS-owned Nordland publishing house, the book displays a so-called candleholder of life. web/fh
Kreismuseum Wewelsburg, inv. no. 4358

No. 4-182
Not shown
Candleholder of life
Wood
This simple candleholder has the shape of a so-called rune of life. web/fh
Kreismuseum Wewelsburg, inv. no. 15685

z.Zt. Gmund am Tegernsee,
4. Januar 1937

U R K U N D E :

Heute, am 4.Januar 1937, hat der SS-Brigadeführer Karl W o l f f in seinem Hause am Schorn zu Rottach-Egern am Tegernsee mir, seinen anwesenden Reichsführer-SS folgende Meldung gemacht:

" Reichsführer-SS: Ich melde Ihnen hiermit unser drittes Kind, das mir meine Ehefrau Frieda, geborene von Römheld als ersten Sohn am 14.Januar 1936, am Schlusse des dritten Jahres des Dritten Deutschen Reiches geboren hat ".

Ich erwiderte darauf:

" Ich danke Ihnen. Ich habe Ihre Meldung vor den Zeugen, den Paten dieses Kindes, also mir selbst, SS-Brigadeführer Weisthor, SS-Gruppenführer Heydrich und SS-Sturmbannführer Diebitsch gehört. Ihr Kind wird in das Geburtenbuch der SS eingetragen und für das Sippenbuch der SS vorgemerkt ".
Brigf.Wolff übergab darauf das Kind der Mutter, die es entgegennahm
Sodann beauftragte ich den SS-Brigadeführer Weisthor die Namensgebung vorzunehmen.

SS-Brigadeführer Weisthor umhüllte das Kind mit dem blauen Lebensbande und sprach dazu die herkömmlichen Worte:

" Das blaue Band der Treue ziehe sich durch Dein ganzes Leben.
Wer deutsch ist und deutsch fühlt, muss treu sein!
Geburt und Ehe, Leben und Tod sind im Sinnbild durch dieses blaue Band verbunden.
Und nun sei dieses Euer Kind, sippen-eigen mit meinem innigen Wunsch, dass es ein rechter deutscher Junge und aufrechter deutscher Mann werde ".

SS-Brigadeführer Weisthor nahm nun den Becher und sprach dazu die herkömmlichen Worte:

" Der Quell alles Lebens ist Got!
Aus Got fliesst Dein Wissen, Deine Aufgaben, Dein Lebenszweck und alle Lebens-Erkenntnis.
Jeder Trunk aus diesem Becher sei Zeugnis, dass Du got - verbunden ".
Den Becher übergab er dann den Vater des Kindes.

SS-Brigadeführer Weisthor nahm nun den Löffel und sprach dazu die herkömmlichen Worte:

" Dieser Löffel nähre Dich hinfort, bis zu Deiner Jünglingsreife. Deine Mutter bezeuge damit ihre Liebe zu Dir und strafe Dich durch Nichtnähren mit ihm bei einem Verstoss gegen die Gesetze Gots ".
Den Löffel übergab er dann der Mutter des Kindes.

SS-Brigadeführer Weisthor nahm dann den Ring und sprach dazu die herkömmlichen Worte:

" Diesen Ring, den Sippen-Ring SS von Wolffs-Geschlecht, sollst Du, Kind, einst tragen, wenn Du Dich als Jüngling der SS und Deiner Sippe wert erwiesen hast.
Und nun gebe ich Dir nach dem Wunsche Deiner Eltern und im Auftrage der SS die Namen T h o r i s m a n, H e i n r i c h, K a r l, R e i n h a r d.
An Euch, Eltern und Namensgoden, liegt es, aus diesem Kinde ein echtes, tapferes, deutsches Herz nach dem Willen Gots zu erziehen.
Dir - liebes Kind - wünsche ich, Du möchtest Dich so bewähren, dass Du bei Deiner Jünglingsreife den stolzen Namen T h o r i s m a n als ersten Vornamen für Dein ganzes Leben erhältst.
DAS WALTE UNSER GOT !!! ".

Ich unterzeichne hiermit diese Urkunde und habe die Namensgoden gebeten, als Zeugen auch ihre Namen einzuzeichnen.

Der Kommandeur:
H. Himmler.

Die Namensgoden:
1. Namensgode: Reichsführer-SS
2. Namensgode: SS-Brigadeführer
3. Namensgode: SS-Gruppenführer
4. Namensgode: SS-Sturmbannführer

No. 4-170
Document for the name consecration (intended as a substitute for baptism) of Karl-Heinz Wolff by Wiligut
January 4, 1937
Translation on page 448

A woman's task was to provide children to the community of kin; the status accorded her in this female role within the National Socialist hierarchy was low. Himmler personally rewarded the birth of children with gifts, which many women perceived as a special honor. Special candleholders called *Lebensleuchter* and ones bearing a frieze of children were initially intended for an SS family's "3rd war child or 4th child." Beginning in 1943, each child born to an SS family received a candleholder. Elaborate gifts from godparents were also common.

A special cult was built up around male children, particularly the eldest, who, as son and heir, secured the continuance of the family and could eventually become a soldier. As future soldiers they were naturally at risk; women, however, were expected not only to bear children, but also to be ready to make sacrifices. In reality, despite all of Himmler's efforts, SS families had below-average birthrates.
web/fh

Jochen von Lang, Der Adjutant. *Karl Wolff, der Mann zwischen Hitler und Himmler* [The Adjutant. Karl Wolff, the Man between Hitler and Himmler], Munich/Berlin, 1985, p. 43 f.

Der Reichsführer-H   Feld-Kommandostelle
Hegewald, d. 15. Aug. 1942   30

H-Befehl an die letzten Söhne.

H-Männer!

1. Ihr seid auf Befehl des Führers als letzte Söhne aus der Front zurückgezogen worden. Diese Massnahme ist erfolgt, weil Volk und Staat ein Interesse daran haben, dass Eure Familien nicht aussterben.

2. Es ist noch niemals die Art von H-Männern gewesen, ein Schicksal hinzunehmen und von sich aus nichts zu seiner Änderung beizutragen. Eure Pflicht ist es, so rasch wie möglich durch Zeugung und Geburt von Kindern guten Blutes dafür zu sorgen, dass Ihr nicht mehr letzte Söhne seid.

3. Seid bestrebt, in einem Jahr das Fortleben Eurer Ahnen und Eurer Familien zu gewährleisten, damit Ihr wiederum für den Kampf in der vordersten Front zur Verfügung steht.

H. Himmler

No. 4-173
SS order to the last surviving sons
August 15, 1942
Translation on page 449
Bundesarchiv Berlin, NS19/3904, p. 30

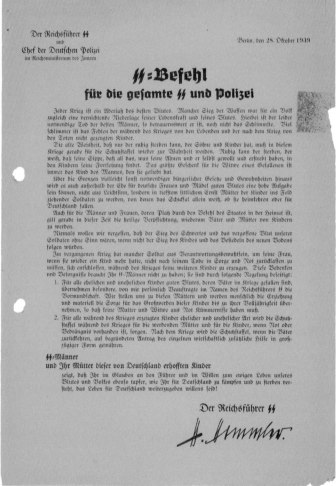

No. 4-174
"Average number of children in SS families"
Statistisches Jahrbuch der Schutzstaffel der NSDAP
[Statistical Almanac for the Schutzstaffel of the NSDAP], vol. 3, Berlin, 1937
Universitatsbibliothek Mainz

No. 4-177
SS order to all SS and police October 28, 1939
Bundesarchiv Berlin, NS 2/276

No. 4-178
"To all men of the SS and police," Himmler's comments on the command of October 28, 1939 January 30, 1940
Himmler's delusional notion that Germany's racial elite need sire as many children as possible led to a bizarre order at the start of the war. Here, the *Reichsführer-SS* promised that after the conflict, the SS would provide for the moral and material needs of the children of dead soldiers. In keeping with Himmler's conceptions, the order succeeded in encouraging out-of-wedlock pregnancies, which contemporary society vehemently rejected. The following passage offering insight into Himmler's inner world met with particularly strong disapproval: "Looking beyond otherwise necessary bourgeois laws and conventions, it may prove a noble task for German women and girls of good blood – not light-heartedly but out of a deep moral seriousness – to become mothers to the children of soldiers bound for the front, of whom fate alone knows whether they shall return or die for Germany." web/fh
Bundesarchiv Berlin, 2/276

An SS Business Venture for the "Protection of the German Soul": Allach Porcelain Manufactory

Im Ausstellungsraum der SS=Porzellan=Manufaktur Allach

Der Reichsführer SS und Chef der Deutschen Polizei bei einer Besichtigung der Ausstellungs= und Verkaufsräume der SS=Porzellan=Manufaktur Allach in Berlin W 9, Hermann=Göring=Straße 2/3. Links der künstlerische Leiter der SS=Porzellan=Manufaktur Allach, SS=Obersturmbannführer Diebitsch.

No. 4-190

Heinrich Himmler and Karl Diebitsch on the sales floor of the Allach Porcelain Manufactory in Berlin
Nordland, vol. 1938, series 24
(December 15, 1938)
Karl Diebitsch (1899–before 1992), graduate of Munich Art Academy and one of four founders of the Allach Porcelain Manufactory, was its artistic director. Diebitsch joined the NSDAP in 1920, early enough to qualify him as an "old fighter." However, after the party was banned from 1923 to 1925, he did not rejoin until 1937, enrolling instead in the SS in 1933, where a year later he became Himmler's artistic adviser. In 1940 he was awarded an honorary professorship; two years later he was granted his own department within the SS, in which he oversaw artistic and architectural affairs. For Allach, Diebitsch designed vases and candelabras, along with coats of arms, wooden coffins, stamps, tapestries, and logos; he also tried his hand at painting. He succeeded in recruiting renowned artists for the porcelain manufactory, including Theodor Kärner (1884–1966), Richard Förster (1873–1956) and Ottmar Obermeier (1883–1958), who had already worked for the Rosenthal and Nymphenburg manufactories. web/fh

Lippische Landesbibliothek, Detmold, 2 St 2315

No. 4-189

Karl Diebitsch, *Almetal*
Probably 1942–1943
Commissioned by Himmler, the painting depicts the view from Wewelsburg onto a wintry Alme Valley. The whereabouts of this painting are presently unknown. web/fh

Kreismuseum Wewelsburg, Fotoarchiv

No. 4-191
Not shown

Catalog of the Allach-Munich Porcelain Manufactory GmbH, with a product register
1938/1939
Artists at the Allach manufactory attempted to develop a new National Socialist style. Their focus was on durable cultural artifacts, with consideration given to their potential as objects of future archeological study. Using figurative models they employed naturalistic representation to restore to man the harmony they felt had been lost. The use of non-representative models meant an increased reliance on symbols, such as runes, for example. These signs were to speak to the "initiated," guiding their sensibilities to related conceptions of race, blood, soil, and Germanic heroism. However, it soon became clear that the typical buyers of Allach porcelain were middle class and preferred classical models. Even the many SS men who purchased Allach products or received them as gifts were partial to animal figurines or simple vases. web/fh

Kreismuseum Wewelsburg, inv. no. 4551

No. 4-185
Not shown

Karl Adolf Gross, *Zweitausend Tage Dachau. Erlebnisse eines Christenmenschen unter Herrenmenschen und Herdenmenschen. Berichte und Tagebücher des Häftlings Nr. 16921* [Two Thousand Days at Dachau: Experiences of a Christian Man Among Men of the Master Race and Men of the Herd. Reports and Diaries of Prisoner No. 16921]
Munich, 1946

Kreismuseum Wewelsburg, inv. no. 16535

No. 4-186
Not shown

Karl Adolf Gross, *Fünf Minuten vor Zwölf. Des ersten Jahrtausends letzte Tage unter Herrenmenschen und Herdenmenschen. Dachauer Tagebücher des Häftlings 16921* [Five Minutes to Twelve: The Last Days of the First Millennium Among Men of the Master Race and Men of the Herd. Dachau Diaries of Prisoner No. 16921]
Munich, 1946

Kreismuseum Wewelsburg, inv. no. 16576

No. 4-188
Not shown

Leo Maduschka, *Die Technik schwerster Eisfahrten* [Navigation Techniques in Severe Ice Conditions], Munich, 1942
The cover design is by Karl Diebitsch, who also served as artistic director at the Allach Porcelain Manufactory. web/fh

Kreismuseum Wewelsburg, inv. no. 15630

No. 4-192
Floor vase, after a design by
Franz Nagy
Ceramic, brown glazing with
recessed swastika frets, stars and
other ornamentation
Produced as of 1937
Kreismuseum Wewelsburg,
inv. no. 15426

No. 4-194
Seydlitz cuirassier officer, after a
design by Theodor Kärner
Porcelain, colored, glazed
Between 1936 and 1945
Kreismuseum Wewelsburg,
inv. no. 16799

No. 4-187
Not shown
Site map of SS facilities at Dachau
with plottings by Hans Landauer.
The Porcelain Manufactory building has
been sketched in directly to the right
of the railroad tracks.
On January 3, 1936, four businessmen,
straw men for Heinrich Himmler, founded
the Allach-Munich Porcelain Manufactory
GmbH (PMA). Like other SS businesses,
the PMA soon came under the control of
the SS Main Economic and Administrative
Department. The business was not oriented
primarily towards financial profit; rather,
Himmler aimed to bring "beauty ... to the
working man in his daily surroundings."
First and foremost, this meant SS personnel, the supposed elite of working men.
The company lost money each year until
1939.

In 1937 production was transferred to
the former gun powder factory at Dachau
Concentration Camp. Porcelain was
manufactured there until the end of the
war, while the ceramics business returned
to Allach in 1940. From 1939, and increasingly as of 1942, production was maintained by prison labor. One inmate, Karl
Adolf Gross, conveyed his experiences
through diaries. web/fh

G. Huber, *Die Porzellanmanufaktur Allach*,
Marburg, 1991, p. 21

No. 4-195
Hitler youth with drum
Porcelain, white, glazed, after a design
by Richard Förster
1936

Kreismuseum Wewelsburg,
inv. no. 15967

No. 4-193
Not shown
Advertisement for Allach Porcelain
Manufactory touting its "Germanic
ceramics"
Nordland, vol. 1939, series 11
(March 18, 1939)

The SS were ever stoking the fantasy of
the supposed pure and strong Germanic
man. Himmler in particular had a predilec-
tion for anything remotely Germanic. As
a result, the Allach product range offered
so-called Germanic ceramics. A line of
eight models featured swastika patterns,
runes, and other purportedly Germanic
symbols. In 1936, with hopes of lending the
PMA a scientific veneer, Wolfram Sievers,
business manager of the SS-Ahnenerbe
research society, ordered prehistoric relics to be collected from museums as
models. Yet, PMA artists almost always
altered these models, as forms and ornamentation were reconstituted.

The pieces, including the vase displayed here, were extensively reported
upon in various SS publications, con-
tributing to the dissemination of related
Germanic ideology within the SS. web/fh

Lippische Landesbibliothek, Detmold, 2 St 2315

No. 4-196
B[und] D[eutscher] M[ädel]
[League of German Girls] girl
Porcelain, white, glazed, after a design by
Richard Förster
1936

The National Socialists were convinced
that art should feature national symbols.
Glorification of the "new era" in the
product line of the Allach Porcelain Manufactory primarily found expression in its
"Figures of the Movement," depicting
National Socialist prototypes. Besides SS
men, standard-bearers and soldiers,
these also included Hitler youths and BDM
girls. All figures were to emphasize the
importance of new roles. Designs were
sometimes rejected for not meeting this
standard. Moreover, all figures exuded
martial form. The drumming and marching
Hitler youths were among the PMA's most
popular figures. web/fh

Kreismuseum Wewelsburg,
inv. no. 17045

Josef Vietze   SS-Gruppenführer Heydrich

No. 4-198
Reinhard Heydrich with the PMA's Fencer
Postcard of a painting by Josef Vietze, 1941
Josef Vietze was a professor at the Prague art academy and presented the painting in 1941 at the Great German Art Exhibition in Munich. web/fh

Bayerische Staatsbibliothek,
Munich, hoff-70103

No. 4-197
SS Fencer
Bisque porcelain, white, after a design by Ottmar Obermeier
1938

Kreismuseum Wewelsburg,
inv. no. 16800

Sports under the Third Reich were often considered military training (*Wehr-ertüchtigung*). Consequently, sports that prepared participants for battle – fencing, for example – were particularly popular in the SS; the guard building at Wewelsburg even contained a fencing hall and gymnasium. Victors in various athletic contests were to be awarded prizes, such as the SS Fencer produced by Allach Porcelain Manufactory (PMA). In accordance with National Socialist notions of art, the fencer's athletic torso is almost nude; he is wearing nothing more than three-quarter-length slacks. This "naked ideal" was to lay bare before the beholder the "superlative race." Reinhard Heydrich (1904 – 1942) was considered a very good fencer as well as the ideal type of Aryan man. The painting by Josef Vietze shows him sitting beside PMA's SS Fencer. Vietze had wanted to paint two figures, each in its way embodying the true Aryan. web/fh

No. 4-199
The Frisian
Porcelain, colored, partially silver-coated, after a design by Ottmar Obermeier
1938
The Allach Porcelain Manufactory produced a series of figures in traditional costume, such as The Frisian. The National Socialists considered traditional costume the visible expression of an ultimately immutable order determined by racial identity. Traditional costume proclaims the wearer's ethnic character, "tribal affiliation," and, in the eyes of the National Socialists, an adherence to Blood and Soil (*Blut und Boden*) ideology. Indeed, these concepts were explicitly propagated in the Third Reich; however, Jews were prohibited from wearing traditional costume. The PMA figures, although pretty at first sight, thus reflect the racialist foundations of National Socialist ideology. web/fh

Kreismuseum Wewelsburg,
inv. no. 15684

No. 4-200, No. 4-201
Two dog figures: a dachshund and a German shepherd
Porcelain, white, glazed, after designs by Theodor Kärner
As of 1936
Kreismuseum Wewelsburg, inv. nos. 11454 and 11012

No. 4-202
Not shown
Fox Terrier ("Foxl")
Porcelain, white, glazed, after a design by Theodor Kärner
As of 1936
Kreismuseum Wewelsburg, inv. no. 10283

Nature should be the taskmaster of art, or so professed the National Socialists, thereby condemning the developments in art over the preceding decades, Expressionism above all. Germans were thought to possess an innate love of nature that was compatible only with "true" representation.

To speak to the special German soul, animals – including those made from porcelain – should always be represented as naturalistically as possible. Moreover, (human) character traits were ascribed to animals, such as loyalty and obedience to shepherd dogs.

The traits attributed to German shepherds made them especially popular as watchdogs among SS concentration camp guards. However, what seemed of primary importance to purchasers of Allach porcelain dogs was to possess an effigy of their "best friend." Thus only breeds of dogs common at that time were available in effigy, and these sold very well indeed. web/fh

No. 4-204
Candelabrum
Porcelain, white, glazed, after a design by Karl Diebitsch
1938
The SS porcelain manufactory also produced everyday objects, including plain vases and candleholders. But only a relatively small selection of such pieces was on offer. Although artifacts of this type conformed in form and construction to a fundamental aesthetic acceptable to National Socialists, they were hardly suitable as conveyors of a new, unique National Socialist style. After the animal figures, these were the best-selling products. A great many buyers of PMA porcelain thus evaded Himmler's sweeping concepts of a national art. As such, several firms continued offering several PMA models, even after 1945, without customers associating them with the SS. web/fh
Kreismuseum Wewelsburg, inv. no. 16740

No. 4-203
Vase
Porcelain, white, with circumferential colored stripes, glazed, after a design by Franz Nagy
1938
Kreismuseum Wewelsburg, inv. no. 15136

No. 4-206
Not shown
Vase for the German Red Cross
Porcelain, white, glazed
As early as 1939, special orders accounted for about half of production at Allach Porcelain Manufactory. These were mainly for Himmler or clients such as the German Red Cross. The largest special order by a considerable margin was the *Julleuchter* (Yule lantern), yet there were also production runs of very low quantity. Himmler often used special orders for presents to friends, patrons, and SS families, allowing him to offer exclusive gifts. For many families it was a very special honor to receive gifts from the *Reichsführer-SS* in person. web/fh
Kreismuseum Wewelsburg, inv. no. 15270

No. 4-208
Insert for a floor vase
Porcelain, white, glazed
Bohemia Porcelain
Manufactory
Kreismuseum Wewelsburg,
inv. no. 15887

No. 4-207
Yule plate belonging to Oswald Pohl, head of the SS Main Economic and Administrative Department
Porcelain, glazed
Produced at the Bohemia subsidiary of PMA, 1944
The front features a quote from Friedrich Hebbel: "Consecration of the Night" in circumferential design (blue crocuses); the back bears a dedication with a facsimile of Pohl's signature.

In the development of new customs for the SS, along with the Yule lantern a Yule plate was introduced as a key element. Each child was to receive such a plate as a gift from his or her parents or godparents and keep it for life. It was intended as a donation plate during Yule, St. Nicholas' Day (Wodan's Day in SS terminology), birthdays, and New Year. Both Himmler and his head of economic affairs, Oswald Pohl, ordered their own Yule plates from the PMA to present as gifts. Because the factories in Allach and Dachau were unable to produce such plates in large numbers, delivery was delayed until the 1940 acquisition of the Bohemia plant in Czechoslovakia. There alone, 6,000 Yule plates were produced in 1943. Each year a new plate was designed for Himmler as well as for Pohl. Himmler's Yule plates were white and bore runes, Germanic symbols, swords, and eagles, while Pohl's featured colorful floral designs. web/fh
Kreismuseum Wewelsburg, inv. no. 9636

No. 4-205
Porcelain plaque: Athletic Roll Call of the Companies (*Sportappell der Betriebe*)
Bisque porcelain, white with raised lettering
Distributed by the German Labor Front, 1939

Kreismuseum Wewelsburg, inv. no. 13447

No. 4-209
Side bowl, quatrefoil
Porcelain, white, glazed, underside featuring the Victoria Manufactory insignia and the *Waffen-SS* seal
As the Allach Porcelain Manufactory was not profitable, following the invasion of Czechoslovakia the SS resolved to secure one of that country's world-renowned manufactories.

In 1939, the Bohemia Manufactory in Neurohlau, near Karlsbad, was acquired for about one-third of its actual value. The renowned firm, founded in 1921, had been under Jewish ownership, thus the SS needed only to compensate the German shareholders, who were awarded a part of the business. The PMA used the location to produce special orders; during the war its primary function was the manufacture of mess hall crockery for the *Wehrmacht* and facilities operated by the SS and German Red Cross (DRK). However, it was the selling off of the large inventory stored at the Bohemia warehouse that would save the PMA financially.

There was also a push to acquire the Victoria Manufactory in Altrohlau. Although the deal eventually fell through, the PMA took advantage of the temporary takeover of Victoria to sell off its entire stock and produce some individual items at the location. web/fh
Kreismuseum Wewelsburg, inv. no. 16450

In September 1934, the SS leased Wewelsburg Castle from what was then the district of Büren. Reconstruction work began with Voluntary Labour Service workers (subsequently the Reich Labour Service). The facility, officially known since 1935 as the "SS Schule Haus Wewelsburg" (Wewelsburg SS School), was provided with a library, a museum, guest rooms, and a specially created interior design. The castle administration consisted of SS academics pursuing their ideologically driven research. Over the years, however, Heinrich Himmler, together with his architect, Hermann Bartels, elaborated more far reaching concepts to turn the castle into a prestigious venue for the highest SS leadership. Very early on, the village of Wewelsburg itself became the target of SS planning. On one hand, it was to serve as a showcase for National Socialist ideology of a racial or ethnic community. On the other, however, it hampered the SS's tendency to expansion; its ever-growing demand for space.

5
The Castle
and Village of
Wewelsburg
1933 – 1939

5.1
Wewelsburg Castle
1933 – 1939

In 1933, the SS national leadership embarked on the search for a "castle stronghold" in Lippe and Westphalia. According to the thinking of the people around Richard Walther Darré, then the SS's leading ideologue, it was to serve the advanced ideological training of SS leaders. Under the influence of architect Hermann Bartels, the choice of *Reichsführer-SS* Heinrich Himmler fell on Wewelsburg. However, beyond establishment of an SS indoctrination center, another notion soon surfaced. Very early on, Himmler pursued the aim of having Bartels transform the castle into a meeting point for higher SS officers, a venue as grand as it was to be discreet. Against a background of the SS's general evolution, the objective of developing the castle into a prestigious focal point of SS society exerted increasing sway.

No. 5-4

Images of the construction work at Wewelsburg Castle in 1934
On September 22, 1934, after protracted leasing negotiations, the district of Büren, which held the property rights to Wewelsburg, officially transferred the castle to the *Reichsführer-SS*. In January 1934, a unit of the Voluntary Labor Service (FAD) had already begun work to convert it. The first order of the day was excavating the castle moat, which had been filled in. The bridge to the castle's inner courtyard was rebuilt, the castle gardens rehabilitated and a footbridge built to the quarters of the *Reichsführer-SS* in the southwestern tower. Workers also had to remove the outer layer of plaster from the castle's exterior façades. The exposed stones were intended to lend the building the appearance of a medieval castle. mm
Kreismuseum Wewelsburg, Fotoarchiv

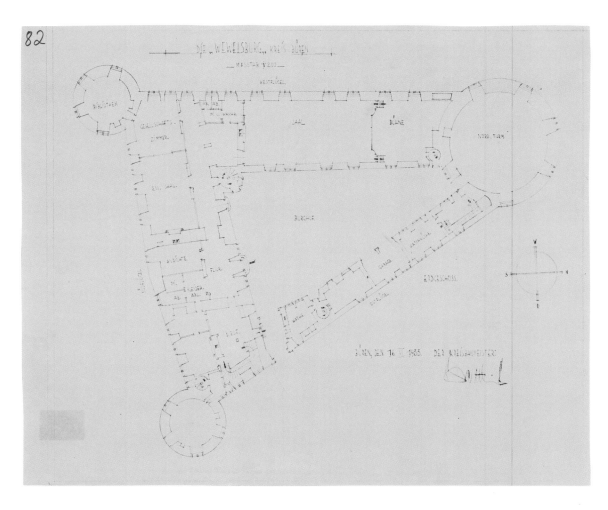

No. 5-5
Not shown
"Fireplace in the dining room at Wewelsburg SS Leadership School," blueprint with pencil corrections and round stamp "Wewelsburg SS School Construction Management" Scale 1:10
Kreismuseum Wewelsburg, inv. no. 12200

No. 5-1
Not shown
Structural drawing of Wewelsburg, basement level Hermann Bartels/Karl Breithaupt Blueprint on paper December 16, 1933 Scale 1:200
Kreismuseum Wewelsburg, Plan 84

No. 5-3
Not shown
Structural drawing of Wewelsburg, upper floor Hermann Bartels/Karl Breithaupt Blueprint on paper December 16, 1933 Scale 1:200
Kreismuseum Wewelsburg, Plan 81

No. 5-2
Structural drawing of Wewelsburg Castle, ground floor Hermann Bartels/Karl Breithaupt Blueprint on paper December 16, 1933 Scale 1:200

Heinrich Himmler first visited Wewelsburg Castle on November 6, 1933. The same day, he commissioned the architect Hermann Bartels to submit blueprints for a conversion of the castle, and Bartels sent Himmler his project the following month. For his part, Bartels was able to rely on extensive preliminary work by Karl Breithaupt, a local architect from Büren. A museum, an officers' mess, and the kitchen were to be situated on the basement level. A library and a series of halls and lounges were added on the ground floor. On the upper floor, Bartels planned quarters for the *Reichsführer-SS* and the family of the chief castle administrator. Eleven cell-like double and single rooms were to be available to visitors. In contrast, classrooms were entirely absent. With this initial allocation of space, Bartels was thus already implicitly calling into question Wewelsburg Castle's ostensible function as an SS school. mm
Kreismuseum Wewelsburg, Plan 82

5.1.2
The SS Library, the Museum, and the Guest Rooms

Library reading room in the southwestern tower
Mid-1930s

Kreismuseum Wewelsburg, Fotoarchiv

A book from the "SS Library" collection at Wewelsburg Castle

On the ground floor of the southwestern tower, Bartels planned an area to house a reference library. This collection serving – at best – the intellectual edification of castle guests changed in character when the academic librarian Dr. Hans Peter des Coudres assumed his duties in April 1935. Des Coudres boosted the number of volumes in the "SS Library" to 16,000, including many works from the sixteenth to the twentieth centuries on (Indo-) Germanic pre- and protohistory; religious, cultural, and legal history; and West-phalian local history. In the eyes of its director, the library would provide the basis for research activity at an "advanced school of the SS" in Wewelsburg Castle. However, by 1938, Himmler already wished to dispose of the book collection. During the war, the volumes were negligently stacked in the SS Staff Building next to Wewelsburg Castle. mm

Loan from the Erzbischöfliche Akademische Bibliothek, Paderborn
Kreismuseum Wewelsburg, inv. no. 17101

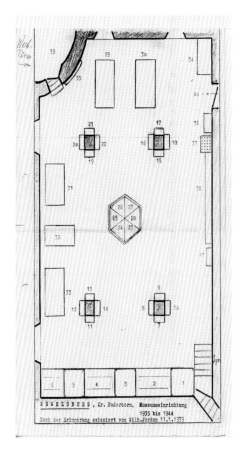

No. 5-6
Sketch of the museum's interior arrangement at the Wewelsburg SS School, drawn from memory by Wilhelm Jordan
January 11, 1979
In 1935, Wilhelm Jordan, the Wewelsburg SS School's archeologist, founded a museum on the premises of the former Büren local history museum, on the basement level of the west wing. In keeping with the professional interests of its curator, the collection was mainly oriented to prehistory and early history, as well as geology and paleontology. During World War II – not least as a result of Himmler's personal involvement – a growing number of significant objects for cultural history, acquired or plundered by the SS from across Europe, also found their way here. The initial teaching collection, which served ideological indoctrination, now increasingly became a collection of trophies stemming from the SS's militaristic expansionist policies. mm
Kreismuseum Wewelsburg, sign. 70/1/2/14

No. 5-10
Spectacle brooch
Bronze
Early Iron Age
This piece of jewelry from the early Iron Age was displayed in the archeological collection of the Wewelsburg SS School museum. mm
Loan from the Verein für Geschichte und Altertumskunde Westfalens, Abt. Paderborn
Kreismuseum Wewelsburg, inv. no. 7633

No. 5-7
Interior decoration of a guest room
Mid-1930s
The SS planners named many rooms at Wewelsburg Castle after historical and mythological figures or concepts. The furnishings were intended to impress upon guests the significance of the eponym for the SS's self-image. The rooms bore names such as "*Reichsführer* Room," "Aryan," "Seasons and Runes," "Westphalia," "Teutonic Knights," "Fredericus," "Duke of Brunswick-Lüneburg" "Grail," "Feme," and "German Language." From the beginning, competition in questions of design arose between the von Knobelsdorffs and Hermann Bartels, Himmler's chosen architect. The chief castle administrator and his wife felt that Bartels took insufficient account of the "Nordic" ideas of their relative, SS indoctrination leader Richard Walther Darré, and of their second ideological influence, Karl Maria Wiligut, in his interior design decisions at Wewelsburg Castle. mm
Kreismuseum Wewelsburg, Fotoarchiv

No. 5-12
Spiral staircase with "Nordic" decoration leading from the vestibule on the ground floor to the private quarters of the chief castle administrator at the eastern end of Wewelsburg Castle's south wing
Photograph: Hardeweg, Velen, ca. 1935
It was in the realm of interior decoration that the von Knobelsdorff couple, and their architectural advisor, Walter Franzius, managed to leave their most lasting mark on Wewelsburg Castle. Numerous pieces of furniture, decorative elements and ceramic objects at the Wewelsburg SS School were adorned with "Nordic" symbols, swastikas, and runes. The spiral staircase became a bone of contention typical of the struggle between the von Knobelsdorffs and Hermann Bartels. While the architect strove to satisfy his client, Himmler, with "Germanized," pseudo-historical styling in a high standard of craftsmanship, the von Knobelsdorffs reported to their relative, Darré, that the insertion of "Nordic" woodcarvings on the staircase was a victory in their long-running, "blood-based" opposition to Bartels. mm
Kreismuseum Wewelsburg, Fotoarchiv

No. 5-11
Chair with armrests in the SS dining room in Wewelsburg Castle's South Wing
Ash (rattan)
After 1935
Kreismuseum Wewelsburg, inv. no. 4697

No. 5-14
Lamp with two-footed base
Wrought iron, shaft covered in leather and six-sided vellum lampshade, Bakelite light bulb fitting
Made in the artist blacksmith's shop at the Wewelsburg SS School, 1935 – 1939
Kreismuseum Wewelsburg, inv. no. 3256

No. 5-13
Candlestick with four massive legs; ornamentation: sun wheel motifs, candle holder encircled with zigzag pattern and circles
Wrought iron
Made in the artist blacksmith's shop at the Wewelsburg SS School, 1935 – 1939
Kreismuseum Wewelsburg, inv. no. 638

In October 1935, Hermann Bartels hired four wrought-iron craftsmen from the Werkkunstschule, a craft school in Dortmund. The SS construction management set up its own artist blacksmith shop on the ground floor of the ruined northern tower. Here, numerous wrought-iron furnishings were produced for Wewelsburg Castle, including lamps, candlesticks, door handles, railings, and fittings. The objects conformed to the formal language in demand at Wewelsburg SS School: design suggestive of medieval and old-German styles blended with ostensibly "Nordic" decorative motifs.

Occasionally, the Wewelsburg artist blacksmith shop also produced privately commissioned objects for SS leaders. In 1939, in the course of the northern tower reconstruction, the blacksmith shop was relocated to the SS construction site at the Externsteine rock formation. It returned to Wewelsburg in 1942, to be housed in a barn near the newly erected Construction Management offices. mm

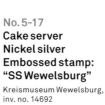

No. 5-15
SS rune in a circle, decorative element on the Wewelsburg Castle gate (until 1945)
Wrought iron
Made in the artist blacksmith shop at the Wewelsburg SS School, 1935 – 1939
Kreismuseum Wewelsburg, inv. no. 7513

No. 5-16
Swastika in a circle, decorative element on the Wewelsburg Castle gate (until 1945)
Wrought iron
Made in the artist blacksmith shop at the Wewelsburg SS School, 1935 – 1939
Kreismuseum Wewelsburg, inv. no. 7511

No. 5-17
Cake server
Nickel silver
Embossed stamp: "SS Wewelsburg"
Kreismuseum Wewelsburg, inv. no. 14692

No. 5-18
Sugar bowl with lid
Nickel silver
Embossed stamp: "SS Wewelsburg"
Kreismuseum Wewelsburg, inv. no. 1609

Cutlery for the Wewelsburg SS School was provided in the second half of the 1930s by the WMF company. It was not custom-made, but a standard catalog product, embossed with the personalized stamp: "Wewelsburg SS." The same applied to the other metal tableware. The material is a nickel-copper-zinc alloy, also known as hotel silver. Scratch marks on certain stamps resulted from use by private individuals after World War II. mm

No. 5-21
Small coffee cup with saucer, glazed, painted
Seelos & Rottka workshop, Dießen am Ammersee
Mid-1930s
Kreismuseum Wewelsburg, inv. no. 1074

No. 5-22
Eggcup, glazed, painted
Seelos & Rottka workshop, Dießen am Ammersee
Mid-1930s
Kreismuseum Wewelsburg, inv. no. 1073

No. 5-23
Teapot, glazed, painted
Seelos & Rottka workshop, Dießen am Ammersee
Mid-1930s
Kreismuseum Wewelsburg, inv. no. 846

No. 5-24
Sugar bowl, glazed, painted
Seelos & Rottka workshop, Dießen am Ammersee
Mid-1930s
Kreismuseum Wewelsburg, inv. no. 13985

No. 5-20
Plate with flat mirror, glazed, painted
Mid-1930s
Kreismuseum Wewelsburg, inv. no. 14413

No. 5-19
Plate, glazed, painted
Seelos & Rottka workshop, Dießen am Ammersee
Mid-1930s
Kreismuseum Wewelsburg, inv. no. 8983

The crockery used at the Wewelsburg SS School was red firing earthenware with cobalt and copper decorations and a zinc glaze. Certain items bore a mark attributable to the Seelos and Rottka art pottery workshop in Dießen am Ammersee. With their *Wolfsangel* designs, double and spiral swastikas, and man and yr runes, the decorative elements supported the total ideological experience the SS sought to create at Wewelsburg Castle. These ceramic objects came to the Kreismuseum Wewelsburg through private collections. They were presumably gathered from the Wewelsburg Castle ruins by onlookers following the SS's demolition of the castle on March 31, 1945. mm

"I intend to introduce and schedule two regular major meetings of *Gruppenführer*, one on November 8, here in Munich …, and the other, which will handle other matters, each spring at the Wewelsburg."

"In future … , I will perform the swearing-in ceremony of uninitiated *Gruppenführer* at Wewelsburg Castle. Next year I will also invite to that event at Wewelsburg Castle the *Gruppenführer*, who through their covenant as *Gruppenführer* have forever committed their lives to upholding the laws of Race and Blood."

No. 5-29
Heraldic shield for Richard Walther Darré
Sheet metal with enamel
1934
As was generally the case during the initial phase of the SS's Wewelsburg project, Heinrich Himmler's congruence of views with Richard Walther Darré's was also evident in the coats of arms discussion. Well before 1933, the "Blood and Soil" ideologue Darré had emphasized the significance of coats of arms for the recreation of a peasant-"Aryan" "new aristocracy." As Reich Farmers' Leader, he wished to provide the members of the Reich Farmers' Council with a coat of arms to be exhibited in a future council "Hall of Honor" in Goslar. This shield was presumably also intended to find its place there. Darré's and Himmler's ideological counselor, Karl Maria Wiligut, was working both on plans for a "peasant coat of arms" and for a coat of arms for the *SS-Gruppenführer*. In 1935, Darré agreed with Himmler to treat their similar purposes regarding coats of arms as confidential. mm

Loan from the Stadtarchiv Goslar
Kreismuseum Wewelsburg, inv. no. 17143

No. 5-25
Heinrich Himmler's announcement of the spring sessions and swearing-in of *SS-Gruppenführer* at Wewelsburg Castle; quotes from a speech to *SS-Gruppenführer* in Munich
November 8, 1938
On the eve of the annual National Socialist Party commemoration of the dead associated with the 1923 Hitler Putsch in Munich, and the start of the November pogrom against the Jewish population throughout Germany, Himmler specified his ideas concerning regular plenary meetings of *SS-Gruppenführer*. Because the fall meeting took place in direct connection with an important event of the SS's parent party, Wewelsburg Castle offered the *SS-Gruppenführer* the luxury of remaining entirely amongst themselves at the planned spring meeting.

Swearing-in of the *SS-Gruppenführer* was designed to highlight the preeminent position of this elite within the SS hierarchy. By relocating the initiation ritual to Wewelsburg Castle, Himmler wished to emphasize the exclusivity and comradeship the castle was intended to foster among the *SS-Gruppenführer*. mm

Quoted in Bradley F. Smith and Agnes F. Peterson (eds.),
Heinrich Himmler – Geheimreden 1933 – 1945,
Frankfurt/Main, 1974, pp. 26 and 43 f.

No. 5-28
Not shown
Family coat of arms of *SS-Gruppenführer* Erich von dem Bach-Zelewski (1899 – 1972) in a version prepared by Karl Maria Wiligut
October 1934
As early as 1934, Heinrich Himmler planned to exhibit the family coats of arms of higher SS leaders at Wewelsburg Castle. In this, he was advised by Karl Maria Wiligut. However, few of the SS leaders with aristocratic backgrounds actually possessed one.

Erich von dem Bach-Zelewski was descended from Prussian landed nobility. In 1939, he dropped the "Zelewski" part of his name, because it sounded too Slavic.

As a rule, Himmler's representatives had to design a new coat of arms for the SS leaders – in imitation of putative "Germanic" examples. After the outbreak of war, efforts concerning the *SS-Gruppenführer* coats of arms came to a standstill. There are indications that Himmler wished to establish a "heraldic office" to deal with the coats of arms issue within the SS after Germany's "final victory." mm

Bundesarchiv Berlin, Dahlwitz-Hoppegarten,
BStU/SAPMO-Bibliothek MfS, HA IX/11, 62/750/61

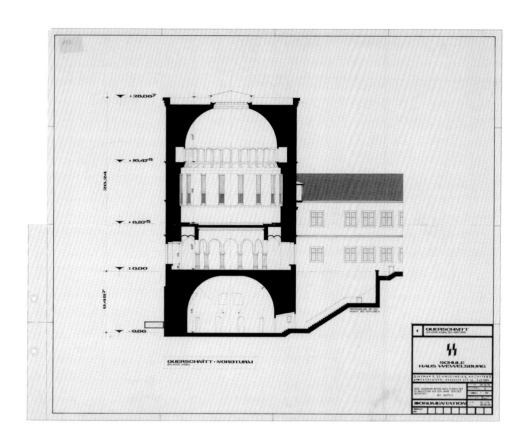

No. 5-26
Cross-section drawing for the conversion of the northern tower, with steps to the interior courtyard
Scale 1:100
December 1939, tracing 1979
From December 1938, the ruin of the northern tower became the focus of SS construction activity in Wewelsburg. In December 1939, Hermann Bartels submitted his initial plan for conversion of the tower. He envisioned a cupola-like underground vault, a hall with twelve columns on the ground floor, along with a domed hall on the upper story. At the time, the upper cupola was still intended to rise within the external walls. Although the rooms had not yet received their final designations of "crypt," "*Obergruppenführer* Hall," and "*Gruppenführer* Hall," there can be no doubt as to their allocation for the *SS-Gruppenführer*. For access, Bartels wanted to build steps from the inner castle courtyard to the underground vault. However, objections from the highest Prussian preservation agency prevented implementation of this plan.
mm
Kreismuseum Wewelsburg, Plan 197

No. 5-30
SS death's head ring, engraved inside:
"S. lb. [to his dear] Baltes 21.6.43
H. Himmler"
Silver, relief decoration on the exterior
Kreismuseum Wewelsburg, inv. no. 15907

No. 5-31
Replica of an SS death's head ring
Silver
After 1945
Kreismuseum Wewelsburg, inv. no. 4097

Until 1945, around sixteen thousand death's head rings were awarded to SS officers. The inscription on the inside, with the award date, expressed the personal loyalty intended between the *Reichsführer-SS* and the wearer. After the capture of Wewelsburg, on Easter 1945, numerous SS death's head rings were said to have been taken by American soldiers from the smoldering ruins of the castle. Since the end of World War II, a staggering number of counterfeit and imitation death's head rings have surfaced at legitimate auctions and in the military collectibles trade, as well as on the black market for SS memorabilia. mm

Abschrift.

Der Reichsführer-SS   Berlin, den 20.4.36.

An ᛋᛋ-Standartenführer Paul Zimmermann, ᛋᛋ-Nr. 276 856.

Ich verleihe Ihnen den Totenkopfring der SS.

    Er soll sein:
    Ein Zeichen unserer Treue zum Führer, unseres unwandel-
baren Gehorsams gegen unsere Vorgesetzten und unserer
unerschütterlichen Zusammengehörigkeit und Kameradschaft.

    Der Totenkopf ist die Mahnung, jederzeit bereit zu sein,
das Leben unseres Ichs einzusetzen für das Leben der Ge-
samtheit.

    Die Runen dem Totenkopf gegenüber sind Heilszeichen un-
serer Vergangenheit, mit der wir durch die Weltanschauung des Nationalsozialismus erneut verbunden sind.

    Die beiden Sigrunen versinnbilden den Namen unserer
Schutzstaffel.

    Hakenkreuz und Hagall-Rune sollen uns den nicht zu er-
schütternden Glauben an den Sieg unserer Weltanschauung
vor Augen halten.

    Umkränzt ist der Ring von Eichenlaub, den Blättern des
alten deutschen Baumes.

    Dieser Ring ist käuflich nicht erwerbbar und darf nie
in fremde Hände kommen.

    Mit Ihrem Ausscheiden aus der SS oder aus dem Leben
geht dieser Ring zurück an den Reichsführer-SS.

    Abbildungen und Nachahmungen sind strafbar und Sie haben
dieselben zu verhüten.

    Tragen Sie den Ring in Ehren!

      Siegel.   gez. H.Himmler.

No. 5-33
SS report, mentioning storage of death's head rings at Wewelsburg Castle
January 1, 1945
Translation on page 449
National Archives, Washington, D.C.,
F175, roll 191

No. 5-32
Certificate attesting to the award of a death's head ring to SS-*Standartenführer* Paul Zimmermann on April 20, 1936
Translation on page 450
Kreisarchiv Paderborn, AS 190 0

A certificate expounded on the symbolism of the death's head ring to its wearer. The ornamentation was designed by Karl Maria Wiligut as commissioned by Heinrich Himmler. The interpretation of the death's head and runic signs did not seek to be historically accurate, but rather, ideologically convincing in both the present and the future. The death's head ring, with its ostensible revisiting of Germanic tradition, was intended to help make its wearer a committed warrior for the National Socialist cause. The collection of rings at Wewelsburg Castle was supposed to have the same effect on guests as the castle itself. mm

Niederschrift über die Besprechung mit Gauleiter Terbowen
und dem Maler Painer auf der Wewelsburg.

Ich habe um folgende Dinge gebeten:

1.) Bild eines Lebensbaumes, einer Lebenesche für den G⊕richts-saal.

2.) Bild von der Marienburg für das Zimmer mit der Problem-stellung Deutscher Orden

3.) großes Triptychon für den Vorplatz vor der Führerwohnung mit folgenden drei Einzelteilen:

a) Der Angriff einen ᛋᛋ-Truppe im Krieg, bei dem ich mir sogar vorstelle, daß ein gefallener oder zu Tode ver-wundeter alter ᛋᛋ-Mann, der verheiratet ist, mit dargestellt wird, um zu zeigen, daß aus dem Tode selbst eines verhei-rateten Mannes trotzdem neues Leben sprießt.

b) Ein Acker im neuen Land, der von einem Wehrbauern, einem ᛋᛋ-Mann, geoflügt wird.

c) Das neugegründete Dorf mit der Familie und zahlreichen Kindern.

d)

4.) Den Hoheitsadler des Gerichtszimmers in keramischer Arbeit. (Allach bereits in Auftrag gegeben.)

5.) Einen großen Teppich in grauer Grundfarbe und rotem Rand-muster aus Zellwolle für das Gerichtszimmer.

6.) Weiterhin, wenn es möglich ist, einen langen schmalen Gobelin für das Zimmer des Reichsführer-ᛋᛋ mit der Figur eines voll erwachsenen jungfräulichen Mädchens, einer künftigen Mutter.

Im Gegensatz dazu soll – nicht von Terbowen gestiftet- aus dem Steinbossen im Burgsaal die Figur einer Mutter mit einem halberwachsenen Knaben, der ein werdender Mann ist, ge-schaffen werden. (Anmerkg.v.ᛋᛋ-Obersturmbannf.Diebitsch: Bildhauer Otmar Obermeier,München, mit Anfertigung einer Skizze beauftragt.)

No. 5-27

Excerpt from the undated log of a meeting in Wewelsburg Castle of Heinrich Himmler with the artistic advisor in the Personal Staff of the *Reichsführer-SS*, Karl Diebitsch, and the head of the "Hermann Göring Master School of Painting" in Kronenburg/Eifel, Werner Peiner, among others; presumably between January 15 and 18, 1939

Translation on page 449

A few months before the beginning of World War II, Heinrich Himmler commissioned a number of works of art intended to decorate Wewelsburg Castle. Their descriptions yield a thematic cross-section of his ideological program for the SS in general, and the *SS-Gruppenführer* castle in particular. The justifying and tradition-founding appeal of Northern European-Germanic mythology and of medieval German history would now be given artistic expression. The same applied to the leading role the SS claimed in the aggressive National Socialist policy of conquest in Eastern Europe. Similarly, Wewelsburg Castle could not be lacking in references to the SS's will to power, or its death and mother cults. mm

Bundesarchiv Berlin, NS 19/1446

No. 5-35

Hans Lohbeck (1909 – 1974): *Peace*, design for a Wewelsburg triptych Gouache on paper 1939 – 1941

The painter Hans Lohbeck produced two designs for the triptych, which Himmler commissioned in 1939. The salient visual elements are nearly identical in both versions: the SS settler family is shown at the center, while SS "soldier farmers" clear land on the right panel, along with the SS standard-bearer and SS man with a child on the left. In the present design, Wewelsburg Castle has been shifted to the left, screened by the riders and standard-bearers of the SS. In the middle section, SS units march from the left and right, converging on the National Socialist Party's (NSDAP) Nuremberg rally grounds in the background. Factories are visible at the far upper right. The other design features an SS unit in combat on the left, with Wewelsburg Castle, as a symbol of the SS, placed at the upper edge of the central panel. One possible visual mes-sage of both designs is that the SS recog-nized the leading position of the NSDAP in the industrialized "Old Reich," but saw itself playing a central role in the conquest and rule of the new – rural – colonized territories. mm

Kreismuseum Wewelsburg, inv. no. 13635

No. 5-36
Heinz Hindorf (1909 – 1990), *Gerichtsesche* **[The Ash of Justice] study for a painting Tempera and gold leaf on paper and wood 1939**

During his stay at Wewelsburg in January 1939, Heinrich Himmler commissioned, among other works, a painting with the theme of the "tree of life, an ash of life." It was to hang in the castle's courtroom. Its execution was entrusted to the painter Heinz Hindorf, from the "Hermann Göring Masters' School of Painting" in Kronenburg/Eifel. Under the title *The Ash of Justice*, Hindorf produced a preliminary design and a finished version of the painting. The latter has been lost.

In Nordic mythology, the ash, as the "world tree," embodies creation and the cosmos bridging heaven and earth. The image of the *Ash of Justice* was intended to establish a relationship between Germanic mythology and the racist "Nordic-Aryan" self-image of the SS. The background in gold leaf makes reference to early medieval altarpieces and aims to elicit a receptive, reverential attitude to the visual motif. mm

Loan from private collection
Kreismuseum Wewelsburg, inv. no. 17252

No. 5-34
Ernst Rötteken (1882 – 1945), *Study for a View of Wewelsburg Castle from the West* **Oil on canvas 1936**

Heinrich Himmler became aware of the Detmold artist Ernst Rötteken in 1935, when a local official gave him a painting of the Externsteine by the artist. Himmler commissioned the painter to produce an oil painting of Wewelsburg Castle. In early 1936, Rötteken submitted several studies to Himmler, presumably including this view of the castle from the west. Himmler selected a view from the north. The ensuing painting has been lost. Besides Wewelsburg Castle and the Externsteine, Rötteken painted other sites administered by the SS subsidiary Society for the Promotion and Care of German Cultural Monuments, such as the Sachsenhain in Verden an der Aller and the Collegiate Church in Quedlinburg. mm

Kreismuseum Wewelsburg, inv. no. 5192

5.2
The Village of Wewelsburg
1933 – 1939

The SS's treatment of Wewelsburg and its population evolved in parallel with the overall Wewelsburg project. The staff of Wewelsburg SS School wanted to appropriate the village as a part of a National Socialist national and ethnic community (*Volksgemeinschaft*). However, as planning progressed, Himmler was increasingly at pains to shield his project from outside interference.

Initially, the castle administration tried to win over the villagers for the SS ideology. For instance, a community center was built for the village, idealized by Walter Franzius in various publications as the epitome of National Socialist village architecture. Yet, architect Hermann Bartels's ever more grandiose plans soon presented the village solely as an obstacle. It was with this mindset that Bartels began to expand his planning and construction project beyond the castle itself, to include the village as well.

Wewelsburg between a National Socialist Ideology
of Ethnic Community and Displacement by the SS

No. 5-37
The Reich Agricultural Organization –
Blood and Soil – The Local Leader of the
Farmers' Organization
Metal sign, enameled
Breslau, mid-1930s
The Reich Agricultural Organization
(*Reichsnährstand*) was a corporative
National Socialist organization led by
Richard Walther Darré. From 1933,
membership was mandatory for all individuals and businesses involved in the
production and sale of agricultural
products. According to a 1934 survey,
51 percent of the Wewelsburg population
were members. Assisted by its local
representatives, the local leaders of the
farmers' organization (*Ortsbauernführer*),
the Reich Agricultural Organization
regulated the livelihood of its members.
Moreover, it also served to promote the
racist "Blood and Soil" ideology among the
rural population. The village of Wewelsburg was caught in the crosshairs of
National Socialist ideology from two
sides, as certain Wewelsburg SS School
staff sought to implement the ideas of
their mentor, Darré, with even more zeal
than the local leaders of the farmers'
organization. mm
Kreismuseum Wewelsburg, inv. no. 13506

No. 5-38
Construction sheds, banners,
and posters in front of
Wewelsburg Castle
February/March 1936
Kreismuseum Wewelsburg,
Fotoarchiv

No. 5-40
Not shown
"The Führer has given us
freedom and honor! Thank
him with your vote on
March 29"
Poster for the Reichstag
election of March 29, 1936
Institut für Zeitungsforschung,
Dortmund, F24/3

No. 5-39
"Germany has become more
beautiful," *Deutsche Arbeits-*
front **(German Labor Front)**
Poster, 1936
Institut für Zeitungsforschung,
Dortmund, F22/44

By the mid-1930s, banners proclaiming
"We're building here, thanks to the Führer"
decorated numerous German construction sites. However, the reconstruction of
the castle initiated by the SS yielded little
work for tradesmen from Wewelsburg and
its environs. Construction manager
Hermann Bartels only complied grudgingly
and sporadically with the SS's initial
assurance that local firms would receive
preferential treatment when jobs were
assigned.
    The poster on the construction shed
to the left urges people to vote in the
Reichstag election on March 1936.
In Wewelsburg, merely two eligible voters
cast their ballot against the National
Socialist Party (NSDAP), the only party to
run in that "election." In view of recent
political successes, such as the occupation of the Rhineland a few weeks earlier,
many villagers may well have believed the
NSDAP propaganda that Germany had
become "more beautiful" since 1933, as
claimed by the poster on the construction
shed in the middle. Certainly, fear of
retribution for voting against the NSDAP
played a part in securing the almost one
hundred percent result for the Führer,
Adolf Hitler. mm

Am 31. März 1935 übergab S.S.-Obersturmführer von Knobelsdorff im Nordturm der Wewelsburg dem neugegründeten „Fähnlein Wewelsburg" des Deutschen Jungvolks die vom Reichsführer-SS gestifteten Trommeln und Fanfaren. Die Feier wurde umrahmt von Fanfarenmärschen der Spielschar des Jungvolks Paderborn. Unser Bild zeigt den Ausmarsch des Jungvolks aus dem Hauptportal der S.S.-Schule „Haus Wewelsburg".

No. 5-41
SS Chief Castle Administrator Manfred von Knobelsdorff distributes trumpets and drums donated by *Reichsführer-SS* Heinrich Himmler to the newly founded Wewelsburg Young Folk (*Jungvolk*) patrol
Das Schwarze Korps, vol. 1 (May 8, 1935)
Kreismuseum Wewelsburg, inv. no. 5481

No. 5-42
The Wewelsburg Storm Detachment (*Sturmabteilung* or SA)
Ca. 1934
Kreismuseum Wewelsburg, Fotoarchiv

By the end of 1933, around thirty, mostly young men from Wewelsburg had joined the SA. A local chapter of the NSDAP was founded relatively late in 1938, and the number of SS members from Wewelsburg continued to be extremely small. Nevertheless, the youth of Wewelsburg only rarely escaped mandatory membership in the Hitler Youth (*Hitlerjugend*). The rural population's relationship to National Socialism was strongly shaped by common social and cultural divisions; for example, between young and old, farmers and salaried workers, the well-to-do and the lower classes, and churchgoers and the unchurched. From the outset, all these factors were at play in Wewelsburg, where National Socialism arrived in the guise of the Wewelsburg SS School, an external institution that instantly exerted an enormous influence on life in the village. In this respect, the drums and trumpets donated to the Young Folk (*Jungvolk*) by the *Reichsführer-SS* were mainly symbolic.

No. 5-43
Everyday scene of life in Wewelsburg: a local woman and an SS member with a baby carriage
Second half of the 1930s
The presence of the Wewelsburg SS School posed a challenge for the almost exclusively Catholic village population, and not just from an ideological or local-political point of view. The villagers needed to adjust to the SS men and their families, their new neighbors, with whom they sometimes lived under the same roof. At times, the urban cultural traits and behavior of the SS – compounded by its ideological prejudice against the "black" (i.e., Catholic) Paderborn district – led to conflict with the local population, who accused the "strangers" of being arrogant and condescending. On the other hand, trusting and amicable relationships also developed between members of the SS and the citizens of Wewelsburg.

The thoughts and feelings a woman from Wewelsburg might have had at the sight of an SS member and his (?) family with their stylish, "modern" baby carriage would therefore have strongly depended on external circumstances, as well as her own background. mm
Kreismuseum Wewelsburg, Fotoarchiv

No. 5-44
***Die Meckerer nach Palästina* [Send the Whiners to Palestine]; SS float with anti-Semitic decorations for a May Day procession in the inner courtyard of Wewelsburg Castle**
Second half of the 1930s
Kreismuseum Wewelsburg, Fotochiv

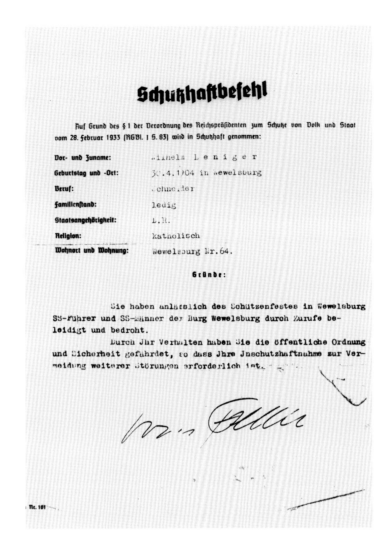

Schußhaftbefehl

Auf Grund des § 1 der Verordnung des Reichspräsidenten zum Schuhe von Volk und Staat vom 28. Februar 1933 (RGBl. I S. 83) wird in Schußhaft genommen:

Vor- und Zuname:	Wilhelm Leniger
Geburtstag und -Ort:	30.4.1904 in Wewelsburg
Beruf:	Schneider
Familienstand:	ledig
Staatsangehörigkeit:	D.R.
Religion:	katholisch
Wohnort und Wohnung:	Wewelsburg Nr.64.

Gründe:

Sie haben anläßlich des Schützenfestes in Wewelsburg SS-Führer und SS-Männer der Burg Wewelsburg durch Zurufe beleidigt und bedroht.

Durch Ihr Verhalten haben Sie die öffentliche Ordnung und Sicherheit gefährdet, so dass Ihre Inschutzhaftnahme zur Vermeidung weiterer Störungen erforderlich ist.

Nr. 101

Among the highlights of the National Socialist festival calendar was the first of May, which was renamed National Labor Day and declared a public holiday in the Third Reich. A regular feature was the formal procession in which local associations and National Socialist organizations took part. In Wewelsburg, the SS School used these occasions to spread anti-Semitic propaganda (although the village did not have a single Jewish inhabitant). Wewelsburg was one of the first localities in the area to post signs on its outskirts declaring Jews "undesirable." This initiative presumably originated at the Wewelsburg SS School, which sought to convey the image of a National Socialist model village to visiting SS and NSDAP dignitaries. mm

No. 5-46
Protective Custody order for Wilhelm Leniger following a marksmen's festival in 1937
Bielefeld, June 18, 1937
Kreismuseum Wewelsburg, Fotoarchiv

No. 5-45
Not shown
Wewelsburg Celebrations on May 1, 1937
Kreismuseum Wewelsburg, Fotoarchiv

From 1934, the Wewelsburg SS School tried to involve the villagers in a never-ending cycle of publicly celebrated National Socialist festivals, myths, and symbols. The inhabitants of Wewelsburg were to learn to see themselves as the farming element of the National Socialist *Volksgemeinschaft*. They were torn between feeling fascinated and patronized. It was against this background that an SS member severely beat an SA man from Wewelsburg at a May Day dance. A major altercation between Wewelsburg residents and SS men from the castle administration at a subsequent marksmen's festival was only narrowly averted. However, this time the authorities became involved, with the Gestapo taking five Wewelsburg men into protective custody for days and even weeks. On the SS side, the overchallenged chief castle administrator Manfred von Knobelsdorff left Wewelsburg soon thereafter. mm

5.2.2
The Guard Building and Village Community Center

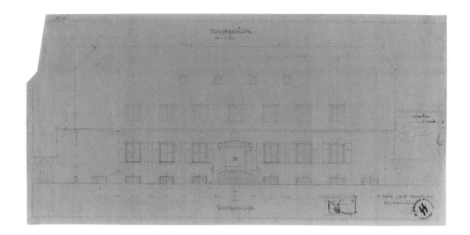

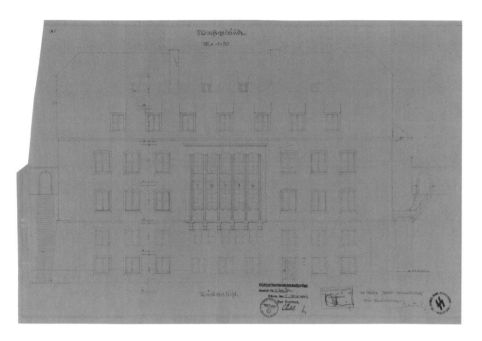

No. 5-49
Architectural drawing of the front view of the Guard Building
Blueprint, paper, red stamp "SS School Construction Management" and stamp of the district administrator as the approval agency
Hermann Bartels
Scale 1:50
Kreismuseum Wewelsburg, Plan 136

No. 5-50
Architectural Drawing of the rear view of the Guard Building
Blueprint, paper, red stamp "SS School Construction Management" with stamp of the district administrator as the responsible approval agency
Hermann Bartels
Scale 1:50
1936
Kreismuseum Wewelsburg, Plan No. 165

In 1936/1937, the SS property development entity in Wewelsburg, the Society for the Promotion and Care of German Cultural Monuments (Gesellschaft zur Förderung und Pflege deutscher Kulturdenkmäler e. V.), bought up houses on the eastern side of the castle hill in front of the entrance, and had them torn down. The "Society" gave the affected homeowners other sites in the village to build on, and subsidized the construction costs for the new buildings.

Without waiting for official permission, SS construction manager Hermann Bartels began with the construction of a large, multi-storey building, which was to house the Wewelsburg Castle SS guards, a mess, and recreation facilities. This freed up space in the castle, which could then be made available to visitors. It also enabled the SS to expand the area in Wewelsburg under its direct control. mm

No. 5-51
Not shown
Architectural drawing of the ground floor of the Guard Building
Blueprint, paper, red stamp "SS School Construction Management" and stamp of the district administrator as the approval agency
Hermann Bartels
Scale 1:50
1936
Although the first SS chief castle administrator, Manfred von Knobelsdorff, and his family had lived in the castle, his successor, Siegfried Taubert, took up quarters on the ground floor of the newly constructed Guard Building in 1938. Unmarried SS men, who until then had also lived in the castle, were accommodated in the new building on the castle forecourt that also provided space for an officers' mess and a combined gym and fencing hall. The administrative offices of the Wewelsburg SS School were located on the upper floor, and until 1942 the SS Construction Management occupied the first basement level. mm
Kreismuseum Wewelsburg, inv. no. 16615

No. 5-52
Armchair from the village community center with a carved Odal rune on the backrest
Oak, rattan seat
1937
Kreismuseum Wewelsburg, inv. no. 15282

No. 5-47
Not shown
Model of Wewelsburg Castle, showing the houses later torn down and the church
Ca. 1934
Kreismuseum Wewelsburg, Fotoarchiv

No. 5-48
Not shown
Photographs of the construction of the Guard Building
1936–1937
Kreismuseum Wewelsburg, Fotoarchiv

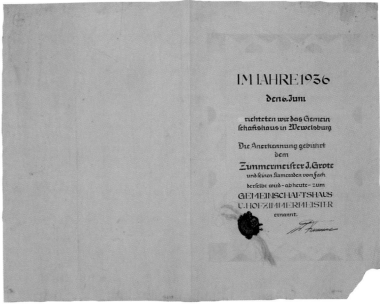

No. 5-53
**Photographs of the construction
and inauguration of the Wewelsburg
community center
1936 – 1937**
Kreismuseum Wewelsburg, Fotoarchiv

Under the direction of architect and SS
indoctrination leader Walter Franzius, the
three-hundred-year-old Ottens Hof in
Wewelsburg was transformed from 1935
to 1937 into the "first National Socialist
village hall in Westphalia." Villagers, SS
castle administration staff, and members
of the Reich Labor Service (RAD) unit
stationed in Wewelsburg all took part in its
construction. The building was officially
inaugurated in the presence of Himmler on
May 8, 1937. It was to provide the villagers
with a new cultural focal point, steeped
in National Socialist ideology, to make up
for the now inaccessible castle. mm

No. 5-54
**Humorous certificate appointing Wewels-
burg master carpenter Johannes Grote
"Master Carpenter of the Village
Community Center and of the Court,"
issued by Walter Franzius, SS construction
manager for the village community center
Cardboard, colored ink, sealing wax
June 6, 1936**
Unlike Hermann Bartels, the SS construction manager at the castle, SS
architect Walter Franzius considered it
crucial to include the Wewelsburg
population in the construction of the
village community center. His aim was to
win over the village for the ideals of
National Socialism and the objectives of
the SS in Wewelsburg. His practical
experience helped him build useful relationships with the local craftsmen.

By contrast, Bartels and his client
Himmler's plans for converting Wewelsburg Castle focused as much as possible
on isolating its inhabitants from all activity beyond its walls. mm
Kreismuseum Wewelsburg, inv. no. 16235

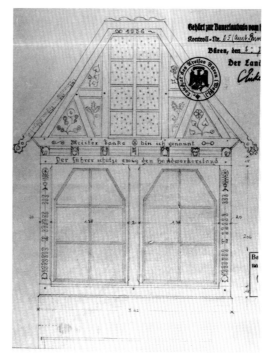

No. 5-55

Bench end from the community center decorated with a heraldic lion's head and skull
Oak, carved

Kreismuseum Wewelsburg,
inv. no. 1119

National Socialist symbols carved in wood or made of iron, as well as other emblems deemed by Franzius to be "Germanic" – such as this decorated bench end – can still be seen in and on the former Wewelsburg community center and its porch.

The stamp on the cutlery was intended to emphasize the exclusiveness of the Wewelsburg community center. The deeper, racist dimension of this exclusivity lay in the fact that Jews and other people branded "strangers to the community" by the National Socialists were barred from entering the community center. mm

No. 5-56

Sugar tongs stamped "Wewelsburg Community Center"
Silver
1937

Kreismuseum Wewelsburg,
inv. no. 14691

No. 5-57

Not shown

Soup spoon stamped "Wewelsburg Community Center"
Silver
1937

Kreismuseum Wewelsburg,
inv. no. 8780

No. 5-58

SS architect Walter Franzius's design proposal for the bay window in the Saake house, facing the village community center
1936

Kreisarchiv Paderborn,
B 5 40/53/1W I-IV

No. 5-59

Completed bay window
1980s

Kreismuseum Wewelsburg,
Fotoarchiv

No. 5-60

Yuletide festival in front of the building that would later become the village community center
Mid-1930s

Kreismuseum Wewelsburg,
Fotoarchiv

Beyond his work on the community center, Walter Franzius hoped to "beautify" the entire village of Wewelsburg in National Socialist terms. The opportunity arrived in the guise of a Reich-wide "village beautification" campaign by the *Deutsche Arbeitsfront* (DAF; German Labor Front). He met with the village elders to discuss planting flowerbeds, cleaning streets, and building gutters. Above the restored bay window of the building facing the community center, he wanted to affix the following inscription (framed by runes and "Germanic" ornamentation): "My name is Master Saake. May the Führer forever protect the order of craftsmen." But in the end, presumably at the insistence of Wewelsburg Catholic priest Franz-Josef Tusch (1887 – 1971), the following lines in Low German were chosen: "Whatever man creates in the glory of the Lord is a seed that never dies. The work of man achieved in God's name cannot be erased by time. As life ebbs and flows, God is with us everywhere." mm

5.2.3
The Voluntary Labor Service (FAD) and the Reich Labor Service (RAD)

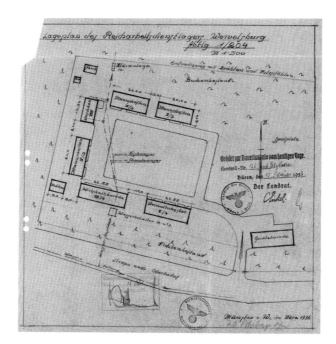

No. 5-65
Reich Labor Service unit taking leave in front of the village community center July 10, 1936

Kreismuseum Wewelsburg, Fotoarchiv

No. 5-61
Map of the Wewelsburg Reich Labor Service camp, dept. 1/204

Kreisarchiv Paderborn, Bür A 1413

No. 5-64
The Reich Labor Service camp at Kleiner Hellweg 1935 – 1938

Kreismuseum Wewelsburg, Fotoarchiv

No. 5-62
Not shown
Topographic map with the Reich Labor Service camp penciled in at Hellweg 1935 – 1938

Kreisarchiv Paderborn, Bür A 1415

Until the SS began with the reconstruction in 1935, up to 110 Labor Service workers had been housed in the east wing of Wewelsburg Castle. A camp was subsequently built at Kleiner Hellweg, near Oberntudorf, for the Wewelsburg unit of the Reich Labor Service. It remained in operation until June 1938, when the unit was transferred to the Eifel region to work on the Siegfried Line. mm

No. 5-63
Not shown
Reich Labor Service unit at work in the inner courtyard of Wewelsburg Castle 1936

Kreismuseum Wewelsburg, Fotoarchiv

The introduction of a compulsory six-month service with the Reich Labor Service in June 1935 was an important corner stone of National Socialist indoctrination. The concentration of Labor Service men in permanent camps, the wearing of uniforms, the incessant marching and drills, and paramilitary way in which the work was organized served to prepare them psychologically and physically for war. The Reich Labor Service was the National Socialist version of a forced labor camp for all citizens. In 1939, the SS replaced the Reich Labor Service camp in Wewelsburg with a concentration camp. "Work" no longer just served to prepare for war, but instead became a means of waging war against prisoners who were excluded from the National Socialist *Volksgemeinschaft*, the national and ethnic community. mm

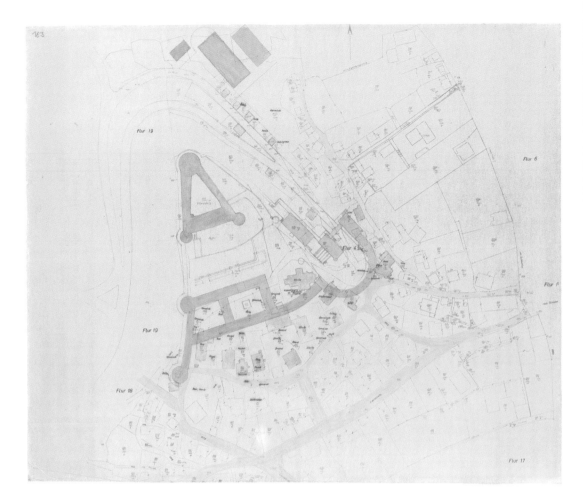

No. 5-66

Plan for the construction of a palace complex in the center of Wewelsburg "Construction Management, Wewelsburg SS School"
1939

In June 1936, Adolf Hitler named Heinrich Himmler "chief of the German police." The *Reichsführer-SS* had thus seized a pivotal position of power in the Third Reich. It was against this background that the SS in Wewelsburg began extending their construction plans to include the existing village.

The Catholic parish church and the presbytery in the immediate vicinity of the castle gardens were the first hurdles they faced. In June 1939, after almost two years of negotiations with the archiepiscopal vicariate general and the parish priest Franz-Josef Tusch, the SS acquired the church buildings, which were meant to be torn down and rebuilt at another location. At about the same time, Hermann Bartels was developing plans for a palace-like complex in the form of a hasp, which would cover the parish church grounds and extend between the castle and the village. mm

Kreismuseum Wewelsburg, Plan 163

No. 5-68
Not shown

Excerpt from the log of the Wewelsburg church council meeting of October 25, 1937
Priest Franz-Josef Tusch reports on negotiations with the SS regarding the relocation of the church buildings
Pfarrarchiv Wewelsburg,
Kirchenvorstandsprotokolle, p. 44 f.

No. 5-69
Not shown

Excerpt from the log of the Wewelsburg church council meeting of May 23, 1939
Determination of the price for the church buildings
Pfarrarchiv Wewelsburg,
Kirchenvorstandsprotokolle, p. 52 f.

No. 5-67

Franz-Josef Tusch (1883 – 1971), Catholic priest in Wewelsburg from 1934 to 1958
Priest Franz-Josef Tusch was adamantly opposed to the SS when it came to the interests of the Catholic Church in Wewelsburg. During negotiations over the sale and relocation of the parish church, he insisted on a sales price of 250,000 Reichsmarks. It was only when he was threatened with expropriation, and directly instructed by the Paderborn archbishop Kaspar Klein, that he agreed to the sum of 200,000 Reichsmarks offered by Himmler. As can be seen from the logs of the Wewelsburg church council, the SS had entrusted Minden District President Adolf von Oeynhausen to conduct the purchase negotiations on its behalf.
In January 1933, Oeynhausen had hosted Adolf Hitler and Heinrich Himmler at his Grevenburg castle during the Lippe state elections, thus presumably providing the initial stimulus for the SS search for a castle. In 1937, Himmler bestowed upon him the rank of an honorary *SS-Sturmbannführer*. mm

Kreismuseum Wewelsburg, Fotoarchiv

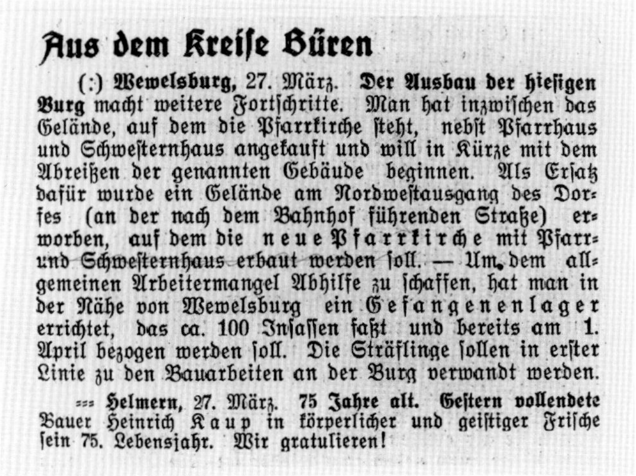

Aus dem Kreise Büren

(:) Wewelsburg, 27. März. Der Ausbau der hiesigen Burg macht weitere Fortschritte. Man hat inzwischen das Gelände, auf dem die Pfarrkirche steht, nebst Pfarrhaus und Schwesternhaus angekauft und will in Kürze mit dem Abreißen der genannten Gebäude beginnen. Als Ersatz dafür wurde ein Gelände am Nordwestausgang des Dorfes (an der nach dem Bahnhof führenden Straße) erworben, auf dem die neue Pfarrkirche mit Pfarr- und Schwesternhaus erbaut werden soll. — Um, dem allgemeinen Arbeitermangel Abhilfe zu schaffen, hat man in der Nähe von Wewelsburg ein Gefangenenlager errichtet, das ca. 100 Insassen faßt und bereits am 1. April bezogen werden soll. Die Sträflinge sollen in erster Linie zu den Bauarbeiten an der Burg verwandt werden.

≡≡≡ Helmern, 27. März. 75 Jahre alt. Gestern vollendete Bauer Heinrich Kaup in körperlicher und geistiger Frische sein 75. Lebensjahr. Wir gratulieren!

No. 5-70

First news report on the construction of a prison camp in Wewelsburg
Bürener Zeitung, March 27, 1939

By the end of the prewar phase of the Third Reich, a first, temporary concentration camp had been constructed in Almetal, below the castle. Contrary to what was stated in the *Bürener Zeitung,* the transfer of 100 prisoners from Sachsenhausen Concentration Camp near Berlin to Wewelsburg, guarded by 50 SS members of the Death's Head Unit, actually took place on May 10, 1939.

Prior to the arrival of the concentration camp prisoners, construction at Wewelsburg had largely been at a standstill since the local Reich Labor Service unit had been withdrawn in June 1938. Together with Bartels's plan for a hasp-shaped, palace-like complex, the construction of the first concentration camp marked a new dimension in the SS's claims to power in Wewelsburg, even before the onset of World War II. The planned expansion of the castle took less and less account of the existing structures of the village. The SS was absolutely ruthless in its treatment of anyone it could force to work on its projects in Wewelsburg. mm

Kreisarchiv Paderborn

From Büren District

(:) Wewelsburg, March 27. Improvements on the local castle are making good progress. The land on which the parish church, the nunnery and presbytery stand has been purchased, and demolition of the buildings is to begin shortly. In exchange, a property has been acquired at the northwest entrance to the village (on the road leading to the railway station), where the new parish church, along with the presbytery and nunnery, shall be rebuilt. – To remedy the general shortage of labor, a prison camp that can house around 100 inmates has been erected in the vicinity of Wewelsburg, to be occupied as early as April 1. The prisoners will be employed primarily for construction work on the castle.

Translation of a transcription

The outbreak of World War II in 1939 fully unleashed
the National Socialist reign of terror. Together with
the police, the SS played a pivotal role in imposing
German rule on the conquered nations.
That which Himmler's organization had initiated
within the more restrictive national framework could
now be pursued by the SS with the entire rigor of their
ideology. Following the slogan "The East belongs to
the SS," the SS and police implemented their conception of the absolute disposal over land, property,
and human life, particularly in Eastern Europe.
The result was resettlement and expulsion in the
name of a "greater Germanic" nationalist policy,
looting of property and cultural artifacts, forced
labor, and the murder of millions of people. The SS
also shed the last vestiges of moral and legal
restraint within the borders of the German Reich.

6
Crimes of the SS during World War II

Das neue Europa im Werden

Stand am 1. September 1941 nach 2 Jahren

Polenfeldzug

In einem Feldzug von 18 Tagen wurde die polnische Wehrmacht zerschlagen, die polnischen Divisionen vernichtet und das Gebiet des ehemals polnischen Staates bis zur deutsch-russischen Interessengrenze besetzt.

Norwegenfeldzug

Mit dem kühnsten Unternehmen der deutschen Kriegsgeschichte wurde der Plan der Alliierten, Deutschland von Norden her anzugreifen, zunichte gemacht.
In zähen Kämpfen, unter denen das Wort Narvik für immer als herrliches Zeugnis deutschen Heldentums leuchtet, wurden unter Überwindung größter klimatischer und geographischer Schwierigkeiten die feindlichen Streitkräfte geschlagen, die Engländer unter schwersten Verlusten aus dem Lande vertrieben und ganz Norwegen besetzt. Damit war zwei Monate nach Beginn der Operationen die englische Blockadefront zerbrochen und Groß-Deutschland im Besitz der strategisch wichtigen Flankenstellung gegenüber Englands Ostküste.

Westfeldzug

Nach einem Kampf von knapp 5 Tagen war die Kapitulation von Holland erzwungen.
Nach 18 Tagen kapitulierte die belgische Armee.
Nach nur 6 wöchigem Kampf waren die französischen Armeen zerschlagen und Frankreich mußte sich die gesamte Waffenstillstand bitten.
Über 1,9 Millionen Gefangene. Die gesamte Waffen- und Geräteausstattung von rd. 130 feindlichen Divisionen mit Geschützen bis zu den schwersten Kalibern, Panzerwagen und Kraftfahrzeuge aller Art wurden erbeutet oder zerstört. Unter der Beute befand sich die gesamte Bewaffnung und Ausrüstung der Maginot-Linie und der übrigen Befestigungen und fast die gesamte schwere und schwerste französische Artillerie. Die feindliche Luftwaffe verlor über 4300 Flugzeuge.

Balkanfeldzug

Kaum zwei Wochen nach Beginn der Aktion war der jugoslawische Staat, der von einer Handvoll gedungener Putschisten gegen das Großdeutsche Reich in den Krieg getrieben wurde, vernichtet. Die britischen Truppen selbst waren drei Wochen später in Griechenland entweder gefallen, verwundet, gefangen, ertrunken oder verjagt. Die Insel Kreta, auf sich ein Teil der aus Griechenland vertriebenen Briten geflüchtet hatte, und die nach Aussage Churchills bis zum äußersten verteidigt werden sollte, wurde in kühnstem Einsatz deutscher Fallschirm- und Luftlandetruppen gegen stärkste feindliche Übermacht erobert.

In den Kämpfen dieses Feldzuges wurden

über 570 000 Gefangene eingebracht. Erbeutet wurden: über 1500 Geschütze, rd. 600 000 Handfeuerwaffen, viele Tausend Maschinengewehre, Flakwaffen, Mörser, Hunderte von gepanzerten und anderen Kraftfahrzeugen, große Mengen an Munition zahlloses sonstiges Kriegsgerät sowie große Vorräte aller Art.

No. 6-1

War poster from the NSDAP Reich Propaganda Section: "The Emerging New Europe: Status of September 1, 1941"
Widespread anxiety and skepticism reigned in the German population at the prospect of another war. These doubts were often dispelled, however, by the *Wehrmacht*'s overwhelming military successes. Propaganda exploiting these victories was meant to win over the population for the war and heighten its acceptance. This poster presents the geographical dimension of victories by Germany and its allies in the first two years of the war. It was to convince viewers of Germany's power and bring them around to the "New Europe," which was to be led by an economically autonomous "Greater Germanic Reich." The "value" of European peoples was ranked according to racist criteria. Together with the *Wehrmacht*, Heinrich Himmler's SS and police apparatus was of central importance in realizing these plans.
mp

Kreismuseum Wewelsburg, inv. no. 4043

6.1
The Organized Terror of Occupation

German occupation rule over the conquered territories of Europe involved numerous institutions and organizations, including the *Wehrmacht*, the SS and police, party agencies, civilian administrations, private and semi-public interest groups, and local residents who collaborated with the Germans.

Despite a certain degree of competition, German occupation authorities shared a common purpose: they aspired to an economically self-sufficient "Greater Germanic Reich," in Central and Eastern Europe, surrounded by subjugated protectorates, where only "racially valuable people" would remain, and, if needed, a limited number of non-Aryan slaves. Heinrich Himmler's SS and police apparatus played a crucial role in implementing these plans.

No. 6-2
Hanns Johst, *Ruf des Reiches – Echo des Volkes! Eine Ostfahrt* [Call of the Reich – Echo of the People! An Eastward Journey] Franz Eher Nachf., Munich, 1940
Kreismuseum Wewelsburg, inv. no. 16581

No. 6-3
Not shown
Helmuth Koschorke, *Polizei greift ein! Kriegsberichte aus Ost, West und Nord* [Police in Action! War reports from East, West and North] Commissioned by the chief of the Order Police; book decorations by Dorul von der Heide, Berlin Print run 21,000 – 43,000 Franz Schneider Verlag, Leipzig, 1941
Kreismuseum Wewelsburg, inv. no. 16539

No. 6-4
Not shown
***Freigemachtes Grenzland. Erlebnisberichte von Günther Rumler, Major der Schutzpolizei und SS-Sturmbannführer, und Otto Holzmann, Oberwachtmeister der Schutzpolizei der Reserve* [Cleared Frontier Area: First-hand accounts by Günther Rumler, Police Major and SS-Sturmbannführer, and Otto Holzmann, Police Sergeant in the Reserve] Nordland-Verlag, Berlin, 1942**
Kreismuseum Wewelsburg, inv. no. 16534

Only a few months into World War II, there appeared the first of a new, quite strange type of travelogue. Members of the *Waffen-SS* and police propaganda services or writers such as Himmler friend Hanns Johst provided glowing accounts of their visits to the territories captured by German troops.

This "literature of conquest" revealed the deep-seated prejudices and attitudes of superiority shared by its authors and the German occupying power in general. The books reveal that the SS and police apparatus charged with combating enemies behind the lines flouted all generally accepted standards concerning wartime security measures, especially in its treatment of the civilian population.

Himmler had succeeded in securing extensive powers for his organization to "cleanse" and control the conquered territories. For him, the ruthless occupation represented the direct preparation for the long-term establishment of the coming "Greater Germanic Reich." mh

No. 6-5
The start of World War II: German soldiers demolish a border barrier between Zoppot (near Danzig) and Gdingen in Poland.
Colorized propaganda photo, September 1 or 2, 1939
Ullstein Bilderdienst, 00622576

No. 6-7
Erich von dem Bach-Zelewski (Higher SS and Police Leader for Russia Center), Major General Max von Schenckendorff (commander of the army rear area Center) and Major Gottlieb Nagel (battalion commander) (from left to right), inspect Police Battalion 322
Warsaw, June 28, 1941
Staatsarchiv Freiburg (Breisgau), F 176/13-1424-14a16

No. 6-6
Execution of Polish hostages by an *SS-Einsatzgruppe* in Kursnik/Kóruik (1939 – 1945, Burgstadt), Posen/Wartheland Reichsgau
October 20, 1939
Bundesarchiv Koblenz, Bildarchiv, Bild 146-1968-034-19A

No. 6-8
A member of Police Battalion 318 with fixed bayonet guards a man digging a hole. The original caption reads: "August 17, 1941. Someone digging their own grave: a captured partisan, about to be shot."
From the photo album of Josef Vogel, a member of Police Battalion 318
Private collection of Winfried Vogel, Bad Breisig

No. 6-9
Members of Dortmund Reserve Police Battalion 61, in Warsaw, at the "Krochmalna Bar," the officers' mess, which the unit set up in its quarters on the premises of Warsaw University. The walls are covered with anti-Semitic caricatures and slogans.
Warsaw, 1942
Landesarchiv NRW, Abteilung Westfalen, Münster, Primavesi, No. 145

With the outbreak of war, Himmler and the SS extended to the conquered territories their concepts of "internal security," which they had previously been developing in Germany since 1933. Wide swaths of Eastern and Southeastern Europe were viewed as future territory of the Reich that was to be "cleansed" of political and ideological "enemies" and "undesirable" population groups and prepared for extensive settlement operations.

It was essentially those institutions already tasked with the persecution of alleged or real adversaries within the German Reich that participated: the Reich Main Security Office (especially the Gestapo and SD), the Order Police, and new formations specifically created for the eventual outbreak of war, such as the police battalions of the Order Police, the *Waffen-SS*, or the SS Deployment Groups (*Einsatzgruppen*). Himmler's occupation policy was coordinated by the Higher SS and Police Leaders (HSSPF), who were directly responsible to him and enjoyed broad authority to issue directives to the police as well as to the *Allgemeine* SS and *Waffen-SS*. The HSSPF were responsible for carrying out settlement and extermination policy and coordinated the operations of the SS, police, and *Wehrmacht* after the invasion of the Soviet Union. Himmler personally selected his HSSPF. In his eyes, men such as Erich von dem Bach-Zelewski embodied the ideal of a fighter, who, unencumbered by moral codes and the regular chain of command, makes his decisions on his own and never shrinks from acts of violence against the civilian population. mh

An important component of the Order Police, in other words, the uniformed police, was the police and reserve police battalions. They had been specifically established as mobile units under military command for "foreign deployment" and were first used on a wide scale in Poland, and then primarily following the invasion of the Soviet Union.

These units not only performed general security tasks in the army rear areas, such as guarding material and buildings or maintaining public order, but also worked in conjunction with the Security Police to achieve the National Socialist regime's ideological and settlement objectives. Police battalions guarded the ghettos and deportation trains, carried out confiscations, fought partisans, evicted local inhabitants, and conscripted forced laborers. They also took part in mass executions of Jews, Sinti and Roma, and Soviet prisoners of war. Order Police constituted not least of all the bulk of the SS Deployment Groups.

Of the 125 German police battalions in existence from 1939 to 1945, at least 75 are proven to have taken direct or indirect part in war crimes. Alone, or in conjunction with the SS and *Wehrmacht*, police units murdered no less than 520,000 people. mh

No. 6-10
Two "Trawniki men" during the crushing of the Warsaw Ghetto Uprising in spring 1943
Warsaw, April/May 1943
The "Trawnikis" were members of "auxiliary units of foreign peoples" who had gone through the SS training camp at Trawniki (southeast of Lublin, Poland) and stood under SS command. The photograph is from a report by *SS-Brigadeführer* Jürgen Stroop, from Detmold, on the liquidation under his command of the Warsaw Ghetto in May 1943. mh
U.S. Holocaust Memorial Museum, Photo Archives, Washington D.C., 51008

No. 6-11
Guards from a Ukrainian police unit with German patrolmen (left)
Photograph: Scherer, Sarig, in the Kiev district, December 1942
Bundesarchiv Koblenz, Bildarchiv, Bild 121-1500

No. 6-13
Blowing up a village in an area suspected of harboring partisans
Belarus, 1944
Museum Karlshorst, Reg0541

No. 6-12
Sign posted by the *Wehrmacht*: "When the partisan rears his head – don't hesitate to fill it with lead"
Crimea, late 1941
Bibliothek für Zeitgeschichte Stuttgart, DC 125.2

The imposition and consolidation of German rule in the immense territories behind the front lines would have been practically impossible without support from indigenous forces. Motives for collaboration with the Germans varied. Personal advantage could play as big a role as opposition to Bolshevism or the hope for national independence. In addition, the German occupation offered the opportunity to violently act out old prejudices and hatreds against other population groups, especially the Jews.

Foreign volunteers fought as soldiers in the *Wehrmacht* and the *Waffen-SS*, they formed death squads of the Order Police, worked in investigative units of the Security Police and Security Service (SD) or, like the so-called Trawnikis, guarded extermination camps.

The expanding use of "willing alien helpers" for occupation duties especially in Eastern Europe was initially opposed within the SS for ideological reasons. The ever-growing need for more troops, however, saw these reservations increasingly subordinated as of 1941. Over 360,000 men served alone in indigenous police force (*Schutzmannschaft*) battalions and police volunteer units attached to the Order Police. In certain occupied regions, they accounted for the majority of police personnel. mh

One of the principal tasks of SS, police, and *Wehrmacht* units deployed behind the lines in Eastern and Southeastern Europe was combating partisans, in other words, armed resistance fighters in the enemy interior. Protections for such irregular combatants – already very weak under international law – were largely ignored by the German occupiers. Captured real or suspected partisans were frequently shot on the spot. Mere suspicion of supporting partisans often sufficed for the indiscriminate murder of civilians and the annihilation of entire village populations. In the parlance of the occupying forces, and also in official use from the summer of 1942, the expression "partisans" was largely supplanted by the more vague and contemptuous term of "bandits."

During the war against the Soviet Union, a serious threat from partisans first developed only as a result of unremittingly harsh, ever more oppressive occupation policies. The SS took over control of combating partisans in the fall of 1942, under the command of HSSPF for Russia Center Erich von dem Bach-Zelewski, whom Himmler appointed "Authorized Representative of the *Reichsführer-SS* for Bandit Control." Under his leadership, units of the SS, police, and *Wehrmacht* killed close to 350,000 people in Belarus alone – the focus of the partisan war. mh

Die Polizei als Freund und Helfer im Märchenwald
Die Hexe wird zugunsten von Hänsel und Gretel aus ihrem Knusperhäuschen zwangs-
evakuiert   Zeichnung: Will Halle

No. 6-14
Liquidation of the Krakow Ghetto
Krakow, March 1943
Visible in the background are
members of an Order Police unit
involved with deportations from
the ghetto. The possessions of the
deported Jews are strewn along
the street. mh

U. S. Holocaust Memorial Museum,
Washington D.C., Photo Archives, 39066

No. 6-15
"The police as friend and helper in the en-
chanted forest. The wicked witch is evicted
from her gingerbread house for the benefit
of Hansel and Gretel"
A caricature in the November 15, 1943 issue
of *Die Deutsche Polizei*, a periodical published for the RFSS and the Chief of the
German Police by the Fraternal Order of the
German Police
Drawing: Will Halle
The sign on the door reads "Seized for our
children. The police."

Die Deutsche Polizei, issue 11, no. 22
(November 15, 1943)

Raids in the Jewish ghettos and deportations were generally accompanied
by looting by German policemen, soldiers, and SS members. On occasion, the
plunder was surrendered at official collection points; frequently, however,
it was simply stolen for personal use – an act that technically carried the
death penalty.

For German occupying forces, World War II constituted an inexhaustible
source of collective as well as personal enrichment. Numerous bureaucracies
and organizations were busy managing the exploitation of labor; seizing
foodstuffs, land, and consumer goods; and carrying off valuable cultural artifacts, including whole libraries and museum collections, to the German Reich.

The cartoon (shown above) out of a trade and fraternal police newspaper
from 1943 gives insight into the invaders' view of themselves. Derisively, the
image transposes the reality of occupation onto the fairy tale of Hansel and
Gretel. The witch in the drawing represents those people forcibly "evacuated"
from their homes to make way for the ethnic Germans (*Volksdeutsche*)
represented by Hansel and Gretel. The positive slogan describing the police
as "your friend and helper" was meant to lend the violent measure an
appearance of legality.

Most readers of this newspaper would have been aware that "mandatory
evacuation" no longer simply referred to the expulsion from one's home, but –
particularly in the case of the Jews – to deportation to the extermination
camps. mh

6.2
SS Settlement Policies and Crimes

In the worldview of Heinrich Himmler and early SS settlement theoretician Richard Walther Darré, the concepts of "blood and soil," "race," and "living space" (*Lebensraum*) were inseparable. National Socialist Germany's strategy of conquest was thus accompanied by an SS settlement policy based on racist criteria. At least part of the conquered territories was to be "Germanized" and incorporated into a "Greater Germanic Reich." This plan stipulated German and ethnic German settlers, who the SS classified on ideological grounds. Those in the local population judged to be "alien" were to be subjugated, driven out, or murdered. The SS aspired to an entirely new social and ethnic order in Central and Eastern Europe.

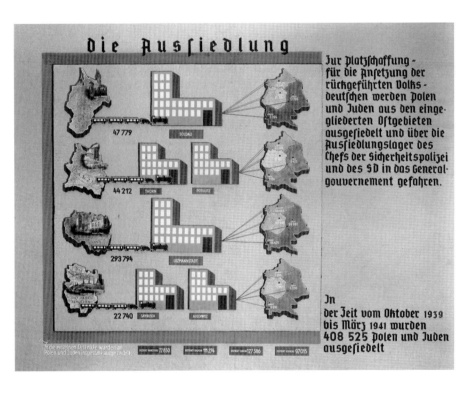

No. 6-16
Photograph of a chart from the exhibition "*Planung und Aufbau im Osten*" (Planning and Reconstruction in the East). The chart illustrates the expulsion of Poles and Jews from "incorporated eastern territories" for the benefit of ethnic German settlers up to March 1941. The exhibition was developed by the Staff Main Office of the Reich Commissar for the Strengthening of German Nationhood, an agency controlled by Himmler and the SS.
Photograph: M. Krajewesky, ca. 1941

The SS elaborated plans for German settlement of Poland and the Soviet Union on a gigantic scale. Initially, ethnic Germans from various eastern and southeastern European countries were brought to the German Reich. Receiving or settlement areas were primarily the "incorporated eastern territories," in other words, formerly Polish territory annexed by the German Reich in October 1939. These settlement actions were always accompanied at a minimum by the expulsion of the local population, and in many cases, their murder. An illustrated chart from the exhibition "Planning and Reconstruction in the East" precisely recorded the relationship between settlement and expulsion. By March 1941, 408,525 Poles and Jews had been driven out of their homes and into the remaining part of Poland controlled by the Germans under the name *Generalgouvernement*, or "General Government."
jes

Bundesarchiv Koblenz, Bildarchiv, R49 Bild-0025

The Reich Commissar for the Strengthening of German Nationhood

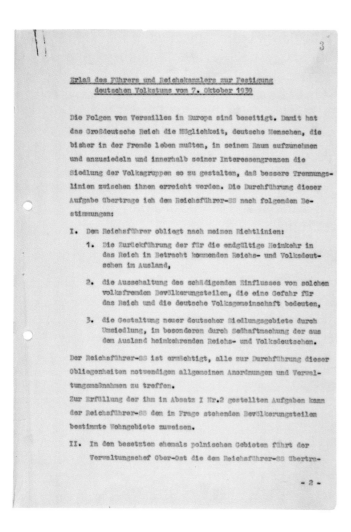

No. 6-17
Decree by Hitler entrusting Heinrich Himmler with the "Strengthening of German Nationhood"
October 7, 1939
Translation on page 450
The decree wording in itself indicates that settlement operations were accompanied by crimes against the local population, including their "elimination." jes
Bundesarchiv Koblenz, R 49/2 (p. 1)

No. 6-18
Office of the Immigration Central Office North-East in Lodz (Łódź, Poland, 1940 – 1945 Litzmann-stadt), ca. 1939 – 1941
Bundesarchiv Koblenz,
R 49 Bild-0108

No. 6-19
***SS-Gruppenführer* Ulrich Greifelt, Head of the Reich Commisar for the Strengthening of German Nationhood from 1941 – 1945**
Bundesarchiv Berlin,
SSO Ulrich Greifelt

On October 7, 1939, Adolf Hitler put Himmler in charge of "Strengthening German Nationhood." The *Reichsführer-SS* was to handle the resettlement of Baltic Germans to areas annexed by Germany in western Poland. The Baltic Germans had been forced to emigrate as a consequence of the "Hitler-Stalin Pact." This task gained Himmler wide-ranging influence over the treatment of the indigenous Polish and Polish-Jewish population. These new powers allowed him to expropriate their property and drive them out of the settlement areas. Himmler himself adopted the title of a Reich Commissar for the Strengthening of German Nationhood (RKF).

Centrally he established the institution of the Staff Main Office RFK, under *SS-Gruppenführer* Ulrich Greifelt. Locally, the Immigration Center (EWZ) was responsible for reviewing the ethnic Germans. In the course of World War II, Himmler extended his influence as Reich Commissar to include additional occupied territories, primarily in Eastern Europe. This also served in making the SS one of the most important factors in German occupation policy. jes

No. 6-20
Heinrich Himmler inaugurates the exhibition "Planning and Reconstruction in the East" at the State University of Fine Arts, Hardenberg Straße, Berlin
Present, among others, are Rudolf Hess, Hitler's deputy (center), Philipp Bouhler, head of the Führer chancellery (at left, next to Heß), and Prof. Konrad Meyer-Hetling.
March 20, 1941
Ullstein Bildarchiv, 00024539

"According to the [Reich Main Security Office] plan, these 8,000,000 German [settlers in East Central, and Eastern Europe] will now be facing 45 million aliens, of which 31 million are to be relocated. … Only if one assumes that the approximately 5 to 6 million Jews living in this area will already have been eliminated before the evacuation, does one arrive at the figure of 45 million aliens mentioned in the plan."

No. 6-21
Remarks and thoughts of Dr. Erhard Wetzel from the Ministry for the East on the *Reichsführer-SS*'s General Plan for the East
April 27, 1942
Nuremberg Document NG-2325-2325

The General Plan for the East was a far-reaching blueprint for German settlement and reshaping of Poland and the western Soviet Union. It was developed by Konrad Meyer-Hetling, an *SS-Oberführer* and a professor at the University of Berlin. A prominent planning and settlement authority, he was a member of the Staff Main Office of the Reich Commissar for the Strengthening of German Nationhood. In June 1942, Meyer-Hetling submitted the plan to Himmler. The immense territories involved were to be "Germanized" within 27 years, with it being an unspoken assumption that the local populations would first be driven out or killed.

Concerning costs, Meyer-Hetling arrived at the huge sum of 66.6 million Reichsmarks. Construction operations would initially require 450,000 workers, mostly forced laborers. SS and police bases would secure the occupied area. The preliminary plans from 1941 provide an impression of these fortresses. For Himmler, however, the plans did not go far enough. He demanded even wider-ranging settlement measures. jes

The SS's settlement plans radicalized considerations to exploit and murder the local populations. Reinhard Heydrich's Reich Main Security Office was also involved in the development of the General Plan for the East. Civilian ministers in the National Socialist regime were informed of the plans. According to a report by the Ministry for the East, at least 31 million persons were to be driven out or murdered. The report openly stated that Jews could be "eliminated."

For Himmler, the settlement plans presented an opportunity to bring great numbers of forced laborers under SS control. They were to construct the structures needed in the settlement zones. Himmler indicated that the planned settlements would not see the light of day "unless we fill our camps with slaves, … with slave laborers who regardless of their losses will build our cities, our villages, our farms." Lublin-Majdanek and Auschwitz-Birkenau Concentration Camps were initially planned as camps for such forced laborers. The settlement plans thus prepared the extermination of the Jews and other population groups by yet another avenue. jes

No. 6-22
Expelled Poles on their way to the train station
Photograph: Wilhelm Holtfreter, Schwarzenau bei Gnesen
Ca. 1939 – 1941

Bundesarchiv Koblenz, Bildarchiv, R 49, Bild 0131

No. 6-23
SS-Gruppenführer Odilo Globocnik, *Gauleiter* (National Socialist Party leader) of Vienna; 1939 – 1943, SS and Police Leader of Lublin, with responsibility for Operation Reinhard, which included the extermination of Polish Jews as well as the settlement of Germans in Zamość; 1943, Higher SS and Police Leader, Trieste

Bayerische Staatsbibliothek, Munich, Fotoarchiv Heinrich Hoffmann, hoff-1161

No. 6-24
German settlers move into a farm in Wartheland that was expropriated from its former Polish owner
Photograph: Scherl, ca. 1940 – 1944

Süddeutsche Zeitung Photo, 33359

No. 6-25
The Ethnic German Liaison Office resettlement camp in Wewelsburg Winter 1943 – 1944

Kreismuseum Wewelsburg, Fotoarchiv

Soon after the occupation of Poland, Poles and Polish Jews began to be driven out of the annexed territory, with the expulsions resulting from the SS plans for settlement. Especially in Lublin District, the local head of the SS and police, Odilo Globocnik, was quick to use Jews as forced laborers. In retrospect, the expulsions proved to be a preliminary stage to the murder of the Polish Jews.

After the invasion of the Soviet Union, Jews were forced to work there under appalling conditions on German infrastructure projects. The SS attempted for a time to establish two prototype German settlements in the "Hegewald" area, near the Ukrainian town of Zhytomyr, and in Zamość in the Lublin district. Part of the Polish population of Zamość was imprisoned in Lublin Concentration Camp. Expulsions, forced labor, and murder were inextricably linked to the settlement policy. jes

The SS Ethnic German Liaison Main Office (VOMI) under *SS-Obergruppenführer* Werner Lorenz was responsible for German-speaking minorities living outside the German Reich; it therefore played a key role in the SS settlement policy. As a central office, the VOMI managed and distributed all funds for the "work for race and nation" (*Volkstumsarbeit*). In addition, it organized housing and support services for the ethnic German settlers who were brought from their former homelands to the German Reich or the annexed territories. Actually, the SS agencies did not initially establish the settlers in the intended areas, but assigned them to resettlement camps specially built for that purpose. In the end, there were 1,590 VOMI camps, 1,248 of which were permanently used. From 1939 to 1941, 500,000 persons had already been resettled, with another 400,000 joining them by 1944.

Particularly in the resettlement camps, ethnic German settlers were subjected to an assessment based on racist criteria that was crucial to their fate. The process classified them into "O cases" (to be resettled in the East), "A cases" (to be placed in the "Old Reich" because of their poor "quality") and "S cases" (to be rejected from the "national community"). After disbandment of the concentration camp at Wewelsburg, the SS also used its grounds and barracks as a resettlement camp of the Ethnic German Liaison Office. ne

6.3
The Murder of Soviet Prisoners of War

Soviet prisoners of war constituted one of the largest groups of victims in World War II. From the beginning, the German attack on the Soviet Union, conceived as a war of extermination, never aimed to "spare the enemy" (Adolf Hitler). The death of millions of people was cold calculation. During their advance, the *Wehrmacht* and *Waffen-SS* captured upwards of 5.7 million Red Army soldiers; of these, between 3 and 3.5 million perished in German captivity.

Responsibility for the Soviet prisoners of war rested with the Army High Command. The majority of prisoners died in camps established for Red Army soldiers or on labor details and deployments. The SS, however, was also responsible for the death of tens of thousands of Soviet prisoners of war.

No. 6-26
Der Reichsführer-SS, SS-Hauptamt: *Der Untermensch* [*The Reichsführer-SS*, SS Main Administrative Office, The Subhuman] Nordland-Verlag, Berlin, 1942

A particularly drastic example of National Socialist hate propaganda, *The Subhuman*, appeared a year into the German invasion on the Soviet Union. The brochure was published on order of the *Reichsführer-SS*, who personally and repeatedly intervened in its production. Published by the SS's own Nordland publishing house, four million copies of the booklet were printed in 15 languages.

The term *subhuman* was applied as an expression of the National Socialists' belief in their own biological and cultural superiority. From the mid-1930s, the term played an important role in their campaign against Bolshevism, with a primarily anti-Semitic and anti-Russian slant.

The brochure's title page displays Soviet prisoners of war. After the Jews, they represented the largest group of victims of the National Socialist policies of extermination. More than half of all Red Army prisoners of war – over three million – perished in German captivity. In addition to the *Wehrmacht*, the SS and police bore primary responsibility for this. mh
Kreismuseum Wewelsburg, inv. no. 16310

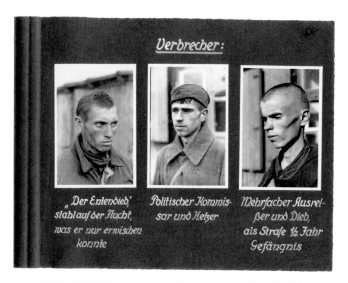

No. 6-28
**Private photo album of a *Wehr-
macht* soldier, defaming Soviet
prisoners of war as criminals**
Archiv Dokumentationsstätte Stalag
326 (VI K) Senne

No. 6-27
**Thousands of Red Army soldiers
are taken prisoner by the Germans
near Tcharkov, May 1942**
Bildarchiv Preußischer Kulturbesitz,
Berlin, 30010669

No. 6-29
**Air-tight containers holding
Zyklon B poison gas crystals,
produced by IG Farben AG for
Auschwitz Extermination Camp**
Bildarchiv Preußischer Kulturbesitz,
Berlin, 30002970

Even before the attack on the Soviet Union, the "Commissar Order" of June 6, 1941, demanded the "selection," or summary execution, of all captured Soviet political commissars. Villainized as the actual drivers of the resistance, they were explicitly not to be taken prisoner. In July 1941, the category of persons slated for murder was expanded to include those identified as "intolerable" because of the assumed "racial" or "ideological" threat they posed. This included government and party officials, leaders of business and commerce, members of the intelligentsia, Jews, and anyone suspected of resistance.

The *Wehrmacht*, in whose "care" the Soviet prisoners of war found themselves, worked closely with the SS. *Wehrmacht* soldiers either executed the selected prisoners of war themselves, or handed these over to the SS, which murdered their victims near the front or in concentration camps. For this, the SS also employed specially designed killing apparatus enabling them to shoot the unknowing prisoner in the back of the head. According to current knowledge, about 36,000 Soviet soldiers were murdered within the first year of the invasion. By July 1942, at least 40,000 Red Army soldiers had been murdered in concentration camps, including some 19,000 at Buchenwald and Sachsenhausen. mm/on

In order to render the National Socialist mass murders psychologically "less burdensome" for the executioners – as well as more efficient, various killing methods were tested, with numerous Soviet prisoners being murdered in such experiments. In early September 1941, the SS first employed the pesticide Zyklon B (active agent: cyanide) for mass killing. This is thought to have occurred under the supervision of "protective detention" camp deputy commandant Karl Fritzsch, when 250 prisoners reported as "ill" and 600 Soviet prisoners of war were gassed in the basement cells of the camp prison (Block 11) at Auschwitz I Concentration Camp, the main camp in the Auschwitz complex. That same month, the camp SS killed another 900 Soviet prisoners of war – this time in the crematorium morgue at Auschwitz I.

Zyklon B was employed for the systematic mass-killing of people from all over Europe as of the spring of 1942, in what at first were provisionally erected gas chambers, in particular at Auschwitz-Birkenau, also know as Auschwitz II. Prisoners were also killed with this poison gas at Majdanek, Neuengamme, and Stutthof concentration camps. The final toll of Soviet prisoners of war murdered with Zyklon B remains unknown. mm/on

No. 6-30
Heinrich Himmler (third from right)
inspecting a prisoner of war camp near
Minsk in the Soviet Union
August 15, 1941
To the left of Himmler, *SS-Sturmbannführer* Dr. Otto Bradfisch (in forage cap),
whose Deployment Commando 8
(*Einsatzkommando 8*) daily carried out
selections and executions of camp
prisoners. mm/on
Bildarchiv Preußischer Kulturbesitz, Berlin,
50074070

No. 6-31
Title page of a *Wehrmacht*
propaganda newspaper showing
Soviet prisoners of war being taken
away in freight cars
October 1941
Archiv Dokumentationsstätte
Stalag 326 (VI K) Senne

In September 1941, the SS began setting up their own labor camps for Soviet
prisoners of war at Sachsenhausen and Mauthausen. The Lublin-Majdanek
camps, along with the camp being built at Auschwitz-Birkenau, were initially
intended to be used entirely as SS prisoner of war camps. In September 1941,
Hitler also approved the transfer of 200,000 prisoners of war to the SS. It was
planned to put most of these prisoners to work as "labor Russians" on SS
construction and settlement projects in the occupied eastern territories.
Himmler also foresaw the use of the prisoners in the SS's own businesses.
    Soviet prisoners of war were in the custody of the Armed Forces High
Command (OKW), which worked closely with the SS – by "selections" as well.
That same month, the OKW assented to the transfer or discharge of 100,000
Soviet prisoners of war to the SS. Within days, 25,000 prisoners were
conveyed from *Wehrmacht* prisoners of war camps to the SS labor camps.
According to current knowledge, the OKW transferred some 30,000 Soviet
prisoners to the SS in 1941, and 5,000 in 1942 – 1943. Very few Soviet prisoners
of war survived even the following months because of the inhuman conditions. Of 10,000 Red Army prisoners who entered Auschwitz I in November
1941, only 945 were still alive in March 1942. Of 2,500 prisoners of war at
Groß-Rosen Concentration Camp, only 89 survived until January 1942.
At Mauthausen, 1,600 prisoners of war died in just the month of March 1942.
mm/on

Soviet Prisoners of War as Concentration Camp Prisoners

Medical Experiments on Soviet Prisoners of War

No. 6-32
Prisoner ID chart for Soviet prisoner of war Ivan J. from Niederhagen Concentration Camp in Wewelsburg
The red triangle with the letters "RK" in the upper right corner identified him as a political prisoner and Soviet prisoner of war. mm/on
Internationaler Suchdienst, Bad Arolsen, Umschlag Iwan J.

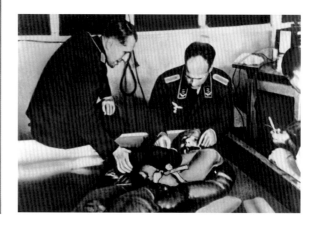

No. 6-33
Dr. Ernest Holzlöhner (left) and Dr. Sigmund Rascher (right) conduct a hypothermia experiment on a prisoner in a life jacket and protective suit at Dachau Concentration Camp
1943
Ullstein Bilderdienst, 00041203

Tens of thousands of Soviet prisoners of war were sent to concentration camps. Removed from the *Wehrmacht*'s responsibility, they were no longer administered as prisoners of war, but as concentration camp inmates. The most commonly given grounds for transfer to a concentration camp were "attempted escape," "refusal to work," "rebellion," and "relations with German women."

The decision to divest a Red Army soldier of his status as prisoner of war and transfer him to a concentration camp rested with the commander of the respective prisoner of war camp. In most cases, the Gestapo took charge of the expelled prisoner of war and decided, based on the severity of his "crime," whether he was to be executed in the concentration camp or assigned to a labor detail there. Because of the ongoing war and the resulting labor shortage, ever more prisoners of war were needed as forced laborers.

Just how many Soviet prisoners of war ultimately fell victim to executions or slave labor in concentration camps is largely unknown. mm/on

Human experiments were performed by SS members, or took place in collaboration with German scientists, physicians, and the *Wehrmacht*. For racist reasons, the SS frequently selected Soviet prisoners of war, considered "Bolshevik subhumans," as test subjects. Hypothermia and altitude sickness experiments were conducted at Dachau Concentration Camp. In charge, or deeply involved, was physician and SS medical officer Dr. Sigmund Rascher. In the case of the hypothermia experiments, test subjects were immersed for hours in a tank filled with ice water, or had to lie naked outside in subzero temperatures. In many cases, their body temperature fell below 25°C (77°F). Afterwards, the prisoners were administered various substances intended to restore their normal body temperature. The *Luftwaffe* (Air Force) hoped to gain knowledge about how long shot-down flyers could survive in the sea, and which methods could be used following rescue.

Rascher expected observation of prisoners' death throes and their subsequent autopsies to yield insight into physiological processes such as the behavior of brain, heart, and lungs. To this day, it is not known how many Soviet prisoners of war or concentration camp prisoners were subjected to these experiments and how many died as a result, or survived with severe physical or psychological disabilities. mm/on

6.4
The Genocide of the Jews

The exclusion, persecution, and, ultimately, murder of the Jews did not proceed according to a pre-established plan. The individual stages of disenfranchisement and deportation sometimes developed in parallel. With a growing radicalization during the war, the final step to homicide and mass murder occurred ever more quickly. Nevertheless, it is possible to distinguish specific phases that advanced the process to the point of a generalized slaughter of the Jewish population. Members of the SS participated in most of these phases. The SS intensified the persecution of the Jews more than any other National Socialist organization. To 1945, at least 5.3 million, but probably more than 6 million Jews perished in the genocide.

No. 6-33a
Yellow badge belonging to Mr. and Mrs. Leven of Krefeld-Hüls
Photograph: Anja Lienemann, 2011

The "yellow badge" was one of the most visible signs of discrimination and exclusion of the Jewish population. In German-occupied Poland, as of December 1, 1939, all Jewish residents had to wear a white armband with a blue, six-pointed star. Within the German Reich, mandatory identification entered into force on September 19, 1941. From then on, all Jewish residents had to wear a yellow badge, officially known as a "Jewish star." At its center, in black lettering parodying the Hebraic alphabet appeared the inscription "Jew." The badge was to be "firmly sewn" to the left side of the garment, at chest level. Stigmatization and isolation were steps leading to the deportation and subsequent murder of the Jews. In most occupied countries, German officials, especially the SS, sought to impose a marking of the Jewish population. jes
Kreismuseum Wewelsburg, inv. no. 17474

Stigmatization

Ghettoization

No. 6-34
Two German policemen with a woman wearing a Star of David armband at a market in northern Poland
Photograph: Wirthgen, PK (propaganda unit) 637, May 1941

Bundesarchiv Koblenz, Bildarchiv, Bild 101I-019-1224-10

No. 6-35
Sentry at the entrance to the Lodz ghetto (Łódź, Poland, 1940 – 1945 Litzmannstadt)
Photograph: Zermin PK (propaganda unit) 689, 1941

Bundesarchiv Koblenz, Bildarchiv, Bild 101I-133-0703-30

No. 6-36
View of Krisciukaicio Street in the Kaunas ghetto (Lithuania)
Photograph: George Kadish (born Zvi Kadushin), between 1941 and 1944

U. S. Holocaust Memorial Museum, Washington D.C., Photo Archives, 81143

The marking of Jewish people was not invented by National Socialist functionaries. As early as the Middle Ages, Jews were made to wear certain prescribed garments. These regulations had only finally disappeared in the nineteenth century. Soon after the invasion of Poland on September 1, 1939, local offices of the German *Wehrmacht* decreed that Jewish shops be marked. The German civil administration quickly followed suit. From December 1, 1939, all Jews in the *Generalgouvernement* – as parts of the occupied Poland territory were designated – had to wear an armband with a blue Star of David.

The introduction of the public wearing this marking in the German Reich occurred under close coordination between the Reich Main Security Office (RSHA) and the Reich Ministry of the Interior. On September 19, 1941, a police decree took effect ordering all Jewish residents over the age of six to wear the yellow badge. Adolf Eichmann and his colleagues, in particular, tried to make the marking of Jews compulsory in France, Belgium and the Netherlands. Decrees to that effect were imposed in all three countries in 1942. This stigmatization completed a process of social exclusion and prepared the way for deportation. jes

Ghettos in the form of isolated residential districts for Jews were already known in the Middle Ages. In 1939 the Gestapo began establishing *Judenhäuser* in the German Reich where Jews were forced to live crowded together in extremely tight quarters. In the occupied areas, above all in Poland, ghettos encompassed entire town districts. Here, too, space was extremely cramped. Hygienic conditions and health care were catastrophic. There was permanent famine. German civilian ghetto administrations and the SS used the Jewish representation of the ghetto population, the so-called Jewish Council, to implement their decrees. Local and German police guarded the ghetto perimeter, with murders and deportations by the SS, police, and local collaborators being commonplace. The local Gestapo offices, in particular, decided directly about whether ghetto residents lived or died. Deportations were carried out in close collaboration with the German civilian administration.

From 1942, the ghettos were progressively disbanded, their inhabitants shot or transported to extermination camps. In April 1943, Jewish resistance groups staged an uprising in the Warsaw Ghetto. After almost a month of fighting, it was crushed by *Waffen-SS* and police units under the command of *SS-Brigadeführer* Jürgen Stroop. jes

Plunder and Forced Labor

Deportation

No. 6-37
Household items being auctioned off following the deportation of Jewish residents in Hanau, 1942
Bildarchiv Preußischer Kulturbesitz, Berlin, 30003501

No. 6-38
Backbreaking labor by female prisoners at Krakow-Plaszow Concentration Camp, 1944
Bildarchiv Preußischer Kulturbesitz, Berlin, 30012732

No. 6-39
Deportation of German Jews from Ludwigshafen to the Gurs camp in the south of France October 22, 1940
Stadtarchiv Ludwigshafen, 11786079

No. 6-40
Deportation of Dutch Jews to Westerbork police transit camp, 1942
U. S. Holocaust Memorial Museum, Washington D.C., Photo Archives, 15338

Wide segments of the German population took part in the "aryanization" of Jewish property, or profited indirectly from it. Government agencies, the National Socialist Party, business people, and private individuals all enriched themselves from uncompensated expropriations and purchases far below market value. Assets, companies, houses, property, apartments, and furnishings were simply taken away from their Jewish owners.

But the Jews were not only robbed of their property. They also had to work for free or at a derisory wage. All over German-occupied Europe, as in the Reich itself, Jews worked as forced laborers. Many succumbed to inhuman working conditions. A gigantic forced-labor camp was established in Krakow-Plaszow (Kraków Płaszów). Run as a concentration camp as of 1944, it held as many as 22,000 to 24,000 prisoners, mainly survivors of the Krakow ghetto, but also Hungarian Jews and Polish resistance fighters. Plaszow Concentration Camp and its SS commandant Amon Goeth became widely known through the film *Schindler's List*.

Mass murder was also exploited for profit. The last personal belongings in the victims' possession were collected at Auschwitz-Birkenau and Lublin-Majdanek as well as at the death camps of Operation Reinhard (Belzec, Sobibor, and Treblinka). This final phase of the looting of Jewish property was managed by the SS Economic and Administrative Main Office (WVHA). Corruption blossomed at the extermination camp collection points for valuables, as SS officials working there sought to enrich themselves. jes

On January 20, 1942, at the meeting know as the Wannsee Conference presided over by Reinhard Heydrich, representatives of the principal Reich ministries were informed about upcoming deportations. Transports of Jews to the extermination camps, primarily from Western, Southern, and Southeastern Europe, were coordinated by Department IV B 4 (Jewish affairs, evacuations) of the Reich Main Security Office (RSHA), under the direction of Adolf Eichmann. His department maintained offices in the countries where the Jewish populations were being deported.

To manage these deportations, Eichmann and his on-site support staff relied on local agencies and police forces. Eichmann's department constituted only the top echelon of the deportation organization. Municipal administrations and police assisted in the identification of Jewish residents and escorted them to assembly points, from where they were transported to the extermination camps. The *Reichsbahn* (German national railway), the Ministry of Transportation, and the SS collaborated closely in organizing the deportations. On August 13, 1942, *SS-Obergruppenführer* Karl Wolff thanked the State Secretary at the Reich Ministry of Transportation, Albert Ganzenmüller, that "for 14 days now, a train with 5,000 members of the chosen people has been departing daily for Treblinka." jes

No. 6-41
"Executions of Jews performed by Einsatzgruppe A (Deployment Group A)," from the report filed by *Einsatzgruppe A* on the Jews killed in the Baltic States and Belarus up to January 31, 1942; known as the second Stahlecker report, it was named after the commander of *Einsatzgruppe A*, Dr. Franz Walter Stahlecker, an *SS-Brigadeführer* and police major general

U. S. Holocaust Memorial Museum, Washington D.C.,
Photo Archives, 03550

No. 6-42
SS-Gruppenführer Franz Walter Stahlecker, commander of *Einsatzgruppe A*, killed March 22, 1942, south of Leningrad (St. Petersburg)

Die Deutsche Polizei,
issue 10, no. 8 (April 15, 1942), p. 114

The number of victims of the genocide of the Jews

The German Reich	160,000	minimum figure
Austria	65,459	
Luxemburg	1,200	
France	76,124	including foreign nationals
Belgium	28,518	including foreign nationals
The Netherlands	102,000	
Denmark	116	
Norway	758	minimum figure
Italy	6,513	
Albany	591	deported
Greece	59,185	
Bulgaria	11,393	deported from occupied Bulgarian territories; all Bulgarian Jews were saved
Yugoslavia	60,000 – 65,000	
Hungary	550,000	
Czechoslovakia	143,000	territory of the Reich Protectorate of Bohemia and Moravia, as well as Slovakia
Romania	211,214	
Poland	2,700,000	
The Soviet Union	2,100,000	

No. 6-43
Wolfgang Benz, "Die Dimension des Völkermords," *idem* (ed.), Dimension des Völkermords. Die Zahl der jüdischen Opfer des Nationalsozialismus, Munich, 1996, p. 15 f.

The prewar years had already seen politically and racially-motivated murders of Jews. The war brought a radicalization of this policy. As early as 1939, SS units in Poland killed tens of thousands of Polish civilians, most of them Jews. Then, in 1941, within a period of a few months, the attack on the Soviet Union brought about yet another escalation of the violence and, step by step, an all-out genocide of the Jewish population. *SS-Einsatzgruppen*, police battalions, and the *Kommandostab* (Commando Staff) *Reichsführer-SS*, in particular were all escalating the process of radicalization.

The *Wehrmacht*, German civilian administrations, and local volunteers also participated in the mass executions. The reports submitted by the *Einsatzgruppen* contain detailed data on the dimensions of the mass-murder. The 990-man *Einsatzgruppe D* alone reported killing 218,050 persons by the end of January 1942. In 1941/1942 the mass murder spread to almost all of Europe. In addition to the mobile death squads, extermination camps were now being established as places of systematic mass murder. At these sites alone, 2.5 million people perished, nearly half of the estimated 5.3 to more than 6 million murdered Jews. jes

6.5
The Extermination Camps

In the fall of 1941, the SS began building stationary extermination sites. These were predominantly sited in Central and Eastern Europe. There, from 1942, people, above all Jews, were murdered systematically in great numbers, mostly by poison gas. The killing facilities varied: Auschwitz-Birkenau and Lublin-Majdanek covered large areas and were used by the SS as both concentration and extermination camps. At Kulmhof (Chełmno), the SS murdered their victims in gas vans. The Operation Reinhard extermination sites (Belzec, Sobibor, and Treblinka) were hardly camps in the usual sense, meaning places where people were imprisoned over longer periods of time, but rather killing sites, where the SS and their helpers murdered most of their victims immediately upon arrival.

No. 6-46
Covert photograph of the area near Crematorium No. 5 at Auschwitz-Birkenau
Photograph: Alex (surname unknown), member of the prisoner *Sonderkommando*, August 1944

From late April to July 1944, some 430,000 Hungarian Jews were deported to Auschwitz. Over 300,000 of them died in the gas chambers. Members of a *Sonderkommando* of Auschwitz prisoners had to burn the corpses of the victims. Four photographs secretly taken by members of this detachment in August 1944 document the undressing of the victims before the gassing and the burning of the corpses outside Crematorium No. 5 at Auschwitz-Birkenau. In May 1944, when the capacity of the crematoria proved insufficient, cremation trenches were dug.

These photos constitute an absolute exception. They show the extermination process from the perspective of the prisoners. As a rule, only SS personnel were allowed to take photographs. The photographer of these four images was a Greek Jew known as Alex, surname unknown. Nowadays often not printed in their entirety, the uncropped photographs reveal the difficult and dangerous conditions under which they originated. Two photographs were taken through the door of Crematorium No. 5 at the north gas chamber. Two others were taken outdoors, with the photographer evidently unable to use the viewfinder. The film roll was smuggled out of the camp a few days later. The first contact prints were made in Krakow (Kraków) as early as 1944. They were distributed to members of the Polish resistance. jes
Auschwitz-Birkenau State Museum, 280

No. 6-44
Photographic portrait of *SS-Sturmbannführer* Christian Wirth
In 1940, Wirth was inspector of the "euthanasia" killing centers in the German Reich; in 1942, he was inspector of the Belzec, Treblinka, and Sobibor extermination camps in occupied Poland. mp
Landesarchiv Baden-Württemberg, Hauptstaatsarchiv Stuttgart, E 151/21, Bü. 1684

No. 6-45
Photograph of Hadamar Regional Sanatorium, near Limburg 1941
In Hadamar, over ten thousand people were murdered in a gas chamber and their corpses subsequently burned. The rising plume of smoke indicates that the crematorium is in operation. mp
Süddeutsche Zeitung Photo, 74968

No. 6-47
The entrance building at Auschwitz-Birkenau Concentration and Extermination Camp
The photograph was probably taken after the war, as the railroad tracks into the camp only went into operation in 1944. jes
Bundesarchiv Koblenz, Image Archives, 175-04413

No. 6-48
Rudolf Höß, commandant of Auschwitz Concentration Camp from 1940 to 1943. From 1943 to 1945 he was Department Head of *Amtsgruppe D* (concentration camps) of the SS Main Economic and Administrative Department
U. S. Holocaust Memorial Museum, Washington, D.C., Photo Archives, 34811

The first sites of systematic mass murder carried out by the National Socialist regime were not located at the periphery, or in territory conquered after 1939, but at the center of the German Reich. Within the framework of the National Socialist program for murdering the sick, the first gas chambers for the mass killing of human beings were constructed beginning in 1939 and 1940 at state hospitals and sanatoria in Bernburg, Brandenburg, Pirna Sonnenstein, Hartheim, Grafeneck, and Hadamar. By the end of 1941, tens of thousands of handicapped and mentally ill patients had been murdered in these facilities by poison gas; their corpses were subsequently burned in crematoria.

As of 1941, the personnel at the institutions engaged in killing the sick played a decisive role in establishing and operating the extermination camps at Belzec, Treblinka, and Sobibor, in Poland. Those responsible were men such as *SS-Sturmbannführer* Christian Wirth, *SS-Hauptsturmführer* Franz Stangl (head administrator at Hartheim and Bernburg, commandant of Sobibor and Treblinka), and *SS-Hauptsturmführer* Franz Reichleitner (Hartheim, Sobibor). Together with over a hundred men already involved in killing the sick, they now organized and supervised the genocide of the European Jews within the framework of Operation Reinhard. mp

In April 1940, Himmler decided to establish a concentration camp at a former army base in eastern Upper Silesia, at Auschwitz (Oświęcim). It was initially to serve primarily as a detention facility for Poles. Himmler appointed Rudolf Höß as commandant. In 1941, IG Farben AG began construction of a hydrogenation plant for the manufacture of rubber substitutes (Buna) at nearby Monowitz. From October 1943, the forced laborers for this enterprise were housed at the Monowitz subcamp (Auschwitz III) established there. As of September 1941, the SS further expanded the Auschwitz complex by having another camp built at neighboring Birkenau (Auschwitz II). This new facility was initially intended to hold Soviet prisoners of war, who were also the first victims of poison gas at the main camp (Auschwitz I) in September 1941.

Jews were deported to Auschwitz-Birkenau beginning in the spring of 1942. At first, they were murdered in provisional gas chambers. From mid-1942 on, camp SS officials sorted the people arriving in railway cars into "fit for work" or "unfit for work," in a procedure known as "selection." Those deemed "unfit for work" were immediately put to death, as of 1943, in newly constructed gas chambers connected to four large crematoria. Over twenty thousand Sinti and Roma, who had been imprisoned in a separate camp section at Auschwitz-Birkenau, were also murdered there.

About 1.1 million people died at Auschwitz, including approximately 1 million Jews. jes

Lublin-Majdanek

Chełmno (Kulmhof)

No. 6-49
Crematoria at Lublin-Majdanek Concentration and Extermination Camp
August 1944
Bildarchiv Preußischer Kulturbesitz, Berlin, 30016988

No. 6-50
Local headquarters of the *SS-Sonderkommando* at Kulmhof/Chełmno
Yad Vashem, Jerusalem, Photo Archives, 1007/10

While visiting Lublin on July 20, 1941, Himmler ordered construction of a new concentration camp in proximity to the Majdan Tatarski district. It was to hold forced laborers for the planned SS settlement of the East. As of September 1941 the concentration camp was repurposed to hold Soviet prisoners of war. As of spring 1942 the SS increasingly imprisoned Jews at the camp. Between 250,000 and 300,000 people were incarcerated at Lublin Concentration Camp, as it was again known beginning in February 1943. Gas chambers began operating there in the fall of 1942.

Besides Auschwitz, Lublin-Majdanek was the second camp to serve both as a concentration and extermination camp. On November 3, 1943, a large number of the surviving Polish Jews were murdered there as part of *Aktion Erntefest* (Operation Harvest Festival). In July 1944, the SS cleared the camp. Immediately after the liberation, a Polish-Soviet commission began investigating the crimes committed at the camp. Current estimates of the number of victims range from 78,000 to 250,000. jes

Jews from the Warthegau (annexed western Poland) were the primary murder victims at Kulmhof/Chełmno. The killings were carried out in mobile gas-vans operated by an *SS-Sonderkommando*, which was initially under the command of *SS-Hauptsturmführer* Herbert Lange. The gassings were ordered by *Gauleiter* Arthur Greiser in coordination with Heinrich Himmler. The killing operation, which began in December 1941, targeted Jews from rural areas of the Warthegau, and especially those from the ghetto in Lodz (Łódź, 1940 – 1945 Litzmannstadt).

In March 1943 the SS temporarily halted the murders. Camp personnel were transferred to the SS Mountain Division "Prinz Eugen" in Yugoslavia. In early summer of 1944 the SS reactivated Chełmno to kill the surviving Jews from the Lodz ghetto. At least 152,000 people died in the gas-vans. Beginning in the fall of 1944, the SS attempted to eliminate all traces of the mass murders. jes

Belzec, Sobibor, Treblinka:
The Extermination Camps of Operation Reinhard

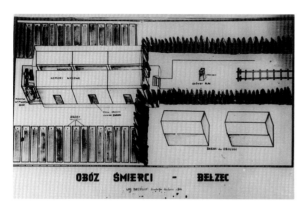

No. 6-51

Postwar diagram of the Belzec extermination center by Rudolf Reder, one of only three known survivors of the camp 1945 – 1946

U. S. Holocaust Memorial Museum, Washington D.C., Photo Archives, 27228

No. 6-52

SS guards outside the commandant's building at the Belzec camp. From right to left: *SS-Rottenführer* Heinrich Barbl and *SS-Oberwachtmeister* Arthur Dachsel; second row: *SS-Hauptscharführer* Lorenz Hackenholt, *SS-Unterscharführer* Ernst Zierke, *SS-Untersturmführer* Karl Gringers (front) and *SS-Untersturmführer* Fritz Tauscher (second from left), 1942

U. S. Holocaust Memorial Museum, Washington D.C., Photo Archives, 87764

Operation Reinhard (or Operation Reinhardt) denoted the program of planned murder responsible for killing a large section of the Polish Jewish population from March 1942 onward. Jews from other European countries were also among the victims. At the Treblinka, Sobibor (Sobibór) and Belzec (Bełżec) extermination centers it is estimated that over 1.5 million individuals were murdered with poison gas. Less than 150 deportees are thought to have survived these three killing centers.

The murder operation was named after *SS-Obergruppenführer* Reinhard Heydrich, who died on June 4, 1942, following an assassination attempt. Operation Reinhard was led by Odilo Globocnik, the SS and police chief of Lublin. The murder facilities were under the command of the police officer and *SS-Führer* Christian Wirth. Like the majority of Germans engaged in the murder, Wirth had initially been active at the German "euthanasia" centers. The guards recruited primarily from former Ukrainian prisoners of war were known as Trawnikis, for the location of their training camp, and stood under the command of German SS officers. Belzec was shut down at the end of 1942 and a prisoner uprising on August 2, 1943, marked the end of Treblinka. On October 14, 1943, prisoners at Sobibor also revolted and succeeded in killing several members of the SS.

At the conclusion of Operation Reinhard, Globocnik, Wirth, and some of their subordinates were transferred to Trieste, in Italy, where they set up another terror and killing center in the former San Sabba rice mill. jes

6.6
The Persecution and Murder of Sinti and Roma

Wide-ranging persecution of Sinti and Roma by the National Socialist regime had already begun prior to 1939. With the beginning of World War II, race-driven, anti-Gypsy policy became ever more extreme, eventually culminating in genocide. SS and police units shot thousands of members of this minority behind the front lines. Sinti and Roma were deported from all over Europe and interned in ghettos and concentration camps. Many were exploited as forced laborers. Auschwitz-Birkenau had a separate "Gypsy camp," from which thousands were sent to the gas chamber. Moreover, medical experiments were frequently performed on Sinti and Roma. The exact number of Sinti and Roma murdered by 1945 remains unknown. Estimates range from the tens of thousands to as many as a half a million victims.

No. 6-53
Letter from an imprisoned Sinti girl, Adelgunde Rose, to her family in Stettin, written at Buchenwald Concentration Camp
Postmarked November 23, 1944
Beginning in late July 1937, the Criminal Police repeatedly used protective detention orders to send Sinti and Roma to concentration camps. With the onset of war Himmler's apparatus sought to purge the German Reich of all Sinti and Roma, who were "settled" in collection camps and, beginning in May 1940, deported to various ghettos and concentration camps in the occupied areas of Eastern Central Europe. The "Gypsy camp" established in Auschwitz at the end of 1942 primarily held Sinti and Roma from the German Reich, most of whom died as a result of the appalling living conditions or medical experiments. A majority of the survivors were murdered by gas when the camp was disbanded in August 1944. *Wehrmacht*, *SS-Einsatzgruppen*, and police units had previously rounded up and executed great numbers of indigenous Roma throughout the conquered areas of Poland, the Soviet Union, and the Balkans.

Prior to writing this letter, the young Sinti girl, Adelgunde Rose, had been transferred from the Ravensbrück concentration camp for women to Buchenwald. She survived the persecution by National Socialists. Her younger brother, Alman, died at Niederhagen Concentration Camp.
mh
Kreismuseum Wewelsburg, inv. no. 17160

Dear Parents, Brothers and Sisters, Your letters were forwarded to me, which has made me very happy. You write of packages; I haven't received any packages since July 15. So look into it and write to the postal censors at Ravensbrück, as my packages have been snatched by the block chiefs of Block 19. They forwarded the letters, but so far no package. Please be so kind as to send me a pair of shoes, socks, warm underwear, skirt, and blouse, or a dress, and a scarf, and please send them as quickly as possible, and toothpaste, toothbrush, hairpins, rollers and all kinds of toiletries, don't worry about me, couldn't write any earlier. Greetings from your daughter.

Translation of a transcription

No. 6-55
Execution of Sinti and Roma in the
***Generalgouvernement*, most likely**
by the SS and *Ordnungspolizei*
(Order Police)

The Institute of National Remembrance,
Warsaw, 61958 and/or AR/073/19/00

No. 6-56
Deportation of Remscheid Sinti
and Roma to Auschwitz, March 1943

Historisches Zentrum Remscheid

No. 6-54
The young Sinti girl, Settela
Steinbach, during transfer
to Auschwitz from Westerbork
Concentration Camp in the
Netherlands on May 19, 1944

Image Bank WW2, Amsterdam,
NIOD 66085

The Deployment Groups (*Einsatzgruppen*) of the Security Police (*Sicherheitspolizei*) and SD were special mobile units of the SS under the command of the head of the Reich Main Security Office, Reinhard Heydrich. The role of this force of roughly 3,000 men was to identify, arrest, and kill political and ideological adversaries. Especially during the war against Poland in 1939 and following the invasion of the Soviet Union in June 1941, the *Einsatzgruppen* actively engaged in mass murder in the army rear area, in the wake of combat units. With respect to movement, provisioning, and accommodations, they were subordinate to the *Wehrmacht*, which provided assistance with the executions. The *Einsatzgruppen* murdered a total of up to 1.5 million people.

Along with Jews, communists, partisans, the alleged mentally ill, and other "undesired elements," Sinti and Roma also fell victim to the *SS-Einsatzgruppen*, police battalions, and *Wehrmacht* units. In Eastern Europe, traveling Sinti and Roma were singled out for persecution and murdered as "spying Gypsies." In the Soviet Union and in the *Generalgouvernement*, more Sinti and Roma were shot by mobile death squads than were murdered in concentration and extermination camps. mp

In Eastern Europe, nonsedentary, itinerant Sinti and Roma – "spying Gypsies" in the eyes of the SS and *Wehrmacht* – were sought out for execution by *SS-Einsatzgruppen*. In Western Europe, by contrast, persecution primarily fell on the sedentary, assimilated members of this minority. Sinti and Roma were deported in several waves: for example, to the *Generalgouvernement* in 1940, to Lodz in 1941, to Bialystock in 1942, and to Auschwitz-Birkenau in 1943.

On December 16, 1942, Heinrich Himmler issued a deportation order resulting in the deportation to the "Gypsy camp" at Auschwitz-Birkenau of roughly 22,600 Sinti and Roma from Germany, Austria, Bohemia, Moravia, the Netherlands, Belgium, and northern France. In particular it was the local branches of the Criminal Police and municipal agencies that would ultimately use their discretionary powers to expel as many Sinti and Roma as possible from their localities. The deportation of Sinti and Roma from the German Reich was carried out publicly in the full light of day. mp

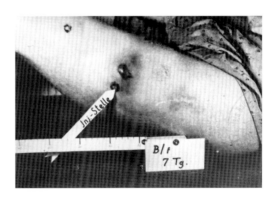

No. 6-57
**View of the "Gypsy ghetto" in Lodz
(Łódź, Poland, 1940 – 1945
Litzmannstadt) surrounded
by a double barbed-wire fence
Probably 1941**

Jüdisches Museum Frankfurt,
Lodz-A371

No. 6-58
**Sinti and Roma in the
Belzec forced labor camp
1940**

U. S. Holocaust Memorial Museum,
Washington, D.C., Photo Archives, 74705

No. 6-59
**(From left to right): Dr. Josef Men-
gele (concentration camp physician at Auschwitz), Rudolf Höß
(former Auschwitz commandant),
Josef Kramer (commandant of
Birkenau) and Anton Thurmann at
the Solahütte SS recreation center
near Auschwitz
1944**

U. S. Holocaust Memorial Museum,
Washington D.C., Photo Archives, 34755

No. 6-60
**Arm following an injection as part
of a medical experiment**

Auschwitz-Birkenau State Museum,
neg. 448

The persecution of Sinti and Roma varied considerably depending on geographic location and administrative jurisdiction. The general trend, however,
was to detain members of the minority at centralized locations to limit their
freedom of movement. Sinti and Roma were interned in, for example, ghettos
as well as in transit, labor and concentration camps. Most ghettos established for Jews in the *Generalgouvernement* also held Sinti and Roma living
in appalling conditions.

In 1941, a separate "Gypsy ghetto" was established inside the Jewish
ghetto at Lodz. About 5,000 Sinti and Roma from the Austrian province
of Burgenland were interned there. Within a few weeks most of the people
penned in there had succumbed to disease, hunger, and exhaustion. In early
1942 the SS brought the survivors of the "Gypsy ghetto" to Kulmhof (Chelmno)
extermination camp, where they were murdered in gas chambers. Not one
of the Sinti and Roma deported from Burgenland to Lodz survived.

While confined in ghettos and various camps, Sinti and Roma were frequently exploited as forced laborers, often for local industries, earthworks,
and construction, at quarries, or in armaments production. Sinti and Roma
were also exploited as forced laborers at the concentration camp in Wewelsburg. mp

Medical experiments were performed on prisoners in numerous concentration camps. Because they were considered "indolent Gypsies" by the SS
and because their alleged "congenericity," promised especially meaningful
results, Sinti and Roma were frequently selected for such exploitation.
Certain experiments were intended to substantiate National Socialist racial
doctrine, while others aimed to find treatments for perceived or actual
health threats to German soldiers. Thus, concentration camp prisoners were
injected with a variety of pathogens to serve as guinea pigs for vaccines
and therapies, submitted to seawater and hypothermia experiments, and
made the object of experiments testing mass-sterilization methods. The possible crippling or even death of prisoners was accepted as a matter of course.
In many cases the subjects were deliberately killed for the purpose of conducting autopsies.

The infamous Dr. Josef Mengele, concentration camp physician at
Auschwitz-Birkenau, frequently used Sinti and Roma twins for his experiments. With funding from the German Research Foundation, he sought to
prove that racial characteristics were rooted in genetics. Mengele personally
chose his victims among the new arrivals on the selection ramp at Auschwitz-
Birkenau. Those whom the SS considered unfit for forced labor or medical
experimentation were immediately put to death in the gas chambers. mp

The "Gypsy Camp" at Auschwitz-Birkenau

No. 6-61
View of Block II at Auschwitz-Birkenau, which also included a "Gypsy camp" (Block B II e) with stable barracks

Auschwitz-Birkenau State Museum, neg. 20995-398

No. 6-62
Portraits of Sinti and Roma prisoners from the "Gypsy camp" at Auschwitz-Birkenau, which a Jewish prisoner, Dinah Gottliebova, was forced to paint on orders from Josef Mengele

Auschwitz-Birkenau State Museum, PMO-l-1-111 and 113

Sinti and Roma were held at Auschwitz-Birkenau Extermination Camp from as early as mid-1941. Around the end of 1942, the camp was enlarged to include a new Block II. Designated "B II e," this new "Gypsy camp" was roughly 600 meters long and 120 meters wide and housed 32 wooden barracks. In July 1943 the "Gypsy camp" was cordoned by an electric fence.

Following Himmler's deportation order of December 16, 1942, Sinti and Roma from various Western European countries arrived at Block II e. By the end of 1943 seventy percent of the prisoners at the "Gypsy camp" had died from the appalling living conditions or from abuse by the SS guards.

In the summer of 1944 the SS was awaiting the arrival of hundreds of thousands of Hungarian Jews at Birkenau and needed space for newcomers, who were to be spared immediate gassing and put to work instead. These were the circumstances that led to the decision to disband the "Gypsy camp" and kill all its occupants. The desperate resistance of the prisoners thwarted an initial attempt, but over the course of the night of August 2, 1944, the remaining Sinti and Roma were murdered in the gas chambers. Of the roughly 22,600 Sinti and Roma imprisoned at the Auschwitz-Birkenau "Gypsy camp" during its 17-month existence, over 19,300 perished. mp

6.7
The Concentration
Camp System
1939 – 1945

Although it evolved from the prewar constellation of camps, the concentration camp system of exploitation and terror during World War II bore only limited resemblance to its origins. Systematic murder in the camps began with the war. The concentration camp system was constantly taking in new and larger groups of prisoners. Beginning in the fall of 1942, concentration camps provided a rapidly rising number of prisoners as forced laborers to the armaments industry. Most prisoners no longer came from Germany, but from occupied territories, creating a multinational society of prisoners. Countless subcamps were established and a gigantic archipelago of camps emerged.

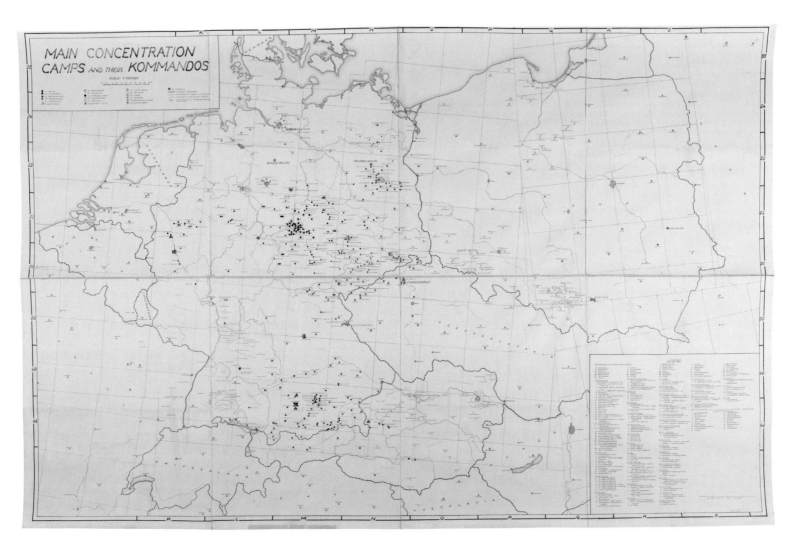

No. 6-63
Main Concentration Camps and their Commandos, **probably prepared by the Documents Intelligence Section Record Branch, International Tracing Service June 28, 1950**

The concentration camp system expanded continuously during World War II. In addition to new main camps, the focus of this expansion in the second half of the war was on external work detachments and subcamps, where prisoners primarily worked at private armament plants. Although the SS Economic and Administrative Main Office remained in control of the concentration camp network, private industry played a major role in its expansion and in determining the geographic distribution of the camps over all of Germany and neighboring occupied countries. There were at least 662 subcamps as of January 1945.

The map indicates camp locations to the extent that these were known at the end of the war. In some instances, successive camps are shown at the same location, as in the Wewelsburg example. jes
Kreismuseum Wewelsburg, inv. no. 16439

No. 6-64
Letter from IG Farbenindustrie AG, Behringwerke Division, regarding a typhus vaccine for human experiments
January 14, 1942
Translation on page 450

Bildarchiv Preußischer Kulturbesitz, Berlin, 30023196

Camp	8. 1943	1. 8. 1944	15. 1. 1945
Auschwitz	74,000		31,746
Auschwitz III (Monowitz)	–		35,081
Bergen-Belsen	3,300		22,286
Buchenwald	17,600		110,556
Dachau	17,300		55,247
Flossenbürg	4,800		39,704
Groß-Rosen	5,000		77,904
Herzogenbusch	2,500		–
Kauen	–	–	–
Krakau-Plaszow	–		–
Lublin	15,400		–
Mauthausen	21,100		73,380
Mittelbau-Dora	–	–	29,323
Natzweiler	2,200		22,170
Neuengamme	9,800		48,164
Ravensbrück	17,200		53,918
Riga-Kaiserwald	3,000		–
Sachsenhausen	26,500		66,097
Stutthof	4,300		48,635
Vaivara	–	–	
Warsaw	–	–	
Total	**224,000**	**524,286**	**714,211**

No. 6-69
Prisoner numbers at concentration camps 1943 – 1945
Concentration camps that did not exist, no longer existed, or were not yet managed as main camps when the prisoner numbers were gathered are marked with a dash (–). Spaces were left blank beside concentration camps for which no exact figures were available for the relevant point in time.jes

The outbreak of war meant not only a halt to prisoner discharges, but also the transformation of concentration camps into centers for systematic murder. This included executions by order of the Gestapo, the killing of sick prisoners under the designation "Operation 14 f 13," the systematic murder of Soviet prisoners of war, and human experiments in which the death of test subjects was oftentimes part of the program. Niederhagen Concentration Camp in Wewelsburg was also used by the Gestapo as an execution site and its ailing prisoners were shipped to "euthanasia" killing centers.

Human experiments at concentration camps involved large numbers of National Socialist officials, members of the SS, soldiers, physicians, and scientists. Although the victims came from concentration camps and the experiments were usually carried out there, those who ordered the experiments often sat at military headquarters, scientific institutes, or pharmaceutical companies. Malaria trials and experiments on hypothermia and death from altitude sickness, for instance, were conducted at Dachau. Typhus experiments at Buchenwald killed at least 250 of about 1,000 test subjects. The experimentation originated as a collaboration between the SS Hygiene Institute in Berlin, a *Wehrmacht* typhus institute in Warsaw, the Robert Koch Institute, and the Behringwerke of IG Farben AG. Human experiments were also conducted at Auschwitz. jes

World War II transformed the concentration camp system, which developed into a detention and terror complex targeting people from all countries controlled by the National Socialist regime. Prisoners were interned for political, ideological, racist, and economic reasons. Following Germany's devastating material and psychological defeat at Stalingrad, the SS, and especially the Gestapo, increasingly transferred people to the camps arbitrarily seized in Eastern Europe and abducted as forced laborers.

As of 1942, German prisoners constituted a minority at the concentration camps. In the prevailing hierarchical social system at the camps, foreign prisoners generally had a lower status than Germans, who often acted as foremen or occupied somewhat privileged positions. All prisoners, however, remained at the mercy of the camp SS. The lowest rung on the social ladder was occupied by the Jewish, Sinti and Roma, and Slavic inmates. In many cases, chances for survival in a concentration camp depended heavily on one's position within the camp hierarchy. jes

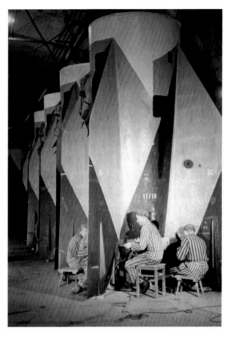

No. 6-66
SS-Standartenführer Gerhard
Maurer (1907 – 1953) managed the
deployment of concentration camp
labor from the concentration camp
headquarters in Oranienburg
(Subdepartment D II, Department D
of the SS Economic and Administrative Main Office)
Bundesarchiv Berlin, formerly the Berlin
Document Center, SSO Gerhard Maurer

No. 6-65
Dachau Concentration Camp
prisoners working in an
armaments plant
1943
Bildarchiv Preußischer Kulturbesitz,
Berlin, 30023281

No. 6-67
A hall at the Mittelwerk rocket
factory; prisoners from Mittelbau-
Dora Concentration Camp at work
on serial production of the V2
(also called A4)
Photograph: Walter Frentz, 1944
Ullstein Bilderdienst, 00416719

No. 6-68
SS-Gruppenführer Dr. Hans Kammler (1901 – 1945), Head of SS
Construction, was responsible for
the underground relocation of
industry using concentration camp
labor and for the deployment of
the V2 rocket.
Bundesarchiv Berlin, formerly the Berlin
Document Center, SSO Hans Kammler

Until 1941, most concentration camp prisoners worked for SS enterprises.
Beginning in the fall of 1942, and especially the fall of 1943, prisoners were
increasingly exploited by private armaments firms. In order to satisfy
industry's demand for forced labor from concentration camps and to allow
for a centralized deployment of prisoners, an office dedicated to the deployment of prisoner labor was created within the SS Economic and Administrative Main Office, under the designation "D II."

One of the first armaments firms to exploit the forced labor of concentration camp prisoners was IG Farbenindustrie AG. As of 1941 it had been
constructing a factory for the production of synthetic rubber, or Buna, in the
vicinity of Auschwitz Concentration Camp. A subcamp for this specific
purpose was established at Monowitz. In 1941 prisoners also began working
at the Heinkel plant in Oranienburg. In 1942 the Volkswagen factory at Fal-
lersleben began sourcing forced labor from concentration camp prisoners.
According to data provided by armaments minister Albert Speer, by early
1943, nearly two-thirds of concentration camp prisoners worked in the war
industries. In the following years, almost every industrial sector required
concentration camp prisoners. This included businesses from the aviation,
motor vehicle, electrical, chemical, metal goods, mining, and heavy
industries. jes

Beginning in 1943, the potentially devastating effects of Allied air raids required that critical manufacturing facilities, especially those producing
German aircraft, be relocated underground. Concentration camp prisoners
were forced to work on the expansion of caves and mining shafts. In some
cases concentration camp labor was also deployed for production at the
relocated businesses. The grueling excavation work, which resulted in
innumerable casualties among the weakened prisoners, was considered a
death sentence.

Early on, production processes for the *Vergeltungswaffe 2* (reprisal
weapon 2), or V2, were relocated underground. This weapon was intended to
counterbalance the material superiority of the Allies and – so hoped the
National Socialist leadership and *Wehrmacht* – bring a turnaround in the war.
Mittelwerk GmbH was established as a production site in the Harz Mountains
and overseen by the Ministry for Armaments. The prisoner construction brigades employed there were under the command of *SS-Brigadeführer*
Dr. Hans Kammler, head of Division C (Construction) at the SS Economic and
Administrative Main Office. The Mittelbau-Dora Concentration Camp was
soon formed from these construction brigades. The large-scale relocation of
industrial plants began in the spring of 1944. Kammler quickly became
indispensable to the Ministry of Armaments and the *Wehrmacht*; he eventually became responsible for commanding the launch of V2 rockets. The
merciless exploitation of concentration camp prisoners, whose death and
suffering were taken for granted, afforded Kammler wide-ranging influence
in the collapsing Reich. jes

241

6.8
Crimes of the *Waffen-SS*

Waffen-SS was the term used from 1939 to designate armed formations of the SS, which, together with the *Wehrmacht*, were deployed as combat troops in nearly every campaign of the war. In organizational terms, the SS remained separate from the *Wehrmacht*. As "political soldiers," members of the SS were to be especially steeped in the racist and anti-Semitic ideology of National Socialism. Due to inadequate training, their initial losses were very high. On all fronts throughout Europe, as well as in the army rear area, units of the *Waffen-SS* committed innumerable crimes against prisoners of war and civilian populations, as well as mass murder in the conquered territories of Eastern Europe. The atrocities cited below are just a few examples.

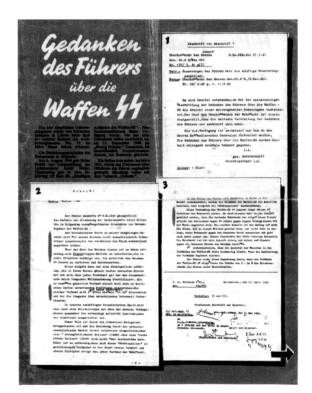 

No. 6-70
Thoughts of the *Führer* on the *Waffen-SS* – Hitler's carte blanche to the SS
Allied aerial leaflet, 1943
Front and back

In early 1943, the Allies began using leaflets to inform the German population of the criminal nature of the National Socialist regime. This handout used captured documents to demonstrate Hitler's objectives for the *Waffen-SS* in a future "Greater German Reich." They would not merely be used as combat troops, the flyer warned, but also as a police apparatus against subjugated populations as well as against politically unreliable compatriots.

In actuality the *Waffen-SS* had never been a purely military organization, but rather a pillar of Himmler's ideological war. Thus, units of the *Waffen-SS* participated in the persecution and murder of local civilian populations, especially Jews, in Eastern Europe. The *Waffen-SS* revealed its criminal character during conventional military operations as well: in nearly every theater of war where it was deployed, its units committed massacres of civilians and prisoners of war. Concentration camp guards also belonged to the *Waffen-SS*. mh

Kreismuseum Wewelsburg, inv. nos. 2910 and 8870

No. 6-72
Photographic portrait of *SS-Ober-sturmbannführer* Fritz Knöchlein, the officer responsible for the massacre at Le Paradis
Bundesarchiv Berlin,
SSO Fritz Knöchlein

No. 6-73
**Soldiers of *Waffen-SS-Division Totenkopf* during the advance on the northern French town of Bethune, near Le Paradis
Photograph: Hermann Ege, May 24 or 25, 1940**
Bundesarchiv Koblenz, Bildarchiv, Bild 101III-Ege-030-14

No. 6-71
**Aerial photograph of the southern French village of Oradour-sur-Glane following its destruction by soldiers of the *Waffen-SS*
August 10, 1945**
Ullstein Bilderdienst, 80190294

West of Lille on May 27, 1940, following a particularly costly battle, the 4th Company of the 1st Battalion, 2nd *SS-Totenkopf* Regiment, committed arguably the worst war crime of the German advance through France. After stubborn resistance, about one hundred British soldiers finally surrendered to the SS company near the village of Le Paradis, becoming prisoners of war. Company leader *SS-Obersturmführer* Fritz Knöchlein ordered that the prisoners be lined up against a barn wall and machine gunned. Those that still showed signs of life were bayoneted or shot in the head. Only two British prisoners survived badly wounded and managed to hide themselves away.

A day after the massacre at Le Paradis, on May 28, 1940, soldiers of the *Leibstandarte Adolf Hitler* murdered about eighty British prisoners of war at the northern French town of Wormhoudt. mm

Following the Allied landing in Normandy, on June 6, 1944, the French Resistance markedly intensified its activities in the south of France. The *Wehrmacht* leadership attempted to crush the partisans with reprisals, which were sometimes explicitly designated as "counter-terror" strikes. *Waffen-SS* units also committed war crimes in this context. In the town of Tulle, soldiers of the 2nd SS Tank Division "Das Reich" arbitrarily hung 99 male civilians after discovering the apparent mutilation of the bodies of German soldiers killed in a partisan attack.

On June 10, 1944, units of that same SS division razed the village of Oradour-sur-Glane. Women and children were locked into the church, which was set on fire. Those trying to escape the flames were shot. The male villagers were murdered by machine gun. The houses were torched. A total of 642 people died in the massacre. Despite criticism from *Wehrmacht* officials and even some *Waffen-SS* superiors, the crimes went unpunished. Instead, such atrocities continued during the remaining months of the war. mm

No. 6-76
**Italian partisans burying
an executed comrade
Marzabotto, 1944**
Süddeutsche Zeitung Photo, 579233

No. 6-78
***Waffen-SS* soldiers carrying out
anti-partisan operations against
the civilian population in Greece
1943 or 1944**
The photograph was long believed
to show the village of Distomo on
the day of the German massacre of
June 10, 1944, but this is now considered questionable. The photograph was seized from a captured
German soldier by Greek partisans
in 1945. mm

Sammlung Dieter Begemann, Herford

From early September 1943 to the end of April 1945, German troops in Italy
fought the Allies advancing from the South, as well as numerous Italian
partisan groups operating in the hinterlands. As part of the *Wehrmacht*
leadership's ruthless "anti-bandit" policy, German units committed numerous war crimes with the significant involvement of the (*Waffen-*) SS.
The following are some of the more well-known examples:
– The massacre on March 24, 1944, in the Ardeatine caves near Rome, of
335 Italian hostages by elements of the Security Police and SD in retaliation
for a partisan attack the previous day. The caves were subsequently
dynamited.
– The Sant'Anna di Stazzema massacre in Tuscany. On August 12, 1944,
villagers were herded together in the church square and at several farms by
four companies of the *Reichsführer-SS*, the 16th Division of the *SS-Panzer-
grenadier* (Armored Infantry). The SS then threw hand grenades into the
crowd and fired randomly at the victims, after which the village was set on
fire. 560 people were killed.
– The Marzabotto massacre (southwest of Bologna) on September 29, 1944,
and the subsequent few days, once again involved men of the 16th SS Division, who used the pretext of combating partisans to murder over 700 civilians
in the villages around Marzabotto. mm

On June 10, 1944, the same day that the residents of Oradour-sur-Glane were
murdered by a *Waffen-SS* unit and their village burned to the ground, members of the 2nd Company of the 7th *Panzergrenadier-Regiment*, 4th *SS-
Polizei-Panzergrenadier-Division*, murdered 218 inhabitants of Distomo, a
village near Delphi. Once more, the massacre in which many women, children,
and elderly were killed was justified by its perpetrators as a retaliatory
operation for recent casualties at the hands of local partisans.
    Two months earlier, on April 5, 1944, units of the same 7th *SS-Panzer-
grenadier-Regiment* had invaded the Macedonian village of Klissoura. Two
SS soldiers had been killed in an earlier engagement nearby. As retaliation
the SS armored infantry proceeded to slaughter at least 215 villagers,
primarily women, children, and old men. mm

No. 6-74
Alleged communists under guard, shortly before their execution by members of the 1st SS Cavalry Regiment Turky, the Soviet Union, August 1941
Bundesarchiv Ludwigsburg, 202 AR-Z 42/62, LO IV Zeugenvernehmungen, Teilakte II m., p. 29

No. 6-75
Members of the *Waffen-SS* Cavalry Brigade on horseback
Photograph: Peter Adendorf, the Soviet Union, Summer 1941
Bundesarchiv Koblenz, Bildarchiv, Bild 101III-Adendorf-002-17A

In the war against the Soviet Union – which Germany proclaimed a "struggle of annihilation" against the "Jewish-Bolshevik system" – the SS had nearly unlimited freedom of action in pursuing the objectives set by Germany's government and military leaders. The SS would also develop its own wide-ranging initiative within the given ideological framework. Units of the *Reichs-führer-SS* Operations Staff, under the direct command of Heinrich Himmler, played a decisive role in expanding mass executions in the Soviet Union. From July to the end of 1941, their murder campaigns behind the front lines killed at least 57,000 Jewish men, women, and children. Bernhard Frank and Rudi Bergmann, SS personnel stationed at Wewelsburg, were deployed to the Commando Staff in the Soviet Union.

Millions of Soviet soldiers perished in the prisoner of war camps controlled by the *Waffen-SS* and *Wehrmacht*. Moreover, members of the *Waffen-SS* perpetrated countless war crimes on the front. After 1941, troops of the Commando Staff and other *Waffen-SS* units continued to murder thousands of Jewish and non-Jewish civilians, for instance during "counterinsurgency" measures. The *Waffen-SS* also participated in the liquidation of numerous ghettos in Eastern Europe and the suppression of the Warsaw Ghetto Uprising (April–May 1943). mm

6.9
Exploitation and Violence in the Collapsing Reich

In the summer of 1943, as signs of the German Reich's military defeat began to mount, the SS experienced one final increase of power. Near the end of the war, Heinrich Himmler managed to unify all of the National Socialist state's essential means of violence. Besides the exploitation and destruction of the occupied territories, SS violence and terror were now increasingly directed at Germany's own population. The SS played a fundamental role in insuring that the German Reich did not collapse from within, but only after its near complete conquest and utter devastation. Continuation of the war over its last eighteen months cost Germany more millions in military and civilian dead than in the four preceding years combined.

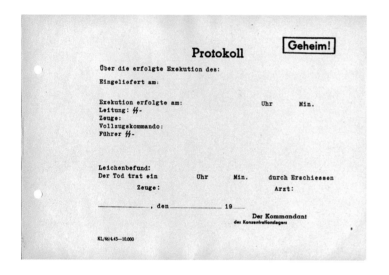

No. 6-79
Concentration camp execution log
Form from the estate of a former SS leader
Amid looming military defeat, Himmler's apparatus of repression and surveillance underwent its last increase in power. In particular, the tasks and responsibilities of the Gestapo were once again considerably expanded. Beyond the hunt for adversaries of the regime, it was now able to punish violations of labor discipline by sending offenders to "labor education camps." Similarly, the Criminal Police detained "problem" youth in "youth protection camps."

Those subject to the closest scrutiny were the numerous foreign and forced laborers, along with concentration camp prisoners, whose numbers had increased sharply with Germany's immense armament efforts, even within the narrower borders of the Reich. These groups were categorically suspected of sabotage and intent to escape. Even the most trifling offenses were harshly punished. Ever more often, it was the Gestapo that – lacking any judicial process – carried out the sentences. The executions were sometimes carried out in public, and sometimes within concentration camps. mh
Kreismuseum Wewelsburg, inv. no. 14574

No. 6-81
Scorched earth tactics by German troops, presumably *Waffen-SS*
The original caption by the photographer, SS war correspondent Hermann Grönert, assigned at the time of the photograph to the 3rd SS Tank Division *Totenkopf*, reads: "The last security forces leave the region, which has been destroyed according to plan."
October 1943

Ullstein Bilderdienst, 00282041

No. 6-82
During their retreat from the area around Vitebsk, in the Soviet Union, German units deploy a railroad plow to destroy rail infrastructure.
March 1944

Bundesarchiv Koblenz,
Bild 101I-279-0901-32

No. 6-83
Public execution of eleven foreign workers of various nationalities by members of the Gestapo Cologne-Ehrenfeld,
October 25, 1944

Bildarchiv Preußischer Kulturbesitz, Berlin, 30017538

No. 6-84
A mobile drumhead court martial comprised of SS members reads out the death sentences for "traitors and deserters"
1944 or 1945

Ullstein Bilderdienst, 00020825

The large-scale retreat of the German army from occupied areas of the Soviet Union, begun in early 1943, inaugurated a comprehensive scorched earth policy. The advance of the Red Army was to be slowed by destroying all infrastructure and material goods, and leaving behind neither food nor labor force.

The SS played a major part in this destruction. In September 1943, Himmler issued orders to the Higher SS and Police Leader in charge, Hans-Adolf Prützmann, that "upon evacuation of areas of the Ukraine, no man, cattle, hundredweight of grain, or railroad track shall remain … The enemy must encounter a truly scorched and ravaged land."

Upon their retreat, *Wehrmacht* and SS troops left a wide swathe of devastation: buildings and entire villages were torched, factories and bridges destroyed, roads and railroad tracks rendered impassable; foodstuffs, crops and cattle were seized; and as much of the local population deported as possible. Depending on the speed of the retreat and the amount of time remaining for destruction, veritable wastelands were created. In his notorious Nero Decree of March 1945, Hitler ordered that the scorched earth policy be extended to include territories of the German Reich. mp

During the war, fear of collapse on the home front haunted the German leadership. It was a National Socialist article of faith that German defeat in World War I had been caused solely by lack of domestic support for the war effort. This time, to ensure internal security under all circumstances Himmler's SS and police apparatus used savage brutality to suppress any signs of war weariness, fatalism or opposition. The SS and police pursued alleged slackers, traitors, defeatists, and those thought to be subverting the war effort, drawing on countless denunciations from the general population. As battle lines drew near, civilians who expressed their readiness to capitulate by hoisting white flags faced punishment by the *Wehrmacht* or SS. In addition, roughly fifteen thousand death sentences were carried out against accused deserters in the final months of the war. By comparison, only 18 German soldiers were executed for desertion during all of World War I.

In the eyes of the SS, the millions of prisoners of war and foreign workers laboring in the German Reich posed a security problem. The slightest offense could mean internment in a labor education camp or concentration camp. Toward the end of the war, thousands of foreign workers were shot or hanged. No later than February 1945, authority to order such executions fell directly to local offices of the Gestapo. mp

No. 6-86
Leaflet of the Edelweiss Pirates, a group from Wuppertal
Fall 1942
Hauptstaatsarchiv Düsseldorf, Gestapo-Personalunterlagen, 3692

No. 6-85
Members of the White Rose (from left): Hans Scholl, Sophie Scholl, Christoph Probst
All three were murdered by the Gestapo on February 22, 1943.
July 22, 1942
Ullstein Bilderdienst, 00003714

No. 6-87
Himmler in conversation with Hitler at the Wolf's Lair – the Führer's headquarters near Rastenburg in East Prussia – a few hours after the failed assassination attempt by Colonel Stauffenberg
In the background are Benito Mussolini and Hermann Göring.
July 20, 1944
Ullstein Bilderdienst, 00051662

Young people were to undergo an early National Socialist indoctrination in terms of nationalist and racist dogma. In addition to family and school, serving in National Socialist youth organizations constituted a central element of the socialization process. Despite all government efforts lavished on cooption, many young people did not wish to assimilate to the National Socialist youth ideal. Non-conformist youths varied considerably in terms of their social origins, interests, and degrees of rebellion. In some cases they organized themselves into loose groupings and clubs based on common interests, such as worker youths, Christian associations, illegal outdoors or scouting groups, Swing Kids, or the Edelweiss Pirates. Police and Gestapo heavily suppressed these young people. Thousands were imprisoned in concentration camps euphemistically designated "youth protection camps," which were located in Moringen, Uckermark, and Lodz (Łódź, Poland, 1940–1945 Litzmannstadt).

The oppositional activity of non-conformist youths intensified markedly during the course of the war, sometimes culminating in concrete political action. Especially during the last phases of the war, acts of political resistance, such as distributing leaflets or harboring Jews and prisoners of war, were often punished by the SS or Gestapo with the death penalty. Well-known examples include the Munich students around Hans and Sophie Scholl (The White Rose) or other groupings involving Bartholomäus Schink and Hans Steinbrück (the Edelweiss Pirates and the Ehrenfeld Group). mp

The near assassination of Adolf Hitler on July 20, 1944, represents the most significant coup attempt during the National Socialist dictatorship. It originated with a broad opposition of military figures, political conservatives, and former trade unionists. Himmler's SS and police apparatus was tasked with investigating the conspiracy and hunting down those involved. A 400-member special commission of the Reich Main Security Office, under the direct authority of Gestapo chief Heinrich Müller, was established specifically for this purpose. In the weeks following the failed assassination attempt, several thousand people were arrested; many were tortured and eventually prosecuted before the People's Court. At least 110 were sentenced to death and executed as participants, accessories, or sympathizers.

Numerous family members of July 20th conspirators fell victim to the principles of collective punishment and guilt by association and were confined to prisons or concentration camps. Children of plotters were often sent to community or juvenile homes. Even in the very last days of the war, leading figures of the resistance were targeted for execution, among them, Dietrich Bonhoeffer, Hans Oster, and Wilhelm Canaris in Flossenbürg and, at Dachau, Georg Elser, who early on had attempted to assassinate Hitler. mp

No. 6-80
SS soldiers take control of the Bendlerblock in Berlin on July 21, 1944, following the failed coup attempt
Süddeutsche Zeitung Photo, 19787

No. 6-88
**Peter Graf Yorck von Wartenburg, a defendant in the July 20th conspiracy trial, is led by two policemen into the People's Court.
August 7 or 8, 1944**
Ullstein Bilderdienst, 00260330

No. 6-90
**Alleged members of the Werewolf underground, ages 8 to 14, in custody of U.S. forces near Aachen
1945**
Bildarchiv Preußischer Kulturbesitz, Berlin, 30020173

No. 6-89
**Proclamation by an Upper Bavarian Werewolf group, which cites central motifs of SS ideology – loyalty, family, and village community – and is signed with a wolf-angel, the symbol of the underground movement
April 25, 1945**
Translation on page 451
The population is threatened with death as retaliation for any help afforded the Allies in their advance, or for any display of white flags as a sign of capitulation. mp
Süddeutsche Zeitung Photo, 323268

The "Werewolf" underground movement was brought into existence by *SS-Obergruppenführer* Hans Adolf Prützmann, on behalf of Heinrich Himmler, in September 1944. As partisans, the "Werewolves" were to commit acts of sabotage and terror against the Allies after the occupation of Germany, and were to murder the "traitors to the people" among the German population, in other words, those who collaborated with the Allies. "Wolf packs" often comprised young, inexperienced SS men, and fanatical members of the Hitler Youth and the League of German Girls.

A few sensational acts of terrorism attributed to the Werewolf – such as the murder of Mayor Franz Oppenhoff of Aachen on March 25, 1945, and the "Penzberg Murder Night" on April 28, 1945 – stirred considerable fear among the Allies and the civilian population of a sizable guerrilla movement. Although attacks persisted into 1947, causing the death of hundreds of Allied soldiers and German "collaborators," the Werewolf underground failed to develop into a broad-based mass movement and had no significant impact on the course of the war. What proved more potent, however, were the myths fostered by Himmler, and especially Joseph Goebbels, the Reich propaganda minister.mp

During World War II, ideological research at Wewelsburg Castle ceased, although construction work there proceeded. Spurred by the initial successes of the war, the plans submitted by the SS Construction Management became ever more grandiose. Up to the end of the war, SS architects went about planning a vast complex with the castle's northern tower at its center. None of it was actually ever completed, and today just two – unfinished – rooms located in the northern tower exist, to provide some insight into the planners' conceptual world. In the course of the war, Construction Management's designs expanded to completely appropriate the village of Wewelsburg. Their implementation would have seen the whole village destroyed. Meanwhile, the locality was being impacted by a growing number of National Socialist camps with different functions.

7 Wewelsburg Castle during the War

7.1
Wewelsburg Castle in World War II: Its People, Tasks, and Objectives

At the start of World War II, the situation that had been developing for the Wewelsburg SS castle administration since 1938 intensified: ideological research practically ceased and the tasks of the SS castle administration, which now included a few disabled Waffen-SS veterans, were largely curtailed between 1939 and 1945 to management of the building. At the local level, Construction Management of the Wewelsburg SS School, led by Hermann Bartels, became the dominant authority, and work on this colossal architectural project became the uncontested focus of SS efforts. Concurrently, the SS used Wewelsburg Castle as a repository for stolen cultural and artistic objects taken from countries throughout occupied Europe.

No. 7-1

Willy ter Hell, *Landschaft am Netzebruch* [Landscape at the Noteć Marsches]
Oil on canvas
1941
Heinrich Himmler acquired this work by painter Willy ter Hell (1883 – 1947) in 1941, at the "Great German Art Exhibition" (GDK). The back of the painting bears a sticker with the following information: "Catalog no. 412, hall no. 11; return address; first and last name: Heinrich Himmler; title: *Reichsführer-SS*; place of residence: Berlin SW 11; Prinz Albrechtstraße 8; stated insured value; RM 3,000.–"

Belying its quiet composition, the landscape depicted bore considerable political significance at the time. The Notec (German: Netze) River in Pomerania flows through the German-Polish borderland that had seen settlement from Prussia since the seventeenth century. Wewelsburg Castle's painting collection, built up through strategic purchases, often mirrored core areas of the SS worldview: Thus, the acquisition of this work should also be considered in connection with the SS vision of settlement east of the German Reich. The Allies seized the painting at Wewelsburg in 1945 and it subsequently became the property of the State of North Rhine-Westphalia in 1952. ds

Kreismuseum Wewelsburg, inv. no. 5199

12

Anläßlich seines Besuches auf der Wewelsburg in der Zeit
vom 15. bis 18.1.1939 äußerte der Reichsführer-SS u.a:

Bei der Besichtigung der einzelnen Burgzimmer
fragte SS-Gruppenführer Taubert, wie er sich bei der Anfrage,
ob die Burg besichtigt werden könne, verhalten soll. Der
Reichsführer-SS meinte darauf, eine Besichtigung der Burg käme
nicht in Frage. Wenn jemand eingeladen würde, müßte das eine
ganz besondere Ehre für den Betreffenden sein. z.B. würde
später einmal der eine oder andere General eingeladen werden.
Weiterhin müßten die Reichsleiter gelegentlich eingeladen werden, da sie nicht schlechter gestellt werden dürften, als die
SS-Gruppenführer.
Auf die Frage, ob über die Burg etwas veröffent-
licht werden sollte, erklärte der Reichsführer-SS entschieden,
daß dies auf gar keinen Fall in Frage käme. Der Hyänepresse
würde dieses Kleinod nicht zur Veröffentlichung freigegeben
werden.
Der Reichsführer-SS äußerte gegenüber SS-Gruppenführer
Taubert, daß er auf der Burg eine besondere Anlage für Gold
und Silberschätze wünsche, erstens aus Tradition und zweitens,
– darüber müsse man sich klar sein – als Notgroschen für
schlechte Zeiten.
In einem Zimmer des 1.Stockwerkes sagte der Reichsführer-SS: Ich habe einen Gedanken, dessen Ausführung allerdings
sehr teuer ist, Die Ausführung meiner Gedanken ist im überhaupt sehr teuer. Ich möchte auf der Burg ein Planetarium
einrichten. (Über die Frage, wo das Planetarium hinkommen
sollte, war sich der Reichsführer-SS noch nicht klar.)

185

A/101/151

Dem Präsidenten der Forschungs- und
Lehrgemeinschaft "Das Ahnenerbe",
Reichsführer-SS Heinrich Himmler
zum 7. Oktober 1942

R e i c h s f ü h r e r !

In treuer Gefolgschaft entbietet Ihnen das "Ahnenerbe"
an Ihrem Geburtstag die herzlichsten Glückwünsche; sie
seien verbunden mit einer Gabe, die von den Ufern des
Kuban stammt, den unsere Truppen unlängst siegreich über-
schritten. Skythenstämme, die in den ersten Jahrhunderten
nach Zeitwechsel dort ansässig waren, haben ihren Toten
diese kostbaren Schmuckstücke mit ins Grab gegeben als
Zeugnis ihrer hohen und eigenartigen Kultur, die zu
erforschen gerade jetzt Sie, Reichsführer, befohlen haben.

Schon vor Jahren wurden diese Stücke, die nur e i n her-
vorragendes Beispiel aus einer grösseren Anzahl Funde
darstellen, aus Kurganen geborgen. Als SS-Obersturmbannführer
Sievers, von Ihnen beauftragt, mit Mitarbeitern des
"Ahnenerbes" im Winter 1940 nach Polen kam, um dort
wertvolles Kulturgut vor der Vernichtung zu retten, fanden
Ihre Männer im Staub eines Magazins diesen Schatz. Er
wäre wohl würdig, dereinst nach Abschluss seiner wissenschaftlichen Bearbeitung auf der Wewelsburg seinen endgültigen
Platz zu finden.

Heil Hitler !

Ihre

gez. W. Wüst
SS-Standartenführer

gez. W. Sievers
SS-Obersturmbannführer

No. 7-3
**Log of Heinrich Himmler's visit to
Wewelsburg Castle
January 1939**
This log was kept by Heinrich Himmler's
personal assistant, Dr. Rudolf Brandt, to
document a visit to Wewelsburg Castle by
the *Reichsführer-SS* in January 1939.
Himmler's statements to Siegfried
Taubert, the chief castle administrator,
were programmatic in nature. The decision to also use Wewelsburg Castle as an
SS treasure chamber caused large quantities of cultural artifacts – including
paintings, furniture, porcelain, antique
weapons, rare books, archaeological
finds, and jewelry – to be brought there
from occupied countries. The SS either
robbed these objects outright, or they
exploited the distress of owners to acquire
the works below market value. ds
Bundesarchiv Berlin, NS 19/1446, p. 12

No. 7-2
**Letter of congratulations from the SS-Ahnenerbe
[Ancestral Heritage] Society to Heinrich Himmler
October 7, 1942**
Translation on page 451
The letter of congratulations from the SS
Ancestral Heritage Society on the occasion of
Reichsführer-SS Heinrich Himmler's 42nd
birthday clearly indicates that only exceptional,
valuable objects were intended for Wewelsburg
Castle. It also illustrates the indifference with
which the SS looted cultural artifacts from
occupied countries, in violation of the regula-
tions of the Hague Convention on the protection
of cultural property in place since 1907.
SS Ancestral Heritage personnel were
deeply involved in the pillage, especially in
Eastern Europe. They plundered museums and
private collections, removed cultural assets, and
even conducted archaeological digs. In 1942,
Ancestral Heritage was incorporated into the
Personal Staff of the *Reichsführer-SS* Main
Office; it reached it greatest dimensions in
1943 – 1944, when it included more than forty
research departments. ds
Bundesarchiv Berlin, formerly the Berlin Document Center,
Ahnenerbe PA Wolfram Sievers, p. 185

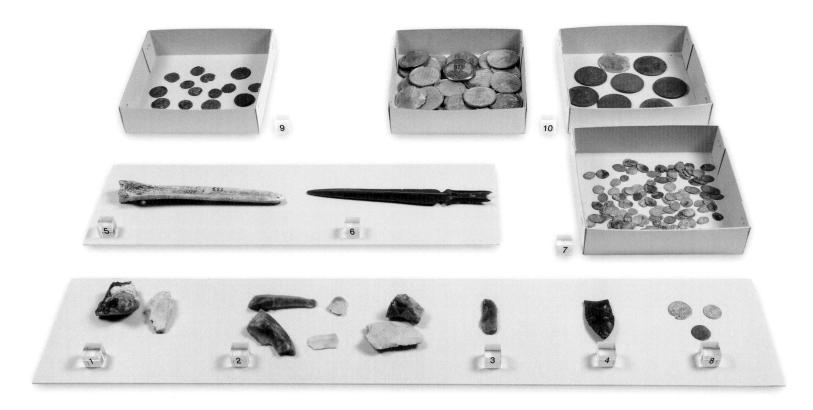

No. 7-4
**Remnants of the archaeo-
logical collection from the SS
museum at Wewelsburg**

1

**Two Stone Age flint artifacts
with the inscription "Alt-
Modsele"**
The location of Alt-Modsele
is unknown.
Loan from the Verein für Geschichte und
Altertumskunde Westfalens, Abteilung
Paderborn, PB-AV-la 49

2

**Six Stone Age flint artifacts
with the inscription
"Niwkowo, near Wizna on the
Narew"**
Niwkowo is located in North-
western Poland, ca. fifty kilo-
meters (ca. thirty-one miles)
from the town of Białystok.
Loan from the Verein für Geschichte und
Altertumskunde Westfalens, Abteilung
Paderborn, PB-AV-la 49

3

**Stone Age flint end scraper
with Cyrillic inscription;
allegedly discovered at
Ringelstein Forest**
Kreismuseum Wewelsburg, inv. no. 3546

4

Folsom style spear point
This type of spear point is
from North America, where
it was in use from 9,000 to
8,000 B.C.
Kreismuseum Wewelsburg, inv. no. 7667

5

**Bone dagger (?) with
Cyrillic inscription**
Kreismuseum Wewelsburg, inv. no. 692

6

**Bronze Age tang handle
dagger, Northern Italy**
Kreismuseum Wewelsburg, inv. no. 7652

7

**Russian wire kopecks
18th century**
Kreismuseum Wewelsburg,
inv. nos. 8100 – 8217

8

Three Polish coins
Kreismuseum Wewelsburg,
inv. nos. 7903 – 7905

9

Fourteen Byzantine coins
Kreismuseum Wewelsburg,
inv. nos. 7906 – 7919

10

**Thirty-one Ukrainian coins
and medals**
Kreismuseum Wewelsburg,
inv. nos. 6546 – 6576 and 6760 – 6766

The artifacts displayed here are from the
collections of the SS museum at Wewelsburg Castle. They present numerous
marks of provenance from the collections
that once owned them, providing clues to
their countries of origin. Some of the
objects were recovered from the debris of
the castle, demolished by the SS in 1945.
Others were scavenged by Wewelsburg
residents after the demolition and donated years later to the Kreismuseum
Wewelsburg or the Verein für Geschichte
und Altertumskunde Westfalens, Abteilung Paderborn (Association for History
and Antiquities of Westphalia). ds

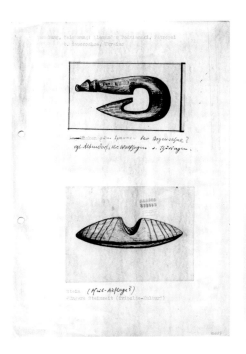

No. 7-6
Drawings of archaeological objects from the collection of A. Bodnianski, Petropol, near Zaporodjie/Ukraine, with subsequent explanations
Probably 1942 – 1944
Kreismuseum Wewelsburg
inv. no. 16689

No. 7-5
Photographs of Hutsuls, a Carpathian people, from a Kiev folklore collection, brought by Wilhelm Jordan in 1944
Kreismuseum Wewelsburg,
Nachlass Wilhelm Jordan, inv. no. 16633

Assigned a covert mission by Heinrich Himmler, Wewelsburg archaeologist and museum director Wilhelm Jordan took an active part in the removal of cultural assets from the Ukraine. As an SS military geologist, Jordan was officially tasked with locating mineral resources of military significance in the Ukraine. In addition, he conducted research on the inventories of archaeological and geological collections. With other National Socialist agencies having already laid claim to most of the Ukrainian museums, Jordan sought out private collectors, offering them food in exchange for their most valuable objects, exploiting the famine unleashed by the Germans' harsh occupation policy. It was only after Germany's position in the war had deteriorated and its government agencies had begun progressively withdrawing from the Ukraine that Jordan was also able to get his hands on museum inventories and send these to Germany.

The objects displayed here are from Wilhelm Jordan's own estate. They illustrate that he also conducted private studies within Ukrainian collections, removing objects that he found interesting. Yet, he always sent any valuable objects to the SS, along with a note stating that they could be incorporated into "his" museum at Wewelsburg Castle if no other purpose was found for them.ds

No. 7-9
Altomonte Hall at the St. Florian Monastery of the Augustinian Canons Regular in Linz
Oberdonau. Querschnitt durch Kultur und Schaffen im Heimatgau des Führers
[Upper Danube: A Cross-Section of Culture and Creation in the Führer's Home District]
Vol. 1, 1941, no. 4, p. 37
Ca. 1940
Heinrich Himmler made a request to August Eigruber, the Gauleiter of Upper Austria, that a grand circular carpet from the St. Florian Monastery in Linz be made a "gift" to Wewelsburg Castle. It is likely that the conversation took place in May 1941 and that the carpet in question is the one shown here.

Like nearly every other monastery in Upper Austria, the important Baroque monastic complex of St. Florian in Linz, built upon the saint's grave, was seized by the Gestapo and expropriated to the benefit of the Reichsgau Oberdonau. Its significant cultural and historical collections were sequestered. During a visit to Wewelsburg Castle in June 1942, however, Heinrich Himmler noticed that the carpet still had not arrived. Once the Viennese security service got involved, the carpet promptly appeared at Wewelsburg Castle, in August 1942. ds
Oberösterreichische Landesmuseen/
Schlossmuseum Linz

- 2 -

No. 1014 Tapisserie 300 x 300 Wildschweinjagd, Maquet, Paris
No. 1021 Tapisserie 350 x 384 Brüssel, 17.Jahrhundert
          Amazonen Königin, Albin, Paris

Dr. Kai MÜHLMANN

Vgl. Regn: Vleie S. 106!
  + S. 113
  + S. 116
  + S. 125/126

274

Der ehemalige Reichsführer der SS Heinrich Himmler hat für
Wewelsburg (Paderborn) nachstehende Kunstgegenstände von der
Dienststelle Dr. Mühlamnn erworben:

No. 565   Bartholomäus van der Elst, Zeichnung "Figurengruppe"
          Leegenhoek, Paris
No. 587   Kleiner Nussholzschrank mit Holzfigur und Nische
          Maquet Paris
No. 594   Nussholzschrank, Französische 16.Jahrhundert mit
          Reliefs, Taillemas, Paris
No. 624   Baudewyn "Baumlandschaft"
          Taillemas, Paris
No. 901   Sebastian Vrancks "Gefolge eines Feldherrn"
          Nicoll, Paris
No. 905   Italienische Truhe, Nussholz 16.Jahrhundert Monnier,
          Cannes
No. 913   Gotische Tür mit 2 Flügeln, Französisch 15. Jahrh.
          Maquet, Paris
No. 918   Kredenz, Deutsch um 1600,3 Türen
          Maquet, Paris
No. 921   Holzfigur, Französisch 15. Jahrh."St. Adrian als Ritter"
          Lagrande, Brüssel
No. 946   Gotische Truhe, Eiche, Französisch um 1500
          Meder, Paris
No. 950   Italienische Truhe 16.Jahrh.
          Meder, Paris
No. 951   Tisch, Französisch 16.Jahrh. Nussholz, Meder, Paris
No. 983   Truhe, Eiche, 1739 datiert, grün bemalt vlämisch
          Smeets, Antwerpen
No. 985   Holländischer Schrank, 2 große Türen darüber je 1 Lade
          Smeets, Antwerpen.
No. 989   Holländischer Schrank, Rosenholz, 2 Türen, 3 Pilaster
          Lagrande, Brüssel
No. 995   Holländischer Schrank, 4 Türen, 2 Laden, Diamantquaderung
          Wiehart, Brüssel
No.1008   Jan Wenix "Baumstamm mit Hase" Nicoll, Paris

No. 7-7
Cultural assets safeguarded by the Allies at Gut Böddeken
April/May 1945
On April 2, 1945, Allied troops reached Wewelsburg. They found the castle demolished by the SS and looted by the local community, yet they managed to secure a great number of cultural artifacts. When the British major Sydney Frank Markham, from the Allied artistic preservation unit Monuments, Fine Arts, and Archives (MFAA), arrived in Wewelsburg on May 14, 1945, works of art were stored in the burned-out castle and at the SS staff building. There was also another storage site for artworks in the camp laundry, set up on the initiative of former concentration camp prisoner Wettin Müller, who had sought the return of plundered property. Moreover, as early as 1943, the SS had had many objects packed by concentration camp prisoners and brought to Gut Böddeken, two kilometers (ca. 1.2 miles) from Wewelsburg, to protect them from air raids. The photograph documents that depot following looting that had also occurred there.

The British artistic preservation officer Markham initially established a provisional inventory of recovered objects. These were then transferred to an Allied Central Collection Point at Nordkirchen Castle, near Münster. From there, they were moved in September 1947 to Dyck Castle, near Grevenbroich. The greater part of what came to be referred to as the "Himmler Collection" was returned to its owners; however, only requests for restitution from state entities were honored, none from individuals. In 1952, still unclaimed inventory of the collection became the property of the State of North Rhine-Westphalia. ds
Kreismuseum Wewelsburg, Fotoarchiv

No. 7-8
List of works of art acquired by SS architect Hermann Bartels for Wewelsburg through the Mühlmann Office (last of four pages)
1942
Translation on page 451
On September 28, 1942, Wewelsburg's head architect Hermann Bartels was urged by the SS Raw Materials Department to select works of art for Wewelsburg Castle from the collections purchased by the Mühlmann Office. Bartels subsequently acquired artifacts valued at 206,193 Reichsmarks. The Mühlmann Office, named after its head, *SS-Oberführer* Kajetan Mühlmann, was established in 1940 at The Hague, with additional offices in Berlin and Paris. Its role was to gather information on the art collections of France and The Nether-lands, to produce reports on seized objects, and to acquire significant works of art on the art market, as well as from "enemy assets," most often Jewish property. Personnel of the Mühlmann Office assembled these various objects in warehouses to transport them to Germany for sale, either to high-ranking National Socialist politicians, or to museums and auction houses. ds
Bundesarchiv Koblenz, B 323/200

Himmler's Architect in Wewelsburg: Hermann Bartels

No. 7-11

Detail of a page of photographs with three images, including one showing Bartels in SS uniform and cap

After Heinrich Himmler, architect Hermann Bartels exercised the greatest influence on the SS project in Wewelsburg from 1933 to 1945. The state inspector for the Westphalian Office of Historical Preservation and regional NSDAP functionary was a major influence in swaying Himmler to choose Wewelsburg Castle in 1933.

From the first day of his tenure to the last, Bartels, as head of the Construction Management entity in Wewelsburg, gave architectural expression to Himmler's vision of an exclusive meeting point for high-ranking SS officers. In pursuing his objectives, he never shied away from exploiting concentration camp labor managed by the SS.

Bartels was always keen on leveraging his work for the National Socialist Party and SS to promote his civil service career. The subsequent provincial head architect did not become a member of the SS until 1938, when Himmler appointed him an honorary *SS-Sturmbannführer*. mm

Bundesarchiv Berlin, formerly the Berlin Document Center, RS Bartels

Hermann Bartels (1900 – 1989)
Architect, Head of Construction Management at the Wewelsburg SS School, 1934 – 1945

April 14, 1900
Born in Minden, the son of a provincial official, four years of primary and five of secondary education in Münster

1916 – 1919
Attended the *Staatsbauschule* (state architectural college) in Münster

1918
Non-combat military service

1920
Began employment as a technician for the state office of historical preservation at the Westphalian Provincial Association in Münster

1922 – 1925
Member of the local Münster chapter of the *Jungdeutscher Orden*, a very popular nationalistic association inspired by medieval Teutonic Knights

1928
Appointed a lifetime civil servant as technical regional secretary at the Westphalian Provincial Association

1930
Led the restoration of Ramsdorf Castle, near Velen in the Münsterland region

September 1, 1932
Joined the NSDAP; employed on the staff of Dr. Alfred Meyer, *Gauleiter* for Westphalia-North in Münster

January 1933
Rejection of his application for appointment to "head regional architect" by his supervising department

Summer 1933
Appointed district cultural supervisor and NSDAP district administrative director for Westphalia-North

July 1933
Inauguration of Beverungen Castle, which had been restored under his authority for use as an SA military sports academy

1933 – 1934
Managed the conversion of Velen Castle to an SA military sports academy

Second half of 1933
Consultant in the SS Race and Settlement Office's search for a "castle" for the SS

September 1933
Encounter with *Reichsführer-SS* Heinrich Himmler at the National Socialist Party's (NSDAP) Nuremberg rally

November 3, 1933
Accompanied Himmler on a visit to Wewelsburg Castle and was immediately commissioned by him to design plans for its conversion

Spring 1934
Appointed by Himmler as head of construction for the SS at Wewelsburg

September 1934
Appointed "Head Regional Architect" by the Provincial Association at the urging of *NSDAP-Gauleiter* Dr. Meyer; provisionally released from his civil servant responsibilities three days a week to perform his duties at Wewelsburg

April 1936
Assumed duties in the service of the newly established SS building development office at Wewelsburg, the "Society for the Promotion and Care of German Cultural Monuments," while preserving his status as a lifetime civil servant

June 1, 1936
Began a leave of absence from the Westphalian Provincial Association, renewed annually until 1945

1937 – 1940
Won the competition for design of a major National Socialist building project on Hiddeser Berg, near Detmold, and for redesign of the city of Münster as *Gauhauptstadt* (National Socialist regional capital). Adolf Hitler and Albert Speer were among the jurors.

April 20, 1938
Date of membership in the SS, with the rank of a *Sturmbannführer*

February 1939
Married the daughter of a Büren physician; they had three children

1939
Design of a barrier-like palace complex for the SS at Wewelsburg

1939 – 1942
Construction of his family villa (Führerhaus I) at Wewelsburg using prisoner labor from Niederhagen Concentration Camp

August 5, 1940
Approval by Himmler of the earliest known design for a circular, multi-building castle complex at Wewelsburg

November 9, 1940
Promotion to *SS-Obersturmbannführer*

June 1, 1941
Appointed "head provincial architect" (an upper civil service post) at the urging of the local NSDAP leadership

June 21, 1942
Promotion to *SS-Standartenführer* on the occasion of Himmler's last known visit to Wewelsburg

October 1942
Toured the granite plant at Flossenbürg Concentration Camp to obtain building material for Wewelsburg

1944
Elaborated at least two new design versions for the circular castle complex at Wewelsburg

Late 1944
Met with Dr. Hans Kammler, the head of Department C (Construction) at the SS Economic and Administrative Main Office, *SS-Gruppenführer*, and lieutenant general of the Waffen-SS; on the "development of SS-Cities," for which Bartels had several designs

May 1945 – 1947
Arrested and imprisoned in the British internment camp at Staumühle

thereafter
Worked as an independent architect

January 13, 1989
Death in Essen mm

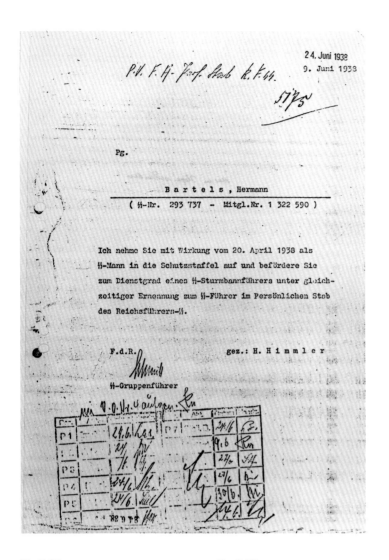

No. 7-15
Official copy of the announcement of Bartels's membership in the SS, effective April 20, 1938
June 9 and 24, 1938
Bundesarchiv Berlin, formerly the Berlin Document Center, SSO Bartels

No. 7-10
(From left to right) Hermann Bartels in Party uniform, building developer Fritz Scherpeltz, and Heinrich Himmler in Wewelsburg
After 1938
Kreismuseum Wewelsburg, Fotoarchiv

No. 7-14
"Reichsführer-SS Himmler lässt sich im Gauhaus (von Hermann Bartels) in Münster den Plan zur Neugestaltung der Stadt Münster erklären"
[*Reichsführer-SS* Himmler has Hermann Bartels explain plans for redesigning the city of Münster at the NSDAP district headquarters (*Gauhaus*) in Münster]
Hermann Bartels (third from the left), Heinrich Himmler (fourth from the left), the district leader (*Gauleiter*) Dr. Alfred Meyer (on the right)
Until 1936, state-licensed conservator and NSDAP district cultural supervisor (*Gaukulturwart*) Bartels only worked extraofficially for the SS in Wewelsburg. While still retaining his civil service status, he took leave from the Westphalian provincial administration to work for the SS property development entity in Wewelsburg, the Society for the Promotion and Care of German Cultural Monuments. In 1937 – 1938, Bartels won a competition held by the NSDAP for the planning and construction of a large National Socialist memorial on Hiddeser Berg near Detmold, and for the redesign of his home city of Münster as a district capital (*Gauhauptstadt*). Adolf Hitler and his architect, Albert Speer, were the jurors. In the summer of 1938, evidently in order to preclude possible co-option by other Party agencies and to bind Bartels more closely to the SS, Himmler made him an honorary officer in the SS. As an *SS-Sturmbannführer*, Bartels was now the highest-ranking SS officer in Wewelsburg, junior only to the chief administrator of Wewelsburg Castle Taubert. mm

Arno Schröder: *Mit der Partei vorwärts! Zehn Jahre Gau Westfalen-Nord* [Forward with the Party! Ten years of the Westphalia-North District], Detmold, 1940

No. 7-12
Not shown
Letter of thanks from Himmler to Bartels for the Wewelsburg development plans
Munich, January 2, 1934
Bundesarchiv Berlin, formerly the Berlin Document Center, SSO Bartels

No. 7-13
Not shown
"Der Gauleiter auf der Wewelsburg. Gauleiter Dr. Meyer lässt sich von Gaukulturwart Bartels den Bauplan erläutern" [The *Gauleiter* at Wewelsburg Castle: *Gaukulturwart* [Hermann] Bartels explains the construction plan to *Gauleiter* Dr. Meyer]
March 31, 1934
Der Filter (Paderborn National Socialist newspaper) Kreisarchiv Paderborn

From their first joint visit to Wewelsburg Castle on November 3, 1933, a special bond of trust developed between Bartels and Himmler. The architect from Münster was immediately put in charge of developing conversion plans for the castle, with Himmler thanking him immediately for their receipt. Even before the SS officially took over Wewelsburg Castle, Bartels had already been named head of construction by Himmler, with sole responsibility for the project.

Westphalian *NSDAP-Gauleiter* Dr. Alfred Meyer was another of Bartels's patrons, in competition with Himmler as a sponsor of the architect, and doing his best to secure Party construction projects for his close colleague from Münster. Moreover, Meyer used his political influence to support Bartels for promotion and leaves of absence at the Westphalian provincial administration. mm

No. 7-20
Preliminary drawings by Hermann Bartels for the planned SS castle complex in Wewelsburg, including related buildings and designs for the cities of Arolsen and Höxter (here: illustration 2)
Presumably from 1943 – 1945; the original plans are missing
Kreismuseum Wewelsburg, Fotoarchiv

No. 7-16
Not shown
Letter from Hermann Bartels to Dr. Alfred Meyer, the NSDAP district leader (*Gauleiter*) of the North Westphalia district (*Gau*) and president of the province of Westphalia, concerning the prolongation of his leave of absence from the civil service
May 15, 1939
Archiv des Landschaftsverbands Westfalen-Lippe, C 11 A Nr. 132, p. 140 f.

No. 7-17
Not shown
Hermann Bartels and Wewelsburg master carpenter Johannes Grote at the topping-off ceremony for the staff building
September 25, 1940
Kreismuseum Wewelsburg, Fotoarchiv

Almost every year until 1945, Bartels was obliged to request extensions of his leave from the provincial administration, relying on the intercession of high-ranking NSDAP and SS officials. In his application letter of May 15, 1939, to Westphalian district leader (*Gauleiter*) Meyer, he presented himself as a National Socialist and true Westphalian, who was involved with the SS only to the extent that his regional consciousness allowed. In fact, Himmler offered him the opportunity of unimpeded professional and personal fulfillment – although the staff building of 1940 – 1941 was one of Bartels's few projects to see completion before the end of National Socialist rule. mm

No. 7-18
Hermann Bartels greets Heinrich Himmler at Paderborn-Mönkeloh airfield on the *Reichsführer-SS*'s last known visit to Wewelsburg; in the background, the chief administrator of Wewelsburg Castle, Siegfried Taubert
June 18, 1942
U. S. Holocaust Memorial Museum, Washington D.C., Photo Archives, 60467

No. 7-19
Führerhaus 1 (Villa Bartels)
From 1942 to 1945
Hermann Bartels enjoyed a large degree of freedom in Wewelsburg. As head of the Construction Management entity at the SS Wewelsburg School, he was not answerable to the chief administrator of Wewelsburg Castle, Siegfried Taubert. Rather, it was the latter who was obliged to help with procuring building materials and manpower for the Wewelsburg project. With the full support of the architect, this workforce was largely drawn from prisoners at Niederhagen Concentration Camp during World War II. From 1939 to 1942, when Bartels had his own villa (Führerhaus 1) built at Kuhkampsberg within view of Wewelsburg Castle, much of the work was performed by concentration camp prisoners. mm
Kreismuseum Wewelsburg, Fotoarchiv

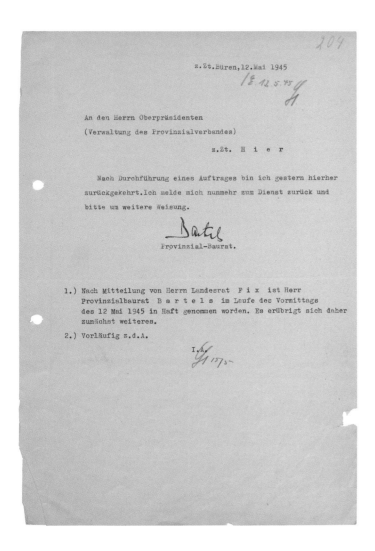

z.Zt.Büren,12.Mai 1945

An den Herrn Oberpräsidenten

(Verwaltung des Provinzialverbandes)

z.Zt. H i e r

Nach Durchführung eines Auftrages bin ich gestern hierher
zurückgekehrt.Ich melde mich nunmehr zum Dienst zurück und
bitte um weitere Weisung.

Provinzial-Baurat.

1.) Nach Mitteilung von Herrn Landesrat F i x ist Herr
Provinzialbaurat B a r t e l s im Laufe des Vormittags
des 12 Mai 1945 in Haft genommen worden. Es erübrigt sich daher
zunächst weiteres.

2.) Vorläufig z.d.A.

No. 7-21

Letter from Bartels to the administration of the Westphalian Provincial Association, regarding resumption of his duties, with a note announcing his arrest the same day May 12, 1945

Archiv des Landschaftsverbands Westfalen-Lippe, C 11 A No. 132, p. 204

By 1944 at the latest, the gigantic castle complex at Wewelsburg was not the only local planning project that Hermann Bartels was overseeing for the SS. He also designed an "SS city" for 10,000 inhabitants, as well as three SS residential developments in central Germany. It is unclear whether the general plans for the cities of Arolsen and Höxter were also part of this assignment.

As late as February 1945, the Reich Ministry of the Interior extended Bartels's leave from the Westphalian Provincial Association by another year, to the benefit of the SS. Himmler's architect continued working in Wewelsburg until the flight of the SS castle administration on March 30, 1945. Bartels then vanished, until four days after Germany's unconditional surrender, when he reported for duty with his – formerly disdained – state employer. That same day, he was arrested by Allied military authorities. mm

7.1.3
The SS Center of Control in Wewelsburg from 1939 to 1945:
The Construction Management Organization

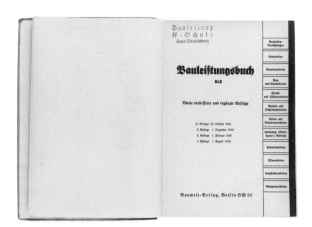

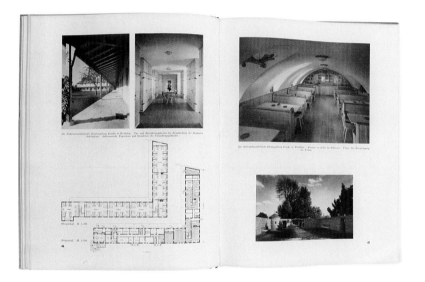

No. 7-30
Bauleistungsbuch BLB [Building Service Specifications], fourth, revised and expanded edition, Berlin 1940, with ink stamp "Construction Management, Wewelsburg SS School"
1940
Kreismuseum Wewelsburg, Nachlass Wettin Müller, inv. no. 15750

No. 7-29
Not shown
Ludwig Baumeister, *Preisermittlung und Veranschlagen* [Costing and Pricing], Berlin 1941, stamped "Construction Management, SS Wewelsburg School"
Although an affiliation is implied in its official title, the Construction Management of SS Wewelsburg School was not a department of the SS school, but an independent institution with its own administration. The books from this department, therefore, did not comprise a subsection of the SS school library, but were managed by specially assigned registrars and bore the Construction Management inventory mark and stamp. mm
Kreismuseum Wewelsburg, Nachlass Wettin Müller, inv. no. 15755

No. 7-27
Construction code manuals from the collection of Construction Management of the SS Wewelsburg School before 1945 (selection)
In April 1945, after the end of National Socialist rule in Wewelsburg, Wettin Müller, a former prisoner and clerk at Niederhagen Concentration Camp, gathered numerous objects from the former SS institutions in Wewelsburg and stored them at his home. Among these was a sizeable collection of volumes from the inventories of the erstwhile SS Construction Management. Besides books on building law and civil engineering, there were works in which Hermann Bartels and his collaborators had sought ideological inspiration, as well as models for their National Socialist building projects in Wewelsburg. mm
Kreismuseum Wewelsburg, Nachlass Wettin Müller, inv. no. 15724

No. 7-23
Report on the activity of Department W (Economic Enterprises) VIII (Special Tasks) of the SS Economic and Administrative Main Office for the year 1941
January 10, 1942
Translation on page 451
Landesarchiv NRW, Abteilung Ostwestfalen-Lippe, Detmold, D70, no. 160

No. 7-22
Not shown
Carbon copy of a letter from Hermann Bartels, the head of Construction Management of the SS Wewelsburg School, to Siegfried Taubert, the SS chief administrator of Wewelsburg Castle and inspector of the Reinforced Death's Head Regiments, addressing, among other things, a request that his application for more prisoners be presented favorably to Heinrich Himmler
March 1, 1940
"Construction Management for the Wewelsburg SS School" was the executive entity headed by Hermann Bartels responsible for planning and project development. During World War II, Bartels endeavored not to lose his male employees to the military draft.

From 1939, Bartels was a driving force behind the establishment and expansion of the concentration camp in Wewelsburg. As in this case from March 1940, he sought to increase the number of prisoners to be able to continue and expand projects of his Construction Management. Here, he enlisted the support of the SS's chief administrator of Wewelsburg Castle, Siegfried Taubert, who temporarily held an important position in the SS's central concentration camp administration as Inspector of the Reinforced Death's Head Regiments. mm
Landesarchiv NRW, Abteilung Ostwestfalen-Lippe, Detmold, D27, BKA 507-19-22-23-file 17-S-a62

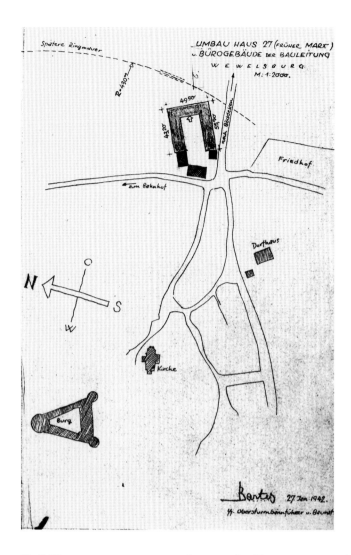

No. 7-25
Site plan for conversion of the Marx farm (Hof Marx) to an office building for Construction Management of the Wewelsburg SS School with indication of the planned curtain wall around Wewelsburg Castle
January 27, 1942
Kreisarchiv Paderborn

Construction Management was located in Wewelsburg castle until 1937 – 1938. It was then moved into the basement of a newly erected guard building on the castle forecourt. In 1942, Construction Management had farm buildings located in the center of Wewelsburg previously owned by the Marx family (who had resettled to Silesia) converted for its use, including the addition of a large, modern office barracks. Former concentration camp prisoners who had to work on this project described the "Marx house detail" as one of the most feared work assignments in Wewelsburg.

As the diagram indicates, the "U"-shaped barracks was located just inside the circular curtain wall, which Hermann Bartels wanted to erect around the Wewelsburg Castle northern tower at a distance of 430 meters (ca. 1410 ft.). The relocation of Construction Management to the Marx farm was, therefore, only seen as a temporary measure, because the construction of the planned castle complex would have required moving the office once again. mm

No. 7-31
Photograph from the estate of a former office employee of Construction Management of the Wewelsburg SS School
Private collection, 1942 – 1944
Not all employees of Construction Management were men, or members of the SS. Besides male architects, engineers, draftsmen, and administrative personnel; there were also women, employed mostly as simple office clerks. These photographs from the estate of an administrative employee show male and female Construction Management employees posing in front of their successive work sites, the guard building and the former Marx farm.

There appear to have generally been more civilian employees than SS members on the Construction Management staff. In monthly reports of the Society for the Promotion and Care of German Cultural Monuments, employees of private companies working for the SS in Wewelsburg were counted as Construction Management personnel. Thus, in September 1942, the Construction Management payroll included 10 SS members, 14 male and 6 female civilian employees, and 35 laborers. mm

Kreismuseum Wewelsburg, Fotoarchiv

No. 7-24
The office building of Construction Management of the Wewelsburg SS School at the Marx farm
1942 – 1943
Kreismuseum Wewelsburg, Fotoarchiv

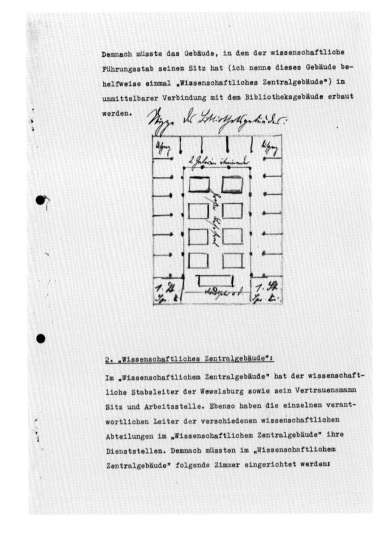

No. 7-26
Not shown
Translated excerpts from the monthly reports by Department W 1 of the SS Economic and Administrative Main Office for August and October 1942, with mention of Bartels's visit to the Deutsche Erd- und Steinwerke GmbH (DESt) granite plant at Flossenbürg Concentration Camp, and Wewelsburg Construction Management's awarding of a contract worth 50,000 Reichsmarks

In Wewelsburg, Construction Management for the Wewelsburg SS School also oversaw construction at the local concentration camp until 1942. From 1939, Construction Management's operations depended on its ability to draw on concentration camp prisoner labor. But the integration of the Wewelsburg Construction Management into the concentration camp system went beyond the local scope. In 1942, Hermann Bartels visited Flossenbürg Concentration Camp and its granite processing plant, a branch of the SS business venture Deutsche Erd- und Steinwerke GmbH. Cut stone worth almost 50,000 Reichsmarks was delivered from the camp to Wewelsburg, where the stone won through the exploitation of prisoners at Flossenbürg Concentration Camp was used for, among other things, the construction of the north terrace structure of the guard building by prisoners from Niederhagen Concentration Camp. mm

Bundesarchiv Berlin, NS. 3-1347

No. 7-28
**Drafting tools from the inventory of Construction Management for the Wewelsburg SS School
Before 1945**

**Fountain pen stand with inkwell
Black marble, nonferrous metal**
Kreismuseum Wewelsburg,
inv. no. 5712

Not shown
**Angle
Wood**
Kreismuseum Wewelsburg,
inv. no. 5709

Not shown
**Protractor
Wood**
Kreismuseum Wewelsburg,
inv. no. 5710

Not shown
**Ruler
Plastic, metal**
Kreismuseum Wewelsburg,
inv. no. 5721

Not shown
**Triangle
Plastic, metal**
Kreismuseum Wewelsburg,
inv. no. 5711

No. 7-33
**Memorandum from Dr. Bernhard Frank with suggestions for final planning of academic buildings in Wewelsburg (excerpt)
January 20, 1941**

By 1939, many of the original indoctrination leaders and researchers had left the Wewelsburg SS School. The outbreak of World War II prevented the desired renewal of the research personnel and approach. Established and prospective researchers were drafted into the *Waffen-SS* or the *Wehrmacht*. The SS Castle Administration was reduced solely to administrative personnel, which included some war-injured.

In early 1941, Wewelsburg SS folklorist Dr. Bernhard Frank, who had been granted leave from the *Waffen-SS* for the task, was entrusted with developing a scenario whereby parts of the planned gigantic SS castle could be used for academic purposes. Implementation of his vague ideas would have involved numerous additional SS researchers moving to Wewelsburg, but the subsequent course of the war prevented this. mm

Bundesarchiv Berlin, NS 48/16

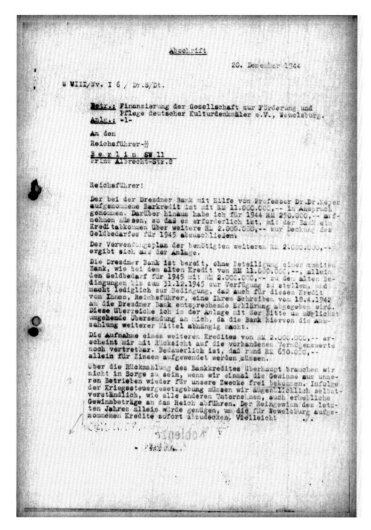
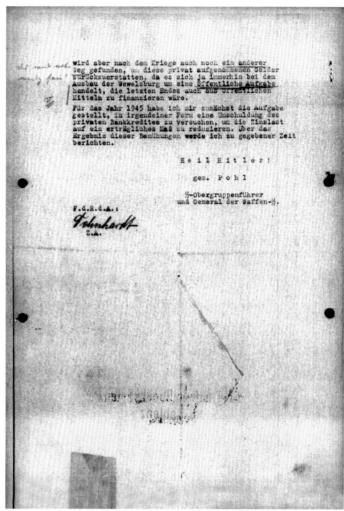

No. 7-36

Letter from the head of the SS Economic and Administrative Main Office, Oswald Pohl, to *Reichsführer-SS* Heinrich Himmler, about the Dresdner Bank's willingness to grant an additional credit of 2 million Reichsmarks to finance the activities of the Society for the Promotion and Care of German Cultural Monuments in Wewelsburg
December 20, 1944

By late 1944, the Society for the Preservation and Cultivation of German Cultural Monuments and Wewelsburg Construction Management had expended the loan of 11 million Reichsmarks taken out with the Dresdner Bank three years earlier. The head of the SS Economic and Administrative Main Office, Oswald Pohl, sought a follow-up loan of 2 million Reichsmarks for 1945, but nothing came of this. Six months before the final collapse of the Third Reich, Pohl was still fantasizing about repaying the loans with profits from the SS's prisoner businesses.

Around the same time, Hermann Bartels estimated the total costs for the completion of his colossal building project in Wewelsburg at 250 million Reichsmarks, with this figure assuming the continued use of prisoner labor, which was largely without cost to the SS. According to Bartels, building operations would take another twenty years following a German "final victory." mm

Internationaler Suchdienst, Bad Arolsen, Historischer Ordner 6, SS-WVHA 6

Der Reichsführer-ß
RF/M. 23/6/44 g

Feld-Kommandostelle, den 26. Febr. 44

Lieber Taubert!

Trotz der vielen Arbeit hat man natürlich
Zeit über das oder jenes nachzudenken. Ich möchte
nun nicht, daß einzelne Einfälle oder Gedanken, die
ich mir über die Zukunft auch der Wewelsburg mache,
vergessen werden.

Im Rahmen dieser Gedanken fiel mir ein, daß
wir die Wewelsburg im Frieden allenfalls folgender-
maßen bezeichnen können:

"Wewelsburg - Reichshaus der ß-Gruppenführer".

Ich bitte Sie, diese Niederschrift mir bei
"Friedensausbruch" wieder vorzulegen.

Heil Hitler !
Ihr

2. an den
Chef des ß-Hauptamtes
ß-Obergruppenführer Berger
durchschriftlich mit der Bitte um Kenntnisnahme übersandt.

i.A.

ß-Hauptsturmführer

No. 7-32
**Housekeeper Elfriede Wippermann
(second from right) with "castle girls" in
the Wewelsburg moat
Ca. 1939 or 1940**
At Wewelsburg, select groups of SS men
were to be encouraged in their sense of
entitlement to reshape history, their own
society, and the world according to their
racist worldview. In their castle stronghold, the SS men had themselves looked
after by women – the so-called castle
maids or castle girls. Many of these young
women were referred to the Wewelsburg
SS School by employment agencies to ab-
solve their "year of service" (a compulsory
year of work in agriculture or house-
keeping instituted in Germany in 1938 for
all racially "irreproachable" women under
the age of 25). Housekeeper Elfriede
Wippermann (1889 – 1980) was responsible
for the domestic management of the
castle and the longest-serving senior staff
member at the Wewelsburg SS School
after the chief castle administrator
Siegfried Taubert. mm

Kreismuseum Wewelsburg, Fotoarchiv

No. 7-35
Not shown
**Wewelsburg with camouflage
pattern
1944**
As time progressed – after the *Gruppenführer* meeting of June 1941,
after Himmler's final visit to Wewelsburg in July 1942, and ultimately
with the cessation of building operations in April 1943 – the duties of
the SS castle administration became
increasingly limited to receiving
additional works of art on behalf of
the *Reichsführer-SS* and guarding
the amply-stocked storerooms of
the Wewelsburg SS School. The chief
castle administrator, SS-*Obergruppenführer*, and general in the
Waffen-SS Siegfried Taubert nonetheless had the opportunity to
prove himself as head air raid
warden of Wewelsburg village and
ordered prisoners assigned to the
external work detachment of
Buchenwald Concentration Camp
still stationed in Wewelsburg to
paint the SS castle with camouflage.
mm

Kreismuseum Wewelsburg, Fotoarchiv

No. 7-34
**Letter from Heinrich Himmler to Wewels-
burg Chief Castle Administrator Siegfried
Taubert on the official naming of Wewelsburg Castle as the "Reich House of the
SS-Gruppenführer"
Field Command Post
February 26, 1944**
Translation on page 452
The more hopeless Germany's position
in the war became, the more the National
Socialists conjured up belief in a total,
"final victory." They envisioned this
ultimate triumph against all odds as the
solution to every political and social
problem through National Socialist
means. Himmler's thoughts of February
1944 on the future designation of the
Wewelsburg seem to have sprung from
just such a "final victory" fantasy. mm

Bundesarchiv Berlin, NS 19/3355

7.2
Unbridled Claims to Power and Architectural Megalomania: SS Building Plans for Wewelsburg in World War II

In November 1938, Himmler announced to the assembled *SS-Gruppenführer* that Germany's future was the "Greater Germanic Empire, or nothingness." Ten months later, on September 1, 1939, the war began, conducted by the German Reich's National Socialist leadership in the spirit of this alternative. Another eleven months later, in August 1940, Himmler's Wewelsburg architect submitted a plan obliterating the entire village of Wewelsburg for the construction of a gigantic SS castle complex. The size and form of the projected SS facility embodied Himmler's notions of the role and significance of the SS in the coming "Greater Germanic Reich." In Wewelsburg, the northern tower, with its ceremonial halls for the *SS-Gruppenführer*, would rise in the midst of a vast, heavily fortified "SS castle." In like manner, the highest-ranking leaders of the SS were to constitute the center of power in a colossal Reich under German rule.

Until the end of the war in May 1945, Bartels varied that vision of a castle for the *SS-Gruppenführer* through successive drafts.

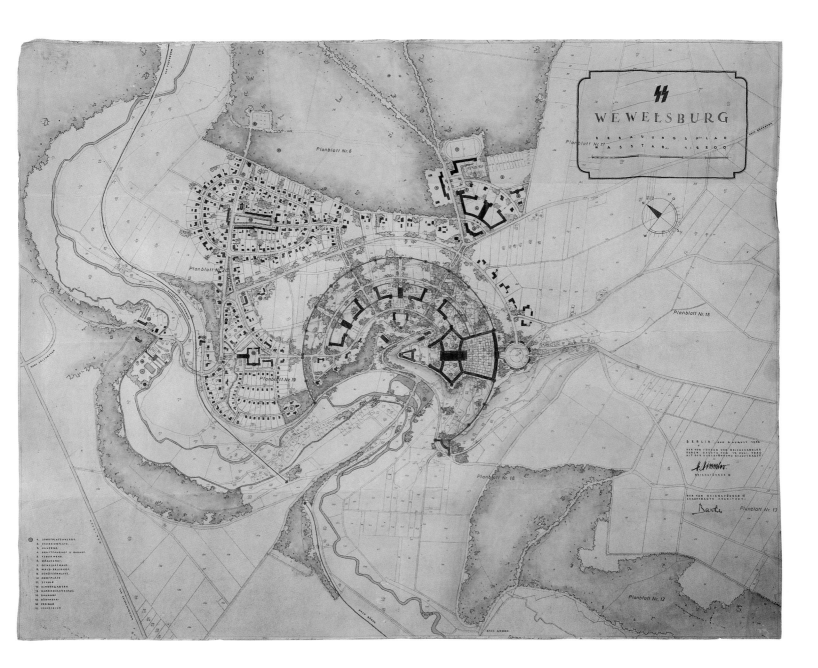

No. 7-37
Diazo print of the Wewelsburg cadaster map, with a superimposed plan in India ink and pencil, hand-colored; original signatures of Heinrich Himmler and Hermann Bartels
Paper, mounted on fabric
Scale: 1:2,500
Hermann Bartels, August 5, 1940

Taking into account geographic conditions, Bartels planned to create a circular castle grounds reaching three quarters of the way around the northern tower, surrounded at a distance of 430 meters (ca. 1,410 ft.) by a wall with eighteen towers and four entrances. The buildings within the walled area were exclusively for the – not further defined – use of the *SS-Reichsführer*. In early 1941, Wewelsburg SS researcher Dr. Bernhard Frank outlined how certain of these buildings could have been used for academic purposes. Beyond the castle walls (going counterclockwise) there were to be an SS barracks, a settlement of private residences for high-ranking SS officers, a new village of Wewelsburg, a housing development for additional SS personnel, and various logistical facilities. mm

Kreismuseum Wewelsburg, Nachlass Wettin Müller, inv. no. 15545

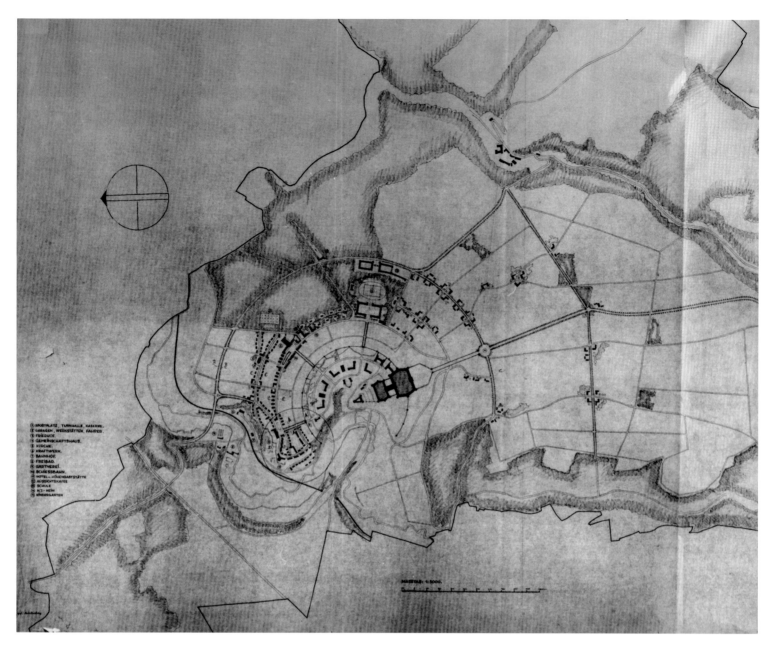

No. 7-38
**Development plan, Wewels-burg castle and village, India ink on velum
Scale 1:5,000
"Construction Management, Wewelsburg SS School"
April 23, 1941**

The SS wanted to convince some of the Wewelsburg population to resettle in eastern regions of Germany or in the occupied areas. However, living space for a certain number of residents was to be created in a new village of Wewelsburg. In the second known planning stage from April 1941, Bartels and his staff replaced the initially envisioned village arranged around a central common with a narrow development situated along streets. The resulting reduction in the number of houses was to be compensated by a series of outlying farmsteads in the Wewelsburg countryside. Conceivably, the Wewelsburg architects were inspired here by the soldier-peasant concept central to SS settlement plans for the "East."

The main access road to Wewelsburg was now to run for two kilometers (ca. one and a quarter miles) straight toward the northern tower, laid out as a grand avenue lined with four rows of trees. mm

Kreismuseum Wewelsburg, Plan 198

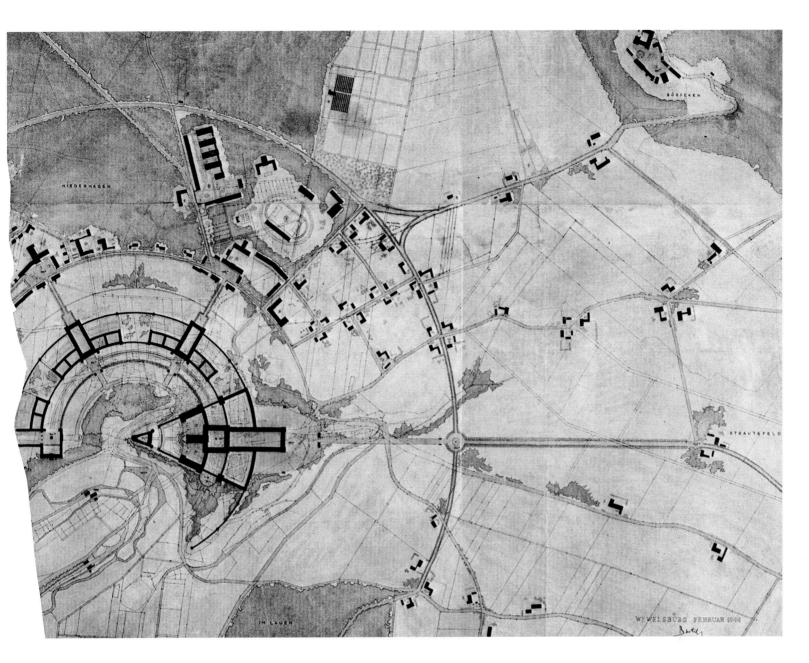

No. 7-40
Development plan, Wewelsburg
castle complex and locality,
showing village properties
Fragment, paper, colored
Hermann Bartels, February 1944

By February 1944, construction operations in Wewelsburg had been at a standstill for nine months. In the interim, National Socialist Germany's military position had further deteriorated. Ideologically driven affirmations of a coming "final victory" increasingly replaced realistic assessment of Germany's prospects. Amid this loosening grip on reality, Bartels was allowed to proceed with his grandiose Wewelsburg plans.

The main building complex in front of the castle was now to extend the lateral alignments of the historical Wewelsburg castle more explicitly than in earlier drafts. Bartels's alterations thus emphasized the northern tower's central status even more.
mm

Kreismuseum Wewelsburg, inv. no. 1697

No. 7-39
Model of the building complex in the alignment of the Wewelsburg Castle north-south axis; planning status of April 23, 1941, view from the northeast
Before 1945

LWL-Amt für Denkmalpflege, Münster

No. 7-41
Model of the projected castle complex, planning status of 1944, view from the south
Before 1945

LWL-Amt für Denkmalpflege, Münster

No. 7-42
Model of the projected castle complex, planning status of 1944, view from the east
Before 1945

LWL-Amt für Denkmalpflege, Münster

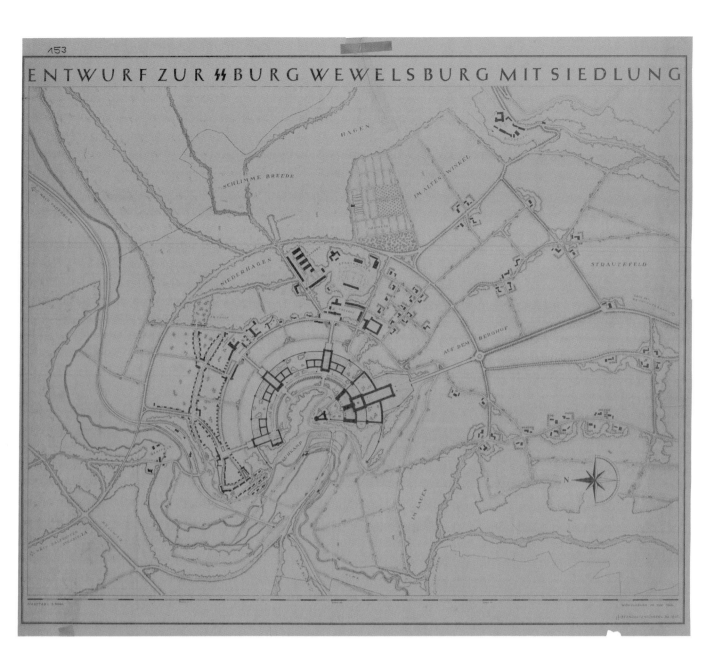

ENTWURF ZUR SSBURG WEWELSBURG MIT SIEDLUNG

No. 7-43
"Plan for SS Castle Wewelsburg, with residential development"
India ink on paper; scale: 1:5,000
Hermann Bartels, June 1944
Whereas the plan fragment from February 1944 is missing the area of the northwestern SS housing development and the larger part of the village, this draft from June 1944 provides a complete view. The omission of a church in the village area in contrast to earlier drawings is of note. mm
Kreismuseum Wewelsburg, Plan 153

7.3
Redesign and Resettlement: The Village of Wewelsburg and its Population as Objects of SS Planning 1939 – 1945

In the plans of architect Hermann Bartels and his client, Heinrich Himmler, a colossal SS castle complex replaced the historical village of Wewelsburg during World War II. On its periphery, Bartels now envisioned a new village of Wewelsburg, squeezed between an SS barracks and a housing development for SS leadership. This would have left many residents of Wewelsburg with no place to live.

The National Socialist leadership, however, was dependent on the support of the German population during the war. This compelled the SS to treat the inhabitants of Wewelsburg with a certain consideration. They sought to obtain space in Wewelsburg by legal means, while also hoping that larger replacement farms in the "East" would convince as many residents as possible to voluntarily resettle. However, it was an offer that only three Wewelsburg families accepted.

genau so wird es nötig sein,für die weichenden Dorfbewohner
das endgültige Schicksal zu bestimmen. Sie müssen entweder-
was das Beste ist- nach dem Osten umgesiedelt oder in einer
kleinen Dorflage an anderer Stelle angesetzt werden.

Wewelsburg/Westf.

No. 7-46

**Memorandum about
Wewelsburg Castle by
District President von
Oeynhausen (excerpt)
July 10, 1940**

Kreisarchiv Paderborn, Bauamt Büren
B 5 40/53/1 W –I—IV; Allgemeiner
Schriftwechsel

No. 7-44

**Aerial photograph of the castle and the
locality of Wewelsburg from the north
1920s or 1930s**

Ever since the SS took over Wewelsburg
Castle in 1934, Himmler and his subordinates had had to concern themselves with
the village of the same name and its
inhabitants, whether they wanted to or
not. Initially, there was talk of making the
existing locality into a National Socialist
model village. With its growing power in
the Third Reich, the SS claimed ever more
space beyond the castle walls in Wewelsburg. At the latest with the unleashing of
war, the historically evolved old village
became little more than a demolition zone
in the imagination of Himmler and his
architect, Hermann Bartels. In this vein,
a satellite community with the name
Wewelsburg was to result hundreds of
meters away from Wewelsburg Castle, at
the edge of the planned SS complex, with
its form and structure entirely subject to
the whim of SS planners. mm

Kreismuseum Wewelsburg, Fotoarchiv

No. 7-45

Reichsgesetzlatt [Reich Law Gazette],
**1940, Part I, No. 127
"Decree of the Führer and Reich Chancellor
on Building Measures in the Area of
Wewelsburg Castle"
July 12, 1940**

In the euphoria following the victorious
campaign against France and the Benelux
Countries, Adolf Hitler signed a decree on
July 12, 1940, granting Himmler the powers to reshape the castle and township of
Wewelsburg according to his ideas. Before
this, in late March 1940, Hitler's favored
architect and principal adviser in questions of National Socialist urban planning,
Albert Speer, had conferred with Himmler
and his architect Hermann Bartels in Wewelsburg. On August 5, 1940, the SS head
approved the initial general plan, in which
Bartels foresaw a gigantic castle for the
SS-Gruppenführer overwhelming the village of Wewelsburg. mm

Kreisarchiv Paderborn

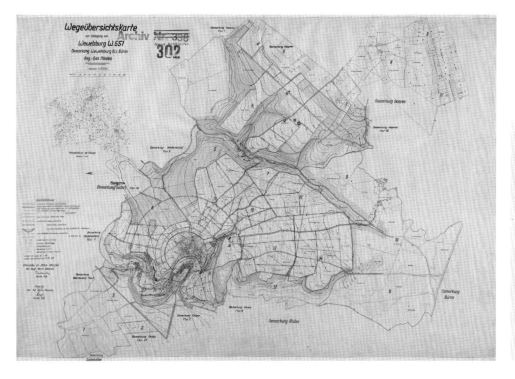

"Wewelsburg, 2. Dez. Abschied von Bauer Marx. In diesen Tagen verzieht der weit und breit bekannte Bauer Fritz Marx nach Immendorf (Kreis Wohlau in Schlesien), um sich dort neu anzusiedeln. Anläßlich einer außerordentlichen Sitzung der Gemeinderäte, zu der auch viele Ehrengäste geladen waren, nahm die Gemeinde Wewelsburg von dem um das Gemeinwohl hochverdienten Mitbürger Abschied. In verschiedenen Ansprachen wurde seiner langjährigen Tätigkeit als Gemeinderat, Orts- und Bezirksbauernführer, Amtsbeigeordneter usw. ehrend und dankbar gedacht. Ortsgruppenleiter und Bürgermeister Dierkes überreichte dem Scheidenden im Namen der Gemeinde zwei von Tischlermeister Josef Saake kunstvoll geschnitzte Wandtafeln, die ihn stets an seine alte Heimat erinnern sollen."Wewelsburg, 2. Dez. Abschied von Bauer Marx. In diesen Tagen verzieht der weit und breit bekannte Bauer Fritz Marx nach Immendorf (Kreis Wohlau in Schlesien), um sich dort neu anzusiedeln. Anläßlich einer außerordentlichen Sitzung der Gemeinderäte, zu der auch viele Ehrengäste geladen waren, nahm die Gemeinde Wewelsburg von dem um das Gemeinwohl hochverdienten Mitbürger Abschied. In verschiedenen Ansprachen wurde seiner langjährigen Tätigkeit als Gemeinderat, Orts- und Bezirksbauernführer, Amtsbeigeordneter usw. ehrend und dankbar gedacht. Ortsgruppenleiter und Bürgermeister Dierkes überreichte dem Scheidenden im Namen der Gemeinde zwei von Tischlermeister Josef Saake kunstvoll geschnitzte Wandtafeln, die ihn stets an seine alte Heimat erinnern sollen.

No. 7-47
Not shown
Excerpt from the Soest Cultural Office application to the upper president of Westphalia as the competent reallocation agency
December 24, 1940
In the fall of 1940, SS Construction Management in Wewelsburg applied to the local board of agricultural affairs for the initiation of reallocation proceedings with the aim of resettling the entire village. The Soest Cultural Office transmitted the application to the upper president of Westphalia province, the responsible reallocation agency. That office authorized the proceeding on January 31, 1941. Similar to the status of people living in a designated strip-mining area, the inhabitants of Wewelsburg now had to reckon with being expropriated and resettled. mm

Landesarchiv NRW, Abteilung Ostwestfalen-Lippe, Detmold, D 32 A no. 13591–13604

No. 7-49
Newspaper article in the *Bürener Zeitung*: "Farewell to Farmer Marx"
December 3, 1941
The place of resettlement is erroneously reported as Immendorf, instead of correctly as Thiemendorf. mm

Kreisarchiv Paderborn

Wewelsburg, Dec. 2. Farewell to Farmer Marx. Farmer Fritz Marx, known far and wide in these parts, is moving to Immendorf (Wohlau District in Silesia) to start a new life. On the occasion of an extraordinary session of the Municipal Council, also attended by many invited guests of honor, the community of Wewelsburg took leave of this fellow citizen who contributed so much to the common good. Various speeches recalled fond memories of his longtime service to a grateful community, as municipal counselor, local and district farmer representative, and so on. In the name of the community, Herr Dierkes, *Ortsgruppenleiter* (local National Socialist leader) and Mayor (of Wewelsburg), bestowed upon the departing Marx a pair of finely carved wooden wall panels by master cabinetmaker Josef Saake, to remind him of his old home.

Translation of a transcription

No. 7-48
General map of roads and byways for the Wewelsburg reallocation proceedings, 1941–1945
Landesarchiv NRW, Abteilung Ostwestfalen-Lippe, Detmold, D 73, Tit. 10, no. 9892

No. 7-51
Not shown
Postcard with a view of Thiemendorf, Wohlau District
Before 1945
Museum für schlesische Landeskunde im Haus Schlesien, Königswinter

No. 7-50
Not shown
Section of an office directive from the upper president of the province of Westphalia, with a declaration of support for the efforts of Construction Management of the Wewelsburg SS School to provide replacement farms for Wewelsburg residents
April 16, 1941
Landesarchiv NRW, Abteilung Ostwestfalen-Lippe, Detmold, D 32 A no. 13591–13604

State-sponsored resettlement programs had already existed during the German Empire and the Weimar Republic, serving to settle willing rural residents from western Germany – including Wewelsburg – in Silesia, in particular. The three Wewelsburg families who took the SS up on its offers of eastern resettlement also moved to larger replacement farms in Silesia, in the localities of Martinwaldau and Thiemendorf. In the *Bürener Zeitung* report of December 3, 1941, the name of the second village was misspelled. In 1945, the families returned to Wewelsburg as displaced persons. mm

No. 7-52
Not shown
Colorized postcard with views of Martinwaldau, Bunzlau District
Before 1945
Kreismuseum Wewelsburg, Fotoarchiv

275

7.4
Wewelsburg as the Site of National Socialist Camps

The camps operated at various locations in the village from 1933 to 1945 are part of the history of the SS project in Wewelsburg.

Reich Labor Service camps, like the concentration camps erected after 1939, were sources of labor for the SS. Following the closure of Niederhagen Concentration Camp in 1943, its Wewelsburg grounds were the site of other SS activities. The former prisoner barracks served as a resettlement camp for the Ethnic German Liaison Office, a key agency of the racist SS settlement policy. *Waffen-SS* members took over the pre-military training at a Hitler Youth preparedness camp established in the former SS guard barracks in 1944.

In Wewelsburg the *Wehrmacht* also ran a camp for French prisoners of war.

The Prisoner of War Camp

The Ethnic German Liaison Office Resettlement Camp

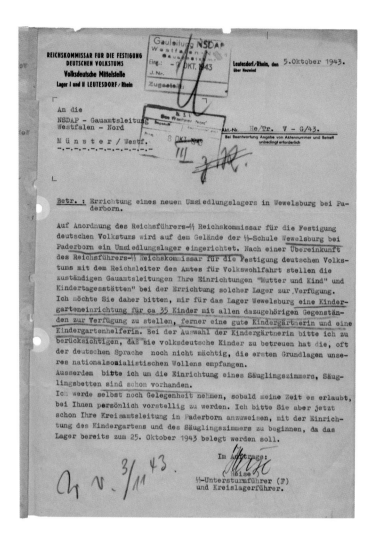

No. 7-53

Photographs from the estate of Frenchman Corentin LeGoff (1917 – 1993), from his time as a prisoner of war and "civilian laborer" in Wewelsburg

1940 – 1945

During the German invasion of France and the Benelux Countries in May and June 1940, many soldiers from these countries were taken prisoner of war. In the second half of 1940, a group of twenty French prisoners of war arrived in Wewelsburg from larger camps in Westphalia. They were housed in a room at the Neumann Inn, near the guard building, guarded by two *Wehrmacht* soldiers. The prisoners of war had to work for farmers in Wewelsburg throughout the day, until they returned in the evening to their confinement at the inn.

The Wewelsburg prisoner of war camp was disbanded on June 4, 1943; the Frenchmen were dispersed among local farmsteads as "civilian laborers." The arrival of American troops on April 2, 1945, brought them freedom. mm

Kreismuseum Wewelsburg, Fotoarchiv

No. 7-54

Establishment of a new resettlement camp in Wewelsburg, near Paderborn; projected occupancy on October 25, 1943

October 5, 1943

Translation on page 452

Landesarchiv NRW, Abteilung Westfalen, Gauleitung Westfalen Nord, Gauamt für Volkswohlfahrt, Bd. 666t

The Wewelsburg resettlement camp was established in October 1943 on the grounds of the former concentration camp in Niederhagen, and stood under the authority of the Ethnic German Liaison Office (VOMI). This SS Main Office was responsible for housing primarily Eastern European nationals of German ancestry in resettlement camps. Following their racial, political, and health vetting, the ethnic Germans (*Volksdeutsche*) awaited their deployment as settlers to locations in the "old Reich," or in the annexed eastern territories.

Degraded by the SS to the status of "raw material" for the implementation of its "greater Germanic" claim to power, the prospective settlers at the Wewelsburg camp came predominantly from Yugoslavia, Poland, and Ukraine. Alongside the women and old men, children were so numerous that a kindergarten was established in one of the camp barracks. mm

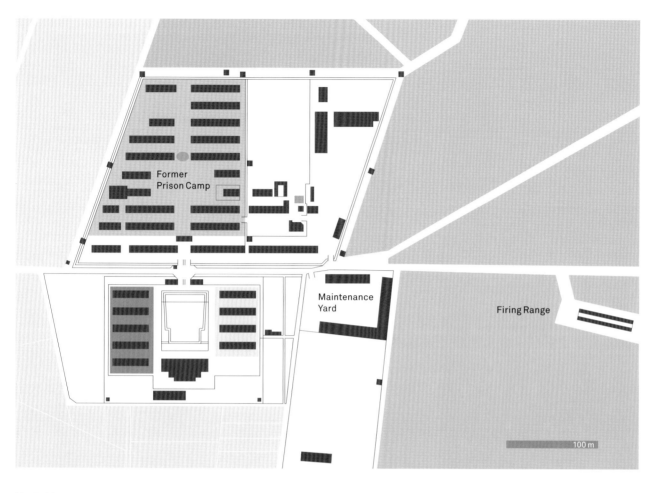

Former
Prison Camp

Maintenance
Yard

Firing Range

100 m

No. 7-56

Map of the Ethnic German Liaison Office (VOMI) Resettlement Camp and of the Hitler Youth Military Preparedness Camp on the grounds of the former Niederhagen Concentration Camp in Wewelsburg

The Wewelsburg Resettlement Camp was housed for a year in several of the SS camp guard barracks of the former concentration camp. During this period, 1,200 to 2,000 people passed through the camp. They each stayed just a few weeks and were assigned work outside the camp during the day.

In October 1944, the VOMI camp was moved across Tudorfer Straße into former inmate barracks of the now converted concentration camp. Ethnic Germans from larger evacuations out of Eastern Europe who now arrived at Wewelsburg remained there until the end of the war. They were only allowed out of the camp one hour per day.

A Hitler Youth military preparedness training camp began operating in January 1944 in the former SS camp barracks not used by the VOMI camp. mm

Plan: Kreismuseum Wewelsburg

No. 7-58
Not shown

Carbon copy of a letter from Construction Management of the Wewelsburg SS School to the Society for the Promotion and Care of German Cultural Monuments regarding insurance for ethnic German (*volksdeutsche*) settlers employed by Construction Management
July 10, 1944

Construction Management of the Wewelsburg SS School assumed oversight of building operations at the camp. The "building conversions" for which the Brenken carpenter was solicited in April 1944 were presumably related to the impending transfer of the resettlement camp to the former inmate section of the concentration camp.

Construction Management of the Wewelsburg SS School used the resettlement camp to its advantage, able until October 1944 to recruit labor from the camp residents for its work sites, such as the SS tree farm or nurseries. The settlers worked side-by-side with a remaining continent of prisoners, which, as of 1943, was housed in the barracks of an industrial yard next to the inmate section of the concentration camp. mm

Landesarchiv NRW, Abteilung Ostwestfalen-Lippe, D 27, BKA_507-19-22-23-S- a7

No. 7-55
Not shown

Ethnic German Liaison Office Resettlement Camp I, Wewelsburg Winter 1943 – 1944

Kreismuseum Wewelsburg, Fotoarchiv

No. 7-57
Not shown

Carbon copy of a letter from the Construction Management of the Wewelsburg SS School to Paderborn military district headquarters concerning the "indispensable" ("U.K.") status of Bernhard K., a carpenter from Brenken, for renovation work at the VOMI camp
April 4, 1944

Landesarchiv NRW, Abteilung Ostwestfalen-Lippe, D 27, BKA_507-1-22-23-S-a14

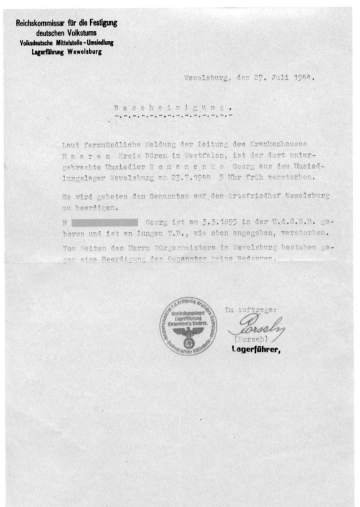

No. 7-59
Death certificate, including cause of death, issued by camp leader Porsch for the evacuee from Soviet territory, Georg R., who died on July 23, 1944
July 27, 1944
Kreismuseum Wewelsburg, 70/4/2/8

No. 7-60
Not shown
Death certificate, including cause of death, issued by camp leader Porsch for the evacuee from Slovenia, Anna L., who died on September 24, 1944
September 28, 1944
Kreismuseum Wewelsburg, 70/4/2/9

Three adults and seven children died at the Wewelsburg resettlement camp and were buried in the village cemetery. Although the death certificate from July 1944 was merely stamped, two months later the camp administration had begun using its own stationary with embossed letterhead – an indication that the Wewelsburg VOMI (Ethnic German Liaison Office) camp was intended to remain in operation for some time. The camp leader also had to ensure that the premises could at any time be converted for re-use as a concentration camp. In assuming the office of Reich Commissar for the Strengthening of German Nationhood, *Reichsführer-SS* Heinrich Himmler played a leading role in formulating the aggressive and racist settlement policies of the Third Reich. The SS Main Ethnic German Liaison Office was one of several SS institutions active in the resettlement program. mm

No. 7-61
Suitcase
Wood, pressboard, leather, metal
Produced at Wewelsburg resettlement camp, with the following inscription on the inside of the lid: "Klara Blech Wewelsburg Paderborn resettlement camp"
Kreismuseum Wewelsburg, inv. no. 14590

No. 7-64
Children's chair from the kindergarten at Wewelsburg resettlement camp
Wood, metal, painted white, assembled with metal brackets
Kreismuseum Wewelsburg, inv. no. 15276

No. 7-62
Not shown
Suitcase
Wood, leather, metal
Produced at Wewelsburg resettlement camp
Kreismuseum Wewelsburg, inv. no. 14589

No. 7-63
Not shown
Brush
Wood, horsehair
Produced by ethnic German (*volksdeutsche*) evacuees from Slovenia at Wewelsburg resettlement camp between late 1943 and early 1945
Kreismuseum Wewelsburg, inv. no. 16229

The food supply at Wewelsburg resettlement camp was dismal, and grew worse especially after relocating to the former concentration camp inmate section. The residents used rare moments of contact with villagers to barter for food. In exchange they offered self-made objects for everyday use, such as this brush. Former evacuees described the locals as unfailingly open and helpful.

The small wooden chair found use in the resettlement camp kindergarten. Two kindergarten staff from the Münster office of National Socialist People's Welfare looked after the numerous preschoolers in a barracks within the camp. mm

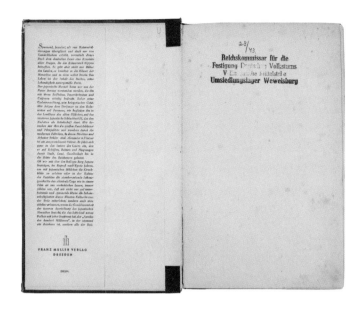

No. 7-66
Book with stamp from the Wewelsburg resettlement camp: Alexander von Thayer, *Die Familien der 100 Millionen. Japan gestern und heute* [Families of the 100 Million: Japan Yesterday and Today], Dresden, 1943

Kreismuseum Wewelsburg, inv. no. 13661

No. 7-65
Not shown
***Behelfsmöbel in Selbstherstellung* [Building Your Own Temporary Furniture] Brochure published by the Reich Commissar for the Strengthening of German Nationhood 1944**

Former residents of the Wewelsburg resettlement camp cannot recall that they or their relatives had any time for reading while at the camp. Nor is there any evidence of the existence of a camp library. This cultural history travel book may have belonged to one of the camp's three successive leaders.

Behelfsmöbel in Selbstherstellung, published by the Reich Commissar for the Strengthening of German Nationhood, was not aimed at the situation of the resettlement camp residents, although the inhabitants did require considerable capacity for improvisation just to manage their daily lives. Rather, the models were intended to foster National Socialist domestic culture in the Eastern European areas, which – following the expulsion and extermination of their Jewish and Slavic populations – were designated for ethnic German settlement. mm

Kreismuseum Wewelsburg, inv. no. 15672

No. 7-67
Announcement of an acceptance examination for the *Waffen-SS* at the Wewelsburg military preparedness camp *Bürener Zeitung*, January 21, 1944

Kreisarchiv Paderborn

No. 7-68
Not shown
Announcement of an acceptance examination for the *Waffen-SS* at the Wewelsburg military preparedness camp *Bürener Zeitung*, March 16, 1944

Kreisarchiv Paderborn

No. 7-69
Not shown
Announcement of an acceptance examination for the *Waffen-SS* at the Wewelsburg military preparedness camp *Bürener Zeitung*, May 18, 1944

Kreisarchiv Paderborn

Wewelsburg, June 8. The forthcoming acceptance examinations for the *Waffen-SS* will take place on Tuesday, June 20, at 8 a.m. at the WE camp in Wewelsburg, and at 2 p.m. at the Paderborn town hall. Applicants must bring their employment records and military service record. Eligible candidates are to register for the acceptance examination; men who have already passed a *Wehrmacht* medical exam may also apply, provided they have not already been called up. Conditions of enlistment are enumerated in a detailed information sheet available at all offices of the *Allgemeine SS*, police, gendarmerie and, in particular, at the *Waffen-SS* Recruitment Office West (VI), Düsseldorf, Freytagstraße 7-9.

Translation of a transcription

The youths at the Wewelsburg military preparedness camp came from the Münsterland and Ostwestfalen-Lippe regions. Newspaper announcements, such as these in the *Bürener Zeitung*, represented one form of recruitment. As in many other military preparedness camps, the instructors belonged to the *Waffen-SS*. After completing the course, the youths were expected to join the *Waffen-SS*. The Wewelsburg camp heavily promoted the 12th SS Tank Division *Hitlerjugend*. Many "volunteers" simply to escape mistreatment at the hands of the camp instructors. mm

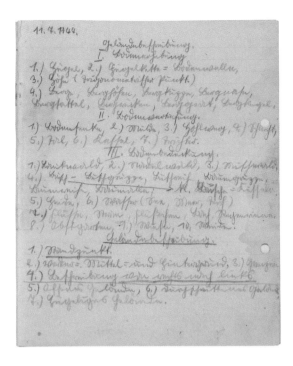

No. 7-70
Not shown
Conscription order to the Wewelsburg military preparedness camp from July 9 to 30, 1944, for Harro H. of Bielefeld, stating that he was "obligated to youth service"
July 30, 1944
Loan from private collection
Kreismuseum Wewelsburg, inv. no. 17109

No. 7-71
Handwritten report book: "Hitler Youth Harro H.; Military Preparedness Camp Wewelsburg II (9); Instructor: *SS-Unterscharführer* Gerwinat, Group 2, Troop 5 (barracks 5, room 1a); Camp leader: *Stammführer Jakobs*."
(original inscription on title page, in translation)
July 1944
The report book of Harro H. – age 16, from Bielefeld – documenting his time at Wewelsburg military preparedness camp in July 1944. It primarily comprises entries on topography, instructions on map reading, weapons and uniforms, and a few soldier songs. Ideology plays only a marginal role. However, the final entry reads:
"Thursday, July 20, 1944
On July 20, 1944, there was an assassination attempt on Führer Adolf Hitler by Colonel Count von Stauffenberg. Fortunately, the Führer sustained only light injuries and was already able to address the German people the following evening, 7/21/1944." mm
Loan from private collection
Kreismuseum Wewelsburg, inv. no. 17108

7/11/1944

Terrain description
I. Elevations,
1.) Hill, 2.) Chain of hills = bump
3.) Elevation (triangulation point.)
4.) Mountains, highlands, mountain knoll ledge, saddle, ridge, peak,
II. Depressions
1.) Trough, 2.) Syncline, 3.) Gully,
4.) Ravine, 5.) Valley, 6.) Basin, 7.) Crater.
III. Ground cover
1.) Deciduous forest, 2.) Evergreen forest,
3.) Mixed forest, 4.) Bushes – bush group, bush row, group of trees, row of trees, grove, sm. bushes = [?]
5.) Heath, 6. Water (lake, sea, pond)
7.) Rivers, large, small, brook - - -
8.) Orchard, 9.) Meadow, 10.) Pasture

Terrain description
1.) Survey point
2.) Fore-, middle- and background,
3.) Borders
4.) Description from right to left
5.) Open terrain
6.) Broken terrain
7.) Hilly terrain
Translation of a transcription

No. 7-73
Not shown
Participation certificate for training at the Wewelsburg military preparedness camp from July 9 – 30, 1944
July 30, 1944
Loan from private collection
Kreismuseum Wewelsburg, inv. no. 17110

No. 7-72
Not shown
Reich swimming certificate for Harro H. from his time at the Wewelsburg military preparedness camp
July 27, 1944
Loan from private collection
Kreismuseum Wewelsburg, inv. no. 17111

After his course at the Wewelsburg military preparedness camp, Harro H. was assigned to work digging trenches for the Westphalian Rampart (*Westfalenwall*), an entirely futile line of defense in the western Münsterland region.
In the final weeks of the war he was deployed as a messenger for the people's militia (*Volkssturm*) in Bielefeld. He was never inducted into the *Waffen-SS*. mm

7.5
The Northern Tower: The Crypt

The domed hall in the northern tower basement, cast in concrete and faced in natural stone, was presumably intended by the SS as a venue for funerals. SS blueprints show this space labeled as "crypt" (*Gruft*). Its form recalls Mycenaean burial sites; the sunken center of floor may have been intended to hold an "eternal flame." Prisoners from Niederhagen Concentration Camp were used for its construction. The crypt was not completed and never saw use by the SS.

As of June 1950, at the initiative of a former Büren district administrator, this room served as a memorial site for the victims of National Socialism. However, the ten works painted for the memorial by Büren artist Josef Glahé found little public notice and were damaged by the room's high humidity. They were removed in 1973 on order of the Büren district chief administrator. Numerous legends arose as to the crypt's alleged uses by the SS.

The Crypt in the Northern Tower – From SS Funeral Site to Memorial

No. 7-74
View of the northern tower basement before its alteration
1934
Westfälisches Amt für Denkmalpflege, Münster

No. 7-75
The Glahé cycle of paintings in the crypt
Postcard, after 1953
Kreismuseum Wewelsburg, Fotoarchiv

With his architect, Hermann Bartels, *Reichsführer-SS* Heinrich Himmler had planned to establish a higher academy of National Socialist ideology for SS officers at Wewelsburg. The northern tower, already scaffolded, was to play a central role. Bartels designed three halls along historical lines that were to serve as venues for ceremonies involving *SS-Gruppenführer*: a basement-level crypt, an *Obergruppenführer* Hall at the ground level, and at the very top, a classical *Gruppenführer* Hall crowned with a large dome, which was never built.

Construction on the northern tower was mostly carried out by prisoners from Niederhagen Concentration Camp, which was specifically established for this purpose. Work began in 1939 with a deepening of the basement. For the planned crypt, the prisoners removed some five meters (ca. 16 ft.) of bedrock to create a space almost nine meters (ca. 30 ft.) high. The crypt recalls the interior of an ancient Greek tumulus; in SS documents, it is also sometimes referred to as a "funeral hall," a space with special acoustics. The window wells direct exterior light to a central basin. The visible ends of metal pipes suggest that an "eternal flame" was to burn at the center of the crypt floor, as is

common at many burial and memorial sites for soldiers. Twelve round pedestals are positioned around the walls. The niches behind these pedestals were most likely already closed off during the construction phase. The walls are of cast concrete faced with natural stone. The keystone of the cupola is a meander swastika. The purpose of the four openings in the swastika remains unknown.

Above the crypt rose the *Obergruppenführer* Hall, with its *Sonnenrad*, or sun wheel, and columned hall designed after medieval models for use by SS generals. Detailed descriptions of the planned functions do not exist for any of the rooms in the northern tower, and evidence shows that none of the rooms was ever used. At the end of the war Himmler ordered the castle be demolished – his final act – to prevent it from falling into foreign hands. Five years later, in June 1950, its reopening as the youth hostel and local history museum was feted with a country fair. There was celebration outside, yet head-scratching within: the public greeted the memorial by Büren artist Josef Glahé with skepticism. The former crypt in the northern tower basement now stood as a memorial to the victims of National Socialism.

The paintings quickly fell into oblivion and were officially removed in 1973. The population proved not yet ready to face the history of the SS. Public debate on the National Socialist past in Wewelsburg would only begin in the late 1970s. The reopening of the memorial in April 2010 included the return of Glahé's paintings to their original location. mm

Translated excerpts from the documentary film *Die „Gruft" im Nordturm – Vom „Totenfeierraum" der SS zum Mahnmal* [The Northern Tower Crypt – From SS Funeral Site to Memorial], dokumentARfilm, 2010

No. 7-76
The crypt
Photograph: Gisbert Gramberg, 1981
Kreismuseum Wewelsburg, Fotoarchiv

From the beginning, the SS sought to cloud its castle in an aura of mystery. After the war this led to wild speculation:

Castle warden Wilhelm Kemper on West German television
1978 (quote)
"I'm standing here in the middle of Valhalla, hallowed ground for the SS, built during the war, from 1934 to 1939. Right here, in the middle, where I'm standing now, they set up a copper cauldron that was kept full with oil. After the death of the twelve officers chosen for the *Lebensborn*, not the body was to be burned, but the knight's coat of arms. And from the coat of arms, the soul would rise up to Valhalla, which is marked up there in the vault by the Germanic sun wheel, but is mostly expressed by the swastika. Here you see four openings: North, East, South, and West. Here, the soul was to escape to so-called Valhalla. They also set up an artificial inlet here, where children were baptized, and where they handed out salt, water, and bread at weddings, as was the custom with the Germanic tribes."

Ancient Germans, Valhalla, shrine of pagan worship: well into our time, abstruse legends coalesce about the goings-on of the SS in Wewelsburg, and what it had planned for the erstwhile palace of the Paderborn prince-bishops. *Reichsführer-SS* Heinrich Himmler himself fed these legends. After he and his SS took possession of the triangular castle, he prohibited any viewings of Wewelsburg Castle. As little as possible was to be made known about the projected meeting place of his *SS-Gruppenführer*.

Beginning in 1939, the SS deployed concentration camp prisoners instead of workers from the Reich Labor Service. In 1944 Himmler had Wewelsburg Castle painted in a camouflage pattern. Finally, in March 1945 he gave the order to blow up the castle: it was not to fall into Allied hands. All traces of his project were to be erased. Speculation and legends about the triangular castle raged all the more after the war. A postcard from the early 1970s equates the crypt with Valhalla. The notion that the SS used the halls for sacral, religious purposes exerts a stubborn fascination.

After the war, a rumor spread among the town of Wewelsburg's predominantly Catholic residents that the anti-Christian SS had used the crypt for Germanic-pagan celebrations of the dead. Many seem to have felt personally exonerated by the idea that the SS dedicated the halls in the northern tower to such purposes. Neo-Nazis, followers of esoterism, and Satanists view the crypt as a mysterious place where purported spiritual forces become perceptible. The spirit of the SS is thought to live on here. In truth, the northern tower was under constant construction until 1945. A cult center for SS ideology never existed at Wewelsburg mm

Translated excerpts from the documentary film *Legenden um Nordturm und "Gruft"* [Legends of the Northern Tower and Crypt], dokumentARfilm, 2010
With thanks to Hessischer Rundfunk

7.6
The Northern Tower: The *Obergruppenführer* Hall

After a fire in 1815, only the outer walls of the northern tower remained standing above the basement level. For this area, SS architect Hermann Bartels envisioned two levels, which he named *Obergruppenführer* Hall and *Gruppenführer* Hall. Of these, only the *Obergruppenführer* Hall, on the ground floor, was largely completed between 1939 and 1943. Although the walls were torn down in preparation for the *Gruppenführer* Hall above, the projected reconstruction of a mighty domed hall never took place. While the architecture of the *Obergruppenführer* Hall references medieval, Romanesque stylistic elements, Bartels wished to employ a classical form with the *Gruppenführer* Hall. There are no contemporary sources that reveal the functions the SS intended these spaces fulfill. The names given to the halls and their configuration suggest that the northern tower was to play a key role in the experience staged at Wewelsburg for the SS-*Gruppenführer*. From 1971 to 1985, the *Obergruppenführer* Hall was used as chapel. The floor ornament at the center of the hall, referred to since the 1990s as the "black sun," has become a popular symbol in esoteric and far-right circles.

Portal der Burgkapelle   Nördlicher Teil des Burghofes   Portal des Treppenhauses
Wewelsburg

No. 7-77
Postcard with views of the northern tower,
taken from the inner courtyard (center),
and of the chapel entrance at its original
location (left)
1934 (unconfirmed)
Kreismuseum Wewelsburg, Fotoarchiv

No. 7-79
Wewelsburg Castle seen
from the north
Photograph: Ophove, ca. 1890
LWL-Amt für Denkmalpflege
in Westfalen, Münster

No. 7-78
The Northern Tower on fire
on January 11, 1815
Wilhelm Stiehl
Kreismuseum Wewelsburg, inv. no. 18

Plans devised by SS architect Hermann Bartels show the ground floor of the northern tower labeled "*Obergruppenführer* Hall." It occupies the level that until the early nineteenth century housed the chapel of the former secondary residence of the prince-bishops of Paderborn.

Wewelsburg Castle in its current form was built from 1603 to 1609. Construction ended with the consecration of the palace chapel on September 8, 1609. The chapel portal leading to the castle's inner courtyard was originally set in the wall of the east wing. The portal dismantled by the SS was reassembled after 1945 and relocated to the center of the tower wall. The inscription in the cornice, *Domus mea domus orationis vocabitur* (my house shall be called a house of prayer), refers to the earlier chapel. The overlaying inscription plate and pediment were added in 1660.

On January 11, 1815, a few years after the end of the Prince-Bishophric of Paderborn and a few months prior to the prolonged occupation of the Paderborn district and Wewelsburg Castle by the Kingdom of Prussia, lightning struck the northern tower, which was gutted by the ensuing fire. The tower lay in ruins for over one hundred and twenty years. In 1925, the Prussian state relinquished control over Wewelsburg Castle to what was then the district of Büren.

In 1932, despite its poor financial standing following the global economic crisis, the local government, at the behest of the Minden district president, began structural work on the northern tower. Damaged sections of the wall were repaired and a ring beam installed to prevent the tower from collapsing. mm

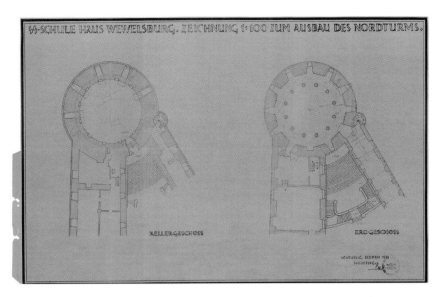

No. 7-80
Interior view of the northern tower
Photograph: Sobizack, 1922
The floor level corresponds to the current ground floor. mm
Stadtarchiv Büren, Fotosammlung

No. 7-81
Floor plans for the expansion of the basement and ground levels in the northern tower
Status of December 1939
Kreismuseum Wewelsburg, plan no. 131

No. 7-84
Stonemasonry sheds in front of the SS guard building on the castle forecourt during work on the *Obergruppenführer* Hall
1941 – 1942
Kreismuseum Wewelsburg, Nachlass Wettin Müller

Beginning in 1938, the northern tower took on a key role in the plans of lead SS architect Hermann Bartels. The bulk of subsequent building operations was carried out by prisoners of Niederhagen Concentration Camp.

First, the foundations were fortified with sprayed concrete. Work began in 1939 on the basement level crypt and the *Obergruppenführer* Hall on the ground floor. Neither was completed. Access from the castle's interior court to the crypt via an outside staircase proposed by Bartels was abandoned following objections by the state conservator of Prussia. The shape of the planned northern tower cupola evolved over time. The upper walls of the tower were torn down over 1941 and 1942 to prepare for construction of a dome-like cupola above the *Gruppenführer* Hall.

The intended uses of the *Obergruppenführer* Hall and *Gruppenführer* Hall remain unknown. Neither Himmler nor Bartels are presumed to have had clear views on their function. The acoustics in the existing hall and the grandiloquent architecture of the spaces suggest that they were planned to host solemn rites of the *Gruppenführer*. As a whole, the northern tower was to be the architectural center point of the gigantic new SS castle complex that Bartels planned to build over twenty years following Germany's "final victory" in World War II with the labor of countless additional concentration camp prisoners. According to a statement by Himmler in 1944, the castle would be called "Wewelsburg – Reich House of the *SS-Gruppenführer*." mm

287

No. 7-88
Images depicting the cladding construction and groin vault masonry work in the *Obergruppenführer* Hall ambulatory
1941 – 1942
The wooden scaffolding for shaping the groin vaults was clad from above with wooden slats. The limestone slabs were cut and fixed in such a way as to create an even surface for the exposed ceiling and a stabile structure for the arched roof. mm

Kreismuseum Wewelsburg,
Nachlass Wettin Müller

No. 7-85
View of the scaffolded northern tower along its west side before the demolition of the upper section
1941 – 1942

Kreismuseum Wewelsburg,
Nachlass Wettin Müller

No. 7-87
View of the arcade at the time of its construction
1941 – 1942
The corbels in the cornice above the twelve columns were later removed.
mm

Kreismuseum Wewelsburg,
Nachlass Wettin Müller

No. 7-86
View from inside the *Obergruppenführer* Hall onto the arcade and the brick window recesses behind the work supports in the groin vault of the ambulatory
1941 – 1942

Kreismuseum Wewelsburg,
Nachlass Wettin Müller

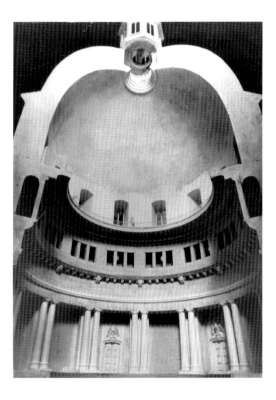

No. 7-82
Photograph of a model showing the interior of the *Gruppenführer* Hall, planned as a classical dome, in the (dismantled) upper floors of the northern tower
Before 1945
Kreismuseum Wewelsburg,
Fotoarchiv

No. 7-83
Views of Wewelsburg Castle Postcard from the early 1970s
Kreismuseum Wewelsburg,
Fotoarchiv

No. 7-89
Illustrations of the Alemannic brooch
D. Renner, *Die durchbrochenen Zierscheiben der Merowingerzeit* [Perforated Phalerae of the Merovingian Period], 1970

The Architecture of the *Obergruppenführer* Hall in the northern tower of Wewelsburg Castle

As Rüdiger Sünner has noted, the *Obergruppenführer* Hall in the ground level of the northern tower recalls the stage decoration for the 1882 Bayreuth premier of Parsifal. However, its design also references local and regional traditions. Like Bartels's current hall built in the empty tower, the prince-bishop's baroque chapel, described only in an early-nineteenth-century source, featured twelve columns. It is unclear whether medieval tradition was an influence here (via copies of the Church of the Holy Sepulchre in Paderborn and Helmarshausen). In fact, nothing is known of Bartels's inspiration for these plans. However, a snapshot taken during construction proves that, as with the crypt, certain details were modified. The columns – of green Anröchte sandstone and connected by an arcade featuring a veneer of the same material – line the border between the groin-vaulted ambulatory and the grand interior space, with its flat, stuccoed ceiling. Each segment of the ambulatory has a niche, eight of which contain a large, newly conceived, rectangular window opening. web

The Floor Ornament in the *Obergruppenführer* Hall

The hall's layout is reflected in the ornamentation at the center of the marble floor: a sun wheel with twelve radii in the form of inverted sig runes, each pointing to a column or a niche. The model for this design is a seventh-century Alemannic brooch belonging to a group of ornamental brooches featuring sun symbols and swastikas. It is thought that these forms, which appeared in late antiquity, had originally possessed religious meaning connected to a Near Eastern worship of light and sun before emerging among the – already Christianized – Alemanni. There is no record of an authentic interpretation of the sun wheel from the period before 1945. web

The history of the concentration camp in Wewelsburg provides insight into the functioning of a National Socialist concentration camp. Its development and organization is described primarily from the perpetrator perspective of the SS administration. Beyond the camp's SS and their management, various aspects of camp life come into focus: the housing and feeding of prisoners, their labor assignments, punishment at the camp, and, finally, the SS's administration of death. The camp was established in 1939 as an external work site of Sachsenhausen Concentration Camp, and made a main camp, Niederhagen, in 1941. After disbandment of the self-administered Niederhagen Concentration Camp in 1943, a group of prisoners in an external work detachment under the control of Buchenwald Concentration Camp remained in Wewelsburg. Although conditions throughout the entire system of National Socialist concentration camps deteriorated dramatically in the last two years of the war, prisoners in Wewelsburg were spared this development. The remaining prisoners were liberated on April 2, 1945.

8 The Concentration Camp in Wewelsburg

8.1
The Development of the Concentration Camp, 1939 – 1943: From an External Work Detachment of Sachsenhausen Concentration Camp to the Self-Administered Niederhagen Concentration Camp

On the order of Heinrich Himmler, the first prisoners from Sachsenhausen Concentration Camp arrived in Wewelsburg in May 1939 to continue construction work on Wewelsburg Castle. Beginning in 1940, the prisoners erected a large concentration camp at the edge of the village of Wewelsburg. On September 1, 1941, the camp, with 480 inmates, was declared an independent main camp under the name Niederhagen/Wewelsburg Concentration Camp.

As of the summer of 1942, the prisoner death rate soared when the SS began increasing the number of prisoners, reducing food rations, and stiffening punishments. Of the roughly 3,900 prisoners interned at Wewelsburg from 1939 to 1945, 1,285 of them – almost one-third of the total – are proved to have died of sickness, hunger, and SS violence.

When the war forced building operations at Wewelsburg Castle to cease in the spring of 1943, Niederhagen Concentration Camp was also closed.

The Organization of the Camp

No. 8-1

Tent camp of the first prisoner detachment
June 1939

The first prisoners from Sachsenhausen
Concentration Camp were interned in a
tent camp below Wewelsburg Castle.
The group consisted of about one hundred
so-called careeer criminals (*Berufsverbrecher*), or career criminals, who
arrived by train, escorted by fifty SS
guards, who were housed in the castle.
One contingent of the Sachsenhausen
external work detachment (*Außenkommando*) continued construction work
on Wewelsburg Castle, while the other
began building the so-called Small Camp
at Kuhkampsberg, a hill opposite the
castle. Construction on Wewelsburg
Castle ceased at the start of the Polish
campaign, on September 1, 1939; the prisoners then returned to Sachsenhausen.
Following the victory over Poland, Himmler decided to resume building operations
and ordered another labor detail of
60 "career criminals" to Wewelsburg.
These inmates arrived by truck and were
guarded by a unit of 35 SS men, headed by
SS-Untersturmführer Wolfgang Plaul. kjs

Kreismuseum Wewelsburg, Fotoarchiv

No. 8-2

The Small Camp at Kuhkampsberg
1939 – 1940

The Small Camp consisted of two prisoner
barracks surrounded by barbed wire, with
another barracks for the SS guards, which
are difficult to make out in the background
of the photograph. In 1940, when an
attempted escape resulted in the death
of two prisoners, the ruthless methods of
unit commander Plaul caused outrage
among the local population. To defuse the
situation, Himmler ordered that the
"career criminal" detail be replaced with
Ernste Bibelforscher, or Ernest Bible
Students: members of the religious community of Jehovah's Witnesses who were
taken into protective detention on
religious grounds and were known for not
attempting escape. The first seventy
Bibelforscher arrived at Wewelsburg by
bus on February 16, 1940. In the following
months, the detail was reinforced by
additional Bible Students from Sachsenhausen and Buchenwald, raising the total
of Jehovah's Witnesses present at Wewelsburg to around two hundred twenty. In the
summer of 1940, the prisoners began
building a larger protective detention camp
in the district of Niederhagen, on the outskirts of Wewelsburg. kjs

Kreismuseum Wewelsburg, Fotoarchiv

No. 8-3

View of the protective detention camp
from the west
Ca. 1940 – 1943

As the new unit commander, *SS-Obersturmführer* Adolf Haas oversaw construction of the concentration camp. In August
the prisoners were moved from the Small
Camp to the new camp, which initially
comprised four barracks. In September
another 280 prisoners, mostly classified
as "antisocial," were moved from Sachsenhausen to Wewelsburg. From then on,
the Bible Students were in the minority.

On January 7, 1941, the Wewelsburg
work detachment was declared a subcamp (*Außenlager*) of Sachsenhausen
Concentration Camp. To improve the
financial situation of the Society for the
Promotion and Care of German Cultural
Monuments, which was responsible for
upkeep of the camp, Himmler altered the
status of the subcamp, with its population
of 480 prisoners, to that of a state-run
main camp (*Hauptlager*): Niederhagen
Concentration Camp. The arrival of further
prisoner transports carrying German and
foreign inmates required expansion of
the camp area. Fourteen housing barracks
and several additional utility barracks
were built. In April 1943, when the over-
crowded camp was shut, it held over
1,300 prisoners. kjs

Kreismuseum Wewelsburg, Fotoarchiv

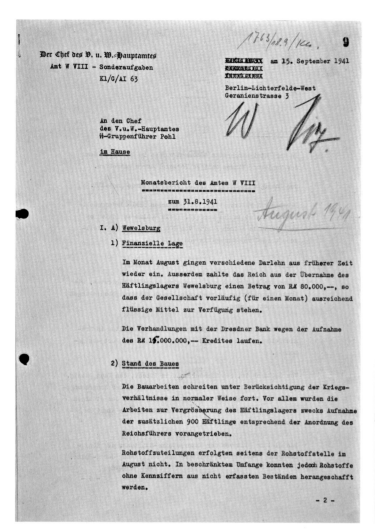

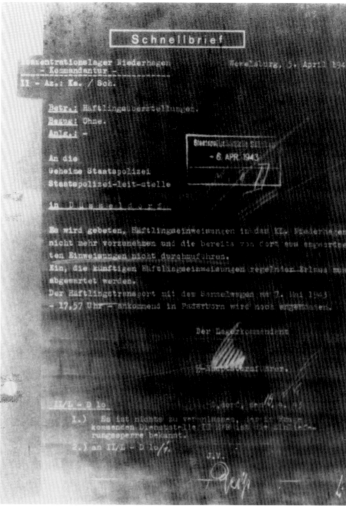

No. 8-6
Not shown
Circular from the head of the security police and SD regarding "increased internments at concentration camps"
March 23, 1943
Gestapo offices in the Rhineland and Westphalia used Niederhagen/Wewelsburg Concentration Camp to intern their prisoners, including large numbers of forced laborers charged with criminal offenses. As early as December 17, 1942, Himmler issued a secret decree requiring at least 35,000 fit-for-work prisoners be sent to concentration camps by late January 1943. Prisons and "labor education camps" were to be scoured for ablebodied inmates. On March 23, 1943, *SS-Oberführer* Heinrich Müller extended the order again, while explicitly excluding Niederhagen. A study to determine the suitability of the camp premises for a weapons plant was also broken off in mid-March without result, making the closure of Niederhagen Concentration Camp all but certain. kjs

Internationaler Suchdienst Bad Arolsen,
HM Niederhagen-Wewelsburg, KL Bu

No. 8-4
Excerpt from the monthly report of the Society for the Promotion and Care of German Cultural Monuments (GEFÖ)
August 1941
Translation on page 453

Bundesarchiv Berlin, NS 3/430
(SS-WVHA, Amt W VIII Sonderaufgaben)

No. 8-5
Express letter from Adolf Haas to the Düsseldorf Gestapo
April 5, 1943

Internationaler Suchdienst Bad Arolsen,
HM KZ Niederhagen-Wewelsburg, KL Bu

A GEFÖ report from July 1941 had already considered elevating the Wewelsburg subcamp to an independent main camp. In August 1941, under financial duress, the Society for the Promotion and Care of German Cultural Monuments sold the concentration camp to the German Reich, which reimbursed the organization for all previous expenses pertaining to construction and upkeep of the camp – a total of 660,000 Reichsmarks. The express letter from April 5, 1943, makes plain that the main camp was to be shut down: Camp Commandant Haas requested that the Düsseldorf Gestapo cease assigning prisoners to Wewelsburg. Following the German defeat at Stalingrad, a stoppage of all building measures not essential to the war effort also halted work on the Wewelsburg Castle project, thus leading to the closure of the main camp. kjs

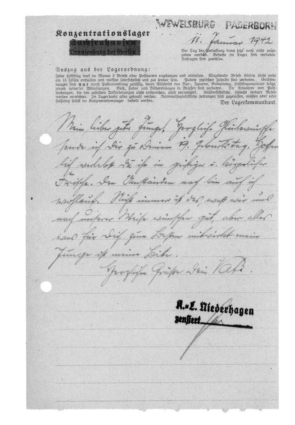

The stages of development of the concentration camp at Wewelsburg can be traced through the changing postcard and letter forms concentration camp prisoners had to use to write to their families.

In March 1941, while Wewelsburg was still a subcamp of Sachsenhausen Concentration Camp, prisoner Georg Klohe wrote a postcard to his son. As a return address he indicated his Sachsenhausen prisoner number and his more precise location as "Block W." "W" was the designation for the Wewelsburg subcamp. In January 1942, four months after Wewelsburg was designated a main camp, Georg Klohe was still using an old letter form from Sachsenhausen, with the name Sachsenhausen struck through and "Wewelsburg Paderborn" stamped next to it. The censorship stamp was also updated to reflect the new status of the camp.
kjs

No. 8-7
Postcard from Georg Klohe to his son Addi, sent from the Wewelsburg subcamp of Sachsenhausen Concentration Camp
March 30, 1941
Loan from the Wachtturm-Gesellschaft der Zeugen Jehovas, Selters
Kreismuseum Wewelsburg, inv. no. 16863

Sachsenhausen Concentration Camp
Oranienburg, Berlin
Excerpt from the camp rules:
Each prisoner may receive and send 2 letters or 2 postcards a month. A letter may not contain more than 4 pages, of 15 lines each, and must be clearly legible. Correspondence not conforming to these requirements will not be conveyed or delivered. No packages may be received, no matter what they contain. Money may be sent, but only via postal money order; sending cash by letter is prohibited. Messages written on postal money orders are prohibited, and will result in rejection of the mail. Everything can be bought at the camp. National Socialist periodicals are allowed, but must be ordered by the prisoner himself via the concentration camp mailroom. Confusing or illegible letters cannot be censored and will be destroyed. Sending pictures or photographs is prohibited.
The Camp Commandant
My exact address:
Georg Klohe
No. 11538 Block W
Oranienburg Concentration Camp near Berlin
Postcard
[with mail censorship stamp, C.C. Sachsenhausen]
To
Mr. Addi Klohe
Henningsdorf (Osth)
Wolterstraße 9
Translation of a transcription

No. 8-8
Letter from Georg Klohe to his son Addi, sent from Niederhagen Concentration Camp
January 11, 1942
Loan from the Wachtturm-Gesellschaft der Zeugen Jehovas, Selters
Kreismuseum Wewelsburg, inv. no. 16864

Sachsenhausen Concentration Camp
[crossed-out]
WEWELSBURG PADERBORN
[printed with stamp]
January 11, 1942
The release date cannot yet be stated. There are no visits to the camp. Inquiries are pointless.
Excerpt from the camp rules:
Each prisoner may receive and send 2 letters or 2 postcards a month. Incoming letters may not contain more than 15 lines and must be clearly legible. Packages are prohibited, no matter what they contain. Money may only be sent via postal money order; these must bear only the first name, last name, date of birth, and prisoner number, but no message whatsoever. Sending cash, photographs, or pictures by letter is prohibited. Mailings which do not conform to these requirements will be rejected. Confusing or illegible letters will be destroyed. Everything can be bought at the camp. National Socialist periodicals are allowed, but must be ordered by the prisoner himself at the concentration camp.
The Camp Commandant
My dear, good boy! I wish you a very happy 19th birthday. I hope you're celebrating it in good physical and spiritual form. I am also well, considering the circumstances. Not everything we hope for is good, but all that is best for you, my boy, is my wish.
Warmest regards, your Dad
Niederhagen C.C.
Censored

Translation of a transcription

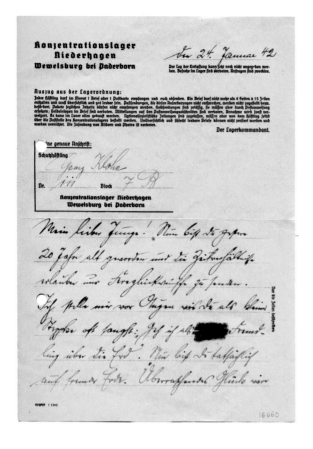

No. 8-9
Letter from Georg Klohe to his son Addi, sent from Niederhagen Concentration Camp
January 24, 1942

For this letter to his son, Addi, who by then had been sent by the Reich Labor Service to work outside Germany, Georg Klohe was already given the printed correspondence form of Niederhagen Concentration Camp. The return address now shows his Wewelsburg prisoner number. kjs

Loan from the Wachtturm-Gesellschaft der Zeugen Jehovas, Selters
Kreismuseum Wewelsburg, inv. no. 16660

Niederhagen Concentration Camp
Wewelsburg, near Paderborn
January 24, '42
The release date cannot yet be stated. There are no visits to the camp. Inquiries are pointless.
Excerpt from the camp rules:
Each prisoner may receive and send 1 letter or 1 postcard a month. A letter may not contain more than 4 pages, of 15 lines each, and must be clearly legible. Mailings not conforming to these requirements will not be conveyed or delivered. No packages may be received, no matter what they contain. Money may be sent, but only via postal money order; sending money by letter is prohibited. Messages written on postal money orders are prohibited and will be rejected. Everything can be bought at the camp. National Socialist periodicals are allowed, but must be ordered by the prisoner himself via the concentration camp mailroom. Confusing or illegible letters cannot be censored and will therefore be destroyed.
Sending pictures or photographs is prohibited.
The Camp Commandant
My exact address:
Protective custody prisoner
Georg Klohe
No. 111 Block 7 B
Niederhagen Concentration Camp
Wewelsburg, near Paderborn
My dear boy! Yesterday you turned 20, yet circumstances only allow for long-distance congratulations. I can still see you as a toddler, when you used to sing "I wander the world as a [made illegible] stranger." And now you're indeed on foreign soil.
It would be surprising luck [reverse side, not shown] if we meet again some day. News from you is anxiously awaited back home. Write your mother if you somehow can. Warmest regards from your father
C.C. Niederhagen
Censored

Translation of a transcription

No. 8-11
Identification Tag
Tin, perforated, stamped

Prisoners in concentration camps used such tags, frequently self-made, to identify their personal belongings. The use of this tag, stamped with "KL Niederhagen" and a number (0184 or 0164), remains uncertain. Where it was found – the former SS shooting range – provides no further clues. kjs

Kreismuseum Wewelsburg, inv. no. 16383

No. 8-10
Baggage label from Kittel & Co., Prague
1939 – 1945

Kittel & Co. was a wholesaler in Prague (Czechoslovakia) for all types of automobile accessories, equipment for auto repair shops, and lighting fixtures. Camp SS personnel presumably ordered spare parts from there for their fleet of vehicles. The address is "Concentration Camp, Wewelsburg, near Paderborn, Westph." kjs

Kreismuseum Wewelsburg, inv. no. 15128

8.1.2
SS Personnel at Niederhagen Concentration Camp

No. 8-13

SS guards in a relaxed mood at Niederhagen Concentration Camp
1942

Kreismuseum Wewelsburg,
Fotoarchiv

No. 8-15

Niederhagen Concentration Camp personnel in front of the guard barracks
1942

Kreismuseum Wewelsburg,
Fotoarchiv

No. 8-14

An SS guard in front of a sentry box at Niederhagen Concentration Camp
1942

Kreismuseum Wewelsburg,
Fotoarchiv

Over its years of existence, well over two hundred SS personnel were deployed at Niederhagen Concentration Camp. Many of them had already served extended assignments at other concentration camps before their transfer to Wewelsburg. Almost all professional backgrounds and social classes were represented among them. As a rule, up to the start of World War II, members of the SS Death's Head Units – the concentration camp guards – volunteered for concentration camp duty. As of late 1939, it was primarily older or combat-unfit members of the *Allgemeine SS* who entered guard duty, as was also the case at Niederhagen Concentration Camp.

A concentration camp's SS determined the living conditions of its prisoners. It organized the prisoners' daily routines, their registration, guarding, housing, and food rations, while driving them mercilessly in forced labor on the SS work sites. Many SS men took part in the routine mistreatment, arbitrary punishment, and execution of prisoners, sometimes without requiring an order to do so. kjs/sk

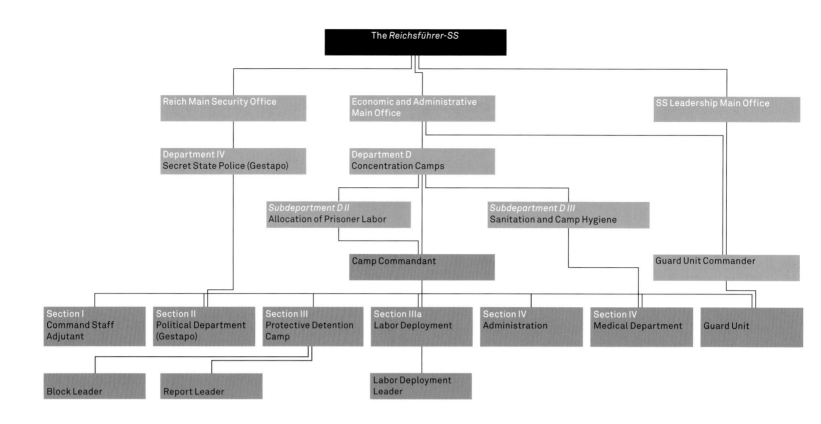

The Reichsführer-SS

Reich Main Security Office — Economic and Administrative Main Office — SS Leadership Main Office

Department IV
Secret State Police (Gestapo)

Department D
Concentration Camps

Subdepartment D II
Allocation of Prisoner Labor

Subdepartment D III
Sanitation and Camp Hygiene

Camp Commandant

Guard Unit Commander

Section I
Command Staff
Adjutant

Section II
Political Department
(Gestapo)

Section III
Protective Detention
Camp

Section IIIa
Labor Deployment

Section IV
Administration

Section IV
Medical Department

Guard Unit

Block Leader

Report Leader

Labor Deployment
Leader

No. 8-12
The organizational structure of the camp SS

The central administrative, command, and control authority for all concentration camps was the Concentration Camp Inspectorate (IKL) and, as of 1942, Department D (*Amtsgruppe D*) of the Economic and Administrative Main Office. The self-administered Niederhagen Concentration Camp, too, was subordinate to the IKL and Department D, and thus organized according to principles common to all concentration camps. The camp SS comprised the guard unit and the command staff. The guard unit was responsible for "exterior" watch duty and provided the chains of sentries for work details deployed outside the camp. The command staff was responsible for the "interior" control of the camp, and consisted of the adjutant's office, protective detention command, and labor deployments departments, as well as administrative, medical, and political ones. kjs/sk

No. 8-16
Adolf Haas, Camp Commandant
Ca. 1941 – 1942

The commandant had final authority within the camp and oversaw the execution of orders by the subordinate SS positions. In June 1940, *SS-Sturmbannführer* Adolf Haas, born in Siegen/Westphalia in 1893, took over command from his predecessor Wolfgang Plaul, who became his deputy. With the reclassification as a main camp, on September 1, 1941, Adolf Haas became camp commandant. He is reported to have described himself to the prisoners as "God Almighty of Wewelsburg." His crude, brutal ways were feared by the prisoners. After the closing of Niederhagen Concentration Camp in April 1943, Haas, along with 90 SS men from Wewelsburg, was transferred to Bergen-Belsen, where he again became camp commandant. In late 1944, he assumed command of the 18th SS Panzergrenadier (armored infantry) Battalion. He vanished after the war. kjs
Kreismuseum Wewelsburg, Fotoarchiv

No. 8-18
SS-Sturmbannführer Wolfgang Plaul, Head of the Protective Detention Camp and Deputy Camp Commander
Ca. 1937

An electrician by trade, Plaul began his activities in the Death's Head Units, in 1935 at Sachsenburg Concentration Camp. Beginning in 1937, he was at Sachsenhausen, first as prisoner block leader, then as prisoner labor duty leader. In December 1939 he escorted the detachment of "career criminals" sent to Wewelsburg, where he assumed command of the Small Camp. In June 1940 he was replaced as camp commandant by Adolf Haas and became head of the protective detention camp and permanent deputy to the camp commandant. Wolfgang Plaul's responsibilities included camp regulations and the daily schedules of the prisoners, who considered him a brutal and ruthless man; he was also unpopular with his SS colleagues. In May 1941 he was transferred to Buchenwald, where he commanded the Hasag Works Leipzig/Schönefeld subcamp. In early May 1945 he made his way to Czechoslovakia, where he was allegedly interned in a prisoner of war camp. He disappeared thereafter. kjs
Bundesarchiv Berlin, formerly the Berlin Document Center, RS Wolfgang Plaul

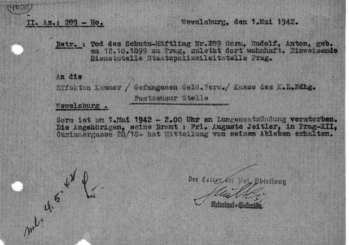

No. 8-20
Ludwig Rehn in uniform
Ca. 1939 – 1945

Labor duty leaders were under the authority of the head of labor deployment. They selected and supervised the work details. Ludwig Rehn, born in 1910, performed these tasks in Wewelsburg from 1940 to 1942. He joined the SS in 1935 and first worked with Wolfgang Plaul on the early prisoner transport of December 1939 from Sachsenhausen to Wewelsburg. In summer 1941 he was charged with setting up an index of prisoner professions, to make prisoner labor assignments more effective.
The prisoners feared the former machinist Ludwig Rehn for his brutality. In summer 1942 he was transferred to Neuengamme Concentration Camp, and later to Lublin and Sachsenhausen. He performed various labor allocation functions for the concentration camps and armament plants, as well as for the SS Economic and Administrative Main Office (WVHA).
kjs

Bundesarchiv Berlin, RS/E 5351

No. 8-17
Death certificate for protective custody prisoner Rudolf Sorm, issued by the head of the Political Department, *SS-Sturmscharführer* Friedrich Schulte
May 1, 1942

As leader of the Political Department, *SS-Sturmscharführer* and Detective Sergeant Friedrich Schulte, born in Hilden in 1890, belonged to the Secret State Police (Gestapo). He was thus not under the authority of the camp commandant, but took his orders directly from Gestapo headquarters in Berlin. Schulte was responsible for the intake, release, and questioning of prisoners. As of 1943, he also led the camp's registry office, whose sole task was to keep a record of deaths at the camp. kjs

Internationaler Suchdienst, Bad Arolsen, Umschlag Rudolf Sorm

No. 8-19
Heinrich Grüter
Listing of encrypted police and SS communications of June 27, 1942, decoded by the British Secret Intelligence Service

In May 1941, *SS-Untersturmführer* Heinrich Grüter, born in 1887, became head of labor deployment. A cabinetmaker by trade, Grüter joined the NSDAP and SS in 1932. Grüter came to Wewelsburg in April 1940 by way of Buchenwald Concentration Camp and remained until the camp's closure in 1943. Occasionally Grüter also performed the duties of interim camp commander. In this capacity he was responsible for sending radio messages from the Niederhagen Concentration Camp command staff to the Concentration Camps Inspectorate in Oranienburg. The British Secret Intelligence Service succeeded early on in intercepting and deciphering these communications. Camp prisoners described Grüter as a humane, quiet SS man. After disbandment of the camp, he initially headed the resettlement camp of the Ethnic German Liaison Office (VOMI) in Ilseberg/Harz before being transferred to Bergen-Belsen. kjs

National Archives Kew, Government Code and Cypher School: German Police Section: Decrypts of German Police Communications during the Second World War, 1939 – 1945, HW 16/19 (ZIP/GPDD 143/30.6.42)

No. 8-21
Labor duty form noting the handoff of prisoners
January 10, 1943
Prisoner labor assignments were bureaucratically regulated and documented. This form records the assignment of five protective detention prisoners to work at the command staff garage on January 10, 1943, from 1:00 p.m. to 4:00 p.m. The labor duty leader signed off on the transfer of the five prisoners to the sentry, who in turn signed off on having received the prisoners and then once again on having returned all of them at the conclusion of the work. The prisoners were received by the block leader, who also signed the form. Finally, the labor duty leader confirmed his having checked the process with yet another signature. kjs

Loan from the Wachtturm-Gesellschaft der Zeugen Jehovas, Selters
Kreismuseum Wewelsburg, inv. no. 16858

No. 8-23
Death certificate for Jakob Schafronow, issued by camp physician Dr. Franz Metzger
November 17, 1942
The camp physician (Section V) was responsible for all medical issues at the concentration camp. From October 1941 to December 1942, the duties of camp physician were assumed by *SS-Untersturmführer* Dr. Franz Metzger. In this capacity he was also responsible for issuing death certificates. Dr. Metzger, born in 1911, had worked at Neuengamme Concentration Camp since October 1940, before being transferred to Wewelsburg. He was subsequently assigned to the SS armored infantry Division *Totenkopf*. Dr. Rudolf Hennings and Dr. Willi Frank were responsible for dental care in Wewelsburg. There is no evidence of medical experiments on prisoners at Wewelsburg. kjs

Internationaler Suchdienst, Bad Arolsen, Umschlag Jakob Schafronow

No. 8-22
Hermann Michl
Section IV of the camp command was responsible for the administration of the concentration camp. This involved the housing and feeding of both SS guards and prisoners. The heads of administration showed little interest in providing adequate food and clothing for prisoners and shared responsibility for the poor living conditions at the camp. The first administrative head at Wewelsburg was *SS-Obersturmführer* Hermann Michl, who held the post from November 1941 to December 1942. After joining the SS in 1933, he began his concentration camp career in 1934 at Lichtenburg Concentration Camp. He then worked on command staff at Buchenwald and at Groß-Rosen Concentration Camp. After his assignment at Wewelsburg, he was transferred to an SS cavalry division on the Eastern Front. He held various administrative leadership posts, most notably at Riga, Litzmannstadt, and Lublin Concentration Camps. He was killed near Lublin in 1944. kjs

Bundesarchiv Berlin, RS Hermann Michl

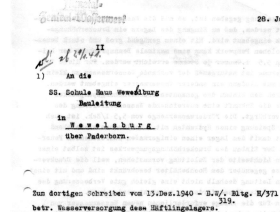

No. 8-24
Dr. Heinrich Hagel, Camp Physician
Ca. 1937
The Small Camp at Kuhkampsberg did not have its own camp doctor, so the prisoners were treated by Dr. Heinrich Hagel (b. 1875), from Büren. On October 10, 1940, he was drafted into the *Waffen-SS* as a concentration camp physician with the rank of *SS-Hauptsturmführer*, a position he held until September 1941. At age 65, he was one of the oldest SS members at the camp in 1940. After Metzger's departure, Hagel was again in charge of providing medical care to the prisoners, a responsibility he also held during the period when Wewelsburg was an external work detachment of Buchenwald from 1943 until the camp's liberation on April 2, 1945. kjs

Bundesarchiv Berlin, RS Heinrich Hagel

No. 8-25
SS-Unterscharführer Wilhelm Otte, guard
1939 – 1945
The camp's 150-man SS guard unit was drawn from SS Death's Head Units stationed in Wewelsburg, which constituted the 1st SS Death's Head Battalion (*Sturmbann*) under the command of Gustav Strese, who took his orders from the SS Operations Main Office. *SS-Unterscharführer* Wilhelm Otte, born in 1905, was assigned to the battalion at Wewelsburg. Drafted in 1939, the former financial clerk was a member of the Death's Head Units as of 1940. He was initially assigned to the Gusen subcamp of Mauthausen Concentration Camp before being assigned to Wewelsburg in 1942. In April 1943 he was assigned to Bergen-Belsen as a deputy report leader. The guards units received precise instructions on how to act toward the concentration camp prisoners. Under the dreadful conditions prevailing at the camps, few guards followed these orders, with arbitrary and abusive treatment a daily occurrence. Although Wilhelm Otte was considered a dedicated member of the NSDAP, he was not known to physically abuse prisoners. kjs

Landesarchiv NRW, Abteilung Ostwestfalen-Lippe, Detmold, D 26/2441_22

No. 8-30
Not shown
Letter from the Niederhagen Concentration Camp administration to Alme Valley Central Waterworks regarding a water-meter shaft
May 28, 1942
Kreismuseum Wewelsburg, inv. no. 16872

No. 8-29
Letter from Alme Valley Central Waterworks to Construction Management of the Wewelsburg SS School about the water supply in the prisoner section
January 28, 1941
Kreismuseum Wewelsburg, inv. no. 16873

Over a period of several years letters were exchanged between the Niederhagen Concentration Camp administration, which was responsible for the camp water main, SS Construction Management, which oversaw construction of the camp, and Alme Valley Central Waterworks, which administered the camp's water supply, concerning the poor water supply in the prisoner section of the concentration camp. The complaints of insufficient water pressure suggest some of the difficulties faced by the prisoners in their daily lives. Water pressure was so low that not all prisoners could wash at the same time. kjs

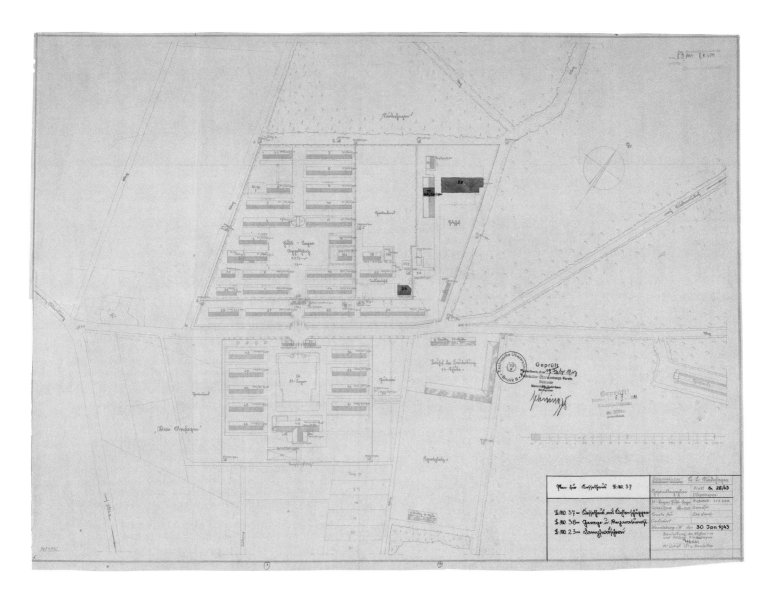

No. 8-28

**Boiler room construction plan from
the SS Construction Management
site plan**
January 30, 1943
With the Allied aerial photograph as
contrast, the site plan from January 30, 1943, provides a very
detailed view of the camp's state of
development in the period when
Wewelsburg functioned as a main
camp. The two rows of barracks
in front of the roll call area are
clearly distinguishable; one had
already been torn down by the time
the aerial photograph was taken in
1945. The plan also shows the precise location of fences, water lines,
and cesspits. kjs
Kreisarchiv Paderborn, BürA 1447

No. 8-31
Not shown
**Building plan of a Reich Labor
Service barracks**
October 1, 1939
Housing barracks for both SS personnel and prisoners were similar
to those of the Reich Labor Service,
which could be assembled from
prefabricated components. A barracks consisted of two wings and
was accessible in the middle, where
there was a collective wash and
toilet area flanked on each side by a
common room. The sleeping quarters were located at the outer ends.
Each wing was 50 meters (ca. 164 ft.)
long and 8 meters (ca. 26 ft.) wide.
kjs
Stadtarchiv Soest, D 1990

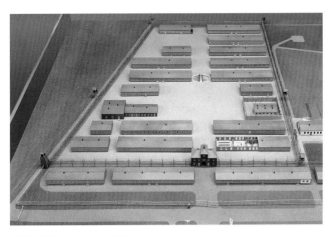

No.8-26
Detail from a U.S. aerial reconnaissance photograph
March 23, 1945
The Allied air reconnaissance photograph from March 1945 clearly shows the camp's geometric ground plan. In front of the roll call area, two of the barracks seen in the 1943 camp plan have been torn down. Only the foundations remain visible. kjs

The Aerial Reconnaissance Archives (TARA), Edinburgh

1 Gatehouse
2 Roll call area
3 Prisoner kitchen
4 Prisoner barracks
5 Bunker
6 Sick bay
7 Fire pond
8 Watchtower
9 Crematorium
10 SS garages
11 Workshop barracks
12 Air raid bunker
13 SS barracks
14 Laundry facility
15 Potato kitchen
16 SS camp
17 SS Maintenance yard
18 Shooting range

No.8-27
Model of Niederhagen Concentration Camp
Plastic, wood, glass
The concentration camp consisted of four clearly defined areas: the protective detention camp and industrial area on one side of the road, and the SS maintenance yard and SS camp on the other. In its layout, the protective detention camp followed the architectural guidelines of the first prototype concentration camp at Dachau ("Dachau Model"). In addition to housing barracks for the prisoners and the gatehouse, it featured a prisoner kitchen, a detention bunker, and a sick bay. In front of the camp entrance, there were four SS barracks. The industrial area included workshops, SS garages, an air raid bunker for SS personnel, stables, kennels, a laundry facility, and a crematorium. In 1941, SS barracks and a maintenance yard were built on the other side of the road. Only a portion of the nine planned stone-foundation barracks were ready for use by April 1943. kjs

Model construction: E. Christiani, 1982, revised in 2010
Kreismuseum Wewelsburg, inv. no. 17445

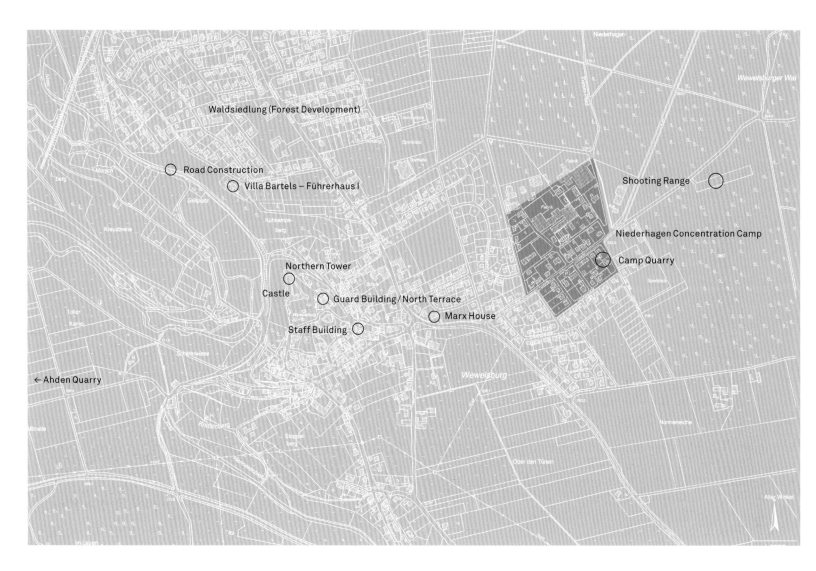

Waldsiedlung (Forest Development)

Road Construction

Villa Bartels – Führerhaus I

Shooting Range

Niederhagen Concentration Camp

Camp Quarry

Northern Tower

Castle

Guard Building / North Terrace

Marx House

Staff Building

← Ahden Quarry

No. 8-32
**Overview of prisoner labor details
in the village of Wewelsburg**

Because prisoner labor details were spread across the entire village, residents saw the columns of prisoners marching through the village each day. In addition to construction at Wewelsburg Castle and work in the quarries, other details were assigned to the Villa Bartels/Führerhaus I, the Marx house, the guard building/terrace and staff building, the Waldsiedlung (Forest Development), and the plant nurseries at the train station and Nonneneiche.

Prisoners were also assigned to road construction and various labor details on the concentration camp grounds, including camp construction, kitchen detail, the crematorium, the laundry, and the tailor shop, as well as the sock-darning detail, for the weakened prisoners. kjs
General map of Wewelsburg (scale 1:5000)

No. 8-35
**Prisoner at work on the northern tower
of Wewelsburg Castle
Between 1939 and 1943**
This is the only known photograph of a concentration camp prisoner working on the castle. Work on the northern tower was especially punishing for prisoners, who were forced to excavate the basement vault for the crypt. Before being used to clad the newly cast concrete cupola, the stone extracted from the quarry was processed in wooden sheds located in the castle moat. The deepening of the basement foundations by more than four meters (ca. thirteen ft.) was comparable to outdoor work in the quarry and consisted of strenuous physical labor in the cold and dark. kjs
Kreismuseum Wewelsburg, Fotoarchiv

No. 8-33
**Concentration camp prisoners at work
in the quarry below Wewelsburg Castle
1939 – 1943**
Work in the quarries below Wewelsburg Castle, at the train station, in the SS camp and in the neighboring village of Ahden was among the most punishing for concentration camp prisoners. They had to work outside, unprotected, in all types of weather, sometimes without proper shoes or gloves, quarrying stones and transporting them to the building sites. Explosives were rare. Tipcarts were used in the quarry below the castle. The prisoners pushed the carts filled with rock along rails up to the castle, resulting in numerous serious accidents.

 As with those assigned to roadwork, prisoners in the quarry details suffered extreme physical exhaustion and emaciation. It was not uncommon for details to return to the camp in the evenings carrying dead or gravely injured prisoners. kjs
Kreismuseum Wewelsburg, Fotoarchiv

No. 8-34
**Prisoners during construction of the
Bartels villa (Führerhaus I)
1940/1941**
When the war-induced moratorium on construction ended in the summer of 1940, building operations on the northern tower, staff building, and Führerhaus I resumed. In his building permit application from July 4, 1940, architect Hermann Bartels indicated that concentration camp prisoners would be used to construct the Führerhaus I, a luxurious, *Heimatschutz*-style residence where he would subsequently reside with his family.

 Below the Führerhaus I, the SS-Waldsiedlung (Forest Development) was built between 1941 and 1943. It consisted of seven residential buildings for families of SS personnel. For six months during its construction, the SS redesignated the Waldsiedlung labor detail as a disciplinary detail, where SS guards and kapos singled out prisoners for systematic beatings and abuse. kjs
Kreismuseum Wewelsburg, Fotoarchiv

- 9 -

280

Vor dem Fall des Erschlagens des Brotdiebes bin ich mit aufge-
fordert worden, einen Häftling namens Westfal, der früher Kapo
gewesen war, und sehr unbeliebt war, mit zu verprügeln. Der
Häftling ist daran gestorben. Ich habe mich nicht beteiligt.
Paetzelt hatte mit diesem Fall aber nichts zu tun.

Der Zeuge wurde vereidigt und im allseitigen Einverständnis
entlassen.

6. Zeuge:
Dr. med. Franz Metzger aus Saarbrücken, Arzt, 59 Jahre alt, mit
den Angeklagten nicht verwandt und nicht verschwägert.
z.S.:
Ich war von Ende September 1941 bis Mitte Dezember 1942 Lager-
arzt im Konzentrationslager Wewelsburg, sowohl für die SS-Leute
als auch für die Häftlinge. Bei meiner Ankunft hatte ich ca. 300
Personen zu betreuen, als ich wegging waren es ca. 600 Personen.
Als Hilfe hatte ich einen Häftling als Pfleger und einen weiteren
polnischen Häftling. Die kranken Häftlinge mußten sich beim Lager-
ältesten melden und wurden mir dann im Revier vorgestellt, unter-
sucht und behandelt. Im Revier standen 2o bis 3o Betten zur Verfügung. Es kam vor, daß Häftlinge wegen Überfüllung des Reviers
in den Blocks lagen. Anfangs war der Gesundheitszustand der Häftlinge ausreichend, später war er bedlagenswert, weil die Häftlinge
teilweise schon krank und unterernährt ins Lager kamen. Die Ver-
pflegung war in keiner Weise ausreichend, sie betrug pro Person
ca. 600 bis 700 Kalorien am Tag. Die häufigsten Erkrankungen
waren Durchfallerkrankungen, Erkältungserkrankungen und Unfälle.
Es ist möglich, daß die angegebenen Unfälle teilweise auf Miß-
handlungen zurückzuführen waren. Mir ist auch bekannt, daß Häftlinge so mißhandelt wurden, daß sie von mir behandelt werden
mußten. Wer ihnen diese Verletzungen zugefügt hatte, habe ich
nicht erfahren. Es kam häufig vor, daß Todesfälle, die auf Miß-
handlungen zurückzuführen waren, mir als Todesfälle durch Unfall
gemeldet wurden.
An Rehn habe ich noch eine geringe Erinnerung. An Friedsam habe
ich keine Erinnerung mehr. An Paetzelt kann ich mich dem Gesicht
nach entsinnen. Schüller kenne ich nicht.

Wewelsburg, 9. Februar 1943

Frau
Hilde S c h u m a n n
C h e m n i t z
Zschopauerstr. 26
Sehr geehrte Frau Schumann !
Wie Ihnen bereits durch die Geheime Staatspolizei - Staatspoli-
zeistelle Chemnitz - mitgeteilt, ist Ihr Vater Paul Ulbricht,
geboren am 13. März 1887 in Freiberg/Sachsen, an den Folgen
einer Herzschwäche und Darmkatarrhs verstorben.

Ihr Vater meldete sich am 31. Januar 1943 krank und wurde dar-
aufhin unter Aufnahme im Krankenbau in ärztliche Behandlung genommen. Es wurde ihm die bestmögliche medikamentöse und pfle-
gerische Behandlung zuteil. Trotz aller ärztlichen Bemühungen
gelang es nicht, der Krankheit Herr zu werden.

Ich spreche Ihnen zu diesem Verlust mein Beileid aus.

Ihr Vater hat keine letzten Wünsche geäußert.

Ich habe die Effekten-Kammer meines Lagers angewiesen, den Nachlass an Ihre Anschrift zu senden.

Der Lagerkommandant

SS-Hauptsturmführer.

No. 8-36
**Testimony of camp physician Dr. Franz Metzger
on the nutritional status of prisoners;
excerpt of investigative documents from the
second Wewelsburg trial
1970/1971**
Translation on page 453

In his testimony at the second Wewelsburg trial,
even the former SS camp physician confirmed
the deficiency of food rations for prisoners
at Wewelsburg. The SS was not interested in
improving the food situation of the prisoners.
Rather, it purposely starved them as a method
of physical and psychological debilitation; the
pigsty that provided meat for the SS was located
within close view of the protective detention
camp and its undernourished inmates.

From 1941 on, the food situation steadily
worsened. The prisoners suffered permanent
hunger, resulting in nutritional deficiencies,
severe exhaustion, and famine edema to the
point of death. In the summer of 1942, prisoners
on nettle detail collected nettles, and later beet
leaves, for the preparation of barely edible soups.
Packages from relatives helped improve the
rations of a few prisoners. kjs

Hauptstaatsarchiv Düsseldorf, Zweigarchiv Kalkum,
trial documents concerning Niederhagen-Wewelsburg
Concentration Camp, AZ: 24JS 2/69 (Z), Rep. 118, no. 855-93

No. 8-37
**Letter from the camp commandant
Adolf Haas to Hilde Schumann
February 9, 1943**
Translation on page 453

Two weeks prior to this letter, Paul Ulbricht's
daughter had received the news that her father
had died of "heart failure and intestinal catarrh."
In this second letter, the camp commandant
cynically emphasized the purported medical
efforts to save her father. Whether his death in
the sick bay was attributable to "natural" causes
or violence can no longer be determined, but the
first-class medical care he was reported to have
received in the sick bay was most certainly a
sham. SS physicians and prisoner medics never
had access to sufficient medication and no
effort was made to improve sanitary conditions.

The sick bay was a feared place, where prisoners knew that patients were commonly "hosed
down," in other words, subjected to a cold jet of
water in the washroom until they died of
circulatory failure or cardiac arrest. kjs

Original privately owned

8.1.6.
Operation 14 f 13

"FOR PRESS ONLY"

DOC. NO. - 1151-C-PS

Tgb.-Nr. 163/41.

Der Reichsfuehrer-SS
Der Inspekteur der Konzentrationslager.
-Pol./Az.: 14 f 13 /Ot./S.-
Geheim Tgb.-Nr. 269/41

Konzentrationslager Gross-Rosen
Kommandantur
Eingang: 12. Dez.1941

Betreff: Aerzte-Kommission.

Bezug: Hiesig. Schreiben vom 12.11.41, 14 f 13 Ot/U.z.

Anlagen: - 1 -

Geheime Reichssache!
Ausfertigung.

An die
Lagerkommandanten der
Konzentrationslager

Dachau, Sachsenhausen, Buchenwald, Mauthausen, Auschwitz, Flossenbuerg, Gross-Rosen, Neuengamme, Niederhagen.

Wie den Lagerkommandanten der Konzentrationslager

Dachau, Sachsenhausen, Buchenwald, Mauthausen und Auschwitz

mit dem Bezugsschreiben mitgeteilt wurde, wird in der naechsten Zeit die Aerzte-Kommission die vorgenannten Konzentrationslager zur Ausmusterung von Haeftlingen aufsuchen.

Fuer die Konzentrationslager Flossenbuerg, Gross-Rosen, Neuengamme und Niederhagen ist die 1. Januarhaelfte 1942 fuer diese Ueberpruefung vorgesehen.

Da die zur Verfuegung stehenden Aerzte sehr stark in Anspruch genommen sind, muessen die Ueberpruefungsarbeiten in den Konzentrationslagern, soweit es irgend geht, abgekuerzt werden.

In der Anlage wird Muster eines Meldebogens als Vorlage zur Vorarbeit uebersandt. Diese Formblaetter sind im Abzugsverfahren herzustellen und auszufuellen. Auf diesem Muster ist die Beantwortung einzelner Fragen vorgenommen, dieselben sind ausserdem rot unterstrichen, nur diese Fragen brauchen beantwortet werden. Bezueglich einzelner Fragen werden noch folgende Erlaeuterungen gegeben:

Die Frage "Koerperl. unheilb. Leiden" ist nach Moeglichkeit nicht nur mit Ja oder Nein, sondern mit kurzer Angabe der Diagnose zu beantworten. Ausserdem ist auch die Frage der Kriegsbeschaedigung festzustellen, weil diese eine wesentliche Erleichterung bei der Ueberpruefungsarbeit der Aerztekommission gewaehrleistet. Wenn der Raum bei den Fragen "Delikt" und "Fruehere Straftaten" nicht ausreicht, ist die Beantwortung auf der

-2- DOC.NO.- 1151-C-PS contd.

Rueckseite des Meldebogens vorzunehmen, wie es auf dem Muster vermerkt ist. Einzelne Vorstrafen sind nicht aufzuzaehlen, es ist nur ueber die hauptsaechlichsten Vorstrafen kurz zu berichten, die einzelnen Delikte sind nur kurz aufzufuehren. Welche Haeftlinge fuer die Vorfuehrung in Frage kommen, ist aus den im Fragebogen gestellten Fragen ersichtlich.

Saemtliche vorhandene Akten und Krankenblaetter sind der Kommission auf Verlangen zur Einsichtnahme zur Verfuegung zu stellen.

Die Adjutanten der Konzentrationslager

Flossenbuerg, Gross-Rosen und Neuengamme werden zwecks muendlicher Anweisung in dieser Angelegenheit zur gegebenen Zeit nach hier befohlen werden.

Nach Abschluss der Untersuchungen ist dem Inspekteur der Konzentrationslager Bericht zu erstatten, dabei ist die Zahl der der Sonderbehandlung "14 f 13" zugefuehrten Haeftlinge zu melden. Der genaue Zeitpunkt des Eintreffens der Aerzte-Kommission wird rechtzeitig bekanntgegeben.

i.V.

gez. Liebehenschel

SS-Obersturmbannfuehrer.

Certified true copy.

No. 8-38
Circular from the Concentration Camp Inspector to the commandants of concentration camps, including Niederhagen, announcing the visit of a medical commission
December 10, 1941
Translation on page 454
In contrast to other concentration camps, no medical experiments were performed on prisoners at Niederhagen. However, Niederhagen was among the camps participating in Operation 14 f 13, the codename for the euthanasia campaigns conducted in concentration camps, which aimed at the "eradication of unworthy life." The designation was derived from the reference codes "14," for deaths at concentration camps, and "13," for death by gassing. Beginning in April 1941, SS physicians selected prisoners with mental illness or serious physical conditions – those deemed unfit for labor – to be killed using poison gas at selected clinics and institutions. As the "service exemptions" issued by the medical commissions escalated, the Economic and Administrative Main Office decreed that, as of 1942, the operation be restricted to prisoners that were truly unable to work. In 1943 Himmler again narrowed the operation's scope to the genuinely "mentally ill." kjs

Reprinted in: Alexander Mitscherlich, Fred Mielke, *Das Diktat der Menschenverachtung. Eine Dokumentation* [Dictating Contempt for Mankind. A Documentation], Heidelberg, 1947, p. 137 f.

Prov. Obermedizinalrat
Direktor Dr. Mennecke
Landesheilanstalt Eichberg (Rheingau)

Eichberg i. Rhg. ü/ Eltville., den 4. April 1942.

Herrn
Weingutsbesitzer
E m i l W
Ortsbauernführer,

L o r c h a/Rhein.

Sehr geehrter Herr W

Ich bitte um Absendung der folgenden Weinkisten auf meine Rechnung:

1) Eine 20er-Kiste an : SS-Gruppenführer Erwin Rösener, M.d.R. Salzburg I, Kapitelplatz 2.
10 Flaschen
Nr. 1 1940er Lorcher Schlossberg, natur, à Mk 1,80 = Mk: 18,00
10 Flaschen
Nr. 2 1940er Lorcher Kapellenberg, natur " " 1,90 = " 19,00

2) Eine 12er Kiste an : SS-Obersturmbannführer K. Künstler, K.L. Flossenbürg b/Weiden (Oberpfalz).
6 Flaschen
Nr. 1 1940er Lorcher Schlossberg, natur à Mk 1,80 = " 10,80
6 Flaschen
Nr. 2 1940er Lorcher Kapellenberg, natur " " 1,90 = " 11,40

3) Eine 12er Kiste an : SS-Hauptsturmführer Adolf Haas, K.L. Wewelsburg b/Paderborn i/W.
wie zu 2). " 22,20

Mk: 81,40

Auch die Frachtkosten bitte ich mir in Rechnung zu stellen. Bei der Avisierung bitte ich den obigen Empfängern mitzuteilen, dass die Übersendung in meinem Auftrage erfolgt. Ich stelle Ihnen anheim, in allen 3 Fällen die leeren Flaschen und Kisten zurückzuerbitten.

Heil Hitler!

Prov. Obermedizinalrat

No. 8-39
Letter from Dr. Mennecke to Emil W., a winemaker
April 4, 1942
After the circular from December 10, 1941, announcing the visit of a medical commission during the following year, a doctor from Hadamar arrived in Wewelsburg in early 1942 to select ailing prisoners for the "special treatment." In April 1942, the head of the operation, the medical director of Eichberg State Mental Hospital Dr. Mennecke, sent a case of wine to camp commandant Haas. The gift was likely a gesture of appreciation, as the commandants of other concentration camps participating in the operation also received wine as a gift. The total number of Wewelsburg prisoners who fell victim to the operation is unknown. The return of the clothing of the selected prisoners to Niederhagen meant that the purpose of the extermination transports did not remain unknown to the prisoners at Wewelsburg. kjs

Hauptstaatsarchiv Wiesbaden, 46123 442, vol. 2

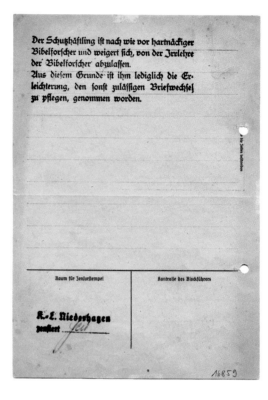

No. 8-40
Letter from Maria Viertlbauer to her son-in-law, Alois Moser, detained at Niederhagen Concentration Camp as a Jehovah's Witness
January 20, 1943
Loan from the Wachtturm-Gesellschaft der Zeugen Jehovas, Selters Kreismuseum Wewelsburg, inv. no. 16664

Moser Alois
Born 7/17/1900
No. 161 Block 3a
Niederhagen Concentration Camp
Wewelsburg, near Paderborn
Translation of a transcription

Packages and letters were subject to strict censorship under supervision of camp leader Wolfgang Plaul. Letters had to be legible and in German. Concentration camp prisoners were allowed only limited correspondence with their families; sometimes they were only permitted to write one letter a month, or even less. Correspondence privileges were sometimes taken away entirely as punishment, or on a purely arbitrary basis. The receiving of letters was also strictly controlled. This letter was sent back to Maria Viertlbauer, stamped "Return to Sender." Another stamp, on the back, stated: "The letter cannot be delivered as the addressee has already received the allotted number of letters for January." kjs

No. 8-41
Letter from Erich Polster to his family, written from Niederhagen Concentration Camp
March 22, 1942
Erich Polster was taken into protective detention because of his activity for the banned International Bible Students Association. Members of the religious community of Jehovah's Witnesses were at times placed under increased pressure in the concentration camp, with their allowance of letters even more restricted in number and length. The stamp offers the rationale: "The protective detention prisoner stubbornly remains a Bible Student and refuses to abandon the false doctrines of the Bible Students. For this reason he has been deprived of the otherwise permitted relief afforded by correspondence." kjs

Loan from the Wachtturm-Gesellschaft der Zeugen Jehovas, Selters Kreismuseum Wewelsburg, inv. no. 16859

No. 8-42
Announcement by the camp commandant concerning the sending of warm clothing
Winter 1942 – 1943
Translation on page 454
Over the course of the war, the allotment of clothing for concentration camp prisoners was continuously reduced, because all resources were directed to supplying the armed forces. In winter 1942 – 1943, to remedy the worsening lack of clothing, prisoners were officially allowed to receive warm underwear and food through the mail. These packages became indispensable for everyday survival. Prisoners without families, or foreign inmates whose families could not be reached by mail, suffered from the lack of such additional packages. kjs

Kreismuseum Wewelsburg, Nachlass Wettin Müller, inv. no. 16681

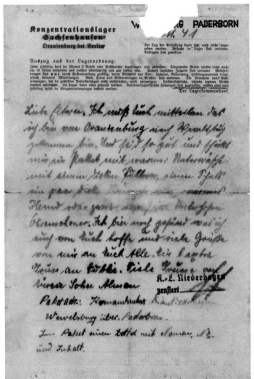

No. 8-44
Portrait of Alman Rose
(1922 – 1941)
Ca. 1935 – 1940
Kreismuseum Wewelsburg,
inv. no. 17454

No. 8-43
Letter from Alman Rose to his
parents via Mr. Ewald Adler in
Stettin
November 7, 1941
Alman Rose, a Sinto, was sent to
Niederhagen Concentration Camp
via Oranienburg. Having never
learned to write, he depended on
fellow prisoners for help with correspondence. In this letter, he
requested additional underwear for
the coming winter. The prohibition
on packages was occasionally lifted
to allow prisoners to receive warm
winter clothing. kjs

Loan from private collection
Kreismuseum Wewelsburg, inv. no. 16921

11/?/41,
Dear parents. I need to let you know that
I've come from Oranienburg to Wewelsburg. And be so good and send me a package with warm underwear, with a warm
thick sweater, a scarf, a pair of thick
socks, a warm shirt or two, a pair of underwear, earmuffs. I'm still healthy, which I
hope for you, too, and many regards from
me to you all. An extra hello to Tubki [?]. All
the best, your son Alman.
Package addr.: Office of the Commandant
Niederhagen Wewelsburg C.C.
via Paderborn
Place a tag in the package with name, no.
and contents.

Translation of a transcription

No. 8-46
Not shown
Letter from Karl Truckenbrodt
to his wife Laura
January 10, 1943
Karl Truckenbrodt, a Jehovah's Witness,
was permitted to receive regular money
and packages from his wife. Prisoners
could purchase some poor quality items
in the concentration camp. Two postal
receipts, for a value of 10 Reichsmarks,
have been preserved. In his letter, Karl
Truckenbrodt also mentions two packages
and deliveries of underwear. In the excerpt
from the camp regulations printed on the
letterhead, the added prohibition on the
sending of packages was crossed out.
However, Karl Truckenbrodt continued to
be under the special restriction limiting
each letter to seven lines. As a "stubborn
Bible Student," he was not allowed to
write on the back of the letter. kjs

Wachtturm-Gesellschaft der Zeugen Jehovas, Selters
Kreismuseum Wewelsburg, inv. no. 16895

No. 8-45
Not shown
Delivery receipt for Karl
Truckenbrodt for 10 Reichsmarks
April 2, 1942

Loan from the Wachtturm-Gesellschaft der
Zeugen Jehovas, Selters
Kreismuseum Wewelsburg, inv. no. 16866

No. 8-49
Alois Moser with his wife and parents-in-law
1930s

Alois Moser, born in 1900 in Schalchen, near Mattighofen (Austria), was arrested in 1939 for his membership in the banned Jehovah's Witnesses religious community and sent to Dachau Concentration Camp. Over the course of his six years of imprisonment, he passed through several main camps and subcamps before his liberation in Schwerin. It took him another four months to return to his family in Braunau am Inn. His wife had also been taken into protective detention. He therefore conducted his correspondence via his parents-in-law. kjs

Wachtturm-Gesellschaft der Zeugen Jehovas, Geschichtsarchiv, Selters

No. 8-50
The journey of Alois Moser (b. 1900), an Austrian Jehovah's Witness, through the National Socialist concentration camp system

April 4, 1939	Arrested by the Gestapo at a commemorative meal Imprisoned in Linz
April 20, 1939	Transferred from Linz to the Gestapo prison in Munich
April 21, 1939	Imprisoned at Dachau Concentration Camp (prisoner number 1339)
September 27, 1939	Transferred to Mauthausen Concentration Camp, Gusen subcamp
February 18, 1940	Returned to Dachau as a *Muselmann* (derogatory term used in the concentration camps for a severely emaciated and listless prisoner)
September 1940	Transferred to Sudelfeld subcamp (Bayrisch-Zell)
November 15, 1940	Transferred from Sudelfeld to Dachau
December 8, 1940	Transferred from Dachau to Buchenwald Concentration Camp
March 8, 1941	Transferred to Wewelsburg, a subcamp of Sachsenhausen Concentration Camp
April 6, 1943	Disbandment of Niederhagen Concentration Camp; transferred to Ravensbrück Concentration Camp
July 7, 1943	Transferred to the subcamp at Gut Comthurey
March 6, 1944	Transferred to Hohenlychen Sanatorium
February 27, 1945	Transferred to the subcamp at Dömnitz an der Elbe
April 14, 1945	Transported to women's camp at Neustadt-Glewe
April 15, 1945	Returned to Ravensbrück Concentration Camp Death march
May 4, 1945	Liberated in Schwerin
September 25, 1945	Returned home and reunited with his family

No. 8-47
Not shown
Postcard from Alois Moser to his family, written from Buchenwald Concentration Camp
March 6, 1941

Loan from the Wachtturm-Gesellschaft der Zeugen Jehovas, Selters
Kreismuseum Wewelsburg, inv. no. 16666

No. 8-48
Not shown
Postcard from Alois Moser to his family, written from Ravensbrück Concentration Camp
April 15, 1943

Loan from the Wachtturm-Gesellschaft der Zeugen Jehovas, Selters
Kreismuseum Wewelsburg, inv. no. 16665

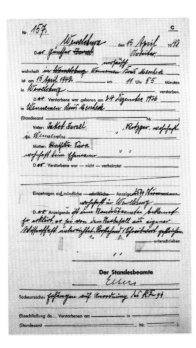

No.8-53
Death certificate of Günther Ransenberg
April 15, 1942
Günther Ransenberg, just 15 years old, was one of 56 Gestapo prisoners transported to Niederhagen Concentration Camp for execution, either by hanging (42 prisoners) or shooting (14 prisoners). With the outbreak of war, the Gestapo was empowered to execute people without legal proceedings. The cases suggested by the Gestapo for "special treatment," the euphemism for such extrajudicial killings, were reported to Berlin. Himmler reserved the right to order executions.

From April 1942 to March 1943, Niederhagen Concentration Camp, like other main camps, served as execution grounds for local Gestapo offices. Until late 1942, death certificates stated the cause of death as "hanging by order of the *Reichsführer-SS*." After the establishment of the camp's own registry office in January 1943, executions – even then with only fabricated legality – were coded as "death by asphyxiation." kjs

Standesamt Büren, Sterberegister 1943
(partly anonymous)

No.8-51
Not shown
Günther Ransenberg with his sister Inge
March 1938
Günther Ransenberg, born in 1926 in Wennemen, Meschede district, grew up in an assimilated Jewish family. His father lost his job as a butcher in the campaign of persecution against the Jewish population. He then found a new position with an Arnsberg construction company, which also hired Günther in 1941, after his graduation. In March 1942 Günther was assigned to a railroad construction near Bestwig. During a breakfast break he took part in a snowball fight between the laborers, in the course of which he threw a snowball at some passing girls. Günther was recognizable as a Jew by the yellow Star of David he wore. One of the girls told her father, an *SS-Obersturmführer*. The very same day, the Gestapo arrested him at the worksite. On April 15, 1942, Günther Ransenberg was hanged for "race defilement." He had thrown a snowball at an Aryan girl. kjs

Kreismuseum Wewelsburg, Fotoarchiv

No.8-52
Günther Ransenberg (center) with his family (mother, Mathilde, at far left; sister, Inge, below)
March 1938
Günther Ransenberg's family learned of his fate only after his execution. His mother died two weeks later of a heart attack. In late 1942, his father and three younger siblings were deported from Dortmund to the ghetto in Theresienstadt. In the fall of 1944, they were transported to Auschwitz and murdered. Günther's older brother, Friedel, was transported directly to Auschwitz in 1942 and assigned to IG Farben's "Buna Works" construction detail. In January 1945, he was transferred to Mittelbau-Dora Concentration Camp, and from there to Bergen-Belsen. He survived and emigrated to the United States to join his oldest brother, Rolf, who had left Germany before the war. kjs

Kreismuseum Wewelsburg, Fotoarchiv

No. 8-54
Detail of a class photograph with Jelena Kekachina
Ca. 1928
Jelena Polikarpowna Kekachina, born in 1920 in Staroredkino, Omsk district, Siberia, lost her mother at age 5 and grew up in poverty. When her father also died, she traveled to Omsk in 1938, and then to Mariupol, in Ukraine, to find work. She arrived in Germany as a *Ostarbeiterin* (forced laborer from the East) and was probably assigned to a Paderborn company. It appears that she was molested there by her German superior and resisted him. Jelena Kekachina was then arrested by the Gestapo and remanded to Nieder-hagen Concentration Camp, where she was hanged for "insubordination" at 12:10 p.m. on March 8, 1943. Her death certificate gave the official cause of death as "asphyxiation." Her hanging was secretly observed by concentration camp pris-oners and long a topic of discussion. kjs
Kreismuseum Wewelsburg, Fotoarchiv

No. 8-55
Death certificate of Jelena Kekachina
March 8, 1943
Standesamt Büren,
Sterberegister 1943, no. 172

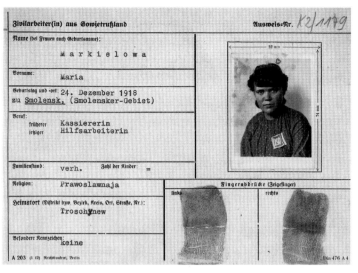

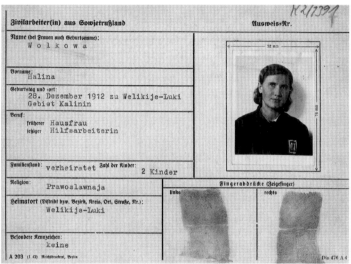

Die Deutsche Arbeitsfront.
Kreisverwaltung Altena-Lüdenscheid

Rundschreiben Nr. 41/42   Lüdenscheid, den 11.12.1942

Abt.: Soziale Selbstverant-
      wortung und Gestaltung
      B./Mü.

                              An alle
                              Lagerführer der Ostarbeiterläger
                              im Kreise Altena-Lüdenscheid

Betrifft: Exekution von zwei Ostarbeiterinnen im Konzentrations-
          lager Paderborn.

Nachdem bereits am 18. November 1942 ein Ostarbeiter wegen Mordes
und Beraubung das Wachmannes Homrighausen in der Firma Lüdenschei-
der Metallwerke Busch-Jäger in Lüdenscheid durch den Strang hingerichtet wurde, sind nunmehr auch – in einer Tagung wurde Ihnen bereits über diesen Fall berichtet – die zwei Ostarbeiterinnen, die
aus dem Lager der Firma Wilh. Schade, Plettenberg, geflohen waren
und dann in Balve einen Mordversuch an einem deutschen Mann, der
sie wieder aufgreifen wollte, unternahmen, am Freitag, den 4. Dezember d.J., in der Nähe von Paderborn in einem Konzentrationslager in der gleichen Weise hingerichtet worden.

Im Einvernehmen mit allen Partei- und Behördenstellen, in Sonder-
heit auf Wunsch der Geheimen Staatspolizei, soll dieses den in
Ihrem Lager befindlichen Ostarbeitern bezw. Ostarbeiterinnen in
geeigneter Form bekanntgegeben werden. Es erscheint hier ange-
bracht, daß Sie sich hier eines Dolmetschers bedienen, der diesen kurz von dem Vorbesagten Kenntnis gibt mit der Mahnung,
Fluchtversuche zu unterlassen und sich vor allen Dingen im Lager
diszipliniert und ordnungsgemäß aufzuführen.

                         H e i l   H i t l e r !

                         Kreissozialwalter

No. 8-56
Registration card for Halina Wolkowa

Halina Wolkowa, born in 1912 in Kalinin, north of Moscow, already had two children when she was sent to the German Reich as a forced laborer. There is no information on the fate of her children. At age 29, Halina was relatively old, considering the average age of female forced laborers from the east was between 18 and 20. As of August 24, 1942, she worked with Maria Markielowa at the Schade company, one of several Plettenberg metal-processing firms, which, as suppliers to the armaments industry, were crucial to war production. Foreign laborers were lodged in a separate barracks camp on the factory grounds, with a capacity of 250 people. Besides French and Belgian prisoners of war, it was above all the female laborers from the East who were housed separately from the German population. Their daily life was marked by hard physical labor and inadequate food and clothing. kjs/an

Stadtarchiv Plettenberg

No. 8-58
Registration card for Maria Markielowa

In late fall 1942, Maria Markielowa, born in 1918 in Smolensk, fled the factory premises of the Schade company with her co-worker, Halina Wolkowa. They presumably hoped to find better work on a farm. In Balve, about sixteen km (ca. nine miles) north of Plettenberg, they were detained by a German, and then arrested by the police. Their attempt to escape from the man was portrayed as attempted murder. On November 7, 1942, they were incarcerated in Steinwache Prison in Dortmund. In lieu of regular legal proceedings, Gestapo officials petitioned the *Reichsführer-SS* to allow "special treatment." They were then sentenced to death with no opportunity to defend themselves. On December 2, they were sent in a prisoner transport to Niederhagen Concentration Camp for execution. Upon arrival they were hanged in front of the concentration camp detention building. The camp physician pronounced them dead at 11:30 a.m. and 11:35 a.m. kjs/an

Stadtarchiv Plettenberg

No. 8-57
Circular from the German Labor Front (DAF), Altena-Lüdenscheid district office, to all leaders of the district's camps for forced laborers from the East
December 11, 1942

Like their male counterparts, female laborers from the East who resisted the multiple humiliations of their everyday lives, or attempted escape, were sentenced by the Gestapo without the benefit of legal proceedings. Women also received extreme punishments for the most trifling offenses. Maria Markielowa and Halina Wolkowa, who fell victim to "special treatment" in the fall of 1942 and were executed at Niederhagen Concentration Camp on December 2, 1942, are two examples.

Although the Gestapo became less likely to perform public executions of foreign forced laborers over the course of the war, not least because of protests from the population, they intended the two women's death to serve as a deterrent. By publicizing the executions in the camps for forced labor from the East, the Gestapo hoped to shock the laborers into submission. kjs/an

Stadtarchiv Meinerzhagen

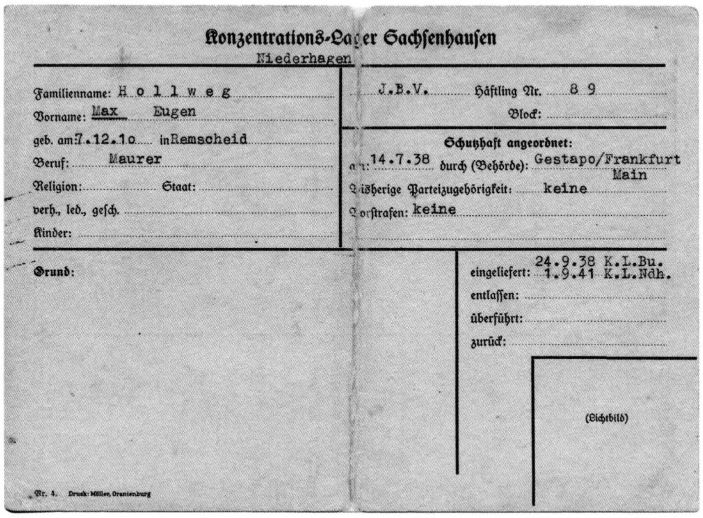

Konzentrations-Lager Sachsenhausen
Niederhagen

Familienname: H o l l w e g   J.B.V.   Häftling Nr.   8 9
Vorname: Max Eugen   Block:
geb. am 7.12.10 in Remscheid
Beruf: Maurer   Schutzhaft angeordnet:
Religion: Staat: am 14.7.38 durch (Behörde): Gestapo/Frankfurt Main
verh., led., gesch.:   bisherige Parteizugehörigkeit: keine
Kinder: Vorstrafen: keine

Grund: eingeliefert: 24.9.38 K.L.Bu.
1.9.41 K.L.Ndh.
entlassen:
überführt:
zurück:

(Lichtbild)

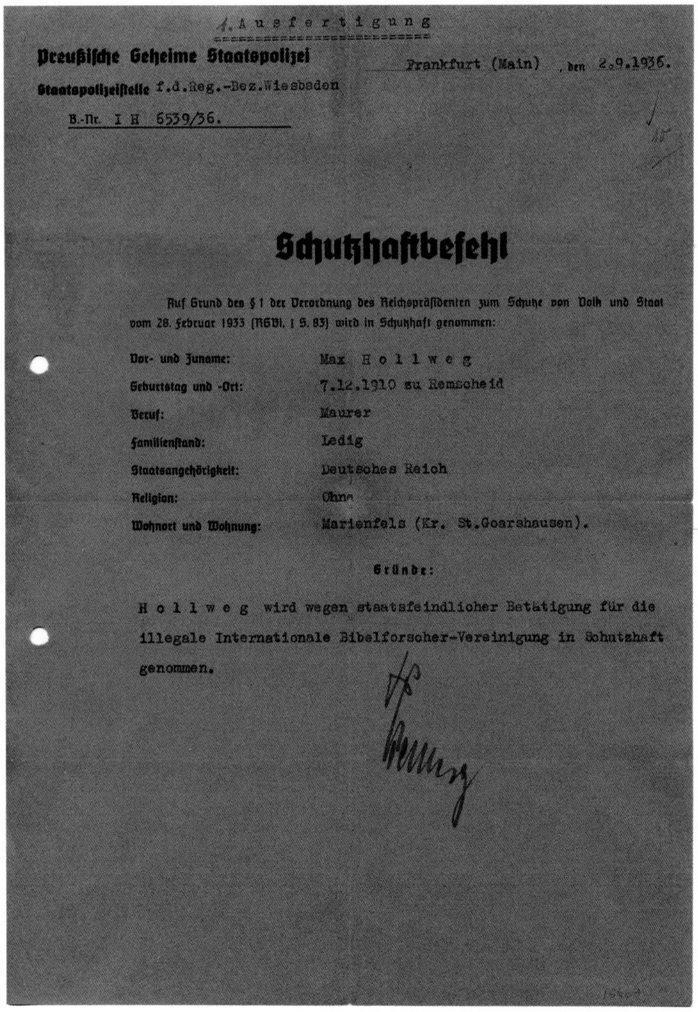

1.Ausfertigung

Preußische Geheime Staatspolizei   Frankfurt (Main), den 2.9.1936.
Staatspolizeistelle f.d.Reg.-Bez.Wiesbaden

B.-Nr. I H 6539/36.

Schutzhaftbefehl

Auf Grund des § 1 der Verordnung des Reichspräsidenten zum Schutze von Volk und Staat
vom 28. Februar 1933 (RGBl. I S. 83) wird in Schutzhaft genommen:

Vor- und Zuname: Max H o l l w e g
Geburtstag und -Ort: 7.12.1910 zu Remscheid
Beruf: Maurer
Familienstand: Ledig
Staatsangehörigkeit: Deutsches Reich
Religion: Ohne
Wohnort und Wohnung: Marienfels (Kr. St.Goarshausen).

Gründe:

H o l l w e g wird wegen staatsfeindlicher Betätigung für die
illegale Internationale Bibelforscher-Vereinigung in Schutzhaft
genommen.

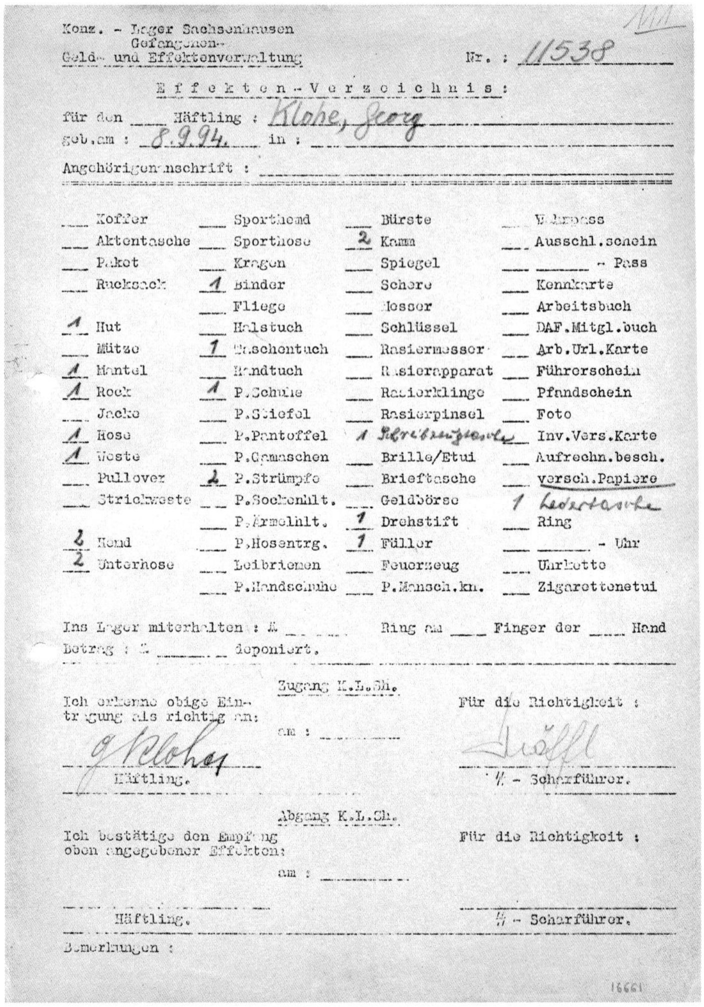

Konz. - Lager Sachsenhausen
Gefangenen-
Geld- und Effektenverwaltung   Nr.: 11538

Effekten-Verzeichnis:

für den   Häftling: Klohe, Georg
geb. am: 8.9.94. in:

Angehörigenanschrift:

Koffer	Sporthemd	Bürste	Wehrpass
Aktentasche	Sporthose	2 Kamm	Ausschl.schein
Paket	Kragen	Spiegel	Pass
Rucksack	1 Binder	Schere	Kennkarte
	Fliege	Messer	Arbeitsbuch
1 Hut	Halstuch	Schlüssel	DAF.Mitgl.buch
Mütze	1 Taschentuch	Rasiermesser	Arb.Url.Karte
1 Mantel	Handtuch	Rasierapparat	Führerschein
1 Rock	1 P.Schuhe	Rasierklinge	Pfandschein
Jacke	P.Stiefel	Rasierpinsel	Foto
1 Hose	P.Pantoffel	1 Schreibzeug	Inv.Vers.Karte
1 Weste	P.Gamaschen	Brille/Etui	Aufrechn.besch.
Pullover	2 P.Strümpfe	Brieftasche	versch.Papiere
Strickweste	P.Sockenhlt.	Geldbörse	1 Ledertasche
	P.Armelhlt.	1 Drehstift	Ring
2 Hemd	P.Hosentrg.	1 Füller	Uhr
2 Unterhose	Leibriemen	Feuerzeug	Uhrkette
	P.Handschuhe	P.Mansch.kn.	Zigarettenetui

Ins Lager mitbehalten: M   Ring am   Finger der   Hand
Betrag: M   deponiert.

Zugang K.L.Sh.

Ich erkenne obige Ein-   Für die Richtigkeit:
tragung als richtig an:
am:
Häftling.   4 - Scharführer.

Abgang K.L.Sh.

Ich bestätige den Empfang   Für die Richtigkeit:
obon angegebener Effekten:
am:
Häftling.   4 - Scharführer.

Bemerkungen:

No. 8-59
Protective detention order for Max Hollweg, Jehovah's Witness September 2, 1936

The SS did not merely use protective detention as an extrajudicial means of neutralizing political opponents; it also applied the measure when it found sentences handed down by the courts were too lenient. Thus, the SS frequently took into protective detention people who had just finished serving their sentences: they walked out the prison gates only to be sent to a concentration camp. The Gestapo twice ordered protective detention for Max Hollweg, a Bible Student. Following his first arrest, on September 2, 1936, by the Wiesbaden Gestapo, for "subversive activity for the illegal International Association of Bible Students," he was initially released again. After his second arrest, on July 14, 1938, by the Gestapo in Frankfurt am Main, he was sent to Buchenwald Concentration Camp in September 1938. Although he arrived in Wewelsburg in May 1940, his presence at the camp, recorded in the document shown here, was only officially registered after Niederhagen attained the status of a main camp. kjs

Loan from the Wachtturm-Gesellschaft der Zeugen Jehovas, Selters Kreismuseum Wewelsburg, inv. no. 16668

No. 8-60
Prisoner record for Max Hollweg
Loan from the Wachtturm-Gesellschaft der Zeugen Jehovas, Selters Kreismuseum Wewelsburg, inv. no. 16667

No. 8-61
List of possessions for Georg Klohe
Loan from the Wachtturm-Gesellschaft der Zeugen Jehovas, Selters Kreismuseum Wewelsburg, inv. no. 16661

Administrative offices at concentration camps maintained various standard forms for each prisoner. Prisoner records contained their personal data, grounds for detention, and a physical description. Punishments in the camp were also entered into the prisoner records. In the clothes depot, prisoner functionaries maintained personal property cards, which cataloged the valuables and articles of clothing that the prisoners were made to surrender upon arrival at the camp. Every change was noted.

When Georg Klohe was transferred from Sachsenhausen to Wewelsburg, along with his possessions he also carried his personal property card, which was then administered at Wewelsburg. kjs

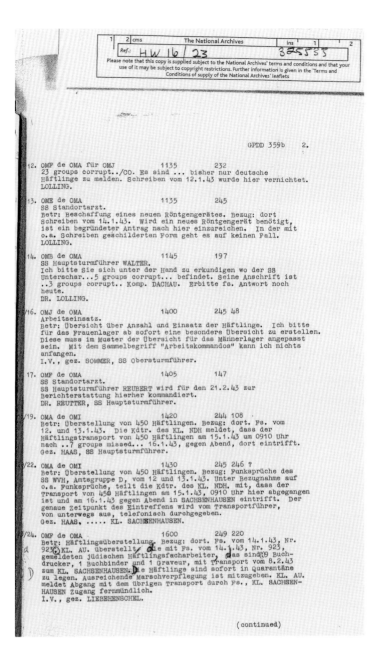

GPDD 359b   2.

12. OMF de OMA für OMJ   1135   232
23 groups corrupt../CO. Es sind ... bisher nur deutsche
Häftlinge zu melden. Schreiben vom 12.1.43 wurde hier vernichtet.
LOLLING.

13. OME de OMA   1135   245
SS Standortarzt.
Betr: Beschaffung eines neuen Röntgengerätes. Bezug: dort
Schreiben vom 14.1.43. Wird ein neues Röntgengerät benötigt,
ist ein begründeter Antrag nach hier einzureichen. In der mit
o.a. Schreiben geschilderten Form geht es auf keinen Fall.
LOLLING.

14. OMB de OMA   1145   197
SS Hauptsturmführer WALTER.
Ich bitte Sie sich unter der Hand zu erkundigen wo der SS
Unterschar...5 groups corrupt... befindet. Seine Anschrift ist
..3 groups corrupt.. Komp. DACHAU. Erbitte fs. Antwort noch
heute.
DR. LOLLING.

16. OMJ de OMA   1400   245 48
Arbeitseinsatz.
Betr: Übersicht über Anzahl und Einsatz der Häftlinge. Ich bitte
für das Frauenlager ab sofort eine besondere Übersicht zu erstellen.
Diese muss im Muster der Übersicht für das Männerlager angepasst
sein. Mit dem Sammelbegriff "Arbeitskommandos" kann ich nichts
anfangen.
I.V., gez. SOMMER, SS Obersturmführer.

17. OMF de OMA   1405   147
SS Standortarzt.
SS Hauptsturmführer REUBERT wird für den 21.2.43 zur
Berichterstattung hierher kommandiert.
DR. REUTTER, SS Hauptsturmführer.

19. OMA de OMI   1420   244 108
Betr: Überstellung von 450 Häftlingen. Bezug: dort. Fs. vom
12. und 13.1.43. Die Kdtr. des KL. NDH meldet, dass der
Häftlingstransport von 450 Häftlingen am 15.1.43 um 0910 Uhr
nach ..7 groups missed... 16.1.43, gegen Abend, dort eintrifft.
Gez. HAAS, SS Hauptsturmführer.

22. OMA de OMI   1430   245 246 ?
Betr: Überstellung von 450 Häftlingen. Bezug: Funksprüche des
SS WVH, Amtsgruppe D, vom 12 und 13.1.43. Unter Bezugnahme auf
o.a. Funksprüche, teilt die Kdtr. des KL. NDH. mit, dass der
Transport von 450 Häftlingen am 15.1.43, 0910 Uhr hat abgegangen
ist und am 16.1.43 gegen Abend in SACHSENHAUSEN eintrifft. Der
genaue Zeitpunkt des Eintreffens wird vom Transportführer,
von unterwegs aus, telefonisch durchgegeben.
Gez. HAAS, ... KL. SACHSENHAUSEN.

24. OMF de OMA   1600   249 220
Betr: Häftlingsüberstellung. Bezug: dort. Fs. vom 14.1.43, Nr.
923 KL. AU. überstellt die mit Fs. vom 14.1.43, Nr. 923,
gemeldeten jüdischen Häftlingsfacharbeiter, das sind 9 Buch-
drucker, 1 Buchbinder und 1 Graveur, mit Transport vom 8.2.43
zum KL. SACHSENHAUSEN. Die Häftlinge sind sofort in Quarantäne
zu legen. Ausreichende Marschverpflegung ist mitzugeben. KL. AU.
meldet Abgang mit dem übrigen Transport durch Fs., KL. SACHSEN-
HAUSEN Zugang fernmündlich.
I.V., gez. LIEBEHENSCHEL.

(continued)

CONFIDENTIAL   1

Konzentrationslager Niederhagen   K.Z.
eingerichtet am 12. Dezember 1939   60 Berufsverbrecher aus Oranienburg.
Diese Art der Häftlinge wurde am
16. Febr. 40 wegen Fluchtversuche
mit Erschießung von 2 Häftlingen
ersetzt durch einen Transport von
70 Bibelforschern.

Vergrößerung des "Arbeitslagers"
durch weitere Zugänge: aus K.L.   20. Febr. 40 = 30 Bibelforscher,
Oranienburg, ...   12. März 40 = 20   dto.
aus K.L. Buchenwald ....   25. Mai 40 = 100   dto.

aus K.L. Oranienburg............   22. Sept. 40 = 287 Asoziale
aus K.L. Buchenwald............   8. März 41 ≠ 90 Bibelforscher
aus K.L. Oranienburg............   27. Juni 41 = 56 Aso. und Politische
aus K.L. Dachau.................   30. Juli 41 = 3 Polische (Friseure)

Dieses Arbeitskommando wurde anfangs von dem Untersturmführer Plaul als
Kommandoführer geleitet und war dem K.L. Sachsenhausen (Oranienburg) un-
terstellt. Die am 16. Febr. 40 nach Sachsenhausen abtransportierten
Häftlinge wurden in der dortigen Strafisolierung innerhalb von 14 Ta-
gen zum größten Teil umgebracht.
Verantwortliche Blockführer der Isolierung in Sachsenhausen waren zu
der Zeit: Kuhn, Josef; Knittler ; Bogdalla; Winnig .
In dieser Isolierung wurden unter der Leitung dieser vorstehenden
Blockführer schwere Grausamkeiten verübt.1/4 der Häftlinge dieser
Isolierung starb monatlich durch Hunger, Kälte, Mißhandlung, übermäßige
Arbeitsforderungen.

Am 1. September 1941 wurde das Arbeitskommando zum selbständigen Lager
erklärt und erhielt den Namen K.L. Niederhagen, und blieb bis zum 12.
April 1943 als solches bestehen.
Die Führung dieses Lagers erhielt der inzwischen überwiesene Oberstf.
Adolf Haas, als Kommandant. Der bisherige Kommandoführer Plaul verblieb
als Lagerführer mit an verantwortlicher Stelle. Der schon oben erwähnte Oberschf. Kuhn aus Sachsenhausen brachte einen Transport Häftlinge
und blieb dann als Rapportführer in Niederhagen. Den Posten des Ar-
beitsdienstführers versah der Unterscharf. Ludwig Rehn. Der 2. Arbeitsdienstführer wurde ein Rottenführer Fritz Rau.
An weiteren Zugängen waren folgende: 23. Okt. 41 = 100 Berufsverbrecher
ferner aus Oranienburg: ....   24. Okt. 41 = 150 dto.u. Politische
aus Sachsenhausen...............   31. März 42 = 300 Juden, Polen, Deutsche u.s.w.

Vom September 40 an traten furchtbare Verhältnisse für alle Lagerein-
gesessenen ein, sodaß allein von den 287 Asozialen in wenigen Wochen

CONFIDENTIAL   2

In der Zeit vom 10.6.42 bis 22.12.42 = 818 Russen und anderer Natio-
nalitäten.
In derselben Zeit ließen von diesen Gefangenen 531 ihr Leben.
Bis zum 5. April 43 als Durchgangstransport   281   Russen

Nach Abzug von Häftlingen, die anderen Lägern zugeführt wurden,
verbleibt folgende Übersicht:
Von 306 Bibelforscherhäftlingen starben 19 im Lager
"   903 Reichsdeutsche (Aso, Poli., B.V.)
        Belgier, Holländer u.a. gingen 455 im Lager zu Grunde,
" 1933 Russen, Belgier, Franzosen "   709 "   "   "   "

Die geringe Sterbeziffer der Bibelforscher erklärt sich durch
biblische Glaubensstellung. Innere Haltung, Sauberkeit, Enthaltsam-
keit von Tabak und verkehrten geschlechtlichen Reizungen.

Unbeschreibliche Nöte entstanden durch jahrelangen Entzug von Familie und Heimat. Geringe und schlechte Ernährung und Bekleidung
brachten die zu schwerer Arbeit getriebenen Geschöpfe zur Verzweif-
lung. Einige krochen zu den mit Elektrizität geladenen Stachel-
drähten, wo sie verbrannten und von schießwütigen Posten von den
Türmen beschossen wurden. Andere liefen auf den Arbeitsplätzen über
die Postenketten um die tötliche Kugel zu erhalten. Die Erschlafften
wurden ins Lager gebracht und den grausamen Mithäftlingen übergeben,
die durch Schläge oder Kaltwasserbäder (der Wasserschlauch wurde
solange auf das Herz gehalten, bis das Opfer verstarb) das Leben be-
endeten. Die zur Ausrottung bestimmten Häftlinge wurden in den

No. 8-63
Radio message concerning the transfer of 450 prisoners from Wewelsburg to Sachsenhausen; listing of coded police and SS radio messages deciphered by the British Secret Intelligence Service
January 15, 1943
Translation on page 455

National Archives, Kew, Government Code and Cypher School: German Police Section: Decrypts of German Police Communications during Second World War, 1939–1945, HW 16/23

No. 8-62
Not shown
Excerpt from the daily population reports sent by the Niederhagen Concentration Camp administration to the Concentration Camps Inspectorate; listing of coded police and SS radio messages deciphered by the British Secret Intelligence Service
January 1943

National Archives, Kew, Government Code and Cypher School: German Police Section: Decrypts of German Police Communications during Second World War, 1939–1945, HW 16/10

The administrative offices of National Socialist concentration camps were charged with reporting the daily popu-lation levels of their respective camps to the Concentration Camps Inspectorate at Oranienburg. The British Secret Intelli-gence Service was capable of intercepting and deciphering these radio communi-cations. Its precise records thus document the evolution of prisoner totals at Nieder-hagen Concentration Camp. A steady rise in the number of prisoners is apparent for January 1943, as more and more forced laborers were transferred from Gestapo prisons.

General radio communications were also intercepted and deciphered. These contain references to the transport of 450 prisoners from Wewelsburg to Sach-senhausen Concentration Camp on January 15, 1943. kjs

No. 8-67
Excerpt from the transports listing by camp prisoner clerk, Wettin Müller
May 4, 1945
Translation on page 455

The former camp clerk, Wettin Müller, produced a report for the U.S. military authorities, who were seeking to docu-ment events at the liberated concen-tration camps. As the majority of camp records had been destroyed by the SS, he had to rely on his own notes and memory. This resulted in a contemporary listing of the transports. Of note is the reference to major transports in early 1943, because their repeated mention in reports by con-temporary witnesses could not be con-firmed by surviving camp records. kjs

National Archives, Washington D.C., NND 775032, p. 1 f.

No.8-64

Larger prisoner transports from other concentration camps to Wewelsburg
With few records having survived from the Wewelsburg Concentration Camp administrative office, data were compiled from various sources at other archives.

May 1939
100 "career criminal" prisoners from Sachsenhausen Concentration Camp
December 12, 1939
60 "career criminal" prisoners from Sachsenhausen Concentration Camp
February 16, 1940
70 Bible Student prisoners from Sachsenhausen Concentration Camp
February 20, 1940
30 Bible Student prisoners from Sachsenhausen Concentration Camp
March 12, 1940
20 Bible Student prisoners from Sachsenhausen Concentration Camp
May 25, 1940
100 Bible Student prisoners from Sachsenhausen Concentration Camp
September 22, 1940
287 German prisoners from Buchenwald Concentration Camp
March 8, 1941
90 German prisoners from Buchenwald Concentration Camp
June 27, 1941
56 German prisoners from Sachsenhausen Concentration Camp
October 22, 1941
100 German, Polish, French, Czech, stateless, and Yugoslavian prisoners from Sachsenhausen Concentration Camp
October 23, 1941
150 German, Polish, French, Czech, and Yugoslavian prisoners from Sachsenhausen Concentration Camp
March 28, 1942
300 German and Polish prisoners from Sachsenhausen Concentration Camp
February 2, 1943
10 German and Polish prisoners from Sachsenhausen Concentration Camp

No.8-65

Transfers of forced civilian laborers from Westphalian and Rhenish State Police Headquarters to Niederhagen Concentration Camp

---

June 10, 1942 to early April 1943
Over 1,500 prisoners from Bielefeld State Police Headquarters, with a majority of Soviet prisoners
June 10, 1942 to early April 1943
Over 1,000 prisoners from Dortmund State Police Headquarters, with a majority of Soviet prisoners
January 1, 1943 to January 31, 1943
105 Eastern European forced laborers, from Düsseldorf State Police Headquarters (from labor education camps)

No.8-66

Prisoner transfers from Wewelsburg to other concentration camps

---

September 1, 1939
98 "career criminal" prisoners to Sachsenhausen Concentration Camp
February 16, 1940
58 "career criminal" prisoners to Sachsenhausen Concentration Camp
February 10, 1941
10 German prisoners to Sachsenhausen Concentration Camp
June 29, 1941
40 German prisoners to Sachsenhausen Concentration Camp
August 1942
126 German, Polish, and Soviet prisoners to Dachau Concentration Camp
January 17, 1943
450 prisoners, including Soviets and Germans, to Sachsenhausen Concentration Camp
January 30, 1943
587 Polish, French, German, Dutch, Belgian, and Serbian prisoners to Sachsenhausen Concentration Camp
February 26, 1943
69 French and Belgian prisoners to Dachau Concentration Camp
April 1943
Ca. 400 prisoners to Ravensbrück Concentration Camp
April 1943
Ca. 200 prisoners to Dachau Concentration Camp
April 12, 1943
339 Soviet and German prisoners to Buchenwald Concentration Camp
May 7, 1943
Ca. 150 prisoners to Bergen-Belsen Concentration Camp
May 30, 1943
2 Bible Student prisoners to Bergen-Belsen Concentration Camp
June 2, 1943
3 Bible Student prisoners to Bergen-Belsen Concentration Camp kjs

---

No.8-70
Not shown
Excerpt from the Paderborn police prison register
January – February 1943
Besides personal data, registers at police prisons listed each prisoner's arrest grounds, detention period, and subsequent destination. On several occasions, the police register's "end of detention" column is marked "Niederhagen C.C." The page from the Paderborn police register displayed in the exhibition shows three entries. Two Soviet and one Polish forced laborer were sent from the police prison to Niederhagen Concentration Camp on January 27 and February 3, 1943. The grounds for arrest were listed as "fugitive" or "abandonment of work post." This shows that protective detention was also imposed upon forced laborers in Paderborn and that they were imprisoned at Niederhagen Concentration Camp. kjs/an

Landesarchiv NRW, Abteilung Ostwestfalen-Lippe, Detmold, D 2C Paderborn, no. 3, p. 69 f.

No.8-69
Not shown
Excerpt from the Dortmund police prison register
June 1942
The page from the Dortmund police prison register shown in the exhibition documents the initial internment of two Soviet prisoners in Wewelsburg after transfer from a Gestapo prison. On June 10, 1942, the two Soviet forced laborers, aged 16 and 18, arrived in Wewelsburg. The grounds for detention was cited simply as "political." While Peter Ivanzov, age 18, died in Wewelsburg, the fate of Dimitri T., age 16, remains unknown.

Niederhagen Concentration Camp thus became an internment and disciplinary camp for Gestapo offices in the Rhineland and in Westphalia. Additional incarcerations on the initiative of state police headquarters in Bielefeld, Düsseldorf, Paderborn, and Osnabrück are documented, as well as several from Cologne. A majority of the forced laborers had previously worked in the Ruhr Region. The civilian forced laborers were predominantly from Ukraine, the designated recruitment basin for the Westphalia labor office. kjs/an

Landesarchiv NRW, Abteilung Westfalen, Münster, Polizeipräsidium Dortmund, Haftbuch, p. 240 f.

No.8-71
Not shown
Gestapo file of the Soviet prisoner of war Wassil E., Osnabrück Gestapo headquarters
January 1943
The Gestapo offices created a specific file for each prisoner, indicating personal data, the grounds for detention, and the prisoner's subsequent destination. In addition to this file, the Gestapo generated personal records, including a precise log of the prisoner's interrogation. However, these personal records are missing for the Osnabrück Gestapo headquarters, which created this file on Soviet prisoner of war Wassil E., born in 1919 in Kirov. He presumably attempted to escape in the winter of 1942 – 1943 to go into hiding as a foreign laborer. He was apprehended and arrested by the Gestapo. On January 14, 1943, he was sent to Niederhagen Concentration Camp per order of the head of the Security Police and the SD on December 16, 1942. After disbandment of the camp, he was transferred to Buchenwald Concentration Camp. His subsequent fate is unknown. kjs

Stadtarchiv Osnabrück, Gestapo-Eingangskartei

Geheime Staatspolizei
Staatspolizeileitstelle
M ü n s t e r ^estf.   Münster,den   1943
II E 3 Nr. 111/42 g -

1.) Gemäss Erlass des RSHA. vom 17.12.42 - IV - 656/42 g-
     sind vertragsbrüchige fremdvölkische Arbeiter unmittel=
     bar dem nächstgelegenen Konzentrationslager zu über=
     weisen. Für die hiesige Dienststelle kommt das Kl.-
     _____in Betracht.

·2.) _____ist am_____1943 mit
     Sammeltransport vom Polizeigefängnis Münster dem Kl.-
     _____überstellt worden.

3.) Schreiben: An das
                 Polizeipräsidium - Ausländerabtl.-
           dem Herrn
                 Landrat - Ausländerabtl.-
                 in _____
     Betrifft: Ostarbeiter_____
               geboren am:_____in:_____
     Vorgang: Ohne.

                 _____ist wegen Vertragsbruchs
           und _____für längere Zeit
           einem Konzentrationslager überstellt worden.

4.) Schreiben: An das
                 Arbeitsamt
                 in_____
     Betrifft: Wie Ziffer 2.)
     Vorgang: Ohne.

                 Text wie Ziffer 2.)
                      J.A.

No. 8-68
Form used by the Münster Gestapo for internment in a concentration camp
Soviet laborers were at the mercy of the arbitrary measures of the Gestapo. This led to a rapid rise in the internment of laborers from the East (*Ostarbeiter*) at German concentration camps. To streamline mass internments, the Münster Gestapo devised a pre-printed form listing the eight processing steps that the Gestapo official had to carry out. These essentially consisted of reports to the competent police stations and employment offices. The process was formalized to the point where only the *Ostarbeiter*'s date and place of birth needed to be entered, along with the relevant concentration camp and internment date. kjs/an
Landesarchiv NRW, Abteilung Westfalen, Münster, Politische Polizei, Driller Buch, no. 362

No. 8-72
Whipping bench
Corporal punishment was meted out on a whipping bench. The prisoner was placed over the wooden whipping bench and restrained at the legs and upper body. The lashes were administered by SS personnel or a prisoner functionary using a bull whip; 25 blows was customary. The prisoner was forced to count out the blows. Prisoners only rarely received medical care following a beating, so injuries to the back an d kidneys were slow to heal. kjs
Auschwitz-Birkenau State Museum, Oświęcim, Poland. Object no. 854

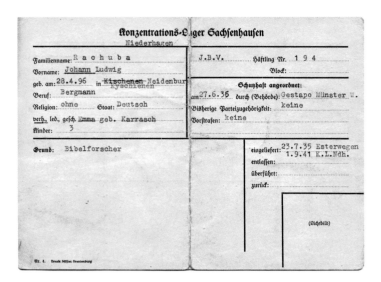

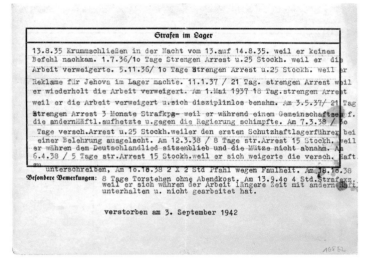

No. 8-75
Not shown
Prisoner file for Georg Klohe

Over the course of his concentration camp captivity, Georg Klohe, a Bible Student, was officially punished three times. At Sachsenhausen Concentration Camp, he was given three days of strict lockdown for having allegedly "done poor work despite a warning." Six days later, on August 30, 1939, he was sentenced to hang from a stake for 30 minutes for "not working." At Niederhagen Concentration Camp, he was subjected to 25 lashes for having contact with an *SS-Unterführer*, through whom he had hoped to obtain a musical instrument.

Georg Klohe was known for his musicality; he was thus frequently had to direct the prisoner singing on the concentration camp roll call area. Finally, in 1944, at the external work detachment in Wewelsburg, he managed in his capacity as a maintenance workshop foreman to officially obtain materials to build a cello through SS Construction Management, and to actually build the instrument. kjs

Leihgabe der Wachtturm-Gesellschaft der Zeugen Jehovas, Selters
Kreismuseum Wewelsburg, inv. no. 16662

No. 8-73
Prisoner file for Johann Rachuba
Translation on page 456

Loan from the Wachtturm-Gesellschaft der Zeugen Jehovas, Selters
Kreismuseum Wewelsburg, inv. no. 16862

No. 8-74
Johann Rachuba with his wife, Emma
Before 1935

Wachtturm-Gesellschaft der Zeugen Jehovas, Geschichtsarchiv, Selters

Johann Rachuba, born in 1896 in Ryschiene-Neidenburg, was taken into protective detention in 1935 because of his religious affiliation with the Bible Students. He was then imprisoned at Esterwegen Concentration Camp and later transferred to Sachsenhausen Concentration Camp. In 1940 he was moved to Wewelsburg. The SS guards felt provoked by his unshakeable faith and steadfast manner, resulting in his subjection to no less than twelve camp punishments and countless instances of abuse in all the camps he passed through. The SS thought it could break his faith with violence, yet its attempt to make an example of him failed. To the contrary, Bible Students honored Johann Rachuba as a martyr; even inmates from other prisoner groups respected him for his attitude. Johann Rachuba finally succumbed on September 3, 1942. The official cause of his death was "physical weakness." kjs

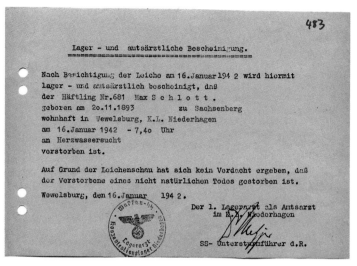

No. 8-77
Letter from the Büren district administrator to the Wewelsburg registrar
January 8, 1942
Translation on page 456
As early as January 1942 and in compliance with new service guidelines for registry offices, the district of Büren ordered terms such as "prisoner," "concentration camp," "prison camp," and other similar expressions be stricken from the death register of the Wewelsburg registry office. The impression of imprisonment was to be avoided. Similarly, in writing camp and administrative medical reports, the camp physician was to disguise the role of mistreatment in camp deaths by using standard phrases such as "suicide by hanging," or "shot while trying to escape." This procedure eliminated the need to notify the district attorney's office, legally required in suspected cases of unnatural death. kjs
Kreisarchiv Paderborn, B 417

No. 8-76
Camp and administrative medical report for Max Schlott
January 16, 1942
Loan from Standesamt Büren, Leichenpässe, Bl. 483
Kreismuseum Wewelsburg, inv. no. 16888

No. 8-78
Telegram from Camp Commandant Adolf Hass announcing the death of Alman Rose
February 6, 1942
Alman Rose, a Sinto prisoner, died on February 5, 1942, at Niederhagen Concentration Camp. The official cause of his death was heart failure. As notification for his relatives, the camp commandant Adolf Haas sent a telegram to the address: "Trailer, Franciscan Meadow, Stettin." kjs
Kreismuseum Wewelsburg, inv. no. 16922

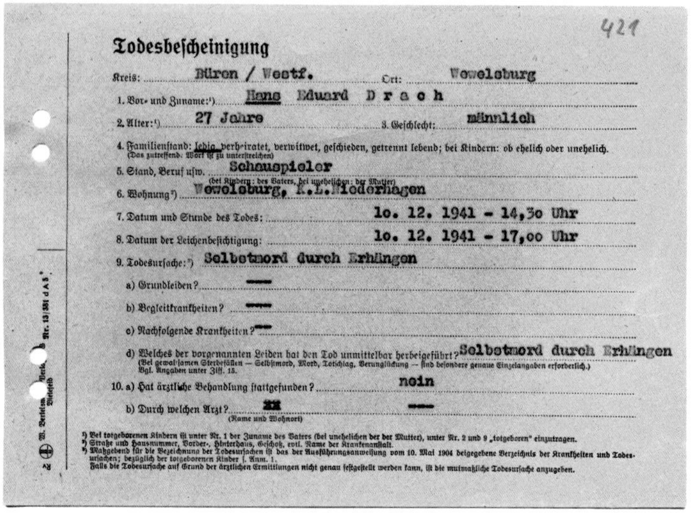

421

Todesbescheinigung

Kreis: Büren / Westf. Ort: Wewelsburg

1. Vor- und Zuname:¹) Hans Eduard Drach
2. Alter:¹) 27 Jahre 3. Geschlecht: männlich
4. Familienstand: ledig, verheiratet, verwitwet, geschieden, getrennt lebend; bei Kindern: ob ehelich oder unehelich. (Das zutreffende Wort ist zu unterstreichen)
5. Stand, Beruf usw. Schauspieler (bei Kindern: des Vaters, bei unehelichen: der Mutter)
6. Wohnung²) Wewelsburg, K.L. Niederhagen
7. Datum und Stunde des Todes: 10. 12. 1941 – 14,30 Uhr
8. Datum der Leichenbesichtigung: 10. 12. 1941 – 17,00 Uhr
9. Todesursache:³) Selbstmord durch Erhängen
   a) Grundleiden? —
   b) Begleitkrankheiten? —
   c) Nachfolgende Krankheiten? —
   d) Welches der vorgenannten Leiden hat den Tod unmittelbar herbeigeführt? Selbstmord durch Erhängen (Bei gewaltsamen Sterbefällen — Selbstmord, Mord, Totschlag, Verunglückung — sind besondere genaue Einzelangaben erforderlich.) Vgl. Angaben unter Ziff. 15.
10. a) Hat ärztliche Behandlung stattgefunden? nein
    b) Durch welchen Arzt? — (Name und Wohnort)

¹) Bei totgeborenen Kindern ist unter Nr. 1 der Zuname des Vaters (bei unehelichen der der Mutter), unter Nr. 2 und 9 „totgeboren" einzutragen.
²) Straße und Hausnummer, Vorder-, Hinterhaus, Geschoß, evtl. Name der Krankenanstalt.
³) Maßgebend für die Bezeichnung der Todesursachen ist das der Ausführungsanweisung vom 10. Mai 1904 beigegebene Verzeichnis der Krankheiten und Todesursachen; bezüglich der totgeborenen Kinder s. Anm. 1.
Falls die Todesursache auf Grund der ärztlichen Ermittlungen nicht genau festgestellt werden kann, ist die mutmaßliche Todesursache anzugeben.

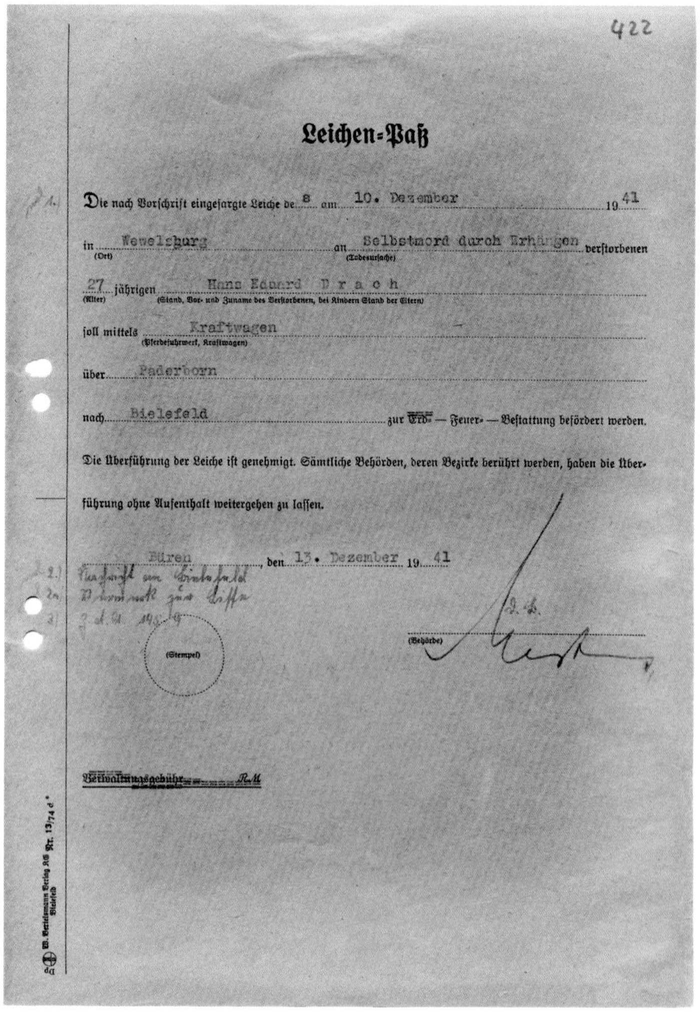

422

Leichen-Paß

Die nach Vorschrift eingesargte Leiche des am 10. Dezember 1941 in Wewelsburg (Ort) an Selbstmord durch Erhängen (Todesursache) verstorbenen 27 (Alter) jährigen Hans Eduard Drach (Stand, Vor- und Zuname des Verstorbenen, bei Kindern Stand der Eltern) soll mittels Kraftwagen (Pferdefuhrwerk, Kraftwagen) über Paderborn nach Bielefeld zur ~~Erd-~~ — Feuer- — Bestattung befördert werden.

Die Überführung der Leiche ist genehmigt. Sämtliche Behörden, deren Bezirke berührt werden, haben die Überführung ohne Aufenthalt weitergehen zu lassen.

Büren, den 13. Dezember 1941

(Stempel) (Behörde)

~~Verwaltungsgebühr~~ RM

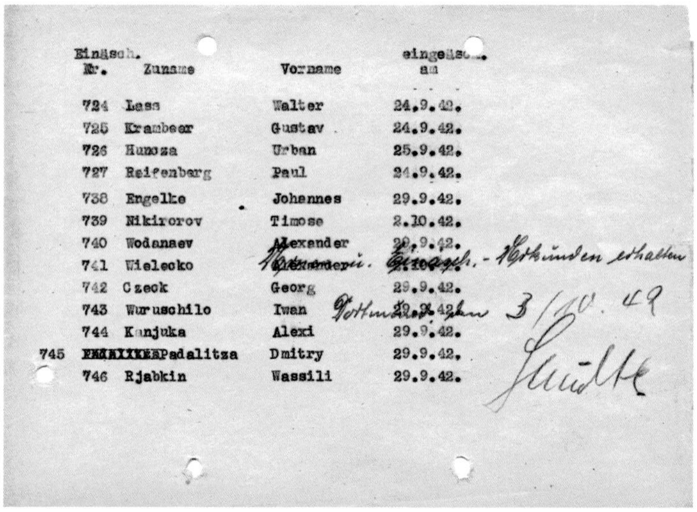

Einäsch. Nr.	Zuname	Vorname	eingeäsch. am
724	Lass	Walter	24.9.42.
725	Krambeer	Gustav	24.9.42.
726	Humsza	Urban	25.9.42.
727	Reifenberg	Paul	24.9.42.
738	Engelke	Johannes	29.9.42.
739	Nikirorov	Timose	2.10.42.
740	Wodanaev	Alexander	29.9.42.
741	Wielecko	Alexander	29.9.42.
742	Czeck	Georg	29.9.42.
743	Wuruschilo	Iwan	29.9.42.
744	Kanjuka	Alexi	29.9.42.
745	Padalitza	Dmitry	29.9.42.
746	Rjabkin	Wassili	29.9.42.

3/10.42 Schulte

No. 8-79

Part of a receipt signed by *SS-Sturmscharführer* Friedrich Schulte after the transport of funerary urns and related documents from Dortmund crematorium to Wewelsburg
October 3, 1942

The corpses of prisoners were cremated in Berlin-Treptow, Bielefeld-Brackwede, Bochum, or Dortmund. This receipt shows that *SS-Sturmscharführer* Friedrich Schulte signed off on receiving 53 urns and associated documents sent from Dortmund to Wewelsburg. Although a place of burial, including a parcel number, was officially identified after the war in administrative correspondence, no one remembers the carrying out of burials. Presumably, the ashes of the deceased were simply scattered. With the number of dead constantly growing and the numerous corpse transports drawing public attention, the camp leadership ordered construction of an on-site crematorium at the back of the industrial area. It appears that a mobile cremation oven was initially employed before the crematorium went into operation in October 1942; it was used until disbandment of the camp in spring 1943. kjs

Kreismuseum Wewelsburg, inv. no. 16909

No. 8-80

Death certificate for Hans Drach

Loan from Standesamt Büren, Leichenpässe, Bl. 421
Kreismuseum Wewelsburg, inv. no. 16869

No. 8-81

Corpse transport permit for Hans Drach for transfer to Bielefeld

Loan from Standesamt Büren, Leichenpässe, Bl. 422
Kreismuseum Wewelsburg, inv. no. 16870

Hans Drach, born in 1914 in Geneva, Switzerland, joined the socialist movement and agitprop group, Kolonne Links, in Berlin. Presumably on orders from the communist party, the writer emigrated to the Soviet Union to escape the Gestapo. On the application for membership in the club of foreign workers, his date of arrival is stated as 1934. Together with other noteworthy artists in exile, he founded the German Kolkhoz Theater in Dnepropetrovsk, where he wrote his popular song, "Mein Vater wird gesucht" ("They're Looking for my Father"). In December 1936, Hans Drach was arrested as a suspected spy. Following the Hitler-Stalin pact of 1939, he and other exiled Germans were handed over to the Gestapo. By way of Sachsenhausen, he ultimately arrived in Wewelsburg on October 22, 1941. kjs

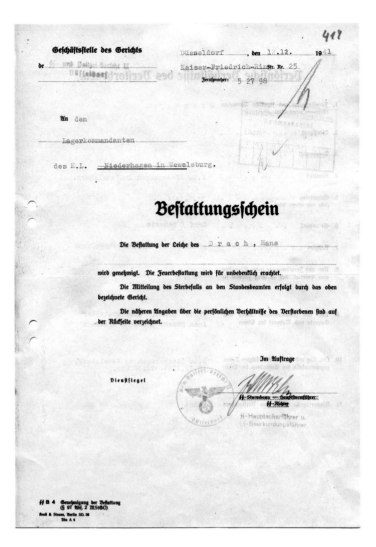

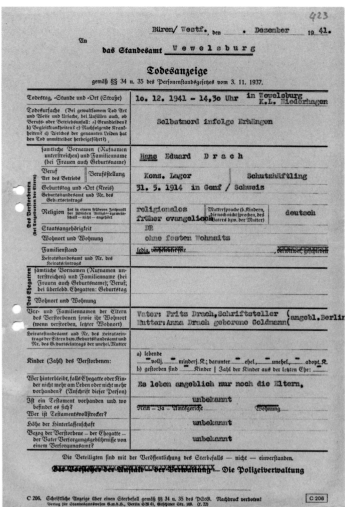

No. 8-82
Burial certificate for Hans Drach, issued by the SS and Police Court II in Düsseldorf December 12, 1941

Loan from the Standesamt Büren, Leichenpässe, Bl. 419
Kreismuseum Wewelsburg, inv. no. 16867

No. 8-83
Death notice for Hans Drach

Loan from the Standesamt Büren, Leichenpässe, Bl. 423
Kreismuseum Wewelsburg, inv. no. 16871

Hans Drach died only seven weeks after his arrival in Wewelsburg, on December 10, 1941. In the numerous documents generated following his death and cremation, the official cause of death was stated as "suicide by hanging." The real cause of his death is unknown. The possibility should not be excluded that the SS murdered Drach, in imitation of his song, "They're Looking for my Father." In the song, a communist is murdered by SA men, and his death is then portrayed in official documents as a suicide. There are significant parallels to Hans Drach's actual fate. The mass of documents generated after his death shows the considerable bureaucratic energy expended on the dead prisoners, in contrast to the inhumane conditions they suffered under in the concentration camps while alive. kjs

8.2
Wewelsburg as an External Work Detachment of Buchenwald Concentration Camp 1943 – 1945

After the disbandment of Niederhagen Concentration Camp in April 1943, 42 prisoners remained in Wewelsburg: 40 Bible Students and 2 political prisoners. They were moved to the workshop barracks in the industrial area and placed under the authority of Buchenwald Concentration Camp. The external work detachment was guarded by only five SS men.

The daily death of prisoners came to a halt. The inmates took on small jobs in the village and at Wewelsburg Castle; to some degree they could even move about freely.

During the last two years before the camp's liberation on April 2, 1945, living and working conditions at Wewelsburg were vastly different than at other concentration camps, where punishing labor in the armaments industry, death marches, and mass mortality prevailed.

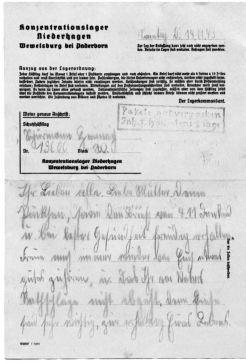

No. 8-84
Letter from Heinrich Schürmann to his family
November 14, 1943
Although by November 1943 the camp was long since organizationally a part of Buchenwald Concentration Camp, correspondence by external work detachment prisoners was still carried out on letter forms of the disbanded Niederhagen Concentration Camp. Presumably, leftover supplies had to be used up. The affiliation to Buchenwald Concentration Camp is apparent in both the high prisoner number (13600) and the inclusion of "Block W" in the return address field. Block W designated the Wewelsburg external work detachment.

Despite censorship, Heinrich Schürmann dared to allude to their common faith with a reference to "fatherly advice." By this time Bible Student prisoners were again allowed more than the seven lines per letter, the additional penalty they had had to bear for years as a result of their religious faith. kjs

Loan from the Wachtturm-Gesellschaft der Zeugen Jehovas, Selters
Kreismuseum Wewelsburg, inv. no. 16860

Niederhagen Concentration Camp Wewelsburg, near Paderborn
Sunday, 14 November, 1943
Excerpt from the camp rules:
Each prisoner may receive and send 1 letter or 1 postcard a month. A letter may not contain more than 4 pages of 15 lines each, and must be clearly legible. Correspondence not conforming to these requirements will not be conveyed or delivered. No packages may be received, no matter what they contain. Money may be sent, but only via postal money order; sending cash by letter is prohibited. Messages written on postal money orders are prohibited, and will result in rejection of the mail. Everything can be bought at the camp. National Socialist periodicals are allowed, but must be ordered by the prisoner himself via the concentration camp mailroom. Confusing or illegible letters cannot be censored and will therefore be destroyed. Sending pictures or photographs is prohibited.
The Camp Commandant
[stamp] Wrap packages firmly contents f. max 2 days

My exact address:
Protective detention prisoner
Schürmann, Heinrich
No. 13600 Block W
Niederhagen Concentration Camp
Wewelsburg, near Paderborn
My dear loved ones! Dear mother. I gratefully received your little package, along with the letter of 11 April, with joy and in the best of health. I'm always happy to hear something good from you, and that you have not strayed from father's advice, as this is important to preserve your lives. [back of page]
Greetings to Paula. Packages all gratefully received. Greetings to Willy and Hugo as well as all other relatives and friends. Dear mother, if Rudi and Hugo can use any of my underwear or suits or shoes, give them to them. When I return we'll get new ones. With all my love, warmest regards to all of you, in the hope of seeing you all again in fine health from your happy Heinz
Greetings to Viktor
[stamp] censored mail

Translation of a transcription

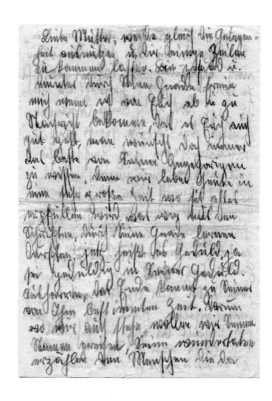

No. 8-85

Letter from Heinrich Schürmann
Undated
Heinrich Schürmann, a Jehovah's
Witness, managed to evade mail
censorship when sending this letter; the SS would never have tolerated a letter of such religious tenor.
Via a hiding place in the plant
nursery near the train station where
a Bible Student prisoner worked,
members of the external work
detachment succeeded in smuggling letters out of the camp to
contact their families.

These conspiratorial efforts
went so far as to allow prisoners to
have secret visits from wives and
parents. They even managed to
periodically switch off the electric
fence surrounding the camp,
allowing the prisoners to leave the
concentration camp grounds at
night or to receive visits without
alerting the SS guards. Because it
was known that Bible Student prisoners for religious reasons would
not attempt escape, they were
guarded with less vigilance. kjs

Loan from the Wachtturm-Gesellschaft
der Zeugen Jehovas, Selters
Kreismuseum Wewelsburg, inv. no. 16861

Dear Mother, I'll use this chance to quickly
write you a few lines. I'm healthy and in
good spirits through His grace. I'm happy
to now and again get news from all of you
that things are alright; it's natural to
always wish the best for one's family, as
we're living in important times, in which
we will see fulfilled everything we have
gathered from scripture through His
grace; what we need now is patience; yes
be patient in His patience. Endure,
the End will come at His appointed hour.
Hence, whatever comes to us, let us praise
His name, spread word of His miracles
to those who hunger and thirst before us.

Translation of a transcription

No. 8-87
Not shown

Draft of a letter from Max Hollweg
to a friend, written in shorthand
Winter 1944 – 1945
Loan from the Wachtturm-Gesellschaft
der Zeugen Jehovas, Selters
Kreismuseum Wewelsburg, inv. no. 16910

No. 8-86
Not shown

Envelope of the letter from Anna
Hollweg to her brother Max
January 9, 1945
When Anna Hollweg wrote to her
brother Max at the camp, she used
the old designation, "Niederhagen
Concentration Camp," which had long
since been disbanded. The proper
procedure would have been to write
to the main camp at Buchenwald, so
that the letter would be forwarded
from there to the subcamp. Presumably because of the camp's earlier
autonomy, it remained possible to
write there directly. Yet, she added
the correct designation, "Block W,"
to indicate the Wewelsburg subcamp.
The high prisoner number also indicates the affiliation with Buchenwald.
kjs

Loan from the Wachtturm-Gesellschaft
der Zeugen Jehovas, Selters
Kreismuseum Wewelsburg, inv. no. 16855/1

My dear Willi,
It's with mixed feelings that I address you
as such. My life experience up to this point
has brought me to an earnest conception
of friendship.

I'm open and I do not like hypocrisy,
and self-delusion even less. The lines of
such warmth and kindness which you
wrote to me on 10 September now prove
beyond any doubt that you appreciate
straight talk and will not take offense at
this introduction to my letter. I'm very glad
that you feel well living with my relatives,
and render thanks for this to the Source of
all life. I can well understand that I'm
often the subject of conversation, though
this should be attributed to my circumstances more than to the excellence of my
person. Without my God, who without fail
surrounds me with His protection, I am
the most wretched creature you could
imagine. Understanding this, I forcefully
direct all respect and honor to Him who is
worthy of respect and honor. As I mentioned in earlier letters, I received the
package of 18 September. Dear Anna's
bicycle accident has certainly made life
difficult for her. I wish for your friendship
with Erwin to grow and deepen and would
love to surprise you one day in person.
But that time has yet to come. I believe
rather in your commitment, although it is
hardly to be coveted. As to your splendid
endeavor, I salute you as a colleague, yet
with a rather different point of view. I don't
believe, for example, that the Highest
would lend his power and support to any
military formation, of whatever
nationality.

Translation of a transcription

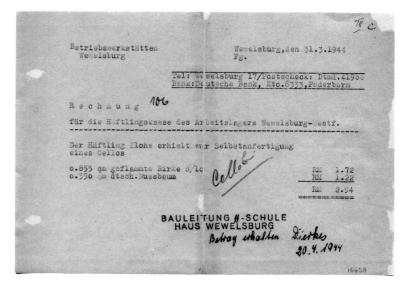

No. 8-88
Draft of a letter from Max Hollweg to his brother, Artur, written in shorthand
Winter 1944 – 1945

During the period when Wewelsburg was an external work detachment, Max Hollweg frequently drafted his letters in shorthand. An interesting detail in the letter is his reference to listening to the zither and cello. In the summer of 1944, a fellow prisoner, Georg Klohe, ordered materials to build a cello. In the winter, members of the external work detachment evidently had the opportunity to sit together and play music. kjs

Wachtturm-Gesellschaft der Zeugen Jehovas, Selters, Nachlass Max Hollweg

Dear Artur,
I'm sitting here, listening to zither and cello music but can't fully enjoy it because it's been so long since I've heard from you. I'm throwing my ideas on the page in shorthand and will write them out for you tomorrow. The mail from home is terribly slow. Today I received a letter from 10 September. Although I write every eight days, sometimes I have to wait a quarter of a year for an answer. Our soldier, Willi, who stayed with my family for a time, wrote me that everyone is still doing well. He seems a fine young fellow. Our Anna is back in the hospital with a hematoma on her knee after that fall from the bike; with good treatment, she's bound to heal quickly. Mother manages to get by, more or less, a real miracle at that age. I still hope to see her again, that would be her greatest joy in life. Her letters show an overwhelming love for me. God will certainly reward her selfless care.

Personally, I'm still doing well and I hope the same for you; please give me a sign of life. One of my letters to you was returned; I hope the address is still valid. One makes such an effort with all that writing, and is happy if only half of it gets to those it's intended to reach. But many obstacles are gone now; things seem to be improving. I wish you now a Happy New Year and a healthy reunion.
All the best, your brother Max.

Translation of a transcription

No. 8-89
Invoice for the purchase of wood used to build a cello
March 31, 1944

Loan from the Wachtturm-Gesellschaft der Zeugen Jehovas, Selters
Kreismuseum Wewelsburg, inv. no. 16658

No. 8-91
Georg Klohe with his cello
Ca. 1960s

Kreismuseum Wewelsburg, Fotoarchiv

No. 8-90
Not shown
Invoice for machine work to build a cello
June 15, 1944

Loan from the Wachtturm-Gesellschaft der Zeugen Jehovas, Selters
Kreismuseum Wewelsburg, inv. no. 16659

At the small, more manageable external work detachment, the SS exerted markedly less pressure on the prisoners than in Niederhagen Concentration Camp. The degree to which relations between prisoners and the SS had relaxed at the external work detachment is apparent from the following: In 1944, Georg Klohe, as a Bible Student prisoner, headed the camp's maintenance workshop and succeeded in obtaining materials to build a cello officially through the office of SS Construction Management. The invoices for the purchase of the materials have survived. In 1942, his efforts at securing a musical instrument through an SS personnel had earned him 25 lashes. The cello survived the concentration camp, and Georg Klohe played it for the rest of his life. The instrument is now preserved at the Watchtower Society in Selters. kjs

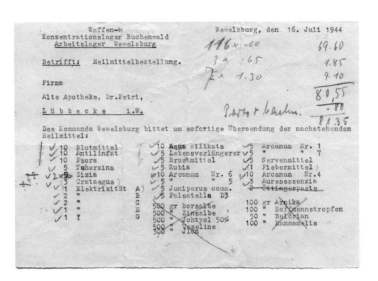

No. 8-94

Letter from Wewelsburg Labor Camp to Dr. Petri, Alte Apotheke (Old Pharmacy), Lübbecke, regarding an order of medical items July 16, 1944

Loan from the Wachtturm-Gesellschaft der Zeugen Jehovas, Selters
Kreismuseum Wewelsburg, inv. no. 16854

No. 8-96
Not shown

Letter to the "Former pharmaceutical factory, Jos. Leifel, Cologne, Klettenberg" July 16, 1944

Loan from the Wachtturm-Gesellschaft der Zeugen Jehovas, Selters
Kreismuseum Wewelsburg, inv. no. 16894

No. 8-93
Not shown

Letter from Wewelsburg Labor Camp to Dr. Petri, Alte Apotheke (Old Pharmacy), Lübbecke, regarding an order of medical items June 3, 1944

Loan from the Wachtturm-Gesellschaft der Zeugen Jehovas, Selters
Kreismuseum Wewelsburg, inv. no. 16853

No. 8-95
Not shown

Cash-on-delivery stub for Dr. Petri, Alte Apotheke (Old Pharmacy), Lübbecke August 26, 1944

Loan from the Wachtturm-Gesellschaft der Zeugen Jehovas, Selters
Kreismuseum Wewelsburg, inv. no. 16857

No. 8-92
Not shown

Handwritten list of required medications for Dr. Petri April 13, 1944

Loan from the Wachtturm-Gesellschaft der Zeugen Jehovas, Selters
Kreismuseum Wewelsburg, inv. no. 16850

Former pharm. factory Jos. Leifel
Cologne–Klettenberg
Petersberger Straße
Please immediately send the following, cash-on-delivery, and under the original terms
10 x Leifozon oxygen p.
10 x Pharmidolax
10 x Lecithin Zell. nutritional salts
3 x Iodine health drops
each 50 gr.
July 16, 1944

Translation of a transcription

No. 8-99

Max Hollweg's notebook, with entries for prisoners in the sick bay and their treatments May 1943 to February 1945

With meticulous care, Max Hollweg recorded in his notebooks the illnesses of his fellow prisoners and the treatments they received. The prisoners were frequently beset by various types of colds, inflammation (boils) and injuries. Although not nearly as subject to stress and mistreatment from the SS guards as they had once been at Niederhagen Concentration Camp, prisoners continued to suffer from injuries, emaciation, infirmity, and malnutrition. kjs

Loan from the Wachtturm-Gesellschaft der Zeugen Jehovas, Selters
Kreismuseum Wewelsburg, inv. no. 16669

No. 8-98
Not shown

Handwritten list of illnesses afflicting SS guards and prisoners Early March to the end of April, no year given [1944]

Loan from the Wachtturm-Gesellschaft der Zeugen Jehovas, Selters
Kreismuseum Wewelsburg, inv. no. 16856

Beginning of March – e. April
2 SS guards pneumonia
2 „ „ stomach and intestinal gastritis
1 „ „ heart problems
2 „ „ flu and bronchitis
Prisoner ailments
during this time
Joint and muscle rheumatism 9
Eczema 3 ... 4
Stomach and/or intestine 9
Bladder and/or kidneys 3
Flu 2
Pneumonia 2
Constipation (chronic)
Heart and nerve conditions 4
Plus daily hand and foot injuries
From quarry work etc.

Translation of a transcription

No. 8-97
Not shown

Listing and deliveries of medications from the prisoner infirmary and pharmacy at Buchenwald to Wewelsburg Labor Camp February 19, 1945

Camp Physician Dr. Hagel provided information on prisoner illnesses and accidents in his monthly reports to the Buchenwald Concentration Camp medical administration, from which he regularly obtained drugs for treatment of SS personnel and prisoners. kjs

Loan from the Wachtturm-Gesellschaft der Zeugen Jehovas, Selters
Kreismuseum Wewelsburg, inv. no. 16917

Medical care at the Wewelsburg external work detachment of Buchenwald Concentration Camp once again fell under the responsibility of the aged Dr. Hagel, from Büren, who had previously provided assistance at the concentration camp. Max Hollweg, who had previously worked as a prisoner medic in the Niederhagen sick bay, aided him in treating illnesses and keeping track of medical stores. Missing medications were ordered from various pharmacies in Lübbecke and Cologne, or procured from Buchenwald Concentration Camp.

Although *Außenkommando* (external work detachment) was the organizationally accurate designation for the camp in Wewelsburg, contemporary documents most often refer to "Wewelsburg Labor Camp." The term *Restkommando* (remaining detachment) became common after the war. kjs

This chapter focuses primarily on the prisoners' experience at the concentration camp. The various grounds for detention provide valuable insight into the prisoners' backgrounds and standpoints, while the hierarchical classification of prisoners exposes the perfidious sophistication of SS camp rule. The Soviet and Jehovah's Witnesses prisoner groups played an important role in the life of the camp and are therefore given particular attention.

Few objects or original written sources from daily life at the camp have survived. Several of the rare remaining items are placed in the context of the former prisoners' memories of their living and working conditions. Lastly, the villagers' ambivalent attitude toward the concentration camp and the prisoners is explored.

9 Concentration Camp Prisoners in Wewelsburg

9.1
Prisoners at the Concentration Camp in Wewelsburg

The German prisoners at Niederhagen Concentration Camp came from various social strata. The course of the war caused a sharp increase in the number of foreign prisoners. From 1942, Soviet prisoners, both forced laborers and prisoners of war, arrived at the camp in increasing numbers. They constituted the largest category of prisoners, with the highest death rate. Jehovah's Witnesses, then also known as Ernest Bible Students, made up a small group at the camp, but were nonetheless decisive in the evolution of the camp. In the early phase of the camp in Wewelsburg, they sometimes represented the only prisoner group and were therefore compelled to take on many of the functionary positions within the camp administration of the prisoners set up by the SS.

The SS developed a rigidly hierarchical system of social rank that intensified existing social disparities and antagonisms between prisoner groups at the camp.

Paul Ulbricht

Max Schlott

No. 9-2
Paul Ulbricht with his son-in-law,
Albert Schumann, and grandson Klaus
Ca. 1936
In 1933, active Social Democrat and administrative inspector Paul Ulbricht, born 1887 in Freiberg, Saxony, was caught up in the first wave of arrests by the National Socialists following their accession to power. Though quickly released, he remained under observation. In 1940, he was informed on and sentenced to a year in prison by the Dresden Special Court for "seditious statements" under provisions of the Treachery Act. He was also expelled from the civil service and stripped of his pension. His daughter Hildegard's legal efforts to reestablish his pension rights failed. Instead, after serving his sentence, Ulbricht was taken into protective detention and sent to Sachsenhausen Concentration Camp in May 1941. In early 1942, Paul Ulbricht arrived in Wewelsburg, where he died on February 8, 1943, from "cardiac insufficiency and gastroenteritis." kjs
Kreismuseum Wewelsburg, Fotoarchiv

No. 9-1
Max Schlott
1930 – 1938
After serving a jail sentence, mechanic Max Anton Schlott, born 1893 in Sachsenberg, Saxony, was again arrested in Rostock for alleged "forgery of official documents." The father of three was then taken into preventive detention by the Gestapo and sent to Sachsenhausen Concentration Camp.

He arrived at Niederhagen Concentration Camp on January 1, 1941, and was assigned the green triangle of the "career criminal." Max Schlott died on January 16, 1942; the official cause of death was "cardiac edema." kjs
Kreismuseum Wewelsburg, Fotoarchiv

Fritz Skirde

Otto Preuss

No. 9-3
Fritz Skirde
Before 1938
For a remark critical of the regime made at work, industrial draftsman Fritz Skirde, born 1895 in Hamburg, was reported by a co-worker and arrested by the Gestapo. During his interrogation, the committed Social Democrat openly criticized the Führer and the political situation in Germany. In August 1938, the Special Court sentenced Fritz Skirde to two years' imprisonment for "violation of the Treachery Act." His brother and brother-in-law were also arrested at this time for illegal political expression. Having served his sentence, Skirde was taken into protective detention by the Gestapo and sent to Sachsenhausen Concentration Camp in May 1940. On March 28, 1942, he was transported to Wewelsburg. A few days later, on April 3, 1942, Fritz Skirde died there; the cause of death was given as "edema." kjs
Kreismuseum Wewelsburg, Fotoarchiv

No. 9-4
Otto Preuss (third from left) with his Belgian agitation and propaganda group, "Roode Rebellen"
Ca. 1936
Otto Preuss, born 1913 in Hamborn, was early involved in the Socialist Workers' Youth and joined the Young Communist League. In the spring of 1933, the mason by trade was briefly arrested in Herford; a search of his home had uncovered flyers from the German Communist Party (KPD). In July 1933, he avoided arrest by fleeing to Belgium. Here, in 1934, he joined the agitprop group "Roode Rebellen," performing at various locations around the country. Following the National Socialist invasion of Belgium, Otto Preuss was arrested in October 1940 and brought to Germany. Unbeknownst to him, his German citizenship had been revoked in 1938. On March 25, 1941, he was imprisoned at Sachsenhausen Concentration Camp as a stateless political prisoner; from there, he arrived in Wewelsburg on October 24, 1941. kjs
Kreismuseum Wewelsburg, Fotoarchiv

Heinrich Auf der Heide

Max Böhmer

No. 9-5
Heinrich Auf der Heide with fellow-students
at agronomy school
1920s
Heinrich Auf der Heide, born 1907, in Kalkriese,
took over the family farm from his parents in
1928 and continued working it after the outbreak
of war. He fell in love with Polish farmworker
Anna Podtstawek, sent to his farm as a forced
laborer. Their mutual child, who died soon after
birth in February 1941, earned him six months of
protective detention at Sachsenhausen Concentration Camp. After his release, the farmer
sought to marry the young Polish woman. This
wish brought him into conflict with the head of
the regional National Socialist farmers' association, who intended to transfer the farm to Auf
der Heide's brother Wilhelm. Heinrich Auf der
Heide was taken into protective detention by the
Osnabrück Gestapo for "race defilement" and
sent to Niederhagen Concentration Camp. Anna
Podtstawek's fate is unknown. Heinrich Auf der
Heide died on July 12, 1942 in Wewelsburg, of
"heart failure." kjs

Excerpted from a newspaper article on Heinrich Auf der Heide
by Volker Issmer in the *Bramscher Nachrichten*, December 22, 2001

No. 9-6
Max Böhmer
Before 1941
Laborer Max Böhmer, born September 19, 1894,
in Golm, formerly Bornim, Osthavelland district,
presumably landed in the "Gypsy Camp Berlin-
Marzahn Rastplatz" in the course of the nation-
wide wave of persecution unleashed against
Sinti and Roma following the so-called Antisocial
Decree of 1937 for the "preemptive combating of
criminality." From there, he was sent to Sachsenhausen Concentration Camp on June 17, 1938,
where he wore the black triangle of prisoners
classified as "antisocial." His transfer to Wewelsburg came before September 1941. Max Böhmer
died on March 7, 1942, officially of "weakness
and circulatory insufficiency." At the time, his
wife was still interned at the "Gypsy camp" in
Marzahn. kjs

Dokumentations- und Kulturzentrum deutscher Sinti und Roma

Rudi L.

Gerrit Visser

No. 9-7
Niederhagen Concentration Camp prisoner identification card for Rudi L.
1941 – 1943
Butler Rudi L., born 1912 in Coswig, near Dresden, presumably came to the SS's attention after 1935, with the increased severity of Paragraph 175 of the penal code, criminalizing all contact between men, which, "objectively, and according to common public sentiment, is sexually offensive to virtue and decency." There followed large-scale raids in 1936 and 1937, in the course of which homosexual men were taken into protective detention. Rudi L. was convicted on four occasions for "illicit sexual relations," before being taken into protective detention under the heading "homosexual," and sent to Sachsenhausen Concentration Camp. From there, he was transferred to Niederhagen Concentration Camp on October 24, 1941. Here, unlike other prisoners classified as homosexual, he did not wear the pink triangle, but the green one of the "career criminals." kjs
Internationaler Suchdienst, Bad Arolsen, Umschlag Rudi L.

No. 9-8
Gerrit Visser
Ca. 1941
Social Democrat and metalworker Gerrit Visser, born 1894 in Oud-Beijerland in the Netherlands, held the office of local union leader for the district of Hengelo in the Dutch Association of Labor Unions. When the Nationaal Socialistische Beweging, the Dutch National Socialist party, took control of the association of unions, in 1940, Gerrit Visser, refused to cooperate with it. In March 1941, he informed the union association that the National Socialists' political ideas ran contrary to his own democratic political convictions. In May, he was arrested, allegedly for inciting metalworkers to strike and for sabotage; two months later, he was transferred to the German police prison in Schoorl, and from there to Scheveningen internment camp. In late Ocober 1941, he was sent to Sachsenhausen Concentration Camp. In the spring of 1942, he arrived at Niederhagen, where he died on June 29, 1942, of "physiological weakness." kjs
Kreismuseum Wewelsburg, Fotoarchiv

Mark Weidman

Rudolf Sorm

No. 9-9
Mark Weidman
Ca. 1941 – 1942
Mark Weidman was born in 1923 to a Jewish
family of the district of Lemberg, Poland, now
Ukraine. The rising persecution of the Jewish
population during the period of Soviet occupation prevented him from going to university, as he
had planned. After the conquest of Lemberg by
the Germans, he was conscripted into forced
labor by the Gestapo. To escape looming deportation to Belzec extermination camp, Mark Weidman decided in the fall of 1942 to flee to the
German Reich. With the vacation pass of a Catholic Pole and under the assumed name Stefan
Galuszka, he made his way to the Ruhr Region.
There, for lack of working papers, he was
detained by the Bochum Gestapo. He lived in
constant fear that his true, Jewish identity would
be discovered. In January 1943, after five weeks
of detention, he arrived at Niederhagen Concentration Camp. kjs
Kreismuseum Wewelsburg, Fotoarchiv

No. 9-10
Rudolf Sorm
Ca. 1935 – 1940
In 1939, when the *Wehrmacht* occupied Bohemia
and Moravia, former career officer Rudolf Sorm,
born 1899 in Prague, was working as a real estate
agent. He was arrested in 1940 for suspected
illegal activity in the service of the Czech govern-
ment-in-exile. Prague Gestapo headquarters
took him into protective detention and sent him
to Buchenwald Concentration Camp on November 5, 1940. From here, he arrived in Wewelsburg in March 1941. He wore the red triangle of
political prisoners. In early December 1941, the
Gestapo brought him back to Prague for renewed
questioning. He was returned to Niederhagen
Concentration Camp on March 20, 1942. He died
there six weeks later. His death certificate of
May 1, 1942, states the cause of death as
"pneumonia." kjs
Kreismuseum Wewelsburg, Fotoarchiv

Jan Rokicki

Zbigniew Jaworski

No. 9-11
**Jan Rokicki with his wife Wladislawa
and their daughters Irena and Zofia
1938**
Jan Rokicki was born in 1900 in Swaryszów
(Poland). From 1918 to 1922, he volunteered in
the army of the newly forming Polish state; from
1928, he worked as a technician for the Jedrzejów
district (Poland) building department. Here, he
also served as head of the local militia. With his
wife, he had two children. After the German
invasion of Poland in September 1939, Jan Rokicki
was detained for six weeks in a prisoner of war
camp. Then, in early June 1940, he was arrested,
along with 50 other citizens of Jedrzejów, for
alleged membership in a partisan group. It is
unclear whether he really was active in the underground or had been falsely informed on. On
July 17, 1940, Jan Rokicki was transferred from
Kielce to Sachsenhausen Concentration Camp
as a political prisoner. From there, he came to
Wewelsburg on March 28, 1942. Jan Rokicki died
there on June 17, 1942, of "pneumonia." kjs
Kreismuseum Wewelsburg, Fotoarchiv

No. 9-12
**Zbigniew Jaworski after his
detention as a prisoner of war
1939**
As a young Polish soldier, Zbigniew Jaworski,
born 1921 in Kaski, near Warsaw, was imprisoned
in a German prisoner of war camp during the
German invasion of his country. He was later
rearrested while attempting to cross the border
into Lithuania. On November 9, 1940, the
Gestapo sent him to Sachsenhausen Concentration Camp as a political protective detention
prisoner. From there, he was transferred to
Wewelsburg in 1941. kjs
Kreismuseum Wewelsburg, Fotoarchiv

Alexander Schtscherbinin

Yuri Zavadski

No. 9-13
Alexander Schtscherbinin
Before 1942
Alexander Schtscherbinin was born in 1927 in
Obozovka, district of Kirovograd (Ukraine).
In 1942, after his village of Novoschachtinsk had
been occupied by the German army, he was
summoned to the local employment office. Then,
together with about one hundred men, he was
deported from his village. The group was forced
to walk the first sixty kilometers, after which it
was transported by freight train to Cologne,
where he was assigned to work in a factory. As he
attempted to flee aboard a freight train, policemen arrested him and took him to the Gestapo
prison in Hamm. From there, he was sent to
Niederhagen Concentration Camp, where he
wore the red triangle of a political prisoner,
with an "R" for "Russian." kjs
Kreismuseum Wewelsburg, Fotoarchiv

No. 9-14
Yuri Zavadski as a graduate of the 3rd Artillery
Military Academy in Leningrad
Ca. 1941
Born in 1923, the son of a school director in a village near Kiev (Ukraine), Yuri Zavadski attended
artillery school in Kiev and later the Military
Academy in Leningrad. He fought in the Red Army
with the rank of lieutenant. In January 1943,
he was captured by the Germans. During transit
to the German Reich, he escaped from a train and
sought refuge with a farmer. Here, however, he
was arrested by a German policeman. Claiming to
be a forced laborer, Yuri Zavadski landed in a
Gestapo prison in Cologne. From there, he was
sent to Niederhagen Concentration Camp. kjs
Kreismuseum Wewelsburg, Fotoarchiv

Georg Klohe

Joachim Escher

No. 9-15
**Georg Klohe as a soldier in World War I
Ca. 1914**
Georg Klohe, born 1894 in Berlin, volunteered in
World War I. From 1920, he worked as a salesman
for the electrical company Allgemeine Elektri-
zitäts-Gesellschaft (AEG) in Berlin. Converted to
the teachings of the International Association of
Bible Students (IBSA), he was baptized in the
faith in 1921. After 1933, problems began to mount
for him at AEG, when he refused to take part in
company marches. Ultimately, he was fired in
1936. After this, he worked as a traveling soap
salesman; this allowed him to serve as a courier
for the IBSA. In 1936, Georg Klohe was caught in
the first nation-wide roundup of IBSA members.
During his interrogation at Columbia House
Gestapo prison in Berlin, he was severely beaten.
The Berlin Special Court sentenced him to two
and a half years in prison because of his activity
for the banned IBSA. After he had served his
sentence, the Gestapo took him into protective
detention and sent him to Sachsenhausen
Concentration Camp. Georg Klohe was in the
first group of Jehovah's Witnesses transported
to Wewelsburg, in February 1940. kjs
Kreismuseum Wewelsburg, Fotoarchiv

No. 9-16
**Joachim Escher
1935**
Joachim Escher, born 1915 in Schalksmühle,
learned about the teachings of the International
Association of Bible Students (IBSA) from his
parents at an early age. After school, he went into
agriculture in 1933, hoping thereby to escape
pressure from the National Socialist Party
(NSDAP). In 1937, he refused to take the oath to
the Führer at his induction into the military in
Ulm, for which he was sentenced to nine months
in military prison. Because of his persistent
refusal to give the "Hitler salute" and render
standard military honors, he was examined at a
local military hospital regarding his mental
status. The Superior Military Tribunal in Wiesbaden subsequently sentenced him to two years'
imprisonment and a dishonorable discharge for
insubordination and incitement to mutiny. On his
release in 1939, the Gestapo took him into
protective detention and sent him to Sachsenhausen Concentration Camp. He arrived in
Wewelsburg on February 16, 1940, with the first
group of Bible Students transported there. kjs
Kreismuseum Wewelsburg, Fotoarchiv

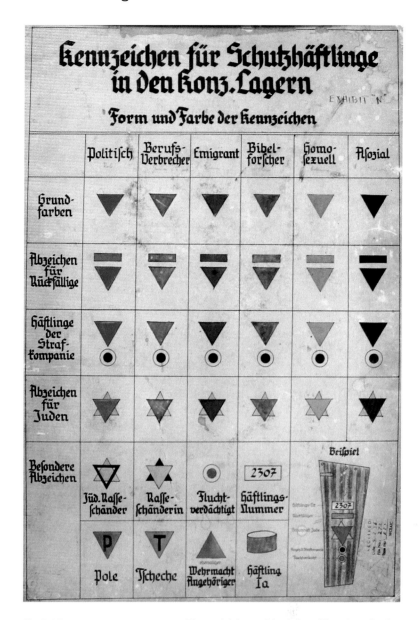

No. 9-17
**Chart of concentration
camp badges
1939 – 1945**
Internationaler Suchdienst, Bad Arolsen

Through hierarchical classification of prisoner groups, the SS elaborated a system for the social and ideologically based racial differentiation of the camp population. The method of marking the prisoner groups was not initially standardized. An official version eventually emerged, as shown by this identification table for SS guards. Political prisoners received a red cloth triangle (*Winkel*) with foreign prisoners' triangles also bearing the initial of their country of origin. Criminal prisoners were designated as "career criminals" and wore a green triangle; those classified as "antisocial" a black triangle, while Sinti and Roma were either branded as "antisocial" or received a brown triangle. The pink triangle was reserved for homosexual prisoners, though there is no evidence of its use at Niederhagen Concentration Camp. Here, prisoners who had been arrested under Paragraph 175 either wore the green or black triangle. Bible Students (Jehovah's Witnesses) were assigned a purple triangle. Jewish prisoners had to wear their colored triangle over a yellow badge. kjs

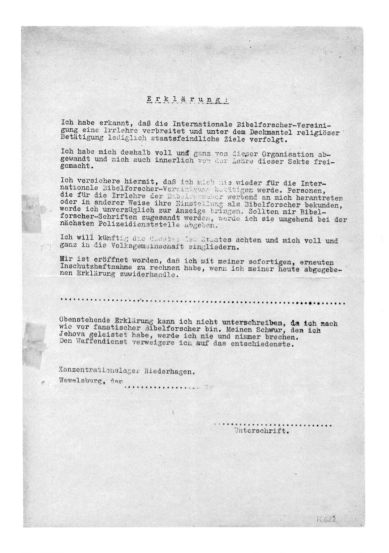

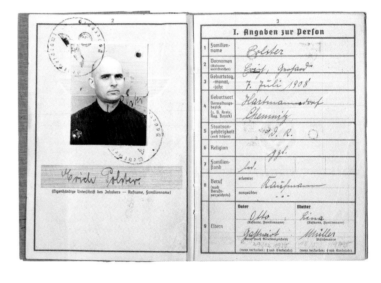

No.9-18
Niederhagen Concentration Camp declaration (*Revers*) for imprisoned Jehovah's Witnesses to renounce their faith
1940 – 1945
Translation on page 456

The religious community of Bible Students (also known since 1931 as Jehovah's Witnesses), founded in the United States in 1881, is a community living in the expectation of a soon-to-come "Kingdom of God" on earth. It is characterized by intense missionary activity and strict adherence to biblical rules. The Jehovah's Witnesses' unwillingness to submit to worldly leaders exposed them to persecution by the National Socialists. They refused to give the "Hitler salute," swear a military oath, or take part in elections; and for this, they were ready to forfeit their jobs, pensions, and custody of their children. They were also fined and sentenced to prison terms. Once the religious community was banned throughout the Reich, in 1935, punishments grew more severe. The SS increasingly applied protective detention. From 1935, while incarcerated in prisons and concentration camps, Jehovah's Witnesses were presented with a declaration form (*Revers*) to sign, by which they were to renounce their faith. The declaration shown here is from Niederhagen/Wewelsburg Concentration Camp.

Thus, in contrast to other persecuted groups, Bible Students had the option – in theory at least – of recovering their freedom of their own accord and rejoining the "national community." But few of the prisoners yielded to the pressure by the SS; most remained true to their faith. Moreover, signing the renunciation would have meant losing the solidarity and support of the religious community. kjs

Loan from the Wachtturm-Gesellschaft
der Zeugen Jehovas, Selters
Kreismuseum Wewelsburg, inv. no. 16682

No.9-19
Military service book of Erich Polster
October 25, 1940

Since the outbreak of war, Bible Students, who categorically refused military service on religious grounds, were subject to the "ordinance for completion of penal provisions in protection of the defense capacity of the German people" of November 25, 1939. Under this special wartime criminal statute, they could be sentenced to death for "degradation of defense capabilities." Bible Students who were already in protective detention, and thus within the Gestapo's sphere of influence, found themselves beyond the reach of the *Wehrmacht* and therefore of its looming death sentences. The some three hundred Bible Students at Wewelsburg included twenty-seven prisoners who had already refused military service, and declined to sign the renunciation declaration while interned at Buchenwald Concentration Camp. In October 1940, they underwent another physical in Wewelsburg and were given their military papers. Once more, they refused to sign the declaration. In January 1941, they received their conscription orders and were transferred to the *Wehrmacht*. kjs

Loan from the Wachtturm-Gesellschaft
der Zeugen Jehovas, Selters
Kreismuseum Wewelsburg, inv. no. 16655

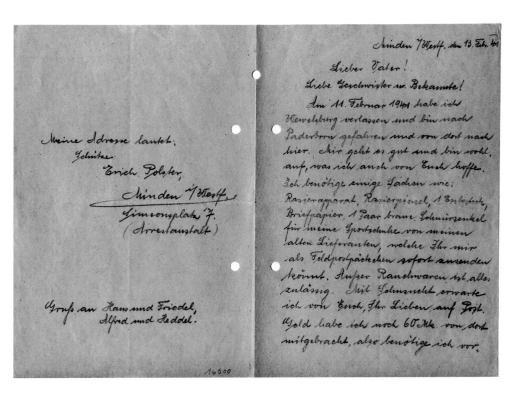

No. 9-20
Letter from Erich Polster to his family, Minden army camp detention center
February 13, 1941

Erich Polster was among the 27 conscientious objectors transferred to the *Wehrmacht* in February 1941. Dressed in civilian clothing, the Jehovah's Witnesses were driven by bus to Paderborn, whence they were distributed in small groups to the garrisons in Gütersloh, Minden, and Iserlohn. Another group remained in Paderborn. They were incarcerated in different military prisons, where they remained for four to five weeks. Only one Bible Student was prevailed upon to enter military service, while the rest remained firm in the precepts of their faith and refused to take up arms. After a court decision relieving the *Wehrmacht* of further responsibility for the objectors, they were returned to Niederhagen Concentration Camp. kjs

Loan from the Wachtturm-Gesellschaft der Zeugen Jehovas, Selters Kreismuseum Wewelsburg, inv. no. 16900

My address is as follows:
Private
Erich Polster
Minden, Westphalia
7 Simeon Square (detention center)
Greetings to Hans and Friedel, Alfred and Heddel

Minden/Westphalia, February 13, 41
Dear Father!
Dear brothers, sisters and friends!
On February 11, 1941, I left Wewelsburg and rode up to Paderborn, then to here. I am well and in good spirits, which I hope you are also. I need a few things such as a razor, a shaving brush, cutlery, writing paper, and 1 pair of brown laces for my athletic shoes, all of which you can send me immediately per military mail. Besides tobacco products, everything can be sent. I long to hear from you by mail, my dears. I still have 60 marks that I brought along from there, so I
[*reverse*]
don't need any more for now. I received an employee card, and I have it with me. The stamps for 1940 have been stuck on (6 of them at 40). Greeting to Karl and Max, Fritz, and Albert.
Dear brother, how are you, and what's your family up to? I have to say, you've written very little as of late. Dear Marie, many thanks for your kind letters, which never fail to bring me joy. I'd so love to see you all again some day, but there's the war.
I'll stop here for today.
All the best, dear father, brothers, sisters and friends,
from your old Erich

Translation of a transcription

No. 9-21
Not shown
Letter with envelope from Gottfried Mehlhorn, written from Paderborn army barracks to Anna Hollweg, mother of Max Hollweg
February 19, 1941

Jehovah's Witness Gottfried Mehlhorn used the period of his detention at the Paderborn army barracks to write uncensored letters. He contacted the mother of fellow prisoner Max Hollweg to let her know that her son was well. In this letter he disregarded the prohibition on revealing anything of camp conditions. Unsparingly, he reports the circumstances Bible Students faced at Buchenwald Concentration Camp. kjs

Loan from the Wachtturm-Gesellschaft der Zeugen Jehovas, Selters Kreismuseum Wewelsburg, inv. nos. 16897 and 16898/2

[*page 1*]
Paderborn, 2.19.1941
Dear Sister Hollweg,
Dear spiritual sister and mother of your well mannered son Max, what you have not yet experienced in this life, you may now experience with the greatest joy. Just think, I'm to send warmest greetings from your son Max. He is in fine health and good spirits. And how could it be otherwise, with your and my heart and entire understanding tuned to our great God Jehovah. You can truly be assured. Jehovah and our leader Jesus Christ are always with us. I will now commit to paper two horrid
[*page 2*]
examples of what they did to us. As I am a true Jehovah's Witness, you may believe me. 1938 on 12.16., 2 prisoners escaped and the whole camp was punished for it. From 4 o'clock in the afternoon, at minus 14–16°C (–6.8°F), until 9 in the evening, at minus 22°C (–7.6°F), we had to stand still on the roll call area. Among us Bible Students, 400 men, there was not a single death, while among the other prisoners over 30 lay dead on the ground and another 100 died as a result in the following days. 2. Another time some prisoners secretly slaughtered a pig, but this came out because someone snitched and so over 10,000 prisoners got nothing to eat or drink for 3 days and 3 nights but still [had] to work.
[*page 3*]
How many here fall by the wayside can't even be said in words. Among us Bible Students, however, no one is ill or dead. And now about me. Twenty-seven Bible Students took the physical at the camp on 11.25.40 and all were declared fit for duty. We were discharged from the camp on 2.13.1941 and transferred under heavy guard to military district headquarters in Paderborn. When they wanted to dress us in uniforms, we refused. We're still wearing our civilian clothes and now perform quite a bit of work around here. Unloading potatoes, cleaning the barracks yard, splitting firewood, and so forth. The case is now before the military tribunal and
[*page 4*]
the outcome remains to be seen. So my dear sister, let us remain true, our Jehovah is always with us. If you can, send your Max a few marks. The food is pretty good, considering the situation, but there's not much of it. Every 14 days Max manages to buy a loaf of bread. Up to now, he's always gotten some from his brothers, because we all share everything. And your cake was absolutely first-rate.
With much love and kisses from your earthly and spiritual son Max, I remain in spirit
Your Brother
Gottfried u. Kurt Feustel

Translation of a transcription

No.9-22

Gramophone record made by Georg Klohe, with the lecture "Rebellion"
Das Goldene Zeitalter [The Golden Age], Bern, no. 299, vol. XIII, March 1, 1935
Shellac
1935 – 1936

In August 1936, ahead of the International Congress of Jehovah's Witnesses in Lucerne, the Gestapo launched a nation-wide dragnet, in which Georg Klohe was arrested. He had already lost his job for refusing to give the "Hitler salute," and had worked since then as a traveling soap salesman. Going house to house, he was also able to distribute religious literature. By 1935, he had begun recording self-produced records. With his son, Addi, he set up a recording studio in a tool shed behind his rented apartment. Here, he was able to cut up to five records simulta-neously, after which the still-soft records were hardened in the oven of a baker friend.

For the record displayed here, Georg Klohe chose "Rebellion," one of four lec-tures by Joseph F. Rutherford already being distributed in record form and which appeared in printed form in the Swiss edition of *The Golden Age* in March 1935.
kjs

Loan from the Wachtturm-Gesellschaft
der Zeugen Jehovas, Selters
Kreismuseum Wewelsburg, inv. no. 16406

No.9-23

Portable gramophone
Ca. 1930

The Ernest Bible Students were early adopters of gramophones and film projectors to spread their message. In 1934, the Watchtower Society began producing portable gramophones and publishing series of records with lectures by the president of the Association of Bible Students, Joseph F. Rutherford. The Bible Students, whose preaching took them house to house, were thus able to spread their "message of the Kingdom." Following a Germany-wide ban on the Jehovah's Witnesses, in 1935, church members went underground, attempting to carry on their bible classes and mis-sionary activities in secret. Despite persecution, they sought to preserve their network. Texts were smuggled into Ger-many and distributed. Frequently, periodicals were transcribed and records rerecorded and duplicated. kjs

Loan from the Wachtturm-Gesellschaft
der Zeugen Jehovas, Selters
Kreismuseum Wewelsburg, inv. no. 16405

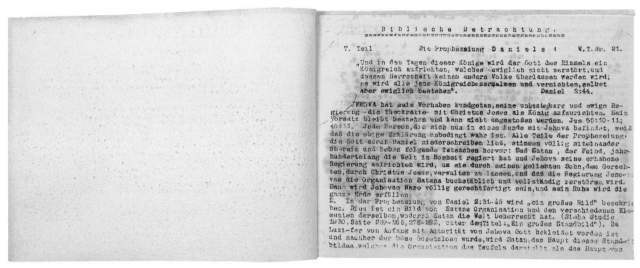

"Now I get to Bad Salzuflen, to Grandma [Schulz]'s. And all of a sudden, here comes this young girl, who's from around there, but not a Jehovah's Witness. She's also looking for Mrs. Schulz. She'd been to Wewelsburg. … She'd been friends with Heinrich Schürmann, a Jehovah's Witness. … Met him [at the concentration camp], then met several brothers. … And they requested that she meet with other Jehovah's Witnesses, to make sure they got the literature. …
So we're sitting there, eating, and discussing what we should do. …
The three of us, Grandma Schulz and Paula, … and I. And I said 'Yes. You've come to the right place. I've got enough magazines available. You can have those. But how do we get them in there? I can't just drive to Wewelsburg every four weeks and bring the magazines.' But the brothers had already told her that. Okay, in Wewelsburg there's a nursery. And it's located – I think, somewhere near the woods on the way to Salzkotten. … There's two Jehovah's Witnesses who work at the nursery. … They were brought out there every morning, and picked up again in the evening. And they worked there on their own. … There was a wall around the nursery, and along the wall, a spot where there was this big rock, just sitting there. And under that rock, that's where the magazines and such were stashed. The rock had to be rolled to the side, the magazines put underneath, and the rock rolled back in place. … Sandor Bayer and Martha Tünker, they pretended to be a married couple. … They'd travel Saturday evenings with the last train from Salzuflen to Salzkotten. That's where they got off, hiked over Salzkotten Hill, right to the nursery, climbed the wall, hid the literature underneath. And there'd already be letters under the stone that the brothers had secretly written, that no one was supposed to read. And then they brought the letters back with them."

No. 9-24
Copy of *Der Wachtturm*
[The Watchtower], issue no. 17
January 15, 1942
Lining wallpaper, paper
Between late 1942 and March 1945
From December 1942, female coreligionists secretly provided Bible Student prisoners with religious literature. The texts were hidden at the plant nursery nearby the train station, where Jehovah's Witness Hermann Struthoff worked. The latter could then smuggle the material into the camp.

After the operators of the Jehovah's Witnesses' clandestine print shop in Oberhausen were arrested in winter 1943, Bible Student prisoners took over their tasks. They received the needed materials via the "dead letter box" at the nursery. Correspondence and the smuggling out of newly printed religious publications also occurred via the "mailbox." This copy of *The Watchtower*, bound in lining wallpaper, is one of the few surviving specimens of illegal printing at Wewelsburg. kjs

Loan from the Wachtturm-Gesellschaft der Zeugen Jehovas, Selters
Kreismuseum Wewelsburg, inv. no. 16408

No. 9-29
On the smuggling of religious texts to the external work detachment (*Außenkommando*) of Buchenwald Concentration Camp stationed in Wewelsburg from 1943 to 1945 Sophie Horstmeier, translation of an excerpt from an interview on March 5, 2004

Kreismuseum Wewelsburg,
Tonarchiv 87-TC-O I+II

No. 9-28
Not shown
Sophie Horstmeier (third from the left) as a Young Pioneer with her group
1930s

Wachtturm-Gesellschaft
der Zeugen Jehovas, Selters

No. 9-27
Sophie Horstmeier
Postwar photograph
Cigar-maker Sophie Horstmeier, born 1903 in Hille-Eickhorst, was a devout Jehovah's Witness who stood up for the banned religious community. She helped to secretly distribute the religious texts produced in the clandestine print shop in Oberhausen. She thus had access to copies to pass on to prisoners at Niederhagen Concentration Camp via a contact in Bad Salzuflen. When the SS's discovery of the printing press in Oberhausen in 1943 led to death sentences for eight of those involved, Sophie Horstmeier also came under pressure. She was arrested, and sentenced in October 1944 to four year's penitentiary for "degradation of defense capabilities." Sophie Horstmeier's arrest also brought suspicion on the Bible Student prisoners in Wewelsburg when letters from concentration camp prisoner Georg Klohe were found at her home. Yet, nothing could be proved against them. kjs

Wachtturm-Gesellschaft der Zeugen Jehovas, Selters

Willi Wilke
7712 Blumberg
Im Winkel 33

Willi Wilke
7712 Blumberg
Im Winkel 33   Blumberg, den

Bericht Blatt 5

Es kamen sehr schwere Zeiten, der Sommer 42 hieß der Brennesselsommer.
Jeden Tag gingen 2 Brüder mit Sense und Säcken los um Brennesseln für
das Mittagessen zu mähen. In diesem Sommer war die Sterblichkeit in
Wewelsburg besonders groß. Einige Zahlen mögen dies veranschaulichen:
Vom 1o.6. bis zum 22.12 kamen 818 Neuzugänge und inderselben Zeit waren
von diesen schon wieder 531 gestorben. Auch die anderen Häftlinge hatte
eine Sterblichkeitsquote von 55%, wir dagegen nur 1/2%.
So können wir erkennen, wie unser Vater trotz mancher Mängel und ungute/
Dinge unter seinen Kindern sie trotzdem in seiner Güte bewahrte, weil
sie durch all die Jahre bewiesen, daß sie IHM treu bleiben wollten.

1943 kam dann der Befehl:Wwelsburg wird bis auf kleines Kommando aufgelöst. Es blieb nur ein kleiner Rest Brüder zurück um die Burg, das
Verwaltungsgebäude, das Lager usw. zu erhalten. Trotz der Drohung des
Kommandoführers er würde uns alle noch durch den Schornstein jagen
begann wieder eine Zeit wo ohne Schläge und schreien gearbeitet wurde.

Auch war jetzt wieder völlige Einheit in Glaubensdingen da, denn vorher
gab es einige extreme Gruppen z.B. Pape,Korn usw. die eigene Ansichten
verbreiten wollten. Einer schrieb sogar selbst einen Artikel über den
Baum der Erkenntnis.
Jetzt wurde auch die Verbindung nach aussen besser und wir erhielten
die gegenwärtigen Wahrheiten ins Lager, die ja auch für unsere Brüder
die nicht eingesperrt waren sehr schwer zu beschaffen waren.

Als Erich Polster und ich eines Samstags den Burghof fegten fanden wir
eine kleine Gummiwalze mit Stiel. Da kam Bruder Polster ein Gedanke:
"Du, solch eine Walze hatten wir früher im Büro für Vervielfältigungen."
Jetzt stellten die Tischler einen Rahmen her in den die Schlosser
einen Stahlrahmen einpassten. Aus dem Lager wurde Filz aufgebracht.
Von dieser Zeit ab wurden im Lager Abzüge gemacht, wozu Bruder Polster
aus Tapeten die Einband herstellte.Wir hatten viele Rollen Tapetenma-
kulatur im Bauhoflager, davon schnitt ich je 10 mtr. ab sodaß die Roll/
zahl weiterhin stimmte. Georg Klohe besorgte die Matrizen-er war im
Bauhofbüro- er und Bruder Draht schrieben dann Sonntags diese - da sie
ihre Schreibmaschinen zum reinigen mit ins Lager brachten!
Als am 5. Januar 45 ein Teil des Bauhofes abbrante kamen wir an einen
Greif-Vervielfältiger und nun konnte die Produktion von Wachttürmen
noch besser anlaufen. Versteckt war er im Gemüsekeller bei Bruder Krau
Wie das Material herein und wieder herauskam kam in Einzelheiten Bruder
Heinrich Schürmann, der nach 45 in Rinteln wohnte wohl am besten berich
ten, da er im Gärtnerkommando am Bahnhof war. Zu einem in der Gärt-
nerei stehenden Taubenhaus hatten auch die Schwestern einen Schlüssel
die den Austausch vornahmen.

Am 2, April 45 kamen dann die Amerikaner. Wieder war es wunderbare
Überwaltung von Jehova, daß es der SS nicht mehr gelang uns in die
Luft zu sprengen oder wie die Hasen im Wald abzu-schießen.

Von den Amerikanern erhielten wir dann die Genehmigung, mit einem
Opel-Blitz (Holzkocher) unsere persönlichen Effekten von Buchenwald
zu holen.
Mit diesem Wagen wurden dann auch die Brüder nach und nach heimgefahren
bis Bruder Draht und ich uns als fast letzte auf den Weg nach Magdeburg
machten.

Ausser den nachstehend aufgeführten Transporten, soweit ich sie noch
zusammen bekam, gab es auch noch Facharbeiter Zugänge von 1-5 Brüdern
Dann die schon im Bericht erwähnte Zugangszahl von 818 vom 1o.6 bis
22.12.42 mit einer Todeszahl von 531 in derselben Zeit. Waren meist
Ausländer. Unsere am 11.2.41 zur Wehrmacht gesandten Brüder kamen bis
zum 26.3.41 wieder ins Lager zurück

Kloke

Bruder Georg Klohe geb. 8.9.94 berichtet wie es den Brüdern im
KZ Niederhagen möglich wurde WT Abschriften herzustellen und
außerhalb des Lagers zur Verteilung zu bringen.

Nachdem das KZ Lager Niederhagen im Frühjahr 1943 als wirtschaft-
lich eigenständige Einrichtung unter Kommandant Haas aufgelöst
wurde,blieben auf Anweisung des Oberführers Tauber (ein Freund
Himmlers) für die SS-Schule 40 Bibelforscher und zwei politische
Häftlinge als Arbeitskommando unter der Aufsicht KZ Buchenwald
im Bereich der sogenannten Wewelsburg.

Die Aufsicht hatten 10 neueingekleidete Männer bei denen es an
der raffinierten Schikane fehlte, soda? es uns möglich wurde mehr
unsere geistigen Bedürfnisse zu stillen.

Dies wurde auch möglich,weil wir auf illegalen Wege briefliche Be-
ziehungen zu Schwestern aus Wetfahlen (Schw. Schulz,Salzuflen;
Schw. Seck, Schw. Horstmeier,Eickhorst) aufnehmen konnten.

Bruder Struthof der als Gärtner in Garten des Oberführers und
auf den Friedhof seine Arbeitszuweisungen hatte, brachte allabend-
lich einen Sack Grünfutter für die Kaninchen der SS-Männer mit in
das Lager.
Durch den illegalen Briefverkehr wurde dann ein bestimmtes Grab
bestimmt,wo wir geistige Speise erwarteten. In dem Futtersack
wurden die WT-Abschriften eingebracht. Wir wurden so sehr gestärckt
da? wir zur Tätigkeit angespornt wurden. Aber wie?

Auf dem Werstättenhof der SS lagen Holz-und andere Werte von 1/2
Million RM. In einer Nacht war Feueralarm und die Werkstätten brann
ten. Wir wurden an der Löschung beteiligt und schnell räumten wir
und löschten das Feuer.
Beim Bergen der Werte kam die Büroschreibmaschine abhanden. Sie
konnte nicht verbrannt sein, aber sie war unauffindbar.

Nach einer Woche bat mich Bruder Struthof mit ihm in den Kartoffel-
keller zu gehen. Er zeigte mir die Maschine in einer Kiste mit
Säcken verhängt . Auf einer kleineren Kiste lag neben der Maschine
das Schriftenmaterial und devor ein Sitzplatz. Es fiel kein Wort
und ich setzte mich und schrieb mit entsprechendem Kopierband den
WT-Inhalt ab.
In den Futtersack fand sich auch das Gelantinematerial zum Atziehe
und Bruder Polster schuf die erforderliche Haltevorrichtung.
Jehova hatte seine Hand über diese Arbeit, denn es klappte gut.

Die Schwestern kamen vor dem Morgengrauen und sorgten für Stoff.
Sie nahmen die Abzüge, es waren je WT ungefähr 50 Exemplare mit
in ihr Gebiet . Sie kamen zu freudigen Arbeitern die vervielfältig
und kehrten zurück zu denkbaren Empfängern.

Als ich plötzlich vom Arbeitsplatz aus dem Werkstätten in das Büro
der SS gerufen wurde, es war ein Tag wo wir gerade wieder etwas
unter dem Grabstein gelegt hatten, stand ich plötzlich vor dem
Gestapomann der Burg mit Namen Knappert. Der illegale Briefverkehr
war entdeckt worden denn bei Schwester Horstmeier, die verhaftet
worden war fand sich ein Brief von mir,der aber zufällig harmloser
Natur war. Welchen Schreck bekamen die Brüder, als sie mich mit de
Gestapomann kommen sahen, der aus unseren Schränken Schriftproben
nahm. Aber, weil der Oberführer der Kommando nicht hoch gehen lass
wollte blieb alles beim Alten. Wir konnte Vervielfältigen bis die
Tore der Gefangenschaft in April 1945 öffneten.

No.9-25
**Excerpt from a recollection by
Willi Wilke on the production
of *Watchtower* editions bound in
lining wallpaper
Late 1960s**
Translation on page 457
Several former prisoners from the
remaining labor detachment
(attached to Buchenwald) stationed
in Wewelsburg after Niederhagen
Concentration Camp was disbanded recount how religious texts
were copied and duplicated at the
camp. To avoid discovery, the
activities were kept as secret as
possible, even among the prison
population. kjs
Wachtturm-Gesellschaft der Zeugen Jehovas,
Selters

No.9-26
**Autobiographical chronicle by
Georg Klohe, typewritten account of
the duplication of *The Watchtower*
at Niederhagen Concentration
Camp and its distribution outside
the camp
April 6, 1971**
Translation on page 458
Wachtturm-Gesellschaft der Zeugen Jehovas,
Selters

No. 9-30
Roman Jefimenko
Pencil drawing
November 17, 1944

Central State Museum for Contemporary History, Moscow (negative no. H/1014, Gedenkstätte Buchenwald)

No. 9-31
Roman Jefimenko
Papa, **pencil drawing**
November 28, 1944

Central State Museum for Contemporary History, Moscow (negative no. H/1001, Gedenkstätte Buchenwald)

No. 9-32
Roman Jefimenko
Pencil drawing
November 6, 1944

Central State Museum for Contemporary History, Moscow (negative no. H/997, Gedenkstätte Buchenwald)

Roman Jefimenko, born 1916 in Klepali (Sumy district, Ukraine), appears to have come to the German Reich as a forced laborer. For reasons that are unclear, on October 28, 1942, he was sent by the Cologne Gestapo to Niederhagen Concentration Camp. His camp identification card stated his occupation as "farmworker." What set him apart, however, was his artistic talent, evident in numerous drawings. After disbandment of Niederhagen Concentration Camp in April 1943, Roman Jefimenko was transferred to Buchenwald Concentration Camp.

Many drawings have survived from his time there, documenting conditions at the concentration camp. The cramped barracks, the exhaustion and desperation of the fellow-prisoners are given clear, powerful expression in his drawings. There are no known works from his time in Wewelsburg. kjs

No.9-33
Prisoner belongings card for Roman Jefimenko from Niederhagen Concentration Camp
1942/1943
Ukrainian forced laborer Roman Jefimenko was one of more than 2,200 Soviet prisoners entered in the Niederhagen Concentration Camp files. Seven hundred thirty-four died of exhaustion, illness, hunger, and gross mistreatment at the hands of the SS guards.

Soviet prisoners included both prisoners of war and forced laborers arrested by the Gestapo. Special decrees prescribed the ruthless treatment of Soviet prisoners of war. Reinhard Heydrich's operational order of July 17, 1941, instituted mass executions, euphemistically designated "cleansing of prisoner camps occupied by Soviet Russians," carried out by specially formed commandos. From September 1941, German concentration camps were also approved as execution sites by the Reich Security Main Office (RSHA). At Niederhagen Concentration Camp, 14 Soviet prisoners of war interned by the Gestapo are known to have been executed.

Though the use of Soviet prisoners of war in German armaments production was initially banned, the labor shortage in German industry led to the approval of their deployment in November 1941. Soviet prisoners of war were to be exploited to absolute limits of their work capacity. More civilian laborers were recruited or forcibly deported from occupied Soviet areas. The "Eastern Laborer Decrees" of February 20, 1942, regulated the use of laborers from the east (*Ostarbeiter*) in German industry. "Russian departments" were established at Gestapo offices to monitor these labor deployments. Forced laborers accused of wrongdoing were taken into protective detention by the Gestapo and sent to concentration camps. From June 10, 1942, Niederhagen Concentration Camp received forced laborers from the police prison in Dortmund, later also from Cologne, Osnabrück, Bielefeld, and Paderborn. kjs

Internationaler Suchdienst, Bad Arolsen,
Umschlag Roman Jefimenko

No.9-35
Decorated box with lid
Wood, straw
In 1942, a Soviet forced laborer gave Klara Ottensmeier this small wooden box. As a child, she lived on her parent's farm Thewes, on the Lippe River, in the Delbrück region. Soviet forced laborers housed in a barn at a neighboring village worked on the riverbank. After their day's work, they helped out on the family farm and for this received additional food from the mother. In thanks, one of the men gave Klara Ottensmeier this small box decorated with straw. For years, she used it to hold her jewelry. In 2008, she donated it to the Kreismuseum Wewelsburg. kjs

Kreismuseum Wewelsburg, inv. no. 16269

No.9-34
Not shown
Decorative basket with lid
Woven straw and aluminum foil, lining of red paper
1942 – 1945
Kreismuseum Wewelsburg, inv. no. 11295

No.9-37
Not shown
Decorative box with lid
Wood
1942 – 1945
Kreismuseum Wewelsburg, inv. no. 11296

No.9-36
Not shown
Decorative basket with lid
Woven straw, lining of blue cloth
1942 – 1945
Carefully crafted objects, like those known as "Russian" boxes or baskets suggest encounters between Eastern European forced laborers and the German population beyond ideological barriers. Despite prohibitions, a lively bartering system emerged, against which party and police were powerless. Polish or Soviet forced laborers and prisoners of war skilled in handicrafts frequently created baskets, boxes, and toys in the work or prison camps that they used for barter or as means of payment.

In this way, they secured additional food rations and clothing from the German population. These three containers are from a farm in the Delbrück-Ostenland region. The baskets were woven of straw and lined with cloth or paper. The small wooden boxes feature straw intarsia.
kjs/an

Kreismuseum Wewelsburg, inv. no. 14272

Prisoner Functionaries

> "If you're familiar with the way a concentration camp works, then you know the SS often kept away from the dirty work and left that to prisoners, primarily the 'antisocial' and the career criminals, whom they used as foremen."

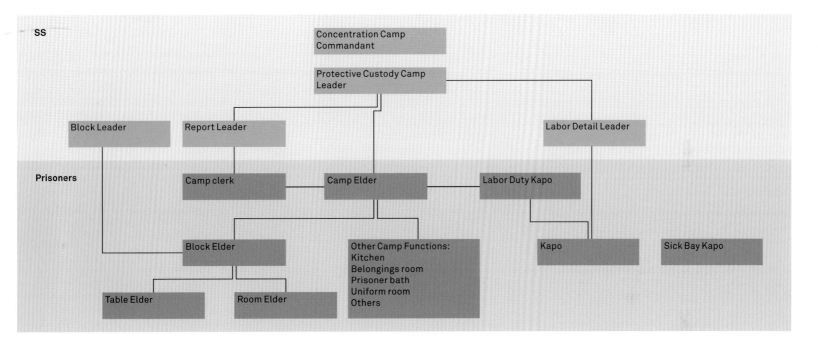

No. 9-38
Organizational chart of prisoner self-administration
To introduce further gradations into the social hierarchy among camp prisoners, the SS assigned various administrative and supervisory tasks to selected prisoners and established the "prisoner self-administration." In contrast to other concentration camps, in Wewelsburg Bible Students took on the responsible positions, such as camp elder and camp clerk. The positions of block elder, room elder, or kapo (foreman) were also assigned to political, "antisocial," or "career criminal" prisoners. Prisoner functionaries used the latitude afforded them by their positions in the camp hierarchy according to their conscience and sense of responsibility. Some prisoner functionaries selfishly improved their own situation, while others tried to protect fellow prisoners from the SS and to help their comrades. kjs

No. 9-39
Testimony of Willi Wilke, former camp elder at Niederhagen Concentration Camp, on the relationship between the SS and the prisoner functionaries (investigation documents from the second Wewelsburg trial 1970 – 1971)

Landesarchiv Nordrhein-Westfalen, Hauptstaatsarchiv Düsseldorf, Zweigarchiv Kalkum
Prozessunterlagen betr. KL Niederhagen-Wewelsburg, AZ: 24JS 2/69 (Z), Sign. Rep. 118-919

No. 9-40
Niederhagen Concentration Camp prisoner identification card for Kurt Paetzelt 1941 – 1943
Political prisoner Kurt Paetzelt occupied the functions of block elder and kapo in Wewelsburg, including at the "SS camp." His brutality toward prisoners led to charges against him after the war, in the second Wewelsburg trial.

The SS primarily appointed German inmates to act as prisoner functionaries, who received better clothing and more food. Depending on their work detail, the functionaries were granted extra rations or easier working conditions. Prisoners who worked indoors (administration, workshops, kitchen) had better chances of survival than prisoners who had to perform heavy labor (quarrying, roadwork) in all kinds of weather. Racist ideology largely barred Soviet or Jewish prisoners from functionary positions or the better work details kjs

Internationaler Suchdienst, Bad Arolsen, Umschlag Kurt Paetzelt

9.2
Prisoner Experiences at the Camp

Neither surviving objects nor documents from the camp administration reveal the personal perspectives of the victims; even the informational value of prisoner letters is limited by SS censorship. There are no known clandestine records of camp conditions at Wewelsburg. Under these circumstances, one line of approach is via former prisoners' memories, which are linked to selected objects of the camp world, such as a barrack wall. Henkel brand glue, available in Ukraine, reminded one concentration camp survivor of his hunger. Other subjects, such as illness and death, are discussed by survivors without reference to specific objects.

Regarding memories, it should be noted that survivors' accounts of what they went through at the camp are also shaped by their subsequent experiences and interpretations. The focus of the narratives is therefore less on how the prisoners' lives in the camp were, but rather on how the survivors remember their time at the camp.

"We were to build a new camp in Westphalia, not far from Paderborn. A couple of days later, we were loaded onto two buses. In the evening, between 8 and 10 o'clock, we were there. Each of us carried a blanket, cooking utensils, and a spoon. That was it – we'd already eaten our bread. Then we heard: 'Out of the bus! Fall in!'"

No. 9-41
Herbert Baron, translated excerpt from an interview on May 16, 1992
Kreismuseum Wewelsburg, Tonarchiv, 011-TC-O

"I immediately noticed the crematorium smokestack and the smell of burning human hair and so forth. You can imagine my feelings and first impression."

No. 9-42
Mark Weidman, excerpt from his autobiographical account of August 15, 1995
Kreismuseum Wewelsburg, Tonarchiv, 039-TC-O

No. 9-43
Summer jacket of prisoner Max Schubert from the Sachsenhausen Concentration Camp external work detachment stationed in Wewelsburg
Blue-and-white-striped cotton drill with purple cloth triangle and sewn-on prisoner number 13598, metal buttons
1943 – 1945

The clothing assigned to prisoners at the concentration camp shocked and humiliated the new arrivals. The "zebra-stripe" uniforms were meant to make prisoners look like common criminals. With the ill-fitting garments in poor repair, the SS made them look just like the "subhumans" they sought to eradicate. In contrast, the SS guards presented themselves in their impeccable, close-fitting uniforms as the "master race." The newly arrived prisoners' handover of their civilian clothing meant that they were also in effect surrendering their names, to become just a number in the mass of prisoners.

The jacket shown here belonged to Max Schubert, who came to Wewelsburg in 1940 and worked mostly in the uniform room. From 1943, he was a member of the Wewelsburg external work detachment attached to Buchenwald Concentration Camp. This is indicated by the high prisoner number 13598. As a Jehovah's Witness, Max Schubert wore the purple triangle. kjs

Kreismuseum Wewelsburg,
Nachlass Wettin Müller, inv. no. 15534

Life in the Barracks

"… so, with four men sharing a single towel for both the face and feet, it was just awful. And then the stench; so many men in one room, each with their own foul breath. What a stink that was; a pigsty was nothing in comparison."

No. 9-44
Friedrich Klingenberg, translated excerpt from an interview on May 16, 1992
Kreismuseum Wewelsburg, Tonarchiv, 016-TC-O

"But we also had to work hard. And that spring there had been quite a bit of rain; in the evenings you'd be drenched to the bone, and the next morning you'd have to get back into your wet rags, because you couldn't dry anything in there. In the barrack, there was just this little stove in the middle; you could hardly even warm up by it."

No. 9-45
Joachim Escher, translated excerpt from an interview on September 25, 1991
Kreismuseum Wewelsburg, Tonarchiv, 010-TC-O

No. 9-46
**Section of a barrack from the
Wewelsburg concentration camp
Wood, glass, metal
1940 – 1945**
The exterior walls and roof of the barracks were poorly insulated, so the buildings were bitterly cold in the winter and stiflingly hot in the summer.

The prisoner's daily routine was strictly regulated: at 6:00 a.m. the block leaders unlocked the doors. The prisoners then had an hour to rise, wash, go to the latrines, carefully fold the sheets on the straw mattresses, and eat breakfast. Given the cramped conditions in the over-crowded barracks, this was an almost impossible task. Next came the morning roll call; the prisoners then marched off to their work details. In the evening, roll call was followed by food distribution. After this, there was little free time left before the lights went out at 10:00 p.m. and the barracks were locked up. kjs
Kreismuseum Wewelsburg, inv. no. 16341

9.2.3
Clothing

No. 9-48
Winter jacket of a concentration camp prisoner
Recovered wool (wool, cotton, rayon) with blue stripes and purple cloth triangle, Bakelite buttons
1943 – 1945
The Concentration Camps Inspectorate first introduced the striped "zebra clothing" to the concentration camp system in 1938. Initially, private textile firms, including clothing testing businesses at Dachau, operated with prisoner labor, produced the uniforms. From 1940, they were made primarily by the SS's own "German Textile and Leather Processing Company" (Texled), based at Ravensbrück Concentration Camp. After 1942, production declined as the need for *Wehrmacht* uniforms rose, so civilian jackets and uniforms from Soviet prisoners of war were increasingly issued until the end of the war. In the winter, prisoners were allowed to receive additional knit garments by mail.

The winter jacket displayed here shows an ink-spot on the breast pocket, presumably from a fountain pen. kjs

Kreismuseum Wewelsburg,
Nachlass Wettin Müller, inv. no. 15533

No. 9-49
Winter trousers of Heinrich Knie, a prisoner from the Buchenwald Concentration Camp external work detachment stationed in Wewelsburg
Recovered wool (rayon, cotton, wool) with blue stripes, purple triangle, and sewn-on prisoner number 13579
1943 – 1945
Winter clothing was made of scratchy recovered wool, which, depending on availability of materials, consisted of a little wool mixed with rayon and cotton. The unlined uniforms offered little warmth and dried slowly. They were printed inside and outside, to prevent prisoners from simply reversing their uniforms while attempting escape.

The frequent damage to uniforms was mended by hand or with the sewing machine. A tailor detail could perform professional-quality repairs. Patches were rarely of the same material, but often of cotton mixed with hemp or linen. The heavily worn seat of this pair of winter pants was even repaired with a knitted wool patch. The trousers bear the prisoner number 13579, assigned to Jehovah's Witness Heinrich Knie. He was imprisoned in Wewelsburg from 1940 to 1945. kjs

Kreismuseum Wewelsburg,
Nachlass Wettin Müller, inv. no. 15537

No. 9-50
Summer jacket of a concentration camp prisoner
Cotton drill, with blue stripes, purple cloth triangle, metal buttons
1943 – 1945
The SS decided when the prisoners switched from their winter garments to summer clothing. Summer uniforms were of cotton drill, a special kind of twill. The blue stripes were produced using colored warp thread. The uniforms shown here conform to the standard concentration camp jacket pattern, with five buttons and tucks under the arms. This summer jacket shows clear signs of wear and tear, including numerous rust and oil stains. The pocket contained a mortar remnant. Prisoners were responsible for attaching the colored cloth triangle and making smaller mends. The uniform room provided needle and thread for prisoners to repair their clothes during their scarce free time. kjs

Kreismuseum Wewelsburg,
Nachlass Wettin Müller, inv. no. 15535

No. 9-51
Summer trousers of a concentration camp prisoner
Cotton drill, with blue stripes
1943 – 1945
All garments displayed are from prisoners assigned to the Buchenwald Concentration Camp external work detachment stationed in Wewelsburg from 1943 to 1945. The cotton summer trousers show signs of heavy wear and much mended damage. Though of a different fabric (mostly cotton with hemp), the patches are sewn on in line with the stripes. Traces of a prisoner number and a worn purple triangle are discernible on the side. Obvious dirt smudges are evident on the pant legs in particular.

With the uniform, prisoners were issued a shirt, socks, and underwear, which could only rarely be washed. As footwear, prisoners were given wooden clogs or used shoes, frequently mismatched. kjs

Kreismuseum Wewelsburg,
Nachlass Wettin Müller, inv. no. 15540

"We had to glue together these 5 mm (1/5 inch) straps with a strong adhesive. Nowadays, you can buy that glue in Russia – it's called 'Moment.' Some prisoners made little clumps of it, chewed them and got high. There was the urge to chew something because our rations were so scant. Some chewed glue, others scrounged about for bones."

No. 9-52
Nikolai Beltschenko, translated excerpt from an interview on April 4, 2000
Kreismuseum Wewelsburg, Tonarchiv, 047-TC-0

No. 9-53
Tube of glue, Ukrainian brand
"Moment" by Henkel
Metal tube with plastic cap, adhesive
2000
Ukrainian forced laborer Nikolai Beltschenko was sent to Niederhagen Concentration Camp from the Dortmund Steinwache prison on September 30, 1942. He suffered greatly from the backbreaking labor at the quarries and in road construction. Emaciated and exhausted, he was assigned to Block 2, for the ill and the *Muselmänner*, as the totally emaciated prisoners were derogatorily known. Here, he had to glue together cloth bands and straps. Many prisoners chewed clumps of the adhesive or sniffed its toxic vapors to deaden their hunger. More than fifty years later, he could still remember the glue's odor. On his visit to the memorial site in the year 2000, he brought along a tube, sold under the Moment brand in Ukraine, which brought back the smell of the glue from that time. The Ukrainian product is similar to the German Pattex brand adhesive. kjs

Kreismuseum Wewelsburg, inv. no. 16369

"I've got abscesses on my knees and can hardly walk … They tell me to report to sick bay. There're two other fellow-sufferers in the room … One has fixed, glassy eyes; he doesn't know what he's doing anymore. His fingers are frost-bitten, rotted, gnawed-through; because in his fits of hunger he bites the flesh off his fingers and chews it. When the SS medical orderly sees this, he whacks him on the fingers with a stick. Uncomprehending and whimpering, the dying man just looks at the SS man."

No. 9-54
Paul Buder, translated excerpt from an personal account, 1976
Kreismuseum Wewelsburg, inv. no. 17074

"Yes, the work, that was very hard. Because it was rainy, and sometimes you caught a cold. And one time, I also had dysentery. That was just awful, for three days. And so they brought me to work by force. But because I simply couldn't do anything anymore, at the quarry – I collapsed – the SS had the others take me to this shed, some shack made of boards, and in there were materials, such as hammers, pliers, and old nails. And so they had me take those bent nails, which were lying all over the place there, and I had to bang them straight again, in spite of the dysentery."

No. 9-55
Herbert Baron, translated excerpt from an interview on May 16, 1992
Kreismuseum Wewelsburg, Tonarchiv, 011-TC-0

"We had some in there, who had phlegmon, where pus develops under the skin, then all of that tissue dies off, until it starts affecting the deeper layers. We couldn't do anything about that, because we didn't have operating facilities. The [prisoners] were [injured] from getting kicked and having stones thrown at them and mistreatment, their injuries began to fester and then it went right over the buttocks to the bone marrow. Which would then always be crawling with worms, so we had to scratch those out through the loose skin, bandage it up as well we could. Those guys, they were literally being eaten alive by the worms."

No. 9-56
Max Hollweg, translated excerpt from an interview on May 16, 1992
Kreismuseum Wewelsburg, Tonarchiv, 015-TC-0

9.2.6
Death

"It was winter, with deep snow. Two poor, emaciated figures stagger across the roll call area. Rehn and another SS man order the two prisoners to strip. Then they had to get down on the snow, got completely packed up in snow … After a short while, their faces became as white as masks, first the nose, the lips, eyes as still as glass; and you just stood there, indifferent, apathetic, unmoved. All feeling gets crushed in that demonic death mill."

No. 9-57
Paul Buder, translated excerpt from personal account, 1976
Kreismuseum Wewelsburg, inv. no. 17074

"I see everything as in a fog. When I think about it longer, figures begin to move about in the fog. I can't get any further than that."

No. 9-58
Zbigniew Jaworski, translated excerpt from an interview on June 26, 1987
Kreismuseum Wewelsburg, Tonarchiv, 005-TC-O

"It was forbidden to have a cigarette. And when a new transport with prisoners was supposed to arrive … The people got very little to eat, when they came back from work. Then suddenly, you were able to get cigarettes. And so people smoked. And the nicotine had such an effect on those weakened bodies, that a man would crouch down on the roll call area, fall asleep … and it was over."

No. 9-59
Zbigniew Jaworski, translated excerpt from an interview on April 3, 1998
Kreismuseum Wewelsburg, Tonarchiv, 041-TC-O

9.2.7
Work

"I was mostly in the camp and at the Bartels House … I built the barracks with the others, and then I was camp glazier. One thing that saved me: I had to work up the putty, the window putty. That was this brown stuff. In the cold it was hard as stone; yes, so in winter, you had to put it in the oven."

No. 9-60
Otto Preuss, translated excerpt from a talk with some Wewelsburgers, May 11, 1984
Kreismuseum Wewelsburg, Videoarchiv, 116-O

No.9-61
Double terrace door from the Führerhaus I, architect Hermann Bartel's villa
Wood, glass, metal
1940 – 1941
From 1940, SS Construction Management architect Hermann Bartels had concentration camp prisoners build him a villa on the outskirts of town. Political prisoner Otto Preuss worked there as a glazier, mounting the numerous panes in the window frames. Just a single terrace door at the mansion had 15 panes of glass.

During this work, Otto Preuss could often spend time near the oven, because the window putty needed to be heated before use. He could thus warm up regularly during the cold winter months and avoid getting frostbite. kjs
Kreismuseum Wewelsburg, inv. nos. 15025/1 and 15025/2

"Once, a prisoner succeeded in escaping in very heavy fog. He was gone four, five or six months, until one day, he was there again … Everybody in the camp had to fall in on the square and he was made to stride up and down, with a drum, shouting 'I'm glad to be back,' and so on. Then they put the "escape dot" (*Fluchtpunkt*), a symbol marking the inmate as a fugitive and target for assassination) on his back, and he didn't live long after that."

No. 9-62
Joachim Escher, translated excerpt from an interview on September 25, 1991
Kreismuseum Wewelsburg, Tonarchiv, 010-TC-O

"The foremen started yelling and then the prisoners had to carry the rocks running, one in back, the other in front. And then, along where they had to run, on every corner, there was a foreman waiting, and he'd let them have it with the club. And one of the prisoners – he later also went on disciplinary detail – he had a foot injury. He couldn't run very well, and wasn't so young either. And of course, he was slower getting by the clubs, see? They noticed that. He was beaten black and blue, from up here right down to his calves."

No. 9-63
Josef Rehwald, translated excerpt from an interview on May 16, 1992
Kreismuseum Wewelsburg, Tonarchiv, 018-TC-O

"And when you think about it, those struggles between the groups, it was life or death. If they wanted to get rid of someone, they just shoved a handkerchief in his mouth, so he couldn't scream. Then they dragged him out and held him under the cold shower, until the body lost its natural warmth and his circulation failed. Then, next morning, it was declared that he had suffered a circulatory collapse."

No. 9-64
Max Hollweg, translated excerpt from an interview on May 16, 1992
Kreismuseum Wewelsburg, Tonarchiv, 015-TC-O

"Instinctively, I knew I needed food to survive. That was my main thought. I didn't spend time thinking about anything else."

No. 9-65
Zbigniew Jaworski, translated excerpt from an interview on April 3, 1998
Kreismuseum Wewelsburg, Tonarchiv, 041-TC-O

"In the camp, morale played just as big a role as food. The fact that you knew you were among friends, that we're in this together, we stick together, the other guy's got your back, you can rely on him, that played a very, very big role in the camp."

No. 9-66
Otto Preuss, translated excerpt from an interview on May 11, 1984
Kreismuseum Wewelsburg, Videoarchiv, 116-O

No. 9-67
Paul Buder, *Wald* [Forest]
Oil on fiber board
Ca. 1943
Bible Student Paul Buder was active as a painter at Niederhagen Concentration Camp. Camp commandant Adolf Haas frequently ordered him to produce works, including oil paintings. The SS officer then gave these to friends and family. This piece was painted during Buder's imprisonment at the concentration camp in Wewelsburg; he gave it to his fellow-prisoner Max Hollweg.

Paul Buder's drawing and painting talents worked to his advantage, resulting in privileges from the SS and a reprieve from harassment. kjs

Loan from the Wachtturm-Gesellschaft
der Zeugen Jehovas, Selters
Kreismuseum Wewelsburg, inv. no. 16404

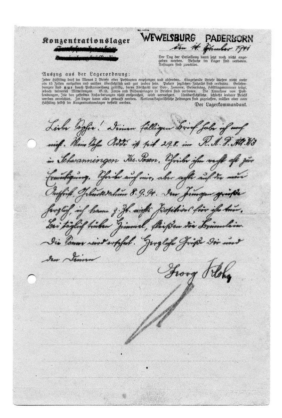

No. 9-68
Letter from Georg Klohe to Sophie Horstmeier, written from Niederhagen Concentration Camp September 14, 1941
After the divorce with his wife, Georg Klohe found a penpal in Bible Student Sophie Horstmeier with whom he maintained a steady correspondence. He had been given her address by a coreligionist. For Georg Klohe, not only was it important to have a contact person on the outside who could take care of his son, but the correspondence with a like-minded person also provided him with spiritual and moral strength. It was this personal correspondence, along with the solidarity among themselves, that – apart from material needs – helped the prisoners assert themselves in the camp and find the courage to survive. kjs

Kreismuseum Wewelsburg, inv. no. 16678

Dear Sophie!
I haven't received your answer to my letter yet. Since 8.29., my son Addi is in the RAD, Bt. W3, Schwanningen, Posen Dist. Please write him often to keep his spirits up. Write to me also, but mind the address; date of birth is 9.8.94. Send my love to the boy. I can't do anything tangible for him at present. Dark skies daily have the springs flowing. We're all waiting for the sun's return.
Best wishes to you and the family, your Georg Klohe

Translation of a transcription

"Siehe ich will zu vielen Fischern senden, spricht Jehova, dass sie sie fischen: und darnach will ich zu vielen Jägern senden, dass sie sie jagen von jedem Berge und von jedem Hügel und aus den Felsenklüften" (Jer.16:16).

1. Jehova kennt die Glieder seines Volkes. Er weiss, wo sie zerstreut worden sind durch die Streitkräfte der Dämonen. "Doch der feste Grund Gottes steht und hat dieses Siegel: Der Herr kennt die sein sind" (2.Tim.2:19). Er enthüllt, dass sein unwiderruflicher und unwiderstehlicher Vorsatz ist, alle intelligenten Geschöpfe, sowohl diejenigen der geistigen Klasse, als auch die der irdischen, welche zusammen Stellung nehmen für die theokratische Regierung unter Christus, als ein einziges Volk zu versammeln. Dieses Versammeln durch den Herrn muss stattfinden vor der Endschlacht von Harmagedon, deshalb müssen diejenigen, die so versammelt sind, die Organisation des Feindes fliehen, und in der Theokratie Zuflucht suchen. Diese Regierung ist jetzt in Tätigkeit, inmitten ihrer Feinde. Die Zeiten sind erfüllt durch das Inkrafttreten der Verwaltung des grossen Messias zur Rechten Gottes. 1918 war der Zeitpunkt, an dem das Versammeln stattgefunden hat, zuerst der geistigen Klasse und nachträglich durch das Versammeln der anderen Klasse welche in immerwährendem Frieden und Glück fortfahren darf, ewig unter der gerechten Überwaltung der Theokratie auf Erden zu leben. "Indem er uns kundgetan hat, das Geheimnis seines Willens nach seinem Wohlgefallen, das er sich vorgesetzt hat in sich selbst für die Verwaltung der Fülle der Zeiten, alles unter ein Haupt zusammensubringen in dem Christus, das was in den Himmeln und was auf der Erde ist, in ihm" (Eph.1:9,10).

2. Der Beginn der gerechten Regierung zeigt an, dass die Nationen der Welt an der "Zeit des Endes" angelangt sind. Diese Zeit fing mit dem "Tag Jehovas" im Jahre 1914 an, und endet in Harmagedon. Dann wird die ursprüngliche Streitfrage betreffend die Universalherrschaft ein für alle Mal entschieden werden. Die Theokratie wird sie richtig entscheiden, d-h- zu Gunsten des grossen Theokraten Jehova, des allmächtigen Gottes. Dieser Sieg wird den Namen Gottes rechtfertigen und allen lebenden Geschöpfen, die Gerechtigkeit und Wahrheit lieben, die Befreiung und Segnung bringen. Jehova ist das höchste und vollkommenste Wesen. Er ist die einzige Quelle des Lebens; er ist gerecht und geordnet und seine theokratische Regierung, welche sich über das ganze Universum, die Erde einbegriffen, erstreckt, ist die einzige rechtmässige Herrschaft.

3. Die Nationen der Erde, besonders solche, die sich "christlich" nennen, sind von Gottes Vorhaben, seine theokratische Regierung durch seinen König Christus Jesus wieder aufzurichten, in Kenntnis gesetzt worden. Dies geschah durch diejenigen, die Gott versammelt und aus welchen er seine Zeugen gemacht hat. Die Nationen haben die treuen Zeugen Gottes mit Verachtung behandelt. Sie haben die durch die treuen Zeugen mit Beharrlichkeit veröffentlichte Botschaft verächtlich zurückgestossen. Sie haben für Gott keine Beachtung gehabt; und um ihre eigenen selbstsüchtigen Pläne, welche die Beherrschung der Welt bezwecken zu begünstigen, haben sie die Dämonenherrschaft gewählt. Bei allen ihren Plänen nehmen sie keine Rücksicht auf den, in seinem Worte ausgedrückten Willen Gottes. Sie haben kein Vertrauen, dass Jehova durch seine Allmacht, seine Regierung der Gerechtigkeit für die Menschheit aufrichten werde. Sie ziehen es vor, selber zu regieren; sie weigern sich, das Königreich anzunehmen, welches durch Jehovas König, Christus Jesus hingestellt wird, und sich demselben zu unterwerfen. Obwohl sie in Anbetracht ihrer religiösen Gebräuche beständig den Namen Gottes im Munde führen, so geht doch aus ihrer Handlungsweise hervor, dass sie Gott vergessen haben. Gottes Urteil über sie lautet: "Es werden zum Scheol umkehren alle Gesetzlosen, alle Nationen die Gott vergessen" (Ps.9:17). In Kurzem wird sie dasselbe Schicksal ereilen, wie das untreue Jerusalem welches, in den Tagen Jeremias, sich der Religion ergab, seinen Bund mit Jehova übertrat und durch Gottes Willensvollstrecker völlig vernichtet wurde. Das Jerusalem des Altertums, war das Vorbild der heutigen "Christenheit". Alle, die darin verbleiben, sie unterstützen und sich ihrer Führung anvertrauen, werden mit ihr zum Schweigen hinabfahren. Sie erleiden dasselbe Schicksal wie die dämonisierten Religionisten von Jerusalem. Der Prophet Jeremia und Ebed-Melech der Äthiopier, sein treuer Gefährte, hatten Gottes Gutheissung. Ebed-Melech war ein Vorbild der "Jonadabe". Sie waren die einzigen, welche entrannten und ihr Leben retteten. Desgleichen werden in Harmagedon nur die Glieder des

---

Oh Wewelsburg, I cannot forget you!

At day's break, before the sun's first rays,
Long columns trudge to the day's toil,
Into the gray morning,
And the rocks are hard, but our step is firm,
And we shoulder our picks and shovels,
And in our hearts, in our hearts, the cares:

Oh Wewelsburg, I cannot forget you,
For you are my fate.
Who has left you begins to fathom
How wonderful is freedom.
Yet Wewelsburg, we neither wail nor weep.
And whatever the future holds,
We'll say yes to life,
For some day the time will come, then we shall be free!

The forest is black, red is the sky,
And we carry little bread in our bag,
And in our hearts, in our hearts, love,
And longing burns
Yet the girl is far, and the wind sighs,
And I love her so,
True, if only she could stay true:
Oh Wewelsburg, I cannot forget you …

The night is short, long is the day,
Yet a song rings out, a song of home,
We won't lose heart now.
Keep in step, comrade, and don't lose heart,
For the will to live courses in our blood,
And in our hearts, in our hearts the faith:
Oh Wewelsburg, I cannot forget you …

No. 9-69
Illegal printed material from the Jehovah's Witnesses, probably produced by prisoners in Wewelsburg
Ca. 1943
In the winter of 1943, Bible Student prisoners launched clandestine copying and duplication of religious texts, which they then smuggled out of the camp. This material is in all likelihood a copy of *The Watchtower* produced at the Wewelsburg camp, distributed illegally in Germany from spring 1943, and in Switzerland under the title "Fishermen and Hunters." The original English-language edition had appeared in February 1942. But it could take months or years until a title was secretly copied and circulated on the "illegal market." These copies bear witness to the strength of the Bible Student prisoners' belief that they brought to bear in their religious resistance under the daunting conditions of the camp. Facing constant threat of discovery by the SS, they consciously took the risk in order to affirm their faith. kjs

Kreismuseum Wewelsburg, inv. no. 16677

No. 9-70
Not shown
Illegal letter from Karl Truckenbrodt
Early 1943
This letter from Karl Truckenbrodt, presumably from 1943, written in a combative tone, and smuggled out of Niederhagen Concentration Camp, shows how crucial the strength of faith was for the Jehovah's Witnesses' survival. Years of concentration camp imprisonment strengthened their religious solidarity and encouraged Karl Truckenbrodt's defiant attitude, with which he supported his coreligionists in resistance and survival. kjs

Loan from the Wachtturm-Gesellschaft der Zeugen Jehovas, Selters
Kreismuseum Wewelsburg, inv. no. 16656

No. 9-73
"Oh Wewelsburg, I cannot forget you"
Wewelsburg prisoner song (translation)
1938 – 1945
The Wewelsburg camp song followed the example of the Buchenwald camp song. There, it was Austrian Fritz Löhner-Breda, a librettist of Franz Lehár, who wrote the lyrics of the original; Vienna cabaret singer Hermann Leopoldi composed the melody. The prisoners frequently had to sing the camp song on the area or while marching to the labor details. Though an official song approved by the SS, many prisoners felt a personal connection to it. kjs

"Sometimes, before the detail moved out, someone would say –
an SS man, that is – quite openly: 'I don't want to see him again
tonight.' So he was 'done in.' That's what they called it."

No. 9-74
Otto Preuss, translated excerpt from an interview in 1996
LWL-Medienzentrum Westfalen, FA 1009 inv 2833

"They were all slowly dying of hunger, fading to less and less. The
stages – you could follow them: Water went into the feet, then they had
elephant feet; when you pressed on them, it'd leave a dent. And then
the phlegmons would get in there. Then came the stage when they'd
stagger around, glassy-eyed, yes. And then, after that, yes, that was
pretty harsh, but that was the language, the hard language of the camp.
When they went into reverse, then you could start the countdown,
to when they would die, yes."

No. 9-75
Otto Preuss, translated excerpt from an interview in 1996
LWL-Medienzentrum Westfalen, FA 1009 inv 2833

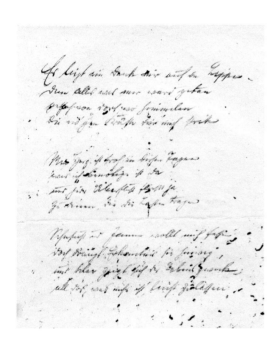

No. 9-71
Poem by Max Hollweg
1943 – 1945

Loan from the Wachtturm-Gesellschaft
der Zeugen Jehovas, Selters
Kreismuseum Wewelsburg, inv. no. 16910

Thanks rises to my lips
Because everything I've suffered came from
there, where heavenward the needed strength
for me did struggle. My heart is glad in these days,
What I require is there and every surplus
flows to those who carry the load
Longing and lament sought to have me,
Yet insight sweeps them aside, and clearly
does life's reason emerge. Everything
that is nothing, is easily left behind.

Translation of a transcription

No. 9-72
Not shown
"The Road Without End"
Song by political prisoner
Otto Preuss
1944
Written at Ravensbrück
Concentration Camp (copy)

Kreismuseum Wewelsburg,
inv. no. 17501

The extreme conditions of camp life left
little time or opportunity for cultural
pursuits. The thoughts of most prisoners
were ruled by hunger, fear, and the desire
to survive. Only those who had secured
their basic material needs could think
of resistance, solidarity, or even poetry
and literature.

Max Hollweg used his precious free
time to write poems expressing his total
religious devotion and unshakeable faith.
The song composed by Otto Preuss also
expresses courage and good cheer, yet is
not characterized by religiosity, but rather
by comradeship and solidarity. kjs

"You were only allowed to write so many lines. There wasn't much to write, anyway. You wrote that everything was okay. What else were you going to write?"

No. 9-76
Joachim Escher, translated excerpt from an interview on September 25, 1991
Kreismuseum Wewelsburg, Tonarchiv, 010-TC-O

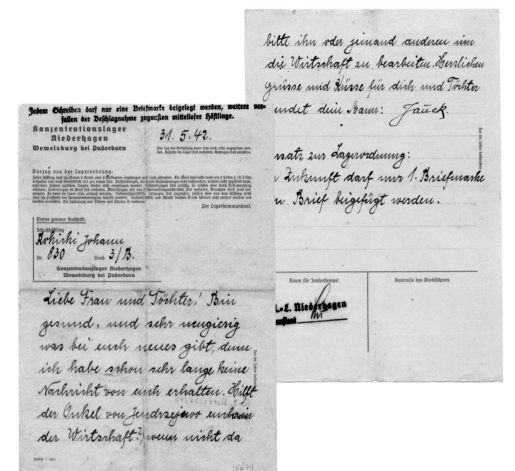

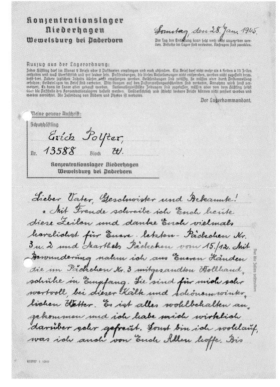

No. 9-77

Letter by Jan Rokicki from Niederhagen Concentration Camp to his wife and two daughters
May 31, 1942

Letters were usually the prisoners' sole link to the outside world, to their families and friends, and were therefore tremendously important. Foreign prisoners also had to write their letters in German. This represented an almost insurmountable obstacle for the majority of foreigners and proved particularly difficult for Soviet prisoners. Before his concentration camp detention, Polish prisoner Jan Rokicki had worked three years in Germany, and was thus able to write this letter to his family on his own. kjs

Kreismuseum Wewelsburg, inv. no. 16679

"Dear Wife and Daughters, I'm healthy and very curious about what's new with you, as I haven't heard from you in such a long time. Is the uncle from Jendrzejów helping you with the business? If not, ask someone else for help in the business. Warm regards and kisses to you and our daughters from your husband: Janek
Addendum to camp rules: in future, only 1 postage stamp may be enclosed in the letter."

Translation of a transcription

No. 9-79

Official letter from Erich Polster, a prisoner with the Buchenwald external work detachment in Wewelsburg, to his family
January 28, 1945

Erich Polster, a German Bible Student prisoner, received regular packages from his family. In this letter, he acknowledges receipt of wool gloves, which he evidently badly needed during the cold winter months. Censorship guidelines in the Buchenwald external work detachment stationed in Wewelsburg had loosened for Bible Student prisoners as well. In this two-page official letter, for which he still used a letter form left over from the disbanded Niederhagen Concentration Camp, Erich Polster openly mentions possible Allied air raids.

kjs

Loan from the Wachtturm-Gesellschaft der Zeugen Jehovas, Selters
Kreismuseum Wewelsburg, inv. no. 16881

Dear Father, Siblings and Friends,
It is with joy that I write these lines to you today and with many thanks for your latest packages nos. 3 and 2 and Marthel's package of December 15. I was delighted to receive the wool gloves you sent me in package no. 3. They are very important for me, with this cold and beautiful winter weather. Everything arrived in perfect order and I was really very happy about it all. Other than that, I'm fine, and wish you the same. Until
[over]
now, there's been no sign of air raids around here. In case of even greater difficulty with postal distribution, please give me a sign of life, as soon as possible. Be filled with faith and of good cheer, watchful, and look to the future with confident hope. My dear father, as I gather from your latest letters, you remain as you were eight years ago, our good father, and I am full of appreciation for your love for your children. Dear Erna and Marie, be a support to our father and I'll be glad when I can take your hands once again in mine, but let us be patient until then. Has Werner written Hedwig – at least once?

Many greetings to all our loved ones. And so to you, my dear family back home, Karl and Marthel's families, all the best and joined in love, your Erich.

Translation of a transcription

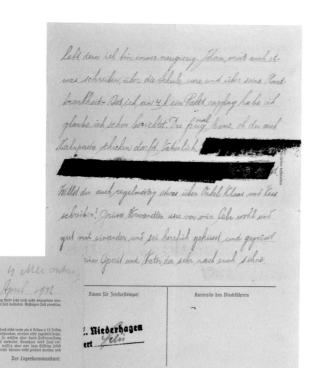

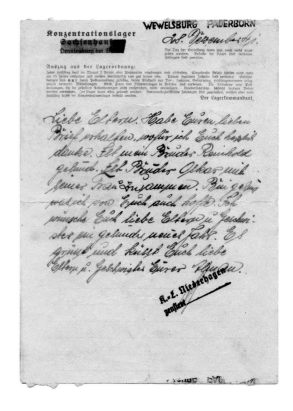

No. 9-78
Official letter from Gerrit Visser from Niederhagen Concentration Camp to his family
April 19, 1942
In his letters, Dutch prisoner Gerrit Visser succeeded in formulating his covert references and inquiries in a way that passed the censorship office. Thus, in this letter, he inquires about "Uncle Klaas and Kees," though in fact he means his colleagues, with whom he had been arrested, and whose fates he did not know. The reference to his son's skin problems is a coded request for information about the course of the war. However, the letter also displays a blacked-out section, rendered illegible by the SS censor.
kjs

Kreismuseum Wewelsburg, Nachlass Gerrit Visser, inv. no. 16617/35-1

Received May 4
April 19, 1942

Prisoner number: 887
Block 5b

My Dear Marie and Johan,
For many weeks, I have received no letter from you. But don't hesitate to write, even if you haven't received a letter from me. For example, 3 weeks after I should have written. – I'm still doing well and I hope you are well also. The latest news was good. – Marie, this time you have to tell about your life, for I'm always curious. Johan also has to write something, about school, etc., and about his skin problems. – I think I've already reported that I received a package on April 4. Marie, please ask whether you can also send toothpaste. Of course.
[censored passage]
Can you also give me some regular news about Uncle Klaas and Kees?
Greetings to relatives, etc., from me.
Live well and in harmony with each other.
Loving kisses and greetings from your Gerrit and father, who longs for you very much.

Translation of a transcription

No. 9-80
Letter from Alman Rose to his family
December 28, 1941
Writing to his parents was especially difficult for the illiterate Alman Rose. He had to ask fellow-prisoners to compose his letters for him. Even though strict censorship guidelines restricted expression, the prisoners did not want to miss out on a chance to give a sign of life to their families and to inquire about their welfare. Even the slightest news from home gave the prisoners a moral and psychological lift. kjs

Loan from private collection
Kreismuseum Wewelsburg, inv. no. 16953

December 28, 41
Dear Parents I received your kind letter, for which I heartily thank you. Is my brother Reinhold healthy. Is brother Oskar together with his wife. I'm healthy, and I wish you the same. I wish you, dear parents and siblings a healthy New Year. Dear parents and siblings, your Alman sends you his love and kisses
Censored Niederhagen C.C

Translation of a transcription

9.3
The Concentration Camp and the Village: A Forced Coexistence

Though the SS did all it could to screen the concentration camp from the public eye, its work details marched through the village daily, quarries and construction sites were partially visible, and the camp crematorium spread a cloying smell whenever prisoner corpses were burned. The direct proximity of the concentration camp to the village of Wewelsburg made it impossible for the SS's inhumane treatment of prisoners to remain hidden from the population.

Although the SS tried to portray the prisoners as dangerous criminals, the villagers remained unconvinced. The Wewelsburg fire department refused to participate in the manhunt for two escaped prisoners, and a farmer even offered one of the fugitives assistance. When the SS shot one escapee in the back, the villagers were dismayed.

At the same time, psychological repression and denial by the population went hand-in-hand with a degree of habituation. Some villagers made timid attempts at assistance, for example, by slipping the prisoners loaves of bread.

No.9-81
Aerial photograph of Wewelsburg
February 22, 1945
The Aerial Reconnaissance Archives
(TARA), Edinburgh

No. 9-82
Excerpt from the municipal chronicle on the first escape attempt by concentration camp prisoners
1939
The first escape, by two concentration camp prisoners, took place a few days after their arrival in Wewelsburg on May 15, 1939. Despite demands by the SS, the local volunteer fire department refused to participate in the manhunt. The impact of SS propaganda is clear in the account of party-loyalist village chronicler and schoolteacher Josef Hartmann: He characterizes the concentration camp as a "prison camp" and condemns the behavior of a farmer who offered one of the fugitives food and clothing, rather than report him immediately. kjs

Stadtarchiv Büren, Gemeindechronik Wewelsburg,
p. 434 f.

[p. 434]
On 5.15., two convicts, Henningsen and Bugla, succeeded in escaping after overpowering, gagging and robbing a guard of a carbine and ammunition. One, Henningsen, was apprehended that same day by SS-Scharführer Listl, suffering a severe gunshot wound to the stomach. He died as a result of his injury the next day at Büren hospital.

Two officers from the Geseke police managed to arrest 29-year-old Paul Bugla from Herten the next day. It is regrettable that the inmate was able to exchange his prisoner uniform for civilian clothing with the help of a farmer living in Geseke district. Rather than assisting the criminal with food and clothing, it would have been this farmer's duty to immediately report the escaped convict to the local police in order to

[p. 435]
support it in its struggle against criminality.

On 6.24, the Dortmund Special Court sentenced Bugla in Salzkotten to a total of 10 years in prison with forfeiture of his civic rights for a period of 10 years for mutiny associated with robbery and jointly attempted murder of a member of the SS. In addition to this sentence, the court authorized police supervision and ordered indeterminate preventive detention.

Translation of a transcription

No. 9-84
Not shown
Radio message with all-points bulletin for Paul Bugla
May 17, 1939
Stadtarchiv Büren, Polizeiakte

Aus dem Kreise

(!) Salzkotten, 27. Juni. Zu zehn Jahren Zuchthaus verurteilt. Das Sondergericht Dortmund verurteilte am 24. Juni 1939 in Salzkotten den 29jährigen Stellmacher Paul Bugla aus Herten als gefährlichen Gewohnheitsverbrecher wegen gemeinschaftlicher schwerer Meuterei in Tateinheit mit gemeinschaftlichem Raub sowie wegen des gemeinschaftlichen Unternehmens der Tötung eines SS-Angehörigen zu einer Gesamtstrafe von 10 Jahren Zuchthaus unter Aberkennung der bürgerlichen Ehrenrechte auf die Dauer von 10 Jahren. Neben der erkannten Strafe wurde Polizeiaufsicht für zulässig erklärt und die Sicherungsverwahrung angeordnet. Bugla war am 15. Mai 1939 zusammen mit dem Häftling Henningsen aus der gegen ihn als Gewohnheitsverbrecher verhängten polizeilichen Vorbeugungshaft nach Ueberwältigung und Knebelung eines Wachtpostens entwichen. Als er auf der Flucht von dem SS-Scharführer Listl an einem Waldrand gestellt wurde, sprang er in ein Kornfeld und wies dem gemeinschaftlich mit ihm handelnden Henningsen, der den dem Wachtposten abgenommenen Karabiner führte, die Schußrichtung. Henningsen legte in seinem Einverständnis den Karabiner auf den Verfolger an, wurde aber von diesem durch einen wohlgezielten Pistolenschuß rechtzeitig am Schießen gehindert. Er ist seinen Verletzungen erlegen, während Bugla am Tag nach seiner Entweichung ergriffen werden konnte.

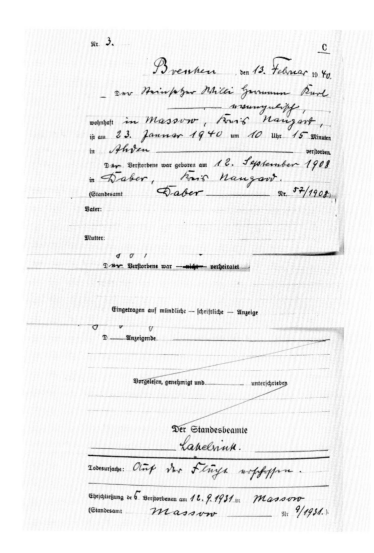

No. 9-85
Newspaper report of June 24, 1939 on the Special Court trial of Paul Bugla in Salzkotten

Despite demands from the SS, the Wewelsburg volunteer fire department refused to participate in the search for Paul Bugla. The SS interpreted this as evidence of the Wewelsburg population's reserved attitude toward them. The commandant of Sachsenhausen Concentration Camp (which at the time ran the Wewelsburg camp as one of its subcamps), *SS-Oberführer* Baranowski, decided, therefore, to travel to Wewelsburg to size up the situation for himself. The SS subsequently spared no effort at a show-trial to portray Paul Bugla as a hardened criminal. The Dortmund Special Court sentenced him to ten years in prison. When, a year later, he again attempted to escape from the prison in Münster, he was sentenced to death for "mutiny as a public enemy." He was executed on September 28, 1940, in Cologne. kjs

Bürener Zeitung, June 28, 1939

No. 9-83
Not shown

Excerpt from the municipal chronicle on the second escape attempt by concentration camp prisoners
January 1940

The second escape attempt occurred in January 1940. Prisoner Karl Wuwer was shot while escaping and died. The other prisoner, Willi Petermann, was apprehended on a farm in the neighboring community of Ahden and, after a one-hour interrogation, shot in the back by unit commander Wolfgang Plaul. Whereas the first escape attempt was widely reported in the press, this time all coverage was forbidden. The chronicler makes only passing reference to it. The SS did all it could to soothe outraged village opinion and to avoid legal consequences. The cause of death in the corpse transport permits was changed to "accidental" to veil the violence. And to prevent further trouble, Himmler had the prisoner labor detachment replaced with a new unit consisting entirely of Ernest Bible Students, who were known not to attempt escape. kjs

Stadtarchiv Büren, Gemeindechronik Wewelsburg, p. 449

No. 9-87
Death certificate of Willi Petermann February 13, 1940

Standesamt Büren-Brenken, Sterberegister No. 3, excerpt

No. 3
Brenken, February 13, 1940
Paver Willi Hermann Karl [*pseudonymized*], protestant, resident of Massow, Naugard district, died January 23, 1940 at 10:15 a.m. in Ahden. The deceased was born on September 12, 1908 in Daber, Naugard district. Daber Registry Office No. 57/1908
Father: [*pseudonymized*]
Mother: [*pseudonymized*]
The deceased was married
Registry officer: Lanebrink
Cause of death: shot while attempting escape
The deceased was married on 9.12.1931 in Massow
(*Standesamt Massow Nr. 9/1931*)

Translation of a transcription

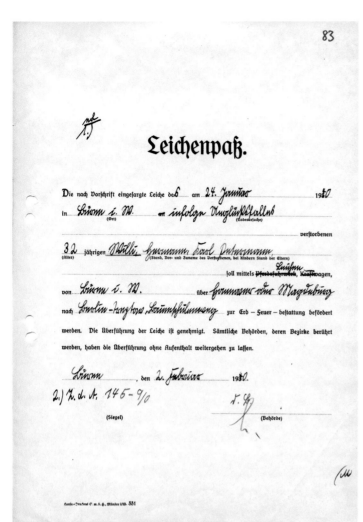

83

Leichenpaß.

Die nach Vorschrift eingesargte Leiche des ___ am 24. Januar ___ 19__

in _Büren i. W._ an _infolge Unglücksfalles_
  (Ort)   (Todesursache)

verstorbenen

_3.2_ jährigen _Willi Hermann Karl Petermann,_
(Alter)   (Stand, Vor- und Zuname des Verstorbenen, bei Kindern Stand der Eltern)

Leichen
soll mittels ~~Pferdefuhrwerk,~~ Kraftwagen,

von _Büren i. W._ über _Hannover oder Magdeburg_

nach _Berlin-Treptow, Baumschulenweg_ zur Erd — Feuer — bestattung befördert

werden. Die Überführung der Leiche ist genehmigt. Sämtliche Behörden, deren Bezirke berührt
werden, haben die Überführung ohne Aufenthalt weitergehen zu lassen.

Büren, den 2. Februar 19__.

2.) K. d. A. 145-9/0

(Siegel)   (Behörde)

84

B ü r e n , den 7.Februar 1940.

An den Herrn Standesbeamten   in Brenken

Anliegend übersende ich einen Personalbogen über den Häftling
Willi Petermann,welcher am 23.v.Mts.auf der Flucht in Ahden er=
schossen wurde.Petermann ist daher eines nicht natürlichen Todes
gestorben.Ich bitte,den Fall zu beurkunden und nach erfolgter Be=
urkundung eine Sterbeurkunde auszufertigen und diese sowie die
anliegende der Kommandantur des Konzentrationslagers Sachsen=
hausen in Oranienburg zu übersenden.Sollten für die Beurkundung
noch weitere Angaben benötigt werden,so bitte ich,sich mit der
vorgenannten Dienststelle in Verbindung zu setzen.

No. 9-86
Not shown
Radio message with all-points bulletin from the Paderborn state police office for prisoners Karl Wuwer and Willi Petermann
January 22, 1940
With this radio message, the state police announced the escape of the two prisoners from the concentration camp and requested assistance in their search. Two *Wehrmacht* soldiers billeted at a farm in Ahden noticed the prisoners searching for a place to hide and apprehended them. After questioning Willi Petermann, *SS-Untersturmführer* Wolfgang Plaul shot him without cause or warning. The death certificate of February 13, 1940, stated that he was "shot while attempting escape." kjs
Stadtarchiv Büren, Polizeiakte Bl. 80

No. 9-89
Corpse transit permit for Willi Petermann
Loan from Stadtarchiv Büren, Polizeiakte
Kreismuseum Wewelsburg, inv. no. 16884

No. 9-88
Order from the mayor to record an "unnatural death"
February 7, 1940
Stadtarchiv Büren, Polizeiakte

To avoid legal complications, the mayor ordered that further administrative steps regarding Willi Petermann's death classify it merely as an "unnatural death." This is the reason why the cause of death on the corpse transit permit was stated as "accidental." Both corpses from the early period of the concentration camp in Wewelsburg were conveyed to the crematorium at Berlin-Treptow. kjs

"So, it was known that the [prisoners] had broken out. … And the place was crawling with search parties, and we had these [soldiers] billeted here [on the family farm]; a division from Hamburg. … And suddenly, the NCO says to my father: 'Mister Stelte, look at that, those fresh tracks running up there.' It had snowed some during the night and those tracks led to our farm, right to this ladder [to the hayloft]. Now both [soldiers] got very nervous; they called up, for them to come down, that there was no escape. Nothing. And all of a sudden, there's this rattling outside. … So the [NCO] walks around the house … and he hits one of them; … He had a stomach wound. Then they first brought up the other one, who had already [run away]. There was straw on the barn floor and they sat him there and my mother brought him coffee and something to eat. …

… Now here comes the SS invasion. … Eventually, this car pulls up. Drove past everyone, drove right up to the door here. That was Plaul. … Short hair, big hulking guy. … Then he immediately screened off [the hallway], wouldn't let any of us in. He wanted to question the [uninjured fugitive]. …

My father was standing here [in the bedroom] and the door opened [to the garden] and the [fugitive] was walking out backwards, with his hands raised. He said Plaul shouldn't shoot, he had a wife and kids. And Plaul told him he wasn't going to shoot him, but he should turn around. But he didn't turn around and he got to about where that cart is, over there. Then he shot him in the face. Hit him in the chin, I think. I mean, that's just what I heard from my father. … How many times he shot him, I don't know either. … So they took out another door from the barn, loaded him on there. Then a truck from the SS pulled up. … And the wounded one, he was now lying on another door, they also brought him to the truck, just dumped him in there. Then one of the SS said 'Hey, take a look at your colleague there, he's already better off than you.' Then they tore off. And that was it."

No. 9-90
Translated excerpt from a letter by Hans Lau to his wife, Henny, about the flight of the two prisoners, Willi Petermann and Karl Wuwer
January 24, 1940
Kreismuseum Wewelsburg, Nachlass Hans Lau, inv. no. 14234/55/1-3

I was awoken suddenly at 2:55 a.m. by the sound of gun shots as well as the clatter of our machine guns. Two prisoners had climbed over the camp gate and disappeared fast as monkeys. Our camp guards immediately fired after them and took up the chase. … I sent out three-man parties to alert the surrounding population. … The Wehrmacht was now also on the scene, to take part in the search. …

I called the castle once again, for further orders. I was told not to take any action for now and to wait. …

At nine a.m., that same office gave us the good news that Wehrmacht soldiers had captured our jailbirds. One of them had tried again to flee and taken a bullet in the stomach. The unit commander immediately set out to welcome the gentlemen. And sure enough, there was the missing pair. During his explanation of the escape route, the unwounded one tried to flee once more, but he had not counted on the unit commander's marksmanship. He let off two pistol shots in quick succession and the beautiful dream of freedom came crashing to an end. Both prisoners were now packed into cars and off they went to the nearest hospital. Here, it was determined that one of the prisoners had died, the other, with the stomach wound, was operated on then put in a secure cell. An SS man remained as a guard. The next day, at 11:30 a.m., he also had made the great escape; he was dead, after confessing various things to our guard. …

I breathed a big sigh of relief when I learned that they had been apprehended. What mischief they could have caused. We spent the whole day yesterday writing reports. In the afternoon, there came an *Obersturmführer* from Oranienburg to officially investigate the whole matter. Each one of us was individually questioned and everything was written down. After that, he drove to the neighboring village with the unit commander to get a view of the scene. The interviews continued today and around four in the afternoon, he returned to Oranienburg. The ambulance came around at about six p.m. to pick up the bodies and that hopefully puts an end to the drama. The whole things sounds like a well-thought-out crime story. But in this case, it's all true. We always considered an escape in winter impossible, because they couldn't remain outside in the cold, but you live and learn. …
Daddy

Translation of a transcription

No. 9-91
Translated excerpts from an interview with Fritz Stelte on the capture of two escaped prisoners at the family farm in January 1940
March 15, 2007
Kreismuseum Wewelsburg, Tonarchiv, 107-MD-O

Wewelsburg, 9. Oktober 1942

Es erscheint Frau Wwe. Elisabeth B█████, geb. K█████,
Wewelsburg Nr. ███
und erklärt:

Bei den Straßenbauarbeiten an der Waldsiedlung und an der Almest
Se haben die Häftlinge das von mir von der gemeinde gepachtete
Grundstück Flur ██, Nr. █████, Teilfläche von 1/4 Morgen ohne
mich vorher zu benachrichtigen, betreten und dort eine Rohrleitu
gelegt. Hierbei ist fast die gesamte aufstehende Ernte an Kohl
verdorben bzw. von den Häftlingen bis auf die Wurzeln aufgefress
worden. Einige Reste haben die Wachmannschaften noch aufsammeln
lassen, diese sind aber alle von den Häftlingen angebissen und z
menschlichen Nahrung nicht mehr brauchbar gewesen.
Ich hatte auf der Fläche Rotkohl, Weißkohl, Wirsing, Rosenkohl u
Wurzeln angebaut und bisher erst eine kleine Menge Weißkohl geer
tet. Meinen Schaden beziffere ich auf RM 20,—.
Diesen Betrag benötige ich, um anderwo dieses Gemüse wiederzukau

Ich bitte deshalb um Erstattung.

Diese Erklärung ist der Erschienenen vorgelesen und von ihr unte
schrieben worden.

No. 9-92
Letter of complaint from a Wewelsburg woman requesting reimbursement for her lost cabbage crop
October 9, 1942
Translation on page 458
In October 1942, a woman from Wewels-burg complained to the concentration camp administration that camp prisoners had ruined her cabbage crop during earthworks. The oral complaint was put in writing and signed by her. What emerges from this document is, on one hand, the unimaginable hunger of the concentration camp prisoners and, on the other, the villager's lack of understanding and indignation about what she saw as the inconsiderate behavior of the prisoners. To what extent the text's choice of words, which betrays a deep contempt for human dignity in its attitude to the starving prisoners, originated with the plaintiff herself, or with the writer of the text – presumably an SS man – remains unknown. kjs
Landesarchiv NRW, Abteilung Ostwestfalen Lippe, Detmold, D 27-BKA-507-19-22-23

" … this wasn't at the castle, it was near the village. And there was a stone wall, I was to bring these stones over to the stonemason. With a cart. I had no strength and fell over, because it was too heavy …
And then [*the kapo*] Schmidt came along and wanted to break my ribs. That's what he did with the prisoners when someone was a '*Muselmann*,' without any strength, because he should just die; and he started pressing on me with his foot, here. That's when I heard a scream; a woman from the village was walking by and saw what he was doing to me, and she started screaming. So right away, the SS guard came and told him to stop, that people were watching … And this woman, she saved my life. So, for me, that's proof that the population was against it, what was happening at the camp."

No. 9-93
Translated excerpt from a contemporary witness interview with former Polish prisoner, Zbigniew Jaworski
1987
Wewelsburg residents felt powerless in the face of the suffering of the prisoners, whom they saw trudging through their village. For fear of punishment by the SS, they did not dare to protest openly against the situation. Some villagers tried to help the prisoners by hiding loaves of bread or other food along their routes to work or at the work sites. The cry of the woman that saved Zbigniew Jaworski's life can be seen as a spontaneous reaction against the inhuman brutality of the prisoner foreman toward a defenseless person. kjs
Kreismuseum Wewelsburg, Tonarchiv, 5 TC-0

The demise of SS rule in Germany was characterized by a complete loss of restraint. The terror within surged once again; prisoners were driven on death marches across all of Germany. Yet, with Heinrich Himmler's suicide, the SS also met its symbolic end. In the last days of the war, Wewelsburg descended into chaos. Explosives set by the SS severely damaged the castle shortly before the arrival of the Allies and the castle administration fled the village with their families.

The liberated prisoners immediately sought a fresh start, sometimes finding work with the Allies. The villagers, however, viewed the American troops as an occupying force.

10
The End of
SS Rule in
Germany and
Wewelsburg

10.1
The Concentration Camps and SS: The Final Phase

In the collapsing Reich, Allied raids and advances spurred an immense mobility. Splintered and marching military units, treks of civilian refugees, bombed-out homeless, escaped forced laborers, columns of prisoners, mobile special courts ("drum-head" court-martials), and marauding SS units roamed the country. Mobilization and social disintegration were part of a further culmination in the campaign of terror and extermination.

Concentration camps now also transformed into mobile facilities. Crammed into trains, relocated as needed, the prisoners were deployed repairing damaged railroad tracks. The SS cleared the larger camps before advancing Allied troops, sending sick and starving inmates on brutal, kilometer-long marches. At least a third of the approximately 700,000 prisoners who had managed to survive the concentration camps now perished. The SS and police seemed more powerful in this phase of the war than ever before. Yet, the unfettered violence proved to be the final surge of radicalization of an apparatus disintegrating in the face of the Allied advance.

No. 10-2
Writing on the door of the former Gestapo "Silver House" prison in Stuttgart, note the inscription "Capo Michat, 7th SS Baubrygady K.L. Auschwitz Gef. nr. 162262 Polak Radom Zeromskiego 3" [Capo … 7th Construction Brigade Auschwitz C. C. prisoner no. 162262 …]
Stadtarchiv Stuttgart, F 4817

No. 10-1
Concentration camp prisoners of Construction Brigade III in Cologne, with the city hall in the background Photograph: Peter Fischer, October 1943
Historisches Archiv der Stadt Köln, Bp 21849

Original planning intended that mobile SS construction brigades of concentration camp prisoners were to be deployed for the SS's settlement projects in East-Central and Eastern Europe. The course of the war, however, changed their scope of activity. Since the fall of 1942, prisoners assisted with rubble removal and bomb disposal following Allied air raids. The prisoner details were a common sight in numerous large cities, such as Cologne, Düsseldorf, Essen, Bremen, or Osnabrück.

One last time, the SS sought with its highly mobile SS railroad construction brigades to present itself as the indispensable crisis manager in this final stage of the war. This attempt cost many prisoners their lives, because they were forced to continue working during Allied air raids or were locked into freight cars. The system of repression functioned even under the mobile deployment conditions. Up until the very last days of the war, SS railroad construction brigades were still remanding individual prisoners to the local Gestapo for punishment. jes

WEAK MEN ARE SHOT DOWN ON THE ROAD.

DER RAPPORTFÜHRER ERSCHIESST EINEN, DER NICHT MEHR SCHRITT HALTEN KANN.

Nos. 10-3 to 5

Alfred Kantor, Drawings, painted over with watercolors, second half of 1945. Created in a displaced persons (DP) camp in Deggendorf (Bavaria)

Das Buch des Alfred Kantor [The Book of Alfred Kantor], 1st ed., Verlag Fritz Molden, Vienna/Munich/Zurich, 1972
(Rights now held by the Jüdischer Verlag of the Suhrkamp Verlag, Frankfurt am Main),
Overleaf of p. 114, overleaf of p. 113, p. 118

At the end of 1944, beginning of 1945, evacuations commenced the final phase of the concentration camp system. Decisions were made primarily at the middle and lower levels. Besides the SS Economic and Administrative Main Office, the decision as to when a concentration camp was to be disbanded rested primarily with the Higher SS and Police Leaders and individual concentration camp commanders, along with local NSDAP party offices. The establishment of hundreds of subcamps had spread the concentration camp system throughout Germany. With the camps now on the move, any locality could become the temporary site of a concentration camp. The guard units escorting these camp evacuations, which are known today as "death marches," committed atrocities and murders on a mass scale.

In powerful drawings, Alfred Kantor recounts an evacuation march that lead from Schwarzheide to Leitmeritz (Litoměřice) and from there to the vicinity of Theresienstadt (Terezín), Czechoslovakia. Kantor (1923–2003) had grown up in a Jewish family in Prague. In 1941, he was sent to Theresienstadt, in 1943 to Auschwitz, and in 1944 he was deported as a forced laborer to Schwarzheide, north of Dresden. He created these drawings at a displaced persons (DP) camp in Deggendorf (Bavaria). DP camps housed persons who, after the end of the war, could not, at least for the moment, return to their native countries. jes

10.1.3
The Liberation of the Concentration
Camps by the Allies

No. 10-6
**U.S. Army troops recover sick
and dead prisoners at the Boelcke
barracks, Mittelbau-Dora
Concentration Camp complex**
KZ-Gedenkstätte Mittelbau-Dora

No. 10-7
**Homeward bound to France:
Children and youths freed from
concentration camps wave to the
camera
June 1945**
National Archives, Washington D.C.,
111-SC-207908

The liberation of the concentration camps did not instantly end the former prisoners' suffering. Weeks later, many were still dying from the effects of their detention. Allied soldiers who entered the camps were confronted with hideous sights. They encountered thousands of dead and dying, prisoners reduced to living skeletons. The soldiers recorded what they witnessed in photographs and films. Few of those liberated were capable of jubilation. Many needed weeks to recover to the point of being able to leave the camp and return – where possible – to their homes.

jes

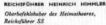

No. 10-8
Allied leaflet *Die Wahl* **[The Choice]**
Single page, front
Second half of 1944
Even with the war now raging on German soil and the defeat of the German Reich in sight, Heinrich Himmler was able to further expand his authority by acquiring ever new powers. Thoroughly convinced of his indispensability, he thought to play an important political role even after the war. From early 1945, he sent feelers out via neutral countries to test the chances of a separate peace with the Western powers, stubbornly refusing to accept that the Allies were not disposed to cut a deal with a nearly defeated National Socialist Germany, and – as the leaflet makes clear – even less so with one of its most-wanted war criminals.

When Adolf Hitler learned of Himmler's independent peace overtures, he stripped his long-time comrade-in-arms of all party and state offices on April 29, 1945. By that point, however, Himmler had relocated with the remnants of his SS empire to northern Germany, where, following Hitler's death, he vainly pressed his services upon the grand admiral Karl Dönitz and his provisional Reich government.

Carrying false papers, Himmler was ultimately apprehended by British armed forces. He took his own life while in custody on May 23, 1945. mh

Loan from private collection
Kreismuseum Wewelsburg, inv. no. 16936/1

No. 10-9
The portal of former Gestapo headquarters on Prinz Albrecht Straße 8, Berlin
Photograph: Yievgeni Chaldei, May 15, 1945
The remnants of Himmler's SS apparatus spread fear and terror until the very last moments of the war. Partly on orders from above, but largely of their own initiative they murdered thousands in early 1945, including many imprisoned surviving regime opponents, such as theologian Dietrich Bonhoeffer or would-be Hitler assassin Georg Elser.

Gestapo commandos were particularly vicious in their havoc; their murder toll alone exceeded ten thousand. The victims were mostly prisoners, foreign laborers, prisoners of war, Jews, and political opponents. The Gestapo's vicious excesses resemble the murderous practices of the earlier Deployment Groups (*Einsatzgruppen*) in Eastern Europe and were largely committed by the same people.

The perpetrators' motives were multiple: Some acted from prejudice and fanatical "final victory" fantasies; others as vengeance for their imminent defeat, or fearing the expected revenge of the persecuted; still others sought to eliminate as many witnesses and traces of their crimes as possible. mh

Ullstein Bilderdienst, 00446022

10.2
Between Chaos and New Beginnings: The End of the War in Wewelsburg

In the spring of 1945, events in Wewelsburg – as in the rest of the collapsing German Reich – came hard and fast. As late as the beginning of March, the Paderborn Gestapo had 15 Soviet and Polish forced laborers executed and hastily buried by the SS at the shooting range in Oberhagen. While youthful members of the military preparedness camp in Wewelsburg engaged the advancing Allies near Paderborn, members of the SS castle administration were already rushing from the village with their families in late March. On March 31, on orders from Himmler, *Waffen-SS-Hauptsturmführer* Heinz Macher attempted to blow up Wewelsburg Castle, with the castle's ruin subsequently being looted. On April 2, 1945, U.S. troops moved into the village and liberated the concentration camp prisoners. In early May, under the American "reeducation policy," former village NSDAP officials were made to exhume the corpses buried in shallow graves at the shooting range in the presence of the villagers and rebury them in the community's cemetery.

No. 10-10
Wewelsburg Castle following its destruction on Easter 1945, view from the north
Photograph: A. Porsch, 1949
On Good Friday, March 30, 1945, the chief castle administrator Siegfried Taubert, together with numerous SS men and their families, hurriedly left Wewelsburg before advancing American troops. At noon, on Saturday, a unit of SS sappers, under the command of *SS-Hauptsturmführer* Heinz Macher, arrived at the village. The previous evening, near Stettin, Himmler himself had given the order to blow up the castle. Yet, the quantity of explosives available was not sufficient to "eradicate" Wewelsburg Castle and the adjacent guard and staff buildings as ordered. The structures merely caught fire. After the SS unit's departure, residents of Wewelsburg and its surroundings, together with inhabitants of the Niederhagen resettlement camp, looted the castle. Rugs, furniture, porcelain, works of art, and untold thousands of bottles of wine were taken from the castle. When the fire reignited on Easter Sunday, April 1, for unknown reasons, leaving only the outer walls of Wewelsburg Castle standing. mm
Kreismuseum Wewelsburg, Fotoarchiv

The Demolition and Looting of Wewelsburg Castle

No. 10-11
Heinz Macher (1919 – 2001)
Ca. 1944
Heinz Macher, from Chemnitz, joined the SS Special Service Troops at eighteen. Since 1939, as a member of the *Waffen-SS*, he had participated in the German invasions of Poland, France, the Benelux Countries, and the Soviet Union. In 1944, he fought in France on the new Western Front. In early 1945, highly decorated, wounded several times in combat, he was ordered by Heinrich Himmler to his staff. Here, Macher was charged with testing new explosives and with the destruction of bridges and other buildings. After the attempted demolition of Wewelsburg Castle, he reported to Himmler, who promoted him to *SS-Sturmbannführer*. Macher accompanied Himmler on his flight and was captured with him by the British armed forces at the Lüneburger Heide on May 22, 1945. After his internment, Macher went into business. For the rest of his life, he remained active in associations of former members of the *Waffen-SS*.mm

Kreismuseum Wewelsburg, Fotoarchiv

No. 10-12
Rug fragment with meander motif
Wool
Ca. 1939 – 1945
During the Wewelsburg Castle fire on the Saturday before Easter, 1945, several villagers sought to save the large rug with a perimeter meander pattern out of the so-called Grand Courtroom. They threw the knotted rug out the window and cut it into several smaller pieces to take home. Like two other sections, this surviving piece of carpet was carefully bound along its edges and used for years as a bedside rug by its past owner. kjs

Kreismuseum Wewelsburg, inv. no. 15023

No. 10-13
Stooped Farmer with Wooden Cart
Oil print on paper, mounted on fiberboard
Kreismuseum Wewelsburg, inv. no. 8097

No. 10-14
Not shown
Plate, glazed and painted
From the inventory of the
Wewelsburg SS School
Seelos & Rottka workshop, Dießen
am Ammersee, mid-1930s
Kreismuseum Wewelsburg, inv. no. 8098

After the explosion, a Wewelsburg woman pulled this oil print along with the ceramic plate from the burning castle. The print was modeled after an original painting by Julius Paul Junghans, shown at the "Great German Art Exhibition" at the "House of German Art" in Munich. The ceramic plates had been ordered by the SS for Wewelsburg from the Seelos & Rottka company. Both objects were donated to the Kreismuseum Wewelsburg by the former owner's daughter. kjs

No. 10-15
Not shown
Soup spoon with (scratched-out) "Wewelsburg" engraving
Silver-coated steel
WMF (Württembergische Metallfabrik)
1939 – 1945
These items of cutlery were among the furnishings of the Wewelsburg SS School. After the explosion, they, too, were taken from the castle by village residents. To hide the pieces' provenance, attempts were made to scratch out their identifying engraving. kjs

Kreismuseum Wewelsburg, inv. no. 14674-14677

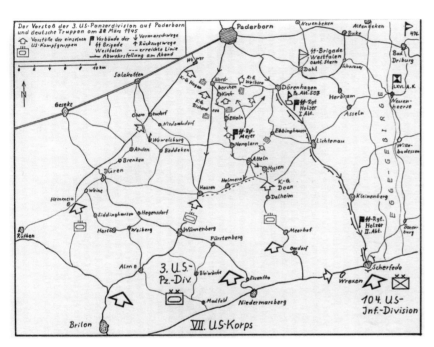

Der Vorstoß der 3. US-Panzerdivision auf Paderborn
und deutsche Truppen am 28 März 1945

3. U.S.-Pz.-Div.

VII. US-Korps

104. US-Inf.-Division

G-2 JOURNAL

HQ 1ST US INF DIV
APO 1, U.S. Army

(From: 1245
Time:
(To :

Date: 2 April

CP: B-667254

TIME	NO	FROM	SYNOPSIS	REC'D VIA	DISPOSITION
1245	30	Lt Lamb	9th Armored received a counterattack, consisting of only two tanks which broke through vicinity 9129, headed south. 2d Battalion of 413th, vicinity 9026 has not seen them yet. 104th Division not worried about it.	Vbal	J M
1310	31	26th	Large ammo dump south of Harth at 5923. About 35 RR cars along east side of woods vicinity 590227 loaded with ammo. Ammo dump being guarded by citizens. We have received no arty or mortar fire.	Tp	J, 4
1315	32	DA	Picked up two PWs from the German air force. They walked from Essen since Wednesday. We traced their path from Ellsen 2927 to 3427, 3827, 4430, 4730 through Buren and they were picked up shortly after.	Tp	J
1335	33	26th	Concentration camp at Wewelsburg. About 1300 people composed of Poles, Russians, German civilians of anti-nazi character, French and others. No arty or mortar being received.	Tp	J
1355	34	VIII Corps	G-2 Periodic Report #286, 30 March.	MC	J
1355	35	75D	G-2 Periodic Report #77, 31 March.	MC	J
1355	36	30Corps(Br)	Intelligence Summary #628, 30 March.	MC	J
1355	37	5AD	G-2 Periodic Report #243, 31 March.	MC	J
1355	38	79D	G-2 Periodic Report #217, 30 March.	MC	J
1355	39	79D	G-2 Periodic Report #218, 31 March.	MC	J
1420	40	4Cav	PW reports Grenadier Replacement Bn 58 moved into town at 535100. Total enemy in town about 300. No tanks or AT guns. Small arms and panzerfaust reported as only weapons. Labor Serv Co and Volkssturm make up remainder of force. (time 0930)	Msg	units Corps J
1420	41	4Cav	Enemy patrol unknown strength at 568090 at 0530A, killed 3 captured 1 (time 0800)	Msg	J, units corps
1420	42	4Cav	Patrols in fire fight with enemy machineguns east edge of Altenburen (time 1105).	Msg	J, units, corps
1420	43	4Cav	Four enemy sighted at 535133 and 2 enemy at 545129. Patrols are investigating. (time 1107)	Msg	J, units, Corps
1420	44	4Cav	Enemy sighted in edge of woods 590116. (time 1153)	Msg	J, units, Corps

NOTE: "Rec'd Via", Tp-telephone; rad-radio; Tgp-telegraph; Tpe-teletype
#, M-map; J-journal; T-troops; CG, C/S, etc.
Revised 3 Jan '44.

No. 10-17
The military situation in the Paderborn-Büren sector on March 30, 1945

In March 1945, moving from the Rhine, Allied forces bypassed the Ruhr Region to the north and south with a pincer movement. On Easter Sunday, April 1, 1945, at Lippstadt, they closed off the so-called Ruhr Pocket, effectively encircling German Army Group B.

On Tuesday, March 27, 1945, a large-scale British-American air raid almost entirely destroyed the town of Paderborn, leaving over three hundred dead. The following weekend, which was Easter, saw heavy engagements between German and American units with high casualties on both sides.

Shortly before the arrival of the Americans in Wewelsburg on April 2, 1945, the local military preparedness camp disbanded. A number of the instructors made their way to southern Germany, to continue fighting there. The majority of the youths attempted to return home on their own. However, a small group with a few instructors mounted a last-ditch defense against U.S. troops, erecting antitank barriers and succeeding in knocking out one U.S. tank. Several youths perished in these clashes. mm

Map: Willi Mues, Erwitte, 1984

No. 10-16
Not shown
Shepherd Mollemeier with his flock and American G.I.s in Alme Valley in front of the ruin of Wewelsburg Castle
April 7, 1945

The demolition represented the final act in Himmler's efforts to pull a pall of secrecy over Wewelsburg Castle. If even during the Third Reich Wewelsburg Castle was only accessible to a few select guests, entry was certainly not going to be allowed enemies of National Socialism.

At the end of National Socialist rule, the residents of Wewelsburg would have liked nothing better than to return to their relatively isolated village life of pre-1933 times, so aptly symbolized by the shepherd and his flock. Yet, now they found themselves plagued by the most recent past, which in the form of the destroyed castle and the concentration camp grounds in Niederhagen had left its indelible mark on the village. As American soldiers marched into Wewelsburg, deeply apprehensive villagers contemplated a future that would face them with the consequences of the war Germany had unleashed and now lost. mm

National Archives, Washington, D.C., U.S. Army Signal Corps, SC 407883

No. 10-18
G-2 Journal of the 1st U.S. Infantry Division
April 2, 1945

National Archives, Washington, D.C., First U.S. Army, 101-2.2

```
Copy No. 1
                    HEADQUARTERS 1st U.S. INFANTRY DIVISION        Auth of CG
                          1ST CIC DETACHMENT                      1st Inf Div
                          APO 1, U.S. ARMY                        Init: Rmw
                                                                  4 Apr 1945

                              FROM: 030800B April 1945
                              TO  : 040800B April 1945

                    CIC DETACHMENT DAILY REPORT
```

Inspected a concentration camp in Wewelsburg which was run by SS troops. Forty religious and two political prisoners (communists) were found in the camp. Many of these prisoners have been in the camp for several years and worked in clerical positions. They furnished a list of 34 SS troops and police who operated part of the camp. This list was submitted to VII Corps CIC for forwarding to higher headquarters. The prisoners at the camp are compiling a list of all SS men at the camp, all administrative personnel and all Party men associated with the camp. According to prisoners many atrocities were committed at this camp. In the process of screening people now living in part of the camp, three SS troopers, Herman SCHROETER, Gerhard BUCZKOWSKI, and Heinz MIETZ, were arrested and sent to MIC via PW channels. The following SS men who worked in the Wewelsburg camp are reported to be at large and possibly in the vicinity:

                    Kurt MACHE
                    LEHMANN
                    CRAMER
                    KNICKDONBERG
                    KNEBELOBERGER
                    KIRSCH

Interrogated and arrested Wilhelm Schneider, SS Sturmbannfuehrer, who was in charge of the concentration camp in Wewelsburg. – sent Subject to MIC. Also arrested and sent to MIC Emil BALLY, an SS man, who was a guard at the camp.

Arrested and sent to MIC Katte NAEGLER who was apprehended crossing the front lines in company with a uniformed Wehrmacht Officer and soldier.

Arrested and evacuated as PWs seven SS members in civilian clothes.

Arrested and evacuated as PWs seven Wehrmacht members in civilian clothes.

```
Copy No. 1
                    HEADQUARTERS 1ST U.S. INFANTRY DIVISION        Auth of CG
                          1ST CIC DETACHMENT                      1st Inf Div
                          APO 1, U.S. ARMY                        Init: Rmw
                                                                  3 Apr 1945

                              FROM: 020800A April 1945
                              TO  : 030800A April 1945

                    CIC DETACHMENT DAILY REPORT
```

Checked the village of Wewelsburg briefly. Closed the telephone office. Received a report that offices of the SS and police leaders of Duesseldorf had moved to this town on 28 March. Mail was found in the post office addressed to HIMMLER'S office. All mail was impounded for examination. The post office was closed. CI work will be continued in this town.

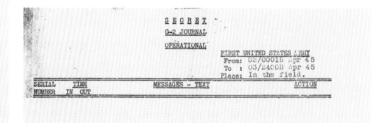

```
                              SECRET
                              G-2 JOURNAL
                              OPERATIONAL
                                           FIRST UNITED STATES ARMY
                                           From: 03/0001B Apr 45
                                           To  : 03/2400B Apr 45
                                           Place: In the field.

SERIAL    TIME        MESSAGES -- TEXT                       ACTION
NUMBER   IN  OUT
```

No. 10-19
Excerpts from the daily reports of the 1st Reconnaissance Section, 1st U.S. Infantry Division as well as the "G-2 journals" of the 1st U.S. Infantry Division
April 2–4, 1945

National Archives, Washington, D.C.,
First U.S. Army, 101-5.6 und 101-2.2

On April 2, 1945, at 1:35 p.m., without taking artillery or mortar fire, soldiers of the 16th U.S. Infantry Regiment reached the grounds of former Niederhagen Concentration Camp. In their initial report to 1st U.S. Infantry Division headquarters, the troops announced encountering 1,300 detainees, including Poles, Russians, Frenchmen, and German regime opponents. Evidently, U.S. front-line troops had initially mistaken Eastern European residents of the resettlement camp and French forced laborers for concentration camp prisoners.

The same day, the Americans searched the newly occupied village of Wewelsburg, shortly after receiving an (erroneous) report that the offices of the Düsseldorf SS and police headquarters had recently been transferred there several days earlier. At the post office, they seized numerous letters addressed to Heinrich Himmler's offices. On April 3, American investigators conducted a closer examination of the concentration camp grounds at Niederhagen, also interviewing the 42 prisoners of the remaining external work detachment (*Restkommando*) from Buchenwald Concentration Camp. That same evening, headquarters of the First U.S. Army were falsely informed that thirty to forty high-ranking SS men were hiding in a castle in Wewelsburg. In the chaos of the Allied advance, the Americans only slowly managed to gain a clearer picture of the situation in Wewelsburg and the SS's legacy there. mm

10.2.3
The Liberated Prisoners

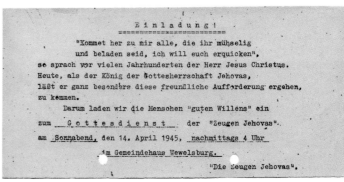

No. 10-21

Written confirmation from the U.S. officer C. H. M. Gould to Ewald Wettin Müller certifying that the prisoners of the external labor detachment (a Buchenwald sub-camp) had handed over works of art to the Allies
May 25, 1945

Kreismuseum Wewelsburg,
Nachlass Wettin Müller, inv. no. 16675

No. 10-20
Not shown

Draft of an Allied decree declaring all SS facilities American spoils of war
To control looting, the U.S. military administration published a decree declaring all SS installations American spoils of war. Evidently distrusting the residents of Wewelsburg, they charged the former concentration camp prisoners with their supervision. In this, they were to be supported by the local police.
kjs

Loan from the Wachtturm-Gesellschaft
der Zeugen Jehovas, Selters
Kreismuseum Wewelsburg, inv. no. 16876

No. 10-22

Members of the external work detachment from Buchenwald Concentration Camp in front of the workshop barracks
May 1945
Before the arrival of U.S. troops, rumors had coursed among the prisoners of the external work detachment of Buchenwald Concentration Camp that they would be executed for their knowledge of hidden art treasures. Although the rumors could never be verified, they live on in oral accounts. Advancing U.S. troops freed the concentration camp prisoners from the workshop barracks on April 2, 1945. To the Allies, who were surprised to discover a concentration camp at this location, the prisoners described the horrifying conditions at Niederhagen Concentration Camp. They were given civilian clothes and allowed to live in former SS houses or barracks. Most of the survivors left the area during the summer, although a few settled in the village and brought their families to Wewelsburg. kjs

Kreismuseum Wewelsburg, Fotoarchiv

No. 10-24

Invitation from the Jehovah's Witnesses to a religious service at the Wewelsburg Community Center on April 14, 1945
Translation on page 459

Loan from the Wachtturm-Gesellschaft
der Zeugen Jehovas, Selters
Kreismuseum Wewelsburg,
inv. no. 16874

No. 10-25
Not shown

Invitation from the Jehovah's Witnesses to a religious service at the Lüke Inn, Tudorf, on April 22, 1945

Loan from the Wachtturm-Gesellschaft
der Zeugen Jehovas, Selters
Kreismuseum Wewelsburg,
inv. no. 16875

As early as April 14, former Bible Student prisoners made invitations to their first public religious service in the village. For the brethren, who had spent many years in concentration camp captivity for their beliefs, it was natural and joyous to gather in open worship directly after their liberation and to hope to win over the villagers to their faith. Max Hollweg, who settled in the village as a practitioner of alternative medicine, made his office available for meetings until a "Kingdom Hall" was built for the Jehovah's Witnesses in Wewelsburg. kjs

No. 10-23

Members of the "remaining detachment" (i.e., external work detachment of Buchenwald Concentration Camp) pose for a commemorative photograph
April/May 1945

The former prisoners did their best to adapt to freedom and begin a new life. Some assisted with disbandment of the resettlement camp. The barracks were also used as temporary housing for displaced persons (e.g., former forced laborers) waiting to return to their home countries. Others endeavored to obtain valid papers to return home as soon as possible. For this, they had passport photos made, and also used the opportunity for group photos to preserve the memory of their shared concentration camp detention. In the photograph, it is apparent that most of the men are already wearing shirts and ties under their prison jackets. kjs

Loan from the Wachtturm-Gesellschaft
der Zeugen Jehovas, Selters
Kreismuseum Wewelsburg, inv. no. 16047

No. 10-26
Not shown

Letter from the Büren district administrator to the registry official in Wewelsburg regarding the marriage of Max Hollweg and Mathilde Uhrig
May 30, 1945

Standesamt Büren

No. 10-27
Not shown

Letter from the Büren district administrator to the registrar in Wewelsburg regarding the marriage of Kurt Hüter and Berta Kerzan
May 12, 1945

Standesamt Büren

The proximity of the workshop barracks housing members of the external work detachment to the resettlement camp had resulted even during the concentration camp period in relationships developing between some of the prisoners and the women in the resettlement camp. Although these contacts were discouraged, there were sufficient opportunities to get to know one another. Max Hollweg, for example, had been responsible for the security of the fireplaces at the resettlement camp barracks. Soon after liberation, former prisoners Max Hollweg and Kurt Hüter married women who had been interned at the resettlement camp. Max Hollweg remained in Wewelsburg, while Kurt Hüter, his new wife, and her child from a first marriage soon moved to southern Germany. kjs

No. 10-33

Pass for Mrs. Minert, Dr. Kaiser, and Wettin Müller to drive to the hospital
May 7, 1945

This pass allowed Dr. Kaiser, a practitioner of alternative medicine who provided medical care in Wewelsburg, and Wettin Müller, who did the driving, to take Mrs. Minert, diagnosed with suspected appendicitis, to the hospital in Büren. kjs

Kreismuseum Wewelsburg,
Nachlass Wettin Müller, inv. no. 16877

No. 10-36
Not shown

Vehicle transit permit for a Mercedes with veh. no. IX 332 148
May to August 1945

Because Wettin Müller, a former prisoner and clerk (*Lagerschreiber*) at Niederhagen Concentration Camp, knew how to drive and spoke English well, he became a driver and courier for the Allied occupation forces in Wewelsburg. With this vehicle transit permit behind the windshield, he was allowed to pass the checkpoints and carry out his tasks. Vehicles and gasoline were strictly rationed in early postwar Germany. Wettin Müller later received this Mercedes automobile in thanks for his services and drove back to his hometown of Bremerhaven in it. kjs

Kreismuseum Wewelsburg,
Nachlass Wettin Müller, inv. no. 16670

7 May 1945
Authority is herby granted Frau Minert and Doctor Kaiser to be absent from their camp to visit Hospital in Buren. Also the driver Muuller [*sic*]. It is believed the case is appendicitis and if so authority is granted to travel to Buren [*sic*] for admission to hospital this date. Car to be driven is IX 162099.
Wilbert L. Jones
Capt. CAC.
Mil. Gov't. Wewelsburg

Transcription

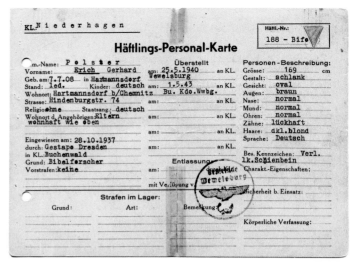

No. 10-28
Prisoner ID card for Max Hollweg
1945

The former prisoners used their old prisoner ID cards from Niederhagen Concentration Camp to obtain new identification documents. On the back of the ID, the new mayor of Wewelsburg vouched for the accuracy of the information. The left side bore an explanation in English to the effect that the bearer – in this case Max Hollweg – had been a concentration camp prisoner, freed on April 2, 1945. It requested that he be given all necessary assistance. The handwritten certification was required for Max Hollweg to move about freely outside the camp while assisting Dr. Kaiser, a practitioner of alternative medicine. kjs

Loan from the Wachtturm-Gesellschaft
der Zeugen Jehovas, Selters
Kreismuseum Wewelsburg, inv. no. 16671

No. 10-30
Not shown
Letter from Max Hollweg to his mother and his brother Erwin
May 2, 1945

Loan from the Wachtturm-Gesellschaft
der Zeugen Jehovas, Selters
Kreismuseum Wewelsburg, inv. no. 16901

No. 10-29
Not shown
Handwritten certification for Max Hollweg
April 27, 1945

Loan from the Wachtturm-Gesellschaft
der Zeugen Jehovas, Selters
Kreismuseum Wewelsburg, inv. no. 16670

No. 10-31
Not shown
List of medications under the letterhead of Construction Management, Wewelsburg SS School
April 16, 1945

Loan from the Wachtturm-Gesellschaft
der Zeugen Jehovas, Selters
Kreismuseum Wewelsburg, inv. no. 16878/1

No. 10-32
Not shown
Letterhead of Construction Management, Wewelsburg SS School
1945

Loan from the Wachtturm-Gesellschaft
der Zeugen Jehovas, Selters
Kreismuseum Wewelsburg, inv. no. 16878/2

In order to provide medical care for the village of Wewelsburg, August Kaiser, a former prisoner and practitioner of alternative medicine, opened up a practice immediately after his release from the camp. Max Hollweg, who had helped out as prisoner medic in the Niederhagen Concentration Camp sick bay and supported the camp physician Dr. Hagel in attending to the remaining detachment, now assisted him. Max Hollweg used the old stationary from the SS Construction Management, which the SS leaders had left behind when they fled Wewelsburg Castle. kjs

No. 10-34
Prisoner ID card for Erich Polster
April 11, 1945

On April 11, 1945, like many erstwhile members of the remaining detachment, former Wewelsburg external labor detachment prisoner Erich Polster received a new ID card on the basis of his concentration camp prisoner card. With this, he was able to leave Wewelsburg in the summer and return to his hometown of Hartmannsdorf, near Chemnitz. In August, the mayor of Hartmannsdorf issued him an additional pass, which was also in Russian for the Soviet occupation soldiers in the region. kjs

Loan from the Wachtturm-Gesellschaft
der Zeugen Jehovas, Selters
Kreismuseum Wewelsburg, inv. no. 16672

No. 10-35
Not shown
Written certification from the mayor of Hartmannsdorf for Erich Polster
May 22, 1945

Loan from the Wachtturm-Gesellschaft
der Zeugen Jehovas, Selters
Kreismuseum Wewelsburg, inv. no. 16680

No. 10-37
Engelbert Kemper (1884 – 1957), Mayor of Wewelsburg
1945 or 1946
Shortly after arriving in Wewelsburg, the Americans dismissed the National-Socialist-era mayor and ordered the farmer Engelbert Kemper to take up the office. He was responsible for holding the oration at the "atonement funeral" on May 4, with its main message being "We must be ashamed to be Germans." The appeal to the Wewelsburgers' sense of shame and responsibility was perceived by most villagers as an accusation of guilt by association and vigorously renounced. mm
Kreismuseum Wewelsburg, Fotoarchiv

No. 10-38
Catholic priest of Wewelsburg, Franz-Josef Tusch, in the vicarage garden
1949
United States occupation officials expected priest Franz-Josef Tusch to hold a sermon at the graves of the Eastern Europeans murdered in Wewelsburg that would address the atrocities of the Germans in the lands they occupied during the World War II. Tusch refused, speaking instead of "the curse of hatred and the blessing of love." In contrast to the newly appointed mayor Kemper, Tusch appeared to the villagers as the defender of the village's honor with respect to the occupying power. The priest became a rallying point for the alleged struggle against every form of "foreign rule," be it at the hands of the National Socialists or the Allies. mm
Kreismuseum Wewelsburg, Fotoarchiv

No. 10-39
Gravestone in the Wewelsburg cemetery for the Eastern European forced laborers executed by the SS in the Wewelsburg forest
1945 – 1961
In late March 1945, members of the SS and Gestapo shot 14 Soviet forced laborers and a Pole at the SS shooting range in Oberhagen. The United States military administration learned of this and on May 4, 1945, it ordered all villagers over the age of nine to attend the exhumation of the bodies and their reburial in the village cemetery. This act, known as an "atonement funeral," was meant to move the population of Wewelsburg to self-critical reflection on the recent past of their locality. However, in view of the SS's resettlement plans, the villagers considered themselves "victims" of the National Socialist dictatorship. Now, they felt that the Allied occupation authorities were placing them on the same level with their former oppressors.

In 1961, after reburial of the remains of the 14 Soviets at Stukenbrock Soviet Military Cemetery and those of the Pole in the cemetery for foreigners in Sennelager, the gravestone in Wewelsburg vanished without a trace. mm
Kreismuseum Wewelsburg, Fotoarchiv

The extreme experiences of the concentration camp left its survivors physically and mentally scarred. Their lives were strongly shaped by the privations and memories of camp life, and efforts to obtain legal and financial redress were usually cumbersome and often without success.

Although the SS was declared a criminal organization at the 1946 Nuremberg trials, and numerous offenders were convicted in subsequent trials by the Allies and in later ones held by the Federal Republic of Germany and the German Democratic Republic (GDR) – most SS perpetrators eluded criminal prosecution. Indeed, former members of the SS frequently managed to transition smoothly into German civil society. They kept a low profile; few were prosecuted. However, many former SS members stayed in contact with their "comrades," even capitalizing on the activities from their time in the SS.

11 Victims and Perpetrators after 1945

11.1
Life after Having Survived: The Former Prisoners

Former prisoners developed various strategies for dealing with their memories: some of them suppressed their experiences for decades, while others began to write them down and speak publicly about them early on. Mementos from the camp, such as a prisoner's jacket, often took on great importance, and were stored carefully at home. Many prisoners who had left Wewelsburg in spring 1943 faced the same uncertain future as those liberated from overcrowded concentration camps or on death marches. In 1945, Eastern European and Jewish inmates were initially accommodated in camps for displaced persons before being sent back to their country of origin. Some feared a return, and sought to emigrate instead.

No. 11-7
Paul Buder: Mosaic of a sailing ship
Glass, wood
1945
A few days after the liberation of the concentration camp, Paul Buder gave wagoneer Johann Wieseler this glass mosaic, titled "Sailing to Freedom," as a token of his gratitude, because he believed Wieseler had saved him from being killed by the SS before the American troops arrived. After their liberation, the prisoners learned that Johann Wieseler had hidden his wagon in the forest from the SS, fearing that an SS man wanted to use it in the execution of prisoners. For years, the glass ship hung in the Wieseler's living room, before being donated to the Kreismuseum in Wewelsburg. kjs
Kreismuseum Wewelsburg, inv. no. 14593

11.1.1
Coping with the Experience

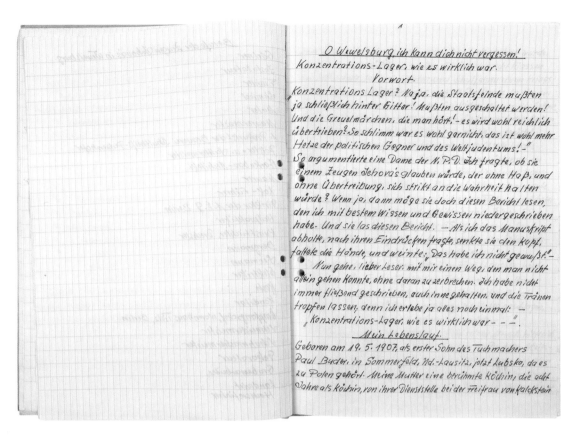

No. 11-5
Recollections by Paul Buder:
"Oh, Wewelsburg, I can't forget you"
Handwritten manuscript
1976
Translation on page 259
In the course of the second Wewelsburg
trial, against two SS men and two kapos,
a number of former prisoners, including
Paul Buder, took the stand as witnesses.
Subsequently, Buder began to write down
his recollections of his persecution and
detention in the concentration camps of
Sachsenhausen and Wewelsburg by the
National Socialists. For many years, the
document known as the Buder Report was
the only written account by a survivor available to the Kreismuseum Wewelsburg for
its research and pedagogical work. kjs
Kreismuseum Wewelsburg, inv. no. 17074

No. 11-2
Paul Buder
Photograph: J. Büttner, 1984
After being freed, Paul Buder, born
1907 in Sommerfeld/Lausitz,
stayed in the region, eventually
settling in Lipperode near Lippstadt,
where he started a painting business. Over the course of investigations stemming from the second
Wewelsburg trial, he began to
examine his own persecution during
the National Socialist era in more
depth, and wrote down his recollections. In 1984, he visited the
"Wewelsburg, 1933–1945. Cult
and Terror Site of the SS" memorial
and documentation center. kjs
Kreismuseum Wewelsburg, Fotoarchiv

No. 11-3
Wettin Müller
Ca. 1955
After being employed as a driver by the American military authorities following his liberation, Wettin Müller returned to his hometown of Bremerhaven with a Mercedes – given him by the Americans for his assistance – and numerous mementos from Wewelsburg. He quickly found work as an architect, his original profession, and married in 1947 for the second time. In the 1960s, Müller severed his close ties with the Jehovah's Witnesses because of his own political activities, yet remained true to his faith.

The extent to which his experience in the camp even influenced his architectural designs is evident in the addition he designed for his parents' house. Ostensibly referencing traditional Westphalian manors, he added a structure with the appearance of a fortified tower next to the existing building. The defiant architectural construct instead awakens memories of a concentration camp watchtower. kjs
Kreismuseum Wewelsburg, Fotoarchiv

No. 11-4
Wettin Müller's house in Bremerhaven, showing the *Wehrturm*
Photograph: K. John-Stucke, 2007
Kreismuseum Wewelsburg, Fotoarchiv

No. 11-10
Not shown
Stoneware eggcup, craquelure glaze, painted, inscription on base underside: Haus Wewelsburg
Workshop of Seelos & Rottka, Dießen am Ammersee, mid-1930s
When Wettin Müller returned to Bremerhaven, he brought with him a number of mementos from Wewelsburg. As an architect, he was particularly interested in the Wewelsburg Castle conversion plans and books from the former SS Construction Management library. This eggcup from the SS castle administration tableware is more of a "trophy." kjs
Kreismuseum Wewelsburg,
Nachlass Wettin Müller, inv. no. 15546

No. 11-12
Not shown
Prisoner's trousers
Striped blue-and-white twill (cotton, rayon, hemp)
Ca. 1940 – 1945
The objects Wettin Müller brought home included 12 items of prison clothing from the Wewelsburg external work detachment (a subcamp of Buchenwald), the so-called "remaining detachment," among which were jackets, trousers, underpants, undershirts, and a cap. Some of the jackets and trousers still bore the sewn-on purple fabric triangles, the identifying mark assigned to Jehovah's Witness prisoners, and individual prisoner numbers, which allowed some items to be traced back to their former wearers. Why Müller did not take only his own clothing, but also that of his fellow inmates is unclear. Conceivably, he wanted the garments as evidence for future generations, because in the early postwar period he worked to raise public awareness by giving political education talks at schools. Perhaps they served as a reminder of his suffering in the concentration camp. kjs
Kreismuseum Wewelsburg,
Nachlass Wettin Müller, inv. no. 15538

No. 11-8
Not shown
Freymüller, Schröder, *Kampf den Bausünden*, **1. Teil [The War on Construction Sins, part 1], the cover bears the stamp of the SS Construction Management library**
Berlin, 1941
Kreismuseum Wewelsburg,
Nachlass Wettin Müller, inv. no. 15763

No. 11-9
Not shown
Nordische Baukunst **[Nordic Architecture]**
1940
Kreismuseum Wewelsburg,
Nachlass Wettin Müller, inv. no. 15737

No. 11-1
Georg Klohe
After 1945
The first person Georg Klohe visited after regaining his freedom was Sophie Horstmeier, in Eickhorst, who had helped prisoners in Wewelsburg obtain religious texts. After Klohe's divorce, she had also maintained contact with his son at the front for him. From Eickhorst, he made his way to Wiesbaden, to the Jehovah's Witnesses' headquarters, where he worked full-time for the religious community. He began early to record his recollections of the past years of persecution by the National Socialists. kjs
Kreismuseum Wewelsburg, Fotoarchiv

No. 11-6
Not shown
Max Hollweg, *Es ist unmöglich, von dem zu schweigen, was ich erlebt habe. Zivilcourage im Dritten Reich* **[I Cannot Remain Quiet About What I Experienced. The Courage to Stand Up in the Third Reich]**
3rd Edition, Mindt, Bielefeld, 2000
The Jehovah's Witnesses in Germany first began to deal with its persecution by the National Socialists quite late, in the 1990s, when they initiated regional touring exhibitions focused mainly on individual cases of persecution. The 1996 documentary film, *Standhaft trotz Verfolgung. Jehovas Zeugen unter dem NS-Regime* [Jehovah's Witnesses Stand Firm against Nazi Assault], sought to establish that the Jehovah's Witnesses had been a victim group singled out for persecution by the National Socialists. It was in the context of these developments that former Niederhagen Concentration Camp prisoner Max Hollweg published his autobiography in 1997, in which he described what he endured during the National Socialist period. kjs
Kreismuseum Wewelsburg, inv. no. 16915

No. 11-13
Otto Preuss in his
prisoner uniform
After 1945
Kreismuseum Wewelsburg, Fotoarchiv

No. 11-11
Not shown
Prisoner's jacket
Striped blue-and-white cotton
fabric, with a red triangle and
sewn-on prisoner number 649
Ca. 1941 – 1945
Kreismuseum Wewelsburg, inv. no. 17060

Former political inmate Otto Preuss, who was imprisoned at Niederhagen Concentration Camp from 1941 to 1943, donated this prisoner jacket to the Kreismuseum Wewelsburg. It is not known whether he had worn it at Niederhagen Concentration Camp; it may have been issued to him later at Ravensbrück or Sachsenhausen Concentration Camp. The jacket bears the number 649, which was also Otto Preuss's inmate number at Wewelsburg. Presumably, he sewed the number onto the jacket after the fact to express his sense of solidarity. Many survivors wore their original prison jackets or replicas thereof at political events and events for former prisoners to show their common fellowship, and as a symbolic reminder of their suffering in the camps. kjs

"A policeman and a non-commissioned officer arrived. We were a big family; the eldest was at the front. They came into our house and said that we were going to go to Germany to work. They gathered a few people together. We all went to the railway station. They scattered straw on the floor of a freight car. Thirty of us rode in each railway car. They bolted the car [doors] and we started off. … They gave us nothing to eat. All we had was what we'd taken with us. [They] stopped the train in Poland so we could relieve ourselves."

No. 11-15
Translated excerpts from
an interview with Ivan Baglikov
April 4, 2005
Interview: Anne Roerkohl
dokumentARfilm GmbH,
Münster
Translation (from Russian to
German): Julia Walser
Kreismuseum Wewelsburg,
DVD inv. no. 297

No. 11-14
Ivan Baglikov, Russia (born 1923)
Photograph: Christoph Gödan, April 2005
Ivan Baglikov was born in 1923 into a family of Russian farmers. From 1929, he lived with his parents and five siblings on a collective farm in Kursk. In 1942, he and his 14-year-old sister were abducted to Germany as forced laborers. After several attempts to escape, the Gestapo sent him to Liebenau an der Weser labor education camp. In October 1942, after having spent two months in police prisons in Hanover and Dortmund, he arrived at Niederhagen Concentration Camp. In April 1943, he was transferred to the men's section of Ravensbrück Concentration Camp. In the spring of 1945, he was sent with a Sachsenhausen Concentration Camp labor detachment to clear bombing debris in Berlin. On May 3, 1945, he was freed by the Red Army while on a death march near Neuruppin. In June 1945, the Red Army sent Ivan Baglikov to the Urals. For the first three months, he had to work in an ore mine as part of a military work detail, after which his unit was placed under the direct control of shaft management. During this period, he was interrogated six times by the military intelligence service SMERSH (Death to Spies) about his time in Germany. He was granted his first leave in September 1946, to see his family in Kursk. Eventually, he was able to return home and marry. kjs

Kreismuseum Wewelsburg, inv. no. 17067

"For years, I couldn't talk about my experiences. I was locked in a shell, I couldn't talk about it. But as I grew older and I realized, I cannot take … I had to share my experiences with future generations. They should know what happened: how the Jewish people suffered, what they went through, how they were destroyed.
To be a warning to the future generation – to prevent it from happening. And I feel that my story – maybe not different from others – but I had to share it and tell the story. It was not easy for me to tell it, but I hope no generation will have to retell such a story again."

No. 11-18
Mark Weidman, USA (1923–2003)
Photograph: Christoph Gödan, April 2000
Mark Weidman was born in 1923 into a prosperous Jewish family in the region of Lviv (German: Lemberg) in Poland (now Ukraine). The outbreak of war in 1939 and the rising persecution of the Jewish population prevented him from studying at university. Instead, the Gestapo conscripted him into forced labor. In the fall of 1942, Mark Weidman escaped his impending deportation by fleeing to the German Reich under the assumed name of Stefan Galuszka, and looked for work in the Ruhr Region, where the Bochum Gestapo arrested him because he had no work papers. He arrived at Niederhagen Concentration Camp on January 1, 1943. In April 1943, he was sent to Ravensbrück Concentration Camp. He managed to escape while on a death march, shortly before the end of the war. In Poland, he reunited with his sister and his father. Fearing anti-Semitic attacks, the family left their Polish homeland. Mark Weidman first studied in Vienna and Paris, and then emigrated with his family to America in 1950. He married in 1952 and had two sons with his wife Dina. Mark Weidman died in 2003. kjs
Kreismuseum Wewelsburg, inv. no. 17062

"Even though the camp was small, it was infamous. I still remember, there was a guy who escaped, whom they [picked up] again … most of them they caught again. And so he was put on display, in the middle of the roll call area with a gaping wound, right here. … He just lay there, and we had to file past the corpse and look at it. Whoever didn't, they'd take two or three [of them] and push their faces right into the blood, like that. Nowadays one can't imagine that kind of thing anymore. So that's why we'd say … when we were still in the camp … we'd often say to each other: 'Well, if we get out now' – at that point, freedom was in sight – 'What are we going to tell other people? They'll never believe us.' … And many of them could never talk about it anyway."

No. 11-21
Translated excerpts from
an interview with Otto Preuss
1996
Interview: Anne Roerkohl
dokumentARfilm GmbH,
Münster
Landesmedienzentrum
Westfalen,
FA 1009 inv 2833

No. 11-20
Otto Preuss, Belgium (1914 –2003)
Photograph: Christoph Gödan, April 2000
Otto Preuss was a political opponent of the National Socialist regime, and a member of the Socialist Worker Youth. He went into exile in Belgium in 1933, and was taken into protective custody by the Gestapo after the country's occupation in 1940. He arrived in Wewelsburg by way of Sachsenhausen, and in the spring of 1943, was transferred to Ravensbrück Concentration Camp. He escaped from the death march. After the war, Otto Preuss initially stayed at the Bernau repatriation camp and returned to Belgium in May 1945. He suffered from long-term pulmonary complications as a direct result of his internment. In 1960, he gained Belgian citizenship. Politically, he was active primarily in the peace movement and at times held leadership positions on the International Sachsenhausen Committee. On his first visit to Wewelsburg in 1970, the locals greeted him with silence and contempt, and relations only thawed gradually. He and his wife Yvonne were regular guests at the memorial site founded in 1982. Otto Preuss died in 2003. kjs
Kreismuseum Wewelsburg, inv. no. 17061

"When you emptied a sack of cement, you had to be careful not to rip it, because it had to be returned, which was actually an advantage. We made a hole at the top … and on the sides, and wore that sack like a jacket. The water couldn't really soak into the paper, or at least it ran off easier than on the jacket. So it provided some protection. … They [the SS] knew about it, and were always checking us: 'Open your jacket!' I also gave in to temptation once. … And one of the SS [men] said: 'He's a Jehovah's Witness, they don't do that kind of thing,' and let me go. The fact that they trusted us so much was lucky; otherwise, they would've tied me to the whipping post."

No. 11-17
Translated excerpts from an interview with Leopold Engleitner
April 2, 2007
Interview: Anne Roerkohl
dokumtARfilm GmbH, Münster
Kreismuseum Wewelsburg,
DVD inv. no. 601

No. 11-16
Leopold Engleitner, Austria (1905 – 2013)
Photograph: Christoph Gödan, April 2000
Leopold Engleitner was born in 1905 in Aigen-Voglhub (municipality of Strobl am Wolfgangsee), Austria. His childhood was marked by illness, poverty, and hunger. At 13, he found work as a farmhand. As a Jehovah's Witness, whose religious community was also outlawed in Austria from 1935, he was arrested repeatedly. Following Austria's incorporation (*Anschluss*) in 1938, the Gestapo took him into protective custody in April 1939. He was sent to Buchenwald Concentration Camp, then transferred to Wewelsburg in March 1941, and ultimately to Ravensbrück Concentration Camp in April 1943. While in the concentration camp, he pledged to work in agriculture for the rest of his life and was consequently released on the initiative of the Reich Security Main Office in the summer of 1943 – without having had to renounce his faith. He then worked on a farm in his home district. However, when Leopold Engleitner received a conscription order on April 17, 1945, days before the end of the war, he fled into the mountains. After the war, he was ostracized by the village for his religious beliefs and for having been a concentration camp prisoner. It was only after 1999, upon the release of a biography and a documentary film about his life, that he received the acknowledgment and social acceptance that for decades had eluded him. Leopold Engleitner died on April 21, 2013.
kjs
Kreismuseum Wewelsburg, inv. no. 17063

"The washroom had hot water, but an SS member came in, took a hose, and doused us with freezing water. I caught a cold, and many others got sick, too. After we washed, we immediately put on the striped clothing and underwear. Then they gave us trousers, a jacket, and a coat. There was a number on the jacket. I was given number 119, category 'R', which stood for 'Russian'. From then on, that's how they told us apart."

No. 11-23
Translated excerpt from an
interview with Valentin Perov
April 4, 2005
Interview: Anne Roerkohl
dokumtARfilm GmbH,
Münster
Translation (from Ukrainian to
German): Elena Kantypenko
Kreismuseum Wewelsburg,
DVD inv. nr. 297

No. 11-22
Valentin Perov, Ukraine (1925 – 2009)
Photograph: Christoph Gödan, April 2005
After his mother died in 1933, Valentin Perov spent the rest of his childhood with his aunt in the Zhitomir District (Ukraine) and in an orphanage. After the start of the German offensive, he was briefly taken prisoner, but managed to make his way back to his aunt. From there, the German police deported him in May 1942 to do forced labor in Cologne. Suspected of stealing food in spring 1943, he was arrested by the Gestapo, and sent to Niederhagen Concentration Camp in early March. A month later, in early April 1943, Valentin Perov was transferred to Ravensbrück, and subsequently to Sachsenhausen Concentration Camp. Before the end of the war, he moved to Neuengamme Concentration Camp and then to Dachau Concentration Camp. On an evacuation march, he was liberated by U.S. soldiers near Penzberg, who brought him to a collection center. Like all forced laborers and freed prisoners of war he was also interrogated by Soviet intelligence, but avoided being exiled. Valentin Perov was allowed to return to Ukraine, and in Kiev he received valid papers and could look for work. Later, he married twice and had three sons. Valentin Perov visited Wewelsburg in 2003 and 2005. He died in 2009. kjs
Kreismuseum Wewelsburg, inv. no. 17068

"I regret that I've forgotten some of the details. My memory has suffered a lot; I was severely malnourished, to an extent – as one doctor told me – that it can lead to a protein deficiency in the brain. And brain cells can be affected, and in my case, it ended up in my memory, you know?"

No. 11-24
Josef Rehwald, Germany (1911 – 2002)
Photograph: Christoph Gödan, April 2000
Josef Rehwald, born 1911 in Königsberg (East Prussia), the fourth child of a Bible Student family, became an auto mechanic after leaving school. Though not yet baptized, he refused military service in 1939 on religious grounds, and was sentenced to a year in military prison. He was subsequently arrested by the Gestapo and sent to Sachsenhausen Concentration Camp. In 1940 he came to Wewelsburg, where he had to work in the quarry, and later he worked in the SS garages. In the spring of 1943, he was transferred to Ravensbrück Concentration Camp, where – for the first time in seven years – he met his mother, who was imprisoned at the Ravensbrück women's camp.

After the American liberation, he went to Berlin, where he was baptized and met his wife-to-be Elli, with whom he had two sons. Josef Rehwald remained active for the Watchtower Society troughout his life. He died on August 28, 2002. kjs

Kreismuseum Wewelsburg, inv. no. 17070

No. 11-25
Translated excerpt from an interview with Josef Rehwald
May 16, 1992
Interview:
Christoph Bitterberg
Kreismuseum Wewelsburg,
Tonarchiv (18-TC-O)

"The camp was disbanded in 1943, except for a remaining detachment of fifty people, who stayed behind. I was transferred to Buchenwald at that time. And when we arrived at Buchenwald from Wewelsburg, our health was so poor that the commandant of Buchenwald ordered a four-week break for our group. We didn't have to work for four weeks, and during the day we could move about freely in the camp."

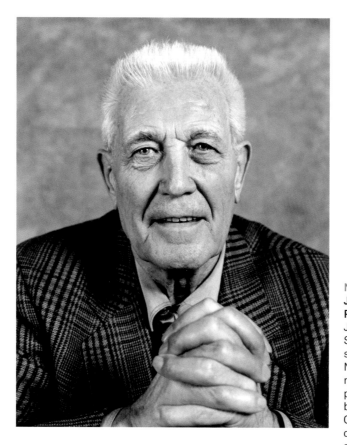

No. 11-26
Joachim Escher, Germany (1915 – 2004)
Photograph: Christoph Gödan, April 2000
Joachim Escher was born in 1915 into a Bible Student family in Schalksmühle. After secondary school, he hoped to escape the impact of the NSDAP by studying agronomy. In 1937, he refused military service, resulting in two years of military prison. Upon his release in 1939, he was detained by the Gestapo, who sent him to Sachsenhausen Concentration Camp. He arrived in Wewelsburg on February 16, 1940. He worked on the expansion of Wewelsburg Castle's northern tower, and as a prisoner functionary or trustee (*Kalfaktor*). In the spring of 1943, he was transferred to Buchenwald Concentration Camp, where he worked as an "assistant" for various prominent prisoners at the "Falkenhof." Following his liberation on April 10, 1945, he married Ruth Töllner, the daughter of a fellow inmate from Buchenwald. After moving to Meinerzhagen, they had four children and Joachim Escher served as the town treasurer. After his retirement, he worked as an alternative health practitioner. He died on September 28, 2004. kjs

Kreismuseum Wewelsburg, inv. no. 17065

No. 11-27
Translated excerpt from an
interview with Joachim Escher
September 23, 1992
Interview:
Wulff E. Brebeck,
Iris Schäferjohann-Bursian
Kreismuseum Wewelsburg,
Tonarchiv (10-TC-0)

11.2
Society's Treatment of the Victims and Perpetrators

Victims' associations assisted survivors after their return from the concentration camp with the laborious applications to receive legal compensation for their persecution. It was only in 1956, with the Federal Compensation Statute, that the Federal Republic of Germany unified payments for German nationals who could prove that they had been persecuted on racial, religious, or political grounds. Certain victims' groups, for example, the Sinti and Roma, the forcibly sterilized, prisoners who had been incarcerated as antisocial, and persecuted citizens from former Eastern Bloc states, were denied all compensation for years. This exclusion from compensation still applies to certain groups. Former forced laborers from Eastern Europe had to wait until 2000 to receive a (generally one-time) payment; for many it came too late.

By contrast, SS members who could not be proven guilty of having committed any crimes on an individual level were already able in 1951 to have their years of concentration camp "service" counted toward their pension payments. Although the SS was declared a criminal organization at the Nuremberg Trials in 1946, and numerous offenders were convicted in subsequent trials by the Allies and in later ones held by the Federal Republic of Germany and the German Democratic Republic (GDR), most SS perpetrators were able to avoid criminal prosecution.

"And one of these [American] officers said to me: 'When you've been in a concentration camp that long, you aren't normal [anymore].' Because it's impossible or someone to survive something like that and be normal. … I wanted to be a normal human being. So I didn't tell anybody that I'd been in a concentration camp. … Then I'd dream, for instance, that I'm in the concentration camp and have to do something. I'd be sweating heavily [from fear]. So, in those situations, I couldn't solve the problem in a normal way, that was the concentration camp side coming out. But I kept it to myself. That's when I understood that the American was right. … It stays with you."

No. 11-28
Zbigniew Jaworski, Poland (1921 – 2002)
Photograph: Christoph Gödan, April 2000
Zbigniew Jaworski, born 1921 in Kaski, near Warsaw, worked as a house painter following his graduation. After the German occupation of Poland in 1939, as a Polish soldier he was interned as prisoner of war. He was captured by the police while trying to escape. On November 9, 1940, the Gestapo sent him to Sachsenhausen Concentration Camp, from where he arrived in Wewelsburg in 1941. Suffering grievously under the horrifying conditions of the concentration camp, he became a *Muselmann* (derogatory term for a terribly emaciated and listless prisoner). Sick and undernourished, he was transferred Dachau Concentration Camp in August 1942, and three months later to Sachsenhausen. In early May 1945, near Schwerin, Zbigniew Jaworski was liberated from a death march by American troops. After returning to Poland, he married. decades, he attempted to suppress his memories of the concentration camps. In the summer of 1987, he returned to Wewelsburg for the first time, and allowed himself to remember. Zbigniew Jaworski died on January 31, 2002. kjs

Kreismuseum Wewelsburg, inv. no. 17069

No. 11-29
Translated excerpts from an interview with Zbigniew Jaworski
April 3, 1998
Interview: Heiner Duppelfeld
Kreismuseum Wewelsburg, Tonarchiv (41-TC-0)

11.2
Society's Treatment of the Victims and Perpetrators

Victims' associations assisted survivors after their return from the concentration camp with the laborious applications to receive legal compensation for their persecution. It was only in 1956, with the Federal Compensation Statute, that the Federal Republic of Germany unified payments for German nationals who could prove that they had been persecuted on racial, religious, or political grounds. Certain victims' groups, for example, the Sinti and Roma, the forcibly sterilized, prisoners who had been incarcerated as antisocial, and persecuted citizens from former Eastern Bloc states, were denied all compensation for years. This exclusion from compensation still applies to certain groups. Former forced laborers from Eastern Europe had to wait until 2000 to receive a (generally one-time) payment; for many it came too late.

By contrast, SS members who could not be proven guilty of having committed any crimes on an individual level were already able in 1951 to have their years of concentration camp "service" counted toward their pension payments. Although the SS was declared a criminal organization at the Nuremberg Trials in 1946, and numerous offenders were convicted in subsequent trials by the Allies and in later ones held by the Federal Republic of Germany and the German Democratic Republic (GDR), most SS perpetrators were able to avoid criminal prosecution.

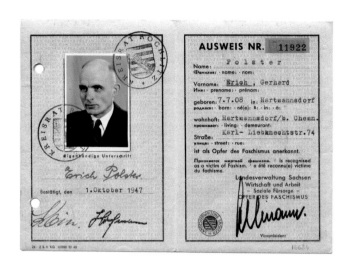

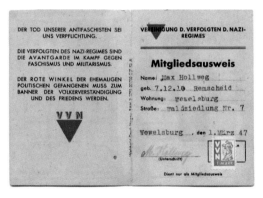

No. 11-34
Erich Polster's Victim of Fascism identification card
1947
Erich Polster, incarcerated for being a Jehovah's Witness, was officially recognized by the state administration of Saxony as a Victim of Fascism (OdF), and received the corresponding ID in October 1947. In the German Democratic Republic (GDR), official "victims of Fascism" were not paid compensatory damages, but as "Persecutees of the Nazi Regime" (VdN) were instead granted an additional pension (known as an "honor pension") at the age of sixty as of the 1960s. Recognition as a VdN proceeded according to clear guidelines: people suffering health problems while still employed also received a partial "honor pension" in addition to their regular wages. Special assistance, such as an annual medical exam and subsidies for children's education, were also allocated. In addition to the Victims of Fascism, the Persecutees of the Nazi Regime also included the "Fighters against Fascism," who were honored with a medal and special allowances. kjs

Loan from the Wachtturm-Gesellschaft der Zeugen Jehovas, Selters
Kreismuseum Wewelsburg, inv. no. 16684

No. 11-33
Max Hollweg's Union of Persecutees of the Nazi Regime membership card
In March 1947, Max Hollweg joined the Union of Persecutees of the Nazi Regime (VVN), which emerged that same year from various victims' associations of former political prisoners. It is a nonpartisan affiliation of resistance fighters and people persecuted by the National Socialist regime. Its guiding principles "peace, freedom, and understanding among all nations" are based on the Oath of Buchenwald, which the liberated prisoners took there in 1945. In the former German Democratic Republic (GDR), the VVN was replaced in 1953 by the Committee of Antifascist Resistance Fighters. In the Federal Republic of Germany, the organization was closely monitored by the intelligence service because of its communist character. In 1971, the VVN broadened into the Association of Antifascists (VVN-BdA), and allowed membership by relatives of people who had been persecuted, as well as interested parties who subscribed to the VVN's antifascist objectives. kjs

Loan from the Wachtturm-Gesellschaft der Zeugen Jehovas, Selters
Kreismuseum Wewelsburg, inv. no. 16676

No. 11-32
Not shown
Letter from the Altena *Kreissonderhilfsausschuss* (District Special Assistance Committee) to Joachim Escher on his official recognition as a victim of religious persecution
December 17, 1948
Joachim Escher, who as of November 1939 spent more than five years in various concentration camps for being a Bible Student (Jehovah's Witness), was officially recognized as a victim of religious persecution on December 17, 1948. To prove that he had been persecuted by the National Socialist regime, he had to submit all available documents relevant to his claim, including his protective custody order, indictments, pronouncements of judgment, and military service record, as well as a sworn statement by a fellow inmate about his time in the concentration camp. kjs

Original privately owned

11.2.2
Reparation and Compensation in Practice

11.2.3
The Treatment of Victims of National Socialist Persecution in their Native Countries

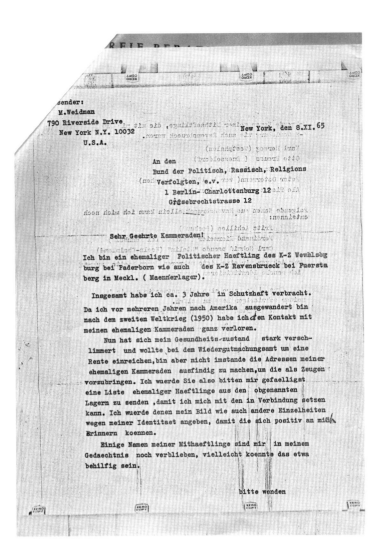

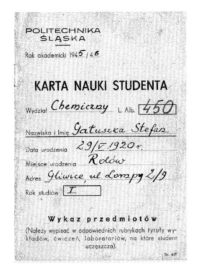

No. 11-37
Not shown
**Sworn statement by Karl Keller-
mann relating to reparation
proceedings for Willi Wilke, original
typewritten carbon copy; n.d.**
In his sworn statement, Karl Keller-
mann, who had been incarcerated
for being a Jehovah's Witness,
confirmed that fellow inmate Willi
Wilke had suffered severe damage
to his health as a result of his incarceration in a concentration camp.
It was often difficult for former concentration camp prisoners to have
their health problems recognized as
a direct result of their detention.
Sworn statements were a useful
addition to the required evidence.
kjs
Loan from the Wachtturm-Gesellschaft
der Zeugen Jehovas, Selters
Kreismuseum Wewelsburg, inv. no. 16898

No. 11-36
**Letter from Mark Weidman, in the
United States, to the Association
of Victims of Political, Racial, and
Religious Persecution
Berlin, November 8, 1965**
Translation on page 459
Despite repeated attempts, Mark
Weidman, a Polish Jew who emigrated to the United States in 1950,
was never compensated for his
three-year internment in concentration camps. In several exchanges
of letters in 1965, he attempted to
locate fellow inmates who could
verify that he had been detained.
The fact that he was listed in the
records under the assumed name of
a Catholic Pole, instead of his own,
caused him difficulties. kjs
Original privately owned

No. 11-35
Not shown
**Claim by Joachim Escher by virtue
of the Federal Act for the
Compensation of the Victims of
National Socialist Persecution (BEG)
September 18, 1953**
Original privately owned

No. 11-39
**Alexander Shtsherbinin
(on the right) with friends
After 1953**
After the war ended, former
Ukrainian forced laborer Alexander
Shtsherbinin was transported with
others back to the Soviet Union.
Like many former Soviet prisoners
of war and forced laborers returning
to their homeland, he was interrogated by Soviet military intelligence SMERSH (Death to Spies),
which suspected him of having been
a spy or traitor in the service of the
Germans. His accounts failed to
convince his interrogators of his
innocence, resulting in his having to
work in coalmines of Shakhty
(southern Russia), along with many
other war repatriates. Some time
later, he was sent to a Gulag (Soviet
prison camp) in Siberia. Near
Irkutsk, he had to clear forests for
the construction of the Tayshet-
Bratsk rail line and build roads. It
was only after Stalin's death that he
was allowed to return to his family
in Krasnyi Luch in 1953, and to begin
professional training. kjs
Kreismuseum Wewelsburg, Fotoarchiv

No. 11-38
**Polish student ID for Mark Weidman,
alias Stefan Galuszka
1945/1946**
In 1945, Mark Weidman enrolled in
the technical university in Gliwice
(Poland) under the assumed name
of Stefan Galuszka. As a Jewish
Pole, he had impersonated a Polish
Catholic during his flight to the
German Reich to escape persecution by the Gestapo. When he
returned to his native country after
the end of the war, he initially
retained his assumed identity, but
soon started attempts to recover
his real name. He was required to
submit numerous documents and
sworn statements by friends
confirming his true identity. Nonetheless, he ended up leaving Poland
for fear of renewed anti-Semitic
assaults and resumed his studies,
first in Vienna, then in Paris, before
emigrating with his father and
sister to the United States. kjs
Original privately owned

Streiflichter vom Konzentrationslager Niederhagen-Wewelsburg.

Sadist ,Lagerkommandant Haas ließ Zigaretten und Zigarren verteilen,
an sog, Vorarbeiter,welche den Auftrag bekamen,dafür die Häftlinge
"fertig"zu machen(fürs Krematorium) .Häftlinge,hungrige Gerippe,bei
schwerster Arbeit im Steinbruch,zu Tode geschlagen,getreten,gewirgt,
von 8 Meter Höhe abgestürzt oder in Jauche-oder Klärgruben geworfen.
Im Revier mit Leichengift abgespritzt. Weil für diese Kranken,sog.
Staatsfeinde,Verbandszeug zu schade war. Schlagwerkzeuge waren:
Mit Sand gefüllte Gummischläuche,Stiele von Hacken und Schaufeln,
Drahtseile,Hämmer,mit Stahldraht umwickelte Ochsenziemer,Hundepeit-
schen.
Häftlinge,geschlagen bis zur Bewustlosigkeit,krochen in ihrer Not
auf dem Bauche zum SS-Posten,und baten um einen gutgezielten Schuß,
oder krochen zum elektrischen Draht. Mancher Tag brachte 5 solcher,
"auf der Flucht erschossener Häftlinge. Wurden Zivilpersonen aufmerk-
sam,sagte der Kommandant abends im Lager zu den Berufsverbrechern-
Vorarbeitern:" Das Schlagen ist verboten! Ich will das nicht sehen!
Verstanden!" Und SS-Lagerführer Plaul anschließend:" Schlagt die
Kerls tot ,aber laßt uns das nicht sehen".
Arbeitsdienstführer Rehn stopfte sterbenden Häftlingen Erde in den
Mund,und sagte lachend:" Guck,der Kerl frißt noch". Häftlinge, bis
aufs Hemd entkleidet,nackend im Schnee sitzend,wurden von Arbeitsdienstführer Rehn eigenhändig bis unter die Arme mit Schnee einge-
packt, und musten so sitzen,bis sie abgestorben waren. Sterbende
Häftlinge, im Revier entkleidet,noch lebend zur Leichenhalle gebracht,erhielten noch lebend die Kennnummer mit Farbe auf den Leib
geschrieben,lagen bis zu drei Stunden auf nassem,kalten Steinboden
bis sie starben.Dauerte der Tod zu lange,so wurde mit Spritzen nachgeholfen. Tote, nachts im Bett gestorben,wurden morgens mit Knüppel
im Bett geschlagen;sie sollten aufstehen zur Arbeit! Unter allgemei-
nem Gelächter hieß es:"Mensch,der ist ja schon tot!"
Eine 18 jährige Russin verteidigte in einer Fabrik ihre Ehre gegen
einen deutschen Schef.Wegen Widerspenstigkeit wurde sie in Wewelsburg gehängt. Vom Verbrennungsmeister SS'Oberscharführer Stolle
wurde dieses tote Mädchen mit einer Eisenstange im Krematorium ge-
schändet. Augenzeuge Häftling Walter Beer (Helfer in der Verbrennungs
station). In den Händen des Verwaltungsführers SS-Oberstf.Michel,lag
die Ernährung der Häftlinge. Mit dem Mehl der Häftlinge wurden die
Schweine der SS-Totenkopfverbände gefüttert.Abends,im Dunkeln,brach-
ten Lastwagen Runkelrüben ins Lager,für die Häftlinge.Von Mai bis
August 1942 gab es jeden Mittag Brennesselsuppe,fast ohne Kartoffeln.
Ein ständiges Arbeitskommando schnitt täglich Brennesseln. Ein Masser
starben war die Folge. Der SS-Offiziersstab hatte des Öfteren Schwein
schlachten und mit dem Zucker,Mehl und Fett aus der Häftlingsküche
wurden Torten gebacken.Wurst und Margarine wurde in Paketen für die
SS-Familien auf Kosten der Häftlinge mitgenommen.Häftlinge sammelten
Regenwürmer und Schnecken während der Arbeit,versuchten diese in
Wasser gebrüht zu essen. Für diese sog,Vergehen gab es abends Straf-
arbeit mit Kostentzug,25.Stockschläge,Pfahl oder Sport:Kniebeuge,
Hüpfen,Rollen,bis zur völligen Erschöpfung,und die Magensäfte aus-
gebrochen wurden.Faustschläge,Fußtritte halfen nach.Gras,Blätter,
Wurzeln wurden während der Arbeit mit Heißhunger gegessen (Hunger-
wahnsinn).

Wewelsburg,den 4. Mai 1945

No. 11-40
Oswald Pohl, former head of the SS Economic and Administrative Main Office (WVHA), as the principal defendant in the so-called Pohl Case (or Case 4) during his concluding statement in Nuremberg
1947

On October 1, 1946, the main war crimes trial of 21 defendants ended with twelve death sentences, three life sentences, four sentences to terms of imprisonment, and three acquittals. Charges of war crimes and crimes against peace and humanity were brought against six groups and organizations, including the SS, SD, and Gestapo. Following the main trial conducted by the International Military Tribunal consisting of representatives of the United States, the Soviet Union, Great Britain, and France; twelve Subsequent Nuremberg Trials were held in the American occupation zone.

Case IV, against the SS-WVHA, involved 18 defendants, including Oswald Pohl, the head of administration. The main charges brought against them were war crimes and crimes against humanity as members of a criminal organization.

On November 3, 1947, Oswald Pohl was sentenced to death. The sentence was enforced on June 7, 1951. kjs

U. S. Holocaust Memorial Museum, Washington, D.C., Photo Archives, 08606

No. 11-41
Reports by Wettin Müller, translated excerpt from the investigation files of the U.S. military administration
May 5, 1945
Translation on page 460

Immediately after the liberation of the concentration camp prisoners, the U.S. military administration began to investigate possible war criminals. Initial reports by American troops already contained lists with names of members of the SS. As a former camp clerk at Niederhagen Concentration Camp, Wettin Müller had good insight into prisoner transfers and the camp command's methods of operation. In early May, he compiled an extensive report on conditions at the camp, which was translated into English and added to the investigators' files. Both the Americans and the British established War Crimes Investigation Teams. In the case of Wewelsburg, their efforts were unsuccessful. It was only in 1970 that a first trial forced members of the camp SS to answer for the crimes they committed at Niederhagen Concentration Camp.kjs

National Archives, College Park, War Crimes Investigation, NND 775032

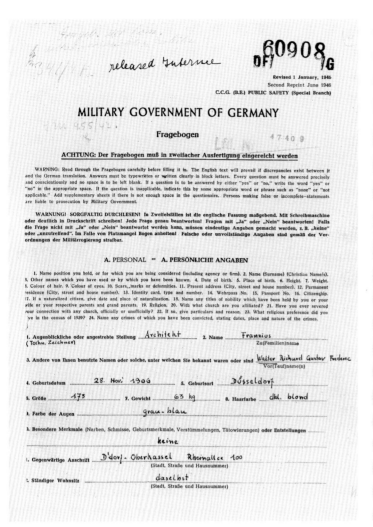

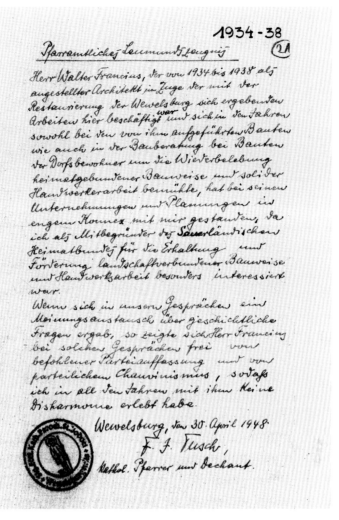

No. 11-42

Translated excerpt from the denazification questionnaire of Walter Franzius, page 1

1945

The denazification process agreed at the Potsdam Conference was comprehensively launched by the four allied powers in July 1945. Germany and Austria were to be freed of all National Socialist influences while also being democratized and demilitarized. The Law for Liberation from National Socialism and Militarism of March 5, 1946, outlined five categories of persons to be prosecuted: major offenders (war criminals), offenders (activists, militarists, profiteers), lesser offenders (probationers), followers, and persons exonerated. Although a questionnaire was created to simplify classification, legislation was often only applied halfheartedly, resulting in the classification of many perpetrators and activists as lesser offenders. Within a few years, many had flourishing careers. The Denazification Closure Law of 1951 ended the process of denazification in the Federal Republic of Germany. kjs

Landesarchiv Nordrhein-Westfalen,
Hauptstaatsarchiv Düsseldorf,
Entnazifizierungsakte, NW 1002-G NR 60908

No. 11-43

Letter from Franz Josef Tusch exonerating the former SS leader of indoctrination Walter Franzius

April 30, 1948

During denazification proceedings, suspected perpetrators could be cleared by presenting positive testimonies provided by victims or former opponents of the National Socialist regime. These exonerating documents were soon known among the German population as a *Persilschein* (referring to a popular brand of laundry detergent), sworn affidavits or letters of support that served to wash the suspected perpetrators clean of all National Socialist sympathies. Any genuine implementation of the denazification statute was thus avoided. Walter Franzius, the architect who had led the conversion of the Ottens Hof into a National Socialist village community center, had priest Franz-Josef Tusch formulate a letter of exoneration for him. They had once strongly disagreed with each other about the ideological use of symbols. kjs

Landesarchiv Nordrhein-Westfalen,
Hauptstaatsarchiv Düsseldorf,
Entnazifizierungsakte, NW 1002-G NR 60908

1934 – 1938

Parochial Certificate –
Character Reference

Herr Walter Francius was hired from 1934 to 1938 as a salaried architect to restore Wewelsburg Castle. In regard to the construction carried out under his guidance, and to his advice to villagers on their own building projects, he was actively involved in reviving traditional building methods and assuring quality building standards. During the planning and implementation of these projects, he worked closely with me. As the co-founder of the Sauerland Regional Association for the Preservation and Promotion of Traditional Architecture and Workmanship, I had a particular interest in these issues. Whenever historical questions arose during our discussions, Mr. Francius proved to be free of imposed party views and partisan prejudices, so that there was never any disharmony in all the years we worked together.

Wewelsburg, April 30, 1948
F. J. Tusch
Catholic Priest and Dean
Translation of a transcription

Ein Folterknecht von unbeschreiblicher Brutalität

Asozialer Häftling tat sich bei grausamen Mißhandlungen hervor — Vier Jahre Gefängnis

Paderborn. Nur mit größtem Abscheu und höchster innerer Empörung konnten die Zuhörer und Prozeßbeteiligten in der Verhandlung am Donnerstag vor dem Paderborner Schwurgericht die Schilderungen der zahlreichen als Zeugen vernommenen ehemaligen Häftlinge des Wewelsburger KZ über die dortigen Zustände und Vorkommnisse in den Jahren 1940 bis 1943 verfolgen. Der Prozeß galt dem jetzt 47 Jahre alten Bauarbeiter und damaligen Vorarbeiter im Wewelsburzer KZ, Otto Schmidt aus Neumünster, der beschuldigt war, sich in mindestens 100 Fällen der vorsätzlichen gefährlichen Körperverletzung mit einem gefährlichen Werkzeug (in einigen Fällen trat der Tod ein), schuldig gemacht zu haben.

Der Angeklagte Otto Schmidt, der seit dem Jahre 1924 insgesamt neunzehmal vorbestraft ist, u. a. wegen Diebstahls, Betrugs, Unterschlagung, Hausfriedensbruchs, Widerstandes, Amtsanmaßung und Unterhaltsentziehung, wurde im Sommer 1939 von der Geheimen Staatspolizei als „Asozialer" in Schutzhaft genommen, in das KZ Sachsenhausen eingewiesen und im Herbst 1941 nach Wewelsburg verlegt. Da er hier schon bald den SS-Wachmannschaften als kräftig und rücksichtslos aufgefallen war, machte man ihn schon nach wenigen Wochen zum Vorarbeiter für eine neu gebildete Arbeitsgruppe.

Dieser Arbeitstrupp umfaßte rund 100 Häftlinge und hatte ein altes Bauernhaus abzureißen und die schweren Ausschachtungsarbeiten für einen Neubau vorzunehmen. Schmidt wurde von zahlreichen dieser Häftlinge beschuldigt, die ihm unterstellten Mithäftlinge schwer mißhandelt zu haben, um sie zu größeren Arbeitsleistungen anzutreiben oder um sie zu strafen, wenn sie infolge Erschöpfung nicht weiter arbeiten konnten.

Die umfangreiche Beweisaufnahme

Im einzelnen haben die Ermittlungen und die Zeugenaussagen in der unter dem Vorsitz von Landgerichtsdirektor Dr. Amedick stehenden Schwurgerichtsverhandlung (Beisitzer Landgerichtsräte Dr. Wurm und Anteß) ergeben: Wie schon in der Anklage angedeutet, hat der Angeklagte in mindestens 100 Fällen Mithäftlinge mit einem Knüppel, einem Ochsenziemer oder Besenstiel schwer mißhandelt. Von den zumeist aus den Kreisen Büren, Lippstadt, Paderborn und Lippe stammenden Zeugen wurde fast übereinstimmend bekundet, daß der Angeklagte zu den brutalsten und gefürchtetsten Vorarbeitern und Antreibern des Lagers gehörte.

Er hätte auch an anderen Exekutionen teilgenommen, z. B. der Verabreichung von je 25 Stockschlägen an Häftlinge, die auf einen Bock gespannt wurden. Er habe so kräftig zugeschlagen, daß die Gepeinigten dann 14 Tage lang nicht sitzen konnten. Andere Häftlinge hat er erst zu Boden geschlagen und dann mit den Stiefeln in die Bauchgegend und in die Rippen getreten, daß sie vom Arbeitsplatz getragen werden mußten.

Zu Tode gequält

Einen Häftling mit Namen Opitz der schon so ausgemergelt war, daß er wie ein Gerippe aussah, schlug er, als er mit seiner Arbeitsleistung nicht zufrieden war, zu Boden. Opitz fiel dabei auf einen Stein und zog sich eine schwere Gehirnerschütterung und einen Schädelbruch zu, an deren Folgen er wenige Tage später verstarb. Zwei andere Häftlinge hat Schmidt ebenfalls niedergeknüppelt und dann noch auf ihnen herumgetreten. Daß einer von ihnen nachher gestorben ist, wie vielfach angenommen wurde, ließ sich nicht mit Sicherheit feststellen.

Durch die Postenkette gejagt

Erwähnenswert ist weiter aus der Aussage eines Zeugen, daß der Angeklagte einem Häftling Graupner gedroht hat, ihn zusammenzuschlagen, wenn er nicht durch die Postenkette liefe. Das tat Graupner auch und wurde von den Posten erschossen. Ein jetzt in Holland lebender Zeuge schilderte den Angeklagten als noch schlechter und brutaler als die SS. Für die Ausführung brutaler Prügelstrafen habe er einige Zigaretten bekommen. Ein anderer Zeuge will gehört haben, daß der Lagerführer zu dem Angeklagten gesagt hätte, ein bestimmter Häftling dürfte abends nicht mehr im Lager erscheinen. Das sollte heißen, ihn derart zu schlagen, daß er bis zum Abend nicht mehr am Leben bliebe. Die Lagerleitung glaubte, sich in dieser Hinsicht auf den Angeklagten verlassen zu können.

Was sonst noch in Wewelsburg geschah

Darüber hinaus berichteten die Zeugen auch allgemein über die im Lager Wewelsburg herrschenden Zustände, Folterungen und die erschreckend vielen Todesfälle. Selbst zwölf- und dreizehnjährige Kinder, Frauen und Mädchen wurden gehängt, viele Häftlinge, wenn sie versuchten, durch die Postenkette zu gelangen, ohne Anruf erschossen. Schwere Arbeiten wie Steinetragen mußten tagelang im Laufschritt verrichtet werden. Wer nicht mehr mitkonnte, dem wurde mit Schlägen und Essensentzug nachgeholfen, bis er schließlich zusammenbrach oder starb.

Bis zum Jahre 1942 wurden bei der Gemeinde Wewelsburg noch 1283 Tote des Wewelsburger KZ registriert, danach durften solche Registrierungen nicht mehr vorgenommen werden, weil die Zahl der Todesfälle beängstigend anstieg.

Mildernde Umstände bei der Urteilsfindung

Staatsanwalt Hennig beantragte gegen den Angeklagten eine Gesamt-Zuchthausstrafe von acht Jahren. Nach zehnstündiger Verhandlungsdauer wurde in den Abendstunden das Urteil gefällt. Es lautete wegen gefährlicher Körperverletzung in mindestens 100 Fällen, dazu in einem Falle wegen Körperverletzung mit Todeserfolg auf vier Jahre Gefängnis.

Der Angeklagte selbst hat die Taten nicht zugegeben, sondern auf die entsprechenden Vorhaltungen immer nur die eine Erklärung gehabt, es müsse sich um eine Verwechselung mit einem anderen Vorarbeiter handeln. Das Gericht hielt den Angeklagten jedoch in den angegebenen Fällen für voll überführt. Bei der Urteilsfindung wurde mildernd berücksichtigt, daß Schmidt eine schlechte Jugend gehabt, daß er auch ein Opfer des damaligen Systems geworden und ins KZ gesteckt, dort ebenfalls wiederholt vorher auf den Bock gespannt und nach 1943 im Kriege noch siebenmal schwer verwundet worden ist.

No. 11-47
"A Torturer of Unspeakable Brutality,"
Newspaper article
Translation on page 460
Westfalen-Zeitung, November 29, 1952

No. 11-44
The Defendant Otto Schmidt
Ca. 1950
Landesarchiv NRW, Abteilung Ostwestfalen-Lippe, Detmold, File D 21 C, access 24/84 no.

Born 1905 in Neumünster, the former kapo Otto Schmidt was the first person to be charged in the Wewelsburg trials in 1952. He had already been arrested numerous times for battery, larceny, and fraud, before being taken into protective custody and being interned at Niederhagen Concentration Camp classified as an "antisocial" prisoner. The initial charge of "crimes against humanity" was later changed to "bodily harm with fatal consequences." His brutal behavior toward other prisoners was confirmed by numerous witnesses. On November 27, 1952, he was sentenced to four years in prison. The district attorney appealed the sentence, and managed to have the prison sentence increased to five years and eight months in the judgment of April 8, 1954. All appeals for clemency were rejected as a result of his "incorrigible behavior" during the period that he was incarcerated. Otto Schmidt died in 1971 in Kiel. kjs

Die Angeklagten müssen mit der moralischen Schuld weiterleben

Freisprüche im Paderborner KZ-Prozeß — Mordvorsatz nicht bewiesen

Paderborn (WB/redna). Vier ehemalige SS-Angehörige und „Kapos" aus dem Konzentrationslager Wewelsburg mußten sich in einem dreimonatigen Prozeß vor dem Paderborner Schwurgericht verantworten. Sie waren angeklagt, am Tode von zahlreichen KZ-Insassen beteiligt gewesen zu sein. Obwohl die Staatsanwaltschaft gegen zwei Angeklagte lebenslange Freiheitsstrafe gefordert hatte, sprach das Gericht unter Vorsitz von Landgerichtsdirektor Safarovic Ludwig Rehn, Josef Friedsam, Ludwig Paetzelt und Max Schüller frei. Das Gericht konnte die moralische Schuld nicht ahnden.

Zu Beginn des letzten Tages im KZ-Prozeß erklärte Friedsam: „Ich habe kein Erinnerungsvermögen mehr an die KZ-Vorgänge." Abschließend bedankte er sich für die faire Behandlung, die er während der Verhandlungsdauer erfahren habe.

Der Anklageverfasser hatte fünf Jahre lang nach NS-Verbrechen aus dem Wewelsburger KZ geforscht. Ausgelöst hatte diese Ermittlungen eine Zeugenaussage im Sachsenhausener-Prozeß. Das Ergebnis der jahrelangen Ermittlungen: Eine fast 300 Seiten umfassende Anklageschrift, die den Angeklagten vollendeten und versuchten Mord vorwarf. Doch die Schuldvorwürfe konnten nicht aufrecht erhalten werden, wie der Vorsitzende in seiner Urteilsbegründung betonte.

Vor 17 Jahren befaßte sich bereits das Paderborner Schwurgericht mit dem KZ-„Kapo" Otto Schmidt, der wegen Körperverletzung in 100 Fällen — einige mit Todesfolge — zu fünf Jahren und acht Monaten Gefängnis verurteilt worden war. Damals war man näher an den Ereignissen. „In diesem Prozeß ging es einzig und allein um die individuelle Schuld der Angeklagten", hob der Vorsitzende hervor. „Jeder Zweifel mußte zugunsten der Angeklagten gewertet werden."

Viele Zeugen sind zum letzten Prozeß geladen worden. Einige hielten leidenschaftliche Verteidigungsreden für den Hauptangeklagten. Bei anderen Zeugen, so betonte der Vorsitzende, hatte man den Eindruck, daß sie es mit der Wahrheit nicht genau genommen haben.

Haß- und Rachegefühle konnten bei manchen Zeugen nicht ausgeschlossen werden. Bei den verschiedenen Körperverletzungen mit Todesfolgen durch die Selbstjustiz der Häftlinge im Lager (Wein- und Brotdiebe) konnte den Angeklagten nach Ansicht des Schwurgerichtes kein Mordversuch nachgewiesen werden. 1300 Häftlinge würden noch leben, wenn sie nicht in das Wewelsburger KZ gekommen wären. „Dieses KZ", meinte der Vorsitzende, „ist ein reines Arbeitslager gewesen. Viele sind an Unterernährung gestorben."

Das Schwurgericht ist der Ansicht, daß bei dem Komplex der Wehrdienstverweigerer, von denen keiner zu Tode gequält wurde, ein Mordvorsatz nicht nachgewiesen werden konnte. Die Staatsanwalt legte Revision ein.

No. 11-48
"Defendants Must Continue to Live with Moral Responsibility"
Newspaper article
Translation on page 461
Westfälisches Volksblatt,
February 6, 1971

No. 11-46
Not shown
"Jury at the Wewelsburg Crime Scene Yesterday. A Witness Testifies: '… and the crematorium was over here;' on-site inspection on the castle forecourt"
Neue Westfälische,
November 11, 1970

Although a guilty verdict could clearly be justified for the defendant in the first Wewelsburg trial, this proved impossible in the second trial in 1971. The four defendants, *SS-Untersturmführer* Ludwig Rehn, *SS-Unterscharführer* Josef Friedsam, and the two kapos Kurt Paetzelt and Max Schüller, were charged with multiple counts of murder and attempted murder. Other offenses, such as criminal assault, had already exceeded the statute of limitations and could thus no longer be included in the charges. Despite a five-year investigation, individual culpability could not be established due to partly unreliable and contradictory testimony. The circumstances of the deaths in question could not be established beyond doubt, resulting in the acquittal of all of the accused. kjs

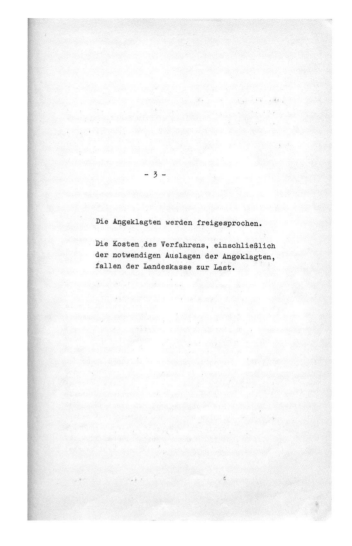

No. 11-45
"Prisoners Battered to Death: Hosed to Death with Water?"
Photograph: Redna
The defendants in the dock at the second Wewelsburg trial; from left to right, Max Schüller, Kurt Paetzelt, Josef Friedsam, Ludwig Rehn
Westfälisches Volksblatt,
November 4, 1970

No. 11-51
Not shown
Translated excerpts from the medical report by Dr. Dotzauer, M.D. regarding the possible forms of abuse that led to the fatalities, investigation files, pp. 6 – 9
1971
The medical expert at the trial, Dr. Dotzauer, M.D., from the Institute of Forensic Medicine at Cologne University, wrote a report on the possible forms of abuse that led to the deaths. Asked whether the hosing down of the affected prisoners in the washroom could directly result in death, he answered that it could, after having considered the difficulties of establishing an opinion based on witness testimony. kjs

Hauptstaatsarchiv Düsseldorf, Zweigarchiv Kalkum, documents from the Zentralstelle im Lande NRW für die Bearbeitung von NS-Massenverbrechen in Konzentrationslagern (North Rhine-Westphalia Central Office for the Investigation of National Socialist Concentration Camp Crimes) Cologne, on the second Wewelsburg trial at the District Court Paderborn, Trial records on the Niederhagen-Wewelsburg CC, AZ_24 JS 2/69 (Z), Rep. 118 no. 855-935

No. 11-50
Not shown
Bill of Indictment at the second Wewelsburg trial
Copy of the typewritten text, bound May 1970
The second Wewelsburg trial was prepared in conjunction with the Auschwitz trial by the North Rhine-Westphalia Central Office for the Investigation of National Socialist Concentration Camp Crimes at the district attorney's office in Cologne. In 1965, the The Central Office of the Judicial Authorities for the Investigation of National Socialist Crimes in Ludwigsburg had begun to investigate all National Socialist concentration camps and their subcamps in an effort to identify a possible group of perpetrators. The office began investigating crimes that had not yet been criminally prosecuted. Following a five-year investigation, the district attorney's office submitted a 250-page indictment containing evidence and statements from over one hundred witnesses. On May 11, 1970, the trial in front of a Paderborn jury court began against two former SS officers and two former kapos on charges of murder and attempted murder. kjs

Kreismuseum Wewelsburg, inv. no. 17075

No. 11-49
Judgment of the second Wewelsburg trial
Copy of the typewritten text, bound February 5, 1971
The judgment of February 5, 1971, handed down by the Paderborn jury court in the criminal proceedings against Ludwig Rehn, Josef Friedsam, Kurt Paetzelt, and Max Schüller is a sobering instance of German jurisprudence. After a nine-month trial, the defendants, who never confessed to any of the crimes, were acquitted because of contradictory witness statements. Nonetheless, the court left no doubt in announcing its judgment as to the moral culpability of the defendants. kjs

Kreismuseum Wewelsburg, inv. no. 17076

11.3
Suppression, Denial, Glorification: Members of the SS after 1945

The SS was formally outlawed by the Allied Control Council on October 10, 1945, and subsequently declared a criminal organization at the Nuremberg trials, along with the Gestapo and SD. During the following years, former SS members were put on trial periodically, but the resulting sentences were generally mild. The majority of erstwhile SS members never had to face legal proceedings; quite a few hid by assuming new identities.

On the surface, the majority of former SS men managed to fit unobtrusively into the new social order. However, personal connections to "old comrades" remained active and useful, for instance when reentering a career, or facing legal difficulties. Former members of the SS cultivated links to their past in various areas: some took a literary or artistic approach to old familiar themes, other "stalwarts" joined right-wing extremist political parties or veterans' associations that openly displayed their fundamental convictions in postwar German society.

No. 11-65
(Right to left) Des Coudres with the writers Ernst von Salomon and Ernst Jünger in front of Jünger's house in Wilflingen
Ca. 1960

Deutsches Literaturarchiv, Marbach, 8963-17

No. 11-63
Not shown
Hans Peter des Coudres: Bibliography of the works of Ernst Jünger

Philobiblon, a quarterly publication for collectors of books and graphic works, 4th year, 3rd issue (1960), pp. 231–266
Kreismuseum Wewelsburg, inv. no. 16454

No. 11-64
Not shown
Max Planck Institute for Comparative and International Private Law; October 29, 1956; articles by Hans Dölle, Hans Peter des Coudres, and Hermann Tausch

Mitteilungen aus der Max-Planck-Gesellschaft, 1956, vol. 6 (October 1956)
Kreismuseum Wewelsburg, inv. no. 16453

No. 11-59
Bernhard Frank, *Als Hitlers Kommandant. Von der Wewelsburg zum Berghof* [As Hitler's Commandant: From Wewelsburg Castle to the Berghof]
Arndt-Verlag, Kiel, 2007

Kreismuseum Wewelsburg, inv. no. 16950

No. 11-58
Not shown
Bernhard Frank, *Die Rettung von Berchtesgaden und der Fall Göring* [Saving Berchtesgaden and the Göring Case]
2nd revised edition, Berchtesgaden, 1987

Kreismuseum Wewelsburg, inv. no. 16963

No. 11-60
Not shown
Bernhard Frank, *Geheime Regierungsstadt Hitlers* [Hitler's Secret Capital]
Berchtesgaden, 2004

Kreismuseum Wewelsburg, inv. no. 16951

No. 11-61
Handwritten slogan: "If I weren't a nationalist, I'd be ashamed to face my forefathers."
After 1950

This note was written by Wilhelm Jordan on the back of a list of statistics from 1950. It demonstrates that even after 1945 Jordan still held fast to his SS convictions – something he would do until his death in 1983. He was involved with various right-wing cultural organizations, and sat on the executive committee of the German Reich Party (DRP) for the state of Rhineland-Palatinate. In the context of the 1960 ban of the DRP in that state, his house was also searched. ds

Kreismuseum Wewelsburg, Nachlass Wilhelm Jordan, inv. no. 16653

Dr. Hans Peter des Coudres (1905 – 1977), the former head of the SS library at Wewelsburg, was interned by the British at Sandbostel Camp, north of Bremen, from November 1945 to February 1948. During the denazification process, he managed to be classified as "exonerated." By 1950, he was working as a librarian again. After a brief period at the Federal Court of Justice library in Karlsruhe, he transferred to the Max Planck Institute for Foreign and International Private Law in Tübingen, and subsequently Hamburg, where he was in charge of the library between 1953 and 1972.

In his private life, des Coudres became a close friend and associate of the elitist and conservative novelist Ernst Jünger (1895 – 1998). Des Coudres enjoyed greater renown as the bibliographer of the brothers Ernst and Friedrich Georg Jünger, and the poet Joachim Ringelnatz, than for his technical publications. mm

The former Wewelsburg SS School folklorist, Dr. Bernhard Frank (1913 – 2011), commanded the *Waffen-SS* units guarding Adolf Hitler's residence at Obersalzberg in Bavaria between 1943 and the end of the war. It was here, at the end of April 1945, that on orders from Hitler he arrested the Third Reich's second-in-command, Reich Marshal Hermann Göring. A few days later, Frank himself was arrested and detained by the Americans for two and a half years for being a member of the SS. His family was still living in Wewelsburg upon his release in January 1948. After returning to his hometown of Frankfurt am Main, he went into business as a salesman. From 1980 on, Frank published a number of autobiographical accounts with the right-wing extremist publishing house Arndt-Verlag, among others. There is no mention or critical assessment of the SS or his own role in it. mm

No. 11-62
Not shown
Public announcement of the federal election results for the Paderborn electoral district
1972

In 1965, the DRP merged with the German National Democratic Party (NPD), which Wilhelm Jordan then dedicated himself to. In 1972, he was the NPD candidate for the National Assembly in Paderborn district, among others against the Christian Democratic Union (CDU) chancellor candidate Rainer Barzel, and the Free Democratic Party (FDP) candidate, *Der Spiegel* publisher Rudolf Augstein. ds

Kreisarchiv Paderborn, PB B-44

No. 11-66

Ludwig Rehn as a defendant in the second Wewelsburg trial

Ludwig Rehn, born 1910, joined the SS in 1935. From 1940 to 1942, he was a prisoner labor duty leader in Wewelsburg. In the summer of 1942, he was transferred to Neuengamme Concentration Camp, and later also to Lublin and Sachsenhausen Concentration Camps.

His activities at Sachsenhausen led to Ludwig Rehn's indictment in the Berlinskij Trial. During this first public Soviet trial of SS personnel at Sachsenhausen Concentration Camp, he was sentenced to life imprisonment at the Soviet Workuta Labor Camp together with other SS officers.

As early as the winter of 1955 – 1956, Rehn was transferred from the Soviet Union to the Federal Republic of Germany as one of about five hundred non-amnestied war criminals handed over to the German government, which was now supposed to handle them in accord with German law as it saw fit. However, legal proceedings subsequently initiated against Rehn were abandoned, with the official explanation that "the preliminary investigation had not provided sufficient grounds to initiate criminal prosecution." kjs/sk

Detail from a photograph in the *Westfälisches Volksblatt* November 4, 1970

No. 11-67
Not shown

Ludwig Rehn's application for additional compensation September 30, 1964

After he returned to the Federal Republic, Rehn faced no social or professional disadvantages as a result of his National Socialist past. As the 1960 letter from the senior public prosecutor's office illustrates, he was not considered to have a criminal record, because the judgment passed by the Soviet court was not legally recognized in the Federal Republic of Germany. The prosecutor's office went so far as to attest to Rehn's good reputation. Like many former SS men, he received financial compensation for his detention at Workuta. Until the end of the 1960s, Rehn worked for the Saarbergwerke, a regional mining company, where he had been employed before working at the concentration camps.

In 1970, Rehn was tried by a Paderborn court. The court case against two SS men, the sole trial for crimes committed exclusively at Niederhagen Concentration Camp, ended in acquittal. Ludwig Rehn died in 1982. kjs/sk

Deutsche Dienststelle (WAST)

No. 11-68

Wilhelm Otte
1951

SS-Unterscharführer Wilhelm Otte, born 1905, worked as a financial clerk before he was drafted in 1939. From 1940, he was a member of the Death's Head Units. He was first sent to Mauthausen Concentration Camp, Gusen subcamp, until his assignment to the Wewelsburg guard batallion (Wachsturmbann) in 1942. In April 1943, he transferred to Bergen-Belsen as a deputy report leader.

In May 1945, Wilhelm Otte was initially held by the British as a prisoner of war, and interned for over two years from January 1946. He was released in July 1948, followed by his denazification in September. He was classified as a Category IV "follower," which led to his assets and bank accounts being frozen. No employment restrictions were imposed on him and Otte applied to be rehired by his former employer, the Bünde tax office. His reemployment was not possible immediately, so he initially received interim payments from the tax office. He was hired back in September 1951, as "concerns regarding his reinstatement ... no longer existed." Just one year after taking up his duties at the tax office, he was awarded civil service status for life. He worked there until his retirement in 1970, and died in early 1992 in Lübbecke. kjs/sk

Landesarchiv NRW, Abteilung Westfalen, Münster, personnel file 340

No. 11-53

General of the *Waffen-SS*, ret., Oswald Pohl, *Credo. Mein Weg zu Gott* [Credo: My Path to God]
Licensed edition
Cover design: H. Jandaurek
Katholische Schriftenmission
Linz, 1952

In this book, the former head of the SS Economic and Administrative Main Office resolves his personal responsibility with general questions of faith, and converts to Catholicism. After being sentenced to death, Oswald Pohl wrote down the story of his life in Landsberg prison for war criminals in 1950. mh

Kreismuseum Wewelsburg,
inv. no. 16934

No. 11-52
Not shown

Kommandant in Auschwitz. Autobiografische Aufzeichnungen von Rudolf Höß [Auschwitz Commandant: The Autobiographical Notes of Rudolf Höß]. **With an introduction and commentary by Martin Broszat**
Quellen und Darstellungen zur Zeitgeschichte [Sources and Depictions of Contemporary History], vol. 5
Deutsche Verlagsanstalt, Stuttgart, 1958

The first commandant of Auschwitz Concentration Camp analyzes his "inner life and experiences," and portrays himself as a sensitive human being. Höß wrote these notes in Polish captivity in early 1947, before he was executed. mh

Kreismuseum Wewelsburg, inv. no. 16540

No. 11-54

Willy Mirbach, *Damit du es später deinem Sohn einmal erzählen kannst … Der autobiografische Bericht eines Luftwaffensoldaten aus dem KZ Mittelbau* (August 1944 – Juli 1945) [So You Can Tell Your Son Some Day … The Autobiographical Account of an Air Force Soldier at Mittelbau Concentration Camp (August 1944 – July 1945)], edited and annotated by Gerd Halmanns
Veröffentlichungen des Historischen Vereins für Geldern und Umgegend [Publications of the Historical Society of Geldern and Surroundings], vol. 98
Historischer Verein für Geldern und Umgegend, Geldern, 1997

An air force soldier assigned to duty as a concentration camp guard attempts to come to terms honestly with the experience. The autobiographical account stemmed from 1946 and has survived as a type-written version from 1960. mh

Kreismuseum Wewelsburg, inv. no. 16532

No. 11-55
Not shown

Paul Hausser, *Soldaten wie andere auch. Der Weg der Waffen-SS* [Soldiers, Like Others, Too. The Path of the Waffen-SS]
Munin-Verlag, Osnabrück, 1966

A general of the *Waffen-SS* defends "his" troops and constructs a grand delusion. mh

Kreismuseum Wewelsburg, inv. no. 16575

No. 11-57

SS service dagger, with sheath and clasp

This dagger was hidden, and subsequently forgotten. It was discovered in the summer of 2004 in the double-walled insulation of a garden shed in Melsungen (northern Hesse). mh

Kreismuseum Wewelsburg, inv. no. 15966/1-3

No. 11-56

Porcelain Yuletide celebration plate of the Mutual Aid Society of Members of the former *Waffen-SS* (HIAG)
The plate exemplifies the continued maintenance of SS traditions among former members of the *Waffen-SS*. mh

Kreismuseum Wewelsburg, inv. no. 14442

No. 11-69
Werner Peiner, *Madonna with Child*
Gouache on cardboard, framed
Undated (after 1945)
Werner Peiner (1897 – 1984), one of Adolf Hitler's favorite artists, and long-time director of the Hermann Göring Master School of Painting in Kronenburg, Eifel, was briefly detained in Recklinghausen in 1945 after the end of the war. By 1946, he was working as an artist again. In 1948, he and his wife bought Haus Vorst, a hilltop castle, at Leichlingen in the Rhineland, where Peiner had his studio until the end of his life. He created monumental paintings and carpets, as he had during the war. Besides landscape and animal representations, he also turned to biblical themes, notably producing several Madonnas such as the one represented here.

The former "state artist" now only received private commissions. Best known are his tapestries, which he produced for the Gerling Group and the Ethiopian emperor Haile Selassie (1892 – 1975). fh
Kreismuseum Wewelsburg, inv. no. 14460

No. 11-70
Amazon
Porcelain, painted, polychrome
Oskar Schaller & Co.,
Windisch-Eschenbach,
after 1947
Apart from Karl Diebitsch, Theodor Kärner (1884 – 1966) was the most prominent artisan of the Allach Porcelain Manufactory (PMA). Kärner primarily produced animal motifs and "political" sculptures (flagbearers, SS men, busts of Hitler). Because of his relatively high honorary SS rank, he was interned in Moosbach from 1945 to 1947. He was subsequently hired by the Oskar Schaller & Co. manufactory in Windisch-Eschenbach as the head of their design department. Kärner's "nonpolitical" PMA designs continued to be produced there under his supervision until 1953. Eventually, the Rosenthal company in Selb took over the Eschenbach design department in 1953, and has continued to produce the former Allach porcelain. Kärner, who was 70 at the time, continued to work there as freelancer.

After World War II, Theodor Kärner was able to seamlessly pick up where he had left off at the SS manufactory; only his "political" figures disappeared from the product range.

Theodor Kärner designed this figure for the Allach Porcelain Manufactory. Before the end of the war, it was only available as a special order. fh
Kreismuseum Wewelsburg, inv. no. 15271

No. 11-71
Plate, based on a design by Franz Nagy
Stoneware, blue, glazed
Allach Porcelain Manufactory,
1937 – 1940
Kreismuseum Wewelsburg, inv. no. 14592

No. 11-72
Not shown
Plate
Stoneware, red
Same model as the object above,
produced by Franz Nagy
Ca. 1950
Franz Nagy Sr. (1888 – 1959) was one of the Allach Porcelain Manufactory's (PMA) first managing directors. The plant was established on his property at Munich-Allach; the workshop was in his house. Nagy designed animals and candle holders in porcelain and plates in stoneware for the PMA, as well as the "great vase with Old Germanic motifs." Like Theodor Kärner, he worked for the Eschenbach manufactory after the war, creating further animal-themed sculptures in porcelain. Until the end of his life, he continued to privately produce various PMA designs. The models remained unchanged, except for the colors, and the Allach SS runes, which Nagy replaced with a rune-like mark bearing the letters NA/GY.

After the war, the German population saw Nagy as an apolitical artist, just like Theodor Kärner. The ornamentation on the edges of the plate was no longer associated with pseudo-Germanic ideology; only the comparison with his "great vase" makes it obvious. fh
Kreismuseum Wewelsburg, inv. no. 14505

Ring
Silber
290,-DM
wenn Rune in Gold
dann + 20,- DM
<=

Brosche/Anhänger
Silber
Lapis Lazuli (blau)
Durchm. ca. 42 mm
350,- DM
=>

"Mutterbrosche"
Silber
Durchm. ca. 55 mm
590,- DM
=>

<=
Brosche/Anhänger
Silber+Karneol(rot)
Durchm. ca. 42 mm
390,- DM
=>

Ring
750/000 Gold
Lapis Lazuli (blau)
1150,- DM
=>

No. 11-75
Brochure of the Peichl company from Nordenham
1980s
Kreismuseum Wewelsburg, inv. no. 16607

No. 11-73
Bangle with the Tree of Life motif
Silver
Peichl workshop, Nordenham
1980s
Molding, supposedly of a Gahr company original, owned by the Karl Wolff family fh
Kreismuseum Wewelsburg, inv. no. 15262

No. 11-76
Brochure of the Rolf Schepmann company, Hörstel
After 1993
Kreismuseum Wewelsburg, inv. no. 16608

No. 11-74
Not shown
Brooch: motif of a Viking ship
Silver, sawn
Peichl workshop, Nordenham
1980s
Karl Martin's original design from 1933 – 1934 resembles the SS's Nordland publisher's signet, which he also designed. fh
Kreismuseum Wewelsburg, inv. no. 15264

After 1945, some artisans deliberately risked continuing with National Socialist traditions. To this day, there are a number of vendors who can readily supply objects from the SS milieu. The sale of SS jewelry has actually increased since the 1980s. This bangle, referred to as an infinity ring, and the brooch with the Viking ship were produced by Berthold Peichl (1920 – 1987) in Nordenham. In one of the company's brochures, Peichl appealed directly to former "comrades," and signed with "former 17th SS Pz. Gr. Div." (*SS-Panzergrenadier-Division*, armored infantry). The company, now run by Peichl's daughter, Elisabeth Nickel, continues to sell these designs to this day. The firm offers additional jewelry items that have been directly copied from the SS supplier Gahr.

But other artisans have also been trying their luck in this market. The Rolf Schepmann company, for example, features the "mother brooch" in its catalog. fh

In many ways, the manner in which local communities and the wider postwar society, the former SS, and victims of the SS dealt with the history of Wewelsburg from 1933 to 1945, legally and with regard to memorial policy, exemplifies in many ways the treatment of the National Socialist era in the Federal Republic of Germany. Debate on how to interpret the past persist to this day. The "struggle over history" has not ended. The multifaceted nature of responsible, democratic action in the present and in the future is explored at the end of the exhibition.

The still-visible signs of SS history in the village of Wewelsburg are also addressed. The intention is to encourage visitors to seek out these sites after viewing the exhibition, as well as to sharpen the gaze for traces of the past in one's own environment.

12 Wewelsburg after 1945: Between Education and Glorification

12.1
National Socialist History in Controversy:
The Wewelsburg Example

No. 12-1
Bunker Door
1936/1937
During construction of the guard building, the SS had the rooms located against the hillside set up as an air raid shelter. As early as 1937, an air raid protection law mandated air raid facilities for new construction. This requirement was satisfied simply by equipping a basement room with gas and shatterproof windows and doors. The guard building also possessed specially reinforced walls and floors. kjs
Kreismuseum Wewelsburg, inv. no. 17078

In their desire for a return to "normalcy," many villagers avoided facing the National Socialist past, all the more because many Wewelsburgers, like numerous ethnic German expellees, saw themselves first and foremost as victims. The traces of the National Socialist past in Wewelsburg could only be secured little by little and in the face of obstacles. In addition to preserving the SS's architectural legacy in the village, the shooting range, meanwhile filled in, played an important role. From 1988 on it was the site of small-scale excavations and conservation measures begun with the help of volunteers. In 2002 researchers were able to examine the contents of a cesspit at the edge of the former concentration camp. The objects discovered there are in and of themselves unspectacular, but their preservation demonstrates the will to uncover the history of Wewelsburg during the Third Reich.

However, simultaneous to these painstaking efforts to secure evidence, right-wing organizations began early on with efforts to exploit Wewelsburg for their own purposes.

12.1.1
Evidence Gathering in the Village of Wewelsburg

No. 12-2
Part of a refugee barracks
Wood, paper
1946 – 1950
The barracks section of the camp was used after the war as a displaced persons (DP) camp for former forced laborers. From 1946, the camp took in displaced persons and refugees. The wooden barracks built by concentration camp prisoners, similar in construction to those of the Reich Labor Service, were modular structures. Refugee families gradually rendered them more habitable. The inner walls, faced with fiberboard, were wallpapered. The barracks wall displayed here bore three layers of wallpaper. The wall section came from a wooden barracks at the Schubert carpentry shop, established on the grounds of the camp in the 1950s. The barracks was sold in 1963 and partly reassembled as a chicken coop on a farm in Büren-Barkhausen. The barracks sections were acquired by the Kreismuseum in 2005. kjs
Kreismuseum Wewelsburg, inv. no. 16341

No. 12-10
View into the collapsed cesspit at the edge of former Niederhagen Concentration Camp
Photograph: R. Gündchen, 2002
Blueprints of the concentration camp from 1943 show three cesspits for the sewage. The rear cesspit survived unnoticed for years in the backyard of a house at the new housing development built on the grounds of the former concentration camp. Finally, in September 2002, heavy rains caused the cesspit cover to collapse, tearing a large hole in the yard. Before the garden was landscaped, the Kreismuseum had the structure measured and secured a container-load of sewage sludge. Examination of the sludge revealed numerous objects, in all likelihood originating from the nearby sick bay. Whether other discovered items stemmed from the concentration camp or the subsequent resettlement and refugee camps cannot be definitely established. kjs
Kreismuseum Wewelsburg, Fotoarchiv

No. 12-3
Not shown
Covers
Plastic
Kreismuseum Wewelsburg,
inv. nos. 14960 and 14962

No. 12-4
Not shown
Needle
Metal
1940 – 1947
Kreismuseum Wewelsburg, inv. no. 14935

No. 12-5
Not shown
Bandage clip
Metal, rubber
Ca. 1940 – 1947
Kreismuseum Wewelsburg, inv. no. 14937

No. 12-6
Not shown
Break-off ampule
Glass, broken
1940 – 1947
Kreismuseum Wewelsburg, inv. no. 14957

No. 12-7
Not shown
Ampules with imprint: Novocain
Glass with rubber stopper
1940 – 1947
Kreismuseum Wewelsburg,
inv. nos. 14974, 14975, 14976

No. 12-8
Not shown
Glass fragment from a tube
Brown glass
1940 – 1947
Kreismuseum Wewelsburg, inv. no. 14985

No. 12-9
Not shown
Charcoal
Ca. 1940 – 1947
Kreismuseum Wewelsburg, inv. no. 15030

The artifacts presented here were presumably washed from the nearby concentration camp sick bay into the cesspit. They are remnants of the medical supplies used to treat camp inmates. Charcoal was a common remedy against diarrhea. The glass ampules were used for storage of medicines. "Novocain," printed on some of the ampules, is a well-known drug first synthesized in 1905 and used for local anesthesia during operations. kjs

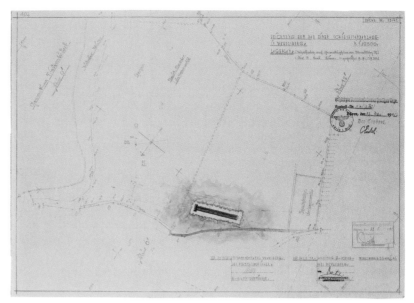

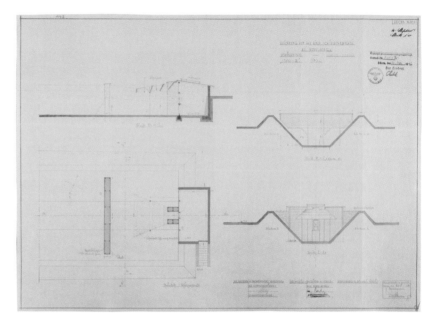

No. 12-11
**Volunteers of Aktion Sühne-
zeichen Friedensdienste e. V.
(Action Reconciliation
Service for Peace) at an inter-
national work camp at the
former SS shooting range
1988**
Kreismuseum Wewelsburg,
Fotoarchiv

No. 12-13
Not shown
**View into the filled-in target
cellar at the end of the
backstop**
Photograph: N. Ellermann,
2004
Kreismuseum Wewelsburg,
Fotoarchiv

No. 12-14
Not shown
**Detail of the shooting range
site plan showing the
discovery sites of cartridges
of various national origins
2005 – 2009**
Kreismuseum Wewelsburg, plan 102

No. 12-12
Not shown
**Participants of a work camp
from the Leo Sympher
Professional College, Minden**
Photograph: N. Ellermann,
2007
Kreismuseum Wewelsburg,
Fotoarchiv

No. 12-15
**Original plan of SS shooting range,
top view
1941**
Kreismuseum Wewelsburg, plan 102

No. 12-16
**Original plan of SS shooting range,
dugout
1941**
Kreismuseum Wewelsburg, plan 148

The shooting range built at Oberhagen by
concentration camp prisoners was used
by the SS for target practice and the
execution of prisoners.

Allied occupation troops also conducted shooting exercises here, before
villagers filled the site with construction
rubble and garbage. The facility only
became the focus of public interest in
1988, when an international youth group
from Action Reconciliation Service for
Peace began clearing the grounds of
weeds. Regular work camps have been
held since then to preserve the premises
and to make them visible once again to the
public as a place of remembrance for the
victims of the executions carried out
there. To this end, the underground rooms
of the target cellar were emptied of sludge
and groundwater, with several items thus
coming to light. Numerous cartridges were
collected from throughout the site. Meanwhile, the clearing of the shooting dugout
fundament and the shooting lane has
begun. kjs

No. 12-17
Target with bullet holes
Metal
1941 – 1945
SS men used the clock face as a target for their target practice. It could be cranked down into the target cellar by a "shooting evaluator." To this end, there was an opening in the floor in front of the backstop. The shooting evaluator counted the hits on the target.

The target was found in 2005 in the sludge of the target cellar by participants in a work camp. kjs
Kreismuseum Wewelsburg, inv. no. 15274

No. 12-19
Cartridge with imprint DWM // 1938 // SS, found at the former Niederhagen Concentration Camp shooting range October 2009
Cartridges of different origins were recovered at the former SS shooting range. Besides German cartridges of various calibers from World War II (including ones from the SS), American, Canadian, and Russian cartridges were also found in the duff along the lane and outside the parapets. The finds confirmed speculation that the shooting range had also been used for target practice by Allied occupation troops. kjs
Kreismuseum Wewelsburg, inv. no. 17459

No. 12-20
Not shown
Fragments of crockery with swastika and Reich eagle
Porcelain
1933 – 1945
Kreismuseum Wewelsburg,
inv. nos. 16338, 16381, 17140/1-6, 17141/1-2
and 17142/1-3

No. 12-21
Not shown
Cutlery
Metal
Ca. 1945
Kreismuseum Wewelsburg, inv. no. 17136/1-3

No. 12-18
Folding table from the target cellar
Wood, metal
1941 – 1945
The folding table was found along a wall of the target cellar, at the back end of the SS shooting range. It could be unfolded from the wall and fixed to the floor with a strut. During target practice, one or two SS men remained in the target cellar. For safety reasons, there was only one entrance, located outside the shooting lane. At the end of target practice, the men cranked the target down into the cellar to count the hits. The table was likely used while recording the results. The parts of the folding table were found in 2004, after the local fire department had pumped out the groundwater in the target cellar to make the cellar accessible for work camp participants. To preserve the wood, the parts were treated with alcohol, stored for several months in peat, and slowly dried. kjs
Kreismuseum Wewelsburg,
inv. nos. 15273/1 and 15273/2

No. 12-22
Not shown
Gas-mask filters
Metal, corroded
Ca. 1945
Kreismuseum Wewelsburg, inv. no. 17139/1-4

No. 12-23
Not shown
Fragments of metal objects, including parts from guns of various types
Metal, corroded
Ca. 1945
Kreismuseum Wewelsburg,
inv. nos. 17134/1-10 and 17138/1-3

During the time when construction rubble was being dumped into the shooting range shortly after the war, inhabitants of Wewelsburg discarded not only pots, cutlery, and other kitchen utensils, but also many plates, dishes, and other pieces of porcelain. The bottoms of the crockery pieces still clearly reveal the swastika and Reicheagle emblems of the period's porcelain marks, from which the people wanted to obviously distance themselves. Gas masks and weapons were also thrown into the construction rubble. kjs

12.1.2
Appropriation by Right-Wing Extremists

No. 12-25
Ceremonial ribbon
Embroidered lettering at right: "To the Bravest Sons of Europe"; at left: "Your Sacrifices – Our Obligation," with horizontal *Wolfsangel* symbol
Synthetic material
2003
Kreismuseum Wewelsburg, inv. no. 14495/2

No. 12-24
Not shown
Ceremonial ribbon
Right inscription: "To our Fallen Comrades"; left inscription: "Foundation for War Graves. When All Our Brothers Remain Silent" and straight-armed cross
Synthetic material
2003
Kreismuseum Wewelsburg, inv. no. 14493/1

In the township of Wewelsburg less than four kilometers (two and a half miles) from the village center, lies the Böddecken Military Cemetery, dedicated in 1953 and known under the name Valley of Peace. Here were buried primarily soldiers who had fallen during the engagements of March 30 to April 1, 1945, and initially had been laid to rest in the village graveyards, or in the countryside. Many belonged to the *Waffen-SS*. Once a year on the People's Day of Mourning (*Volkstrauertag*), a German holiday, a memorial ceremony is held at the cemetery. Since 1978, the cemetery is the site of a memorial by Josef Rikus to all victims of the war.

But the war cemetery has also been misused by right-wing extremist groups and associations. For instance, on the eve of that day of public mourning, the Mutual Aid Association of Former Members of the *Waffen-SS*, HIAG, (later renamed the Federal Association of Former Soldiers of the *Waffen-SS*), would sometimes lay wreaths with all-too-predictable slogans on the graves. Similar slogan-bearing wreaths and symbols also appeared in the military cemetery on other occasions. fh

No. 12-27
Not shown
Georg Christians, *"Die Reihen fest geschlossen." Die FAP – Zu Anatomie und Umfeld einer militant-neofaschistischen Partei in den 80er Jahren* ["The Lines tightly closed." The FAP – Anatomy and Social Environment of a Militant Neo-fascist Party in the 1980s]
Marburg, 1990
The photograph shows participants at the FAP "Gau meeting" 1988 in Wewelsburg; from left: Thomas Hainke, Michael Kühnen, Christian Worch, Thomas Brehl, Walther Matthaei.

In March 1988, under false premises, the neo-Nazi Free German Worker Party (Freiheitliche Deutsche Arbeiter Partei, FAP) succeeded in renting the basement of the Wewelsburg inn, Ottens Hof, the former National Socialist village community center. The FAP, eventually banned in 1995, sought to exploit the site's "aura" in choosing it as a venue for a "Gau meeting" and the founding of a district chapter. The neo-Nazis gained the desired media coverage by inviting the press and staging a "public part" of their meeting. This mainly consisted of an aggressive, xenophobic rant by the FAP's best-known leader of the time, Michael Kühnen (1955 – 1991). The meeting concluded with the singing of political hymns and the "Kühnen salute," a Hitler salute slightly modified to skirt legal strictures. fh
Kreismuseum Wewelsburg, inv. no. 15275

No. 12-26
Candles arrayed as a death rune at Böddeken Military Cemetery
Photograph: Hermann Ohagen, January 1996
Kreismuseum Wewelsburg, inv. no. 14495

No. 12-28
Banner with inscription "Wewelsburg stands up to right-wing extremism"
The banner was carried in Paderborn on January 5, 2002, at the "Wewelsburg against right-wing extremism" counter-demonstration.
In 2002, when the Crimes of the *Wehrmacht* exhibition came to Bielefeld, a right-wing extremist group *Initiative der weißen Art* (Initiative of the White Kind) planned a demonstration in Wewelsburg to promote the "glory and honor of the *Waffen-SS*." Here, its extreme right-wing backers sought to exploit the notoriety of Wewelsburg to gain as much public attention as possible. The march, however, was banned by the authorities. Finally, on January 5, the German Supreme Court as well ruled that such a demonstration in Wewelsburg was clearly illegal. In its ruling, the court noted that a march of right-wing extremists in Wewelsburg would constitute "an injury to the human dignity of the victims." After it became known that the organizers planned to relocate the march to Paderborn town center, the "Paderborn Alliance for Tolerance" announced counter-demonstrations. This, in conjunction with further official bans, finally prevented the march of the neo-Nazis. fh
Kreismuseum Wewelsburg, inv. no. 15258

12.2 Projections

Local legends depicting Wewelsburg Castle as, for example, a "breeding center for Aryan children" developed in parallel to fantastic stories in the popular press describing the castle as the venue of séances by the SS leadership.

Accounts of former SS members had already alleged Himmler's use of Wewelsburg Castle as a site for occult rituals. These reports, however, were transparent attempts at obscuring the men's own involvement through their references to a "deranged" Himmler.

Nevertheless, over time an ever-widening repertoire of tales of bizarre occurrences at Wewelsburg Castle ensued. The themes that arose here spread to books of fantasy and esotericism, as well as Satanic and radical right-wing literature, with fluid borders between the genres.

From the 1990s, with the growing notoriety of the "black sun" (derived from the northern tower intarsia), the Wewelsburg increasingly became the ideal field of projection for a number of far-right-wing, esoteric, and satanic fantasies. The black sun now graces T-shirts, flags, and underwear.

No. 12-32
Trevor Ravenscroft, *Der Speer des Schicksals. Die Geschichte der Heiligen Lanze* [The Spear of Destiny: The History of the Holy Lance]
Universitas Verlag, Munich, 1974
The Spear of Destiny by Trevor Ravenscroft is a classic of speculative literature involving National Socialism. Ravenscroft attributes magical powers to the "holy lance," brought from Vienna to Nuremberg in 1938 as part of the Reich insignia, and reputed to have pierced Christ's body on the cross. The author links Hitler's destiny with the artifact, alleged to impart invincibility. In addition, he claims that Himmler selected Wewelsburg Castle as repository for the lance, but was overridden by Hitler, who wanted it kept at Nuremberg.

To this day, the castle is associated with the "spear of destiny." There are frequent references to a never-implemented SS Construction Management plan from the war years. Many authors insist on discerning the form of a lance in the structure of the buildings, with Wewelsburg Castle at its tip. In an interview, however, the architects of the time categorically rejected this interpretation. ds

Kreismuseum Wewelsburg, inv. no. 16639

No. 12-29
**Walter Schellenberg, *Memoiren*
[Memoirs], Gita Petersen (ed.)
Verlag für Politik und Wirtschaft,
Cologne, 1959**
Walther Schellenberg was employed
in the SS's Security Service (SD)
and from 1942 led the foreign office
of the SS Reich Main Security Office
(RSHA). At the Nuremberg trials of
principal war criminals, he was
indicted but never sentenced
because of his readiness to testify
for the prosecution. In the subsequent "Wilhelmstraße Trial" of 1949,
however, he received six years in
prison. He was released early, in
December 1950, on account of a
liver condition. Schellenberg died of
cancer in Italy on March 31, 1952,
just 42 years old.
    During the almost two years
that Schellenberg spent at the
Landsberg prison for war criminals,
he wrote his memoirs, which in later
years often served as the basis for
historical accounts of the SS. Here,
he claimed that Himmler structured
the SS on the model of the Jesuit
order. His characterization of
Wewelsburg Castle as an "SS monastery" was meant to support his
portrayal of the SS as a strictly
hierarchical, top-down organization. In this manner, he exonerated
himself of all responsibility, while
Himmler – as the order's "general"
demanding absolute obedience –
was presented as the culprit for all
the horrors committed by the SS. ds
Kreismuseum Wewelsburg, inv. no. 16516

No. 12-30
**Felix Kersten, *Totenkopf und Treue.
Heinrich Himmler ohne Uniform*
[Death's Head and Loyalty: Heinrich
Himmler without Uniform]
Mölich Verlag, Hamburg, 1952**
The author, Felix Kersten, Himmler's
personal masseur as of 1939, first
published his memoirs in Sweden in
1947 under the title *Samtal med
Himmler: Minnen från Tredje Riket
1939 – 1945* (Conversation with
Himmler: Memories of the Third
Reich, 1939 – 1945). Its revised edition appeared in Germany in 1952 as
*Death's Head and Loyalty: Heinrich
Himmler without Uniform*. In the
1950s his work became an important source for both historical
researchers and novelists. In fact,
comparison with other historical
sources reveals that many of his
claims are false – rather, the book
serves to exculpate Kersten. For
example, he claims to have achieved
the release of concentration camp
prisoners and to have brought about

negotiations between Himmler and
the World Jewish Congress. Many of
the fictions or half-truths propagated by Felix Kersten became part
of received knowledge about Heinrich Himmler and the SS in the
following years. For example, the
widely held belief that Himmler took
himself to be the reincarnation of
the Saxon king Henry I is only
attested by Kersten. ds
Kreismuseum Wewelsburg, inv. no. 16596

No. 12-31
**Willi Frischauer, *Himmler, the Evil
Genius of the Third Reich*
Odhams Press, London, 1953**
Willi Frischauer, a journalist born in
Vienna, emigrated to London in
1935 and worked as a foreign
correspondent there. After 1945, he
was chief reporter for the London
weekly *Illustrated*. Beginning in the
1950s, he wrote biographies of
Hermann Göring and of Heinrich
Himmler, for which he conducted
wide-ranging interviews with contemporary witnesses – including
the former head of the SS Central
Office of Race and Settlement,
Richard Walther Darré. Although
Frischauer strove to produce a
nuanced account, even criticizing
the Germans for shifting their
responsibility onto the dead Himmler, the exculpating legends of his
witnesses flowed into his own
account. Thus, without bothering to
check, Frischauer states that
Himmler had Wewelsburg Castle
built as a place of meditation over
the ruins of a medieval castle. In the
1960s and 1970s, Frischauer's
account became one of the bases
for further embellishments, which
declared the structure the "castle
of the Holy Grail" or the repository
of the "spear of destiny." ds
Kreismuseum Wewelsburg, inv. no. 16640

Fantasy

As early as the 1950s, many legends emerged about the SS. These primarily originated in the autobiographies of former National Socialist officials that began to appear at that time. Here, there emerged a very specific image of Heinrich Himmler and the SS, with which they sought to whitewash themselves. On this basis grew myths portraying the SS as an occult order in possession of esoteric knowledge and supernatural powers, with its own "monastery" at Wewelsburg Castle. Since the 1960s, conspiracy theories have often been grafted onto those myths, seeking to explain National Socialism as the effect of secret societies operating in the shadows of official politics. It is asserted, for example, that "flying saucers" were produced in the Third Reich, allowing a part of the SS to escape to remote locations.

Fantasy novels and computer games continue to hawk this material to the present day. Over time, Wewelsburg Castle was stylized as the "castle of the SS order" or the "castle of the Holy Grail." These accounts display hardly any points of contact with reality; historical facts are deformed and blended with invention. The concentration camp hardly ever gets mentioned in these myths. ds

Esoterica

The quest for "power locations" is widespread within various esoteric currents. Wewelsburg Castle is often counted among these places, where "lines of energy" are alleged to converge. Added to this is the claim that the site of the northern tower housed a proto-historical Germanic pagan sanctum. None of this can be verified by scientific methods, but must be "intuited." Followers of esoteric doctrines frequently ascribe occult knowledge to the National Socialists, particularly to the SS. This is also alleged to have determined their choice of Wewelsburg Castle as a "cult center." Below the surface, esoteric views are often animated by the racialist-religious ideas of the National Socialist period, without their adherents always being conscious of it. The history of Niederhagen Concentration Camp, however, hardly interests anyone in these circles.

The sun wheel emblem in the floor of the northern tower, known in the right-wing extremist milieu as the "black sun," is also invested by certain occultists with the most varied interpretations. The viewpoints mostly proceed from the current designation and link the symbol to the solar interpretations of various occult doctrines ds

Satanism

The generic term of Satanism covers a number of widely differing phenomena: from a juvenile fascination with graveyards and the occult through serious exploration of anti-Christian thought, right up to ritualistic murder, rape, or pedophilia. Organized Satanism is principally associated with a highly elitist, power-oriented worldview, in which man, by acting out of his desires or through "spiritual" evolution, is to take the place of God.

Against this background, certain satanic groups have developed a specialized interpretation of National Socialism. They view the SS with particular fascination, as the former understood itself as an elite and wielded actual power over others. This fascination also extends to Wewelsburg Castle.

In this context, Wewelsburg Castle's northern tower has been a venue for satanic rituals. Thus, Michael A. Aquino, co-founder of the "Temple of Set," performed a ritual meditation here in 1982 that is referred to as "Wewelsburg Working." In television documentaries of 2001 and 2003, women suffering from multiple-personality disorders as a result of sexual abuse claim to have been the victims of satanic rituals, including rapes and murder of newborn babies in the 1970s. These are alleged to have taken place, among other places, in the castle's northern tower. Until now, however, justice officials have been unable to uncover any evidence that Wewelsburg Castle was in fact the scene of such crimes. ds

Right-wing radicalism

For adherents of extreme-right-wing worldviews, Wewelsburg Castle has significance on two levels: first, they see the castle as the locus of National Socialist tradition, where they seek the traces of Heinrich Himmler and the SS. On another, right-wing circles gravitate to the sun wheel ornament embedded in the floor of the northern tower. This decorative motif consists of three staggered, superimposed swastikas, with their outer ends forming sig runes. With no specific significance during the National Socialist era, it has been adopted by the right-wing extremists as a badge of recognition, legal under German law.

The symbol was popularized in the 1990s by the novel *The Black Sun of Tashi Lhunpo*. Since then, it has become increasingly detached from its location in public perception: Many right-wingers are familiar with the sign, which, in keeping with the neofascist scene's growing association with youth culture, appears on CDs, patches, buttons, T-shirts, jewelry, and many other objects. Frequently, however, they remain unfamiliar with actual historical events in Wewelsburg.

The concentration camp generally does not play a role in the right-wing extremists' view of the place. While right-wing visitors are numerous in Wewelsburg, they are practically never to be seen at the memorial on the former concentration camp's roll call area. ds

**Howard A. Buechner and Wilhelm Bernhart, *Adolf Hitler and the Secrets of the Holy Lance*
1989**

Howard A. Buechner is a physician and former professor of medicine at Louisiana State University. Before this, he was a doctor in the U.S. Army and wrote a book about American involvement in the liberation of Dachau Concentration Camp. In this book, he tells of a former German submarine commander approaching him about the holy lance. He gives the commander the pseudonym of Wilhelm Bernhart.

The lance on exhibit in Vienna, Bernhart explains, is a copy. On Hitler's order, the genuine article was hidden, along with other treasures of the Reich, in Antarctica. In 1979, it was brought back by a National Socialist secret society and is currently somewhere in Europe.

The piece exhibited in Vienna did actually undergo a detailed examination in 2005. This revealed it to be an artifact dating to the eighth century, whose further use could also be scientifically documented. Although the object did not yet exist at the crucifixion of Christ, it is indeed the medieval original. fh

Kreismuseum Wewelsburg, inv. no. 16641

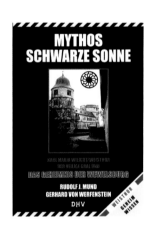

**Russell McCloud, *Die Schwarze Sonne von Tashi Lhunpo* [The Black Sun of Tashi Lhunpo]
Arun Verlag, Engerda, 1991**

The roman à clef *The Black Sun of Tashi Lhunpo* popularized the Wewelsburg sun wheel in the 1990s in right-wing circles. The novel recounts the investigation of journalist Hans Weigert into the background of a series of mysterious murders. Each victim was found with a twelve-spoked sun wheel branded into the forehead; the same symbol, Weigert discovers, as in the marble hall at Wewelsburg Castle. Weigert dubs the symbol "black sun." On a trip to Tibet, he meets a former member of the SS, described as belonging to the *initiated*, and in possession of occult knowledge. From him, Weigert learns that the black sun is the symbol of a secret society, the men of "Agarthi." The Agarthi belong to an original race from Atlantis, just as their opponents, the men of "Shambhala." They fought each other because the Agarthi wished to share the divine knowledge with humankind, while the Shambhala sought to keep this knowledge for themselves and be worshiped as gods. Weigert learns that the members of Agarthi collaborated with the SS in the National Socialist era. The men of Agarthi were once initiated in the "Temple of Wewelsburg" and passed on their knowledge in the postwar era.

The Black Sun of Tashi Lhunpo was the first work to apply the term "black sun," coined by Wilhelm Landig, to the floor ornament in Wewelsburg Castle's *Obergruppenführer* Hall. The book was originally brought out by publisher Arun Verlag, based in Engerda, Germany. The latter popularized the novel in both right-wing and esoteric circles, also spinning off the first related products, thus launching a wave of merchandising for articles linked to the black sun that continues unabated to this day. The novel, published under a pseudonym, has gone through several editions; there is also a screenplay. ds

Kreismuseum Wewelsburg, inv. no. 16499

No. 12-38
Allerseelen: Gotos-Kalanda
CD, Aorta, 1995
Kreismuseum Wewelsburg,
inv. no. 16819

No. 12-47
Not shown
Allerseelen: Gotos-Kalanda
LP, Ahnstern, 2006
Kreismuseum Wewelsburg,
inv. no. 16448

No. 12-36
Miguel Serrano, *Adolf Hitler, el Último Avatāra* [Adolf Hitler. The Last Avatar]
Santiago de Chile, 1984
Miguel Serrano (1917 – 2009), the author of this text, which appeared in 1984, was a former Chilean diplomat, who founded the so-called Esoteric Hitlerism. This worldview considers Adolf Hitler a messiah, who will return as the last of the ten avatars (i.e., incarnations) of the god Vishnu to establish a "golden" age. The notion that in 1945 Hitler was able to flee in the "Reich flying saucer" plays a pivotal role in Seranno's theory. According to this notion, Hitler located in "New Swabia" (a part of Antarctica claimed by Germany in 1938 – 1939) an entrance to the center of Earth, where, rejuvenated, he is awaiting his return, made possible by a certain form of energy, so-called vril energy. The escape was prepared by a secret circle of SS men in the know, who are initiated into the secret mysteries at Wewelsburg Castle. Serrano designates these as "sun people" and "supermen," whose Aryan blood conveys the memory of their divine Aryan forefathers.

In his theories, Serrano clearly takes up notions that Wilhelm Landing had originated in his novels of 1971 and 1980, *Götzen gegen Thule* [Idols against Thule] and *Wolfszeit um Thule* [Wolf Times at Thule]. He extrapolates these and, by integrating additional elements, arrives at a quasi-religious worldview. ds

Kreismuseum Wewelsburg, inv. no. 16476

No. 12-35
Stefan Brönnle, *Landschaften der Seele. Von Mystischen Orten, heiligen Stätten und uralten Kulten* [Landscapes of the Soul: Of Mystical Places, Sacred Sites and Ancient Cults]
Munich, 1994
Landscape ecologist Stefan Brönnle has run his own Institute for Geomancy since 2006, which deals in energy phenomena, divining, and the like. *Landscapes of the Soul* was the first of his meanwhile five published works. All treat nature or the vital environment of man. Here, Brönnle posits a form of spiritual energy that properly trained individuals can perceive and use for themselves.

In *Landscapes of the Soul*, Brönnle introduces places where, he claims, special energy flows. In this connection, he cites Wewelsburg Castle as an example for the activities of National Socialists, who exploited people's spiritual needs.

He characterizes the SS as "Hitler's priesthood." Consequently, he describes the castle at Wewelsburg as their religious headquarters, where Himmler brought together twelve men around a table. Himmler wished to have the "city" rebuilt so as to symbolize the Holy Grail, while the castle was modeled on the Holy Lance. As the center of the whole complex, Brönnle saw the crypt, where an eternal flame was to burn. With all this, the author merely collects various interpretations, which, since the early 1990s, had already appeared in numerous other esoteric texts. fh

Kreismuseum Wewelsburg, inv. no. 16496

No. 12-37
Rudolf J. Mund and Gerhard von Werfenstein, *Mythos Schwarze Sonne. Karl Maria Wiligut/Weisthor, Der Heilige Gral und das Geheimnis der Wewelsburg* [The Myth of the Black Sun. Karl Maria Wiligut/ Weisthor, The Holy Grail, and the Secret of Wewelsburg Castle]
Deutschherrenverlag, Riga/Vienna/ Berlin, 2004
This work, brought out by right-wing-extremist publisher Deutschherrenverlag, is based on older texts by Rudolf J. Mund (1920 – 1985). Mund, along with Wilhelm Landig and Erich Halik, formed a right-wing and esoteric circle known as the Landig, or Vienna Group.

The slender volume mainly offers a defense of Karl Maria Wiligut, alias Weisthor, begun by Mund in earlier works. Here, the reader learns that Otto Rahn found the Holy Grail and brought it to Wewelsburg Castle, where it presumably remains hidden to this day. The black sun thus symbolizes the Grail. Of special mystical importance, according to the text, is the Böddeken Estate near Wewelsburg, expropriated by the SS in 1941. Here, a center for "time research" is alleged to have been established. The secret head of the esoteric scene was Wiligut.

The book's goal is stated unequivocally: To prove the "cultural aptitude of the Germans, unique in the world." A "renaissance of traditional life" is invoked, one which bears a more than coincidental resemblance to National Socialist life. The book concludes with a prophecy that a "rebirth" of Germany lies ahead, and urges all who are sympathetic to vigorously join the effort. fh

Kreismuseum Wewelsburg, inv. no. 14709

No. 12-43
Francis King and Angus Hall, *Mysteries of Prediction*
London, 1978
The "Great Mysteries" series consists of works aiming to introduce various esoteric-mystical themes to a broader public. The volumes are thus profusely illustrated. The work appearing as volume 4, *Mysteries of Prediction*, addresses the question of whether future events can reliably be predicted. Both authors (whose names are apparently pseudonyms) are known in Britain for their authorship of widely varying works. In *Mysteries of Prediction* they attempt to make the case that the future can at least be partly predicted. The Third Reich is held up as a special example of the influence of astrological activity. The authors focus on the – in their view – essentially occult character of the SS. Thus, Himmler only converted Wewelsburg Castle in order to pursue his esoteric predilections. According to King and Hall, a circle of initiates came together, never numbering more than twelve, excluding Himmler. This motif evidently derives from Schellenberg's memoirs, and has been copied numerous times. Although these depictions of Wewelsburg Castle bear little connection to the actual theme of the work, the notion of an occult clique of SS members seems to have been so irresistible that a corresponding illustration (photograph, bottom left) was especially commissioned for this volume. The artist is Gino d'Achille, a well-known Italian book illustrator. fh

Kreismuseum Wewelsburg, inv. no. 16478

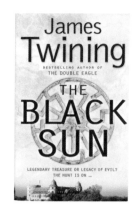

No. 12-34

James Twining, *The Black Sun*
New York, 2006
James Twining (born 1972 in London), a British writer of thrillers, is the author of four novels with Tom Kirk as the hero. *The Black Sun* is the second volume in this series.

In this novel, three curious thefts bring Tom Kirk on the trail of a conspiracy. The culprits turn out to be a secret order under the command of Heinrich Himmler and with the allegiance of twelve knights whose badge of recognition is the black sun. Here, Twining follows the recurring speculations that Himmler founded a secret society.

Though the author clearly portrays the SS and their followers as the "villains," he toys in the novel with the claims of occult dealings by the *Schutzstaffel*. This also applies to other works of fiction in the Anglo-Saxon world and demonstrates a fascination of English-speaking readers for this "dark and mysterious" aspect of the SS. fh

Kreismuseum Wewelsburg, inv. no. 16497

No. 12-45

Medal of Honor, computer game
The computer game "Medal of Honor: Underground" was released in 2000 and constitutes the second part of a first-person shooter series for PlayStation. The game was developed by DreamWorks Interactive, which also released a version for the Game Boy Advance in the United States in 2002. Sale of the game is prohibited in Germany because of violent content.

The player assumes the role of Frenchwoman Manon Batiste, who in 1940 is fighting the Germans in the Resistance. Twenty-one orders must be executed within seven "missions." Mission 4 of the game is the "Wewelsburg Mission": the Resistance has observed that the castle serves as a control center for intelligence service activities. The player must gain access to the castle to gather evidence for a possible war crimes trial. Here, both Wewelsburg Castle's *Obergruppenführer* Hall and its crypt (referred to as "Walhalla") are clearly portrayed. Though the programmers allowed themselves a degree of poetic license, in many details they remained true to the original. ds

Kreismuseum Wewelsburg, inv. no. 17133

No. 12-39

Staatsfeind, *Democrazy*
1998, banned on August 29, 2008
List A
The band Staatsfeind was exclusively a studio band from Chemnitz, Germany. It was active from 1996 to 1998 and released four albums. Its songwriters were evidently highly impressed by the Wewelsburg sun wheel and the 1991 novel, *The Black Sun of Tashi Lhunpo*, for they dedicated songs to both. Their 1998 album *Democrazy*, which features the song "Die Schwarze Sonne" [The Black Sun], was banned in 2008 by the German Federal Review Board for Media Harmful to Minors. ds
Kreismuseum Wewelsburg, inv. no. 16817

No. 12-41

Wewelsburg, *The Antiarchitect*
The Russian National Socialist Black Metal (NSBM) band named Wewelsburg was founded in 2001 – 2002. In addition to three CDs with other bands, it has released four albums on its own. The band glorifies German National Socialism and advocates a collective struggle of the "white race" against the Jews. Lyrics of Wewelsburg songs attempt to propagate National Socialist themes. Wewelsburg Castle has not only inspired the band's name, but also appears in the lyrics of three of their songs. This Russian band should not be confused with a German group of the same name. ds
Photograph: Argumente und Kultur Gegen Rechts e.V., Bielefeld
Kreismuseum Wewelsburg, inv. no. 16838

No. 12-40

Race War: *Stimme des Blutes*
2005
Having undergone frequent personnel changes, the band Race War has been in existence since 1999; it is based in Schwäbisch Gmünd, Germany. Its debut album, *The White Race Will Prevail*, was released in 2002 by the U.S. label, Micetrap Records. The group has since released two more albums, which, like its first album, were banned in Germany by the Federal Review Board for Media Harmful to Minors. Race War was the second band, after Landser, to be condemned in Germany as a criminal organization. In contrast to Landser, however, its punishment was fairly light: the members of Race War merely received suspended sentences.

Since 2008 the band has appeared under the name Heiliger Krieg (Holy War). The album shown here, *Stimme des Blutes* [Voice of the Blood], was released in 2005. The cover features a photograph of Wewelsburg Castle and a black sun; the motif, evidently of great importance to the band, is reproduced on the back cover and on the CD itself. The CD was banned in Germany in 2006. ds
Kreismuseum Wewelsburg, inv. no. 16481

No. 12-42

Wewelsburg: *Endzeit Klänge*, Vol. 2
The German band named Wewelsburg is from Altenburg, Thuringia. It has performed since 1999 and released an initial demo CD in 2000. In 2001 Wewelsburg was featured on the sampler *Endzeit Klänge, Vol. 2 – Wer leben will, der kämpfe* (Endtime Sounds, Vol. 2: Fight for Your Life), which also included tracks by Solution, Störfaktor, and 14 Nothelfer. The CD contains four of the band's songs, one of which is titled *Wewelsburg*. In 2002 the band released an album of its own, but it was limited to 50 copies. ds
Photograph: Argumente und Kultur Gegen Rechts e.V., Bielefeld

No. 12-50

Entry from October 19, 1982, from the first visitor book, Kreismuseum Wewelsburg
June 5, 1982 – May 18, 1983
This 1982 Kreismuseum Wewelsburg visitor book entry is by Michael A. Aquino, who led Wewelsburg Working, a ritual meditation renowned in satanic circles. Aquino is the founder of the Temple of Set, which split off from the Church of Satan in 1975, and was its high priest in 1982. The two groups are among the world's best-known satanic organizations. From 1980 to 1986, Aquino was a professor of political science at Golden Gate University in San Francisco. Until 1994 he worked as a political adviser to the U.S. Military Intelligence Service, with the rank of lieutenant colonel. Aquino used the opportunity of a service-related trip to NATO installations in Britain, Belgium, and Germany to visit Wewelsburg Castle, which was familiar to him from his readings of fantasy literature. In the northern tower crypt, Aquino performed a meditation to clarify for himself certain internal problems that had befallen the Temple of Set. According to Aquino, his choice of Wewelsburg Castle as a venue was possibility to "to summon the 'Powers of Darkness' at their most powerful locus." To this day, the Temple of Set homepage features a photograph of Wewelsburg Castle. ds
Kreismuseum Wewelsburg, inv. no. 16838

No. 12-49

Remnants of a runic ritual in the northern tower crypt
December 1992
In December 1992, the crypt beneath the northern tower of Wewelsburg Castle was broken into; the culprits, who were never identified, switched the locks of the lower tower door and of the iron gate that stood at the time in front of the entrance to the crypt. On each of the twelve stone pedestals, the intruders left white kerchiefs to which runic symbols had been sewn. They had evidently conducted some kind of ritual and wished to make this known. Its ideological orientation, however, remains unclear; it may have had a satanic or a neo-pagan bent. What clearly emerged from this episode, however, is the extent to which some esoteric circles had invested this space with "magic" significance. The circumstances of the maltreated concentration camp prisoners forced to build this very structure have little meaning in this understanding of the world. ds
Kreismuseum Wewelsburg, Fotoarchiv

Von Satanssekte gequält

Gütersloherin sieht sich als Opfer ritueller Praktiken

VON LUDGER OSTERKAMP

Opfer: *Diese Frau soll vor langer Zeit als Mädchen gefoltert worden sein. In der Sendung „Höllenleben" berichtete sie darüber.* FOTO: MD

No. 12-48
T-shirt of right-wing rock band No Alibi

No Alibi is a hardcore rock band from Buffalo, New York, founded in 1986. The band is part of the neo-Nazi-affiliated White Power movement in the United States. The T-shirt shows that Wewelsburg Castle holds significance for No Alibi, as does their CD *Back for Blood and Soil*, which features a track inspired by the castle titled "Knights of the Round."

In 1997 or 1998 No Alibi visited Wewelsburg Castle. In 1998 a photograph of the visit appeared in the German neo-Nazi fanzine *Neue Ordnung* [New Order]. In 2001 the most prominent U.S. neo-Nazi music magazine, Resistance, published two photographs of the band, one in the *Obergruppenführer* Hall posing before the black sun and the other holding a band banner in the castle access area. ds

Kreismuseum Wewelsburg, inv. no. 15398

No. 12-54
Black sun tablecloth

This crocheted tablecloth was offered for 66 euros in the 2002 mail-order catalog of the National Democratic Party of Germany (NPD) newspaper, *Deutsche Stimme* [German voice], which presents the black sun as an accessory for the "radical right-wing dining room." Although the tablecloth is only one of numerous commercial products depicting the Wewelsburg sun wheel, it shows just how far merchandising of this politically charged symbol has progressed within radical right-wing circles. ds

Kreismuseum Wewelsburg, inv. no. 14475

No. 12-55
Thule watch

This wristwatch, described as "Thule watch," is one of many black sun products sold by radical right-wing shops and mail-order businesses. In neofascist circles, these are not merely fashion statements, but identification markers as well.

The enduring popularity of the symbol among right-wing extremists began in 1991 with the novel *Die Schwarze Sonne von Tashi Lhunpo* [The Black Sun of Tashi Lhunpo]. Its publisher, Arun-Verlag, would later market its first item of merchandise, a Thule watch. ds

Kreismuseum Wewelsburg, inv. no. 14483

No. 12-52
Black sun flag

As a prominent symbol of right-wing extremism, the black sun represents explicit allegiance to racist and anti-Semitic ideology. At a 2004 neo-Nazi demonstration protesting the construction of a synagogue in Bochum, the black sun flag was raised beside the Reich war flag, the flag of the National Democratic Party of Germany (NPD) and the latter's youth organization, the Young National Democrats (JN).

In 2000 the band Von Thronstahl also used a black sun flag during its controversial protest appearance at the *Wave-Gotik-Treffen* in Leipzig. ds

Kreismuseum Wewelsburg, inv. no. 14476

No. 12-53
Black sun table ornament

This black sun table ornament is a purely decorative plastic item. In 2002 the NPD's *Deutsche Stimme* (German voice) mail-order catalog offered it as home adornment for 115 euros. For radical right-wing mail-order companies, the popularity of the Wewelsburg sun wheel among neo-fascists is not merely a matter of ideology, but also a welcome opportunity for profits. ds

Kreismuseum Wewelsburg, inv. no. 14474

No. 12-56
Pink panties
2009

These women's panties are from the 2009 catalog of the radical right-wing mail-order company, Enos-Versand. The black sun has been entirely stripped of its context, but in the process has also lost its original elitist connotations. ds

Kreismuseum Wewelsburg, inv. no. 17004

12.3
Controversy over Public Perceptions

In Wewelsburg, a first reckoning with the history of National Socialism took place very early on with the cycle of paintings by Josef Glahé. The work, however, was largely rejected by the public, and eventually taken down in 1973, with few people having taken any notice of it. Other expressions of admonishment were initiated by outside sources and later removed.

A more serious coming-to-terms with Wewelsburg's SS past only properly began in 1975 with a discussion of a memorial. The Paderborn district assembly funded a research project on the establishment of a memorial and documentation center, which opened in 1982. Since then, contact with former concentration camp prisoners, scientific research, and pedagogical work has continued apace. Over the years the memorial site has increasingly dedicated itself to preserving the crime sites, while sometimes facing public protest. The local view of Wewelsburg's past was slow to change. Finally, in 2000, a memorial initiated by the younger generation of townspeople was consecrated on the former concentration camp roll call area.

No. 12-57
Josef Glahé at work on his painting
Verfolgung [Persecution] in his
studio
Angelika Gausmann and Iris Schäferjohann-Bursian, "Das vergessene Mahnmal Josef Glahés. Kunst als Mittel der Auseinandersetzung mit dem Nationalsozialismus im Bürener Land (1949 – 1974)," in *Westfalen – Hefte für Geschichte, Kunst und Volkskunde*, 1993, vol. 71, pp. 121 – 138, ill. 15

Ten paintings by Josef Glahé as a Wewelsburg Castle memorial
Late June 1949 saw the refounding of the Association for the Preservation of Wewelsburg Castle (Verein zur Erhaltung der Wewelsburg), an organization that had existed in the Weimar Republic. Among its members were the district president at the time, the chief district administrator for Büren, and the district undersecretary, Dr. Aloys Vogels, who himself had been Büren district president from 1921 to 1925. In 1949 he recommended the establishment of not only the youth hostel, but also a "political education center in the truly democratic sense." In July of the same year he submitted proposals for a memorial, which would provide a reckoning of National Socialism through a visual history of the regime. On October 4, 1949, on the basis of Vogel's suggestions, Josef Glahé presented five studies to the Association, and shortly afterward was granted the commission to design of the imagery.

Josef Glahé, born on November 3, 1925, in Büren, fought as a soldier on the Eastern Front as of 1943. In late 1945 he resumed his training as a painter; he would subsequently study architecture, graphic arts and painting in Paderborn, Dortmund, and Düsseldorf. In the early 1950s he founded a design and architecture firm in Cologne, which still exists today. From this point on he would go by the name of Jo Glahé.

The memorial with Josef Glahé's paintings was officially consecrated on June 29, 1950. The paintings were originally intended to speak for themselves, thus they remained untitled. However, when the Association took it upon itself to select titles for the paintings without consulting Glahé, the artist felt obligated to provide his own titles, which were each a single word. The cycle comprises five pairs of paintings, with each pair sharing common visual themes. fh

No. 12-58
***Flüchtlinge* [Refugees]**
(Title suggested by the Wewelsburg Castle
Association: *Das Millionenheer der
Flüchtlinge* [The Million-Man Army of
Refugees])

In this and the following painting,
Glahé evokes people who survived the war,
yet lost all their belongings. The foreground shows a woman with two children
and a baby on her arm. The figures appear
rigidly vertical, as if confronting the
viewer. The mother and daughter have fear
in their eyes, while the son looks down in
resignation. The father, who would complete the group, is missing. More people
can be discerned behind the family, arrayed
in an imaginary line. There were masses
of refugees, as the painting makes clear.

In placing the mother at the center of
the image, Glahé drew inspiration from
religious painting. His female figure conforms to models of the Virgin of Mercy
familiar from Gothic art. The face of such
Madonnas is often represented in a yellow-
golden hue – radiating a "heavenly" gold.
In this painting, however, the woman's
face is a sickly yellow.

World War II produced thousands of
refugees. Even during the war, masses of
uprooted people fled across Europe. At
the war's end, Glahé personally experienced the hoards of bombed out, displaced
people. The number of refugees was
enormously high in rural areas, such as
the former prince-bishopric of Paderborn.
After the war, refugees were spread
throughout the Büren area, and even given
shelter in the barracks of the former
Niederhagen Concentration Camp.fh
Kreismuseum Wewelsburg, inv. no. 4905

No. 12-59
Kirchentrümmer [Church Ruins]
(Title suggested by the Wewelsburg Castle Association: *Gotteshäuser zerstört* [Houses of God Destroyed])

The viewer peers through a ruined church onto an equally destroyed belfry. The tower can clearly be identified as that of the Paderborn Cathedral. A figure is dimly seen hanging from the tower; its spectral outline is worked into the painting like Christ on the cross. On one hand, this widens the painting's scope: not only are the buildings destroyed; religion itself has been stricken. On the other, the Christ figure may represent the coherence of guilt and atonement, sin and forgiveness. The painting is executed in clear colors, informing a powerful dynamic. The viewer, standing in the first church and looking through the ruins, is surrounded by teetering pillars, as if the process of destruction were still underway.

The models used by the artist can be clearly discerned. The church in the foreground, offering our view onto the cathedral tower, is the Josef Church on Heierstraße, in Paderborn. Its ruins were torn down in 1953. The cathedral tower is rendered in all its details, making it recognizable to anyone from the area around Paderborn. However, the artist chose to leave out the nave in order to give his painting a greater feeling of depth. fh

Kreismuseum Wewelsburg, inv. no. 4908

No. 12-60

Hunger
(Title suggested by the Wewelsburg Castle Association: *Verschleppt, vergast, ausgelöscht ...* [Deported, Gassed, Extinguished ...])

In this image the artist employs a cubist idiom to elicit a deep spatiality that is also oppressively void of content. At the center of this unfathomable area appears a family: father, mother, and child. Only the child is clothed, with rags; the adults are naked, and thus seemingly defenseless. The child is suffering, with underdeveloped legs and a distended abdomen typical of someone starving. The father carries the weakened child while the mother holds her head in despair. It took only three days for the memorial to be mired in controversy. Young girls complained that *Hunger* showed naked people, resulting in the painting's removal on July 3, 1950. It was possibly the painting's intensity, in combination with its initial title of "Deported, Gassed, Extinguished ...," that caused some to reject it. Or perhaps people did not want such an insistent reminder of the crimes of the Third Reich.

The painting's original message is most likely not conveyed by the title *Hunger*. Perhaps the initially proposed title comes closer to doing so. fh

Kreismuseum Wewelsburg, inv. no. 4909

12.3.2
Disputes over the Commemoration of the Concentration Camp Victims

No. 12-62
Photographic album of the first International Youth Festival in Wewelsburg
Paper, cardboard, leather
1954
On the initiative of traditional dance groups from Büren and refugees from former German territories in the East, the first International Youth Festival was held in Wewelsburg in June 1954. Under the motto "The youth of the world unite in friendship," 120 German youths, along with 67 youths from abroad, came together in Wewelsburg, where they grappled with the political themes of the war and forced migration.

As in the rest of the Federal Republic of Germany, the remembrance of the victims of National Socialist crimes was largely repressed. Many residents of Wewelsburg, including the expellees who had settled there, felt that they themselves were the victims. Mourning was done primarily for one's own war dead, such as at the new war cemetery established in 1953 in Böddeken. It was only in 2002 that youth festival participants first commemorated the concentration camp victims, at a ceremony at the new memorial in Wewelsburg kjs

Kreismuseum Wewelsburg, inv. no. 16361

No. 12-63
Commemorative plaque of the Bund der Verfolgten des Naziregimes
Metal
1965
In 1965, at the urging of Erich Niko-laizig, a former prisoner at the concentration camp in Wewelsburg and president of the Büren chapter of the Bund der Verfolgten des Naziregimes (Union of Persecutees of the Nazi Regime), the District of Büren installed a plaque commemorating the victims of the concentration camp at the stair tower in the interior courtyard of Wewelsburg Castle. The stated number of concentration camp victims omitted two prisoners who were killed while attempting escape.

In the early 1970s, the plaque became the object of public criticism. Concerned that mention of the concentration camp would give visitors to the biennial youth festival the "wrong impression" of Wewelsburg Castle, the Büren district office of educational and cultural affairs requested that the plaque be removed. It was finally taken down in August 1973. That same year, Josef Glahé's memorial cycle was removed from the crypt. Both events went unnoticed by the public. Since 1998, the commemorative plaque has once again been on display at the memorial site. kjs

Kreismuseum Wewelsburg, inv. no. 16362

No. 12-61
Not shown
Plaques from the former contemporary history exhibition "Wewelsburg 1933 – 1945. Cult and Terror Site of the SS," showing the names of the concentration camp victims in Wewelsburg
Wood
1992
On July 6, 1977, after lengthy political discussions and under pressure from regional and national press coverage, the Paderborn district assembly resolved to establish a permanent contemporary history exhibition as a "reminder to the living and in commemoration of the victims of Niederhagen Concentration Camp." Professor Karl Hüser was entrusted with formulating its intellectual foundation. Inaugurated on March 20, 1982, the exhibition underwent an overhaul in the early 1990s, principally to integrate new research into the narrative of the concentration camp and its prisoners. After years of controversy over issues of confidentiality, two wooden plaques bearing the names of the 1,285 people killed at the concentration camp in Wewelsburg could finally be installed. Until the consecration of the memorial at the former roll call area, the plaques served as the place of commemoration for the dead. kjs

Kreismuseum Wewelsburg,
inv. nos. 16363/1 and 16363/2

No. 12-64
Not shown
Sample of stone used in the memorial for victims of SS violence in Wewelsburg
Limestone
2000
The first memorial ceremony for victims of the concentration camp was held in 1995 on the former grounds of the camp. On April 2, 1998, another memorial event took place as the result of an initiative by Wewelsburg youth who joined to form the "April 2 Day of Remembrance" workgroup. This same group, together with former camp prisoners, presented a formal request to the city of Büren for the establishment of a permanent memorial and on April 2, 2000, the memorial was consecrated.

Art students at the University of Paderborn conceived of the prisoner triangle as the overriding design motif for the memorial – a symbol common to all concentration camp prisoners. Flat triangles of local limestone in varying heights are embedded in a triangular concrete frame. The material is a reference to the quarrying work of the concentration camp prisoners. The stones, like this stone sample, came from a quarry near Niederntudorf.
kjs

Kreismuseum Wewelsburg, inv. no. 15024

No. 12-66
Memorial plate by Valentin Perov with the inscription: "In the name of mutual understanding and reconciliation from Valentin Perov, Ukraine, 2005"
Porcelain
April 2005
Former Ukrainian concentration camp prisoner Valentin Perov presented this plate, which he had specially made at a local porcelain manufacture, to the memorial administration on the occasion of his second visit to Wewelsburg – April 2, 2005, the 60th anniversary of the liberation of the concentration camp. The red triangle at the plate's center represents the red prisoner triangle Valentin Perov was forced to wear as a political prisoner.

As a gesture of reconciliation, survivors of Niederhagen Concentration Camp have been invited to Wewelsburg on several occasions, beginning in 1992. Since 1998, Russian and Ukrainian guests have been invited as well. The memorial site attaches great importance to maintaining contact with the victims of SS violence and their families. The memories of former prisoners are recorded and saved, along with personal effects, for coming generations of visitors. kjs

Kreismuseum Wewelsburg, inv. no. 15548

No. 12-65
Das Salzkorn [Grain of Salt], **prize bestowed by the Evangelical Church of Westphalia upon the April 2 Day of Remembrance Association**
Plastic, glass, metal
October 20, 2007
Since its founding in 2000, the activities of the April 2 Day of Remembrance workgroup have been carried on by the "April 2 Day of Remembrance in Wewelsburg – Association Against Forgetting and for Democracy." Among the association's duties are the organization and implementation of the annual memorial ceremony with youth groups at the memorial site, along with other events, such as exhibitions, competitions, readings, and excursions. In 2007 the Evangelical Church of Westphalia bestowed its Grain of Salt prize upon the association "for the perseverance with which the group brought the survivors out of anonymity and its shedding of light upon current problems through its confrontation with the Nazi past" (Peter Ohligschläger, jury member). The distinction is awarded every other year by the Evangelical Church of Westphalia in recognition of projects promoting justice, peace, and the integrity of creation. kjs

Kreismuseum Wewelsburg,
inv. nos. 16792/1 and 16792/2

No. 12-67
Padded chair from the meeting hall at the Paderborn district assembly
Wood, leather, metal, plastic
1975 – 2008
Until 2008 this leather chair stood in the main meeting hall of the Paderborn Assembly House. Ever since the districts of Büren and Paderborn were merged – as part of the 1975 northern Rhine-Westphalian territorial reform – the hall has been used by political committees of the Paderborn district. It was also the location of the district council sessions – filled with heated debate on what form the Wewelsburg memorial should take – that ultimately led to the establishment of the contemporary history exhibition "Wewelsburg 1933 – 1945. Cult and Terror Site of the SS." The chair thus serves to symbolize the political dimension of commemoration in a parliamentary democracy. kjs

Kreismuseum Wewelsburg, inv. no. 16691

Wewelsburg Castle in Science, Pedagogy, and Media

No. 12-72
Karl Hüser, *Wewelsburg 1933 – 1945. Kult und Terrorstätte der SS. Eine Dokumentation* [Wewelsburg 1933 – 1945: Cult and Terror Site of the SS. A Documentation]
Paderborn, 1982

Kreismuseum Wewelsburg, inv. no. 16366

No. 12-73
Kirsten John, "Mein Vater wird gesucht …" Häftlinge des Konzentrationslagers in Wewelsburg ["They're Looking for My Father …" Concentration Camp Prisoners in Wewelsburg]
4th ed., Essen, 2001

Kreismuseum Wewelsburg, inv. no. 16970

No. 12-74
Heinz Höhne, "Der Orden unter dem Totenkopf, The History of The SS" [The Order under the Death's Head, The History of the SS]
Der Spiegel, vol. 20, issue 42, part 1, pp. 94 – 107
October 10, 1966

Kreismuseum Wewelsburg, inv. no. 16946

No. 12-75
Rüdiger Sünner, *Schwarze Sonne. Entfesselung und Missbrauch der Mythen in Nationalsozialismus und rechter Esoterik* [Black Sun. The Unleashing and Abuse of Myths in National Socialism and Right-Wing Esotericism],
2nd ed.
Freiburg i. B., 1999

Kreismuseum Wewelsburg, inv. no. 16977

Initial scientifically researched, historical depictions of Wewelsburg in the Third Reich
For decades after 1945, fantastical accounts, such as those from the memoirs of the former National Socialist foreign intelligence chief Walter Schellenberg and those by Himmler's private physician Felix Kersten, determined the image of Wewelsburg Castle during the Third Reich. In 1965 journalist Heiner Lichtenstein wrote the first research-based article in which Niederhagen Concentration Camp figured prominently. The research commissioned from Professor Karl Hüser by the District of Paderborn and the establishment of the Documentation and Memorial Center in 1982 launched a long-term scientific examination of all aspects of National Socialist history in Wewelsburg. fh

Popular science publications
In the 1980s, former British soldier Stuart Russell, who settled in Wewelsburg, and some of his fellow army comrades developed close contacts with former SS personnel and their families. Altough they succeeded in bringing to light an important group of contemporary witnesses of Wewelsburg under National Socialism, and in securing photographic and source materials, these publications aimed at a wide audience lack the certain skepticism necessary in the self-portrayal of former SS members. fh

Wewelsburg in accounts of regional and national German history
Once Karl Hüser's 1982 publication had laid the foundations for historical research concerning Wewelsburg, scholarly mention of Wewelsburg gradually increased, initially in historical works centered on Eastern Westphalia and on Westphalia generally. Works of a wider geographic scope, within the framework of concentration camp research, would only come much later. Since 2000, Wewelsburg has also attracted more attention as a site of National Socialist crimes. This includes investigations into the structure, inner organization, and mythology of the SS, a field Heinz Höhne began exploring in 1966.

Today, almost all authors working on the history of the concentration camps or the history of the SS address the events that occurred at Wewelsburg. In the English-speaking world, however, the prevailing interest focuses on the mythological aspects of SS history. fh

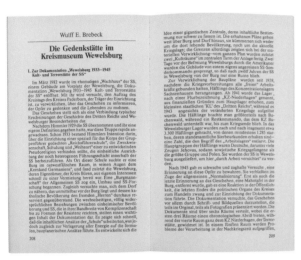

No. 12-68
Detlef Garbe (ed.), *Die verges-
senen KZs? Gedenkstätten
für die Opfer des NS-Terrors
in der Bundesrepublik* [For-
gotten Concentration Camps?
Memorial Sites for Victims of
National Socialist Terror in the
Federal Republic of Germany]
Bornheim-Merten, 1983

Kreismuseum Wewelsburg, inv. no. 17118

No. 12-69
Wulf E. Brebeck, Angela Genger, et al. (eds.),
*Zur Arbeit in Gedenkstätten für die Opfer
des Nationalsozialismus – ein internatio-
naler Überblick* [On the Work at Memorial
Sites for the Victims of National Socialism
– An International Overview]
Action Reconciliation Service for Peace
Göttingen, 1988

Kreismuseum Wewelsburg, inv. no. 17213

No. 12-70
Cornelia Filter, "Wewelsburg
ist überall" [Wewelsburg is every-
where]
Zeitmagazin, supplement
to *Die Zeit*, issue 38
September 14, 1990

Kreismuseum Wewelsburg, Fotoarchiv

No. 12-71
Der Dom [The Cathedral],
Sunday magazine for the Bishopric
of Paderborn, p. 410 f.
October 29, 1961

Kreismuseum Wewelsburg, Fotoarchiv

Publications from and about National Socialist memorial sites

For years, of all former concentration camps in the Federal Republic of Germany, only Dachau, and perhaps Bergen-Belsen, received any notice. With the growing interest in local history during the 1970s and 1980s, a movement that enjoyed considerable civic support, many investigations of local concentration camps developed beyond those within academic research. It was only at this time that the broader public learned that there had been a great number and wide range of camps under the Third Reich. In 1983 Detlef Garbe drew attention to the memorial sites that had thus far been consecrated at various such locations.

The institution that formed in Wewelsburg in 1982 saw itself as one of these early "working memorials," which combined remembrance of the victims, pedagogical functions and scientific research, and soon collaborated in research groups. fh

Memorial site pedagogy and the culture of remembrance

Beyond the actual commemorative aspect of the memorial sites founded since the 1980s for victims of Natio- nal Socialism, their goals have always included the potential for historico-political education. This – along with a socially critical attitude on the part of the founding genera- tion towards a mainstream society that was only very slowly coming to terms with the legacy of National Socialism – engendered a wide spec- trum of activities and publications. In addition to special exhibitions, visits, seminars, lectures and work- shops, local tours, and working camps now constitute a significant part of the program – in Wewelsburg as elsewhere – as do further activ- ities supported by a dense network of publications and media. fh

Wewelsburg Castle through the eyes of popular media

Fantastical literature, which for de- cades constituted the only readily available information on Wewelsburg Castle, gave rise to all sorts of media speculation as to ritual deeds per- formed by the SS andv the use of the existing premises for mystical pur- poses. Only rarely did journalists make the effort to do their own research, or to understand the signi- ficance of the site within the wider context of history. Among the few exceptions are a 1961 article in *Der Dom* [The Cathedral] and a 1990 report in *Zeitmagazin*.

Unfortunately, misleading claims about the mythical uses of the castle in the Third Reich are once again re- ceiving increased publicity. fh

"Evidently, we are being held responsible for the concentration camp. … The concentration camp was our misfortune."

No. 12-76
On May 4, 1945, at the interment of the unknown SS victims executed at the shooting range, a ceremony arranged by the U.S. military administration, Pastor Franz-Josef Tusch rejected any responsibility by the people of Wewelsburg.
(attributed quote)

Wewelsburg Castle must be converted to a "political education center in the truly democratic sense" and "a cautionary Nazi memorial for all northern Rhine-Westphalia."

No. 12-77
On June 29, 1949, former Büren district administrator Dr. Aloys Vogels demanded that public remembrance become part of Wewelsburg Castle's future responsibilities.

The text of the commemorative plaque is "unhistorical." The concentration camp was not located "in Wewelsburg, but, at best, near Wewelsburg."

No. 12-78
On February 19, 1972, local historian Dr. Wilhelm Segin argued for the removal of the commemorative plaque displayed in the inner courtyard of Wewelsburg Castle. It was installed in 1965 by survivors of the concentration camp, with the support of the district of Büren, and removed in 1973.

"Because these SS crimes were closely tied to the conversion of the castle and because the former concentration camp grounds have been built upon, I consider Wewelsburg Castle to be the most appropriate location for the memorial site."

No. 12-79
On September 16, 1976, SPD district assembly representative Hans Rothe justified his request for a memorial plaque in Wewelsburg Castle to the Paderborn district assembly, the responsible authority since the territorial reform of the previous year.

"Continuing to accuse ourselves will certainly not increase the trust foreign countries have in us. We mustn't forget the victims of the Nazis …, but neither should we make a new beginning for our people unnecessarily difficult in the interest of young people."

No. 12-80
At the district assembly meeting on October 11, 1976, CDU representative Reinhold Stücke justified the rejection of the SPD request.

"It's incomprehensible to me how anyone can oppose the memorial with the argument that …, the youth of today shouldn't be burdened with something like that …. What we're talking about here is the recognition of guilt and the readiness to express this acknowledgement."

No. 12-81
Like many others, Bernhard Krane, the writer of this letter to the editor of the *Westfälisches Volksblatt* on October 16, 1976, criticized the district assembly's decision against a memorial plaque.

"The district assembly's decision to prepare a documentary exhibit … cannot dispel our impression that … a publicly visible memorial remains excluded."

No. 12-83
In an open letter on November 9, 1977, SPD national assembly representative Klaus Thüsing justified his independent – and unauthorized – installment of a memorial plaque in the inner courtyard of Wewelsburg Castle.

Thüsing has "reinvoked, for himself and his friends, the Enabling Act, which was abolished in 1945. Democratic decisions mean nothing to Thüsing."

No. 12-84
CDU district assembly representative and acting district administrator Felix Klingenthal sharply attacked Thüsing in a letter to the editor of the *Westfälisches Volksblatt* on November 11, 1977.

Wewelsburg must not be allowed to become a kind of "open-air National Socialist museum." The conviction of the citizen's initiative is "that the memorial site at the former guard building … the commemorative plaque on the castle square, the war memorial at the Catholic church and commemorative stones … at nearby Friedenstal, near Böddeken, are enough for 'our small village.'"

No. 12-86
In a flyer from October 29, 1989, the Niederhagen-Wewelsburg Citizens' Initiative – especially created for this purpose – vehemently opposed the historical preservation of additional SS facilities.

"But … Niederhagen Concentration Camp, the castle itself, the quarries, the shooting range … were the sites of atrocities and terror."

No. 12-87
In his speech, on April 2, 2000, for the dedication of the memorial on the former Niederhagen roll call area, Büren Mayor Wolfgang Runge cited the numerous crime scenes in the village.

"The majority of the task force is … of the opinion that the establishment of a documentary exhibit will achieve more than the establishment of a memorial … The former also encourages reflection and forces intellectual debate."

No. 12-82
On June 30, 1977, following renewed discussion of the issue, CDU district assembly representative Dr. Wilhelm Ahle, as spokesman for the memorial task force, justified the decision for a permanent documentary exhibition rather than a commemorative plaque to the cultural committee. A week later, on July 6, 1977, the district assembly resolves, by majority decision, to establish the exhibit.

"The premises (of the former concentration camp) are of importance not merely for the history of the city of Büren, but possess significance beyond the region, indeed national historical relevance."

No. 12-85
On December 9, 1987, chief conservator Dr. Jahn, of the Westfälisches Amt für Denkmalpflege (Westphalian Office for the Preservation of Historical Monuments), took a public stand in opposition to the planned development of the former roll call area at Niederhagen.

"This memorial must not be seen as the end of the remembrance process, but rather should encourage us and future generations to stand up for human rights and democracy, and to view all individuality as something precious, not as something detrimental."

No. 12-88
On April 2, 2000, Sonja Büttner, spokeswoman for the "April 2" workgroup that initiated the call for the memorial, formulated future tasks for remembrance in Wewelsburg.
All quotations are presented here in translation.

Appendix

Authors

web   Wulff E. Brebeck
Head of the academic project group
Director of the Kreismuseum Wewelsburg
Co-editor of the exhibition catalog

ne   Norbert Ellermann, M.A.
Member of the academic project group (2000 – 2005)
Historian, museum educator at the Kreismuseum Wewelsburg

mh   Matthias Hambrock, Ph.D.
Member of the academic project group (2000 – 2010)
Researcher at the Interdisciplinary Centre
for European Enlightenment Studies
Martin Luther University, Halle-Wittenberg

fh   Frank Huismann, M.A.
Member of the academic project group (2004 – 2005)
Researcher at Scriptorium, Marsberg/Padberg
Co-editor of the exhibition catalog

kjs   Kirsten John-Stucke, M.A.
Deputy head of the academic project group
Director of the Kreismuseum Wewelsburg
Co-editor of the exhibition catalog

sk   Sabine Kritter, M.A. in Political Science
Member of the academic project group (2005 – 2007)
Researcher in the development of a new concept
for the Ravensbrück Concentration Camp Memorial
Doctoral studies since 2015 at the Ruhr-Universität Bochum
as Hans Böckler Foundation scholarship holder

mm   Markus Moors, M.A. in Political Science, M.A. in Archival Studies
Member of the academic project group (2004 – 2010)
Researcher at the Kreismuseum Wewelsburg

on   Oliver Nickel, M.A.
Historian, Director of the Stalag 326 (VI K) Senne
Documentation Center (Stukenbrock)
Museum educator at the Kreismuseum Wewelsburg

an   Andreas Neuwöhner, Ph.D.
Member of the academic project group (2003 – 2005)
Lecturer and instructor at the Department of Educational Science
at the University of Kassel
Researcher at the Paderborn Office of Cultural Studies since 2012

mp   Moritz Pfeiffer, M.A.
Research associate at the Kreismuseum Wewelsburg (2009 – 2011)
Researcher at the Kreismuseum Wewelsburg
Lives and works currently in Tübingen

jp   Jörg Piron, M.A.
Member of the academic project group (2004 – 2010)
Researcher at the Kreismuseum Wewelsburg
Co-editor of the exhibition catalog

ds   Dana Schlegelmilch, M.A.
Member of the academic project group (2007 – 2010)
Doctoral studies at the Philipps University, Marburg
Hans Böckler Foundation scholarship holder

jes   Jan Erik Schulte, Ph.D.
Director of research on the General History of the SS
in the academic project group (2004 – 2010)
Researcher at the Hannah Arendt Institute for Research
on Totalitarianism, Technische Universität Dresden
Director of the Hadamar Memorial since 2014

Translations of German Documents

p. 43
No. 1-26

Excerpt from the 1941 annual report of the Society for the Preservation and Cultivation of German Cultural Monuments

To reduce expenses to the Society [for the Promotion and Care of German Cultural Monuments], Wewelsburg prison camp was taken over by the Reich to become an independent entity under the name Niederhagen Concentration Camp. In accordance with the head of the Main Office, construction management for Niederhagen Concentration Camp remained with SS School Construction Management. The accounting is done by Department W VIII of the Concentration Camps Inspectorate. Although Department II also did not make building materials available during the reporting year for Niederhagen Concentration Camp's construction project, classified at priority level 2 U 1 Münster, construction and extension could proceed with little delay.
Excerpt

p. 69
No. 2-24

The *Schutzstaffel* as Intellectual Shock Troops

Impelled by the conviction that it will be the excellence and skilled use of guns and books that will prove decisive in the coming times of conflict, a mobilization of youth took place in both of these weapons, with its extent to be greeted and increased all the more as the threat to our worldview and ideology grows around the globe.

The army trains the use of weaponry and its preparedness to protect the Reich against external threats. The SS carries and trains the use of weapons to insure the Reich's internal safety. Yet weapons alone can no more defend our hard-won freedom than can knowledge and books by themselves.

While the purpose of the weapon and the sense of its use are obvious, the sense and purpose of books and libraries initially appear to be all too broad and vague. Hence, it is from this universal application of books to any and all conceivable types of thought and empty discourse that we must extract only that category of books that by their very nature serve to fortify. By this is to be understood a type of literature encompassing all areas of thought that safeguard our belief and way of life.

If we think of it more deeply, selecting the literature described above from the deluge of printed material quite resembles the task of the military commander, who must select the strategically significant features for assault and defense from the endless terrain at his disposal. Here, we encounter a military science that evolves over time but which is always bound to the same, perennial principles. We can similarly speak of an art of reading and learning, which, although it is also subject to change and transformation, must remain constant at its essential core. Thus, while the sword may also have yielded to the machine gun, it has remained the symbol of the potent and pure weapon – in the same way that an old book of indispensable truths retains its place among its younger brethren and in our hearts.
Excerpt

p. 76
No. 2-40

Operations Special Order from the Commando Staff of the *Reichsführer-SS*: Guidelines for screening and patrolling swampland by cavalry units; signed by Himmler; countersigned by Frank "for the accuracy [i.e., of the file copy]"
July 28, 1941

Commando Staff RF-SS   HQ, July 28, 1941
Dept. Ia
Daily order No. Ia 18/0/41 secret

Special Order from Headquarters

Re.: Guidelines for combing and patrolling of marshlands by mounted units.

I. Capability of mounted formations

1) It should be noted that cavalry covers less distance in a day, on average, than infantry without gear
…

2) If, from a national standpoint, the population is hostile, racially or humanly inferior, or, as is often the case in marshy areas, consists of resettled criminals, anyone suspected of supporting partisans is to be shot. Women and children are to be deported, cattle and foodstuffs confiscated and secured. Villages shall be burned to the ground.
…

3.) Either the villages and settlements are a network of bases whose inhabitants kill every partisan and marauder of their own initiative and inform us fully, or they shall cease to exist. No enemy shall receive support and sustenance in this area.

                    sign. Heinrich Himmler

F. d. R.
B. Frank
SS-Hauptsturmführer

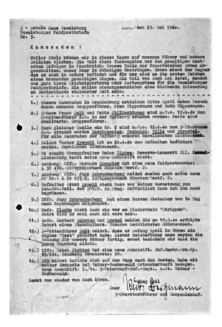

p. 79
No. 2-47
**Wewelsburg Military Postal
Service Letters, No. 3,
written by** *Obersturmführer*
**and company commander Rudi Bergmann
Weimar, May 23, 1940**

SS School Wewelsburg   loc. not given, May 23, 1940.
Wewelsburg Military Postal Service
No. 3.

C o m r a d e s !

These days we can behold our Führer and our soldiers with
great pride. The world is stunned by the massive German
successes in France. Whole sections of the French army
have been isolated and our forces are steadily advancing.
The enemy has now grasped the danger he is in and we can
see the first signs of a coming mighty victory. Some of you
are in the thick of it: send us your very brief first-hand
reports or postcard messages for the Wewelsburg military
mail letters. They will be reprinted to serve as a lasting
memory to Germany's proudest hour.

1.) Our comrades in Oranienburg received distinguished
visitors in mid-April in the persons of our *Gruppenführer*,
Mrs. Wippermann and Ruth Wippermann.

2.) SS man Franz Pult and Fritz Stilkenbäumer were promoted to *SS-Rottenführer* of the reserve in the *Waffen-SS*,
effective 4.12.40. Both are acting *Gruppenführer*.

3.) From the same source, we learn that <u>Karriesmeier</u>,
<u>Wochnick</u>, <u>Wille</u> and <u>Stroebel</u> have been promoted to the
rank of *SS-Sturmmann* of the reserve, effective 4.12.40.
Hearty congratulations to all our comrades of the *Waffen-
SS*.

4.) Private Gustav <u>Kyewski</u> was promoted on 4.20.40 to the
rank of lance corporal. Congratulations.

5.) Does anyone know the whereabouts of Corporal Heinz
<u>Tigges</u>? Reserve III Military Hospital, Kassel-Lindenberg,
does not have his new address.

6.) Attention: NCO Hermann <u>Spengler</u> has a new military
postal code: L 37 416, Air Force Administrative Command
Münster/Westf. 2.

7.) Attention: NCO Jupp <u>Schreckenberg</u> also just reported
his new military postal code as L 24 697/2, Air Force
Administrative Command Münster/Westf. 2.

8.) Corporal Ernst <u>Arnold</u> will shortly be reassigned to San.
Ers.Bat1. of the SS Special Service Troops in Prague. Hope
to see him before he leaves.

9.) NCO Jupp <u>Schreckenberg</u> was just in Copenhagen on
a quick 10-day jaunt.

10.) Lance Corporal <u>Flacke</u> is still pulling the strings on the
Lower Rhine. Looks like he'll have a front row seat now.

11.) Lance Corporal <u>Schroen</u> and <u>Gretel</u> announce the birth
of a son and heir on 3.18.40. Warmest congratulations.

12.) *SS-Rottenführer* <u>Pult</u> announced that he rented his
own "nest" in Büren at the beginning of April. Dear *Reichsführer*, when will the quarters for our men be ready?
Otherwise, we'll soon be settling the whole area on our own.

13.) NCO Erich <u>Richter</u> has a new address. Inf.Nachr.Ers.
Kp. 15/254, Bromberg Memelerstr. 28.

14.) I am presently on my way north myself and have
recently taken up quarters with my company at Weimar-
Buchenwald. My new address: 5./14. SS Deaths Head-Inf.-
reg., currently Weimar-Buchenwald.

Please keep in touch.

Sieg Heil
Yours Truly, Rudi Bergmann
SS-Obersturmführer and Company Leader.

p. 82
No. 2-54

**Instructions to all SS men on conduct
to be adopted toward prisoners
in the concentration camps, issued by the
Inspector of Concentration Camps,
Glücks, and the General Inspector of the
Reinforced SS Death's Head Regiments,
signed by Siegfried Taubert
Oranienburg, January 22, 1940**

THE *REICHSFÜHRER-SS*

Oranienburg, January 22, 1940.

The General Inspector
of the Reinforced Death's Head Regiments
IIa Az. St.Kdt.

Re: Instructions to all SS men regarding proper conduct
toward prisoners.
Ref. None
Enclosure: – 1 –

To all Death's head regiments,
departments, and replacement units

1./ All prisoners interned in concentration camps are
public enemies of the worst sort.

2./ Of late, there have been repeated instances of SS
members availing themselves of the help of prisoners for
making beds, shining boots, and other such services.
On top of that, these criminals were then rewarded by SS
members with gifts of bread, among other things.

3./ Criminals and enemies of the state have been excised
from the national community and put behind bars.
Guarding of these criminals is the responsibility of the
Inspector of the Concentration Camps.

4./ The following is hereby ordered:
a.) All units of the Death's Head regiments, departments
and formations shall be instructed in detail on the
conduct to be adopted toward prisoners.
Instruction is to be repeated every two weeks.
b.) New units are to be instructed in the proper conduct
toward prisoners in the first hour of training.

5./ The following is prohibited:
a.) Members of the SS allowing themselves to be served in
any form by these criminals.
b.) Assigning prisoners to tasks without permission from
the ranking SS men.
c.) Providing any form of gift to the prisoners.
6./ If prisoners are detailed to work assignments for the
Death's Head Units, the former shall be guarded by SS
men of the Death's Head Units if no concentration camp
guards are immediately available. At conclusion of work,
the prisoner must be turned back over to the
concentration camp guard.

7./ Any members of the SS who engage in sentimentality
and fail to see these public enemies and criminals for
what they are will be dealt without mercy.

The Inspector of Concentration Camps
sign. Glücks
SS-Oberführer
F.d.R.d.A.
The Staff Commander:
Klein
SS-Sturmbannführer

The General Inspector
of the Reinforced SS Death's Heads Regiments
sign. Taubert
SS-Gruppenführer

p. 85
No. 2-63

**Letter of complaint from
SS-Obergruppenführer Oswald Pohl
to Adolf Haas, March 30, 1944**

3.30.1944

CH Po/To.

To *SS-Sturmbannführer* Adolf Haas
Camp Commandant, Bergen-Belsen

It has come to my attention that you, along with a certain
number of other SS leaders, have had your portrait
painted by a Jewish prisoner. This fact, which you have not
disputed, is so unworthy of an SS leader as to leave one
almost speechless. Either you have not had the benefit of
ideological training, or you have comprehended very little
of it. Not only can I not understand your and your officers'
behavior, I am absolutely outraged. I am expressing my
sharpest disapproval to you and your officers and
herewith command all paintings produced by the Jew to
be burned, without exception. I order you to communicate
the contents of the present letter to the SS officers
involved as to my opinion in this matter. You are to submit
a report confirming execution of my order to burn the
paintings by April 30, 1944. I hold you personally
responsible for the destruction of all paintings.

sign.: Pohl
SS-Obergruppenführer
and General of the *Waffen-SS*

Copies of this letter have been transmitted
to the Head of Department D and the SS Leadership
and the SS Main Office requesting attention and
communication to the 7th SS Regiment.

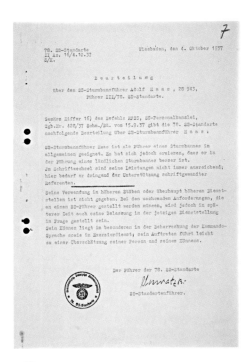

p. 86
No. 2-61
**Official evaluation for SS Major Adolf Haas,
commander of the 3rd SS Battalion,
78th SS Regiment
October 4, 1937**

78th SS Regiment   Wiesbaden, October 4, 1937
II Az. 16/4.10.37
S/K.

Evaluation

of SS-*Sturmbannführer* Adolf H a a s, 28 943,
Commander of III/78th SS Regiment.

Pursuant to Subsection 16) of RFSS Order, SS Personnel
Office, Tgb. No. 428/37 Schm./Bü of 9.15.37, 78th SS
Regiment provides the following evaluation of SS-*Sturm-
bannführer* Haas:

SS-*Sturmbannführer* Haas is generally suited as a commander of an SS battalion. It has nevertheless become
apparent that he is better at leading a rural battalion.
His performance in written correspondence is not always
satisfactory; in this respect, he urgently requires the
support of more literate assistants.

He is generally not suited for higher-level staffs or in
higher-level service. In view of the growing demands
placed upon SS commanders, his placement in the
current post must, however, in the future also be called
into question.
His capabilities lie mainly in the mastery of the language
of command and in drilling; his manner can easily lead to
overestimation of his person and ability.

The Commander of the 78th SS Regiment
[*signed*]
SS-*Standartenführer.*

p.89
No. 2-72
**Letter from Hans Lau to his wife Henny
December 8, 1940**

Wewelsburg, 12.8.1940

Muttchen dearest,

Today, Sunday, I'm back on duty, and since in the meantime
I've received two letters and the package with handkerchiefs, I have to write a letter of thanks to Quickborn, like
it or not. And I'm glad to. So my wife is finally having her
hair permed again; and not a day too soon, because otherwise I wouldn't have taken a step out of the house with
you at Christmas. I'm just not sure how we'll get through
all the visiting. The Michels, the Jüttemeiers, and Erna
also asked that we not forget her this time around. Then
we are also to drop in on the Wendefeuers. It's odd having
all these outsiders decide about my vacation, I'm the only
one who doesn't have a say in the matter. After all, I'm the
one coming home to spend time with my family. Sure, if I
had four weeks, it would be possible to get this and that
done on the side, but the way things stand, with only eight
days, as soon as I'm home I have to start thinking about
going back again. So all the visits have to take place within
two days. I don't want them to take more of my time. All
that was missing is that Erna now also wants to know the
exact day, so that she can invite a bunch of people to show
off with her brother from the *Waffen-SS*.

Today, I also sent off the package in question again,
finally also with your shoes, and everything else I had
around. A pretty impressive package, I have to say. But
this time again, there's only a pound of butter, that's all
the old lady had in store. But she promised us that there'd
be more next week. For Christmas, there won't be any
butter, though, because I'll already be setting out in the
middle of the week, and Ernst W. will also already be
traveling Saturday afternoon. So we'll hold the butter for
the week after Christmas, with this cold weather it'll stay
fresh a long time.
Yesterday, I had an unpleasant run-in with Plaul. I can't
believe that the guy expected me to come back here on the
second day of Christmas, just so he could make it to Chemnitz for his sister-in-law's wedding-eve party. But I really
gave him a piece of my mind, and got a lot of support from
Obersturmführer Haas. That's just like these gentlemen
from the *Waffen-SS*: give them your little finger, and they'll
not only take the whole hand, but the whole man, if they
can. Absolutely no sense of decency whatsoever. But I've
long known what kind of a guy Plaul is, I've been with him
exactly a year now. On 12.11, we're having a small party to
celebrate our first year here. How much has changed
in that year. We came here with 36 men, and 70 prisoners,

and now we've grown to 142 men and 500 prisoners. And
what changes have been made, but only at our camp one
can see that something practical has been achieved. Not
much has been done at other work sites, because for the
longest time Construction Management had no one at the
helm with any sense of responsibility. Money is thrown out
the window, material wasted, and Hermann Göring keeps
calling for further savings in all areas. If he got a look at
the junk that's being put up here by all these architects,
and at a salary of at least 600 RM on top of that, he would
disband the whole outfit and have them all dressed in
striped jackets. I would really like let my anger out on these
guys. These are good times for all those fine gentlemen.
But more about that later.
14 days from today, I'll be back home. Looking forward to
it, all the best to all of you, and finally much love and a long
kiss to you,

my dear Muttchen   Your
dearest Daddy

p. 99

No. 3-15

**Takeover of the concentration camps
by the SS Economic and Administrative Main Office
and the economic tasks of the camps:
Pohl's report to Himmler
April 30, 1942**

The Head of the
SS Economic and Administrative Main Office
Ch.Po/Ha.

Berlin,
Lichterfelde-West
Unter den Eichen 126-135
Telephone; Local call 76 52 61
Long distance call 76 51 01

Re.: Integration of the Concentration Camp Inspectorate
into the SS Economic and Administrative Main Office.

To the *Reichsführer-SS*,
Berlin SW 11,
Prince Albrecht Straße 8

Reichsführer!

Today, I am reporting on the current state of the concentration camps and on measures which I have taken to carry out your order of March 3, 1942.
     I.

1.) Upon the outbreak of war, the following concentration camps were in existence:

a) Dachau	1939	4,000	currently	8,000	prisoners	
b) Sachsen-hausen	"	6,500	"	10,000	"	
c) Buchen-wald	"	5,300	"	9,000	"	
d) Maut-hausen	"	1,500	"	5,500	"	
e) Flossen-bürg	"	1,600	"	4,700	"	
f) Ravens-brück	"	2,500	"	7,500	"	

2.) In the period between 1940 – 1942, nine more concentration camps were established, to wit:

a) Auschwitz
b) Neuengamme
c) Gusen
d) Natzweiler
e) Groß-Rosen
...

p. 99

No. 3-16

**Correspondence concerning the administration
and accounting of valuables stolen
from Jews murdered in Poland
Cover letter for a report
by *SS-Gruppenführer* Odilo Globocnik
1943**

Assets delivered from Operation Reinhard

Assets from Operation "Reinhard" were remitted to the SS Economic and Administrative Main Office in Berlin for transfer to the Reichsbank or to the Reich Ministry of the Economy. These include:

a) Reichsmark amounts for
a total value of   RM   53,013,133.51

b) Foreign currency in banknotes from
all major countries of the world
(of special interest are ½ million Dollars)
for a total value of   "   1,452,904.65

c) Foreign currency in gold coin,
total value   "   843,802.75

d) Precious metals (ca. 1,800 kg of gold
and about 10,000 kg of silver in bars),
for a total value of   "   5,353,943.--

e) Other valuables, such as jewelry items, watches, eyeglasses, etc. (especially noteworthy here is the number of watches, of which ca 16,000 in working order and about 51,000 repairable; these were made available to our troops)   " 26,089,800.--

f) About 1,000 railway cars of textiles,
for a total value of   " 13,294,400.--

Total: RM 100,047,983.91
               ========================

p. 101

No. 3-20

**"Heirats- und Verlobungsbefehl
des Reichsführers SS" [Marriage and
Engagement Order of the Reichsführer-SS],
SS Order A No. 65
December 31, 1931**

The *Reichsführer-SS*   Munich, December 31, 1931

S S – O r d e r A – No. 65.

1.) The SS is a band of German men of Nordic stock chosen according to special criteria.
2.) In accordance with the National-Socialist ideology and realizing that the future of our people rests upon the selection and preservation of racially and genetically sound blood, I hereby institute the "marriage authorization" for all unmarried members of the SS, effective January 1, 1932.
3.) The objective is to insure the hereditarily healthy kin of the German Nordic type.
4.) Marriage authorization shall be granted or denied exclusively on racial and genetic grounds.
5.) Every SS man who intends to marry must request marriage authorization from the *Reichsführer-SS*.
6.) SS members who marry despite having been denied marriage authorization shall be excluded from the SS; they are given the option of resignation.
7.) Proper processing of marriage requests shall be handled by the SS "Race Office."
8.) The SS Race Office maintains the SS "Book of Kin," in which the families of SS members are entered upon approval of the marriage request or granting of the application for entry.
9.) The *Reichsführer-SS*, the head of the Race Office and the experts of this office are sworn to secrecy.
10.) With this order, the SS is fully aware that it has taken a step of great importance. Mockery, scorn and misunderstanding leave us unmoved; The future is ours!

               The *Reichsführer-SS*
               H. Himmler

Enclosures: Implementing regulations
             Model of a genealogical table
             Model of an application for
             marriage authorizations.

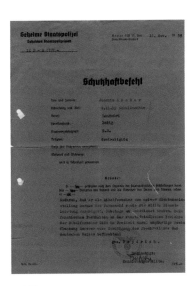

p. 143
No. 4-44
Protective custody order issued by the Berlin Secret State Police office for Joachim Escher, who was temporarily imprisoned at Niederhagen Concentration Camp
November 13, 1939

Secret State Police	Berlin SW 11, Nov. 13, 1939
Secret State Police Office	Prinz Albrecht Straße 8
II D – E 2357 –	

Protective Detention Order

First and family name: Joachim E s c h e r
Date and Place of Birth: 11.9.15 Schalksmühle
Profession: farmer
Marital Status: single
Nationality: R.D. [Reichsdeutsch, German]
Religion: free religious
Race (indicate in case of non-Aryans):
Place of residence and address:
    is taken into protective detention.

Grounds:

The state police has established that through his behavior he endangers the existence and survival of the People and State in that,
because of his religious convictions as a Bible Student he has refused to take the oath of allegiance as well as to serve in the military, and sabotages military service.
His fanatical adherence to the false, subversive doctrine of the Bible Students justifies fears of damage to the defense capabilities of the German people through his detrimental influence upon others if he is allowed to remain free.

Sign. H e y d r i c h.

Certified by: [signed]
Office clerk.   Fri.-

p. 146
No. 4-49
Office of the Dachau Concentration Camp Commandant: Disciplinary and Penal Regulations (copy), excerpt
October 1, 1933

Copy

Dachau Concentration Camp   10.1.1933
Commandant Staff

Disciplinary and Punishment Regulations for the prison camp.

Introduction.

Within the framework of current camp regulations and for the purpose of maintaining discipline and order for the area of Dachau Concentration Camp, the following rules of punishment are enacted.

These provisions apply to all prisoners of Dachau Concentration Camp from the moment of their arrival at the camp until the hour of their release.

Executive penal power resides with the camp commandant, who is personally responsible to the political police commander for enforcement of enacted camp regulations.

Tolerance is weakness. Based on this insight, we shall ruthlessly intervene whenever it appears necessary in the defense of the Fatherland. Our upstanding, long-suffering compatriots will not be affected by these disciplinary provisions. However, you malicious political agitators and intellectual trouble-makers – of whatever political conviction – are warned not to be found out, lest we seize you by the throat and silence you according to your own methods.
pp.

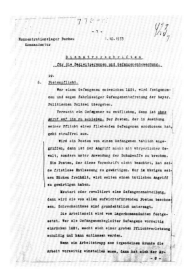

p. 146
No. 4-50
Office of the Dachau Concentration Camp Commandant: Service Regulations for SS Guards (copy), excerpt
October 1, 1933

Dachau Concentration Camp   10.1.1933
Commandant Staff

Service Regulations for escort personnel and prisoner supervision.

pp.

6. Guard duty.

Whoever allows a prisoner to escape shall be arrested and handed over to the Bavarian Political Police for negligently aiding and abetting the escape of a prisoner.

If a prisoner attempts to escape, he is to be shot without warning. A guard who has shot an escaping prisoner in the performance of his duty shall not face disciplinary action.

If a sentry is attacked by a prisoner, the assault is not to be parried with physical force but by the use of firearms. A guard who does not heed these instructions can expect immediate dismissal. Incidentally, whoever keeps up his guard will seldom have to deal with an assault.

If a prisoner section revolts or mutinies, it shall be taken under fire by all guards on duty. Warning shots are absolutely prohibited.

Labor hours are set by the camp commandant. Any prisoner escort who allows prisoners to report back early is guilty of a gross breach of duty and may be dismissed.
...

SS-Männer!
Sippen der SS!

Ich übersende Euch die Julkerze und meine besten Julwünsche für 1945.

Das neue Jahr möge Euch allen Glück und Segen bringen!

1944 hat abermals das gesamte deutsche Volk den härtesten Belastungen ausgesetzt und wiederum haben Heimat und Front die Probe bestanden.

Das Jahr 1945 wird wohl das entscheidende Jahr dieses Krieges sein. Es steht für uns unter der Parole:

„Durch Mütter und Helden —
wird unser der Sieg!"

Wir grüßen in unerschütterlicher Treue und tiefster Dankbarkeit

den uns vom Herrgott gesandten Führer:

ADOLF HITLER!

H. Himmler

Feld-Kommandostelle, 21. Dezember 1944.

SS

Liebe Eltern, Frauen und Kinder,

Bräute und Geschwister,

unserer gefallenen SS-Männer!

Euch, den Gesippen unserer gefallenen lieben Kameraden, die Ihr unserer großen Familie der Schutzstaffel angehört, übersende ich meine herzlichsten Wünsche für das Julfest und für das Jahr 1945.

Heil Hitler!

H. Himmler

Feldkommandostelle, im Dezember 1944

---

p. 148
No. 4-56
Julleuchter (Yule lantern Dedication Certificate with Heinrich Himmler's facsimile signature)
1941

SS Men!
SS Kin!

Along with this Yule Candle, I send you my best Yule wishes for 1945.
May this New Year bring you all fortune and blessing!
1944 again confronted the entire German People with the hardest challenges, and once again homeland and front stood the test.
1945 will likely be the decisive year of this war. It shall stand for us under the motto:
"By mothers and heroes –
The Victory will be ours!"

In unshakable loyalty and deepest gratitude we salute
Our God-sent Führer:
ADOLF HITLER!

H. Himmler

Field Command Post, December 21, 1944.

---

p. 149
No. 4-57
Letter from Himmler accompanying a Shipment of *Julkerzen* (Yule candles) December 21, 1944

SS

Dear parents, wives and children,
fiancés and siblings
of our fallen SS men!

To you, the kin of our dear fallen comrades, who belong to great *Schutzstaffel* family, I send my warmest wishes for the Yuletide festival and the year 1945.
Heil Hitler!
H. Himmler

Field Command Post, December 1944

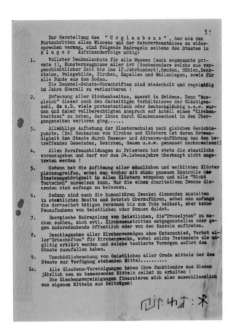

p. 164
No. 4-114
Karl Maria Wiligut, "Zur Herstellung des Urglaubens" [On the Establishment of the Original Faith], with Wiligut's stylized signature
Undated

For the establishment of the "O r i g i n a l F a i t h," which can never stand in contradiction to progress in the sciences and knowledge of the laws of nature, the following measures must be taken by the State in c l e v e r succession:

1. Strict historic preservation of all museums (also of so-called private museums!), artistic productions of all kind (especially those dating from prehistoric times to the 17th century), buildings, caves, monuments, geological formations, churches, chapels and bulwarks, as well as all archeological finds from excavations.
   Rules for the protection of historical monuments are to be publicized at regular intervals throughout the year.

2. Registration of all [Catholic] church property. Then "equalization" of the latter according to current ratios of the number of followers, because, e.g., many have gone over to Protestantism, or the German Faith, etc., and thus have an entirely justified claim to a share of "church property," which they lost through their change of faith in the transitional period …

3. Gradual closure of convent schools on the same basis. (In case of new construction of churches and monasteries, their necessity must be substantiated in exacting detail by submission of names and addresses from the affected parishes, districts, *Gaue*, etc.!)

4. Any training for the priesthood must always be preceded by state education and may not, under any circumstances, begin before the age of 24!

5. Next, the dissolution of all male and female monasteries shall go forward, keeping in mind that this can be preceded by strict verification of nationality at all persons in the monasteries, and expulsion of all "non-Germans." Only those institutions serving some charitable purpose may initially be tolerated.

6. Thereupon, institutions serving humanitarian purposes are also to be transferred to state ownership, although persons in activity there will initially be allowed to remain until their death, but no intake of new clergymen or nuns will be tolerated.

7. Forceful measures against clergy attempting to proselytize, to counter departures from the church or criticize positions at odds with their own, either publicly or from the pulpit.

8. Seizure of all church property, without distinction, prohibition of all "bequests" for church purposes, with all such wills being annulled and their bequeathed property immediately falling to the State.

9. Neutralization of clergy of all ranks using every means available to the State

10. All religious groups shall support their functionaries from these resources, annually subject to new assessment!
    Religious groups will thus finance themselves exclusively from their own means, derived from contributions!

[*signed*]

p. 166
No. 4-122
Letter from Wolfram Sievers, general secretary of the SS-Ahnenerbe, to SS-*Sturmbannführer* Galke
July 12, 1938

2. *SS-Sturmbannführer* Galke requesting attention   July 12, 1938
3. Files "Ahnenerbe"
4. Daily copy

S-K/Ab.

Via
SS-Sturmbannführer G a l k e
To
SS porcelain manufacture Allach
1. B e r l i n – SW 11
Prinz-Albrecht Straße 8

Re.: Reproduction of an ancient Saxon bossed urn

I am hereby sending you the reproduction of an ancient Saxon vessel, found by one of our employees in storage at the Museum der Männer von Morgenstern in Wesermünde.

What we have is a typical old Saxon bossed urn, dated ca. 500 BCE. The bosses were made to wheel crosses exhibiting so-called horseshoes on both sides by cutting over with a cross. Between the usual longitudinal bosses, a sign, which can certainly be considered a sig rune, is reproduced four times on the belly of the vessel. Similar and less definite finds have already been made.
The vessel originates from the well-known burial ground at Westerwanne, Lehe District.
I recommend also reproducing this vessel, which constitutes a beautiful companion piece to the bossed urn reproduced last year. As this is not an exact reproduction but an artistic copy, and because the sig rune occurs running both from the right and the left, there are no reservations about inscribing the sig runes with the familiar form during the reproduction process.

Heil Hitler!
Sievers
SS-Hauptsturmführer

1 enclosure.

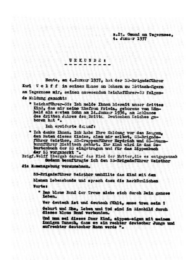

p. 174
No. 4-156
**Letter from the head of the Reich
Security Main Office, Reinhard Heydrich,
to Heinrich Himmler
May 23, 1939**

The *Reichsführer-SS*   May 23, 1939
The Head of the Main Security Administration

II 21 / AZ. 6202/39.
Sp./Kä.

Secret and Confidential!

To the *Reichsführer-SS*   Secret and Confidential!
B e r l i n SW 11
Prinz-Albrecht Straße 8

<u>Re.</u>: Possible detection of a witch in the genealogical
chart of the *Reichsführer-SS*.
File: None
Encl: 1

There is a possibility that, within the framework of the
Main Security Administration's investigation of witchcraft, a female forbear in the H i m m l e r family tree has
been identified as a witch. Enclosed are certain details
from the files available on the burning of Margreth
H i m b l e r from Markelsheim near Mergentheim (1629).
The spelling with "b" definitely corresponds to the new
High German spelling with double "m." The genealogical
lines of the Himmler family extend into this geographic
area. Now, precise comparison with the genealogical
chart would be required to determine what position, if any,
the burned Margreth H i m b l e r assumes in said
genealogical chart.

Heydrich
SS-Gruppenführer.

p. 180
No. 4-170
**Document for the name consecration
(intended as a substitute for baptism)
of Karl-Heinz Wolff by Wiligut,
January 4, 1937**

Currently, Gmund am Tegernsee,
January 4, 1937

C E R T I F I C A T E :

Today, January 4, 1937, at his home in Schorn at Rottach-
Egern on Tegernsee, *SS-Brigadeführer* Karl W o l f f made
the following statement to me, his *Reichsführer*, in my
presence:
"*Reichsführer-SS*: I hereby announce the birth of our
third child, which my wife Frieda, nee von Römheld,
bore me as first son on January 14, 1936, at the end of
the third year of the Third German Reich."
I answered as follows:
"I thank you. I have heard your announcement in the
presence of the witnesses, this child's godfathers,
that is, myself, *SS-Brigadeführer* Weisthor, *SS-
Gruppenführer* Heydrich and *SS-Sturmbannführer*
Diebitsch. Your child will be entered into the SS birth
register and his name noted for the SS Book of Kin."
Brigf. Wolff thereupon gave the child over to his mother,
who received it.
I then charged *SS-Brigadeführer* Weisthor with
performance of the name-giving ceremony.
SS-Brigadeführer Weisthor wrapped the child in the blue
Band of Life, then spoke the customary words:
"The blue Band of Loyalty may stretch through your
entire life.
Whoever is German and feels German must be true!
Birth and marriage, life and death are united in
symbol by this blue Band.
And now, may this child of yours, in keeping with its
kin, answer my heartfelt hope, become a real German
boy and an upright German man."

[p. 2]
SS-Brigadeführer Weisthor now took the cup and spoke
the customary words:

"The source of all life is *Got*!
From *Got* flows your knowledge, your tasks, the
purpose of your life and all life-insights. Let every
draught from this cup bear witness that you [are]
bound to *Got*."
He then handed the cup to the child's father.
SS-Brigadeführer Weisthor now took the spoon and spoke
the customary words:
"Henceforth this spoon shall nourish you, to the prime
of youth. With it, shall your mother show her love for
you and by withholding nourishment punish offense to
the laws of *Got*."
He then handed the spoon to the child's mother.
SS-Brigadeführer Weisthor now took the ring and spoke
the customary words:
"Child, this ring, the SS kin ring of the Wolff lineage,
you shall one day wear, once you have proven yourself
as a youth worthy of the SS and your kin.
And now, according to the wishes of your parents and
in the name of the SS, I name you Thorisman, Heinrich,
Karl, Reinhard. It is your task, parents and
Namensgoden [godfathers], to raise in this child a true,
brave, German heart according to the will of *Got*.
And for you – dear child – I wish you to prove yourself
as such, so that in maturing to manhood you may bear
as your first name the proud
name Thorisman your whole life through.
M A Y O U R *GOT* G R A N T I T B E S O !!!"

I hereby sign this certificate and have requested the
Namensgoden to inscribe theirs as witnesses.

The Commander:
H. Himmler

The *Namensgoden*:

1. *Namensgode:* *Reichsführer-SS* H. Himmler
2. *Namensgode:* *SS-Brigadeführer* K. M. Weisthor
3. *Namensgode:* *SS-Gruppenführer* R. Heydrich
4. *Namensgode:* *SS-Sturmbannführer* Karl Diebitsch

p. 180
No. 4-173
SS order to the last surviving sons
August 15, 1942

The *Reichsführer-SS*   Field Command Post
Hegewald, August 15, 1942

SS order to the last surviving sons.

SS Men!

1.   On the order of the Führer, as last surviving sons, you have been pulled back from the front. This measure has been taken because People and State have an interest in not seeing your families die out.
2.   It has never been the way of SS men to simply accept fate without taking action to change it. It is your duty, through procreation and fathering of children of sound blood, to insure that you do not remain last surviving sons.
3.   In one year, endeavor to insure the perpetuation of your ancestors and your families so that you become available again for the struggle at the front lines.

H. Himmler.

p. 199
No. 5-33
SS report, mentioning storage
of death's head rings at Wewelsburg Castle
January 1, 1945

III. According to the award certificate, the death's head ring is returned to the *Reichsführer-SS* when the ring holder departs the SS or this life.
The rings of fallen or deceased SS members shall be saved by the current *Reichsführer-SS* at a worthy location in the Castle "House Wewelsburg" for the admonition to future generations; the rings of the otherwise departed shall be melted down.
From the 2,431 SS leaders departed until now, 1,562 (= 64 %) death's head rings have been returned to the SS Main Personnel Office. In 236 cases (= 10 %), subsequent investigations revealed that the rings were lost. They were either buried along with the dead SS members or destroyed through enemy action. Hardly any cases of refusal to return the ring in the face of adequate pressure have been reported. Unfortunately, there are cases, …

p. 199
No. 5-32
Certificate attesting to the award of a death's head ring to
***SS-Standartenführer* Paul Zimmermann on April 20, 1936**

Copy.

The *Reichsführer-SS*   Berlin, 4.20.36.

To *SS-Standartenführer* Paul Zimmermann,
SS-No. 276 856.

I confer upon you the death's head ring of the SS.

This is intended as:
A sign of our loyalty to the Führer, of our unwavering obedience to our superiors and our unshakeable esprit-de-corps and camaraderie.
The death's head is an exhortation to be always ready to put our individual lives at the service of the life of the whole.
The runes across from the death's head are signs of salvation from our past, with which the National Socialist world view has once more connected us.
The two sig runes are the visual representation of our Protection Squadron (*Schutzstaffel*) name.
The swastika and hagall rune serve to remind us of our unshakeable faith in the triumph of our worldview.
The ring is garlanded with oak branches, the leaves of the ancient German tree.
This ring is not available for sale and may never fall into the hands of strangers.
When you leave the SS, or this life, this ring is returned to the *Reichsführer-SS*.
Images and imitations of the ring are punishable, and you must prevent these.
Wear this ring with honor!

Seal   Sign. H. Himmler.

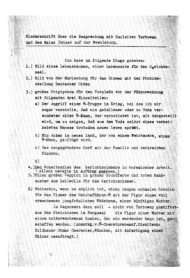

p. 200
No. 5-27
Excerpt from the undated log of a meeting in Wewelsburg Castle of Heinrich Himmler with the artistic advisor in the Personal Staff of the *Reichsführer-SS*, Karl Diebitsch, and the head of the "Hermann Göring Master School of Painting" in Kronenburg/Eifel, Werner Peiner, among others; presumably between January 15 and 18, 1939

Minutes of a discussion with *Gauleiter* Terbowen
<u>and painter Painer on the Wewelsburg.</u>

        I have requested the following:
1.) A picture of a Tree of Life, of an Ash Tree of Life for the Courtroom.
2.) A picture of Marienburg Castle for the hall with the Teutonic Knights theme
3.) A large triptych for the forecourt in front of the leader's quarters with the following three panels:
    a) An assault by an SS unit in battle, for which I can even imagine a fallen or mortally wounded SS stalwart, a married man, to show that new life sprouts even from the death of a married man.
    b) A field in the new lands, being plowed by a soldier farmer, an SS man.
    c) The newly founded village, with the family and numerous children.
4. The Reich Eagle for the Courtroom, in ceramic (already contracted to Allach).
5. A large gray carpet with red edge pattern, made of rayon, for the Courtroom.
6. In addition, when feasible, a long, narrow tapestry for the *Reichsführer-SS* room, with the figure of a fully-grown, virginal girl, a future mother."
    In contrast to this, the figure – not donated by Terbowen – of a mother with a half-grown boy, a nascent man, shall be hewn from the stone bosses in the castle hall. (Note by *SS-Obersturmbannf(ührer)*. Diebitsch: sculptor Otmar Obermeier, Munich, has been commissioned to create a sketch.)

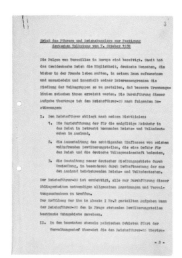

p. 220
No. 6-17
**Decree by Hitler entrusting Heinrich Himmler with the "Strengthening of German Nationhood"
October 7, 1939**

<u>Decree of the Führer and Reich Chancellor
for the Strengthening
of German Nationhood of October 7, 1939</u>

The consequences of Versailles in Europe have been swept aside. With this, the Greater German Reich now has the capacity to take German people who heretofore had been forced to live outside of its borders into its territory and to resettle them, while restructuring the settlement of ethnic groups in its sphere of interest in so as to achieve better lines of separation between them. I am entrusting the execution of this task to the *Reichsführer-SS* according to the following provisions:
I. According to my guidelines, the *Reichsführer* is responsible for:
    1. the return from abroad of Reich and ethnic Germans appropriate for permanent return to the Reich,
    2. the elimination of the harmful influence of those alien population groups that pose a danger to the Reich and the German national community,
    3. the restructuring of new German settlement areas through resettlement, particularly through permanent settlement of Reich and ethnic Germans returning from abroad.
The *Reichsführer-SS* is empowered to issue all general instructions and administrative measures necessary to execution of these duties.
In the performance of the tasks set for him under Paragraph I, No. 2, the *Reichsführer-SS* is empowered to assign specific residential areas to the population groups in question.
...

p. 240
No. 6-64
**Letter from IG Farbenindustrie AG, Behringwerke Division, regarding a typhus vaccine for human experiments
January 14, 1942**

I. G. FARBENINDUSTRIE AKTIENGESELLSCHAFT [CORP.]
BEHRINGWERKE MARBURG-LAHN

To:
SS-Obersturmführer Howen, Camp Physician
Buchenwald Concentration Camp
near Weimar

...   Dr. D/Hp. 6553   1.14.1942

Dear Herr *Obersturmführer*,
Following up on several conversations between our gentlemen and the gentlemen of the *Waffen-SS* Hygiene Institute, Berlin, Knesebek Straße 43/44, we are pleased to send you today per express mail 7 x 25 cc typhus vaccine (for experimental purposes) for 50 persons, at no charge. This vaccine is concentrated and at least twice as powerful as the typhus vaccine that the *Waffen-SS* Hygiene Institute previously received from the signatory at left. As you know, besides the concentrated vaccine sent today and the vaccine we previously produced, trials are also to be conducted on two other vaccines.

Heil Hitler !

I.G. Farbenindustrie Aktiengesellschaft
Department Behringwerke Marburg
[*Signed*]

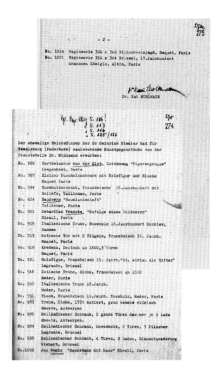

p. 249
No. 6-89
**Proclamation by an Upper Bavarian
Werewolf group, which cites central motifs
of SS ideology – loyalty, family,
and village community – and is signed
with a *Wolfsangel*, the symbol of the
underground movement
April 25, 1945**

"The Werewolf"   to all locations, 4.25.45
Upper Bavaria

Warning
To all traitors and lackeys of the enemy.

The Werewolf of Upper Bavaria preventively warns all
those who would aid and abet the enemy, or threaten or
harass Germans and their families who remained true to
Adolf Hitler.
We warn you! Traitors and criminals acting against the
people shall pay with their lives and the lives of all their
kin.
Villages which sin against our people or show the white
flag will sooner or later suffer terrible punishment.

Our vengeance is deadly!
==================

"The Werewolf"
Upper Bavaria

p. 253
No. 7-2
**Letter of congratulations
from the SS-Ahnenerbe [Ancestral Heritage]
Society to Heinrich Himmler
October 7, 1942**

To the President of the Research and
Teaching Community "Ancestral Heritage,"
Reichsführer-SS Heinrich Himmler
on October 7, 1942

Reichsführer!

In loyal allegiance, "Ancestral Heritage" offers its
warmest congratulations on the occasion of your birthday; let these be bound to a gift from the banks of the
Kuban, which recently our troops victoriously crossed.
Scythe tribes who lived there in the early centuries of the
common era placed these precious articles of jewelry
along with their dead in the tomb as evidence of their high
and unique culture, the study of which you, *Reichsführer*,
have now ordered.
These pieces, which only represent o n e outstanding example from a larger number of finds, were recovered
from Kurgans some years ago. When *SS-Obersturmbannführer* Sievers came to Poland on your orders in the winter
of 1940 with employees of "Ancestral Heritage" to rescue
valuable cultural goods from destruction, your men found
this treasure in a dusty warehouse. It would well deserve,
at some time after its scientific study is complete, to take
its permanent place in Wewelsburg Castle.

Heil Hitler!

Yours truly,

sign. W. Wüst   sign. W. Sievers
SS-Standartenführer   *SS-Obersturmbannführer*

p. 256
No. 7-8
**List of works of art acquired by SS architect Hermann
Bartels for Wewelsburg through the Mühlmann Office
(last of four pages)
1942**

Former *Reichsführer* of the SS Heinrich Himmler acquired
the following works of art for Wewelsburg (Paderborn)
from the Mühlmann Agency:

No. 565   Bartholomäus van der Elst, drawing,
           Group of Figures
           Leegenhoek, Paris
No. 587   Small walnut cabinet with wooden figure and niche
           Maquet, Paris
No. 594   Walnut cabinet, French, 16th century, with reliefs,
           Taillemas, Paris
No. 624   Baudewyn, *Landscape with Trees*
           Taillemas, Paris
No. 901   Sebastian Vrancks,
           Retinue of a Military Commander
           Nicoll, Paris
No. 905   Italian chest, walnut, 16th century
           Monnier, Cannes
No. 913   Gothic door with 2 leaves, French 15th century
           Maquet, Paris
No. 918   Crendeza, German, ca. 1600, 3 doors
           Maquet, Paris
No. 921   Wooden figure, French, 15th century,
           "St. Adrian as Knight"
           Lagrande, Brussels
No. 946   Gothic chest, oak, French, ca. 1500
           Meder, Paris
No. 950   Italian chest, 16th century
           Meder, Paris
No. 951   Table, French, 16th century, walnut
           Meder, Paris
No. 983   Chest, oak, dated 1739, painted green, Flemish
           Smeets, Antwerp
No. 985   Dutch cabinet, 2 large doors, 1 drawer above each
           Smeets, Antwerp
No. 989   Dutch cabinet, rosewood, 2 doors, 3 pilasters
           Lagrande, Brussels
No. 995   Dutch cabinet, 4 doors, 2 drawers,
           diamond pattern
           Wiehart, Brussels
No. 1008   Jan Wenix, *Tree Trunk with Hare*
           Nicoll, Paris
No. 1014   Tapestry, 300 x 300, Wild Boar Hunt
           Maquet, Paris
No. 1021   Tapestry, 350 x 384, Brussels, 17th century,
           Amazon Queen
           Albin, Paris

Dr. Kai MÜHLMANN

p. 261
No. 7-23
Report on the activity of Department W (Economic Enterprises) VIII (Special Tasks) of the SS Economic and Administrative Main Office for the year 1941
January 10, 1942

…

A) Wewelsburg

1) Financial Situation
As shown in the report under I)1), existing sources of financing are exhausted. From the beginning of the year under review, negotiations have been conducted by Office W VIII for the purpose of securing new sources of financing. By decision of the *Reichsführer*, a new loan is to be contracted with Dresdner Bank, sufficient to cover the financial requirements of Wewelsburg Castle for the coming years (assuming maintenance of wartime restrictions on construction). These financial requirements are based on the following estimate, with the usual qualifications:

10.1.1941	Requirement for 1941	RM	500,000
	Redemption of existing loans	"	3,000,000

		RM	3,500,000
			==========

p. 265
No. 7-34
Letter from Heinrich Himmler to Wewelsburg Chief Castle Administrator Siegfried Taubert on the official naming of Wewelsburg Castle as the "Reich House of the *SS-Gruppenführer*"
Field Command Post
February 26, 1944

The *Reichsführer-SS*   Field Command Post, Feb. 26, 44
RF/M.

Secret

My dear Taubert!

In spite of all the work, there's always time to think about this or that. And I would not want that specific ideas or notions which occur to me about the future, including for Wewelsburg Castle, should be forgotten.
In the context of these thoughts, it came to me that we may describe the Wewelsburg in peacetime as follows:

"Wewelsburg – Reich House of the *SS-Gruppenführer*."
I request you remind me of this note upon the "outbreak of peace."

Heil Hitler!

Yours truly,
Heinrich Himmler

2. to the Head of the SS Main Office
SS-Obergruppenführer Berger
sent as a copy requesting attention

p.p.
SS-Hauptsturmführer

p. 277
No. 7-54
Establishment of a new resettlement camp in Wewelsburg, near Paderborn; projected occupancy on October 25, 1943
October 5, 1943

REICH COMMISSIONER FOR THE STRENGTHENING OF GERMAN NATIONHOOD
Ethnic German Liaison Center
Camp I and II, Leutesdorf/Rhein

Leutesdorf/Rhein, October 5, 1943,
via Neuwied

To NSDAP-Gau Headquarters
Westphalia-North
Münster/Westph.

File No. He/Tr. V-G/43

Re.: Establishment of a new resettlement camp in Wewelsburg, near Paderborn.

On the orders of the *Reichsführer-SS*, Reich Commissioner for the Strengthening of German Nationhood, a resettlement camp will be established on the grounds of Wewelsburg SS School, near Paderborn. Pursuant to an agreement reached between the *Reichsführer-SS*, Reich Commissioner for the Strengthening of German Nationhood, and the Reich Leader of the Office of the Welfare Organization, the competent Gau administrative offices will provide their "Mother and Child" and "Kindergarten" facilities for installation of such camps.
For the Wewelsburg camp, I therefore request you to place at my disposal kindergarten facilities for ca. 35 children, with all corresponding equipment, along with a competent kindergarten teacher and assistant. In selecting the kindergarten teacher, please bear in mind that she will be in charge of ethnic German children, often without command of the German language, who will be receiving the first rudiments of our National Socialist purpose.
Furthermore, I request installation of a nursery room; cribs are already present.
As soon as time permits, I will take the opportunity to meet with you personally in this matter. However, I request you promptly instruct the head of your district office in Paderborn to begin the installation of the kindergarten and the nursery, as the camp is to be occupied as early as October 25, 1943.

Per procurationem:
Heise
SS-Untersturmführer (F)
and District Camp Commander.

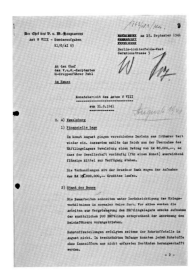

p. 294
No. 8-4
**Excerpt from the monthly report
of the Society for the Promotion
of the Care of German Cultural Monuments (GEFÖ)
August 1941**

The Head of the Economic and Administrative Main Office
Department W VIII – Special Tasks
Kl/G/AI 63   September 15, 1941
                                        Berlin-Lichterfelde-West
                                              Geranien Straße 3

To the head of the Economic
and Administrative Main Office
SS-Gruppenführer Pohl

In-house

                Monthly Report of Department W VIII
                =============================
                            to 8.31.1941
                            =========

I. A) Wewelsburg

1) <u>Financial Situation</u>
During the month of August, various loans taken out
earlier were repaid. In addition, the Reich paid the sum of
RM 80,000 for the takeover of Wewelsburg Prison Camp,
so that the Society currently has sufficient liquidity
(for one month).
Negotiations with the Dresdner Bank for a loan of
RM 15,000,000 are in progress.

2) <u>Status of construction</u>
Construction is progressing at a normal pace, in view of
wartime conditions. Above all, work on expansion of the
prison camp for the accommodation of an additional
900 prisoners, according to the *Reichsführer*'s instructions, is moving forward.
Deliveries of raw materials from the Raw Materials
Department were not made in August. However, to a
limited extent, raw materials without identification
numbers could be secured from unregistered stocks.

p. 306
No. 8-36
**Testimony of camp physician
Dr. Franz Metzge on the nutritional status
of prisoners; excerpt of investigative
documents from the second Wewelsburg trial
1970/1971**

...

<u>6th witness:</u>
Frank Metzger, M.D., from Saarbrücken, physician, age 59,
neither a relative nor an in-law of the defendants.
ad rem/to the point:
I was camp physician at Wewelsburg Concentration Camp
from late September 1941 to mid-December 1942, for SS
members as well as prisoners. On arrival, I was responsible for ca. 300 persons, when I left, it was ca. 600 persons.
To help me, I was assigned a prisoner as a nurse, and
another Polish prisoner. Ill prisoners had to report to the
camp elder and were then brought to me in sick bay to be
examined and treated. 20 to 30 beds were available in the
sick bay. Sometimes, prisoners lay in the blocks because
of sick bay overcrowding. Initially, the health status of the
prisoners was adequate; later on, it was deplorable, partly
because the prisoners arrived at the camp already sick
and malnourished. Food rations were in no way sufficient;
they amounted to 600 to 700 calories per person, per day.
The most common illnesses were diarrheal problems,
colds and accidents. It is possible that reported accidents
could in part be attributed to mistreatment. I also know
that prisoners were mistreated to a point where they
required treatment from me. It was not known to me who
had inflicted these injuries to them. It often happened
that deaths caused by mistreatment were reported to me
as accidental deaths.
I only have a faint memory of Rehn. I have no recollection
of Friedsam. With Paetzelt, I can remember his face.
Schüller, I don't know.

p. 306
No. 8-37
**Letter from the camp commandant
Adolf Haas to Hilde Schumann
February 9, 1943**

                                    Wewelsburg, February 9, 1943

Mrs.
Hilde S c h u m a n n

C h e m n i t z
Zschooauer Straße 26

Dear Mrs. Schumann!

As the Gestapo – Chemnitz State Police office – has
already informed you, your father, Paul Ulbricht, born on
March 13, 1887 in Freiberg/Saxony, died as the result
of cardiac insufficiency and enteritis.
Your father reported sick on January 31, 1943, whereupon
he was admitted to the hospital and given medical treatment. There, he received optimal drug therapy and nursing
care. Despite every effort of the medical staff, it proved
impossible to control the illness.
I send you my condolences for your loss.
Your father did not express any final wishes.
I have ordered the effects room of my camp to send the
remaining effects to your address.

                                    The Camp Commandant,
                                            Haas
                                    SS-Hauptsturmführer

Circular from the Concentration Camp Inspector to the commandants of concentration camps, including Niederhagen, announcing the visit of a medical commission December 10, 1941

Daily Order No. 163/41.

The *Reichsführer-SS*
The Inspector of the Concentration Camps.
–Pol./Az.: 14 f 13 /Ot./S.-
Secret Daily Order No. 269/41
Gross-Rosen Concentration Camp
Command Office
Received: Dec. 12, 1941

Re.: Physicians' Commission
Ref.: Kiesig. Letter of 11.12.41, 14 f 13 Ot/U.z.
Enclosure: – 1 –

Secret Reich Business!
Copy.

To the camp commandants of the concentration camps
Dachau, Sachsenhausen, Buchenwald, Mauthausen, Auschwitz, Flossenbuerg, Gross-Rosen, Neugamme, Niederhagen.

As the camp commandants of
Dachau, Sachsenhausen, Buchenwald, Mauthausen and Auschwitz Concentration Camps
have been informed in the reference letter, the Physicians' Commission will be calling on the above concentration camps for the purpose of sorting out prisoners.
For Flossenbuerg, Gross-Rosen, Neuengamme and Niederhagen Concentration Camps, the first half of January 1942 is planned for this inspection.
As very high demands are placed on all available doctors, examinations in the concentration camps should be kept as short as possible.
Attached, you will find a report form as a template for preparatory processing. These forms must be generated as copies and filled out. On this example, answers to specific questions have been filled in; in addition, they have also been underlined in red; only those questions need be answered. Regarding individual questions, we are providing the following explanations:
The question "Phys. incur. Illness" should, as far as possible, not merely be answered with Yes or No, but with a brief statement of the diagnosis.
Moreover, the question of military injury must be settled, as it provides a considerable decrease in the examination workload for the Physicians' Commission. If space proves

insufficient for the questions "Offence" and "Previous Convictions," the answer should be provided on the back of the form, as indicated on the template. Individual convictions should not be enumerated; only principal convictions should be briefly described and the individual offences briefly listed. Which prisoners are to be considered is apparent from the questions posed in the form.
All available files and medical records must be made available to the commission upon request.
The Adjutants of
Flossenbuerg, Gross-Rosen and Neuengamme Concentration Camps will report here at the appropriate time to be personally briefed in this matter.
Upon conclusion of the examinations, a report is to be submitted to the Inspector of the Concentration Camps, stating the number of prisoners selected for special treatment "14 f 13." The precise arrival time of the Physicians' Commission's arrival will be announced in a timely fashion.

per.proc.
sign. Liebehenschel
SS-Obersturmbannführer.

Announcement by the camp commandant concerning the sending of warm clothing Winter 1942/1943

Niederhagen Concentration Camp –
Wewelsburg, near Paderborn.

For the impeding cold season, the sending of the following personal items of clothing is permitted:
shirts, underpants, gloves, a cardigan or vest, socks or foot clothes, scarves, handkerchiefs.
Applying for ration coupons for the above items is prohibited.
Further, prisoners may receive food packages from their families, and this without limitation. However, the contents must be consumed by the prisoner on the day of reception or on the next day. If this is not possible, distribution will also be made to other prisoners.

The Camp Commandant.

p. 315
No. 8-63
**Radio message concerning the transfer of 450 prisoners from Wewelsburg to Sachsenhausen; listing of coded police and SS radio messages deciphered by the British Secret Intelligence Service
January 15, 1943**

...

18/19
OMA de OMI   1420   244 108
Re: Transfer of 450 prisoners. Ref: radio messages of 1.12.43 and 1.13.43. Comdt. Staff of NDH C.C. reports prisoner transport of 450 prisoners on 1.15.43 at 0910 to … 7 groups missed …. will arrive there toward evening 16.1.43.
Sign. HAAS, *SS-Hauptsturmführer.*

20/22
OMA de OMI   1430   245 246 ?
Re: Transfer of 450 prisoners. Re: radio messages of SS WVH, Office Group D from 1.12.43 and 1.13.43. With reference to above radio messages, Comdt. Staff of NDH C.C. reports transport of 450 prisoners departed here 1.15.43, at 0910, and will arrive at SACHSENHAUSEN on 1.16.43 toward evening. Exact time of arrival to be announced by telephone en route by transport commander.
Sign. HAAS,…… SACHSENHAUSEN C.C.

...

p. 315
No. 8-67
**Excerpt from the transports listing by camp prisoner clerk, Wettin Müller
May 4, 1945**

Niederhagen Concentration Camp
established December 12, 1939
          60 habitual criminals from Oranienburg
          Concentration Camp. This type
          of prisoner was replaced on Feb. 16, 40
          because of attempted escape
          with shooting of 2 prisoners by a transport
          of 70 Bible Students.

Expansion of the "labor camp"
through additional arrivals:
from………… Feb. 20, 40	=	30	Bible Students
Oranien-burg C.C. ……… March 12, 40	=	20	"
from Buchen-wald C.C. ……… May 25, 40	=	100	"
from Oranien-burg C.C. ……… Sept. 22, 40	=	287	antisocials
from Buchen-wald C.C. ……… March 8, 41	=	90	Bible Students
from Oranien-burg C.C………. June 27, 41	=	36	antisocials and politicals
from Dachau C.C…… July 30, 41	=	3	politicals (barbers)

This work detachment was originally led by *Untersturm-führer* Plaul as detachment leader and was subordinate to Sachsenhausen C.C. (Oranienburg). Within two weeks, the prisoners transferred to Sachsenhausen on Feb. 16, 40 were largely murdered in the isolation block there. Responsible block leaders of the isolation area in Sachsenhausen at the time were: Kuhn, Josef; Knittler; Bogdalla; Winnig.
In this isolation area, under the authority of the above block leaders, appalling cruelties were committed. ¼ of the prisoners of this block died every month from hunger, cold, mistreatment, excessive work quotas.

On September 1, 1941, the work detachment was declared an independent concentration camp under the name Niederhagen C.C. and continued in existence as such until April 12, 1943.
Command of the camp was given to *Oberst[urmbannf[ührer].* Adolf Haas, who had been transferred there in the meantime. Plaul, the detachment leader up to that point, remained as a high-level camp leader. The previously-mentioned *Obersch[ar]f[ührer].* Kuhn from Sachsenhausen brought in a prisoner transport, then remained in Nieder-hagen as *Rapportführer.* The post of labor duty leader was occupied by *Unterscharf(ührer).* Ludwig Rehn. The 2nd labor duty leader was taken over by a certain *Rottenführer* Fritz Rau.
Additional arrivals were
as follows: ……. Oct. 23, 41	=	100 career criminals
also, from Oranienburg:….. Oct. 24, 41	=	150 career criminals and politicals
from Sachsen-hausen: ……… March 31, 42	=	300 Jews, Poles, Germans, etc.

In the period from 6.10.42 to 12.22.42	=	818 Russians and other nationalities.

During the same period 531 prisoners lost their lives.
Up to April 5, 43 As transit transport	281 Russians

After subtraction of the prisoners who were sent to other camps, there remains the following overview:
Of 306 Bible Student prisoners, 19 died at the camp
"   903 Reich German prisoners, (antiso., poli., c.c.)
Belgians, Dutch, and others   455 died at the camp
" 1933 Russians, Belgians, French 709 died at the camp
...

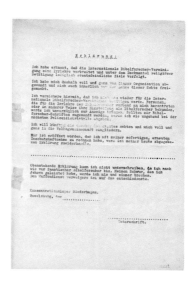

p. 318
No. 8-73
**Prisoner file for
Johann Rachuba**

[front]

Sachsenhausen Concentration Camp
Niederhagen

Family name: R a c h u b a
First name: Johann Ludwig
born on 4.28. 96, in Kyschienen-Neidenburg
Profession: miner
Religion: none   Nationality: German
Marital status: married; Emma, née Karrasch
Children: 3

J.B.V.   Prisoner No. 194
[International Association   Block:
of Bible Students]

Protective detention ordered:
on: 6.27.35 by (office): Gestapo Münster W.
Party affiliation: none
Previous convictions: none
Grounds for arrest: Bible Student
Taken into custody: 7.23.35 Esterwegen
             9.1.41 Ndh. C. C.
Released:
Transferred:
Back:

[back]
Punishments at the camp
8.13.35 bent over the block in shackles on the night of 8.13.
to 14.35 for refusing to follow orders. 7.1.36 / 10 days of
disciplinary arrest and 25 blows for refusing work. 11.5.36
/ 10 days of disciplinary arrest and 25 blows for proselytizing for Jehovah in the camp. 1.11.37 / 21 days of disciplinary arrest for repeatedly refusing to work. May 1, 1937,
18 days of disciplinary arrest for refusing work and being
insubordinate. On 5.3.37 / 21 days of disciplinary arrest,
3 months of disciplinary detail for inciting other prisoners
to mutiny and inveighing against the government during a
meeting with other prisoners. On 3.7.38 / 30 days of severe
arrest and 25 blows for laughing at the protective detention camp leader during a lecture. On 3.12.38 / 8 days of
disciplinary arrest, 15 blows for remaining seated during
the national anthem and not removing his cap. On 4.6.38 /
5 days of disciplinary arrest and 15 blows for refusing to
sign off on strict arrest. On 10.10.38 2 x 2 hours pole-
hanging, for sloth. On 10.18.38, for 8 days, standing with
arms raised until exhaustion, no dinner. On 9.13.40, 4 hrs.
of disciplinary exercise, for consorting at length with
other prisoners during work and not working.
                    Deceased September 3, 1942

p. 319
No. 8-77
**Letter from the Büren district
administrator to the Wewelsburg registrar
January 8, 1942**

The Chief Administrative Officer of Büren District.
(Registry Office Supervision Authority).
                    Büren, January 8, 1942.

To the registrar
    in Wewelsburg.
    via Paderborn

In registrations Nos. 4, 11, 13, 15, 17, 19, 20, 21, 23 and 24 in
the 1940 register of deaths of the local office of vital records, you used the words "prisoner," "in the concentration
camp" or "in the prison camp." When someone has died in
a prison or penal institution, as is the case with the above
registrations, the imprisonment or the relation of the
person making the report to the institution may not be
made evident in the entry. Clearly, you were not aware of
this regulation when registering the listed deaths, so that
the expressions mentioned in the document are to be
viewed as typographical errors. Pursuant to Paragraph
131 of the civil service regulations, I grant authorization to
delete the words "prisoner," "in the prison camp" or "in
the concentration camp" in the mentioned register of
deaths. I thus request you to delete the words in question
and to identify this deletion with a remark on the margin
of the document. The remark itself must mention my
authorization.

The marginal remark may run as follows:

"With authorization of the lower administrative office, the
words . . . . in line . . . are deleted, as the corresponding
designation is improper."

            Wewelsburg, ... 1942.

                    The Registrar:
            _____
                    Signature)

p. 338
No. 9-18
**Niederhagen Concentration Camp
declaration (*Revers*) for imprisoned
Jehovah's Witnesses to renounce their faith
1940 – 1945**

        D E C L A R A T I O N !

I have recognized, that the International Bible Student
Association spreads a false doctrine and pursues
subversive goals under the cloak of religious activity.

I have therefore entirely turned away from this organization and also freed myself inwardly from the teaching of
this sect.
I hereby assert that I shall never again become active in the
International Bible Student Association. I shall immediately report any persons who approach me proselytizing
for the false doctrine of the Bible Students, or otherwise
reveal their viewpoint as Bible Students. Should Bible
Student literature be addressed to me, I shall promptly
submit it to the nearest police station.
In future, I shall observe the laws of the State and fully
integrate into the National Community.
I have been advised that I will immediately be placed again
in protective detention if I act in contradiction to the
declaration I have made today.

. . . .

I cannot sign the above declaration, as I remain a fanatical
Bible Student. I shall never break the oath I have made to
Jehovah. I categorically refuse to enter military service.

Niederhagen Concentration Camp.
Wewelsburg, ...

            . . . .
                    Signature

Willi Wilke
7712 Blumberg
Im Winkel 33

Bericht Blatt 5

Blumberg, den

p. 342
No. 9-25

**Excerpt from a recollection by Willi Wilke
on the production of *Watchtower* editions
bound in lining wallpaper
Late 1960s**

Willi Wilke
7712 Blumberg
Im Winkel 33   Blumberg,

Report Page 5

There came very hard times; the summer of 42 was called the Stinging Nettle Summer. Every day, 2 brothers went off with scythe and sacks to mow nettles for the lunchtime meal. That summer, the mortality rate in Wewelsburg was especially high. Some figures will illustrate this: From 6.10. to 12.22., there were 818 new arrivals, and during this period 531 of these had already died. The other prisoners also had a mortality rate of 55 %, we, on the other hand, of only 1/2 %.

We can thus recognize how our Father, despite some deprivations and negative events among his children nonetheless sustained them in his loving kindness because they showed throughout all those years that they wished to stay true to HIM.

Then, in 1943, the order came: Wewelsburg would be disbanded, except for a small detachment. Only a small group of brothers remained behind to maintain the castle, the administrative building, the camp, etc. Despite the detachment leader's threat that he would yet send us all up the chimney, a time began when once again we worked without blows and screaming.

Once more there was full agreement on articles of faith, because previously there had been some extremist groups, e.g., Pape, Korn, etc., who attempted to spread their own views. One even wrote an article about the Tree of Knowledge.

Now, also connections to the outside world improved, and we at the camp were able to get the true story, which were also very difficult to obtain even for our brothers who were not imprisoned.

One Saturday, as Erich Polster and I were sweeping the castle court, we found a small rubber roller with a handle. Then an idea occurred to Brother Polster: "Hey, we used to have a roller like that at the office, for duplications." Now, the carpenters built a frame to which the metalworkers fit a steel frame. Felt was scrounged up from the camp. From then on, copies were produced in the camp, for which Brother Polster made the covers out of wallpaper. In the maintenance yard storeroom, we had many rolls of lining wallpaper; I cut 10 meters from each, so that the number of rolls remained the same. Georg Klohe provided the stencils – he worked in the maintenance yard office – he and Brother Draht then typed them – as both brought their typewriters with them into the camp to clean them!

When, on January 5, 45, a section of the maintenance yard burned down, we got our hands on a mimeograph machine, and so now production of the Watchtower could run even better. It was kept hidden in the vegetable cellar, with Brother Kraus.

Probably best placed to recount how the material was smuggled in and out is Heinrich Schürmann, who lived in Rinteln after 45, because he worked on the gardener detail at the railway station. The sisters who exchanged things [texts and letters] for us also had a key to a pigeon loft located at the plant nursery.

Then, the Americans came on April 2, 45. Once more, it was by the wonderful grace of Jehovah that the SS never succeeded in blowing us up or shooting us like rabbits in the forest.

We then obtained permission from the Americans to pick up our personal effects from Buchenwald with an Opel Blitz (wood gasifier) [truck].

It was with this vehicle that the brothers were gradually taken back home, until Brother Draht and I, as nearly the last ones, headed off for Magdeburg.

Apart from the transports listed below, as far as I recall there were also arrivals of skilled workers, consisting of 1-5 brothers. Then that arrival figure of 818, from 6.10. to 12.22.42 already mentioned in the report, with 531 deaths during the same period. Most were foreigners. Our brothers sent to the Wehrmacht on 2.11.41 returned to the camp by 3.26.41.

p. 342
No. 9-26
Autobiographical chronicle by Georg Klohe, typewritten account of the duplication of *The Watchtower* at Niederhagen Concentration Camp and its distribution outside the camp
April 6, 1971

Brother Georg Klohe, born 9.8.94, explains how the brothers in Niederhagen Concentration Camp managed to produce copies of the WT [Watchtower] and distribute these outside the camp.

After Niederhagen Concentration Camp was disbanded as an economically independent institution under Commandant Haas, 40 Bible Students and two political prisoners remained in the area of the so-called Wewelsburg [Castle] as a labor detachment for the SS School on order of *Oberführer* Tauber (a friend of Himmler's) and under the authority of Buchenwald Concentration Camp.

Supervision was by 10 newly-minted men, unrefined in the art of harassment, so it became possible to devote ourselves more to our spiritual needs.

This also became possible because we were able to covertly take up correspondence with sisters from Westphalia (Sister Schulz, Salzuflen, Sister Seck, Sister Horstmeier, Eickhorst).

Every evening, Brother Struthof, who was assigned as gardener to the *Oberführer*'s garden and the cemetery, brought a sack of green fodder for the SS men's rabbits into the camp.

Through the covert correspondence a certain grave was then designated, where we awaited our spiritual sustenance. The WT copies were smuggled in the fodder sack. This strengthened us so that we were moved to action. But how?

In the SS maintenance yard, there was lumber and other materials worth ½ million RM. One night, the fire alarm sounded and the workshops were burning. We took part in putting out the fire, quickly clearing the site and getting the fire under control.

While salvaging items of value, the office typewriter got lost. It could not have burned, yet it could not be found. After a week, Brother Stuthof bid me come with him to the potato cellar. He showed me the machine in a box covered with sacks. On a small wooden box next to the machine there were writing materials and in front of it a place to sit. Not a word was spoken; I sat down and began to copy the WT with the necessary stencil.

In the fodder sack, I also found the gelatin material for the reproduction, and Brother Polster devised the device needed to hold it. Jehovah had a hand in this work, because it went smoothly.

The sisters came before dawn and provided subject matter. They took the copies, about 50 per WT edition, to their area. They came to joyous workers who were copying and returned to grateful recipients.

When I was suddenly called from my station in the workshop into the office of the SS – it was a day when we had once again just placed something under the gravestone – I suddenly stood before the castle's Gestapo man, name of Knappert. The illegal exchange of correspondence had been discovered, because a letter from me, by chance harmless in content, was found at sister Horstmeier's, who had been arrested. What a fright the brothers had when they saw me coming with the Gestapo man, who took writing samples from our cabinets. But because the *Oberführer* did not wish to have the detachment disbanded, everything remained the same. We were able to continue copying until the gates of captivity opened in April 1945.

p. 363
No. 9-92
Letter of complaint from a Wewelsburg woman requesting reimbursement for her lost cabbage crop
October 9, 1942

Wewelsburg, October 9, 1942

The widowed Mrs. Elisabeth B, née K, Wewelsburg No. 115, appeared and made the following statement:

During roadwork at the Waldsiedlung [Forest Development] and on Alme Straße, the prisoners entered the lot I lease from the municipality at Parcel - -, No. - -, measuring 1/4 *Morgen* [2,500–3,400 m2 / ca. .6–.9 acres], without previous notification to lay a water line. In the process, almost my entire crop of cabbage was destroyed, or devoured, down to the roots, by the prisoners. The guard detachment had a few remnants gathered, but these had already been bitten into by the prisoners and thus were no longer fit for human consumption.

On this plot, I had planted red cabbage, white cabbage, Savoy cabbage, Brussel sprouts and roots vegetables, and to that point had only harvested a small amount of white cabbage. I estimate my loss at RM 20.00.

I require this amount to buy these vegetables somewhere. I therefore request reimbursement.

This declaration has been read to the appearing party and was signed by her.

[*signed*]

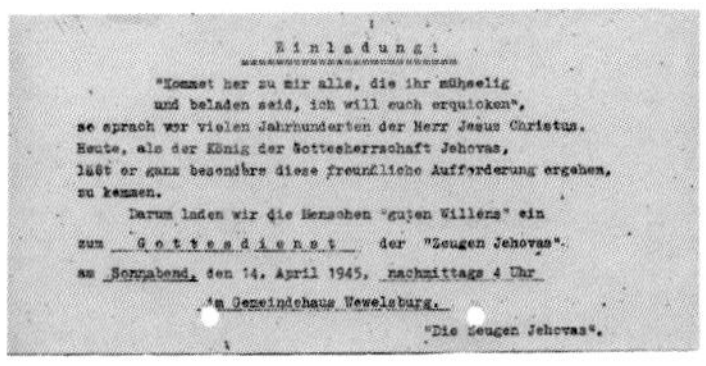

![typewritten invitation document]

p. 375
No. 10–24
**Invitation from the Jehovah's Witnesses
to a religious service at the Wewelsburg
Community Center on April 14, 1945**

Invitation!
= = = = = = = = = = = =

"Come to me, all you who are weary
    and burdened, and I will give you rest."
Thus spoke the Lord Jesus Christ many centuries ago.
Today, as the King of Jehovah's divine reign, he sends this
friendly invitation to come to Him.
    We thus invite people of "good will" to join us for
the church service of the "Jehovah's Witnesses"
on   Saturday,   April 14, 1945,   at 4 p.m.
                    at Wewelsburg Community Hall
                            "The Jehovah's Witnesses."

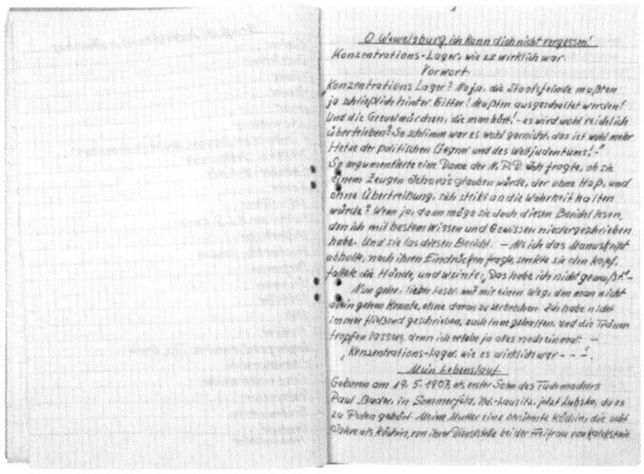

![handwritten manuscript pages]

p. 383
No. 11–5
**Recollections by Paul Buder:
"Oh, Wewelsburg, I can't forget you"
Handwritten manuscript
1976**

O Wewelsburg, I cannot forget you!
Concentration camp: the way it really was.

Preface.
"Concentration camp? – Well, the enemies of the State
had to go behind bars, after all! Had to be put out of action!
And the tales of horror you hear! – Greatly exaggerated,
right? Couldn't have been all that bad; probably more
agitation from political enemies and World Jewry!"
This is how a lady from the NPD. [National Democratic
Party of Germany] argued. I asked her whether she would
believe a Jehovah's Witness, who, without hate, and
without exaggeration, would strictly stick to the truth. If
so, would she read this report, which I wrote to the best of
my knowledge and conscience? So she read the report. –
When I came to collect the manuscript and asked about
her impressions, she dropped her head, folded her hands,
and sobbed: "I didn't know this!"
 So, dear reader, come with me along a path one could not
travel alone without breaking apart. I have not always
written skillfully, and sometimes paused to let the tears
flow; for I relive everything a second time:
    "Concentration camp, the way it really was – – –."

My Life
Born 5.19.1907, the first-born son of textile worker Paul
Buder, in Sommerfeld, Nd.-Lausitz, now Lubsko, as it
belongs to Poland. …

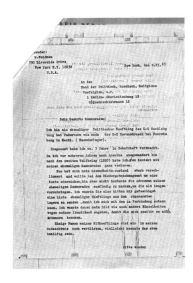

p. 397
No. 11–36
**Letter from Mark Weidman, in the United States,
to the Association of Victims of Political, Racial, and
Religious Persecution
Berlin, November 8, 1965**

Sender:
M. Weidman
790 Riverside Drive   New York, XI.8.65
New York, N.Y. 10032
U.S.A

        To the
        Union of politically, racially, religiously
        Persecuted Persons
        1 Berlin-Charlottenburg
        Giesebrecht Straße 12

    Dear comrades!
I am a former political prisoner of Wewelsburg
Concentration Camp, near Paderborn, as well as of
Ravensbrueck Concentration Camp, near Fuerstenberg in
Meckl. (men's camp).
All told, I spent 3 years in protective detention.
Because I emigrated to America several years ago after
World War II (1950), I completely lost touch with my former
comrades.
Now my health has badly deteriorated and I wanted to
apply for a pension with the reparations office, but am
unable to locate the addresses of my former comrades, in
order to produce them as witnesses. I therefore request
you to be so kind as to send me a list of former prisoners
from the above-mentioned camps, so that I may contact
them. I would send these my photo along with other
details of my identity in order that they may clearly
remember me.
Some names of fellow-prisoners have remained in my
memory; perhaps this could be helpful.
    …

p. 398
No. 11-41
Reports by Wettin Müller, translated excerpt from the investigation files of the U.S. military administration
May 5, 1945

Focus on Niederhagen-Wewelsburg Concentration Camp. Sadistic Camp Commandant Haas had cigarettes and cigars handed out to so-called foremen, who were assigned the task of "doing in" the prisoners (for the crematorium). Prisoners, starving skeletons, performing the hardest of labor in the quarry, were beaten to death, kicked, strangled, thrown from a height of 25 feet, pushed into manure pits or cesspools; or injected with ptomaine in sickbay. Because bandages were too precious for these sick prisoners, so-called public enemies. Instruments for beating were: rubber hoses filled with sand, axe and shovel handles, steel cable, hammers, truncheons wrapped in steel wire, whips.
Prisoners, beaten unconscious, in their distress creeping on their bellies to the SS sentry, pleading for a well-aimed shot, or crawling to the electrical fence. Some days saw 5 such prisoners "shot while attempting escape." If civilians became aware of this, in the evening, the commandant would say to his career criminal foremen: "Beatings are prohibited! I don't want to see that! Understood?" And SS camp leader Plaul would later add: "Beat those guys to death alright, just don't let us see it."
Labor duty commander Rehn stuffed dirt in dying prisoners' mouths and would laughingly say: "See, the guy's still got an appetite." Prisoners, undressed, down to their shirts, were buried in snow up to their arms personally by labor duty commander Rehn, and had to remain there until they died. Dying prisoners, stripped naked in sickbay, brought still living to the morgue, the identification number inscribed with paint on their bodies while still alive, lying up to three hours on the cold, wet stone floor until they died. If death came too slowly, it was helped along with injections. Dead prisoners, who had passed away during the night in bed, were beaten with truncheons in bed; they must get out to work! Then came the word, amid general laughter: "Man, the guy's already dead!"
In a factory, an 18-year-old Russian girl defended her honor against her German boss. She was hanged in Wewelsburg

for insubordination. The body of the dead girl was desecrated with an iron bar by the cremation master *SS-Oberscharführer* Stolle. Prisoner Walter Beer (crematorium assistant) was an eyewitness. Feeding of the prisoners was in the hands of the administration head *SS-Oberst[urmbann]f[ührer]* Michel. The flour for the prisoners served to feed the pigs of the SS Death's Head Units. In the dark of night, trucks delivered mangold beet leaves to the camp, for the prisoners. From May to August 1942, at every lunch there was nettle soup with almost no potatoes. A permanent work detail was charged with cutting nettles daily. Massive numbers of deaths resulted. Frequently, the SS officers had pigs slaughtered, and pies were baked with sugar, flour and fat from the prisoner kitchen. Packages of sausage and margarine were taken away for the SS families at the expense of the prisoners. Prisoners collected worms and snails during work, attempted to consume these scalded in water. This so-called offence was punished by disciplinary labor with denial of food, 25 blows, pole-hanging, or sport: knee bends, jumping jacks, rolling, to complete exhaustion and vomiting. Encouragement was given with punches and kicks. During work prisoners ate grass, leaves, roots, with ravenous hunger (hunger madness).

Wewelsburg, May 4, 1945

p. 400
No. 11-47
"A Torturer of Unspeakable Brutality,"
newspaper article

Antisocial prisoner stands out with appalling mistreatment – four-year prison sentence

Paderborn. At the Thursday hearing before the Paderborn jury court, it was with horror and deep indignation that public and participants in the trial followed the accounts of numerous former prisoners of Wewelsburg Concentration Camp on conditions and events there in the years from 1940 to 1943. The proceedings were directed against 47-year-old construction worker and erstwhile foreman at Wewelsburg Concentration Camp, Otto Schmidt, from Neumünster. The latter stood accused of at least 100 counts of premeditated assault and battery with a deadly weapon (several of which resulted in death).

Defendant Otto Schmidt, who has nineteen previous convictions since 1924, including for theft, fraud, embezzlement, trespassing, resisting arrest, impersonating a public servant and failure to pay child support, was taken into protective detention by the Gestapo in the summer of 1939 as "antisocial" and sent to Sachsenhausen Concentration Camp, then, in the fall of 1941, to Wewelsburg. Here, he soon came to the attention of the SS guard unit as strong and brutal and within a few weeks was named foreman of a newly formed labor detail. This detail of about 100 prisoners was tasked with tearing down an old farmhouse and performing the heavy excavation work for a new building. Schmidt was accused by numerous prisoners of severely mistreating fellow-prisoners to extract more work, or to punish them when they could no longer continue from exhaustion.

Comprehensive hearing of the evidence
The investigation and testimony in the jury trial presided over by regional head judge Dr. Amedick (assisted by regional court counselors Drs. Wurm and Anteß) came to the following individual conclusions:
As stated in the charges, in at least 100 cases, the defendant severely mistreated fellow-prisoners with a club, truncheon, or broomstick. The witnesses, who predominantly hail from the districts of Büren, Lippstadt, Paderborn, and Lippe, almost all testified that the defendant counted among the most brutal and feared foremen and slave-drivers at the camp.
He also took part in other punishments at the camp, e.g., administration of 25 blows to prisoners, who were strapped to a whipping post. He was accused of hitting so hard that victims could not sit for two weeks. Other prisoners were knocked to the ground, then kicked with boots in the abdomen and ribs, to the extent that they had to be carried from the worksite.

Tortured to death

He knocked down one prisoner by the name of Opitz, who was so emaciated he looked like a skeleton, because he was dissatisfied with his work. In falling, Optiz hit a rock, suffering a concussion and skull fracture that he died of a few days later. Schmidt also clubbed down two other prisoners and stomped on them. The subsequent death of one of them, which is generally assumed, could not be proved with certainty.

Forced to run through the line of guards

Also worth noting is the testimony of one witness, that Schmidt threatened to beat another prisoner, Graupner, to death if he did not run through the guard cordon. Graupner did so and was shot to death. A witness currently living in Holland described the accused as even worse and more brutal than the SS. For the execution of savage beating punishments, he was said to have received a few cigarettes. Another witness claimed to have overheard the camp commandant state to the defendant that he did not wish to see a certain prisoner that evening again. This meant to beat him so severely, that he would no longer be alive by evening. The camp leadership evidently believed it could count on the accused for this.

What else happened in Wewelsburg

In addition, witnesses also testified generally about conditions prevailing at the Wewelsburg camp, tortures and the appalling number of deaths. Even twelve- and thirteen-year-old children, women, and young girls were hanged; many prisoners, when they attempted to cross the guard cordon, were shot without warning. Backbreaking labor, such as carrying rocks, had to be performed on the double, for days on end. Whoever could not keep up was helped along with beatings and denial of food, until he broke down or died.

Up to 1942 1,283 deaths at Wewelsburg Concentration Camp were registered at the Wewelsburg office of vital statistics, but thereafter such records were no longer kept, because the number of deaths rose so alarmingly.

Mitigating circumstances at sentencing

District Attorney Hennig requested a sentence of eight years imprisonment for the defendant. In the early evening, after ten hours of deliberations, the verdict was handed down. The defendant was sentenced to four years in prison for over 100 counts of aggravated assault and battery and one count of assault and battery resulting in death.

The defendant never admitted to the charges, answering every accusation with the claim that it was a case of mistaken identity involving another foreman. The court, however, held the defendant's culpability as fully established. As mitigating circumstances in its sentencing, the court took into account Schmidt's difficult childhood, that he had himself been a victim of the National Socialist system, sent to concentration camp, where he, too, had been repeatedly stretched across the whipping block, and later severely wounded seven times at war after 1943.

p. 401
No. 11–48

"Defendants Must Continue to Live with the Moral Responsibility,"
newspaper article

The Defendants Have to Live with the Moral Guilt

Acquittals at the Paderborn concentration camp trial – Premeditated murder not proved

Paderborn (WB/redna). Four former members of the SS and "kapos" from Wewelsburg Concentration Camp had to answer to charges during a 3-month trial before the Paderborn jury court. They stood accused of participating in the murder of numerous concentration camp inmates. Although the District Attorney's office had requested life sentences for two of the defendants, the court, presided over by Chief Judge of the Regional Court Safarovic, acquitted Ludwig Rehn, Josef Friedsam, Ludwig Paetzelt, and Max Schüller. Moral culpability lies outside the court's purview.

At the start of the last day of the concentration camp trial, Friedsam declared: "I have no recollection of events at the concentration camp." He then thanked the court for the fair treatment he received during the trial.

The drafter of the indictment had conducted a five-year investigation of National Socialist crimes at Wewelsburg Concentration Camp. The investigation was launched by testimony from a witness at the Sachsenhausen trial. The results of this multi-year investigation: an indictment of nearly 300 pages charging the defendants with murder and attempted murder. However, the accusations could not be substantiated, as the presiding judge emphasized in his opinion.

Seventeen years earlier, the Paderborn Jury Court had already taken up the case of concentration camp "kapo" Otto Schmidt, who was sentenced to a prison term of five years and eight months for 100 counts of assault and battery – some resulting in death. That trial stood closer in time to the events. "This trial focused exclusively on the individual guilt of the defendants," the presiding judge noted, "any doubts had to work to the advantage of the defendants."

Many witnesses were summoned to this latest trial. Some made impassioned pleas in favor of the principal defendant, while others, so the presiding judge, left one with the impression that they took liberties with the truth. Emotions of hatred and revenge could not be excluded in some witnesses. In the opinion of the jury court, attempted murder on the part of the accused could not be established in the various cases of bodily harm resulting in death from prisoners' self-administered justice at the camp (bread and wine thieves). Today, 1,300 prisoners would still be alive if they had not been sent to the concentration camp at Wewelsburg. "This concentration camp," the presiding judge opined, "was purely a labor camp. Many died of malnourishment."

The jury court found that in the case of the group of conscientious objectors, none of whom were tortured to death, attempted murder could not be established. The district attorney's office has lodged an appeal.

Index of Names

Lenders and Archives

Our thanks to the lenders :
Erzbischöflich Akademische Bibliothek Paderborn
LWL-Freilichtmuseum Detmold –
Westfälisches Landesmuseum für Volkskunde
Stadt Goslar, Stadtarchiv
Stiftung Deutsches Historisches Museum, Berlin
Wachtturm-Gesellschaft Zeugen Jehovas, Selters
and private lenders

Our thank for advice, support, and publication rights go to:
The Aerial Reconnaissance Archives (TARA), Edinburgh
Archiv des Landschaftsverbandes Rheinland
Argumente und Kultur Gegen Rechts e. V. Bielefeld
Bayerisches Hauptstaatsarchiv, München
Bayerische Staatsbibliothek München
Image Bank WO2, Amsterdam
Belarusian State Archives of Films, Photographs
and Sound Recordings, Dzerzhinsk, Minsk
Bibliothek für Zeitgeschichte Stuttgart/
Württembergische Landesbibliothek
Bildarchiv Preußischer Kulturbesitz, Berlin
Bistumsarchiv Münster
Bundesarchiv Berlin
Bundesarchiv Filmarchiv, Berlin
Bundesarchiv Koblenz, Bildarchiv
Bundesarchiv Ludwigsburg
Bundesarchiv Militärarchiv Freiburg
Deutsche Dienststelle (WASt) für die Benachrichtigung
der nächsten Angehörigen von Gefallenen der
ehemaligen deutschen Wehrmacht, Berlin
Deutsche National Bibliothek, Leipzig
Dokumentationsstätte Stalag 326 (VI K) Senne, Stukenbrock
Rainer Fröbe
Gedenkstätte Breitenau, Guxhagen
Gedenkstätte Buchenwald
KZ-Gedenkstätte Dachau
Gedenkstätte Deutscher Widerstand, Berlin
KZ-Gedenkstätte Flossenbürg
Gedenkstätte KZ Lichtenburg, Annaburg
KZ-Gedenkstätte Mittelbau-Dora
KZ-Gedenkstätte Neuengamme
Geschichtsort Villa ten Hompel, Münster
Hauptstaatsarchiv Nürnberg
Hessisches Hauptstaatsarchiv, Wiesbaden
Hessische Landesbibliothek Fulda
Historisches Archiv der Stadt Köln
Historisches Zentrum Remscheid
Stefan Hördler
Humboldt Universität, Berlin
Internationaler Suchdienst, Bad Arolsen
Institut für Zeitgeschichte, München
Institut für Zeitungsforschung, Dortmund
Institute of National Remembrance, Warschau
Harald Jankuhn
Johannes Gutenberg Universität Mainz
Jüdisches Museum Frankfurt/Main
Klingspor-Museum Offenbach
Kommission für Zeitgeschichte, Bonn
Kreisarchiv Paderborn
Landesamt für Denkmalpflege Hessen, Außenstelle Marburg
Landesarchiv Nordrhein-Westfalen,
Abteilung Ostwestfalen-Lippe, Detmold
Landesarchiv Nordrhein-Westfalen,
Abteilung Rheinland, Düsseldorf
Landesarchiv Nordrhein-Westfalen,
Abteilung Westfalen, Münster
Landesarchiv Nordrhein-Westfalen,
Hauptstaatsarchiv Düsseldorf
Landesarchiv Baden-Württemberg,
Hauptstaatsarchiv Stuttgart
Landesarchiv Baden-Württemberg,
Staatsarchiv Ludwigsburg
LangenMüller Verlag
Lippische Landesbibliothek Detmold
LWL-Amt für Denkmalpflege in Westfalen, Münster
LWL-Archivamt für Westfalen, Münster
LWL-Freilichtmuseum Detmold – Westfälisches Landesmuseum
für Volkskunde
LWL-Landesmuseum für Kunst und Kulturgeschichte, Münster
Mahn- und Gedenkstätte Ravensbrück /Stiftung Branden-
burgische Gedenkstätten
Museum Berlin-Karlshorst, Berlin
Museum Gross-Rosen, Rogoźnica
National Archives, Kew
National Archives, Washington, D.C.
Niedersächsisches Landesarchiv, Hauptstaatsarchiv Hannover
Niedersächsisches Landesarchiv – Staatsarchiv Oldenburg
Oberösterreichische Landesmuseen/Schlossmuseum Linz
Pferdemuseum Verden
Philipps-Universität Marburg,
Seminar für Vor- und Frühgeschichte
Ruhr-Universität Bochum
Sammlung Dieter Begemann, Herford
Sammlung Stephen Cook, Andrews
Sammlung Hans W. Kusserow, Köln
Sammlung Winfried Vogel, Bad Breisig

Spiegel-Verlag
Auschwitz-Birkenau State Museum
Staatsarchiv Freiburg/Breisgau
Staatsarchiv Marburg
Staatsbibliothek Berlin
Stadtarchiv Büren
Stadtarchiv Goslar
Stadtarchiv Hof
Stadtarchiv Ludwigshafen
Stadtarchiv Meinerzhagen
Stadtarchiv München
Stadtarchiv Paderborn
Stadtarchiv Plettenberg
Stadtarchiv Reichenbach
Stadtarchiv Soest
Stadtarchiv Stuttgart
Stadtarchiv Würzburg
Stanford University
Standesamt Büren
Steinwache Dortmund
Süddeutscher Verlag, Bilderdienst
THF 33-45, Förderverein für ein Gedenken
an die Naziverbrechen auf dem Tempelhofer Flugfeld e. V.
Thüringisches Hauptstaatsarchiv Weimar
Ullstein Bilderdienst
Universitätsbibliothek Kassel,
Landes- und Murhardsche Bibliothek der Stadt Kassel
Vorgeschichtliches Seminar der Philipps-Universität
Marburg
U. S. Holocaust Memorial Museum, Washington, D.C.
Westfälischer Heimatbund e. V.
Wissenschaftliche Buchgesellschaft, Darmstadt
Yad Vashem, Jerusalem

We have endeavored to identify
the authorized holders of the rights
to all of the images. Should anyone
feel that their copyright has been infringed,
please do not hesitate to advise us of this.

Exhibition Credits

Scholarly Planning
Wulff E. Brebeck
Dr. Matthias Hambrock
Kirsten John-Stucke
Markus Moors
Dana Schlegelmilch
Dr. Jan Erik Schulte

Scholarly and Conceptual Collaboration
Dr. Stephan Berke
Sonja Büttner
Norbert Ellermann
Dina van Faassen
Maja Gujer
Dr. Beate Herring
Frank Huismann
Sabine Kritter
Dr. Andreas Neuwöhner
Andreas Pflock
Daniela Siepe

Academic Advisory Council
Professor Stefan Baumeier
Dr. Detlef Garbe
Angela Genger
Professor Detlef Hoffmann
Professor Hans Ottomeyer
Professor Waltraud Schreiber
Professor Johannes Tuchel
Professor Wolfgang Wippermann

Exhibition Collaboration
Jörg Piron
With assistance from
Sabine Grundke

Pedagogical Consulting
Katharina Dehlinger

Object Documentation and Display Implementation
Doris Bohm

Administration
Heinz-Josef Struckmeier
With assistance from
Heike Richter
Gabriele Both

Marketing
Karin Stelte
With assistance from
Moritz Pfeiffer
Beate Meier

Technical Facility Systems
Johannes Büttner
Franz-Josef Corsmeier

Janitorial Services
Brigitte Leniger
Irmgard Schlüter
Hiltrud Witte

The District of Paderborn
District Administrator
Manfred Müller
District Director
Heinz Köhler
The District Press
and Public Relations Office
Michaela Pitz
Diana Borghoff
Marina Müller

Construction Management
Albert Löhr
Willi Schumann
Ralf Tölle
The District of Paderborn Building
Department

Professional Planning
Gülle Engineering, Bad Lippspringe
Sander Engineering, Paderborn

Lighting
Fahlke und Dettmer, Neustadt

Exhibition Design
ikon, Hannover
Martina Jung
Martina Scheitenberger
With assistance from
Anke Wallenhorst

Graphic Arts
Weidner Händle Atelier, Stuttgart
With assistance from
Tobias Becker

Exhibition Construction
Sehner GmbH, Deckenpfronn
Mühlich GmbH, Laichingen
Hüser Michels, Büren

Exhibition Installation
Martin Dertinger, Paderborn
Peter Strieder, Remscheid
With assistance from
Ingo Friedenberger
Matthias Groppe
Marcus Gryglewski
Rolf Hellmeier
Andy Jung
Jürgen Ratajczak
Iris Wurmser

English Translation
Robin Benson, Berlin

Printing
RLS Jakobsmeyer GmbH, Paderborn

Media Planning
IMS Mediaplan, Wulsbüttel

Film and Media Production
Anne Roerkohl DokumentARfilm GmbH,
Münster
Bässgen AV-Technik GmbH, Freiburg
inSynergie GmbH, Rheinbreitbach
Robert Gündchen, Paderborn

Model Construction
Erhard Christiani, Salzkotten

Restoration
Consulting by the Westphalian Office of
Museums, Münster
Ars colendi, Painting Restoration,
Paderborn
Ars Servandi Restoration Center,
Department of Paper and Leather, Essen
The Workshop for Paper and Book
Restoration, Ratingen
Beier, Freund und Kühler,
Restoration Partnership, Cologne
Johan Anton Kemper, Marienfeld
Anja Lienemann, Ruppichteroth
Runge, Koch, Enge, Restoration Team,
Berlin
The Westphalian Office of Archives,
Münster
ZFB – Center for Book Preservation,
Leipzig

Under the aegis of the
District of Paderborn

Special thanks for financial support from the

Federal Republic of Germany,
Federal Commissioner for Culture and the Media

 Der Beauftragte der Bundesregierung
für Kultur und Medien

State of North Rhine-Westphalia
Ministry of Building and Transport
State Agency of Civic Education

demokratie leben   Landeszentrale
                    für politische Bildung
                    Nordrhein-Westfalen

Regional Association of Westfalen-Lippe, Münster

Für die Menschen.
Für Westfalen-Lippe

Kreismuseum Wewelsburg Support Association